"Profs. Verona and Fox have created a volume which deftly connects theory, research evidence and the implications for crime policy. This is the rare Handbook that will find a home on the shelves of academics, applied researchers and practitioners alike."

Thomas Loughran, *Professor of Sociology, Criminology, and Public Policy at Penn State University & Co-Lead Editor of Criminology*

"Verona and Fox's volume helps justice practitioners meet the challenge of evidence-based crime policy by providing much-needed actionable translations of high-quality scientific research that are useable and accessible."

Cynthia Lum, *University Professor of Criminology, Law and Society at George Mason University, Director of the Center for Evidence-Based Crime Policy, & Co-Editor in Chief of Criminology and Public Policy*

"Criminal justice policy should be driven by evidence and analysis rather than speculation and hunches. This Handbook is an invaluable resource to make our system more effective and our communities safer."

Andrew Warren, *State Attorney for Florida's 13th Judicial Circuit*

ROUTLEDGE HANDBOOK OF EVIDENCE-BASED CRIMINAL JUSTICE PRACTICES

Now more than ever, the criminal justice system, and the programs, policies, and practices within it, are subject to increased public scrutiny, due to well-founded concerns over effectiveness, fairness, and potential unintended consequences. One of the best means to address these concerns is to draw upon evidence-based approaches demonstrated to be effective through empirical research, rather than through anecdote, standard practice, or professional experience alone.

The goal of this book is to describe the most useful, actionable, and evidence-based solutions to many of the most pressing questions in the criminal justice system today. Specifically, this edited volume contains brief and accessible summaries of the best available research, alongside detailed descriptions of evidence-based practices, across different areas of the criminal justice system. It is written so that practitioners and researchers alike can use the text as reference tool in their work and in training the new generation of individuals working to improve the system. Researchers and practitioners in many areas of criminal justice – crime prevention, policing, courts (prosecution, defendants, judges), corrections, sanctions, and sentencing – can reference specific chapters in this book to guide their policy and practice decisions. Although theory is a guide for the practices described, the chapters will address practical issues in implementation and action.

This book overcomes the limitations of previous criminal justice practice books in that it is written as a practice resource and reference guide and spans practices and policies across different sectors of the criminal justice system – from prevention to policing to sanctions and corrections. Each chapter contains a list of action items, based upon the best available scientific research, that can be implemented in practice to address key issues and long-standing challenges in the criminal justice system.

Edelyn Verona is a professor in the Department of Psychology, with a courtesy appointment in the Department of Criminology, at the University of South Florida (USF) and co-director of the Center for Justice Research & Policy. She has authored over 90 peer-reviewed journal articles in high impact journals such as *Journal of Abnormal Psychology, Law & Human Behavior, Psychology of Violence, Journal of Consulting and Clinical Psychology,* and *American Journal of Psychiatry* and has served as PI on several projects funded by the National Institute of Mental Health, National Institute of Drug Abuse, and National Institute of Justice. She received the Early Career Award from the Society for the Scientific Study of Psychopathy (2011), a Mid-Career Research Award at the University of Illinois (2013), and an Excellence in Research Award from USF (2020). She is also a fellow of the Association for Psychological Science. Her research program is in the area of psychology and crime and application of science to help reduce violence and recidivism. Her early work considered biological (e.g., genes, neurophysiology) and psychosocial factors (e.g., stress, early adversity) involved in the development and maintenance of problems of externalizing, and current ongoing work focuses on pathways to incarceration, reentry, and intersections between mental health and criminal justice system involvement.

Bryanna Fox is an associate professor in the Department of Criminology and Faculty Affiliate of the Florida Mental Health Institute at the University of South Florida. Dr. Fox earned her PhD from the University of Cambridge and is a former FBI special agent. Her research focuses on the identification of psychological and developmental risk factors for criminal behavior and prolific offending, experimental field research, and evidence-based policing and crime prevention strategies. She has published more than 40 peer-reviewed articles in outlets such as: *Journal of Research in Crime and Delinquency, Justice Quarterly, Criminal Justice & Behavior, Law & Society Review,* and *Psychological Bulletin.* Dr. Fox is Co-Editor of *Justice Quarterly* and a member of editorial boards for *Criminology & Public Policy, Criminal Justice & Behavior, Youth Violence & Juvenile Justice, Policing: An International Journal*, and the *Journal of Criminal Justice.* She is on the executive board of the American Society of Criminology's Division of Developmental and Life-Course Criminology. She received the 2017 Early Career Award from the American Society of Criminology's Division of Developmental and Life-Course Criminology, the 2019 Outstanding Research Achievement Award from the University of South Florida, the 2014 Nigel Walker Prize for Outstanding PhD Research from the University of Cambridge, and the 2013 Excellence in Law Enforcement Research Award from the International Association of Chiefs of Police.

ROUTLEDGE HANDBOOK OF EVIDENCE-BASED CRIMINAL JUSTICE PRACTICES

Edited by Edelyn Verona and Bryanna Fox

Routledge
Taylor & Francis Group
NEW YORK AND LONDON

Designed cover image: © gettyimages.com

First published 2024
by Routledge
605 Third Avenue, New York, NY 10158

and by Routledge
4 Park Square, Milton Park, Abingdon, Oxon OX14 4RN

Routledge is an imprint of the Taylor & Francis Group, an informa business

British Library Cataloguing-in-Publication Data
A catalogue record for this book is available from the British Library

Library of Congress Cataloging-in-Publication Data
Names: Verona, Edelyn, editor. | Fox, Bryanna, editor.
Title: The handbook of evidence-based criminal justice practices / edited by: Edelyn Verona and Bryanna Fox.
Description: Abingdon, Oxon ; New York, NY : Routledge, [2024] | Series: Routledge international handbooks | "First published 2022 by Routledge." | Includes bibliographical references and index.
Identifiers: LCCN 2023022349 (print) | LCCN 2023022350 (ebook) | ISBN 9781032107349 (hardback) | ISBN 9781032112978 (paperback) | ISBN 9781003219286 (ebook)
Subjects: LCSH: Criminal justice, Administration of.
Classification: LCC HV7419 .H374 2024 (print) | LCC HV7419 (ebook) | DDC 364.068—dc23/eng/20230620
LC record available at https://lccn.loc.gov/2023022349
LC ebook record available at https://lccn.loc.gov/2023022350

ISBN: 978-1-032-10734-9 (hbk)
ISBN: 978-1-032-11297-8 (pbk)
ISBN: 978-1-003-21928-6 (ebk)

DOI: 10.4324/9781003219286

Typeset in Sabon
by Apex CoVantage, LLC

CONTENTS

TABLES

CONTRIBUTORS

Eliana Aronson is a student in the Psychology and Law PhD program at the Graduate Center of the City University of New York, where she studies eyewitness memory and behavior. She received her bachelor's degree in psychology and criminal justice from New York University.

John L. Badalamenti is a United States District Judge for the Middle District of Florida and a former judge on Florida's Second District Court of Appeal. He earned a Bachelor of Arts in Criminology and Law *with Highest Honors* and a Master of Arts in Sociology from the University of Florida and a Juris Doctor with *Honors* from the University of Florida Levin College of Law, where he served on the executive editorial board for the *University of Florida Journal of Law and Public Policy* and as director of its Juvenile Justice Symposium. Judge Badalamenti serves as an adjunct professor of law at the University of Florida Levin College of Law, where he teaches advanced constitutional theory. He has authored articles and lectured on topics including pretrial diversion programs, alternatives to incarceration, federal and Florida state constitutional law, the Federal Sentencing Guidelines, and trial and appellate practice. He serves on the board of directors of Gentlemen's Quest, a not-for-profit organization which serves the academic and professional development needs of high school youth in the Tampa Bay community.

Michael T. Baglivio is the Vice President of Research & Development at Youth Opportunity, with focus on examining the effectiveness of juvenile treatment programming on short- and long-term performance measures and outcomes. He earned his PhD from the College of Criminology, Law, and Society at the University of Florida. For the past 15 years, he has evaluated the effectiveness of juvenile justice reform initiatives throughout Florida. His research interests include the repercussions of adverse childhood experiences exposures, structured decision-making tools, and policy-relevant research.

Timothy C. Barnum is a senior researcher at the Max Planck Institute for the Study of Crime, Security, and Law in the Department of Criminology. His research has focused on the role of choice in sociological and criminological theories of crime. Specifically, his recent works have examined whether and how environmental and social factors shape cognitive evaluations and emotional responses to criminal opportunities.

McKenzie N. Berezin is a fourth-year doctoral candidate in counseling psychology at New York University. Her research seeks to understand and reduce the multi-level impact of systemic inequity on youth through collaborative systems change efforts. McKenzie's research supports local and national initiatives to disrupt youth pathways across child-serving systems in partnership with court- and community-based organizations through the implementation of gender- and trauma-responsive practices and policies. McKenzie also supports the work of local and international programming that aims to investigate the structural drivers of physical, mental, and sexual health disparities among adolescents and how they can be bolstered through community-based programming and policy change. She has cultivated 10 publications and 19 conference or invited presentations to date.

Klejdis Bilali is a clinical psychology graduate student at the University of Central Florida's College of Sciences. Her research and clinical interests include trauma resulting from sexual violence, with a focus on survivors of commercial sexual exploitation.

Szilvia D. Biro is a doctoral student in the College of Criminology and Criminal Justice at Florida State University. Her research interests include trauma, victimization, mass incarceration, and urban sociology with an emphasis on housing instability.

Marcus T. Boccaccini, Ph.D., serves as a professor of psychology in the Sam Houston State Department of Psychology. He maintains an active research program focusing on understudied issues in forensic assessment.

Skye C. Bristol is a doctoral student in the College of Behavioral and Community Sciences at the University of South Florida. She graduated from the University of Florida with a Bachelor of Science in Health Education and Behavior, minoring in Sociology and Nonprofit Organizational Leadership. Her previous research experience includes quantitatively analyzing the correlation between school enrollment status and opioid misuse among justice-involved adolescents in the state of Florida. She also conducted research at the Massachusetts Institute of Technology in the Department of Urban Studies and Planning Community Innovators Lab. Her current research focuses on examining health behavior outcomes such as substance misuse and childhood trauma utilizing the Florida Department of Juvenile Justice data.

Calli M. Cain is an assistant professor in the School of Criminology and Criminal Justice at the Florida Atlantic University. Her research interests include victimization, human trafficking, juvenile delinquency, corrections, and sex offender policy.

Melissa Carlson, B.S., is a project manager in the Department of Mental Health, Law, and Policy at the University of South Florida (USF). She received her Bachelor of Science in Behavioral Healthcare with a concentration in Adult Community Sciences from the University of South Florida. For the past eight years, she has collaborated with principal investigators within the field of mental health and substance use that have served adults, children, and families within the Tampa Bay community. She has served as a project coordinator and project manager on over 15 grant-funded projects. These grant projects have resulted in multiple peer-reviewed publications, technical reports, and professional presentations at local, statewide, and national conferences.

Kaci Crook is a graduate student at the University of South Florida's Rehabilitation and Mental Health counseling program. Her research interests include commercial sexual exploitation, substance abuse, and therapeutic interventions.

Carmen L. Diaz, M.S., is a doctoral student in the Department of Criminal Justice at Indiana University. Broadly, her research interests include issues related to race, ethnicity, and class in the criminal justice system, with a particular focus on pretrial and prosecutorial decision making. Her recent work has appeared in the *Journal of Criminal Justice*.

Anna R. Dixon, Ph.D., C.C.D.I. is Associate Professor of Instruction in Anthropology at University of South Floridas. Dr. Dixon has taught full-time at USF since 2011, with specializations in paleoethnobotany, archaeology, and medical anthropology. She also works at the office of the Capital Collateral Regional Counsel – Middle Region as a post-conviction investigator. In addition to Ph.D., M.A., and B.A. degrees in anthropology, she holds certifications in crime scene technology, criminal defense investigation, and paralegal studies and is a member of the National Defense Investigators Association.

Kevin S. Douglas currently is Professor of Clinical-Forensic Psychology, Department of Psychology, Simon Fraser University, Canada. He is also a researcher at the Helse Bergen-HF (Centre for Research and Education in Forensic Psychiatry) and Senior Research Advisor at the Centre for Research and Education in Forensic Psychiatry, Oslo University Hospital-HF. He was President of the American Psychology-Law Society (Division 41 of the American Psychological Association) in 2018–2019 and Treasurer of the International Association of Forensic Mental Health from 2013–2018. His research and professional activities include violence risk assessment and management, implementation of risk assessment protocols into forensic and correctional systems, psychopathy, the association between mental and disorder and violence, and dynamic risk factors. Dr. Douglas is lead author on the latest (third) version of the HCR-20 violence risk assessment measure, published in 2013, which is the most commonly used violence risk assessment instrument worldwide, used in 45+ countries and translated into 25+ languages. Dr. Douglas has authored over 190 journal articles, books, or book chapters and has given over 250 invited presentations or workshops across 20+ countries.

David P. Farrington, O.B.E., is Emeritus Professor of Psychological Criminology at Cambridge University. He has been President of the American Society of Criminology, President of the European Association of Psychology and Law, President of the British Society of Criminology, and President or Chair of several other organizations. He has received many prizes and awards, including the Stockholm Prize in Criminology and the four major awards of the American Society of Criminology. His major research interest is in developmental criminology, and he is Director of the Cambridge Study in Delinquent Development, which is a prospective longitudinal survey of over 400 London males from age 8 to age 61. In addition to 879 published journal articles and book chapters on criminological and psychological topics, he has published 118 books, monographs, and government publications and 164 shorter publications (total = 1,161). According to Google Scholar on October 25, 2021, his publications have been cited a total of 123,286 times; his h-index was 178, which means that 178 of his publications have each been cited at least 178 times, and his i10-index was 771, which means that 771 of his publications have been cited at least 10 times.

Lauren Fournier, M.A., is a doctoral student in clinical psychology at University of South Florida. Her research focuses on ways in which traumatic brain injury may relate to aggressive, externalizing, and criminal offending behavior. Additionally, Lauren is interested in relationships between mental health problems, traumatic brain injury, and criminal justice-related outcomes, such as recidivism.

Emma E. Fridel is an assistant professor in the College of Criminology and Criminal Justice at Florida State University. She received her Ph.D. in criminology and justice policy from Northeastern University. She primarily studies violence and aggression with a focus on homicide, including gun violence, school violence, homicide–suicide, serial and mass murder, and fatal officer-citizen encounters. Dr. Fridel's work has been published in *Criminology*, *Social Forces*, and *Justice Quarterly*, and she is a co-author of *Extreme Killing: Understanding Serial and Mass Murder*.

Lexi Gill is a doctoral student in the Department of Criminology at the University of South Florida. She earned her Master of Science in Criminal Justice and Criminology from the University of Missouri–Kansas City. Her research interests include gun violence, communities and crime, policing, and social network analysis.

Neil Gowensmith, Ph.D., serves as Director of University of Denver's (DU) Forensic Institute for Research, Service, and Training; Associate Professor in the DU Graduate School of Professional Psychology; and Director of the DU Postdoctoral Fellowship in Forensic Psychology. He is a practicing forensic psychologist who also consults with state systems to improve forensic services.

Kelsey Greenfield, J.D., is a doctoral student in the University of South Florida's College of Behavioral and Community Sciences. In 2018, Ms. Greenfield graduated from the University of Florida Levin College of Law and subsequently served as an assistant public defender in Hillsborough County. Prior to attending law school, Ms. Greenfield worked as a research assistant on the Medicare Current Beneficiary Survey (MCBS) while employed by Westat in Washington, D.C. Her areas of interest include mindfulness intervention, program evaluation, and mental health and the law.

Cory P. Haberman, Ph.D., is an associate professor in the School of Criminal Justice and Director of the Institute of Crime Science at the University of Cincinnati. He studies hotspot policing, community problem–oriented policing, police effectiveness, crime analysis, and crime and place.

L. Maaike Helmus is an assistant professor in Criminology at Simon Fraser University in Vancouver, British Columbia, Canada. She is also the Vice-President (Research) for SAARNA (the Society for the Advancement of Actuarial Risk Needs Assessment). Her research has focused on offender risk assessment, particularly regarding risk scale development and validation, risk communication, and biases in decision-making. She is part of the development team for Static-99R, Static-2002R, BARR-2002R, STABLE-2007, ACUTE-2007, VRAG-R, CPORT, and the Risk of Administrative Segregation Tool (RAST). Dr. Helmus also has a particular interest in meta-analysis and statistical approaches to prediction. She is currently co-editor of the journal *Sexual Offending Theory, Research, and Prevention* and on the editorial board of *Sexual Abuse* and *Psychological Assessment*. A former Banting postdoc scholar, she is also the winner of the Governor General's Gold Medal and the Saleem Sham Early Career Award from the American Psychology Law Society and the American Academy of Forensic Psychology.

Heather Henderson, Ph.D., recently completed her dissertation in applied anthropology. In 2018 she completed her master's degree, where her work focused on stigma, lived experiences, and learned helplessness of patients and providers surrounding opioid use disorder. Her dissertation work utilized those findings to construct an ED medication for the opioid use disorder pathway and a broader harm reduction system including the first syringe exchange in Hillsborough County, Florida.

Kelsey S. Henderson, Ph.D., is an assistant professor of criminology & criminal justice at Portland State University. She conducts research on the American courts system, specifically focusing on how people make decisions within the legal system. Her research focuses on questions such as: How do jurors evaluate confession evidence? What factors influence innocent and guilty individuals' plea decisions? How do judges determine if the defendant is making a voluntary, knowing, and intelligent waiver of their rights? In 2019, she was awarded the Department of Criminology & Criminal Justice Professor of the Year award and the College of Urban & Public Affairs Dean's Award for Scholarly Excellence (junior faculty). Her work has been published in a number of high-impact, peer-reviewed journals, including *Law and Human Behavior*, *Psychology, Public Policy and Law*, and *Policing and Society*.

Raquel A. Hernandez is a doctoral candidate in criminology and criminal justice at the University of Maryland. Her research centers on individual and contextual-level disparities in courtroom decision-making, with a primary focus on racial inequality and prosecution.

Lindsay Holcomb is currently serving as a term law clerk for Judge John L. Badalamenti. She holds degrees from Swarthmore College, Columbia University, and the University of Pennsylvania Law School.

Alexander (Alex) M. Holsinger earned a Ph.D. in criminal justice from the University of Cincinnati in the summer of 1999, joining the faculty at the University of Missouri-Kansas City (UMKC) in the fall of that same year. For nearly 30 years, he has been researching, evaluating, and implementing several aspects of effective correctional interventions and behavioral change. Specific areas of concentration include the development of original, and testing of existing, actuarial risk, need, and responsivity assessments and assisting programs and agencies with case planning protocol. He has also conducted many individual program reviews using instruments such as the CPAI and the CPC, as well as large-scale multi-group research designs to quantitatively test program effectiveness. Other accomplishments include the development of agency-level policy for technical violations to enhance the success of justice-involved individuals. In addition to publishing peer-reviewed articles and teaching courses at UMKC, Alex also provides training to local and state agencies focused on the improvement of correctional interventions in an effort to make programming more effective and systems more just and humane.

Sean Houlihan is a doctoral candidate in criminology and criminal justice at the University of Maryland. His research examines differences in the administration of justice across racial and ethnic groups, with a particular focus on prosecution and sentencing.

Michelle Hua graduated from the University of South Florida with a bachelor's in psychology and a minor in criminology. She previously volunteered as a research assistant in the Disinhibition & Affect Regulation Clinical (DARC) Lab and currently works as a psychometrist in the USF Health Neuropsychology clinic. Her research interests broadly involve cognitive and emotional processing in relation to psychopathology.

Shabnam Javdani is an associate professor of applied psychology and Associate Director of the Prison Education Program at New York University. The goal of her work is to understand and eradicate the individual and community impact of persistent inequality, focusing on mental health and legal problems and study community and institutional responses to these complex challenges, with a focus on policy and community-based change approaches. Her research hopes to advance our understanding of people in context and to identify meaningful individual- and systems-level solutions, with a focus on promoting equality for underserved youth and families, girls, and gender-expansive individuals. She is a recognized leader in juvenile justice research and evidence-based intervention, has published 50+ empirical papers, and is supported by federal (e.g., National Institutes of Health) and private (e.g., Ford Foundation) funding.

Chae M. Jaynes, Ph.D., is an assistant professor within the University of South Florida's Department of Criminology. Her research interests include the relationship between employment and crime, the decision to hire justice-involved job applicants, and factors that influence the decision to offend and to accept a guilty plea bargain.

Brian D. Johnson is Professor of Criminology and Criminal Justice at the University of Maryland. He is a past co-editor of *Criminology* and serves as the gubernatorial-appointed Criminal Justice Policy Expert on the Maryland State Commission on Criminal Sentencing. His research focuses on inequalities in prosecution, plea-bargaining, and sentencing, as well as other issues related to criminal punishment. His published work has appeared in various peer-reviewed journals such as the *American Journal of Sociology*, *Criminology*, and *Justice Quarterly*.

Micah E. Johnson is a sociologist trained in criminology and psychiatric epidemiology. He is an assistant professor in the Department of Mental Health Law and Policy at the University of South Florida. His research centers around childhood trauma, behavioral health, and juvenile justice. Dr. Johnson was awarded nearly 3 million dollars in research grants by the National Institutes of Health. His research was cited by the *New York Times*, Senator Bernie Sanders, Charlamagne Tha God, and others. Dr. Johnson published two books in 2021. He wrote a picture book entitled *Never Had a Friend*, which helps to facilitate discussions of trauma, homelessness, adversity, and resilience. The picture book debuted as the #1 new release in the poverty category on Amazon. Dr. Johnson also co-authored *The Little Book of Police Youth Dialogue: A Restorative Path Toward Justice*, which is a leading resource for conducting dialogues between police officers and community members. Dr. Johnson is a pioneer of forensic sociology, serving in the state and federal court system as an expert witness, leveraging the science of trauma and social disadvantage to empower the justice system to make more informed decisions. Please support Dr. Johnson's work by using #DoctorMicahJohnson or visiting DoctorMicahJohnson.com.

Kelly E. Kortright is a doctoral candidate within the University of South Florida's Department of Criminology. Her research interests include developmental life course criminology, risk factors for offending, and mental health in the criminal justice system.

Margaret Bull Kovera is Presidential Scholar and Professor of Psychology at John Jay College of Criminal Justice and the Graduate Center, City University of New York. She received her B.A. in psychology with departmental honors from Northwestern University and her Ph.D. in social psychology from the University of Minnesota. She is an internationally known expert on eyewitness identification and legal decision making, with 25 years of continuous funding from the National Science Foundation for her research on these topics. She was appointed by the American Psychology-Law Society (APLS) to co-author evidence-based recommendations for best practice in the collection of eyewitness identification, recommendations that were endorsed by APLS. Her research on has been published in *Law and Human Behavior*; *Journal of Applied Research in Memory and Cognition*; *Applied Cognitive Psychology*; and *Psychology, Public Policy, and Law*. She is a past president of the American Psychology-Law Society and former Editor-in-Chief of *Law and Human Behavior*, the premier outlet for scholarship in psychology and law. She is a fellow of the Association for Psychological Science, the American Psychological Association, APLS, and several other scholarly societies. She regularly serves as an expert witness in cases involving eyewitness identification.

Charis E. Kubrin is Professor of Criminology, Law and Society at the University of California, Irvine. Her research examines the neighborhood correlates of crime, with an emphasis on race and violent crime. She studies the intersection of neighborhoods, race, and violence to bring attention to pressing social issues and as a means of clarifying and extending social disorganization theory, which considers the effects of 'kinds of places,' specifically different types of neighborhoods, in creating conditions favorable or unfavorable to crime. In addition to her work in peer-reviewed journals, Charis is co-author of *Researching Theories of Crime and Deviance* and *Privileged Places: Race, Residence, and the Structure of Opportunity* (Lynne Rienner) and co-editor of *Introduction to Criminal Justice: A Sociological Perspective* and *Punishing Immigrants: Policy, Politics, and Injustice*. In 2019, she was named a fellow of the American Society of Criminology.

Jacqueline G. Lee is an assistant professor at Boise State University. She earned her Ph.D. from the University of Maryland and was a research assistant at the National Institute of Justice in Washington, D.C., while completing her doctorate. She has also earned a J.D. from the University of Oklahoma. Her research interests include courts and sentencing; criminal justice policy; integration of social science research with legal research; inequalities in the justice system; and the female experience of violence, offending, and punishment.

Narim Lee, M.A., is a doctoral student in the Department of Criminal Justice at the University of Central Florida. Her research interests include help-seeking behaviors of intimate partner violence and the treatment of victims of intimate partner violence. Her most recent research appears in *The Korean Journal of Woman Psychology* and *Criminal Investigation Studies*.

Evan M. Lowder, Ph.D., is an assistant professor in the Department of Criminology, Law and Society at George Mason University and directs the Early Justice Strategies Lab. Her research focuses on strategies to reduce offending and improve behavioral health outcomes among justice-involved adults, with a particular focus on pretrial release, risk assessment, and diversion programs. Her recent work has been published in outlets including the *Journal of Criminal Justice, Justice Quarterly, Criminology & Public Policy,* and *Criminal Justice and Behavior*.

Lindsay C. Malloy is currently an associate professor at Ontario Tech University. Her research addresses questions concerning children's and adolescents' disclosure of negative or traumatic experiences, cognitive and socio-contextual influences on children's memory and narratives, investigative interviewing and interrogation techniques, and implications of research findings for the legal system. Her scholarship is widely cited in both forensic and developmental psychology and has appeared in amicus briefs submitted to the U.S. Supreme Court. She is also co-editor of a 2011 volume concerning children's testimony for academics and legal practitioners. Dr. Malloy's work has resulted in multiple prestigious early career awards (e.g., from Divisions 37 and 41 of the American Psychological Association) and has been supported by grants from several federal agencies in the United States and Canada. Her TED talk on police interrogations with juvenile suspects has been viewed over 1.5 million times.

Christian A. Meissner is a professor of psychology at Iowa State University. He holds a Ph.D. in cognitive & behavioral science from Florida State University (2001) and conducts empirical studies on the psychological processes underlying investigative interviews, including issues surrounding eyewitness recall and identification, deception detection, and interrogations and confessions. His research has facilitated an understanding of factors that lead to false confessions and to the development of evidence-based techniques for developing rapport and trust, enhancing recollection from memory, and improving assessments of credibility. He is a fellow of the Association for Psychological Science, the American Psychological Association, and the Psychonomic Society.

Greg Midgette is an assistant professor of criminology and criminal justice at the University of Maryland. He received his Ph.D. from the Pardee RAND Graduate School and M.P.P. from UCLA. He specializes in program evaluation, policy analysis, and empirical research methods. His work focuses on alcohol and drugs, illicit markets, community corrections, the impact of public safety policies and practices on public health, and the influence of policy design on disparities.

Amelia Mindthoff received her Ph.D. in legal psychology from Florida International University (2020) and is currently a post-doctoral scholar at Iowa State University. Dr. Mindthoff's research primarily focuses on examining the efficacy of evidence-based investigative interviewing methods. She also studies juror perceptions and decision making regarding various topics (e.g., interrogations, forensic evidence). Dr. Mindthoff's research has been funded by the National Science Foundation and the American Psychology-Law Society and has appeared in journals including *Law & Human Behavior* and *Psychology, Public Policy & Law*.

Meghan M. Mitchell is an assistant professor in the Department of Criminal Justice at the University of Central Florida. Through her current research she examines the areas of corrections, subcultures, reentry, and research methodologies.

Ojmarrh Mitchell is an associate professor in the School of Criminology and Criminal Justice at the Arizona State University. Professor Mitchell earned his Ph.D. in criminology and criminal justice from the University of Maryland with a doctoral minor in measurement, statistics, and evaluation. His research interests center on criminal justice policy, particularly in the areas of drug control, sentencing and corrections, and racial fairness in the criminal justice system. More broadly, Dr. Mitchell studies the effectiveness and fairness of criminal justice sanctions. His research has appeared in many criminology journals, including *Justice Quarterly*, *Journal* *of Experimental Criminology*, *Journal of Quantitative Criminology*, *Journal of Research in Crime and Delinquency*, and *Criminology & Public Policy*.

Kathleen A. Moore, Ph.D., is a research professor in USF's Department of Mental Health, Law, and Policy as well as the Executive Director of the Louis de la Parte Florida Mental Health Institute (FMHI). She received her Ph.D. in health psychology from Kent State University and completed a postdoctoral fellowship at Duke University Medical Center. For the past 22 years, she has collaborated with mental health and substance use agencies as well as different problem-solving courts. Her focus is on program evaluation, bridging the gap between research and practice. She also serves on several committees, both within USF and the community such as Hillsborough County Anti-Drug Alliance and drug court steering committees. Dr. Moore has been Co-PI on numerous NIH-related grants, most recently a CDC R01 grant examining 'Effects of Remote Motivational Enhancement and MySafeRx on Post-Detox Engagement and Retention in Buprenorphine Treatment' and a R25 NIDA-funded training grant for a Summer Research Institute with a focus on mentoring rising seniors in behavioral health research. Additionally, she has been PI on over 12 SAMHSA grant projects within drug court and treatment agencies. These grant projects resulted in peer-reviewed publications, technical reports, and professional presentations at local, statewide, and national conferences.

Daniel C. Murrie, Ph.D., serves as Associate Director of the University of Virginia's (UVA) Institute of Law, Psychiatry, and Public Policy; Professor of Psychiatry in the UVA School of Medicine; and Director of the UVA Postdoctoral Fellowship in Forensic Psychology. He is a practicing forensic psychologist who also consults with state systems to improve forensic services.

Anna Newell is a student at the University of Maryland pursuing degrees in psychology, criminology, and criminal justice, with a minor in statistics. Her research interests include juvenile justice policy, drug policy, and quantitative research methods.

Justin Nix is a Distinguished Associate Professor in the School of Criminology and Criminal Justice at the University of Nebraska at Omaha. He received his Ph.D. in Criminology and Criminal Justice from the University of South Carolina. His research is centered on policing with a focus on legitimacy. His work has recently appeared in *Criminology & Public Policy*, *PLOS ONE*, and *Justice Quarterly*.

Kenneth J. Novak received his Ph.D. in criminal justice from the University of Cincinnati and is currently a professor in the Department of Criminal Justice and Criminology at the University of Missouri–Kansas City. He has published scientific research articles on various topics in policing, including officer decision-making, citizens' attitudes toward the police, racially biased policing, and program evaluation. He has conducted research with several criminal justice agencies, including the Kansas City (MO) Police Department; the Jackson County Prosecutor's Office; the Bureau of Alcohol, Tobacco, Firearms, and Explosives; and the U.S. Attorney for the Western District of Missouri.

Meghan A. Novisky is an assistant professor of Criminology at Cleveland State University. Her research investigates the implications of carceral contact on health and well-being, conditions of confinement, and the collateral consequences of criminal justice policy.

Bradley J. O'Guinn is a doctoral student at the University of Cincinnati's School of Criminal Justice. His research interest includes police effectiveness, crime and place, and police organizations.

Mark E. Olver, Ph.D., is Professor and Registered Doctoral Psychologist in the Clinical Psychology Program at the University of Saskatchewan, Canada, where he is involved in graduate and undergraduate research supervision, teaching, administration, clinical training, and applied forensic research. Prior to his academic appointment, Mark worked as a clinical psychologist in various capacities, including providing assessment, treatment, and consultation services for young offenders in the Saskatoon Health Region and for adult federal offenders in the Correctional Service of Canada. He has published over 170 journal articles and book chapters, and his research interests include risk assessment and correctional treatment, justice-involved youth, psychopathy, variations in human sexuality, and the evaluation of therapeutic change. He is the co-developer of the Violence Risk Scale-Sexual Offense version (VRS-SO) and the Violence Risk Scale-Youth Sexual Offense version (VRS-YSO), and he provides training and consultation services internationally in the assessment and treatment of high psychopathy, sexual, and violent offending populations.

Silas Patterson is a doctoral student in the Department of Criminology at the University of South Florida. He holds a master's in criminal justice (M.A., Boise State University). His research focuses on policing, procedural justice and legitimacy, police culture, and police technology.

Jennifer H. Peck, Ph.D., is an associate professor in the Department of Criminal Justice at the University of Central Florida. Her research interests surround racial/ethnic disparities in the juvenile justice system and the treatment of vulnerable populations in criminal justice settings. Her most recent research appears in *Crime & Delinquency, Criminal Justice and Behavior*, and *Youth Violence & Juvenile Justice*.

Gillian M. Pinchevsky is a violence against women (VAW) scholar whose research primarily focuses on criminal justice and community responses to VAW. She received her Ph.D. in Criminology and Criminal Justice from the University of South Carolina. Her recent work has been published in *Feminist Criminology, Journal of Interpersonal Violence*, and *Criminal Justice Review*.

Greg Pogarsky is a professor in the School of Criminal Justice at SUNY–Albany, where he has been since 2001. His research on offender decision making applies principles from behavioral economics and psychology to refine criminological theories. Recent investigations have focused on situational choice processes involving moral considerations, social dynamics, and risk updating.

Joan A. Reid is an associate professor at the University of South Florida St. Petersburg campus and director of the USF Trafficking in Persons Research Lab. She has authored over 50 publications regarding human trafficking, sexual victimization, and child maltreatment in journals such as *Justice Quarterly*, *Sexual Abuse*, and *Child Maltreatment*.

Tara N. Richards is a Distinguished Associate Professor in the School of Criminology and Criminal Justice at the University of Nebraska at Omaha and Co-Director of the Victimology and Victim Studies Research Lab. She received her Ph.D. in Criminology from the University of South Florida. Her research is centered in victimology, with recent articles appearing in *Criminology & Public Policy*, *Journal of Interpersonal Violence*, and *Psychology of Violence*.

Khary K. Rigg, Ph.D., is an associate professor in the Department of Mental Health Law & Policy at the University of South Florida, with additional appointments in the Department of Criminology, Florida Mental Health Institute, and Center for Justice Research & Policy. He holds a Ph.D. in medical sociology from University of Miami and completed a postdoctoral fellowship in health services research from the University of Pennsylvania School of Medicine. His research aims to improve service provision to people with addictive disorders across criminal justice settings.

Ashley E. Rodriguez is an undergraduate student in the Department of Criminology, Law and Society at George Mason University and a research assistant in the Early Justice Strategies Lab. Her research interests include pretrial processes, judicial decision-making, risk assessments, and criminal justice system disparities.

Lillian A. Rodriguez Steen, Ph.D., is an assistant professor in forensic psychology at the College of Saint Rose. She received her doctorate from Ontario Tech University, where she was a member of the Development, Context, and Communication Lab working under the supervision of Dr. Lindsay C. Malloy. She holds a B.A. in psychology from the University of Toledo. Lillian's research is focused broadly on child witnesses and developmentally appropriate interviewing techniques. Her dissertation focuses on the 'ground rules' portion of investigative interviews with children. Specifically, she is examining methods for encouraging children to tell adults when they do not understand their questions as well as how adults perceive children's ground rule applications within an interview context. Her research has been supported by grants from the American Psychology-Law Society, the Society for Research in Child Development, and the Society for the Psychological Study of Social Issues. She hopes to use her research to inform policymakers and all those who question or work with children (e.g., researchers, teachers, doctors) on best practice guidelines for interviewing youth.

Raquel E. Rose is a fifth-year doctoral candidate in counseling psychology at New York University. Her research seeks to understand the impact of trauma, resource precarity, and deficit-based narratives around ethnic minority youth on psychosocial outcomes; influence the effective implementation and evaluation of participatory programs with youth who are legal system involved; and to inform multi-disciplinary efforts to change systems to promote better service delivery and innovation. Raquel's research supports the integration of culturally respectful approaches implemented through community partnerships to empower youth and families. Raquel has served in multiple leadership roles in clinical, advocacy, and academic settings.

Christine L. Ruva is a professor of psychology and Sarasota-Manatee campus chair at the University of South Florida. In 2001, she obtained her Ph.D. in psychology from the University of South Florida in the area of cognitive and neural sciences, where she focused on the application of cognitive psychology to the legal system. For over 20 years, she has explored the effects of pretrial publicity on jurors' perceptions, emotions, memories, interpretation of trial evidence, deliberation behavior, and verdicts. Her research also explores how individual differences of jurors and defendants influence jurors' perceptions, deliberation behaviors, and verdicts. Additionally, her research explores the effectiveness of remedies available to the courts for reducing juror bias (e.g., deliberation, expert testimony, jury instructions, voir dire, and implicit bias remedies). She utilizes both quantitative and qualitative (i.e., content analysis of jury deliberations) methods. Her research has been published in a variety of high-impact psychology and criminology journals, including the following: *Criminal Justice and Behavior; Journal of Experimental Psychology-Applied*; *Law and Human Behavior*; *Psychology, Crime and Law; Psychology, Public Policy, and Law.*

Mateus R. Santos, Ph.D., is an assistant professor in the Department of Criminology at the University of South Florida. His research focuses on the drivers of crime and criminal justice trends, on the effects of crime policy, and on the applications of quantitative methods to criminology.

Jacob Scocca is a Ph.D. student in criminology and criminal justice at the University of Maryland. His research agenda is focused on LGBT+ topics in criminology, along with various topics at the nexus of psychology and criminology.

Ali Andrew Shakoor, J.D., is a senior attorney at Capital Collateral Regional Counsel with a multifaceted background. He is a post-conviction attorney with nearly 20 years of experience in the criminal law field, and he has over 20 years of experience as a part-time instructor with his family's company, JYS Consultants-PosiPower Concepts, Inc. (www.posipowercomcepts.com). As a practicing attorney, Ali has argued cases before the Florida Supreme Court and the United States Court of Appeals for the Eleventh Circuit. In the past, Ali was an instructor for the University of Phoenix teaching criminal justice and constitutional law. He received his Juris Doctor (cum laude) from Capital University Law School in Columbus, Ohio. He earned his B.A. at The Ohio State University with a major in political science and minors in women's studies and Black studies. Ali served as a volunteer for Big Brothers Big Sisters of America and Boys and Girls Clubs of America and is currently mentoring teens in Hillsborough County Schools. He enjoys training/facilitating and is an inspiring public speaker. He published a book titled *For Black Men Trying to Survive and Thrive in America: A Defense Attorney's Advice and Life Experiences*. Ali is committed to helping to improve the lives of others. He is passionate about criminal justice.

J. Amanda Sharry is a doctoral student in criminology, law, and society at the University of California, Irvine. Her research focuses on the genesis and effects of poverty and inequality, specifically how it relates to social marginality, formerly incarcerated populations, and the labor market.

Kendall Smith, B.A., is a lab coordinator in the Department of Psychology at the University of South Florida, where she also earned her bachelor's degree in psychology and criminology. Her research interests are centered in disinhibition, psychopathy, and psychological intersections within the criminal legal system, including clinical risk assessment and bias.

Keira C. Stockdale, Ph.D., is a registered doctoral psychologist who currently practices in Saskatoon, Saskatchewan, Canada. She is presently employed in an operational capacity with Saskatoon Police Service and serves as an adjunct professor in the Department of Psychology at the University of Saskatchewan. Her clinical experiences have included the provision of assessment and treatment services to violent and high-risk adult and young offenders in both institutional and community settings. She also works with university, government, and police partners to design, implement, and evaluate integrated community safety responses to reduce interpersonal violence and criminal recidivism.

Bryan L. Sykes is an associate professor in the Department of Sociology and the Jeb E. Brooks School of Public Policy at Cornell University. He studies racial inequality, mass incarceration, demography, law and society, population health, and research methodology.

Emily Torres, M.S., is the center coordinator at the Center for Justice Research and Policy (CJRP) at the University of South Florida. Emily holds a master's degree in criminology from Florida State University. Her research interests include corrections, reentry, and criminal justice policy.

Alexander G. Toth is the Dean of the Center for Public Safety at Seminole State College of Florida. Dean Toth earned his Ph.D. in criminology from the University of South Florida and his M.S. in criminal justice from the University of Cincinnati. He has over 30 years of military, local, and federal law enforcement experience. He served as a U.S. Drug Enforcement Administration (DEA) special agent for over 25 years. At the time of his retirement from the DEA, he was in charge of Bolivia, Paraguay, Argentina, Chile, and Brazil. His research interests are in transnational crime, drug enforcement, and policing. His research has appeared in the *Journal of Experimental Criminology*, *Deviant Behavior*, and the *International Journal of Drug Policy*.

Rebecca Tublitz, M.P.P., is a doctoral student in the Department of Criminology, Law & Society at the University of California, Irvine. Her research explores criminal justice reform, inequality, courts, and corrections. She has over 10 years of experience working with state and local governments to conduct applied research, program evaluation, and technical assistance in criminal justice and corrections. Her work has appeared in the peer-reviewed journals *Justice Quarterly* and *PLOS One*.

Jillian J. Turanovic is an associate professor and Director of the Crime Victim Research and Policy Institute in the College of Criminology and Criminal Justice at Florida State University. Her research focuses on various issues in criminological theory and correctional policy, with a special focus on victimization, violence, and youth development.

Ashley L. White is an assistant professor at the University of Wisconsin-Madison. Before her appointment at UW-Madison, Dr. White served as the 2019–2020 Joseph P. Kennedy Public Policy Fellow with the Committee on Education and Labor under Chairman Robert 'Bobby' C. Scott and has worked in several other policy spaces. Before earning her Ph.D. from the University of South Florida, White taught school for 15 years, primarily in special education settings. Dr. White researches the intersectionality of ethno-racial identities and disability across the educational spectrum through the consideration of student and educator experiences in P–postsecondary settings, applicable federal legislation and other policies, related socioeconomic impact with attention to historicized context, and the sociological construct of race. Additionally, Dr. White invests time in working with school districts across the country to advance professional development for teachers related to special education, disability, and intersectional issues. Dr. White also serves as the inaugural Education Fellow for Equity Access and Opportunity with the National Association for the Advancement of Colored People (NAACP).

Jason W. Wilson, M.D., M.A., is an emergency medicine physician and medical anthropologist. He is interested in the direct deployment of social scientists into the clinical space in order to break down entanglements and to consider new assemblages of care in the construction of patient-centered pathways. He serves as the Medical Director of the Clinical Decision Unit, the Research Director for Emergency Medicine, and the Associate Medical Director of the Emergency Department at Tampa General Hospital. He is an associate professor in the University of South Florida Morsani College of Medicine.

Svetlana Yampolskaya is a research professor in the Department of Child & Family Studies, University of South Florida. She is a sociologist by training, but her primary expertise and research interests lie in improvement of well-being for at-risk youth. Within this area of research, Dr. Yampolskaya conducted numerous studies examining issues related to child maltreatment, fatal child abuse, mental health, and involvement with juvenile justice among child welfare–involved youth. Another focus of her work has been the application of advanced statistical methods in behavioral health and child welfare services research, with specific emphasis on the utilization of large administrative data sets or data that have been previously collected. Dr. Yampolskaya's current research interests include prevention of adverse outcomes for youth involved in multiple systems as well as innovative methodological approaches.

Introduction

1

EVIDENCE-BASED APPROACHES AND IMPLEMENTATION CHALLENGES AND SOLUTIONS

Edelyn Verona and Bryanna Fox

Introduction and Overview

The criminal justice system, as well as the programs, policies, and practices within it, is principally responsible for ensuring that justice is served fairly, effectively, and efficiently to those involved in and impacted by the system. However, too many of the current policies used to reduce crime and effectuate justice have been developed from anecdotes, historical practice, political pressure, cultural norms, and unscientific opinion rather than evidence-based approaches demonstrated to be effective through empirical research (Sherman et al., 1998). This has produced massive negative outcomes, such as mass incarceration, conflict between police and the community, ballooning criminal justice costs with limited effect on crime, and other well-founded concerns over bias, ineffectiveness, lack of fairness, and potential long-term negative consequences of justice involvement.

As an example, despite a consistent and significant drop in crime in the United States over the past few decades, more than 12 million Americans are booked into local jails annually, and about 575,000 individuals enter state prisons each year (Minton & Zeng, 2015). However, research consistently shows that this mass incarceration policy has little impact on crime yet causes catastrophic collateral effects on human, community, and financial resources; increases in structural racial, ethnic, and socioeconomic bias; and substantial harm to justice-involved individuals and their families (particularly when diversion approaches for most low-level offenses would yield far better effects; Bratton, 2011; Durlauf & Nagin, 2011). Specifically, studies show that the longer persons are incarcerated, the more likely it is that they will lose housing, employment, and prospects in the labor market (Dobbie et al., 2018; Freudenberg et al., 2005; Snodgrass et al., 2011); experience lasting psychological impact and disrupted social and familial bonds (Sugie & Turney, 2017); and, in the end, still reenter the justice system post-release (Lowenkamp et al., 2012; Subramanian et al., 2015). This leads to the obvious question: given the lack of intended effects and substantial negative consequences of mass incarceration, why would some of these harmful criminal justice practices continue?

The goal of this book is to describe the most useful, actionable, and evidence-based solutions to many of the most pressing questions in the criminal justice system today. These solutions are realized by increasing the volume and quality of research, promoting strong researcher–practitioner partnerships and effective evidence-based practices that emanate from

DOI: 10.4324/9781003219286-2

those collaborations, and reducing the research–practitioner gap by improving accessibility of the best and latest scientific research.

First, this book outlines the practical reasons for agencies and practitioners to implement evidence-based practices and invest in research and evaluation. Criminal justice agencies are routinely provided limited funds to enact their mission, with new questions and issues constantly arising. This book helps practitioners quickly identify which practices work and don't work and where more research is needed. We hope this will help foster collaborations and new research on burgeoning problems to then inform new solutions and evidence-based practices. Further, given the limited resources and the considerable needs of criminal justice agencies, it makes sense to eliminate wasteful and ineffective practices and replace them with those that have been shown to work or are at least promising in solving problems. This book provides recommendations for reducing the reliance on ineffective and/or unfair programs, policies, and practices and decreasing the potential unintended consequences associated with practices that cannot be eliminated completely (e.g., incarceration). Finally, this book speaks to researchers as to the gaps in the literature that need to be filled for research to inform policy and how to adequately address the needs of agencies and systems in their research. We believe that recent world events have underscored both the importance of relying on science to inform policy and practice and the essential need for fairness, justice, and a reliance on evidence-based recommendations.

This book represents the intersection of these goals, with the message that evidence-based research is vital to improve the criminal justice system and to ensure that justice is served fairly, effectively, and efficiently. This edited volume contains brief and accessible summaries of the best available research, alongside detailed descriptions of evidence-based practices, across multiple sectors of the criminal justice system (e.g., crime prevention and criminal justice policy, policing, courts and sanctioning, corrections). Each chapter is written by the top scholars and practitioners in each of the areas of the criminal justice system covered in this book, where the authors attended to accessibility of the content so that practitioners and researchers alike can use the text as reference. We look forward to sharing these chapters but first aim to dive into the criteria to be considered an evidence-based approach and why these policies and practices are so crucial in the criminal justice system.

What Is Evidence-Based Practice?

Evidence-based practice relies on rigorous research and evaluation to guide decisions about policies and practices shown to work for particular problems and persons (Golder et al., 2005). In our view, there are at least three ways in which persons can engage in evidence-based practice. The *first approach* is to *implement* specific programs and practices that have been tested through scientific methods and shown to produce meaningfully positive outcomes for the problems and settings in which one works. This can require practitioners keeping up with the research literature and understanding to some extent the methods behind the science. This task is made easier by resources provided by agencies like the Department of Justice, which hosts the website Crimesolutions.org, providing a list of programs (i.e., typically, packages of practices and activities carried out according to guidelines) and practices (i.e., more general strategies) in the field rated as 'effective', 'promising', and 'no effects'. This is a highly useful resource for practitioners interested in implementing new practices that have been shown to work.

It should be noted that ratings of quality and determinations of effectiveness of programs are weighted in part on the rigor of the research methods used, in which rigorous experiments are considered the best evidence for whether a program or practice works (or not). This is detailed in the Maryland Scientific Methods Scale (Farrington et al., 2003), which consists of a 5-point scale that measures the 'quality' of the research based primarily on the extent to which the methodology involves randomization and minimizes threats to internal validity. Internal validity is higher when you can control for extraneous factors to better determine that the effects of a program are due to the program and not external factors. Higher-quality studies are typically those involving at least a matched comparison group or statistical control for group differences, and the highest-rated would involve random assignment (randomized controlled trial, or RCT).

Because the use of control groups and randomized experiments in the field (e.g., randomizing persons in a prison to receive one type of program and the others another type) is difficult if not prohibitive in criminal justice research, the research base involving these types of rigorous evaluations is small, and there are many settings or problems for which there are few resulting evidence-based practices. Further, the heavy reliance on these assessments of research quality based on having high internal validity has been criticized, because it is often assumed that these experiments represent the true situations we are faced with in the field (Laub & Frisch, 2016; Nagin & Sampson, 2019). In fact, conducting such studies in which we can infer causality often comes at the sacrifice of external validity. External validity is higher when the study procedures reflect how the program or practice will be implemented in actuality in the field. An evaluation can have high internal validity by randomizing participants to groups and by controlling for extraneous factors but it may not work in the setting to which it should be applied because the conditions are so different or 'messier' in the field.

As such, besides working to implement particular programs that have been shown to work for particular problems (*content*), the *second approach* to evidence-based practice involves knowing how to approach problems in a logical and scientific way (*process*) and avoiding the mistake of relying on what has been done for years that has led to the maintenance or exacerbation of the problem. An evidence-based approach to problems in organizations would involve reviewing what is known by research, figuring out ways to use that information to come up with potential solutions, and continuously assessing the strategies implemented in relation to the outcomes desired. This approach does not necessarily involve implementing already-identified programs wholesale, especially if no evaluations of programs or practices for one's particular problem are available, but instead using what is known about general practices or strategies and organizational structures to come up with and internally evaluate solutions within organizations. This is a tall order, of course, but it provides practitioners an opportunity to flexibly integrate approaches that have been shown to produce better outcomes, even when the implementation of full programs is not possible.

Indeed, there are many circumstances where there are barriers to implementing evidence-based policies, even when they are shown to be effective. As is often noted throughout the criminal justice world: we often dislike how it is, but we also hate change. This translates to the reluctance to implement new practices simply because it is a change, even if the change is likely positive to the agency. In this case, demonstrating the benefits of implementing evidence-based policies as opposed to the negative effects of maintaining the status quo can help overcome hesitancy. For instance, this book contains many chapters that present 'cost-benefit' analyses: how much agencies, taxpayers, and the criminal justice system may stand to save if a specific policy is implemented, as opposed to costs of maintaining less effective programs. Typically, enumerating the cost-savings and benefits to the organization and community is highly effective in overcoming resistance to new and unknown evidence-based practices (Cullen et al., 2009). This book aims to assist with that effort.

The *third approach* towards evidence-based practice, which we heavily emphasize in this book, is the advancement of scientist–practitioner collaborations. Several of the chapters in this book address how to make these connections and successfully pursue partnerships that benefit the organization and the field. These collaborations between researchers and policymakers are highly needed if we are to make headway on changing policies that currently do not work or are harmful. Unfortunately, there is evidence that criminal justice policymakers and practitioners rarely consult the research literature when making policy decisions (Lum et al., 2012; Alpert et al., 2013) and tend to rely on their peers or trade organizations for advice. At the same time, researchers often speak only to audiences of other academics, use technical jargon, and publish in venues that are not accessible to practitioners. There is also a lot that researchers can learn from practitioners and policymakers, especially about how programs are actually implemented and what types of practices fit best within organizations. For researchers, implementing and evaluating practices in the field and in collaboration with practitioners is critical to determining what agency structures and climates allow programs to be successful and what challenges are actually encountered in implementation.

We acknowledge the many barriers to these collaborations, often due to differences in perceived alignment of goals and inability to even understand each other at times. We believe that, in the end, we all share the same goal: to improve fairness, effectiveness, and long-term outcomes for all those who engage in or work for the criminal justice system and to improve safety and quality of life for all. As such, we strive in this book to guide readers as to how researchers and criminal justice practitioners can work towards achieving this goal in a symbiotic fashion and to bridge gaps in understanding. That said, there may be times where our goals initially appear to diverge, and this can be overcome. For instance, researchers may seek data and access to implement and evaluate policies as part of their goal to produce research, publish, secure tenure, and gain status in the field. Practitioners may hope to reduce strains on their already over-burdened staff by declining requests for data, prevent criticisms of their agency by refusing the chance to collaborate on a new practice, and avoid transparency if they are asked to collaborate with a researcher they do not trust. These divergencies are notable, but in many ways, they can be overcome if both parties approach the problem in good faith. For instance, researchers willing to take on this work should enter collaborations with the aim to reduce burden on the agency and to prioritize positive impact on the community to gain trust and maximize benefits of the collaboration. Practitioners who really want to gain the most out of the experience should aim to foster relationships with researchers through a spirit of sharing, transparency, and ultimately a focus on what is in the best interest for the public (Burch, 2015). In sum, by demonstrating the benefits of strong researcher–practitioner collaborations, which we believe is the best means of developing and evaluating evidence-based practices, we hope this book will inspire new researcher–practitioner partnerships and the development of the next generation of fair and effective practices in the criminal justice system.

As noted in this section:

- Evidence-based practice can include implementing programs and practices that have been shown to work and testing them in one's particular organization
- Evidence-based practice can also include approaching problems in a systematic and research-based way within organizations, as well as doing internal evaluations of the practices currently being used
- Evidence-based practice can also include engaging in research-agency collaborations to understand practices and policies that work and how they can be implemented successfully, given structural barriers

What's to Come?

It is hoped that this book will serve as an essential guide for researchers and practitioners in the criminal justice field as they apply the latest research evidence to the work that they do every day. This book makes a case to practitioners about the benefits of using empirically tested and validated practices in their work and to public and advocacy organizations about ways to help persons involved in the justice system. Besides making this case, each chapter of the book contains a list of action items based upon the best available scientific research that can be implemented in practice to address key issues and long-standing challenges in the criminal justice system. Although theory is a guide for the practices described, the chapters will address practical issues in implementation and action.

Importantly, the book addresses best practices and recommendations across a range of settings and criminal justice sectors. Researchers and practitioners in many areas of criminal justice – crime prevention, juvenile justice, risk and needs assessment, policing, courts, sanctions and sentencing, corrections, and policy – can reference specific chapters in this book to guide their policy and practice decisions.

Beginning with Part 1 (Crime Prevention) of the book, the chapters explore the practices and overall efficacy of crime prevention initiatives that address critical risk factors for offending. These topics will include multi-component evidence-based strategies that aim to address crime in the community and/or within the justice system. These programs include community-based interventions aimed at improving socio-economic and structural risk factors that are known to disproportionately increase the risk of crime, particularly in urban and impoverished communities. Drug use, unemployment, and mental health issues can also bring individuals in contact with the criminal justice system, and the chapters in this section review evidence-based practices that can deter involvement in the system. Importantly, community-oriented harm reduction programs and a focus on public health strategies have the potential to curb negative outcomes among individuals with medical, mental health, and drug problems. Chapters in this section also address services for potential victims of crime, including how to prevent human trafficking and guidance on navigating the psychological and legal consequences of crime victimization. In sum, these issues and strategies are incredibly important for academics and practitioners alike, and it is no accident that the crime prevention section of the book has several chapters devoted to it.

Part 2 (Juvenile Justice and Early Interventions) follows naturally from the previous section on crime prevention by tackling the multiple issues faced by those who work with youth engaged in or at risk of becoming involved in the juvenile justice system. The chapters in this section focus on formative contexts for prevention and intervention, including the home, school, community, out-of-home placements, and the juvenile justice system itself. This section reviews the most promising practices that help reduce exposure to iatrogenic effects of detention and contact with law enforcement and provide developmentally appropriate and accessible services and enrichment to youth.

Part 3 (Predictors of Crime and Risk Assessment) of the book examines risk factors and assessment instruments that help inform decisions on sanctions, tailor interventions, reduce recidivism, and ensure public safety. Chapters in this section will provide information on early predictors (psychosocial, educational, and cognitive risk factors; risk perceptions), including history of trauma and abuse, as well as discussing validated risk assessments used with populations of interest (e.g., sexual and violent offenders). The implementation science behind the appropriate use of risk assessment instruments across contexts will also be described. Based on the assessment of risk factors, we can implement risk and needs-responsive interventions that have been shown to reduce re-offending and re-incarceration.

Part 4 (Policing) is one of great interest to many readers interested in evidence-based practices in criminal justice, an area with substantial opportunity to improve investigations, crime reduction, and public support for the work. In an era of increased scrutiny of police and public demand for crime reduction, alongside reductions in budgets and quality of relations with the community, law enforcement is often searching for answers to address these combined concerns. The chapters in this section overview evidence-based practices shown to successfully reduce crime and violence such as hotspot policing and use of technology. The chapters also highlight the most effective programs and policies to address salient and widespread crime problems, such as domestic violence and drug enforcement. Finally, this section will provide evidence-based recommendations on issues surrounding engagement with the community and suspects, such as interviewing and interrogation techniques and enhancement of positive police–community relations through procedural justice models.

Part 5 (The Courts) of the book details evidence-based practices that address major issues throughout the court system and sanctions, to include effects of prosecutorial discretion and overwork and burnout among public defenders. The chapters in this section also review the use of competency assessments and strategies for competency restoration, the impact and potential 'blind spots' of eyewitnesses and how to improve eyewitness validity, and advances in juror education to help reduce potential biases in outcomes. The chapters also address the role of judges and their discretion in bond and sentencing decisions. Finally, this section reviews the evidence for problem solving courts, particularly drug court, as alternatives to incarceration, with discussion of the determination of who qualifies for these programs and best practices when implementing them.

Part 6 (Corrections) deals with the correctional system, detention, and community supervision, reviewing their practices and programs and what strategies yield the best outcomes for inmates, returning citizens, and the public. Chapters in this section address the evidence for various in-custody support programs and services and practices that increase inmate safety and reduce negative effects of incarceration. Upon release or in the community, individuals require support and evidence-based strategies to improve reentry success, supervise them through parole and probation services, and help them access treatment for drug use disorder to avoid overdose mortality and continued offending. Details are provided about evidence-based programs or policies that have been shown to improve rehabilitation, reduce in-custody victimization, support successful reentry, and enhance the deterrent effect of community supervision and treatment.

Part 7 (Considerations for Policy Change) culminates with discussions of controversies surrounding some of the most highly impactful policy issues as they relate to the justice system, to include drug laws, the death penalty, firearm regulation, bail reform, and mass incarceration. In light of the increasing attention of the media and the public to the biases and disparities inherent to the criminal justice system, chapters in this section also review research on policies that are often applied inequitably. This research is used to provide guidance for moving in new directions, with chapters that address policy change with regard to anti-racism and equity work across the justice system.

We end with a Conclusions and Integration chapter, summarizing the main points that practitioners and academics should keep in mind as they implement and promote evidence-based practices or shifts in policy in their organizations. This chapter highlights how the previous sections of the book provide helpful guidance on effective programs and practices in specific domains or settings (*content*) and on ways of approaching problems that are backed by research (*process*). It also aims to demonstrate how different practices affect different stages of the system, and we identify how certain approaches may address issues as individuals move through the separate sectors of the justice system. We also weave in examples to illustrate how evidence-based practices implemented at various stages may shape persons' experiences as they go through the criminal justice process.

Conclusion

To conclude, this book aims to address the goal of achieving greater effectiveness, efficiency, fairness, and public safety through criminal justice practices and policies by serving as a reference guide on the evidence-based policies across all sectors of the criminal justice system – from prevention and policing to sentencing and corrections. Given that this book covers the most timely, and timeless, issues across all major domains of the criminal justice system, many audiences could benefit from the material presented. In particular, criminal justice practitioners (e.g., police officers and executives, judges, prosecutors, probation officers, juvenile justice staff, etc.), allied professionals (e.g., social/case workers, child welfare, forensic psychologists), and policymakers (e.g., city mayors; governors; local, state, and federal legislators; their staff) will benefit from the accessible reviews of research as they pursue the development, implementation, and support of the programs, policies, and practices used throughout all aspects of the criminal justice system. At the same time, academics, applied researchers, and trainees/students can find herein the best available literature, which provides a foundation for those researching, evaluating, and recommending programs, policies, and practices in the criminal justice system. Finally, we anticipate that individuals from the public (e.g., advocacy groups, media, and engaged citizens) can benefit from the accessible format of the content and strong interest in these issues by these groups. Each chapter contains a list of action items based upon the best available scientific research that can be implemented in practice to address key issues and long-standing challenges in the criminal justice system. We also hope this book serves as an inspiration to motivate future research to develop evidence-based solutions to tomorrow's criminal justice challenges today.

References

Alpert, G. P., Rojek. J., & Hansen, J. A. (2013). *Building bridges between police researchers and practitioners: Agents of change in a complex world* (Final report submitted to the U.S.). Department of Justice.

Bratton, W. J. (2011). Reducing crime through prevention not incarceration. *Criminology and Public Policy*, *10*(1), 63–68.

Burch II, J. H. (2015). The evolution toward integrating science and evidence in U.S. Department of Justice agencies–An insider's reflections. *Translational Criminology*, *8*, 2–4.

Cullen, F., Myer, A., & Latessa, E. (2009). Eight lessons from moneyball: The high cost of ignoring evidence-based corrections. *Victims and Offenders*, *4*, 197–213.

Dobbie, W., Goldin, J., & Yang, C. S. (2018). The effects of pre-trial detention on conviction, future crime, and employment: Evidence from randomly assigned judges. *American Economic Review*, *108*(2), 201–240.

Durlauf, S., & Nagin, D. (2011). Imprisonment and crime: Can both be reduced? *Criminology and Public Policy*, *10*(1), 13–55.

Farrington, D. P., Gottfredson, D. C., Sherman, L. W., & Welsh, B. C. (2003). The Maryland scientific methods scale. In *Evidence-based crime prevention* (pp. 13–21). Routledge.

Freudenberg, N., Daniels, J., Crum, M., Perkins, T., & Richie, B. E. (2005). Coming home from jail: the social and health consequences of community reentry for women, male adolescents, and their families and communities. *American Journal of Public Health*, *95*(10), 1725–1736.

Golder, S., Ivanoff, A., Cloud, R. N., Besel, K. L., McKiernan, P., Bratt, E., & Bledsoe, L. K. (2005). Evidence-based practice with adults in jails and prisons. *Best Practices in Mental Health*, *1*(2), 100–132.

Laub, J. H., & Frisch, N. E. (2016). Translational criminology: A new path forward. In T. Blomberg, J. M. Brancale, K. M. Beaver, & W. Bales (Eds.), *Advancing criminology and criminal justice policy* (pp. 78–88). Routledge.
Lowenkamp, C. T., Holsinger, A. M., Robinson, C. R., & Cullen, F. T. (2012). When a person isn't a data point: Making evidence-based practice work. *Federal Probation*, *76*, 11.
Lum, C., Telep, C. W., Koper, C. S., & Greico, J. (2012). Receptivity to research in policing. *Justice Research and Policy*, *14*(1), 61–95.
Minton, T. D., & Zeng, Z. (2015). Jail inmates at midyear 2014. *NCJ*, *241264*.
Nagin, D. S., & Sampson, R. J. (2019). The real gold standard: Measuring counterfactual worlds that matter most to social science and policy. *Annual Review of Criminology*, *2*, 123–145.
Sherman, L., Gottfredson, D., MacKenzie, D., Eck, J., Reuter, P., & Bushway, S. (1998). Preventing crime: What works, what doesn't what's promising. National Institute of Justice Research in Brief. Retrieved from www.ncjrs.gov/pdffiles/171676.PDF
Snodgrass, M. G., Blokland, A., Haviland, A., Nieuwbeerta, P., & Nagin, D. (2011). Does the time cause the crime? An examination of the relationship between time served and reoffending in the Netherlands. *Criminology*, *49*(4), 1149–1194.
Subramanian, R., Delaney, R., Roberts, S., Fishman, N., & McGarry, P. (2015). *Incarceration's front door: The misuse of jails in America*. Vera Institute of Justice.
Sugie, N. F., & Turney, K. (2017). Beyond incarceration: Criminal justice contact and mental health. *American Sociological Review*, *82*(4), 719–743.

PART I

Crime Prevention

2
SOCIAL DISORGANIZATION THEORY AND COMMUNITY-BASED INTERVENTIONS

Charis E. Kubrin and Rebecca Tublitz

Social Disorganization Theory

Crime is not randomly distributed; rather, it clusters in certain areas. It is for this reason that some neighborhoods acquire reputations as "good" or "bad." Social disorganization theory, one of only a handful of social structural theories of crime, takes this fact – the non-random distribution of crime across space – as a point of departure and asks: Why is crime higher in some places than others?

The answer, according to the theory, is that some communities are unable to realize common goals and solve local problems, like crime (Kornhauser, 1978; Bursik, 1988). Underscoring this is the notion that we do not need communities so much to satisfy our private needs, which are best met elsewhere, but to express and realize *common* values and standards.

The theory posits communities exist along a spectrum of organization, with socially organized neighborhoods on one end and socially disorganized neighborhoods on the other. The former is marked by solidarity (internal consensus on norms and values such as a crime-free community), cohesion (strong bonds among neighbors), and integration (social interaction among residents) (Kubrin & Wo, 2016, p. 122). The latter, however, lack these characteristics, and thus have higher crime rates.

The connection between social organization and crime has to do with informal social control, defined as the scope of collective action a community directs toward local problems (Kornhauser, 1978; Shaw & McKay, 1969). Where formal social control refers to practices of authorities (i.e., police) to maintain order and enforce the law, informal social control reflects residents' efforts to prevent or sanction criminal conduct through informal surveillance of the streets and direct intervention in problems, such as questioning persons about suspicious activity, admonishing those who are misbehaving, and informing parents about their children's misconduct (Kubrin & Weitzer, 2003, pp. 375–76). When residents act as the "eyes and ears" of the community, their informal surveillance – and even simple presence – can deter others from committing crime (Kubrin & Wo, 2016, p. 122). Social disorganization theory privileges informal control because it is community based and more central to preventing crime, whereas formal social control is often exercised by institutions based outside the neighborhood, which typically respond only after a crime has occurred (Kubrin & Weitzer, 2003, p. 381).

DOI: 10.4324/9781003219286-4

In determining which structural characteristics impact informal social control, early theorists focused on the effects of neighborhood poverty, residential instability, and racial and ethnic heterogeneity. Consider residential instability, or the frequency with which residents move in and out of neighborhoods. Some communities are stable, with residents living in the same homes for decades, while others are unstable and experience significant turnover. Residential instability can disrupt a neighborhood's network of social relations. As residents move in and out, it becomes harder for them to know, trust, and interact with one another, reducing informal social control. Thus, communities marked by high rates of turnover should experience high crime rates, precisely because these communities suffer from low levels of informal social control, a finding demonstrated in the literature (Bellair, 2000; Chamlin, 1989; Kubrin, 2000; Sampson & Groves, 1989; Warner & Rountree, 1997). Scholars have examined a range of structural sources of social disorganization, including unemployment and joblessness, immigration, family disruption (i.e., divorce and single-parent households), population density, and land use characteristics.

Early empirical tests reveal support for social disorganization theory (Sampson & Groves, 1989), yet findings from more recent evaluations question the claim that strong social ties generate informal social control, which, in turn, prevents crime. Research on the impact of social ties reveals that even infrequent interaction among residents can reduce crime (Bellair, 1997; Warner & Rountree, 1997; see also Granovetter, 1973). Moreover, dense networks of strong ties may not be sufficient, in and of themselves, to fulfill social control functions, as originally thought (Browning et al., 2004; Kubrin & Weitzer, 2003; Pattillo, 1998; Sampson, 2006). Social ties thus help *or* hinder social organization, depending on the actors involved and their interests.

In a study of a middle-class Black neighborhood in Chicago, Pattillo (1998) finds that residents are highly connected to one another and that these strong ties are characterized by emotional investment and frequent interaction. As a result, the neighborhood is able to keep crime to a relatively acceptable level through the supervision of youth, identification of strangers, and mobilization of community organizations. Yet the value of these ties comes with a trade-off, as they connect law-abiding residents with those breaking the law in the neighborhood; residents are often reluctant to publicly shame or legally sanction those with whom they are closely tied, even when they witness illegal behavior. In short, social ties are not automatically equated with effective social control because: 1) weak ties can be equally important in the activation of informal social control; 2) strong ties can undermine social control efforts; and, 3) social ties may connect law-abiding citizens with criminals and vice versa (Sampson, 2006).

Social ties must be activated, and resources mobilized, in order to enhance social control (Sampson et al., 1997). For this to occur, residents must develop a willingness to take action, which depends on conditions of mutual trust and solidarity among neighbors. The concept of "collective efficacy" captures this linkage of mutual trust and the willingness to intervene for the common good (Sampson, 1997; Sampson et al., 1999). Collective efficacy advances previous theorizing by accounting for mechanisms of social action that may be facilitated by, but do not necessarily require, an interconnected network of strong ties (Sampson, 2006, p. 152).

In their study of Chicago neighborhoods, Sampson and colleagues (1997) empirically demonstrate that collective efficacy is negatively associated with violent crime and that associations of concentrated disadvantage and residential instability with violent crime are largely mediated by collective efficacy. Studies generally document support for the role of collective efficacy (Browning, 2009; Browning et al., 2004; Mazerolle et al., 2010; Sampson & Raudenbush, 1999).

From this discussion, takeaways to consider for evidence-based programs, policies, or practices derived from social disorganization theory include:

- Social disorganization theory is a "kinds of places" rather than "kinds of people" theory;
- Social disorganization is a property of neighborhoods, not individuals. As such, residents of a neighborhood are not disorganized; rather, the community in which they reside is disorganized;
- Neighborhood ecological conditions shape crime rates over and above the characteristics of individual residents;
- Ecological characteristics such as poverty and residential instability are related to crime largely *indirectly* through neighborhood processes such as collective efficacy, which emphasize the linkage of mutual trust and the willingness to intervene for the common good;
- These insights point to crime control interventions that bolster communities' capacity to develop and sustain collective efficacy and generate pro-social norms.

Evidence-Based Community-Centered Interventions

Social disorganization theory has informed community crime prevention initiatives since its earliest days (Bursik & Grasmick, 1993). Most famously, it informed the Chicago Area Project, a program established in the 1930s by one of the theory's originators that sought to address juvenile delinquency in disadvantaged Chicago neighborhoods (Kobrin, 1959). The Chicago Area Project focused on two goals: strengthening local institutions, such as the family, community organizations, and religious and school groups, and developing conventional norms and values (Schlossman & Sedlak, 1983). Central to this approach was allowing local institutions and leaders to design and deliver crime prevention strategies, which included street outreach and counseling to youth at high risk of committing delinquency, organized recreational activities, and advocacy for youth involved with formal social welfare and juvenile justice systems. Despite intentions, little evidence for its effectiveness exists (Bursik & Grasmick, 1993; Kobrin, 1959) and the program ultimately failed to build community institutions able to sustain themselves without external support (Hope, 1995; Wickes, 2017).

Subsequent community crime prevention efforts draw from the Chicago Area Project model and social disorganization theory, incorporating elements of community mobilization, direct service, tenant involvement, modification of the built environment, and increasing informal surveillance, among other strategies (for a comprehensive review, see Hope, 1995). However, crime prevention programs that rely primarily on local communities to address crime and delinquency without external support (e.g., funding from government or foundations) rarely yield positive results (Hope, 1995). These efforts are often mired by implementation and resource challenges; studies that lack sufficient data or research designs to yield rigorous evidence; and, more fundamentally, by the inability of community institutions to address macro-structural conditions, such as poverty and inequality, that weaken social organization (Hope, 1995; Sherman et al., 1997; Welsh & Hoshi, 2003). Relying on community mobilization and action alone may be insufficient to address local crime problems. Without large-scale interventions that address structural conditions such as concentrated disadvantage and residential instability, among others, community-led interventions may yield only modest results for the most entrenched crime problems (Sherman et al., 1997; Wickes, 2017).

Despite this, promising community-centered approaches to crime do exist. Here, we review evidence on community-centered and place-based interventions that target social process mechanisms identified in social disorganization theory: social ties, collective efficacy, and informal social control. We limit our review to interventions that do not position law enforcement in a central role, consistent with the theory's emphasis on informal, rather than formal, social control. Policy discourses on community crime control often focus on interventions, like community policing, that center law enforcement. While we acknowledge that police do occupy a role in crime control, social disorganization theory's philosophy is more closely aligned with community-centered, peacemaking, and restorative justice interventions than with police-led community collaborations or surveillance-focused initiatives (Warner, Beck & Ohmer, 2010). In the following, we describe three types of crime prevention strategies that align conceptually with the lessons learned from social disorganization theory: community violence outreach programs, community-based mentoring and after-school programs for youth, and place-based improvements to the physical environment.

Approach 1: Community-Led Outreach to Intervene in Community and Retaliatory Violence

Although violent crime declined substantially from its peak in the early 1990s, it remains stubbornly persistent in some communities, especially as gun violence and homicide spiked during the COVID-19 pandemic (Lopez, 2021). In addition to well-documented negative effects of violence on individuals (Sharkey, 2018), communities suffer from violence, too: high levels may drive residents out of neighborhoods and depress investments in residential and retail spaces (Skogan, 1986), processes which can destabilize social ties and community cohesion, leading to further declines in social organization and collective efficacy (Kubrin & Weitzer, 2003). Exposure to police violence and aggressive policing tactics is also linked to negative health outcomes (Bor et al., 2018; Geller et al., 2014). As such, solutions that do not rely on law enforcement are promising alternatives to police-focused interventions.

Community violence outreach programs (CVOs), known as street outreach programs, are anti-gun violence interventions that incorporate sustained community outreach (Butts et al., 2015; Skogan et al., 2009). Strategies involving outreach workers have a long history in health interventions (Mack et al., 2006) and crime prevention, particularly with respect to gang violence (Decker et al., 2008). CVOs combine several types of interventions aimed at addressing both individual- and group-level drivers of violence, including sustained engagement with individuals at high-risk of violence to identify and intervene in interpersonal conflicts, connections to pro-social activities and social services, and broader outreach to enhance anti-violence community norms.

Contemporary community outreach interventions view violent behavior through an epidemiological lens, which frames violence as transmissible between people, akin to communicable diseases (Slutkin & Ransford, 2020). Like other behavior, violent behavior is shaped, in part, by community norms and values that support violence as a means to resolve interpersonal conflict (Butts et al., 2015; Hemenway, 2013). While not explicitly derived from a social disorganization lens, both the epidemiological framework and social disorganization theory position the role of informal social controls, social ties, and community norms as instrumental in combatting violence.

CVOs vary in their program models but share similarities in their target populations and goals (Butts et al., 2015; Corburn et al., 2021). First, CVOs target individuals and communities that experience, or are at highest-risk for experiencing, gun or group-based violence. These groups are reluctant to engage with formal service providers and lack trust in outsiders (Decker et al., 2008). Second, CVOs are operated by community-based organizations, either alone or in partnership with other community-based organizations. Third, CVOs deploy paid outreach workers who are well known in the communities where they work. In many cases, outreach workers have prior experience with the criminal justice system, helping build trust and credibility among the targeted individuals and communities. Finally, CVOs bolster informal social control through direct mediation and conflict resolution in situations either likely to escalate into violence or in the aftermath of violent events and through developing prosocial norms and beliefs (Butts et al., 2014).

The most well-known of such programs, Cure Violence, was developed in Chicago by Gary Slutkin and has been implemented in cities across the nation, including Boston, Pittsburgh, New York, and Baltimore, as well as internationally (Butts et al., 2015). The Cure Violence model incorporates three core elements: 1) employing violence interrupters to identify and mediate potentially violent conflicts before they occur; 2) using outreach workers to connect high-risk participants to community resources, including employment, education, recreation, and housing services; and 3) engaging community through public events, door-to-door canvassing, education campaigns, and partnerships with other community-based organizations to transmit antiviolence messages and build consensus against violence in the community (Butts et al., 2015). Other models draw on similar principles. Advance Peace, implemented in cities in California, uses outreach workers to engage with a small cohort of at-risk individuals through trauma-informed mentorship, support, and service provision over an 18-month period. Staff also work to broker truces between conflicting parties and facilitate conflict resolution through conversations (Corburn et al., 2021). The Urban Peace Institute provides training to street outreach workers for gang outreach, intervention and conflict mediation, and violence, while the United Teen Equality Center uses street outreach to build relationships with youth at risk of engaging in violence (Urban Peace Academy n.d.; UTEC n.d.).

Evidence for the effectiveness of CVOs is mixed but promising. A time series analysis using 16 years of data from Chicago's Cure Violence program (formerly called CeaseFire) examined the program's impact on shootings and homicides and finds the program was associated with significant reductions of shootings in four of the seven sites (where declines were greater than comparison sites) but reveals mixed results with respect to reductions in gang and retaliatory homicides (Skogan et al., 2009). Notably, Cure Violence program clients established trusting relationships with outreach workers, frequently rating the workers as among the most important adults in their lives, and indicating their support for efforts to disseminate anti-violence messaging (Skogan et al., 2009).

Another study evaluating the Baltimore, Maryland, Cure Violence program in four neighborhoods finds significant reductions in either homicides or nonfatal shootings in all four sites; however, results are inconsistent across outcomes and only one site saw reductions in both homicides and nonfatal shootings (Webster et al., 2012a, 2012b). Researchers suggest that inconsistent implementation in program areas, and spillover of program activities into comparison areas, led to difficulties isolating true program impacts. Researchers find the New York City Cure Violence program significantly reduced gun injuries in its two intervention sites and shooting victimizations in one of the sites (Delgado et al., 2017). Young men living in Cure Violence neighborhoods were substantially less likely to report willingness to use violence in response to hypothetical scenarios about interpersonal conflicts relative to those in comparison sites (Delgado et al., 2017). Studies of similar programs in Phoenix, Arizona, and Pittsburgh, Pennsylvania, report mixed evidence of interventions' impacts on violent events, demonstrating reductions in assaults in Phoenix but potential deleterious effects in the Pittsburgh program (Fox et al., 2015; Wilson & Chermak, 2011). However, Butts et al. (2015) argue the Pittsburgh program failed to include core program components and may not be representative of the Cure Violence intervention. An evaluation of Advance Peace in Richmond, California, finds significant reductions in firearm violence, deaths, and hospital visits but small increases in non-firearm violence (Matthay et al., 2019).

As this discussion reveals,

- Community violence outreach programs yield mixed results;
- These programs are promising interventions, as most evaluations document reductions in gun violence and victimization;
- Studies examining the impact of these programs find they bolster social trust and community norms and attitudes against violence, consistent with social disorganization theory.

Approach 2: Engaging Youth to Build Social Ties and Collective Efficacy

Adult criminal careers generally begin in adolescence (Moffitt, 1993; Piquero et al., 2012), marking this period as a key target for crime prevention efforts. Strong ties to parents and other caring adults, as well as monitoring and supervision, are associated with reduced delinquency (DuBois et al., 2011; Farrington et al., 2012; Sampson & Laub, 1993). For youth in disadvantaged neighborhoods, prosocial bonds and activities may be protective against offending (Intravia et al., 2017). We discuss evidence on two interventions that aim to create prosocial spaces for youth, connect at-risk young people with adult mentors, and enhance social ties: community-based mentoring and after-school programs.

Community-based mentoring programs are a common approach for intervening with youth who are at risk of delinquency. Such programs involve adult volunteers who spend time with youth in a "supportive, nonjudgmental manner while acting as role models" (Howell, 1995, p. 90). However, these programs vary widely in terms of setting (e.g., community center, church, school), mentorship approaches (e.g., one-on-one or group-based mentoring), frequency and duration of mentorship relationships, level of mentor training, and structure across mentorship programs (DuBois et al., 2011).

Evidence demonstrates that community-based mentoring yields positive, but modest, effects on academic, social, and emotional outcomes for youth, including reductions in delinquent behavior (DuBois et al., 2011; Jolliffe & Farrington, 2008; Tolan et al., 2014). Studies suggest such programs are more effective for youth who are at high risk of delinquency and where mentor–mentee relationships involve sustained contact and close emotional bonds, yet insufficient evidence exists on which program components are most effective (DuBois et al., 2011; Sullivan & Jolliffe, 2012). One well-known program, Big Brothers/Big Sisters, aims to develop attachment, mutual trust, and social bonds between youth and volunteer adult mentors in community and school settings. An early randomized control trial study shows that youth mentored in the program were less likely to report aggressive or anti-social behavior or drug or alcohol use and were more likely to report improvements in family relationships 18 months following participation (Grossman & Tierney, 1998). Importantly, crime reduction benefits of community-mentoring involvement may be sustained over the long term for certain groups. Female mentees and mentees from racial and ethnic minority groups who had at least a year-long relationship with a Big Brothers/Big Sisters mentor are significantly less likely to be arrested for property crimes many years after the intervention (Dubois et al., 2018). However, not all mentoring programs show positive results; studies document damaging outcomes where close mentor–mentee relationships end abruptly, mentors fail to meet basic expectations of their role, or youth who were not previously involved in delinquent behaviors are exposed to youth who were (Dubois, 2021).

A related community-based intervention, after-school programs – also known as out-of-school time programs – engage young people in the immediate hours following the end of the school day. Such programs target unsupervised time, a risk factor for delinquency (Gottfredson et al., 2001, 2004). Typically taking place between 2 and 6 pm, after-school programs deliver prosocial supervision and peer interaction, social and academic skill development, and leisure activities (Gottfredson et al., 2004).

Research on the effectiveness of after-school programs on delinquency is mixed. Substantial variation across program models, and evaluation rigor, likely explain this. While an early review of research on community-based recreation centers finds positive evidence of their effects on juvenile arrests and drug use, these conclusions are tempered by methodological weakness and a small number of studies (Sherman et al., 1997; Welsh & Hoshi, 2003). Subsequent reviews of after-school programs, which include a wider range of modalities, find these programs do not universally reduce delinquency. A meta-analysis of evaluations of 17 different after-school programs shows a small but non-significant effect on reducing juvenile delinquency (Taheri & Welsh, 2016). However, some research documents significant effects: a rigorous evaluation of 14 programs implemented across Maryland shows that overall, participation in the after-school programs resulted in significant reductions in delinquency but only for middle-school, not elementary-school, youth (Gottfredson et al., 2004). Researchers find that reductions in delinquency were driven by increases in positive peer associations and changes in attitudes around substance use. Effects were greatest for programs that emphasize social skills and character development (Gottfredson et al., 2004). After-school programs that are highly structured, incorporate planned activities and evidence-based practices, hire educated staff, and are smaller in size are associated with greater reductions in juvenile delinquency (Gottfredson et al., 2007).

The research evidence indicates the following:

- Efforts to engage youth, either through developing strong, lasting mentorship relationships or through structured after-school activities focused on skill and character development, hold promise for preventing a broad range of undesirable behaviors, including delinquency;
- The likelihood of success for mentoring and after school programs is related to key aspects of programmatic design, such as the type and quality of mentor–mentee relationships and program size and structure.

Approach 3: Place-Based Physical Environment Improvement Strategies

Social disorganization theory encourages researchers to consider "kinds of places" rather than "kinds of people" for determining why certain communities experience more crime than others. Consistent with this, researchers focus on how physical characteristics of places intersect with their social contexts (Stucky & Ottensmann, 2009). Certain types of land use such as liquor stores and bars, commercial and high-density residential properties, fringe lenders, and vacant lots are associated with higher crime rates (Boessen & Hipp, 2015; Cui & Walsh, 2015; Groff & Lockwood, 2014; Kubrin & Hipp, 2016; LaGrange, 1999).

Physical features may hinder a community's ability to maintain social control by reducing the ability to recognize local residents from others outside the area (Greenberg et al., 1982; Taylor et al., 1995; Wilcox et al., 2004) or by increasing perceptions of neighborhood decline or disorder (McCord et al., 2007; Taylor et al., 1995). Further, visible signs of physical disorder, such as vacant lots, garbage dumped in public spaces, or overgrown vegetation, may signal a lack of control or surveillance to others, leading to higher crime rates (Kubrin & Weitzer, 2003; Skogan, 2015). Conversely, noticeable signs of residents and maintained landscapes and facilities, or "cues to care," may imply community norms of investment and informal surveillance (Greenberg et al., 1982; Nassauer & Raskin, 2014). The relationship between land use and crime is not universal but is shaped by levels of social organization within a community (Kubrin & Hipp, 2016; Stucky & Ottensmann, 2009). Socially organized communities may be able to effectively pressure local police or municipal governments to intervene when problems arise; alternatively, communities that lack institutional resources or collective efficacy may be less able to effectuate formal responses to local crime problems. Improvements to aspects of the physical environment can promote neighborhood stabilization, contributing to the reduction of crime and to creating community cohesion and informal social control, particularly in communities characterized by poverty, inequality, and physical signs of disinvestment, such as vacant or dilapidated properties.

Interventions designed to improve characteristics of places take many forms, including the creation of green spaces, such as adding parks, vegetation, or tree coverage; cleaning debris and vacant lots; improving street lighting; installing CCTV cameras; minimizing abandoned buildings, and preventing foreclosures. While this approach encompasses interventions informed by social disorganization theory and related theoretical frameworks (e.g., Crime Prevention Through Environmental Design (CPTED), crime pattern theory, routine activity theory), we focus attention on interventions directed at a common problem in urban landscapes: vacant, substandard, and abandoned properties (Garvin et al., 2013). Two approaches demonstrate strong or promising impacts on crime while promoting prosocial interactions: vacant lot greening and dilapidated or abandoned property abatement.

Prior research links vacant lots to negative health and crime outcomes (Cohen et al., 2003; Spelman, 1993). Initiatives to clean up debris and turn these lots into green spaces show strong evidence for reducing crime in and around once-vacant properties. A large-scale, randomized control trial study in Philadelphia tested the effects of ameliorating vacant lots on crime (Branas et al., 2018). Treated lots were cleaned and reseeded with new grass and trees to create a park-like atmosphere. Low fencing with ungated entrances was also installed around lot perimeters, allowing residents to use the spaces. Before the intervention, these lots were common locations for drug activity, and neighbors reported rarely confronting drug sellers. After the intervention, treated lots saw significant reductions in all crimes, including gun assaults and burglaries, even for lots receiving only clean-up and regular maintenance. Neighborhood perceptions of crime and fear of crime were reduced, and nearby residents increased their use of lots for leisure and socializing. A follow-up study finds the intervention also reduced shootings by 6.8–9.2 percent (Moyer et al., 2019). Ameliorating once-vacant lots significantly improves residents' perceptions of safety (Garvin et al., 2013), which has been linked to social cohesion (Markowitz et al., 2001).

Quasi-experimental research also supports "cleaning and greening" efforts to ameliorate vacant lots. An initiative in Youngstown, Ohio, to clean and plant vegetation in vacant lots, either through a municipal contractor or community-led "reuse" initiatives, yielded significant declines in crime. The contractor-stabilized lots were associated with significant reductions in burglaries, while the community reuse lots were associated with significant reductions in felony assaults and robberies (Kondo et al., 2016). A similar community-led "Clean & Green" program in Flint, Michigan, was associated with a 40 percent reduction in assaults and violent crimes (Heinze et al., 2018). Evidence of reductions in crime in immediate areas surrounding the greened lots was also documented (Heinze et al., 2018, Johnson et al., 2014).

Physical improvements to abandoned or dilapidated properties also show promise in reducing crime, though the evidence base is more limited. A quasi-experimental study of a Philadelphia ordinance requiring owners of abandoned or unused buildings to install new doors and windows on their properties finds that remediations were associated with significant reductions in crime, including assaults, gun assaults, and nuisance crimes (Kondo et al., 2015). However, increases in drug and property crimes were also documented. Finally, demolition of abandoned properties yields promising effects: a study of a blight removal program aimed at demolishing abandoned and unkept properties in Detroit, Michigan, shows that areas with more demolitions saw significant reductions in violent and property crimes (Larson et al., 2019).

In sum, the following can be said based on this evidence:

- Land use shapes social interactions in ways that create or inhibit conditions that give rise to crime and delinquency;
- Initiatives either led by municipal governments or through collaboration with communities to improve vacant, substandard, or abandoned properties through cleaning and maintenance, facility upgrades, or the creation of communal green spaces are linked with substantial reductions in crime, as well as fear of crime;
- Interventions focused on improvements to the built environment can increase the prosocial use of public spaces, consistent with social disorganization theory.

Conclusion

Crime clusters within broader communities, particularly in neighborhoods characterized by concentrated disadvantage and other social ills. Social disorganization theory asserts these structural conditions undermine community-level social processes, including collective efficacy and prosocial ties, which help control crime and delinquency. In this chapter, we highlighted three promising community-centered crime prevention approaches supported by research: community violent outreach programs, community-based mentoring and after-school programs for youth, and physical improvements to neglected properties. Each approach draws core lessons learned from social disorganization theory and seeks, in part or in whole, to bolster prosocial relationships, build community norms and attitudes that reinforce values of safety, and create spaces for residents to interact. Yet community-centered interventions are no panacea; without attention to broader policy and market forces that generate and entrench neighborhood structural inequalities, and without sustained programmatic investments, community-centered interventions alone remain limited in their ability to alter the neighborhood conditions that cause crime.

References

Bellair, P. E. (1997). Social interaction and community crime: Examining the importance of neighbor networks. *Criminology*, *35*, 677–703.

Bellair, P. E. (2000). Informal surveillance and street crime: A complex relationship. *Criminology*, *38*, 137–167.

Boessen, A., & Hipp, J. R. (2015). Close-ups and the scale of ecology: Land uses and the geography of social context and crime. *Criminology*, *53*(3), 399–426.

Bor, J., Venkataramani, A. S., Williams, D. R., & Tsai, A. C. (2018). Police killings and their spillover effects on the mental health of Black Americans: A population-based, quasi-experimental study. *The Lancet*, *392*(10144), 302–310.
Branas, C. C., South, E., Kondo, M. C., Hohl, B. C., Bourgois, P., Wiebe, D. J., & MacDonald, J. M. (2018). Citywide cluster randomized trial to restore blighted vacant land and its effects on violence, crime, and fear. *Proceedings of the National Academy of Sciences of the United States of America*, *115*(12), 2946–2951.
Browning, C. R. (2009). Illuminating the downside of social capital. *American Behavioral Scientist*, *52*, 1556–1578.
Browning, C. R., Feinberg, S. L., & Dietz, R. D. (2004). The paradox of social organization: Networks, collective efficacy, and violent crime in urban neighborhoods. *Social Forces*, *83*, 503–534.
Bursik, R. J. (1988). Social disorganization and theories of crime and delinquency: Problems and prospects. *Criminology*, *26*, 519–51.
Bursik, R. J., & Grasmick, H. G. (1993). Economic deprivation and neighborhood crime rates, 1960–1980. *Law & Society Review*, *27*, 263–284.
Butts, J., Bostwick, L., & Porter, J. (2014). *Denormalizing violence: Evaluation framework for a public health model of violence prevention*. Research & Evaluation Center, John Jay College of Criminal Justice, City University of New York.
Butts, J. A., Roman, C. G., Bostwick, L., & Porter, J. R. (2015). Cure violence: A public health model to reduce gun violence. *Annual Review of Public Health*, *36*(1), 39–53.
Chamlin, M. B. (1989). A macro social analysis of the change in robbery and homicide rates: Controlling for static and dynamic effects. *Sociological Focus*, *22*, 275–286.
Cohen, D. A., Mason, K., Bedimo, A., Scribner, R., Basolo, V., & Farley, T. A. (2003). Neighborhood physical conditions and health. *American Journal of Public Health*, *93*(3), 467–471.
Corburn, J., Boggan, D. V., Muttaqi, K., Vaughn, S., Houston, J., Thibodeaux, J., & Muhammad, B. (2021). A healing-centered approach to preventing urban gun violence: The advance peace model. *Humanities and Social Sciences Communications*, *8*(1), 4–10.
Cui, L., & Walsh, R. (2015). Foreclosure, vacancy and crime. *Journal of Urban Economics*, *87*, 72–84.
Decker, S. H., Bynum, T. S., McDevitt, J., Farrell, A., & Varano, S. P. (2008). *Street outreach workers: Best practices and lessons learned*. Justice Studies Faculty Publications, Roger Williams University. Retrieved from https://docs.rwu.edu/sjs_fp/15
Delgado, S. A., Alsabahi, L., & Butts, J. A. (2017). *Young men in neighborhoods with cure violence programs adopt attitudes less supportive of violence*. Research and Evaluation Center, John Jay College of Criminal Justice.
DuBois, D. L., Herrera, C., & Rivera, J. (2018). *Investigation of long-term effects of the Big Brothers Big Sisters community-based mentoring program: Final technical report for OJJDP*. OJJDP.
Dubois, D. L. (2021). *Mentoring programs for youth: A promising intervention for delinquency prevention*. U.S. Department of Justice, Office of Justice Programs, National Institute of Justice. Retrieved from: https://nij.ojp.gov/topics/articles/mentoring-programs-youth-promising-intervention-delinquency-prevention
DuBois, D. L., Portillo, N., Rhodes, J. E., Silverthorn, N., & Valentine, J. C. (2011). How effective are mentoring programs for youth? A systematic assessment of the evidence. *Psychological Science in the Public Interest*, *12*(2), 57–91.
Farrington, D. P., Loeber, R., & Ttofi, M. M. (2012). Risk and protective factors for offending. In D. P. Farrington & B. C. Welsh (Eds.), *The Oxford handbook of crime prevention*. Oxford University Press.
Fox, A. M., Katz, C. M., Choate, D. E., & Hedberg, E. C. (2015). Evaluation of the Phoenix truce project: A replication of Chicago CeaseFire. *Justice Quarterly*, *32*(1), 85–115.
Garvin, E. C., Cannuscio, C. C., & Branas, C. C. (2013). Greening vacant lots to reduce violent crime: A randomised controlled trial. *Injury Prevention*, *19*(3), 198–203.
Geller, A., Fagan, J., Tyler, T., & Link, B. G. (2014). Aggressive policing and the mental health of young urban men. *American Journal of Public Health*, *104*(12), 2321–2327.
Gottfredson, D. C., Cross, A., & Soulé, D. A. (2007). Distinguishing characteristics of effective and ineffective after-school programs to prevent delinquency and victimization. *Criminology & Public Policy*, *6*(2), 289–318.
Gottfredson, D. C., Gerstenblith, S. A., Soulé, D. A., Womer, S. C., & Lu, S. (2004). Do after school programs reduce delinquency? *Prevention Science*, *5*(4), 253–266.

Gottfredson, D. C., Gottfredson, G. D., & Weisman, S. A. (2001). The timing of delinquent behavior and its implications for after-school programs. *Criminology & Public Policy*, *1*(1), 61–86.
Greenberg, S. W., Rohe, W. M., & Williams, J. R. (1982). Safety in urban neighborhoods: A comparison of physical characteristics and informal territorial control in high and low crime neighborhoods. *Population and Environment*, *5*(3), 141–165.
Granovetter, M. S. (1973). The strength of weak ties. *American Journal of Sociology*, *78*, 1360–1380.
Groff, E. R., & Lockwood, B. (2014). Criminogenic facilities and crime across street segments in Philadelphia. *Journal of Research in Crime and Delinquency*, *51*(3), 277–314.
Grossman, J. B., & Tierney, J. P. (1998). Does mentoring work: An impact study of the Big Brothers Big Sisters program. *Evaluation Review*, *22*(3), 403–426.
Heinze, J. E., Krusky-Morey, A., Vagi, K. J., Reischl, T. M., Franzen, S., Pruett, N. K., Cunningham, R. M., & Zimmerman, M. A. (2018). Busy streets theory: The effects of community-engaged greening on violence. *American Journal of Community Psychology*, *62*(1–2), 101–119.
Hemenway, D. (2013). Preventing gun violence by changing social norms. *JAMA Internal Medicine*, *173*(13), 1167.
Hope, T. J. (1995). Community crime prevention. In M. Tonry & D. P. Farrington (Eds.), *Building a safer society: Strategic approaches to crime prevention, crime and justice*, Vol. 19. The University of Chicago Press.
Howell, J. C. (1995). *Guide for implementing the comprehensive strategy for serious, violent, and chronic juvenile offenders*. U.S. Department of Justice, Office of Justice Programs, Office of Juvenile Justice and Delinquency Prevention.
Intravia, J., Pelletier, E., Wolff, K. T., & Baglivio, M. T. (2017). Community disadvantage, prosocial bonds, and juvenile reoffending. *Youth Violence and Juvenile Justice*, *15*(3), 240–263.
Johnson, S. D., Guerette, R. T., & Bowers, K. (2014). Crime displacement: What we know, what we don't know, and what it means for crime reduction. *Journal of Experimental Criminology*, *10*(4), 549–571.
Jolliffe, D., & Farrington, D. P. (2008). *The influence of mentoring on reoffending*. The Swedish National Council for Crime Prevention.
Kobrin, S. (1959). The Chicago area project – A 25-year assessment. *The Annals of the American Academy of Political and Social Science*, 322(1), 19–29.
Kondo, M. C., Hohl, B., Han, S. H., & Branas, C. (2016). Effects of greening and community reuse of vacant lots on crime. *Urban Studies*, 53(15), 3279–3295.
Kondo, M. C., Keene, D., Hohl, B. C., MacDonald, J. M., & Branas, C. C. (2015). A difference-in-differences study of the effects of a new abandoned building remediation strategy on safety. *PLoS One*, *10*(8), e0136595.
Kornhauser, R. (1978). *Social sources of delinquency*. University of Chicago Press.
Kubrin, C. E. (2000). Racial heterogeneity and crime: Measuring static and dynamic effects. In D. A. Chekki (Ed.), *Research in community sociology* (Vol. 10, pp. 189–218). JAI Press.
Kubrin, C. E., & Hipp, J. R. (2016). Do fringe banks create fringe neighborhoods? Examining the spatial relationship between fringe banking and neighborhood crime rates. *Justice Quarterly*, *33*, 755–784.
Kubrin, C. E., & Weitzer, R. (2003). New directions in social disorganization theory. *Journal of Research in Crime and Delinquency*, *40*, 374–402.
Kubrin, C. E., & Wo, J. (2016). Social disorganization theory's greatest challenge: Linking structural characteristics to crime in socially disorganized neighborhoods. In A. R. Piquero (Ed.), *Handbook of criminological theory* (pp. 121–136). Wiley-Blackwell.
LaGrange, T. C. (1999). The impact of neighborhoods, schools, and malls on the spatial distribution of property damage. *Journal of Research in Crime and Delinquency*, *36*(4), 393–422.
Larson, M., Xu, Y., Ouellet, L., & Klahm, C. F. (2019). Exploring the impact of 9398 demolitions on neighborhood-level crime in Detroit, Michigan. *Journal of Criminal Justice*, *60*, 57–63.
Lopez, G. (2021). Murders are up. Crime is not. What's going on? Vox.com. Retrieved from www.vox.com/22578430/murder-crime-2020-2021-covid-19-pandemic.
Mack, M., Uken, R., & Van De Mark Powers, J. (2006). People improving the community's health: Community health workers as agents of change. *Journal of Health Care for the Poor and Underserved*, *17*(1), 16–25.
Markowitz, F. E., Bellair, P. E., Liska, A. E., & Liu, J. (2001). Extending social disorganization theory: Modeling the relationships between cohesion, disorder, and fear. *Criminology*, *39*(2), 293–319.

Matthay, E. C., Farkas, K., Rudolph, K. E., Zimmerman, S., Barragan, M., Goin, D. E., & Ahern, J. (2019). Firearm and nonfirearm violence after operation peacemaker fellowship in Richmond, California, 1996–2016. *American Journal of Public Health*, *109*(11), 1605–1611.

Mazerolle, L., Wickes, R., & McBroom, J. (2010). Community variations in violence: The role of social ties and collective efficacy in comparative context. *Journal of Research in Crime and Delinquency*, *47*, 3–30.

McCord, E. S., Ratcliffe, J. H., Garcia, R. M., & Taylor, R. B. (2007). Nonresidential crime attractors and generators elevate perceived neighborhood crime and incivilities. *Journal of Research in Crime and Delinquency*, *44*(3), 295–320.

Moffitt, T. E. (1993). Adolescence-limited and life-course-persistent antisocial behavior: A developmental taxonomy. *Psychological Review*, *100*(4), 674–701.

Moyer, R., MacDonald, J. M., Ridgeway, G., & Branas, C. C. (2019). Effect of remediating blighted vacant land on shootings: A citywide cluster randomized trial. *American Journal of Public Health*, *109*(1), 140–144.

Nassauer, J. I., & Raskin, J. (2014). Urban vacancy and land use legacies: A frontier for urban ecological research, design, and planning. *Landscape and Urban Planning*, *125*, 245–253.

Pattillo, M. E. (1998). Sweet mothers and gangbangers: Managing crime in a Black middle-class neighborhood. *Social Forces*, *76*, 747–774.

Piquero, A. J., Hawkins, D., & Kazemian, L. (2012). Criminal career patterns. In R. Loeber & D. P. Farrington (Eds.), *From Juvenile delinquency to adult crime*. Oxford University Press.

Sampson, R. J. (2006). Collective efficacy theory: Lessons learned and directions for future inquiry. In F. T. Cullen, J. P. Wright, & K. Blevins (Eds.), *Taking stock: The status of criminological theory* (pp. 149–167). Transaction.

Sampson, R. J., & Groves, W. B. (1989). Community structure and crime: Testing social-disorganization theory. *American Journal of Sociology*, *94*, 774–802.

Sampson, R. J., & Laub, J. H. (1993). Crime in the making. *Crime & Delinquency*, *39*(3), 396–396.

Sampson, R. J., Morenoff, J. D., & Earls, F. (1999). Spatial dynamics of collective efficacy for children. *American Sociological Review*, *64*, 633–660.

Sampson, R. J., Raudenbush, S. W., & Earls, F. (1997). Neighborhoods and violent crime. *Science*, *277*, 918–924.

Schlossman, S., & Sedlak, M. (1983). The Chicago area project revisited. *Crime & Delinquency*, *29*(3), 398–462.

Sharkey, P. (2018). The long reach of violence: A broader perspective on data, theory, and evidence on the prevalence and consequences of exposure to violence. *Annual Review of Criminology*, *1*, 85–102.

Shaw, C. R., & McKay, H. (1969). *Juvenile delinquency and urban areas*. University of Chicago Press. (Original work published 1942).

Sherman, L. W., Gottfredson, D., MacKenzie, D. L., Eck, J., Reuter, P., & Bushway, S. D. (1997). *Preventing crime: What works, what doesn't, what's promising*. U.S. Department of Justice, Office of Justice Programs, National Institute of Justice.

Skogan, W. (1986). Fear of crime and neighborhood change. *Crime and Justice*, *8*, 203–229.

Skogan, W. (2015). Disorder and decline: The state of research. *Journal of Research in Crime and Delinquency*, *52*(4), 464–485.

Skogan, W. G., Hartnett, S. M., Bump, N., & Dubois, J. (2009). *Evaluation of CeaseFire-Chicago: Final report to the National Institute of Justice*. U.S. Department of Justice, Office of Justice Programs, National Institute of Justice.

Slutkin, G., & Ransford, C. (2020). Violence is a contagious disease: Theory and practice in the USA and abroad. In M. Siegler & S. O. Rogers Jr. (Eds.), *Violence, trauma, and trauma surgery: Ethical issues, interventions, and innovations* (pp. 67–85). Springer International Publishing.

Spelman, W. (1993). Abandoned buildings: Magnets for crime? *Journal of Criminal Justice*, *21*(5), 481–495.

Stucky, T. D., & Ottensmann, J. R. (2009). Land use and violent crime. *Criminology*, *47*(4), 1223–1264.

Sullivan, C. J., & Jolliffe, D. (2012). Peer influence, mentoring, and the prevention of crime. In D. P. Farrington & B. C. Welsh (Eds.), *The Oxford handbook of crime prevention*. Oxford University Press.

Taheri, S. A., & Welsh, B. C. (2016). After-school programs for delinquency prevention: A systematic review and meta-analysis. *Youth Violence and Juvenile Justice*, *14*(3), 272–290.

Taylor, R. B., Koons, B. A., Kurtz, E. M., Greene, J. R., & Perkins, D. D. (1995). Street blocks with more nonresidential land use have more physical deterioration. *Urban Affairs Review*, *31*(1), 120–136.

Tolan, P. H., Henry, D. B., Schoeny, M. S., Lovegrove, P., & Nichols, E. (2014). Mentoring programs to affect delinquency and associated outcomes of youth at risk: A comprehensive meta-analytic review. *Journal of Experimental Criminology*, *10*(2), 179–206.
Urban Peace Academy. (n.d.). Our work. Retrieved from www.urbanpeaceinstitute.org/our-work-urban-peace-academy.
UTEC. (n.d.). *UTEC: Our programs*. Retrieved from https://utecinc.org/what-we-do/our-programs/
Warner, B. D., & Rountree, P. W. (1997). Local social ties in a community and crime model: Questioning the systemic nature of informal social control. *Social Problems*, *44*, 520–536.
Warner, B. D., Beck, E., & Ohmer, M. L. (2010). Linking informal social control and restorative justice: Moving social disorganization theory beyond community policing. *Contemporary Justice Review*, *13*(4), 355–369.
Webster, D., Jennifer, W., Jon, V., & Elizabeth, P. (2012a). *Evaluation of Baltimore's safe streets program: Effects on attitudes, participants' experiences, and gun violence*. Johns Hopkins Center for the Prevention of Youth Violence.
Webster, D., Jennifer, W., Jon, V., & Frank, C. (2012b). Effects of Baltimore's safe streets program on gun violence: A replication of Chicago's *CeaseFire* program. *Journal of Urban Health*, *90*, 27–40.
Welsh, B. C., & Hoshi, A. (2003). Evidence-based crime prevention. In D. P. Farrington, D. L. MacKenzie, L. W. Sherman, & B. C. Welsh (Eds.), *Evidence-based crime prevention*. Routledge.
Wickes, R. (2017). *Preventing crime and violence* (Eds. B. Teasdale & M. S. Bradley). Springer International Publishing.
Wilcox, P., Quisenberry, N., Cabrera, D. T., & Jones, S. (2004). Busy places and broken windows? Toward defining the role of physical structure and process in community crime models. *The Sociological Quarterly*, *45*(2), 185–207.
Wilson, J. M., & Chermak, S. (2011). Community-driven violence reduction programs. *Criminology & Public Policy*, *10*(4), 993–1027.

3

EVIDENCE-BASED EMPLOYMENT PRACTICES TO REDUCE OFFENDING

Chae M. Jaynes, Kelly E. Kortright, and Mateus R. Santos

Introduction

Justice-involved individuals are a disadvantaged group within the labor market, as they frequently experience joblessness and underemployment. This is a key concern because the association between employment and crime is strongly couched within criminological theory, which has proposed that those who are not working or working in low-quality jobs are more likely to offend (e.g., Merton, 1938; Sampson & Laub, 1993). This hypothesized relationship between employment and offending also guides employment-related programs and policies which commonly target high-risk populations. For example, employment is seen as a key hurdle to successful reentry among state-level Departments of Corrections (La Vigne et al., 2008), and correctional institutions regularly incorporate some form of vocational training into their programming (National Institute of Justice, 2022). Employment is also considered a standard condition of criminal justice supervision (Kimchi, 2019), to the extent that some argue the current environment implies many on community supervision must "get to work or go to jail" (Zatz, 2020). In light of this emphasis on work, countless interventions have been implemented with the goal of reducing recidivism in high-risk populations through employment-related practices. This chapter overviews the state of the literature surrounding the relationship between employment and crime (at the individual level) and suggests evidence-based practices for employment programs striving to reduce recidivism.

Traditional Theoretical Perspectives

Several criminological theories posit a relationship between work and crime. For example, strain theory suggests that crime is the result of blocked legitimate means to opportunity – such as quality employment – where work generates earnings to reduce financial strain that could pressure an individual towards crime (Agnew, 2006; Merton, 1938). Sampson and Laub's (1993) theory of informal social control posits that employment becomes an important protective institution in young adulthood, strengthening one's social bonds and reducing crime. According to routine activities theory (Cohen & Felson, 1979), work can provide structure to one's time and reduce opportunities for offending (Apel & Horney, 2017; Laub & Sampson, 2003). Cumulatively, these theories consistently support the notion that work, especially high-quality work, reduces offending among high-risk populations.

 DOI: 10.4324/9781003219286-5

The Empirical Literature

Periods of Employment

The empirical literature surrounding the relationship between employment and crime is less consistent. While some observational research has found that those who are employed are less likely to offend (a negative association) (e.g., Laub & Sampson, 2003; Loughran et al., 2017; Savolainen, 2009), others have failed to find an association (Jaynes, 2020; Skardhamar & Savolainen, 2014) or found only limited crime-specific or race-specific support (Griffin & Armstrong, 2003; Piquero et al., 2002). Horney and colleagues (1995) even found an unexpected positive association between employment and property crime, where those who were employed were *more* likely to commit crime.

The Role of Job Quality

Research has moved beyond simply focusing on whether someone has a job to focusing on characteristics of that job, as some types may be more protective than others. However, scholarship that has evaluated the role of job characteristics has also reached inconsistent conclusions. For instance, while some research has found that a higher wage/income is negatively associated with offending (e.g., Grogger, 1998; Uggen & Thompson, 2003; Witte, 1980), others found little to no association (e.g., Apel & Horney, 2017; Jaynes, 2020; Sampson & Laub, 1993; Wadsworth, 2006). One study even found that workers who were affected by an increase in the minimum wage were more likely to offend, an association which was exacerbated among those with prior criminal connections (Beuchamp & Chan, 2014). Obtaining jobs with fringe benefits (e.g., health insurance, paid vacation) has also garnered mixed empirical support, with one national (U.S.) study finding that fringe benefits had a negative association with property crime and a marginal negative association with violent crime (Wadsworth, 2006) and another study finding no significant association in a sample of high-risk individuals with past criminal involvement (Jaynes, 2020). Research seems to suggest that improvement in job satisfaction (a subjective measure of job quality) seems to have a more consistent negative association with offending, especially among high-risk populations (e.g., Paternoster et al., 2016; Simons et al., 2002; Uggen, 1999; Wadsworth, 2006). However, one recent study found the effect size was small and race specific (Jaynes, 2020).

Program Evaluations

In addition to these observational studies, most experimental evaluations of employment-related programs have failed to demonstrate joint improvements in participants' labor market outcomes and reductions in offending (Bushway & Apel, 2012; Visher et al., 2008). This surprising lack of empirical support has led scholars to question why "work doesn't work" as a policy lever to reduce crime (Bushway & Apel, 2012) – a question that has underscored potential limitations of prior employment programming implemented with justice-involved individuals that we address directly in our recommendations.

Future Recommendations

1. **Providing reach-in *and* wrap-around services**
2. **Taking a holistic approach**

First, many programs only provide services post-release rather than providing both pre-release correctional programming (reach-in) and post-release (wrap-around) services within the community (Cook et al., 2015). Accordingly, leading scholars now recommend combining reach-in and wrap-around efforts as a foundational aspect of successful reentry programming (Cook et al., 2015; James, 2015; Petersilia, 2003; Travis, 2005).

Second, employment programming *alone* may not be enough to produce reductions in offending. Therefore, employment-based reentry programing should take a more holistic approach, incorporating risk-needs assessments and a plethora of additional support services in areas such as housing, substance abuse, and mental health.

There are at least two successful examples of programs that were designed with these first two elements in mind. The Milwaukee Safe Streets Prison Release Initiative (PRI) provided both reach-in and wrap-around employment-based programming to individuals who were incarcerated for a violent offense (Cook et al., 2015). The program included vocational-skills assessment, soft skills training, vocational training, work release, and access to the Community Corrections Employment Program (CCEP). A coordinated-care team also met with participants pre-release to aid in their job search. Post-release participants were eligible to continue CCEP assistance and to receive subsidized employment for 6 months which included assistance transitioning to unsubsidized employment afterwards. PRI participants were also connected with a host of additional holistic services (both pre- and post-release), including restorative justice circles, cognitive-realist curriculum, alcohol and drug treatment, education and plans for housing, transportation, and securing important documents. Current empirical evidence about the program is promising in that it helped improve employment and earnings of participants as well as reduce recidivism (Cook et al., 2015).

Another promising example is the Minnesota Comprehensive Offender Reentry Plan (MCORP). The goal of MCORP was to increase returning citizens' access to prison programming and community services through enhanced case management collaboration. MCORP's reach-in and wrap-around efforts were quite extensive. They engaged participants in case management and reentry planning, conducted risk-needs assessments, established transition accountability plans, and helped align them with target interventions. MCORP was also holistic and focused on helping returning individuals "access services related to employment, vocational training, education, housing, chemical health, mentoring, faith-based programming, and income support" both inside and outside of the prison (p. 353). Duwe's (2012) research used a randomized controlled trial (RCT) in which the treatment group participated in MCORP at least 60 days pre-release, while the control group received the traditional support without the supplements provided by the MCORP. Program participants saw significant reductions in recidivism, which Duwe (2012, p. 347) attributed to "increase[ing] the extent to which [participants] were employed, involved in community support programming, and able to develop systems of social support" – acknowledging that reductions in recidivism were not singularly an employment effect.

Based on recommended best practices and the initial success of the two overviewed programs, *employment-based programming should aim to be reach-in and wrap-around and take a holistic approach connecting participants with a variety of services.*

3. Improvements in job quality

Participating in work programs may not result in high-risk individuals obtaining the *types of jobs* which most effectively deter crime. Cook and colleagues (2015, p. 378) questioned whether offering "a temporary low-wage menial job" was a strong enough intervention, as high-risk individuals may "require a bigger 'dose' of legitimate opportunity" than most work programs provide. This idea is consistent with the observational research, which found inconsistent support for an association between job quality and offending (e.g., Apel & Horney, 2017; Jaynes, 2020), as it is unlikely that high risk disadvantaged individuals will naturally obtain employment which is particularly "high-quality". It may be that there is little effect of job quality because individuals are not obtaining jobs with a quality that is *high enough* to have a significant impact on their trajectories.

It may also be that employment-based programs have been focusing on the wrong type of "quality". Improvements in wage or income are by far the most common measures of job quality, which is consistent with the assumption that individuals primarily offend for pecuniary reasons (Merton, 1938). However, other perspectives place more emphasis on the role of work in providing "a sense of identity and meaning" in one's life (Laub & Sampson, 2003, p. 47). This is consistent with research suggesting that individuals value less-tangible aspects of a job, such as a sense of usefulness, accomplishment, and autonomy (Clark, 1998; Jencks et al., 1988). We also know that there is variation in the rewards individuals seek to obtain from work (Jencks et al., 1988), and perceptions of these rewards change over time (Kalleberg, 2011). This is further supported by observational findings that when released individuals reported getting a "good job" or "any job they liked" shortly after release, they had significantly longer times until rearrest (Paternoster et al., 2016).

It is also notable that providing better-paying jobs may not always be a feasible policy option, as this can be costly. Helping individuals find jobs that they *like* or that fit their personal interests may be more feasible and is in line with literature that improvements in job satisfaction can reduce offending (Jaynes, 2020; Paternoster et al., 2016; Simons et al., 2002; Uggen, 1999; Wadsworth, 2006). There are also no known findings suggesting that a job that is more satisfying is more criminogenic. Therefore, employment programming should focus on *improving subjective assessments of job quality, such as increasing participant job satisfaction, through pairing individuals with jobs that align more closely with their interests.*

4. Targeting identity change

Most employment-related programs seek to increase employment rates and wages based on the assumption that individuals offend for primarily for financial reasons. This is not consistent with either observational research or program evaluations, which generally find that improvements in income are not consistently associated with reductions in offending. Paternoster and Bushway (2009; see also Bushway, 2022) proposed instead that identity change, rather than "employment", is the main underlying cause of desistance. Specifically, a substantial reduction in offending oftentimes necessitates a prior change in identity which must become prosocial, rather than antisocial. This change is likely to occur over time as the individual comes to see their accumulated failures as a consequence of their life choices. As an individual visualizes their "feared self" and begins to form a prosocial identity that person will increasingly self-select into fitting prosocial roles, such as conventional employment. Hence, while employment may help solidify a prosocial identity, a job is neither the primary cause of desistance from crime nor a necessary condition thereof, as desistance can occur without employment.

This perspective has found support within the desistance literature (e.g., Paternoster et al., 2016). For example, Liu and Bachman (2021) not only found that a prosocial identity decreased offending but also that a prosocial identity amplified the crime-reducing effect of employment. Relatedly, Jaynes (2022) found that problematic work behaviors symbolizing low job commitment (e.g., calling in sick, doing a job poorly, coming to work under the influence) were associated with an increased likelihood of offending (see also Apel & Horney, 2017). These results suggest that commitment to work, which is likely symptomatic of a prosocial identity, leads to reductions in offending. Jaynes (2022) also found that improvements in job quality did not seem to inspire commitment. In other words, a high-quality job is not a prerequisite for commitment to the job. This is consistent with qualitative accounts of individuals being provided high-quality opportunities yet failing to take advantage of them (Shaw, 1930/1966). It is also consistent with findings where gains in employment failed to produce reductions in offending (Bushway & Apel, 2012). If individuals do not have a prosocial identity ready to take advantage of opportunities, just offering these opportunities may not be sufficient to change their offending trajectories. For this reason, *employment-related programs should target prosocial identity formation as a key underlying mechanism and outcome.*

5. Focusing on signaling (program completion) rather than causality

A natural goal of employment programming among high-risk populations is to promote improvements in employment that *cause* reductions in offending. Therefore, it is no surprise that high-level evaluations have sought to evaluate the causal impact of these programs using strong research designs such as RCTs. However, an emerging perspective, referred to as signaling theory, suggests that employment programming does not need to have a causal effect to be beneficial to program participants, to businesses, and to society (Bushway & Apel, 2012; Bushway, 2022).

A signaling perspective acknowledges that individuals tend to self-select into participating in and completing employment-based programs. In other words, those who are most motivated to change, ready to desist, or hardworking (etc.) are more likely to choose to participate in programming. It is then no surprise if these participants find better jobs and have a reduced likelihood of offending, as they had preexisting characteristics that made them more likely to succeed in both endeavors. While RCTs aim to eliminate selection by randomizing participants to treatment and control conditions, a signaling approach to programming would take advantage of selection – allowing candidates to self-select into programs and designing program completion as a reliable "signal" of a commitment to desistance and of one's increased likelihood of success elsewhere. To do this, the program must be rigorous. The signal (program completion), when communicated to prospective employers, can be used by participants on the job market as evidence of lower risk relative to those who did not complete the program. This benefits program participants, as they may be more likely to be hired (DeWitt & Denver, 2020), and rightfully so if they are indeed more motivated and lower risk. It can also be beneficial to employers who use this signal to select a lower-risk applicant. In sum, even if a program does not have a causal effect, it can be a valuable signal on the labor market to both participants (job seekers) and employers. The key is that for a *program to be an effective signal, it must be both voluntary and rigorous.*

Conclusions

In sum, this chapter reviewed the evidence base surrounding the relationship between employment and crime, which for decades has produced weak and/or conflicting evidence, in contrast to theoretical expectations. When then offered five recommendations to aid in the future development of employment-based programming:

1. Programs should be reach-in and wrap-around.
2. Programs should be holistic, addressing a wide variety of participant risks and needs.
3. Programs should focus on improving subjective job satisfaction by pairing individuals with jobs they like or give them meaning.
4. Programs should target identity change toward a prosocial identity.

5. Programs should not be evaluated solely on causality, as they can be beneficial by providing a strong signal on the labor market if they are voluntary and rigorous.

Foremost, our review emphasized the complexity of the relationship between employment and crime, which is certainly much more nuanced than simple direct effects between having a job and offending less. To the contrary, recent studies have recognized that not all jobs are the same and that the role of work in individuals' lives goes beyond simply earning a paycheck. Furthermore, we align with current research (Bushway, 2022) in arguing that even if employment is not itself a necessary cause of desistance, employment-based programs remain a cornerstone of that process by supporting the long-term viability of desistance (in financial terms but also as a source of identity) and as a signal to society that an individual is both willing and able to pursue a new trajectory. Instead of relying exclusively on the causal association between program participation and reductions in recidivism, stakeholders can instead take advantage of program completion as a prosocial signal, as properly designed programs can help to identify which individuals would take advantage of strong opportunities, and support those individuals with an increased chance at successful reintegration.

Future research is needed to continue to evaluate our recommendations as they are implemented in practice. In addition, both researchers and practitioners should carefully consider whether employment-related effects vary among specific subgroups (e.g., race, gender, risk-level), as prior research has documented meaningful differences in findings, which is formally referred to as "treatment effect heterogeneity" (e.g., Jaynes, 2020; Simons et al., 2002; Piquero et al., 2002).

References

Agnew, R. (2006). *Pressured into crime: An overview of general strain theory*. Roxbury.

Apel, R., & Horney, J. (2017). How and why does work matter? Employment conditions, routine actives, and crime among adult male offenders. *Criminology*, *55*(2), 307–343. doi: 10.1111/1745-9125.12134

Beauchamp, A., & Chan, S. (2014). The minimum wage and crime. *The BE Journal of Economic Analysis & Policy*, *14*(3), 1213–1235. doi: 10.1515/bejeap-2013-0130

Bushway, S. (2022). Job-related programs for people on supervision: Reframing the problem. *The ANNALS of the American Academy of Political and Social Science*, *701*(1), 98–113. doi: 10.1177/00027162221115501

Bushway, S. D., & Apel, R. (2012). A signaling perspective on employment-based reentry programming. *Criminology and Public Policy*, *11*(1), 21–50. doi: 10.1111/j.1745-9133.2012.00786.x

Clark, A. E. (1998). *Measures of job satisfaction: What makes a good job? Evidence from OECD countries* (No. 34). OECD Publishing. doi: 10.1787/18151981

Cohen, L. E., & Felson, M. (1979). Social change and crime rate trends: A routine activity approach. *American Sociological Review*, *44*(4), 588–608. http://doi.org/10.2307/2094589

Cook, P. J., Songman, K., Braga, A. A., Ludwig, J., & O'Brien, M. E. (2015). An experimental evaluation of a comprehensive employment-oriented prisoner re-entry program. *Journal of Quantitative Criminology*, *31*, 355–382. doi: 10.1007/s10940-014-9242-5

DeWitt, S. E., & Denver, M. (2020). Criminal records, positive employment credentials, and race. *Journal of Research in Crime and Delinquency*, *57*(3), 333–368. doi: 10.1177/0022427819886111

Duwe, G. (2012). Evaluating the Minnesota comprehensive offender reentry plan (MCORP): Results from a randomized experiment. *Justice Quarterly*, *29*(3), 347–383. doi: 10.1080/07418825.2011.555414

Griffin, M. L., & Armstrong, G. S. (2003). The effect of local life circumstances on female probationers' offending. *Justice Quarterly*, *20*(2), 213–239. doi: 10.1080/07418820300095511

Grogger, J. (1998). Market wages and youth crime. *Journal of Labor Economics*, *16*(4), 756–791. doi: 10.1086/209905

Horney, J. D., Osgood, W., & Marshall, I. H. (1995). Criminal careers in the short-term: Intra-individual variability in crime and its relation to local life circumstances. *American Sociological Review*, *60*(5), 655–673. doi: 10.2307/2096316

James, N. (2015). *Offender reentry: Correctional statistics, reintegration into the community, and recidivism*. Congressional Research Service (CRS). https://sgp.fas.org/crs/misc/RL34287.pdf

Jaynes, C. M. (2020). The relationship between job quality and crime: Examining heterogeneity in treatment and treatment effect. *Journal of Research in Crime and Delinquency*, *57*(6), 693–740. doi: 10.1177/0022427820918899

Jaynes, C. M. (2022). Commitment to work: Assessing heterogeneity in the work-crime relationship from a social control perspective. *Journal of Developmental and Life-Course Criminology*, *8*, 394–418. doi: 10.1007/s40865-022-00188-w

Jencks, C., Perman, L., & Rainwater, L. (1988). What is a good job? A new measure of labor-market success. *American Journal of Sociology*, *93*(6),1322–1357. doi: 10.1086/228903

Kalleberg, A. L. (2011). *Good jobs, bad jobs*. Russell Sage Foundation.

Kimchi, A. (2019). Investigating the assignment of probation conditions: Heterogeneity and the role of race and ethnicity. *Journal of Quantitative Criminology*, *35*, 715–745. doi: 10.1007/s10940-018-9400-2

Laub, J. H., & Sampson, R. J. (2003). *Shared beginnings, divergent lives*. Harvard University Press.

La Vigne, N. L., Davies, E., Palmer, T., & Halberstadt, R. (2008). Release planning for successful reentry. Urban Institute. Retrieved from www.urban.org/sites/default/files/publication/32056/411767-Release-Planning-for-Successful-Reentry.PDF

Liu, L., & Bachman, R. (2021). Self-identity and persistent offending: A quantitative test of identity theory of desistance. *Journal of Offender Rehabilitation*, *60*(5), 341–357. doi: 10.1080/10509674.2021.1931623

Loughran, T. A., Nagin, D. S., & Nguyen, H. (2017). Crime and legal work: A Markovian model of the desistance process. *Social Problems*, *64*(1), 30–52. doi: 10.1093/socpro/spw027

Merton, R. K. (1938). Social structure and anomie. *American Sociological Review*, *3*(5), 672–682. doi: 10.2307/2084686

National Institute of Justice. (2022). Crime solutions: Rated practices. Retrieved from https://crimesolutions.ojp.gov/rated-practices#-2

Paternoster, R., & Bushway, S. (2009). Desistance and the feared self: Toward an identity theory of criminal desistance. *Journal of Criminal Law & Criminology*, *99*(4), 1103–1156. www.jstor.org/stable/20685067

Paternoster, R., Bachman, R., Kerrison, E., O'Connell, D., & Smith, L. (2016). Desistance from crime and identity: An empirical test with survival time. *Criminal Justice and Behavior*, *43*(9), 1204–1224. doi: 10.1177/0093854816651905

Petersilia, J. (2003). *When prisoners come home: Parole and prisoner reentry*. Oxford University Press.

Piquero, A. R., MacDonald, J. M., & Parker, K. F. (2002). Race, local life circumstances, and criminal activity. *Social Science Quarterly*, *83*(3), 654–670. doi: 10.1111/1540-6237.00107

Sampson, R. J., & Laub, J. H. (1993). *Crime in the making: Pathways and turning points through life*. Harvard University Press.

Savolainen, J. (2009). Work, family and criminal desistance: Adult social bonds in a Nordic welfare state. *The British Journal of Criminology*, *49*(3), 285–304. doi: 10.1093/bjc/azn084

Shaw, C. R. (1966 [1930]). *The Jackroller: A delinquent boy's own story*. The University of Chicago Press. (Original work published 1930).

Simons, R. L., Stewart, E., Gordon, L. C., Conger, R. D., & Elder Jr., G. H. (2002). A test of life-course explanations for stability and change in antisocial behavior from adolescence to young adulthood. *Criminology*, *40*(2), 401–434. doi: 10.1111/j.1745-9125.2002.tb00961.x

Skardhamar, T., & Savolainen, J. (2014). Changes in criminal offending around the time of job entry: A study of employment and desistance. *Criminology*, *52*(2), 263–291. doi: 10.1111/1745-9125.12037

Travis, J. (2005). *But they all come back: Facing the challenges of prisoner reentry*. The Urban Institute.

Uggen, C. (1999). Ex-offenders and the conformist alternative: A job quality model of work and crime. *Social Problems*, *46*(1), 127–151. doi: 10.2307/3097165

Uggen, C., & Thompson, M. (2003). The socioeconomic determinants of ill-gotten gains: Within-person changes in drug use and illegal earnings. *American Journal of Sociology*, *109*(1), 146–185. doi: 10.1086/378036

Visher, C. A., Debus, S., & Yahner, J. (2008). *Employment after prison: A longitudinal study of releases in three states*. Urban Institute, Justice Policy Center.

Wadsworth, T. (2006). The meaning of work: Conceptualizing the deterrent effect of employment on crime among young adults. *Sociological Perspectives*, *49*(3), 343–368. doi: 10.1525/sop.2006.49.3.34

Witte, A. D. (1980). Estimating the economic model of crime with individual data. *The Quarterly Journal of Economics*, *94*(1), 57–84. doi: 10.2307/1884604

Zatz, N. D. (2020). Get to work or go to jail: State violence and the racialized production of precarious work. *Law & Social Inquiry*, *45*(2), 304–338. doi: 10.1017/lsi.2019.56

Suggested Readings

Bushway, S. (2022). Job-related programs for people on supervision: Reframing the problem. *The ANNALS of the American Academy of Political and Social Science*, *701*(1), 98–113. doi: 10.1177/00027162221115501

Bushway, S. D., & Apel, R. (2012). A signaling perspective on employment-based reentry programming. *Criminology and Public Policy*, *11*(1), 21–50. doi: 10.1111/j.1745-9133.2012.00786.x

Cook, P. J., Songman, K., Braga, A. A., Ludwig, J., & O'Brien, M. E. (2015). An experimental evaluation of a comprehensive employment-oriented prisoner re-entry program. *Journal of Quantitative Criminology*, *31*, 355–382. doi: 10.1007/s10940-014-9242-5

Duwe, G. (2012). Evaluating the Minnesota comprehensive offender reentry plan (MCORP): Results from a randomized experiment. *Justice Quarterly*, *29*(3), 347–383. doi: 10.1080/07418825.2011.555414

Jaynes, C. M. (2020). The relationship between job quality and crime: Examining heterogeneity in treatment and treatment effect. *Journal of Research in Crime and Delinquency*, *57*(6), 693–740. doi: 10.1177/0022427820918899

Paternoster, R., & Bushway, S. (2009). Desistance and the feared self: Toward an identity theory of criminal desistance. *Journal of Criminal Law & Criminology*, *99*(4), 1103–1156. www.jstor.org/stable/20685067

4

MENTAL HEALTH INTERVENTIONS AND CRISIS RESPONSE TEAMS

Emily Torres, Kendall Smith, Lauren Fournier and Edelyn Verona

Introduction

Research estimates that 37% of state and federal inmates and 44% of jail inmates report a previous mental health diagnosis (Bronson & Berzofsky, 2017). Serious mental illnesses (e.g., major depressive disorder, schizophrenia spectrum disorders, and bipolar disorder) are found among 15% of men and 31% of women in jails (Steadman et al., 2009). The most commonly used explanation for the prevalence of individuals with mental health problems in the criminal justice system is the criminalization hypothesis, which posits that individuals with mental health problems, who would have formerly received psychiatric treatment, are placed in the criminal justice system (Lamb & Bachrach, 2001; Lamb & Weinberger, 1998, 2005; Lamb et al., 2004; Teplin, 1983). Indeed, the widely cited deinstitutionalization movement in the 1950s–60s shifted many individuals with mental illness from a hospital setting to communities without commensurate funding for mental health resources to manage their symptoms closer to home. At the same time, the increase in mental health problems among incarcerated populations is much more complex than deinstitutionalization alone (Mulvey & Schubert, 2017), and several questions remain about the association between mental health and crime. In particular, it is important to know which prevention or intervention programs can be put in place to reduce the number of persons with mental health problems who are processed through the criminal justice system.

Mental Health and Crime

Given the increased rates of mental health problems among incarcerated populations, professionals have attended to the role of psychological disorders (i.e., schizophrenia, bipolar disorder, personality disorders) and mental health problems (symptoms and behaviors associated with psychological distress) in the search for recidivism predictors and offending correlates (Lovell et al., 2002; Skeem et al., 2014; Steiner et al., 2011; Wilson et al., 2011). Research confirms that mental health problems are associated with increased rates of aggression, violence, and recidivism (Becker et al., 2012; Ostermann & Matejowski, 2014; Rosenblatt et al., 2000; Silver et al., 2008; Sullivan et al., 2007). Meta-analyses suggest an effect size of about .8 between serious mental illness, particularly psychotic disorders, and crime and violence (e.g., Brennan et al., 2000). Incarcerated persons with serious mental illness are more likely to

DOI: 10.4324/9781003219286-6

experience multiple incarcerations and substantially decreased time between periods of incarceration (Baillargeon et al., 2009; Cloyes et al., 2010; Skeem et al., 2011).

This summary of relationships between mental health problems and criminal justice involvement does not tell the whole story. First, the increased arrest and recidivism rates among individuals with mental health problems may partially stem from increased contact with law enforcement officers, who are often called for service in mental health crisis situations (Godfredson et al., 2011; Markowitz, 2011; Wood & Watson, 2017). There is also evidence that officers tend to view individuals with mental health problems as more threatening and dangerous (Markowitz, 2011; Watson et al., 2004). Second, mental health problems have been found to add little to criminal risk assessments when compared with the predictive utility of sociodemographic and behavioral risk factors, such as prior history of criminal/juvenile delinquency, younger age, and lower employment/education level (Bonta et al., 1998, 2014; Cunningham et al., 2005; Gendreau et al., 1996; Skeem et al., 2014). These findings refute the model that mental health problems are a direct cause of offending behavior. Instead, prior work suggests that mental health problems interact with a confluence of other compounding variables to exacerbate risk of offending (Douglas et al., 2009; Link et al., 2016; Skeem et al., 2014; Swanson et al., 2002; Witt et al., 2013). That is, individuals with mental health problems have a greater number of general risk factors (i.e., substance use, homelessness, witnessing violence, lower education/employment) for aggression, violence, and offending, and these other risk factors serve to compound risk and contribute to more extensive involvement in the criminal justice system (Bonta et al., 1998; Monahan et al., 2001; Peterson et al., 2014; Skeem et al., 2014; Steadman et al., 1998; Swanson et al., 2002; Walters & Crawford, 2014). Indeed, many of the factors associated with low socioeconomic opportunities overlap with those involved in the development of both mental health problems and crime and delinquency in youth (Toumbourou et al., 2007).

These insights motivate a first set of preliminary recommendations to help guide intervention and prevention:

- Engage mental health promotion efforts among persons living in socioeconomically disadvantaged communities. These efforts are likely to be more effective if enrichment is provided prior to than following involvement with the criminal justice system (Das et al., 2016; Helseth & Frazier, 2018; Toumbourou et al., 2007), with some research showing that access to mental health and substance use treatment among youth in foster care reduced odds of involvement in the juvenile justice system (Cuellar et al., 2004).
- Train law enforcement officers on the needs of persons with mental health problems and overturn myths that link mental illness with violence. This topic is tackled in the next section that focuses on the effects of mental health response programs (e.g., crisis intervention teams) on law enforcement management of persons with mental health problems (Bird & Schemilt, 2019).

Pre-Booking Crisis Response Teams

Self-reported and official arrest rates estimate that 25% of people with mental illness have been arrested at some point in their lifetime (Livingston, 2016). In the last 15 to 20 years, police departments have developed and implemented special programs and practices to assist people with mental illness at the point of contact with law enforcement in the community, typically in response to emergency or disturbance calls (Reul, 2010). This section will explore the current literature on pre-booking crisis response programs.

Crisis Intervention Teams. The most widely implemented specialized response to mental health crises and disturbance calls are crisis intervention teams (CITs) (Deane et al., 1999). Initially developed in Memphis, Tennessee, in 1988 (Cochran et al., 2000), the "Memphis model" serves as a popular prototype (Compton et al., 2008; Rodriguez, 2016). CITs are mainly composed of self-selected officers who complete 40-hour training on mental illness, mental health treatment, and strategies for deescalating mental health crises situations (Cochran et al., 2000; Compton et al., 2014; Skeem & Bibeau, 2008).

Most studies examining CITs are quasi-experimental and use pre- and post-tests or post-test only designs, with only a few studies using control or matched control groups of non-CIT officers. Several meta-analyses conducted in the last 10 years show small to moderate effect sizes of CITs on arrest (range –.09–.42), police use of force (range –.30–.51), and injuries to officers and persons with mental health problems (d = –.04) (Taheri, 2016; Seo et al., 2021). However, larger effect sizes are found for officers' self-reported perceptions of their self-efficacy/confidence (M_d = 1.10) and knowledge of mental illness (M_d = .90), and a moderate effect size for citizen diversion to mental health services (M_d = 0.40; Seo et al., 2021). Officer-reported data on arrests, use of force, and diversion yielded stronger effects in favor of CITs than when official data were used (Taheri, 2016; Seo et al., 2021). Additional reviews found that CIT officers, relative to pre-CIT training or to non-CIT officers, were more likely to transport individuals to mental health services and reported increased feelings of preparedness and increased knowledge relevant to mental illness and related encounters (Compton et al., 2008; Peterson & Densley, 2018). Another study also found that pre-booking diversion programs, most of which were CITs, increased the likelihood of mental health service utilization (i.e., mental health medication and hospitalization) among citizens during 3- and 12-month follow-up periods (Broner et al., 2004).

Thus far, a limited body of evidence shows CITs connect individuals to mental health services, but their effects on public safety outcomes, such as arrests, use of force, and injuries to police officers and the individuals with mental health problems they encounter, seem small and inconsistent. Future research should use both self-reported and official data (Taheri, 2016), longitudinal designs (Hartford et al., 2006; Peterson & Densely, 2018), and stronger experimental designs (Peterson & Densley, 2018).

Co-response models. Co-response models involve collaborative efforts between police departments and community mental health providers (Morabito et al., 2018; Reuland, 2010; Steadman et al., 2000), such that mental health professionals and specially trained police officers both respond to mental health-related calls (Shapiro et al., 2015). Unlike the CIT model, co-response models do not have a single prototype, which makes evaluations difficult (Morabito et al., 2018; Rodriguez, 2016; Teller et al., 2006).

The literature on co-response models is scarce, with approximately 30 quantitative evaluations mainly conducted in Australia, Canada, and the United Kingdom. Most studies only evaluate one model type using quasi-experimental designs that include pre-and post-tests or post-test only designs, with a few studies using control groups of regular police intervention. A recent meta-analysis of 11 studies found that co-response models produced strong effect sizes for outcomes of Section 136 detentions (M_d = .96), which are an emergency police power in the United Kingdom used to transport individuals with mental illness to receive assessments (e.g., local psychiatric hospitals but can include other emergency departments and even jail) (Keown et al., 2016). Moreover, officers' self-reported knowledge of mental illness (M_d = 1.26); ability, techniques, and skills (M_d = 1.64); and attitudes toward mental illness

(M_d = .77) also produced strong effect sizes (Seo et al., 2021). Additionally, outcomes of jail diversion (M_d = .37) and reduced arrests (M_d = .23) had moderate effect sizes. However, these findings should be interpreted with caution due to the small number of studies and sample sizes for each outcome measure (Seo et al., 2021). Several systematic reviews found positive perceptions of co-response models among consumers and family members, but their effects on reduced psychiatric hospital admissions by way of community-based mental health services were mixed (Shapiro et al., 2015; Puntis et al., 2018).

The limited findings on co-response models indicate a positive effect on perceptions among officers and consumers, but outcomes of diversion, arrests, and reduced psychiatric hospital admissions are inconsistent. Additional research is needed to identify how to best assess the efficacy of co-response models using more rigorous evaluations (Morabito et al., 2018; Seo et al., 2021). The following are a few key takeaways and recommendations for pre-booking crisis response programs:

- There is some evidence, albeit inconsistent, that pre-booking crisis response programs divert individuals to mental health services. One common theme in the literature is the importance of community partnerships between law enforcement and mental health service providers and advocates. Other local stakeholders, such as substance abuse service providers, elected officials, housing officials, community representatives, and others should also provide guidance and resources to more wholistically help divert individuals and connect them with services (Council of State Governments Justice Center, 2008).
- The two most widely used pre-booking crisis response programs, described previously, involve law enforcement in their response. Police officer involvement increases contact with individuals with mental health problems and the risk of arrest (Godfredson et al., 2011; Markowitz, 2011; Wood & Watson, 2017). On occasion, these encounters may result in injury or death for persons with mental health problems. This raises the question of whether police intervention is the most appropriate mental health crisis response and whether the officers are trained to deal with these crises.
- Specialized mental health-based crisis response programs that dispatch mental health professionals and social workers to non-criminal calls for service should be considered, as have been implemented in some cities more recently (e.g., St. Petersburg, FL; Denver, CO). Unfortunately, no empirical research has evaluated these or compared them to law enforcement-led crisis response teams.

Post-Booking Recidivism Reduction Programs

Mental health–targeted criminal justice programs have emerged to address the overrepresentation of persons with mental health problems in the criminal justice system. This section will discuss interventions that specifically address mental health problems among individuals involved in the justice system, including mental health courts, correctional programs, and reentry programs.

Mental Health Courts

Mental health courts (MHCs) almost exclusively make up the post-booking programs targeted toward individuals with mental health issues. MHCs typically involve recent arrestees who agree to court-supervised community mental health treatment as a diversion from incarceration with the goal of reducing future system involvement and ameliorating psychological symptoms. There have been approximately 45 evaluations of MHCs on recidivism, and these studies typically employed quasi-experimental designs involving non-matched control groups. Several recent meta-analyses and systematic reviews support the effectiveness of MHCs on recidivism reduction as measured by rearrests, severity of charges, reincarcerations, days incarcerated, and reconvictions (Canada et al., 2019; Dean, 2017; Fox et al., 2021; Lowder et al., 2018). The most recent meta-analysis by Fox and colleagues (2021) indicated a moderate to large effect size ($d = -.74$) of MHC participation on recidivism. However, studies using randomization showed less effectiveness for MHCs (Fox et al., 2021; Lowder et al., 2018). Moreover, individual programs often do not detail the types of services clients are referred to (Cross, 2011), making it difficult to determine which aspects are effective. Many MHCs may also exclude prospective participants if they have a history of violence (Hiday et al., 2016).

Research on MHCs, however, rarely answers whether the mental health treatment and symptom amelioration reduce risk for further criminal justice contact. Han and Redlich (2016) found that increased medication compliance and use of mental health services were linked with a significant reduction in rearrests; however, very few other studies have examined these mechanisms of change. Altogether, MHCs demonstrate effectiveness on recidivism reduction (Canada et al., 2019; Dean, 2017; Fox et al., 2021; Lowder et al., 2018). Future research should continue to examine what aspects of MHCs make them effective through more rigorous evaluations to better inform succeeding programs.

Correctional Programs

One of the most popular correctional programs applied to addressing mental health problems is cognitive behavioral therapy (CBT), which targets negative ways of thinking and encourages more effective behaviors. CBT programs for incarcerated persons with mental health issues aim to reduce psychological symptoms (e.g., depression, anxiety, PTSD, and anger) as well as recidivism. There have been over 100 studies assessing the effect of CBT programs on recidivism for justice-involved persons with mental health problems (the majority of which target anger control), and these studies are usually quasi-experimental designs, with unmatched or matched control groups. These evaluations have demonstrated effectiveness of CBT in reducing recidivism (Khodayarifard et al., 2010; Zlotnick et al., 2009), especially in samples with anger issues (Henwood et al., 2015).

Less is known about whether psychological symptom reduction can serve as a mechanism for recidivism reduction. A recent RCT assessing a modified CBT program (Reasoning and Rehabilitation 2: Short Version for Adults; Ross et al., 2007) found that significant psychological symptom reduction was not linked to recidivism (Kingston et al., 2018), and studies assessing if anger predicts recidivism have failed to find effects (Klepfisz et al., 2014; Loza & Loza-Fanous, 1999). Although results are promising, additional research is needed to make sound conclusions, particularly evaluations of programs not specifically targeted at anger issues and of the extent to which psychological symptom reduction contributes to decreased recidivism.

Reentry Programs

Reentry programs aim to facilitate successful transition from incarceration to the community after individuals are released. There are well over 100 evaluations of the effects of broad reentry programs that help address criminogenic risk factors by connecting individuals to social services upon release (e.g., social support, housing, employment). Although many of these reentry programs include a mental health treatment component, there are few that focus explicitly on individuals with mental health issues. As an exception, some reentry interventions employ adaptions of assertive community treatment, a model of care for the general population that connects individuals with severe mental health problems to community treatment to reduce psychological symptoms, homelessness, and rehospitalizations (Mueser et al., 1998). The forensic assertive community treatment (FACT) adapts this model for justice-involved individuals, including adding probation or parole officers to the treatment team, with the additional aim of reducing recidivism. The methodology of program evaluations varies, but most commonly consist of pre-post designs with no control groups. Findings regarding the effectiveness of FACT programs are mixed, although a recent meta-analysis assessing 16 studies indicates a moderate effect size ($d = -.48$) for recidivism reduction (i.e., rearrests, reincarceration, days incarcerated, reconviction; Goulet et al., 2021).

Lamberti and colleagues (2017) addressed methodological limitations of previous studies through an RCT design when evaluating the Rochester FACT program – a standardized model of FACT targeting criminogenic risk factors. Despite the fact that mental health needs were addressed in the treatment group, as indicated by significant reductions in hospitalizations, there were no significant differences between treatment and control groups for rearrests/incarceration. However, the FACT group did have fewer criminal convictions. Other studies have not examined the role of mental health treatment on recidivism reduction.

Past research indicates some evidence for the ability of reentry programs to decrease recidivism, and effects of these programs appear to be enhanced when they incorporate some mental health treatment components (Ndrecka, 2014). Despite this, fewer programs have focused solely on mental health treatment or services targeted for individuals with mental health issues. FACT programs have partially addressed this but find mixed effects for recidivism. FACT is encouraging for decreasing psychological symptoms but requires much more work to address recidivism.

Based on the limited evidence, post-booking programs for justice-involved individuals with mental health problems should:

- Broadly adhere to the risk-need responsivity (RNR) model, which assesses for and prioritizes level of risk, provides tailored treatment, and is considered the most effective model in reducing recidivism (Andrews et al., 1990; Andrews & Bonta, 2010). Key to this model are eight central risk factors (criminal history, procriminal attitudes, antisocial personality, procriminal peers, education/employment, family/marital, and substance abuse), which apply to all justice-involved persons, regardless of mental health problems (Duwe, 2017).
- Utilize interventions effective in general populations that target this broad range of risk factors (i.e., CBT; Aos et al., 2006).
- Incorporate ways to increase completion rates and time spent in programs as individuals who complete or spend more time in programs tend to demonstrate decreased levels of recidivism (Burns et al., 2013; Canada et al., 2019; Henwood et al., 2015).

Conclusion

Research has established the association between mental health, crime, and violence, although there are many additional factors that may increase the risk of offending. Next steps and recommendations at the community and criminal justice system level are as follows:

- Mental health problems combine with a range of other difficulties among persons (e.g., trauma, economic disadvantage, substance use) which exacerbate the risk of offending. As such, mental health promotion prior to involvement in the criminal justice system should target socioeconomically disadvantaged communities.
- Pre-booking crisis response programs provide training to law enforcement officers on mental health-related topics and show effectiveness in increasing officer knowledge and confidence but have not produced significant effects on public safety outcomes. Mental health-based crisis response programs that do not include law enforcement should be explored further.
- Post-booking recidivism reduction programs are less mental health oriented but show some effectiveness, which increases with the inclusion of mental health treatment components.

References

Andrews, D. A., & Bonta, J. (2010). Rehabilitating criminal justice policy and practice. *Psychology, Public Policy, and Law*, *16*(1), 39–55. doi: 10.1037/a0018362

Andrews, D. A., Zinger, I., Hoge, R. D., Bonta, J., Gendreau, P., & Cullen, F. T. (1990). Does correctional treatment work? A clinically relevant and psychologically informed meta-analysis. *Criminology*, *28*(3), 369–404. doi: 10.1111/j.1745-9125.1990.tb01330.x

Aos, S., Miller, M. G., & Drake, E. (2006). *Evidence-based adult corrections programs: What works and what does not*. Washington State Institute for Public Policy.

Baillargeon, J., Binswanger, I. A., Penn, J. V., Williams, B. A., & Murray, O. J. (2009). Psychiatric disorders and repeat incarcerations: The revolving prison door. *American Journal of Psychiatry*, *166*(1), 103–109.

Becker, S. P., Kerig, P. K., Lim, J. Y., & Ezechukwu, R. N. (2012). Predictors of recidivism among delinquent youth: Interrelations among ethnicity, gender, age, mental health problems, and posttraumatic stress. *Journal of Child & Adolescent Trauma*, *5*(2), 145–160.

Bird, K. S., & Shemilt, I. (2019). The crime, mental health, and economic impacts of prearrest diversion of people with mental health problems: A systematic review. *Criminal Behaviour and Mental Health*, *29*(3), 142–156.

Bonta, J., Blais, J., & Wilson, H. A. (2014). A theoretically informed meta-analysis of the risk for general and violent recidivism for mentally disordered offenders. *Aggression and Violent Behavior*, *19*(3), 278–287.

Bonta, J., Law, M., & Hanson, K. (1998). The prediction of criminal and violent recidivism among mentally disordered offenders: A meta-analysis. *Psychological Bulletin*, *123*(2), 123–142.

Brennan, P. A., Grekin, E. R., & Vanman, E. J. (2000). Major mental disorders and crime in the community. In *Violence among the mentally III* (pp. 3–18). Springer.

Broner, N., Lattimore, P. K., Cowell, A. J., & Schlenger, W. E. (2004). Effects of diversion on adults with co-occurring mental illness and substance use: Outcomes from a national multi-site study. *Behavioral Sciences & the Law*, *22*(4), 519–541. doi: 10.1002/bsl.605

Bronson, J., & Berzofsky, M. (2017). Indicators of mental health problems reported by prisoners and jail inmates, 2011–12. Bureau of Justice Statistics. Retrieved from https://bjs.ojp.gov/content/pub/pdf/imhprpji1112.pdf

Burns, P. J., Hiday, V. A., & Ray, B. (2013). Effectiveness 2 years postexit of a recently established mental health court. *American Behavioral Scientist*, *57*(2), 189–208. doi: 10.1177/0002764212465416

Canada, K., Barrenger, S., & Ray, B. (2019). Bridging mental health and criminal justice systems: A systematic review of the impact of mental health courts on individuals and communities. *Psychology, Public Policy, and Law*, *25*(2), 73–91. doi: 10.1037/law0000194

Cloyes, K. G., Wong, B., Latimer, S., & Abarca, J. (2010). Time to prison return for offenders with serious mental illness released from prison: A survival analysis. *Criminal Justice and Behavior*, *37*(2), 175–187.

Cochran, S., Deane, M. W., & Borum, R. (2000). Improving police response to mentally ill people. *Psychiatric Services*, *51*(10), 1315–1316. doi: 10.1176/appi.ps.51.10.1315

Compton, M. T., Bahora, M., Watson, A. C., & Oliva, J. R. (2008). A comprehensive review of extant research on crisis intervention team (CIT) programs. *Journal of the American Academy of Psychiatry and the Law Online*, *36*(1), 47–55.

Compton, M. T., Bakeman, R., Broussard, B., Hankerson-Dyson, D., Husbands, L., Krishan, S., . . . & Watson, A. C. (2014). The Police-Based Crisis Intervention Team (CIT) model: II. Effects on level of force and resolution, referral, and arrest. *Psychiatric Services*, *65*(4), 523–529. doi: 10.1176/appi.ps.201300108

Council of State Governments Justice Center. (2008). Law enforcement responses to people with mental illnesses: Improving outcomes. Retrieved from https://csgjusticecenter.org/wp-content/uploads/2020/02/le-essentialelements.pdf

Cross, B. (2011). Mental health courts effectiveness in reducing recidivism and improving clinical outcomes: A meta-analysis. Graduate Theses and Dissertations. Retrieved from https://digitalcommons.usf.edu/etd/3052

Cuellar, A. E., Markowitz, S., & Libby, A. M. (2004). Mental health and substance abuse treatment and juvenile crime. *Journal of Mental Health Policy and Economics*, 59–68.

Cunningham, M. D., Sorensen, J. R., & Reidy, T. J. (2005). An actuarial model for assessment of prison violence risk among maximum security inmates. *Assessment*, *12*(1), 40–49.

Das, J. K., Salam, R. A., Lassi, Z. S., Khan, M. N., Mahmood, W., Patel, V., & Bhutta, Z. A. (2016). Interventions for adolescent mental health: An overview of systematic reviews. *Journal of Adolescent Health*, *59*(4), S49–S60.

Dean, R. (2017). What is the impact of mental health courts? A systematic literature review. Retrieved from https://sophia.stkate.edu/msw_papers/721

Deane, M. W., Steadman, H. J., Borum, R., Veysey, B. M., & Morrissey, J. P. (1999). Emerging partnerships between mental health and law enforcement. *Psychiatric Services*, *50*(1), 99–101.

Douglas, K. S., Guy, L. S., & Hart, S. D. (2009). Psychosis as a risk factor for violence to others: A meta-analysis. *Psychological Bulletin*, *135*(5), 679–706.

Duwe, G. (2017). *The use and impact of correctional programming for inmates on pre-and post-release outcomes* (Vol. 48). US Department of Justice, Office of Justice Programs, National Institute of Justice. Retrieved from www.ojp.gov/pdffiles1/nij/250476.pdf

Fox, B., Miley, L. N., Kortright, K. E., & Wetsman, R. J. (2021). Assessing the effect of mental health courts on adult and juvenile recidivism: A meta-analysis. *American Journal of Criminal Justice*, *46*(4), 644–664. doi: 10.1007/s12103-021-09629-6

Gendreau, P., Little, T., & Goggin, C. (1996). A meta-analysis of the predictors of adult offender recidivism: What works!. *Criminology*, *34*(4), 575–608.

Godfredson, J. W., Thomas, S. D., Ogloff, J. R., & Luebbers, S. (2011). Police perceptions of their encounters with individuals experiencing mental illness: A Victorian survey. *Australian & New Zealand Journal of Criminology*, *44*(2), 180–195.

Goulet, M. H., Dellazizzo, L., Lessard-Deschênes, C., Lesage, A., Crocker, A. G., & Dumais, A. (2021). Effectiveness of forensic assertive community treatment on forensic and health outcomes: A systematic review and meta-analysis. *Criminal Justice and Behavior*. doi: 10.1177/00938548211061489

Han, W., & Redlich, A. D. (2016). The impact of community treatment on recidivism among mental health court participants. *Psychiatric Services*, *67*(4), 384–390. doi: 10.1176/appi.ps.201500006

Hartford, K., Carey, R., & Mendonca, J. (2006). Pre-arrest diversion of people with mental illness: Literature review and international survey. *Behavioral Sciences & the Law*, *24*(6), 845–856.

Helseth, S. A., & Frazier, S. L. (2018). Peer-assisted social learning for diverse and low-income youth: Infusing mental health promotion into urban after-school programs. *Administration and Policy in Mental Health and Mental Health Services Research*, *45*(2), 286–301. doi: 10.1007/s10488-017-0823-0

Henwood, K. S., Chou, S., & Browne, K. D. (2015). A systematic review and meta-analysis on the effectiveness of CBT informed anger management. *Aggression and Violent Behavior*, *25*(Part B), 280–292. doi: 10.1016/j.avb.2015.09.011

Hiday, V. A., Ray, B., & Wales, H. (2016). Longer-term impacts of mental health courts: Recidivism two years after exit. *Psychiatric Services*, *67*(4), 378–383.

Keown, P., French, J., Gibson, G., Newton, E., Cull, S., Brown, P., . . . McKinnon, I. (2016). Too much detention? Street Triage and detentions under Section 136 Mental Health Act in the North-East of England: A descriptive study of the effects of a Street Triage intervention. *British Medical Journal Open*, *6*(11), e011837.

Khodayarifard, M., Shokoohi-Yekta, M., & Hamot, G. E. (2010). Effects of individual and group cognitive-behavioral therapy for male prisoners in Iran. *International Journal of Offender Therapy and Comparative Criminology*, *54*(5), 743–755. doi: 10.1177/0306624X09344840

Kingston, D. A., Olver, M. E., McDonald, J., & Cameron, C. (2018). A randomised controlled trial of a cognitive skills programme for offenders with mental illness. *Criminal Behaviour and Mental Health*, *28*(4), 369–382. doi: 10.1002/cbm.2077

Klepfisz, G., O'Brien, K., & Daffern, M. (2014). Violent offenders' within-treatment change in anger, criminal attitudes, and violence risk: Associations with violent recidivism. *The International Journal of Forensic Mental Health*, *13*(4), 348–362. doi: 10.1080/14999013.2014.951107

Lamb, H. R., & Bachrach, L. L. (2001). Some perspectives on deinstitutionalization. *Psychiatric Services*, *52*(8), 1039–1045.

Lamb, H. R., & Weinberger, L. E. (1998). Persons with severe mental illness in jails and prisons: A review. *Psychiatric Services*, *49*(4), 483–492.

Lamb, H. R., & Weinberger, L. E. (2005). The shift of psychiatric inpatient care from hospitals to jails and prisons. *The Journal of the American Academy of Psychiatry and the Law*, *33*(4), 529–534.

Lamb, H. R., Weinberger, L. E., & Gross, B. H. (2004). Mentally ill persons in the criminal justice system: Some perspectives. *Psychiatric Quarterly*, *75*(2), 107–126.

Lamberti, J. S., Weisman, R. L., Cerulli, C., Williams, G. C., Jacobowitz, D. B., Mueser, K. T., Marks, P. D., Strawderman, R. L., Harrington, D., Lamberti, T. A., & Caine, E. D. (2017). A randomized controlled trial of the Rochester forensic assertive community treatment model. *Psychiatric Services*, *68*(10), 1016–1024. doi: 10.1176/appi.ps.201600329

Link, N. W., Cullen, F. T., Agnew, R., & Link, B. G. (2016). Can general strain theory help us understand violent behaviors among people with mental illnesses? *Justice Quarterly*, *33*(4), 729–754.

Livingston, J. D. (2016). Contact between police and people with mental disorders: A review of rates. *Psychiatric Services*, *67*(8), 850–857.

Lovell, D., Gagliardi, G. J., & Peterson, P. D. (2002). Recidivism and use of services among persons with mental illness after release from prison. *Psychiatric Services*, *53*(10), 1290–1296.

Lowder, E. M., Rade, C. B., & Desmarais, S. L. (2018). Effectiveness of mental health courts in reducing recidivism: A meta analysis. *Psychiatric Services*, *69*(1), 15–22. doi: 10.1176/appi.ps.201700107

Loza, W., & Loza-Fanous, A. (1999). Anger and prediction of violent and nonviolent offenders' recidivism. *Journal of Interpersonal Violence*, *14*(10), 1014–1029. doi: 10.1177/088626099014010002

Markowitz, F. E. (2011). Mental illness, crime, and violence: Risk, context, and social control. *Aggression & Violent Behavior*, *16*(1), 36–44.

Monahan, J., Steadman, H. J., Silver, E., Appelbaum, P. S., Robbins, P. C., Mulvey, E. P., . . . Banks, S. (2001). *Rethinking risk assessment: The MacArthur study of mental disorder and violence*. Oxford University Press.

Morabito, M. S., Savage, J., Sneider, L., & Wallace, K. (2018). Police response to people with mental illnesses in a major US city: The Boston experience with the co-responder model. *Victims & Offenders*, *13*(8), 1093–1105.

Mueser, K. T., Bond, G. R., Drake, R. E., & Resnick, S. G. (1998). Models of community care for severe mental illness: A review of research on case management. *Schizophrenia Bulletin*, *24*(1), 37–74. doi: 10.1093/oxfordjournals.schbul.a03331.

Mulvey, E. P., & Schubert, C. A. (2017). Mentally Ill individuals in Jails and Prisons. *Crime and Justice*, *46*(1), 231–277.

Ndrecka, M. (2014a). *The impact of reentry programs on recidivism: A meta-analysis*. University of Cincinnati.

Ndrecka, M. (2014b). The impact of reentry programs on recidivism: A meta-analysis (Unpublished doctoral dissertation). School of Criminal Justice, University of Cincinnati.

Ostermann, M., & Matejkowski, J. (2014). Exploring the intersection of mental health and release status with recidivism. *Justice Quarterly*, *31*(4), 746–766.

Peterson, J. K., & Densley, J. (2018). Is Crisis Intervention Team (CIT) training evidence-based practice? A systematic review. *Journal of Crime and Justice*, *41*(5), 521–534.

Peterson, J. K., Skeem, J., Kennealy, P., Bray, B., & Zvonkovic, A. (2014). How often and how consistently do symptoms directly precede criminal behavior among offenders with mental illness?. *Law and Human Behavior*, *38*(5), 439.

Puntis, S., Perfect, D., Kirubarajan, A., Bolton, S., Davies, F., Hayes, A., Harriss, E., & Molodynski, A. (2018). A systematic review of co-responder models of police mental health 'street' triage. *BMC Psychiatry*, *18*(1). doi: 10.1186/s12888-018-1836-2

Reuland, M. (2010). Tailoring the police response to people with mental illness to community characteristics in the USA. *Police Practice and Research: An International Journal*, *11*(4), 315–329.

Rodriguez, V. M. (2016). *The Impact of Psychiatric Emergency Response Team (PERT) training on law enforcement officers on time and disposition responding to mental health related emergencies in urban, suburban, and rural communities* (PsyD thesis). Alliant International University.

Rosenblatt, J. A., Rosenblatt, A., & Biggs, E. E. (2000). Criminal behavior and emotional disorder: Comparing youth served by the mental health and juvenile justice systems. *The Journal of Behavioral Health Services & Research*, *27*(2), 227–237.

Ross, R. R., Hillborn, J., & Liddle, P. (2007). *Reasoning & rehabilitation 2: Short version for adults*. Cognitive Centre of Canada.

Seo, C., Kim, B., & Kruis, N. E. (2021). A meta-analysis of police response models for handling people with mental illnesses: Cross-country evidence on the effectiveness. *International Criminal Justice Review*, *31*(2), 182–202.

Shapiro, G. K., Cusi, A., Kirst, M., O'Campo, P., Nakhost, A., & Stergiopoulos, V. (2015). Co-responding police-mental health programs: A review. *Administration and Policy in Mental Health and Mental Health Services Research*, *42*(5), 606–620.

Silver, E., Felson, R. B., & Vaneseltine, M. (2008). The relationship between mental health problems and violence among criminal offenders. *Criminal Justice and Behavior*, *35*(4), 405–426.

Skeem, J. L., & Bibeau, L. (2008). How does violence potential relate to crisis intervention team responses to emergencies? *Psychiatric Services*, *59*(2), 201–204. doi: 10.1176/ps.2008.59.2.201

Skeem, J. L., Manchak, S., & Peterson, J. K. (2011). Correctional policy for offenders with mental illness: Creating a new paradigm for recidivism reduction. *Law and Human Behavior*, *35*(2), 110–126. doi: 10.1007/s10979-010-9223-7

Skeem, J. L., Winter, E., Kennealy, P. J., Louden, J. E., Tatar, I. I., & Joseph, R. (2014). Offenders with mental illness have criminogenic needs, too: Toward recidivism reduction. *Law and Human Behavior*, *38*(3), 212.

Steadman, H. J., Deane, M. W., Borum, R., & Morrissey, J. P. (2000). Comparing outcomes of major models of police responses to mental health emergencies. *Psychiatric Services*, *51*(5), 645–649.

Steadman, H. J., Mulvey, E. P., Monahan, J., Robbins, P. C., Appelbaum, P. S., Grisso, T., . . . Silver, E. (1998). Violence by people discharged from acute psychiatric inpatient facilities and by others in the same neighborhoods. *Archives of General Psychiatry*, *55*(5), 393–401.

Steadman, H. J., Osher, F. C., Robbins, P. C., Case, B., & Samuels, S. (2009). Prevalence of serious mental illness among jail inmates. *Psychiatric Services*, *60*(6), 761–765.

Steiner, H., Silverman, M., Karnik, N. S., Huemer, J., Plattner, B., Clark, C. E., Blair, J. R., & Haapanen, R. (2011). Psychopathology, trauma and delinquency: Subtypes of aggression and their relevance for understanding young offenders. *Child and Adolescent Psychiatry and Mental Health*, *5*(1), 21.

Sullivan, C. J., Veysey, B. M., Hamilton, Z. K., & Grillo, M. (2007). Reducing out-of-community placement and recidivism: Diversion of delinquent youth with mental health and substance use problems from the justice system. *International Journal of Offender Therapy and Comparative Criminology*, *51*(5), 555–577.

Swanson, J. W., Swartz, M. S., Essock, S. M., Osher, F. C., Wagner, H. R., Goodman, L. A., Rosenberg, S. D., & Meador, K. G. (2002). The social-environmental context of violent behavior in persons treated for severe mental illness. *American Journal of Public Health*, *92*(9), 1523–1531.

Taheri, S. A. (2016). Do crisis intervention teams reduce arrests and improve officer safety? A systematic review and meta-analysis. *Criminal Justice Policy Review*, *27*(1), 76–96.

Teller, J. L., Munetz, M. R., Gil, K. M., & Ritter, C. (2006). Crisis intervention team training for police officers responding to mental disturbance calls. *Psychiatric Services*, *57*(2), 232–237.

Teplin, L. A. (1983). The criminalization of the mentally ill: Speculation in search of data. *Psychological Bulletin*, *94*(1), 54–67.

Toumbourou, J. W., Hemphill, S. A., Tresidder, J., Humphreys, C., Edwards, J., & Murray, D. (2007). Mental health promotion and socio-economic disadvantage: Lessons from substance abuse, violence and crime prevention and child health. *Health Promotion Journal of Australia*, *18*(3), 184–190.

Walters, G. D., & Crawford, G. (2014). Major mental illness and violence history as predictors of institutional misconduct and recidivism: Main and interaction effects. *Law and Human Behavior*, *38*(3), 238.

Watson, A. C., Corrigan, P. W., & Ottai, V. (2004). Police officer attitudes and decisions regarding persons with mental illness. *Psychiatric Services*, *55*, 46–53.

Wilson, A. B., Draine, J., Hadley, T., Metraux, S., & Evans, A. (2011). Examining the impact of mental illness and substance use on recidivism in a county jail. *International Journal of Law and Psychiatry*, *34*(4), 264–268.

Witt, K., van Dorn, R., & Fazel, S. (2013). Risk factors for violence in psychosis: Systematic review and meta-regression analysis of 110 studies. *PLoS ONE*, *8*(2).

Wood, J. D., & Watson, A. C. (2017). Improving police interventions during mental health- related encounters: Past, present and future. *Policing and Society*, *27*(3), 289–299.

Zlotnick, C., Johnson, J., & Najavits, L. M. (2009). Randomized controlled pilot study of cognitive-behavioral therapy in a sample of incarcerated women with substance use disorder and PTSD. *Behavior Therapy*, *40*(4), 325–336. doi: 10.1016/j.beth.2008.09.004

5

OPIOID USE DISORDER, INFECTIOUS DISEASE, AND COORDINATED HARM REDUCTION IN A MEDICAL SETTING

Jason W. Wilson and Heather Henderson

Introduction

The medical model of addiction has gained increased acceptance over the last decade across healthcare, social science, law enforcement, and the general public. However, drug use largely remains an illegal activity. Within the health care system, criminal justice and legal issues associated with people who use drugs complicate the substance use disorder treatment space in a way not seen in the management of coronary artery disease, stroke, or diabetes. Furthermore, the legacy of stigma associated with drug use and co-occurring infectious diseases (e.g., HIV and HCV) has also perpetuated barriers for medical providers and healthcare systems wanting to design evidence-based treatment programs for persons who use drugs. This chapter will outline the key tenets of a coordinated harm reduction system using a medical model and public health approach. The evidence driving each node of the harm reduction network is reviewed, as well as the concomitant legal and criminal justice issues surrounding implementation. We focus on intersections between opioid use disorder, injection drug use, and infectious diseases. Opioid use disorder, through physiological dependence and escalating dosing, often leads to injection drug use, and, ultimately, injection drug use increases rates of blood-borne virus transmission.

Coordinated harm reduction systems take time to build, especially in local jurisdictions with restrictions prohibiting needle exchange. Linking opioid use disorder to infectious disease elimination in a medical setting provides a pathway to harm reduction that may be easier to move forward in an environment more restrictive to public health program implementation.

The Medical Model of Addiction

Research that positioned the brain as a target of addiction coalesced and changed approaches to addiction as a chronic relapsing brain disorder by the mid-2000s (Keane & Campbell, 2008; DuPont, 1997; Henderson, 2022). The brain disease approach was bolstered through the dopamine hypothesis which posits that ongoing drug use alters neural structures (Lester

DOI: 10.4324/9781003219286-7

and Koob) and neuroimaging studies demonstrate impaired dopamine transmission and hypodopaminergic states in persons who use drugs (Martinez et al., 2007; Melis & Spiga, 2005; Di Chiara & Bassareo, 2007; Henderson, 2022). The effects of addiction are pervasive across the person, as the reward system dysregulation manifests in decision making not just about drug use but in all aspects of life history.

Treatment approaches to addiction have not matched biomedical models of the pathophysiology of disease. While hyperlipidemia is measured specifically through LDL levels in the blood and then treated using statin medication, much of the approach to addiction involves mixes of counseling, religion, and legal motivations for cessation. Evidence for the effectiveness of these approaches are plagued by subjective markers of reporting and unconvincing findings, perpetuating a mismatch in pathophysiological disease and treatment, as there is no objective biomarker test of disease. While these mixed approaches may help with the experience of disease, there is less data that they have been effective in treating disease. Anthropologists have focused on the emergence of suffering in the space between disease: illness disconnection (Kleinman, 1978; Good, 2012).

To decrease stigma around drug use disorders, parity between the drug use medical model and other medical models must be realized. McLellan et al. (2000) demonstrated that relapse in drug addiction (40–60%) was similar to relapsing rates of uncontrolled diabetes (30–50%), hypertension (50–70%), and asthma (50–70%). The medical model of addiction not only centers addiction as biomedical phenomenon but also challenges the medical model itself to further the role of individual choice and social determinants of health (SDOH) in explaining drug use and health outcomes. Case and Deaton (2020) have further linked the opioid epidemic to a broader pain epidemic associated with underemployment and lower education levels that was associated with increased opioid prescriptions and a decrease in life expectancy that began in 2000 (Dowell et al., 2017). In other words, if addiction is a dysregulation of choices within the broader life history, then there are indeed social-level phenomena that perpetuate the disease. This does not mean that addiction does not fit a medical model, but, instead, every medical disease interplays with individual choice and social determinants of health (including past trauma and lived experiences). Our approach to harm reduction considers the disease and illness in design of an evidence-based system encountering biomedical and social determinants of health across the addiction continuum.

The Infectious Disease–Injection Drug Use Connection

A public health approach to drug addiction, especially injection drug use, must recognize and explicitly link the relationship between injection drug use and risk for infectious disease. HCV infection can spread via direct contact with blood residue in injecting supplies such as hollow bore needles. Injection drug use represents the majority of new HCV infections (NIDA Notes, 2020 Website). Sixty-five percent of people who inject drugs (PWID) will contract HCV within 1 year, and our own data gathered from 688 participants in a local harm reduction system demonstrates an HCV prevalence of 76%, matching the national estimate of 76.5% HCV positivity after 6 years of injection drug use (NIDA Notes, 2020 Website). Of 230 participants tested at our syringe exchange program during 1 year, 169 participants had HCV and 4 were HIV positive. One of those participants had both HCV and HIV. The CDC estimates that an injection drug user has a 1/160 chance of acquiring HIV every time they use a needle that has been used by a person with HIV, representing the second most common route of new HIV infection. There are about 36,000 new cases of HCV each year in the United States and approximately 4 million people living with chronic HCV. HCV can lead to liver failure and liver cancer, representing significant morbidity and mortality. This virus also cannot be cleared. Approximately 1.2 million people are living with HIV in the United States.

Establishing local HIV and HCV seropositivity is difficult without high-volume, broad-based screening programs (e.g., emergency department based). Significant changes to the law in 2015 by the Florida legislature allowed for opt-out testing during hospital encounters. Opt-out testing is similar to other diagnostic and treatment services provided during routine hospital encounters after a patient signs a general consent. In addition, counseling requirements were also relaxed. Statute 381.004 specifies that the opt-out approach to testing is suitable for healthcare settings as long as patients are notified orally or in writing (e.g., signage) that HIV testing is being conducted and that they can "opt-out" in writing. Opt-out decisions need to be documented in the medical record but specific written informed consent as part of a larger HIV screening program in a healthcare setting does not need to be uniquely identified during each encounter (FS 381.004, n.d.).

At our site of work, Tampa General Hospital Emergency Department, we implemented opt-out, non-targeted (i.e., everyone who meets CDC guidelines; Branson et al., 2006) screening for HIV and HCV (Schillie et al., 2020) in 2016. Our site links HIV- or HCV-positive patients to downstream care. Through this ED-based program, over 75,000 HIV and 80,000 HCV tests have been conducted, leading to the diagnosis of 4,331 patients with HCV antibody and 750 with HIV between May 2016 and December 2021. From 2016–2018, we were able to link over 90% of patients with HIV to care for antiretroviral therapy (ART). However, we struggled to link (<35%) patients with HCV and to initiate downstream treatment with direct acting antivirals (<3%). During this time period, the prevalence of HCV shifted from a disease in people born between 1946 and 1965 to people born after 1980. Those born after 1980 were more likely to be underinsured and also more likely to have acquired HCV from ongoing injection drug use. In addition, the seropositivity of HCV has increased, with new incidence of HCV rising from 11,500 in 2011 to over 36,000 in 2017. Therefore, in order to manage the escalating epidemic of HCV and opioid use disorder (OUD), these disease states must be understood syndemically (the relationship between social determinants of health, OUD, and HCV).

Medications for Opioid Use Disorder

Eliminating HCV (2030 WHO Goal, Dore & Bajis, 2021) will only be possible by co-managing the social determinants of health and, specifically, the likely ongoing injection drug use leading to new HCV diagnosis. People who inject drugs who present to the ED, either after overdose or in acute withdrawal, are in the ED during a liminal moment of crisis.

D'Onofrio et al. (2015) demonstrated that ED patients presenting with opioid dependence and clinical withdrawal could be given buprenorphine/naloxone [Suboxone] in the ED to increase retention in downstream care. Clinical withdrawal can be gauged using a validated clinical opioid withdrawal scale (COWS, Wesson & Walter, 2003), and buprenorphine/naloxone is available as a sublingual (dissolvable) tablet. The authors found that patients who received only a referral to opioid treatment services had less than a 40% retention in care rate (2015). Providing a brief intervention (e.g., provider affirmation of drug use dangers) only resulted in a modest increase in care retention to just over 40%. However, initiation of buprenorphine led to almost 80% care retention rate at 3 months. Follow-up studies demonstrated continued statically significant higher rates of care retention at 6 and 12 months as well (D'Onofrio et al., 2017). In other work, authors reported that 17,000 patients that presented to Massachusetts EDs after acute overdose had a 1-year mortality rate of 4.7%, and only 33% of patients were ever offered linkage to services for opioid use disorder therapy (Sordo et al., 2017). All-cause mortality decreased by 59% in 1 year in this same population after initiation of a buprenorphine treatment pathway. ED-based buprenorphine programs lead to increased care retention and save lives but are not widely adopted.

In 2022, dispensing and prescribing intravenous and oral opioids remains easier than dispensing and prescribing medications to treat opioid use disorder and decrease mortality. Barriers to use of opioid partial agonist therapy (e.g., buprenorphine and methadone) reifies stigmas in treating opioid use disorder. Buprenorphine is clinically "non-inferior" to methadone; however, our model advocates for scale up of buprenorphine instead of methadone for most patients given similar costs ($126/week for methadone, $115/week for suboxone, NIDA, 2021). While buprenorphine may be easier to divert, there is low-level presence of buprenorphine in overdose death data and the benefits of appropriate use outweigh theoretical concerns for inappropriate diversion (Han et al., 2021). We favor the decreased stigma of buprenorphine utilization (a tablet that can be taken at home), as well as the provider-level ability to dispense and prescribe (compared to a facility dispensation model for liquid methadone), so that it can be integrated into an ED or hospital encounter and prescribed across different spaces of care delivery (hospital; home; other facility such as incarceration, jail, prison). We have reservations regarding use of long-acting agonist medications such as injectable naltrexone (Vivitrol). In a large trial comparing buprenorphine and long-acting naltrexone, participants were less likely to achieve early stabilization and treatment initiation in the naltrexone arm, and doses of buprenorphine in the comparator arm were lower than that used in many clinical settings (Lee et al., 2018).

Medication for Opioid Use Disorder Programs

The Drug Addiction Treatment Act (DATA) in 2000 enacted requirements for physicians to undergo an 8-hour training course in use of buprenorphine (something not required to prescribe morphine, hydromorphone, fentanyl, oxycodone, oxycontin, or other opioids linked to increased mortality). Physicians who underwent training could then apply to obtain a waiver for prescribing buprenorphine, usually called the "X-waiver" given the X-denotation placed in front of a trained provider's DEA number (often all on their own expense). The requirement for X-waiver training has led to healthcare disparities that reflect already existing inequities in healthcare access. The rate of mortality in Black Americans increased 818% from synthetic opioids from between 2014 and 2017 (James et al., 2018). In France, all physicians have been able to prescribe buprenorphine since 1995, leading to a 79% decrease in opioid-related deaths in the following 4-year period (D'Onofrio et al., 2021; Auriocombe et al., 2004).

In 2019, bipartisan legislation, endorsed by multiple medical societies, titled the Mainstreaming Addiction Treatment (MAT) Act, was designed to end the DATA 2000 requirements. However, that legislation did not pass. In 2021, the Department of Health and Human services considered exempting physicians from the DATA 2000 requirements through the Practice Guidelines for the Administration of Buprenorphine for Treating Opioid Use Disorder (HHS, 2021) but reversed course after there were questions surrounding their authority to act. In April 2021, HHS did release new practice guidelines giving providers the ability to forego the additional DATA 2000 training if treating no more than 30 patients at a time (HHS, 2021). Providers must still apply for the X-waiver on the SAMHSA website. Passing of the MAT Act and full removal of the X-waiver would lead to decreased stigma, increase buprenorphine utilization, and decreased mortality.

Based on high rates of HCV infection among persons with inject drugs in our ED, we knew that there was imperative to co-locate pathways for HCV and opiate use disorder identification, stabilization, and linkage to care. Before 2019, we did not have any physicians in our ED with an X-waiver. However, we were able to creatively find a way to launch our program by creating a warm handoff model with a local substance use treatment center after administering emergency dosing of buprenorphine following Title 21, CFR, Part 1306.07(b) This part of the federal regulations states that "one day's medication may be administered to the person. . . . Such emergency treatment may be carried out for not more than three days" (Administering or Dispensing of Narcotic Drugs, 2020). Utilizing the emergency dispensing of buprenorphine, we initiated an ED-based medication assisted program in September 2018.

To avoid the stigmatizing language reflected in the term MAT and the focus on disorder, in 2022, we formally renamed our program from ED Medication for Opioid Use Disorder (MOUD) to ED BRIDGE (Building Recovery Integration for Drug Users) to better reflect our mission and services. Since September 2018, our program has grown substantially and is hard-wired into ED operations. Over a 3-year period, we also added ED-based peer recovery support specialists (people in recovery with specialized training in linkage to treatment services). Peers are an integral aspect of an ED-based medication program for opioid use disorder, as enrollment increases through shared lived experiences (Peers, 2021). During the 3-year period from 2018–2021, 688 unique participants were enrolled in the ED-based program, with take-home nasal spray naloxone offered in 48% of opioid use disorder encounters. Further, 70% of patients followed up and were retained in care, and 76% were identified as HCV positive. At the same time, our department has gone from no physicians with an X-waiver to 13 waivered providers.

Creation and implementation of an ED-based medication program for opioid use disorder requires preliminary community work with potential treatment partners to create memoranda of understanding to allow sharing of patient level data. In addition, operational specifics for follow-up need to be pre-established. Often, federal- and state-level funding (e.g., SAMHSA State Opioid Response grants) can be carved out to pay salaries for peers and to purchase naloxone. Treatment facilities can utilize state and federal dollars more widely available during the opioid crisis for the cost of buprenorphine or methadone. Weekly rounding is an essential aspect of success to ensure provider engagement and stakeholder buy-in. Recently, we have also introduced home-induction buprenorphine strategies for patients who are interested in initiation of partial opioid agonist therapy but are not yet in withdrawal. The large number of X-waivered physicians and trust in peer engagement and follow-up has allowed us to implement that program feature.

Unimagined obstacles have also been present, including differences in definitions across organizations and expectations and requirements for medication-assisted therapy or medication for opioid use disorder programs in an acute healthcare setting (e.g., the ED or hospital) compared to a downstream partner treatment organization. In Florida, the Florida Administrative Code (Code 65D-30) regulates substance use treatment facilities. This code was last updated in 2006, while the science and evidence for ED-based medication for opioid use disorder program have progressed substantially since 2015. There will be disjointed definitions and goals. As an ED-based program, we look at every encounter as an opportunity to initiate treatment, whereas Code 65D-30 specifies requirements for number of days of use and number of days of cessation prior to enrollment. The code is not very applicable to EDs but peers, as well as other interdisciplinary team members, may work at least part of the time in both spaces. These differences in perspective can best be overcome by weekly rounding to facilitate program goals and expectations.

While our program is ED based, medication programs for opioid use disorder have also found success in other settings. For example, a jail-based program demonstrated that buprenorphine utilization led to a 32% decrease in opioid use disorder, rearrest, probation violations, reconvictions, and reincarcerations among participants (Evans et al., 2022). Clearly MOUD programs work to decrease opioid use disorder and related sequelae. However, what are the harm reduction options for people not ready to stop using drugs or willing to enter into institutional or healthcare environments? A complete community-based coordinated harm reduction approach is necessary. Along with large ED-based programs, a needle exchange is critical component of a wraparound strategy to decreasing infectious disease transmission and opioid use disorder.

Syringe Exchange Programs: IDEA Tampa

Syringe exchange programs are an evidence-based approach to reducing opioid overdose deaths as well as rates of HIV and HCV infection (Fernandez et al., 2017; Gibson et al., 2001; Hurley et al., 1997; Barthlomew et al., 2021). Until 2016, there were no syringe exchange programs in Florida. In 2016, the Florida legislature passed SB242 (SB 242. Florida State Senate, n.d.) the Infectious Disease Elimination Act (IDEA). This act allowed one site (University of Miami) to operate a pilot sterile syringe service program. Within 2 years of operation, IDEA Miami identified an HIV risk network among persons who inject drugs, halting transmission of virus and preventing new cases of HIV (Tookes et al., 2020). The success of this program led to expansion of the IDEA legislation in 2019 (FS 381.0038(4), 2019). No tax dollars can be used to fund an exchange; 1:1 syringe exchange has to occur, and the county jurisdiction (e.g., Board of County Commissioners) must approve an exchange agreement with a single non-profit entity. The Department of Health must support the agreement and then collect data on exchange operations and report that back to the county commission. Exchange programs in Florida provide HIV and HCV testing, 1:1 needle exchange, naloxone distribution, STD prevention and education materials, linkage to care to other health system resources, and medical management of infectious diseases such as soft tissue and skin infections from IV drug use.

Tampa General Hospital, in partnership with the University of South Florida, celebrated 1 year of exchange operation in January 2022. IDEA Tampa operates 3 days a week. In year one, 540 unique participants utilized the sterile syringe services program, representing over 1,985 participant encounters and 1,430 repeat exchanges. In total, 117,532 used syringes were brought in, while 114,748 sterile syringes were distributed. Naloxone was widely distributed and utilized: 1,774 doses of nasal spray naloxone were handed out and 1,310 uses of naloxone, preventing or reversing overdose and overdose-related death. In addition, 215 HIV tests were conducted, identifying 4 participants with HIV who were then linked to care. 230 HCV tests were completed, and 169 participants had HCV antibodies and were potentially infectious, requiring follow-up viral load testing for overall HCV status.

There are now over 200 needle exchange programs across 34 states (NASEN, 2022). While there were no exchange sites in Florida in 2015, there are now 5 counties in Florida with operational exchange programs (Hillsborough, Dade, Broward, Palm Beach, Orange). Three additional counties, as of January 2022, have also passed an ordinance and identified an operating entity (Alachua, Pinellas, Manatee), while one other county has taken a preliminary step of passing the ordinance allowing for an exchange (Leon). Sterile syringe service programs are an important aspect of a fully coordinated harm reduction continuum. Our frequent involvement with county agencies and task forces to combat opioids and mental illness and to improve health care in Hillsborough County has been a critical aspect to achieving stakeholder, including law enforcement and city leadership, buy in. Steps for implanting a syringe exchange are outlined in the CDC technical standards manual (Javed et al., 2020).

The Full Harm Reduction Continuum

ED-based HIV and HCV screening programs lead to high volume, rapid scale-up of new HIV and HCV diagnoses. The discovery of high seropositivity further leads to identification of viral transmission mechanisms and the link between HIV, HCV, and opioid use disorder among people who inject drugs. Persons who inject drugs encounter the healthcare system, legal system, or other community check points at different paths in the addiction continuum. A fully coordinated harm reduction continuum engages people where they are along this spectrum. Our implementation of a warm-handoff, peer-led ED BRIDGE program with buprenorphine and the opening of the syringe exchange program all move Hillsborough county closer to coordinated harm reduction. There are a number of remaining barriers to preventing overdose death and infections that must be legally overcome.

In 2016, synthetic opioids overtook heroin as the leading cause of overdose and mortality (CDC, 2021). Fentanyl is the predominant synthetic agent. Drug suppliers utilize fentanyl as part of the opioid product mix because fentanyl is cheaper and more accessible than heroin or other opioids. However, the high potency of fentanyl leads to user dosing errors and unintentional overdose. Persons who inject drugs recognize the threat that synthetic opioids pose and are willing to reject use of fentanyl. However, to identify fentanyl in an opioid supply, test strips are necessary. Federal grants allow for the purchase and distribution of fentanyl tests strips to persons who inject drugs. As of January 2022, however, many states, including Florida, still consider fentanyl test strips illegal drug paraphernalia (FS893.145*)*. Pending state legislation (HB6101/SB1668) would legalize fentanyl test strips and save lives.

Coordinated harm reduction is a communitywide effort that begins before the hospital encounter. To implement a successful program, frontline responders and the criminal justice system must be involved. Prehospital emergency medical responses include training in the use of naloxone. In addition, patients who refuse transport may be served by "leave-behind Narcan" and provision of harm reduction resources (e.g., address and times for syringe exchange operation). Ultimately, we envision prehospital EMS buprenorphine use in acute overdose as well as ED-based syringe prescribing and buprenorphine and direct acting antivirals and antiretroviral therapy. Nuances in community frontline training revolve around when to transport patients into the hospital and went to place patients under a legal hold for their own safety (Marchman Act Florida, 2018). Our ultimate goal is for clear communication across prehospital, ED, and hospital-based care to and through our community partner substance use organizations. Future states envision citywide naloxone supplies and harm reduction vending machines and lockers. While that system is still a potentiality and vision, implementation of our infectious disease harm reduction model has successfully increased diagnosis of HIV and HCV, distribution of naloxone, intake of used syringes, and reversal of overdoses and changed lives through stabilization with buprenorphine.

Conclusions

We suggest the following action steps to establish a coordinated harm reduction system. We believe that linking opioid use disorder to infectious disease elimination provides a pathway to harm reduction that may be easier to move forward in an environment more restrictive to public health program implementation

1. Engage an emergency department champion for infectious disease screening and linkage to care as well as for opioid use disorder. The scale and impact of an engaged ED, and the associated healthcare system, will rapidly drive change through ED volume.
2. Initiate HIV and HCV screening programs following the CDC guidelines. Use the initiation of HIV and HCV screening programs as an opportunity to build a stakeholder network for linkage to care and treatment. That stakeholder network will overlap and be synergistic with an opioid use disorder provider network. Utilize HIV and HCV positive screening encounters to gather further information regarding patient-level use of injection drugs.
3. Through deidentified population data of the HIV/HCV screening program, demonstrate the connection between HIV, HCV, and injection drug use. Work with the medical examiner to integrate data for overdose deaths and demonstrate the ongoing public health overdose and infectious disease crisis related to opioid use disorder.
4. Contact your area entities that manage state opioid response dollars (in Florida, these funds flow through the Department of Children and Families to managing entities, such as the Central Florida Behavioral Health Network) and identify that you are building a coordinated harm reduction system. Work with funding sources to draw down in-kind naloxone supplies for broad distribution to law enforcement, EMS, and emergency departments for leave-behind programs on the frontline and take home at discharge from the ED.
5. Work with the ED champion to develop an ED-based buprenorphine program for patients with a Clinical Opioid Withdrawal Score (COWS) ≥ 4. This can be initiated with non-waivered providers using one-time buprenorphine in the ED. However, the ED champion should encourage providers to apply for their own X-waiver, allowing a bridging prescription at time of discharge.
6. Use the same funding source and stakeholder network for HIV and HCV linkage to care to build a network for follow-up for opioid use disorder. Also lean on this funding source to deploy peers into the ED.
7. Collect follow-up data and share with county jurisdiction and the Department of Health, as well as provider and facility stakeholders.
8. Follow state laws and the syringe exchange technical standards outlined in the CDC manual to initiate a syringe service program. Once a syringe service program is established in the setting of an ongoing ED-based medication for opioid use disorder program, work with county and prehospital systems to fully develop a coordinated harm reduction system.
9. Continue to triangulate data with the Department of Health, medical examiner, and care providers to show a link between decreased overdose deaths, HIV and HCV identification, linkage, and imitation of treatment. Begin to use this data to drive EMS and law enforcement education and enhanced repones strategies (e.g., naloxone in the field), ultimately moving the local region to a fully implemented harm reduction continuum.

Acknowledgments

Our work is made possible through the FOCUS program, the NIH HEAL initiative, the ED-INNOVATION study, cooperation and engagement of partners at USF Morsani College of Medicine, Tampa General Hospital, DACCO (The Cove), ACTS, Central Florida Behavioral Healthcare Network, ED physicians, our peers, and all of our frontline staff.

The FOCUS Program is a public health initiative that enables partners to develop and share best practices in routine blood borne virus (HIV, HCV, HBV) screening, diagnosis, and linkage to care in accordance with screening guidelines promulgated by the U.S. Centers for Disease Control and Prevention (CDC), the U.S. Preventive Services Task Force (USPSTF), and state and local public health departments.

FOCUS funding supports HIV, HCV, and HBV screening and linkage to the first medical appointment after diagnosis. FOCUS partners do not use FOCUS awards for activities beyond linkage to the first medical appointment.

References

Administering or Dispensing of Narcotic Drugs. (2020). eCFR: 21 CFR 1306.07. Ecfr.Gov. Retrieved from www.ecfr.gov/current/title-21/chapter-II/part-1306/subject-group-ECFR1eb5bb3a23fddd0/section-1306.07

Auriacombe, M., Fatséas, M., Dubernet, J., Daulouède, J.-P., & Tignol, J. (2004). French field experience with buprenorphine. *The American Journal on Addictions*, *13*(Suppl. 1), S17–S28. doi: 10.1080/10550490490440780

Bartholomew, T. S., Patel, H., McCollister, K., Feaster, D. J., & Tookes, H. E. (2021). Implementation and first-year operating costs of an academic medical center-based syringe services program. *Harm Reduction Journal*, *18*(1), 116. doi: 10.1186/s12954-021-00563-8

Branson, B. M., Handsfield, H. H., Lampe, M. A., Janssen, R. S., Taylor, A. W., Lyss, S. B., Clark, J. E., & Centers for Disease Control and Prevention (CDC). (2006). Revised recommendations for HIV testing of adults, adolescents, and pregnant women in health-care settings. *Recommendations and Reports: Morbidity and Mortality Weekly Report*, *55*(RR-14), 1–17; quiz CE1–4.

Case, A., Deaton, A., & Stone, A. A. (2020). Decoding the mystery of American pain reveals a warning for the future. *Proceedings of the National Academy of Sciences of the United States of America*, *117*(40), 24785–24789. doi: 10.1073/pnas.2012350117

CDC. (2021, March 11). Overdose death rates involving opioids, by type, United States, 1999–2019. Cdc.gov. Retrieved from https://www.cdc.gov/drugoverdose/data/OD-deaths-2019.html

Di Chiara, G., & Bassareo, V. (2007). Reward system and addiction: What dopamine does and doesn't do. *Current Opinion in Pharmacology*, *7*(1), 69–76. doi: 10.1016/j.coph.2006.11.003

D'Onofrio, G., Hawk, K. F., Herring, A. A., Perrone, J., Cowan, E., McCormack, R. P., Dziura, J., et al. (2021). The design and conduct of a randomized clinical trial comparing emergency department initiation of sublingual versus a 7-day extended-release injection formulation of buprenorphine for opioid use disorder: Project ED innovation. *Contemporary Clinical Trials*. doi: 10.1016/j.cct.2021.106359

D'Onofrio, G., O'Connor, P. G., Pantalon, M. V., Chawarski, M. C., Busch, S. H., Owens, P. H., Bernstein, S. L., & Fiellin, D. A. (2015). Emergency department–initiated buprenorphine/naloxone treatment for opioid dependence: A randomized clinical trial. *JAMA: The Journal of the American Medical Association*, *313*(16), 1636.

Dore, G. J., & Bajis, S. (2021). Hepatitis C virus elimination: Laying the foundation for achieving 2030 targets. *Nature Reviews. Gastroenterology & Hepatology*, *18*(2), 91–92. doi: 10.1038/s41575-020-00392-3

Dowell, D., Arias, E., Kochanek, K., Anderson, R., Guy, G. P., Jr, Losby, J. L., & Baldwin, G. (2017). Contribution of opioid-involved poisoning to the change in life expectancy in the United States, 2000–2015. *JAMA: The Journal of the American Medical Association*, *318*(11), 1065–1067. doi: 10.1001/jama.2017.9308

DuPont, R. (1997). *The selfish brain: Learning from addiction*. American Psychiatric Association.

Evans, E. A., Wilson, D., & Friedmann, P. D. (2022). Recidivism and mortality after in-jail buprenorphine treatment for opioid use disorder. *Drug and Alcohol Dependence*, *231*(109254), 109254. doi: 10.1016/j.drugalcdep.2021.109254

Fernandes, R. M., Cary, M., Duarte, G., Jesus, G., Alarcão, J., Torre, C., Costa, S., Costa, J., & Carneiro, A. V. (2017). Effectiveness of needle and syringe Programmes in people who inject drugs – An overview of systematic reviews. *BMC Public Health*, *17*(1), 309. doi: 10.1186/s12889-017-4210-2

FS 381.0038(4). (2019). Infectious Disease Elimination Act (IDEA), section 381.0038(4), Florida statutes. Statutes & constitution: View statutes: Online sunshine. State.Fl.Us. Retrieved from www.leg.state.

fl.us/Statutes/index.cfm?App_mode=Display_Statute&Search_String=&URL=0300-0399/0381/Sections/0381.0038.html

FS 381.004. (n.d.). Florida HIV Testing Law 381.004. Statutes & constitution: View statutes: Online sunshine. State.Fl.Us. Retrieved from www.leg.state.fl.us/Statutes/index.cfm?App_mode=Display_Statute&URL=0300-0399/0381/Sections/0381.004.html

Gibson, D. R., Flynn, N. M., & Perales, D. (2001). Effectiveness of syringe exchange programs in reducing HIV risk behavior and HIV seroconversion among injecting drug users. *AIDS (London, England)*, *15*(11), 1329–1341. doi: 10.1097/00002030-200107270-00002

Good, B. J. (2012). *Lewis Henry Morgan lectures: Medicine, rationality and experience: An anthropological perspective: An anthropological perspective*. Cambridge University Press. doi: 10.1017/cbo9780511811029

Han, B., Christopher, M. J., Emily, B. E., & Wilson, M. C. (2021). Trends in and characteristics of buprenorphine misuse among adults in the US. *JAMA Network Open*, *4*(10), e2129409.

Health and Human Services Department. (2021). Practice guidelines for the administration of buprenorphine for treating opioid use disorder. In *Federal register* (Vol. 86, pp. 22439–22440). Retrieved form www.federalregister.gov/d/2021-08961

Henderson, H. D. (2022). *Applied anthropology of addiction in clinical spaces: Co-developing and assessing a novel opioid treatment pathway*. University of South Florida.

Hurley, S. F., Jolley, D. J., & Kaldor, J. M. (1997). Effectiveness of needle-exchange programmes for prevention of HIV infection. *Lancet*, *349*(9068), 1797–1800. doi: 10.1016/S0140-6736(96)11380-5

James, K., & Jordan, A. (2018). The opioid crisis in Black communities. *The Journal of Law, Medicine & Ethics: A Journal of the American Society of Law, Medicine & Ethics*, *46*(2), 404–421. doi: 10.1177/1073110518782949

Javed, Z., Burk, K., Facente, S., Pregam, L., Ali, A., & Asher, A. (2020). *Syringe services programs a technical package of effective strategies and approaches for planning, design, and implementation*. CDC.

Keane, H., & Campbell, N. D. (2008). *Discovering addiction: The science and politics of substance abuse research* (p. 336). Ann Arbor: The university of Michigan press [$50.00 (cloth). ISBN 978-0-472-11610-2. *Journal of the History of the Behavioral Sciences*, *44*(4), 370–371. doi: 10.1002/jhbs.20335]

Kleinman, A., Eisenberg, L., & Good, B. (1978). Culture, illness, and care: Clinical lessons from anthropologic and cross-cultural research. *Annals of Internal Medicine*, *88*(2), 251–258. doi: 10.7326/0003-4819-88-2-251

Lee, J. D., Edward, V. N. Jr., Patricia, N., Bachrach, K., Genie, L. B., Bhatt, S., & Farkas, S. (2018). Comparative effectiveness of extended-release naltrexone versus buprenorphine-naloxone for opioid relapse prevention (X:BOT): A multicentre, open-label, randomised controlled trial. *The Lancet*, *391*(10118), 309–318.

Marchman Act Florida. (2018, November 26). Marchman Act Florida. Retrieved from https://marchmanactflorida.com/

Martinez, D., Kim, J.-H., Krystal, J., & Abi-Dargham, A. (2007). Imaging the neurochemistry of alcohol and substance abuse. *Neuroimaging Clinics of North America*, *17*(4), 539–555. doi: 10.1016/j.nic.2007.07.004

McLellan, A. T., Lewis, D. C., O'Brien, C. P., & Kleber, H. D. (2000). Drug dependence, a chronic medical illness: Implications for treatment, insurance, and outcomes evaluation. *JAMA: The Journal of the American Medical Association*, *284*(13), 1689–1695.

Melis, M., Spiga, S., & Diana, M. (2005). The dopamine hypothesis of drug addiction: hypodopaminergic state. *International Review of Neurobiology*, *63*, 101–154. doi: 10.1016/S0074-7742(05)63005-X

NIDA. (2021, April 13.). How much does opioid treatment cost?. Retrieved from https://nida.nih.gov/publications/research-reports/medications-to-treat-opioid-addiction/how-much-does-opioid-treatment-cost

North American Syringe Exchange Network. (n.d.). NASEN. Retrieved from https://nasen.org/

Peers. (2021). Samhsa.Gov. Retrieved from www.samhsa.gov/brss-tacs/recovery-support-tools/peers

SAMHSA. Application for X-Waiver. Retrieved from https://buprenorphine.samhsa.gov/forms/select-practitioner-type.php

SB 242. The Florida Senate. (n.d.). Flsenate.Gov. Retrieved from www.flsenate.gov/Session/Bill/2016/242

Schillie, S., Wester, C., Osborne, M., Wesolowski, L., & Ryerson, A. B. (2020). CDC recommendations for hepatitis C screening among adults – United States, 2020. *Recommendations and Reports. Morbidity and Mortality Weekly Report*, *69*(2), 1–17. doi: 10.15585/mmwr.rr6902a1

Sordo, L., Barrio, G., Bravo, M. J., Indave, B. I., Degenhardt, L., Wiessing, L., Ferri, M., & Pastor-Barriuso, R. (2017). Mortality risk during and after opioid substitution treatment: systematic review and meta-analysis of cohort studies. *BMJ (Clinical Research Ed.)*, *357*, j1550. doi: 10.1136/bmj.j1550

Tookes, H., Bartholomew, T. S., Geary, S., Matthias, J., Poschman, K., Blackmore, C., Philip, C., Suarez, E., Forrest, D. W., Rodriguez, A. E., Kolber, M. A., Knaul, F., Colucci, L., & Spencer, E. (2020). Rapid identification and investigation of an HIV risk network among people who inject drugs – Miami, FL, 2018. *AIDS and Behavior*, *24*(1), 246–256. doi: 10.1007/s10461-019-02680-9

Wesson, D. R., & Walter, L. (2003). The Clinical Opiate Withdrawal Scale (COWS). *Journal of Psychoactive Drugs*, *35*(2), 253–259.

6

ADULT VICTIMS OF VIOLENCE

Outcomes and Services

Jillian J. Turanovic and Szilvia D. Biro

Introduction

Few events are thought to be as traumatic as violent victimization. Research has linked being victimized to a range of health and social problems in the short and long term, including symptoms of depression and post-traumatic stress, poor physical health, substance use, relationship strain, financial hardship, and problems at school or work (Langton & Truman, 2014; Turanovic & Pratt, 2019). These consequences are particularly concerning given that victimization affects millions of Americans each year. Recent estimates from the National Crime Victimization Survey (NCVS) suggest that, in 2020, there were 4.6 million violent incidents involving victims aged 12 or older (Morgan & Thompson, 2021), with rates being highest among victims aged 18–24. And though the bulk of research on violent trauma and its impacts focuses on childhood or adolescence (Turanovic, 2018), victimization in adulthood also carries numerous lasting consequences.

One of the most serious of these consequences is the perpetration of crime. Violent victimization is one of the strongest and most consistent risk factors for criminal behavior (Lauritsen & Laub, 2007), in part because victimization involves the violation of justice norms, is associated with low social control, and can create pressures or incentives for individuals to engage in maladaptive coping (Agnew, 2002). In certain contexts, victimization can also increase motives for revenge or retaliation, which can contribute to a cycle of violence (Pyrooz et al., 2014). Recurrent experiences with violence are common among adult crime victims and research consistently finds that individuals who are victimized once are more likely to be victimized again (Farrell & Pease, 2001; Turanovic & Pratt, 2014).

In efforts to mitigate the consequences that victims experience – including their risks of repeat victimization and criminal involvement – various victim service programs have been developed. Today, over 12,000 programs of various sizes operate throughout the country, providing a range of services to crime victims (Oudekerk et al., 2019). Such services may include referrals to community-based treatment providers, crisis interventions for individuals struggling with post-victimization trauma, emergency aid for victims with immediate needs (e.g., shelter, clothing, food, cash), or court advocacy for victims who are overwhelmed by the complexities of the legal system. Nevertheless, victim service programs vary widely in their

DOI: 10.4324/9781003219286-8

effectiveness and capacity to serve diverse populations of victims of different crime types, and not all adhere to evidence based practices (Lurigio, 2014).

Given this backdrop, the primary goals of this chapter are: (1) to provide an overview of adult violent victimization and its impacts and (2) to review the research on promising practices developed to assist such victims of crime. The chapter proceeds as follows. After briefly discussing the literature on the consequences of adult victimization and trauma, we summarize the research on victim services; discuss promising practices (trauma-informed care, culturally competent services, and trauma-focused cognitive behavioral therapy); and conclude with a discussion of gaps, challenges, and recommendations.

Adult Victimization and Trauma

Violent victimization can be a traumatic experience, regardless of whether it occurs in early or late life. Victimization is often unexpected and unwelcomed, and its negative effects can linger long after the event occurred. Even if there are no physical injuries involved, in the aftermath of a crime, victims may feel confused, afraid, and angry, and suffer hardships in various aspects of life (Turanovic & Pratt, 2019). A recent NCVS report indicated that 68% of victims of serious violent crime (sexual assault/rape, robbery, or aggravated assault) aged 12 years or older experienced socioemotional problems due to their victimization (Langton & Truman, 2014). Socioemotional problems included feelings of moderate to severe distress, significant problems with work or school (such as trouble with a boss, coworkers, or peers), and significant problems with family members or friends (including more arguments, an inability to trust, or not feeling as close). These symptoms were also found to be more severe for those victimized by someone they knew (e.g., an intimate partner, relative, or acquaintance) instead of a stranger (Langton & Truman, 2014).

Depending on how victims cope with their experiences, these symptoms may lessen over time, or they may develop into more serious and long-term problems. Coping strategies can vary widely in response to victimization, where healthy coping techniques – such as participating in therapy, seeking comfort from family or friends, or engaging in positive thinking – tend to be more successful at reducing long-term distress (Ong et al., 2006). Alternatively, unhealthy coping strategies might include behaviors like abusing drugs and alcohol, withdrawing from school or work, acting out aggressively, or socially isolating. Due to the intensity of negative emotions that victims feel, and because healthy coping can take more effort and resources, victims of violent crime often cope with their experiences in unhealthy ways (Turanovic & Pratt, 2019).

Compounding these difficulties are the hardships that victims often face when navigating the criminal justice system. In a system that is built with offenders' rights (rather than victims' rights) in mind, victims often feel left out and excluded from the criminal justice process. Crimes are technically considered offenses against the state, which means that victims are merely viewed as witnesses to a case (Doerner & Lab, 2021). Navigating the criminal justice system can therefore be intimidating, confusing, and frustrating for victims of crime. Many feel "revictimized" by the criminal justice process – especially if they must recount their traumatic experiences multiple times to law enforcement officers and attorneys or if their credibility is questioned throughout various stages of case processing (Campbell, 2008). To provide support and assistance to victims of crime as they heal from trauma and navigate the criminal justice system, victim service programs have been established. The remainder of this chapter will focus on the use and impacts of victim services on adult crime victims.

Takeaways

- Adult violent victimization is associated with numerous negative psychological, health, behavioral, and social problems
- The impacts of victimization can vary according to the nature of violence and victims' coping strategies
- Victims can be retraumatized by the criminal justice process
- Victim services can provide support and coping resources to buffer the harms of victimization

Adult Victim Services

Victims have increasingly been granted a range of rights and protections in the aftermath of a crime. Spurred in part by the crime victims' rights movement and the President's Commission on Crime in 1967, experimental victim-witness programs began to emerge in the 1970s. By 1977, there were more than 100 federally funded victim-witness programs, and by 1979 the number had increased to more than 400 (Blomberg et al., 2002). Most of these early programs were focused on providing witness services to assist in the prosecution of criminal cases.

Today, the many thousands of victim service programs operating across the country provide a range of services to victims, such as victim compensation, individual and group counseling, shelters for victims of domestic violence, rape crisis counseling, death notifications, and support for survivors of homicides. Depending on the type of crime experienced, victims may require a unique set of services and specialized forms of assistance. For example, victims of intimate partner violence may need temporary housing after victimization and help with safety planning, and advocates may conduct a danger assessment. Alternatively, secondary victims of homicide may require emotional support and grief counseling. For those who are traumatized or dealing with severe crimes, a greater dosage of services may also be required.

The National Census of Victim Service Providers (NCVSP) lists approximately 12,200 providers in the United States (Oudekerk et al., 2019), with most being either governmental (43.4%) or non-profit/faith-based organizations (45.1%). A small portion of victim service providers are embedded within hospitals, medical, or emergency locations (2.9%) or located on college campuses or other educational institutions (2.0%). The average rate of victim service providers per 100,000 residents in the United States is 3.7, ranging from 2.1 to 14.8 per state (Oudekerk et al., 2019).

Promising Practices in Victim Services

Although there are many different types of victim service programs across the country that vary in size and scope, there are several general practices, backed by empirical evidence, that can be applied widely. Here, we focus on three key promising practices in victim services: (1) trauma-informed care, (2) culturally competent services, and (3) trauma-focused cognitive behavioral therapy. These are discussed in more detail in the following.

Trauma-Informed Care

Trauma-informed care is a hallmark of effective victim service provision that emphasizes sensitivity to the needs of traumatized individuals (Kusmaul et al., 2019). Trauma after victimization can linger long after the incident and cause debilitating fear, helplessness, and reduced self-regulation (Hopper et al., 2010). The neurological impacts of trauma can lead to health risk behaviors that, in turn, result in serious problems over the lifespan. Trauma can also stem from numerous adverse experiences that are repeated over years of a person's life (Horowitz et al., 1995). For instance, earlier experiences with physical abuse, psychological abuse, repeated abandonments, sudden loss, and the witnessing of violence can compound the trauma of being violently victimized in adulthood.

The Substance Abuse and Mental Health Services Administration (SAMHSA) breaks trauma-informed care down into four tenets: "realizing" the impact of trauma on the individual, "recognizing" trauma symptoms and signs, "responding" with policies that are fully integrated with knowledge about trauma, and "resisting re-traumatization" when interacting with victims (SAMHSA, 2014). The main themes that make trauma-informed care successful are trauma awareness, being safety centered, empowering victims to regain control, and focusing on strengths rather than deficits (Hopper et al., 2010). Victim service providers must focus on the emotional recovery of victims through empowerment and rebuilding a sense of safety while advocating for them and addressing concrete needs (Levenson, 2017).

For victims who participate in the criminal justice process, trauma-informed services can help minimize re-victimization by the system and increase the likelihood of cooperation with criminal justice actors. Victim service providers can develop trauma-informed practices through individual and organizational training, by working to change cultural beliefs and stereotypes that harm victims, by leveling out power differences between victims and providers, and by ongoing empirical evaluations of services and their impacts on victims (Unick et al., 2019).

Culturally Competent Services

Culturally competent victim services are tailored toward the culture of specific groups, such as those defined by race, ethnicity, class, immigrant status, sexual orientation, gender identity, disability status, rurality, or religion. Culture can reflect a mix of folkways, mores, language, spirituality, gender roles, childrearing practices, rituals, healing practices, and behavioral scripts. Culturally competent victim services embrace these elements of culture when treating and responding to victims of crime (Carleton, 2021).

Although many crime victims perceive barriers to help-seeking (e.g., a lack of system responsiveness), those barriers may be exacerbated among victims who belong to traditionally marginalized groups. For example, victims of color may experience racism and discrimination, including microaggressions and microinsults, that dissuade them from forming meaningful connections with service providers (Bell & Mattis, 2000). Culturally competent approaches therefore use language and techniques that do not evoke harmful stereotypes that erode trust and service engagement (Pyles & Kim, 2006).

Culturally competent victim service organizations are often embedded within the communities they serve and provide an array of services (e.g., counseling, crisis intervention, support groups). These culturally specific organizations have existed for decades, yet they have historically not been able to provide empirical evidence for their work (Serrata et al., 2017). With the push toward "evidence-based" practices, however, empirical research is growing. The results thus far confirm that trauma-informed, culturally competent services positively contribute to crime victims' experiences. In a study of Latina survivors of intimate partner violence, for instance, Serrata et al. (2020) found that culturally competent services were linked to improved well-being and other positive changes (e.g., greater self-confidence, ability to recognize the impacts of trauma, improved emotional regulation), even after accounting for survivors' participation in other trauma-informed services.

Emerging research also suggests that culturally competent services can better serve members of the LGBTQIA+ community. Still, some providers subscribe to the belief that "a victim is a victim" and gender and sexual identity should not be relevant when providing services (LaSala & Fedor, 2020). Even among health care professionals there is distrust and uneasiness around trans and gender-expansive patients (Hall & DeLaney, 2021). Studies have found that when serving the queer community, emotional trust (i.e., not having to prove their gender identity), physical safety, collaborative decision-making, and feeling empowered are some of the most important aspects of victim services (Hall & DeLaney, 2021).

Trauma-Focused Cognitive Behavioral Therapy

Cognitive behavioral therapy (CBT) and psychological debriefing are the two most common interventions for victims of violent crimes. A systematic review of studies examining their effectiveness suggested that immediate intervention in the form of psychological debriefing was not effective and sometimes increased psychological distress after victimization (Guay et al., 2019). CBT, on the other hand, was found to improve victims' mental health at one-month and six-month intervals after victimization. Early and prolonged exposure to CBT was noted to be especially helpful when combined with trauma-informed strategies, such as stress management, cognitive restructuring, and exposure therapy (Guay et al., 2019).

Trauma-focused cognitive behavioral therapy (TF-CBT) is a form of CBT developed for treating trauma symptoms that also integrates components of interpersonal and family systems therapy. TF-CBT emphasizes stabilization skills (psychoeducation and parenting skills, relaxation skills, affective expression and modulation skills, cognitive coping skills), trauma narration and processing, in vivo mastery of trauma reminders, and enhancing safety and future development. These components comprise three treatment phases: Phase 1, stabilization skills; Phase 2, trauma narration and cognitive processing of the trauma memories; and Phase 3, integration phases (in vivo mastery, enhancing safety and future development). Therapy typically consists of a minimum of 12 sessions, with up to 25 sessions for more complex cases.

TF-CBT is typically used for children and adolescents (Gutermann et al., 2016), but it shows promise among young adults and adult terrorism victims (Moreno et al., 2019). A recent study by Peters et al. (2021) found that, among transitional aged youth and young adults (aged 15–25) who experienced interpersonal trauma, TF-CBT improved reports of anxiety, depression, and PTSD. Peters et al. (2021) also found that a small portion of participants reported a worsening of anxiety, depression, and PTSD symptoms during the trauma-narration phase of treatment; however, these symptoms resolved by the end of treatment.

Gaps and Challenges

Despite a growing evidence base on promising practices in victim services, many crime victims never seek or receive such services. Based on NCVS estimates, assistance from a victim-service agency was received in only 8% of violent victimizations in 2019 (Morgan & Truman, 2020), and this was a decline from the percentage in 2018 (11%). Previously, Sims et al. (2005) found that, in their survey of victims in Pennsylvania, only 1 in 25 (3%) reported ever using victim services or a victim-witness program – likely because most victims surveyed (57%) were never notified that such programs existed. Other victims reported not using services because they thought it would be a hassle, and others noted that they could receive assistance from friends or family members instead. Sims and colleagues (2005) therefore put forth three recommendations to increase the use of services by crime victims: (1) more efforts should be spent educating the public about such services, (2) victim service programs need to be staffed with well-trained individuals who can meet the needs of crime victims, and (3) the services provided to victims need to be broadened.

The timing and nature of contact with victim services can also play a role in service engagement. Initial contact with victim services too long after the crime occurred can reduce the effectiveness and need for services (Turanovic et al., 2020). Even so, contact too soon after the incident can be overwhelming in the wake of a traumatic event (Bryce et al., 2016). Victim service providers should thus follow up with victims a few days or weeks after the initial incident. Additionally, victims who do not report their crimes to the police may not receive prompt referrals to victim services. Using NCVS data, Zaykowski (2014) found that reporting to the police increased the odds of seeking victim services by 3 times. Distrust in law enforcement and fear of reporting may therefore correspond with low service engagement.

The use of victim services may also be impacted by the type of services that are available and perceived eligibility. Some victims may not be eligible for publicly funded services, which are limited by statutory definitions. For example, victims who may have contributed to the crime, or victims with a violent criminal history, are often excluded from services (Turanovic & Pratt, 2019). Some victim service agencies also only serve a narrow class of victims – usually victims of violence (e.g., homicide, rape, domestic violence, assault, and drunk driving) – given that these crimes are thought to be the most traumatic and financially taxing (Turanovic et al., 2020).

Moreover, victims can "fall through the cracks" of a service network due to weaknesses in communication and a breakdown in collaboration among agencies. Strong linkages are characterized by consistent communication and information sharing between agencies; a clear knowledge of services; referral mechanisms; and trust that referred clients will access services and be treated appropriately (Balaswamy, 2004). For populations that are hard to reach and experience a multitude of health problems and economic struggles, "one-stop shop" victim service organizations may be the most helpful (George et al., 2020). Such organizations are built on principles of comprehensive care and seek to provide not only trauma support but also assistance with medical needs, housing, education, and work opportunities (George et al., 2020). The main benefit of these organizations is that victims do not need to navigate multiple systems spread out in various locations, each with new personnel who are unfamiliar with their needs. Still, the establishment and sustainability of a one-stop, comprehensive victim service organization can be challenging and require a great deal of investment and communication between multiple stakeholder groups that often have competing interests (Blomberg et al., 2002).

Takeaways

- Victim services should be trauma informed and culturally competent
- Trauma-focused cognitive behavioral therapy can be effective for crime victims
- Only a small portion of crime victims contact or receive victim services
- The reporting of crime to police can increase interaction with victim services
- Service providers should make timely contact with victims and follow up within the first few days or weeks after the crime

- Restrictive statutory definitions and eligibility requirements can exclude many victims from receiving services, contributing to service gaps among high risk populations
- One-stop, comprehensive victim service organizations can more effectively target multiple needs of crime victims related to trauma, housing, education, medical care, and employment

Conclusion

Despite the exponential growth of victim service programs over the past several decades, there is much more to learn about "what works" in the field of victim services. Compared to other areas of criminal justice that focus on offender treatment, less research has been produced on the effectiveness of providing support services to victims (Lurigio, 2014). Unfortunately, crime victims and criminal justice personnel often lack knowledge on available victim services and perceive victims' needs as a low priority in a system that is designed primarily to deal with offenders (Englebrecht, 2011). This is troubling since victim services can play a role in crime prevention and disrupting the cycle of violence. Indeed, such services may discourage victims from seeking revenge or retaliation, help to break patterns of repeated abuse and intimate partner violence, or prevent unhealthy coping behaviors (e.g., drug and alcohol use) that increase the likelihood of criminal involvement (Turanovic & Pratt, 2013). Growing research on trauma-informed care, cultural competency, and trauma-focused cognitive behavioral therapy suggest numerous promising practices; yet far more research is needed to establish a literature on evidence-based victim services. Increased resources and attention must be devoted to this area to find ways to better serve and heal victims of crime.

References

Agnew, R. (2002). Experienced, vicarious, and anticipated strain: An exploratory study on physical victimization and delinquency. *Justice Quarterly*, *19*(4), 603–632.

Balaswamy, S. (2004). Rating of interagency working relationship and associated factors in protective services. *Journal of Elder Abuse and Neglect*, *14*, 1–20.

Bell, C. C., & Mattis, J. (2000). The importance of cultural competence in ministering to African American victims of domestic violence. *Violence against Women*, *6*(5), 515–532.

Blomberg, T. G., Waldo, G. P., & Chester, D. (2002). Assessment of the program implementation of comprehensive victim services in a one-stop location. *International Review of Victimology*, *9*, 149–174.

Bryce, J., Brooks, M., Robinson, P., Stokes, R., Irving, M., Graham-Kevan, N., . . . Lowe, M. (2016). A qualitative examination of engagement with support services by victims of violent crime. *International Review of Victimology*, *22*(3), 239–255.

Campbell, R. (2008). The psychological impact of rape victims. *American Psychologist*, *63*, 702.

Carleton, B. (2021). *One size does not fit all: Tailoring victim services for the local native American population in Pennington County, South Dakota*. CNA Analysis & Solutions.

Doerner, W. G., & Lab, S. P. (2021). *Victimology*, 9th ed. Routledge.

Englebrecht, C. M. (2011). The struggle for "ownership of conflict": An exploration of victim participation and voice in the criminal justice system. *Criminal Justice Review*, *36*, 129–151.

Farrell, G., & Pease, K. (Eds.). (2001). *Repeat victimization*. Criminal Justice Press.

George, J. S., Malik, S., Symes, S., Caralis, P., Newport, D. J., Godur, A., . . . Potter, J. E. (2020). Trafficking healthcare resources and intra-disciplinary victim services and education (THRIVE) clinic: A multidisciplinary one-stop shop model of healthcare for survivors of human trafficking. *Journal of Human Trafficking*, *6*(1), 50–60.

Guay, S., Beaulieu-Prévost, D., Sader, J., & Marchand, A. (2019). A systematic literature review of early posttraumatic interventions for victims of violent crime. *Aggression and Violent Behavior*, *46*, 15–24

Gutermann, J., Schreiber, F., Matulis, S., Schwartzkopff, L., Deppe, J., & Steil, R. (2016). Psychological treatments for symptoms of posttraumatic stress disorder in children, adolescents, and young adults: A meta-analysis. *Clinical Child and Family Psychology Review*, *19*(2), 77–93.

Hall, S. F., & DeLaney, M. J. (2021). A trauma-informed exploration of the mental health and community support experiences of transgender and gender-expansive adults. *Journal of Homosexuality, 68*(8), 1278–1297.
Hopper, E. K., Bassuk, E. L., & Olivet, J. (2010). Shelter from the storm: Trauma-informed care in homelessness services settings. *The Open Health Services and Policy Journal, 3*(1).
Horowitz, K., Weine, S., & Jekel, J. (1995). PTSD symptoms in urban adolescent girls: Compounded community trauma. *Journal of the American Academy of Child & Adolescent Psychiatry, 34*(10), 1353–1361.
Kusmaul, N., Wolf, M. R., Sahoo, S., Green, S. A., & Nochajski, T. H. (2019). Client experiences of trauma-informed care in social service agencies. *Journal of Social Service Research, 45*(4), 589–599.
Langton, L., & Truman, J. L. (2014). *Socio-emotional impact of violent crime*. U.S. Department of Justice, Office of Justice Programs, Bureau of Justice Statistics.
LaSala, M. C., & Fedor, J. P. (2020). "A victim is a victim": LGBT blindness among victim assistance workers. *Journal of Qualitative Criminal Justice & Criminology, 9*(1).
Lauritsen, J. L., & Laub, J. H. (2007). Understanding the link between victimization and offending: New reflections on an old idea. In M. Hough & M. Maxfield (Eds.), *Surveying crime in the 21st century: Commemorating the 25th anniversary of the British Crime Survey* (pp. 55–75). Criminal Justice Press.
Levenson, J. (2017). Trauma-informed social work practice. *Social Work, 62*(2), 105–113.
Lurigio, A. J. (2014). *Violent victimization in the United States: Major issues and trends*. National Institute of Justice.
Moreno, N., Sanz Fernández, J., García Vera, M. P., Gesteira Santos, C., Gutiérrez, S., Zapardiel, A., . . . Marotta-Walters, S. (2019). Effectiveness of trauma-focused cognitive behavioral therapy for terrorism victims with very long-term emotional disorders. *Psicothema, 31*(4), 400–406.
Morgan, R. E., & Thompson, A. (2021). *Criminal victimization, 2020*. Bureau of Justice Statistics.
Morgan, R. E., & Truman, J. L. (2020). *Criminal victimization, 2019*. Bureau of Justice Statistics.
Ong, A. D., Bergeman, C. S., Bisconti, T. L., & Wallace, K. A. (2006). Psychological resilience, positive emotions, and successful adaptation to stress in later life. *Journal of Personality and Social Psychology, 91*, 730–749.
Oudekerk, B. A., Warnken, H., & Langton, L. (2019). *Victim service providers in the United States, 2017*. Bureau of Justice Statistics.
Peters, W., Rice, S., Cohen, J., Murray, L., Schley, C., Alvarez-Jimenez, M., & Bendall, S. (2021). Trauma-focused cognitive-behavioral therapy (TF-CBT) for interpersonal trauma in transitional-aged youth. *Psychological Trauma: Theory, Research, Practice, and Policy, 13*, 313–321.
Pyles, L., & Kim, K. M. (2006). A multilevel approach to cultural competence: A study of the community response to underserved domestic violence victims. *Families in Society, 87*, 221–229.
Pyrooz, D. C., Moule, R. K., & Decker, S. H. (2014). The contribution of gang membership to the victim-offender overlap. *Journal of Research in Crime and Delinquency, 51*, 315–348.
Serrata, J. V., Macias, R. L., Rosales, A., Hernandez-Martinez, M., Rodriguez, R., & Perilla, J. L. (2017). Expanding evidence-based practice models for domestic violence initiatives: A community-centered approach. *Psychology of Violence, 7*, 158–165.
Serrata, J. V., Rodriguez, R., Castro, J. E., & Hernandez-Martinez, M. (2020). Well-being of Latina survivors of intimate partner violence and sexual assault receiving trauma-informed and culturally specific services. *Journal of Family Violence, 35*, 169–180.
Sims, B., Yost, B., & Abbott, C. (2005). Use and Nonuse of victim services programs: Implications from a statewide survey of crime victims. *Criminology Public Policy, 4*, 361–384.
Substance Abuse and Mental Health Services Administration. (2014). *SAMHSA's concept of trauma and guidance for a trauma-informed approach*. Author.
Turanovic, J. J. (2018). Toward a life-course theory of victimization. In S. H. Decker & K. A. Wright (Eds.), *Criminology and public policy: Putting theory to work* (2nd ed., pp. 85–103). Temple University Press.
Turanovic, J. J., Blomberg, T. G., Pesta, G. B., Kuper, J. L., & Brancale, J. (2020). *Palm Beach County victim services driving under the influence (DUI) related deaths demonstration project*. Final Report to the Office for Victims of Crime.
Turanovic, J. J., & Pratt, T. C. (2013). The consequences of maladaptive coping: Integrating general strain and self-control theories to specify a causal pathway between victimization and offending. *Journal of Quantitative Criminology, 29*, 321–345.

Turanovic, J. J., & Pratt, T. C. (2014). "Can't stop, won't stop": Self-control, risky lifestyles, and repeat victimization. *Journal of Quantitative Criminology*, *30*, 29–56.
Turanovic, J. J., & Pratt, T. C. (2019). *Thinking about victimization: Context and consequences*. Routledge.
Unick, G. J., Bassuk, E. L., Richard, M. K., & Paquette, K. (2019). Organizational trauma-informed care: Associations with individual and agency factors. *Psychological Services*, *16*(1), 134.
Zaykowski, H. (2014). Mobilizing victim services: The role of reporting to the police. *Journal of Traumatic Stress*, *27*(3), 365–369.

7
TOWARD EVIDENCE-BASED HUMAN TRAFFICKING PREVENTION

Joan A. Reid, Klejdis Bilali, Calli M. Cain, and Kaci Crook

Introduction

Human trafficking is profit-driven exploitation of men, women, or children facilitated by force, fraud, or coercion. Human trafficking exists across many job sectors and industries ranging from agriculture to manufacturing. Key individual and community vulnerability factors for human trafficking include poverty, economic distress, war, lack of social and economic safety net, government corruption, criminal activity, and gender inequality (Shelley, 2010). Global estimates of the number of victims of human trafficking range from 24.9 million to 40.3 million men, women, and children (International Labour Organization, 2017). Advances in globalization and technology facilitate the spread of human trafficking by expanding connections and opportunities for traffickers to recruit and exploit victims (Jeffreys, 2009; Reid & Fox, 2020; Shelley, 2010).

In the past two decades, international protocols and national anti-trafficking laws have authorized law enforcement to protect victims of human trafficking and prosecute traffickers (Gallagher, 2010). The sheer magnitude of human trafficking at the population level qualifies this issue as a serious threat to safety and public health (Peck et al., 2021). Undoubtedly, the exploitation of vulnerable persons also results in significant and often long-term physical and psychological illness and injury, furthering the destructive nature of this widespread problem (Peck et al., 2021). Due to severe consequences of human trafficking for individuals, families, and communities, there is a critical and urgent need for human trafficking prevention programs Kabbash & Ronis, 2021).

Raising-awareness campaigns are commonly used in the anti-human trafficking movement (Bryant & Landman, 2020). A review of 90 raising-awareness campaigns found that about half included some form of evaluation with mixed results. Bryant and Landman (2020) concluded that "the impact of raising awareness campaigns is limited when these are not targeted to specific communities with a clear message" (p. 136). In a recent assessment of the public health efforts related to human trafficking, it was noted there has been an uptick in prevention efforts such as offender diversion programs, red flag awareness campaigns, and training and screening programs for healthcare personnel (Greenbaum et al., 2015; Long et al., 2019). In this chapter we provide an overview of three of the more common types of human trafficking prevention programs-screening tools for identifying victims of human trafficking, prevention

DOI: 10.4324/9781003219286-9

education programs for K–12 schools, and prevention education programs developed for specific populations at greater risk for exploitation in human trafficking.

Human Trafficking Screening Measures and Exploitation Prevention

The development and administration of preventative human trafficking screening measures has garnered much attention from providers across a number of organizations, including law enforcement and child-welfare agencies, psychosocial clinics, healthcare facilities, educational institutions, and residential spaces. Though non-exhaustive, Table 7.1 outlines a number of these trafficking screening tools, utilized across various agencies with the aim of detecting crucial victim vulnerabilities of commercial sexual exploitation (CSE) and labor trafficking, further precluding revictimization (Hershberger et al., 2018; West Coast Children's Clinic, 2015).

Interestingly, one study by Chisolm-Straker and colleagues (2016) found that roughly 68% of trafficking victims had contact with health care providers at least once, yet there was great inconsistency in the frequency in which these victims were actually identified by health care providers. Certainly, the awareness and insight gained through assessor training in the administration of trafficking measures is crucial for further improving victim identification and response.

It should be noted that a great number of extant trafficking identification and prevention tools primarily serve as invalidated guides or protocols for service providers. Despite the widespread use of these measures, the psychometric properties of many screening tools have yet to be empirically evaluated, hence the lack of consensus among service providers for the administration of a single all-encompassing human trafficking screening measure.

The precision with which these tools are able to identify sensitive victim vulnerabilities plays a vital role in the adequate placement of the victim in social services, preventing victim elopement and reducing the likelihood of trafficking reoccurrence. Empirical testing can further allow for the creation of short-form versions of these tools, conducive for application in emergency department and other healthcare settings where victim contact is transitory. Further, most screening tools have only been normed with English-speaking populations, and given that trafficking pervades a number of cultural groups and may involve migration across borders, linguistic barriers are an inevitable issue for service providers implementing these tools (Pascual-Leone et al., 2017). Some screening instructions advise the use of an interpreter during the assessment of non-English speaking victims; however, even such avenues of accommodation are not always feasible for agencies given the lack of interpreters for victims speaking uncommon languages in destination countries. Therefore, it cannot be overstated that empirical testing and measure norming is vital for the prevention of the proliferation of human trafficking.

Take Away Points:

- Though a number of human trafficking screening tools exist, many such measures lack strong empirical support.
- Further research evaluating the effectiveness of screening assessments used for identifying victims in specific settings is needed.
- Standardization of human trafficking screening tools is crucial to identifying and serving victims.

Table 7.1 Human Trafficking Screening Measures

Measure	*Developers/ Reference*	*Service Delivery Sector*	*Targeted Population*	*Exploitation Type*	*Number of Items*	*Strengths*	*Weaknesses*
Commercial Sexual Exploitation Identification Tool (CSE-IT), Version 2.0	WestCoast Children's Clinic (n.d.)	• Most settings (excluding emergency departments with brief victim contact)	• Minors • Young adults	• Commercial sexual exploitation	• 46	• Evidence of psychometric validation • Thorough inclusion of sensitive trafficking vulnerabilities • Reliance on multiple sources of information	• Lengthy • Not ideal for use in emergency departments with limited victim contact • May require extensive time to complete given reliance on multiple sources of information
Quick Youth Indicators of Trafficking (QYIT)	Covenant House; Chisolm-Straker et al. (2019)	• Any setting	• Young adults (18–26) at-risk of elopement and homelessness	• Commercial sexual exploitation • Labor trafficking	• 4	• Evidence of psychometric validation • Brief • Direct, closed-ended questions (Yes/No) • Trafficking expert is not necessary for measure administration	• Given the brevity of the tool, general training on human trafficking may be useful to inform adequate judgement of victim identification • Follow-up use of a more comprehensive assessment may be necessary for providers with longer victim contact to identify nuanced trafficking vulnerabilities

(*Continued*)

Table 7.1 (Continued)

Measure	*Developers/ Reference*	*Service Delivery Sector*	*Targeted Population*	*Exploitation Type*	*Number of Items*	*Strengths*	*Weaknesses*
CSEC Screening Protocol	Asian Health Services and Banteay Srei; Chang et al. (2015)	• Primary care outpatient clinical setting	• Minors • Young adults	• Commercial sexual exploitation	• Varies on question modification	• Ideal for medical settings • Major indicators of exploitations for patients between ages 11-18 are clearly delineated • Screening protocol advises the assessor to inquire if victim needs further services (e.g., referrals to mental health professionals)	• Requires question modifications in order to administer in a trauma-informed manner • No evidence of psychometric validation
CSEC Screening Tool	CSEC Collaborative Response Team, San Luis Obispo County (2014)	• Child welfare service agencies	• Minors	• Commercial sexual exploitation	• 22	• Relatively brief, (Yes/ No/Unknown questions) • Reliance on multiple sources of information	• No evidence of psychometric validation • No instructions for trauma-informed interviewing • May require extensive time to complete given reliance on multiple sources of information

CSEC/CST 6-item Screening Tool	Greenbaum et al. (2018)	• Pediatric emergency departments	• Minors	• Commercial sexual exploitation	• 6	• Brief • Easily applicable in emergency departments settings • Evidence of adequate item sensitivity	• Follow-up use of a more comprehensive assessment may be necessary for providers with longer victim contact to identify nuanced trafficking vulnerabilities
Human Trafficking Interview and Assessment Measure (HTIAM-14)	Covenant House; Bigelson et al. (2013)	• Any setting	• Older youth • Young adults, particularly homeless populations	• Commercial sexual exploitation • Labor trafficking	• 20+ (affirmative responses to some questions leads to further questioning)	• Evidence of psychometric validation • Clear, specific wording of assessor instructions when probing for information • Can be administered in research and clinical settings • Allows for assessment of victim verbal and non-verbal communication • Clear scoring instructions	• Requires 45+ minutes to administer • Requires an expert with human trafficking knowledge • Questions require modification if administering assessment to younger victims

(*Continued*)

Table 7.1 (Continued)

Measure	*Developers/ Reference*	*Service Delivery Sector*	*Targeted Population*	*Exploitation Type*	*Number of Items*	*Strengths*	*Weaknesses*
Rapid Screening Tool (RST) for Child Trafficking	Center for the Human Rights for Children, Loyola University Chicago, International Organization for Adolescents (IOFA); Walts et al. (2011)	• Any setting	• Minors	• Commercial sexual exploitation • Labor trafficking	• 12	• Brief questions (Yes/No) • Assessment is general enough to tailor to most agency protocols	• No evidence of psychometric validation • Great reliance on assessor judgement call • Little direction provided on how to administer in a clinical setting • Follow-up use of a more comprehensive identification tool may be necessary
Comprehensive Screening and Safety Tool (CSST) for Child Trafficking	Center for the Human Rights for Children, Loyola University Chicago, International Organization for Adolescents (IOFA); Walts et al. (2011)	• Any setting with extensive victim contact or agencies conducting in-depth victim case investigations	• Minors	• Commercial sexual exploitation • Labor trafficking	• 54 (excluding the Rapid Screening Tool administered beforehand)	• Includes the Child Trafficking Indicator Questionnaire and Child Trafficking Safety Assessment Form for a comprehensive identification process • Clear, specific instructions for interview administration and assessor action based on victim reports	• Lengthy • Difficult to generalize to interviewees who do not identify as victims or those who trafficked themselves • No evidence of psychometric validation

Human Trafficking of Children Indicator Tool	State of Florida Department of Children & Families (2009)	• Child welfare agencies/child protective investigators • Ideal for settings with extensive victim contact	• Minors	• Commercial sexual exploitation • Labor trafficking	• Varies on question modification	• Major trafficking indicators and special considerations provided for guidance • Special considerations for interviewing trafficked population are delineated	• Lack of specific question items • May require an extensive amount of time to complete when relying on information from sources beyond victim reports • No evidence of psychometric validation
Rapid Human Trafficking Assessment (RHTA)	New Jersey Department of Children and Families (n.d.)	• Any setting	• Minors	• Commercial sexual exploitation • Labor trafficking	• 11	• Brief, Yes/No questions • Victim and third-party individual may report	• Several major trafficking indicators are missing such as an indication that the victim is trafficking themselves and/or does not identify as a victim • No evidence of psychometric validation
Child Trafficking Decision Map	Connecticut Department of Children & Families, Human Anti-trafficking Response Team (HART) (2021)	• Child welfare agencies	• Minors	• Commercial sexual exploitation • Labor trafficking	• 36	• Relies on multiple sources of information beyond victim • Incorporates victim verbal and nonverbal communication	• Lengthy • No evidence of psychometric validation

(*Continued*)

Table 7.1 (Continued)

Measure	*Developers/ Reference*	*Service Delivery Sector*	*Targeted Population*	*Exploitation Type*	*Number of Items*	*Strengths*	*Weaknesses*
Domestic Minor Sex Trafficking (DMST) Practitioner Guide and Intake Tool	Shared Hope International (2010)	• Any setting, particularly child advocacy and mental health centers	• Minors	• Commercial sexual exploitation	• 34 (tier 1) • 48 (tier 2)	• Great emphasis on trauma-informed care • Considers a number of correlates to exploitation (e.g., development, homelessness, abuse/neglect endured in the victim's home • Contributes to development of a therapeutic alliance	• Lengthy • No evidence of psychometric validation
Human Trafficking Screening Tool (HTST; original and short form versions)	Urban Institute (2017)	• Any setting	• Presently ideal for young adults	• Commercial sexual exploitation • Labor trafficking	• 19 (original) • 6 (short form)	• Evidence of psychometric validation • Assesses for exploitation endured in the past as well as in the last year	• Further evaluation of sensitivity and specificity of tool to detect victims versus nonvictims is advised by authors for victims under the age of 18 and youth in child-welfare settings

Trafficking Victim Identification Tool (TVIT; original and short form versions)	Vera Institute of Justice (2013)	• Any setting	• Adults • Transnational victims	• Commercial sexual exploitation • Labor trafficking	• 50+ (original) • 20+ (short form)	• Evidence of psychometric validation • Ideal for comprehensive trafficking investigations	• Lengthy and may require extensive time to administer • Question modifications are necessary for use with youth
Comprehensive Human Trafficking Assessment	National Human Trafficking Resource Center (NHTRC), Polaris Project (2011a)	• Any setting	• Adults	• Commercial sexual exploitation • Labor trafficking	• 100+	• Thorough inclusion of sensitive trafficking vulnerabilities • Clearly delineated considerations when working with victims • May be applicable to most settings	• Lengthy • Not ideal for emergency department or crisis services • No evidence of psychometric validation • Unclear how to score assessment
Medical Assessment Tool for Human Trafficking	National Human Trafficking Resource Center (NHTRC), Polaris Project (2010)	• Healthcare settings	• Unspecified	• Commercial sexual exploitation • Labor trafficking	• 6	• Brief decision tree ideal for medical settings • Major signs of exploitation are delineated	• No evidence of psychometric validation • Assessment itself does not include more nuanced indicators of trafficking • Lack of instructions on how to administer questions in a trauma-informed manner

(Continued)

Table 7.1 (Continued)

Measure	*Developers/ Reference*	*Service Delivery Sector*	*Targeted Population*	*Exploitation Type*	*Number of Items*	*Strengths*	*Weaknesses*
Human Trafficking Assessment for Domestic Workers	Polaris project (2011b)	• Any setting with access to domestic workers	• Adult domestic workers	• Domestic labor trafficking	• 28	• Manual includes major indicators and red flags of domestic labor trafficking • Assessment may be tailored to any setting	• No evidence of psychometric validation • Great reliance on assessor's judgement call • Unclear scoring instructions
Adult Human Trafficking Screening Tool (AHTST)	National Human Trafficking Training & Technical Assistance Center (2018)	• Any setting	• Adults	• Commercial sexual exploitation • Labor trafficking	• 8	• Available in Spanish • Manual provides detailed instructions on trauma- and survivor informed care and considerations for building a relationship with victim • Less expertise	• No evidence of psychometric validation • Given the brevity of the tool, general training on human trafficking may be useful to inform adequate judgement of victim identification
San Diego Labor Trafficking Survey Questionnaire	San Diego State University; Zhang (2012)	• Research settings	• Adult migrant agricultural workers	• Labor trafficking	• 100+	• Ideal for research purposes • Spanish version available • Clear, specific wording of instructions, useful when probing for information	• Lengthy • No evidence of psychometric validation for clinical application • Requires question modifications to generalize

Human Trafficking Prevention Curricula in Schools

The internet and K–12 schools are active recruiting grounds for traffickers looking to lure minors into sexual exploitation (e.g., Blum et al., 2018; Carpenter & Gates, 2016; Smith et al., 2009). For example, Pooler and colleagues (2022) found that nearly one out of five central Texas high school students reported being approached by a trafficker or were trafficked. Additionally, Smith and colleagues (2009) found the average age of entry into prostitution (sex trafficking) is 13. Thus, there is a dire need for human trafficking prevention education in schools and with those who work with minors (U.S. Department of Education [DOE], 2021). As the number of school-aged youth who are trafficked continues to increase, raising awareness and increasing knowledge about human trafficking among teachers, students, and parents has become a priority in the United States (DOE, 2021; National Center for Homeless Education [NCHE], 2014; Rizo et al., 2019). Several states have mandated prevention education programs/workshops for school personnel so they can identify and report suspected cases of child trafficking (Pooler et al., 2022; Rizo et al., 2021; Salas & Didier, 2020). Yet, educating school personnel alone is not enough; students themselves must also be educated to enhance youth awareness, build resilience, and prevent potential victimization (DOE, 2021).

The DOE (2021) provides a framework for trafficking prevention in America's schools that highlights prevention efforts at the primary, secondary, and tertiary tiers (developed by the Department of Health and Human Services [DHHS], 2019). The primary tier (or universal prevention) involves creating environments and fostering skills in children that prevent victimization. Primary prevention involves training all staff on the risk factors and indicators of trafficking, while for students it may involve various programming depending on their age (DOE, 2021). For example, primary prevention for students can include enrichment programs for preschool aged kids, social-emotional skills education for K–5th graders, and safe dating and relationship education for 6–12th graders (DOE, 2021). Some programs can be provided to students regardless of age, such as online safety education, mentoring programs, and after-school programs. Several school districts across the nation have added a human trafficking prevention curriculum to existing classes or provided assembly-style training to educate students and school personnel on the issue, yet there is little research to date regarding *how* to best educate youth and school staff about human trafficking (Rizo et al., 2019).

A few states have passed laws via their state legislature or department of education to mandate various forms for human trafficking prevention curricula for students and/or school personnel (Lesak et al., 2021). For example, California was the first state legislature to pass a law mandating anti-trafficking education be added to the 7–12th grade public school curriculum (Salas & Didier, 2020). The California state legislature recognized it was important to have education programs to help students and teachers recognize signs of human trafficking and teach students about healthy boundaries and relationships. Florida became the first state to mandate all students, K–12, to receive human trafficking prevention education. School districts may customize such programs for their students, though most districts are trying to build this prevention education into regular health curricula for K–12 students (Florida Department of Education [FLDOE], 2019). The FLDOE has worked to produce age-appropriate training, presentations, and resources for school staff, parents, and students, often partnering with local anti-trafficking non-profit organizations. Additionally, the Florida Department of Health has partnered with FLDOE to conduct a trafficking awareness survey of school health personnel and to develop annual training for school nurses.

Other school districts where there is no state mandate for human trafficking prevention education have taken it upon themselves to provide awareness and training to students and teachers (Rizo et al., 2021). Pooler and colleagues (2022) found that as little as a one-hour assembly training for high school students in Central Texas schools (using Keeping Students Safe [KSS] curriculum; Peters, 2012) was effective in increasing students' knowledge and awareness about human trafficking. Their findings are crucial because many school districts may be reluctant to add new curriculum for students and teachers to an already full schedule, especially when the budget for creating a new curriculum are limited or in rural areas where there is still a denial of child sex trafficking (e.g., Blum et al., 2018).

Youth are more vulnerable to human trafficking than adults, largely because they are still in the psychosocial developmental stage of adolescence, which means they may be more easily manipulated (Gardner & Steinberg, 2005; Reed et al., 2019). Traffickers exploit vulnerability; thus increasing youths' awareness about human trafficking risks or red flags could help reduce those vulnerabilities. In short, schools have several responsibilities: to increase staff awareness on the nature of trafficking and which youth are most vulnerable, to increase parent and student awareness of the risks and realities of trafficking, and to develop district or schoolwide policies and protocols for identifying and supporting trafficking victims (Albert, 2021; DOE, 2021; Lesak et al., 2021; Taylor, 2018; Zhu et al., 2020). Although increasing student and teacher awareness of human trafficking does not guarantee that they will not be trafficked, it does provide them with tools to protect themselves and others from potential threats or from people trying to exploit them, whether online or in person. Prevention and awareness curricula may also validate a student's victimization experience, given that they may not have initially identified such experiences as exploitative, as many victims of human trafficking do not always see themselves as victims. Such newfound insight may prompt them to seek help (Albert, 2021; Lesak et al., 2021).

Take Away Points:

- Students should receive age-appropriate education on healthy relationships/boundaries and online safety to enhance their awareness of potential threats, build resilience, and prevent potential exploitation.
- Parents of school-aged children should receive training or resources so they know the risks and realities of trafficking, are equipped to protect their child online, and know how to talk to their children about healthy relationships.
- School personnel should be educated on the nature of human trafficking and which youth are most vulnerable, so they are prepared to identify and report suspected cases of youth trafficking.
- School districts (or states) should develop policies and protocols for identifying and supporting trafficking victims.

Prevention Programs for Special Populations

Table 7.2 summarizes some of the available prevention projects for sex trafficking and CSE in general. This table focuses on CSE rather than labor trafficking due to a lack of prevention programs targeting labor trafficking prevention. A majority of the presented programs are aimed at adolescents and young adults, with an average age range of 12–18 years. Of the presented prevention programs, six focus primarily on females, and five are aimed at all genders.

Table 7.2 Human Trafficking Programs for Vulnerable Populations

Name of Program	*Reference*	*Ages*	*Gender*	*Target Population*	*Evaluation/ Effectiveness*	*Intervention Type*	*Topics Covered*
My Life, My Choice	Rothman et al. (2020, 2021); My Life My Choice: Empowering Youth, Ending Exploitation (n.d.)	12–18	Mostly females	At risk youth, or survivors exiting the life	Evaluated, significant reduction of substance use, delinquency; 40% increased CSE awareness	Survivor mentor program	Substance use, delinquent behavior, social support, coping skills. leadership development. job readiness skills
Shared Hope	Shared Hope International (n.d.)	Adults	All	Parents, teachers, and child workers	Not yet evaluated	Comprehensive tools, tips online	Popular apps, video games and esports, sexting, how to talk to kids about online interactions
Love 146 (Not a Number)	Pooler et al. (2022); Love 146 (n.d.)	12–18	All	Middle and high school students	Not yet evaluated	Classroom setting	Introduction to human trafficking, society and culture, red flags and relationships, vulnerability and resilience, reducing risky behavior and getting help

(*Continued*)

Table 7.2 (Continued)

Name of Program	*Reference*	*Ages*	*Gender*	*Target Population*	*Evaluation/ Effectiveness*	*Intervention Type*	*Topics Covered*
Prevention Project	Human Trafficking Prevention Education (Prevention Project, n.d.)	Adolescents	All	Middle and high school students	Not yet evaluated	Classroom setting	Introduction and international human trafficking, sex trafficking in the U.S., profile of a pimp, decreasing demand, media literacy and the over-sexualization of our culture, student empowerment and impact, self-worth, technology safety, steps to prevention
Phoenix Project	Pierce (2012)	Adolescents	Female	Native American	Evaluated through surveys, results show program is effective	Outreach to high schools	Commercial sexual exploitation, targeting of vulnerable girls, recruitment tactics of traffickers
GEMS	Girls Educational & Mentoring Services (n.d.)	12–24	Female	Trafficked girls and women	Not yet evaluated	Advocate, awareness training	Understanding and addressing demand, understanding trauma bonds, long-term prevention efforts. developing a strengths-based program, motivational interviewing with survivors

Project STARFISH	Project STARFISH Education (n.d.)	Adolescents	All	Middle and high school students	Not yet evaluated, partnered with ASU to be evaluated	Resources for educators to create lessons	Terminology, analysis of literature and media supply and demand in the sex trafficking, historical events, trends in sex trafficking
Word on the Street	Murphy (2016)	13–18	Female	Foster youth	Not yet evaluated	Training sessions	What is commercial sexual exploitation of children, recruitment tactics, survivor stories, healthy relationships, empowerment
PREVENT	Kruger et al. (2016)	10–16	Female	Black Students	Not yet evaluated	Focus groups	Decision making, coping strategies, relationship with peers and family
PROTECT Now	An Educated Student is a PROTECTED student (n.d.)	Youth	All	K–12	Not yet evaluated	Classroom setting	Developing personal boundaries, child abuse and forms of human trafficking, understanding and recognizing human trafficking, linking historical and modern-day slavery
Ending the Game	Usacheva et al. (2021)	Youth and adults	Female	Trafficked youth	Increased knowledge, improved self-worth, positive attitude	Community-based, peer support model	False promises, isolation, dissociation, self-defeating thoughts, emotional intensity, self-defeating behavior, identity disturbance, phobias, shame

The presented programs vary in format and include survivor mentorship programs, classroom curricula, websites, apps, focus groups, and training sessions. Most of these programs are intended to work directly with at-risk populations and students in general, but one program is aimed to educate parents, teachers, and others who are working *with* children. Two of the presented programs are also designed to work with youth and adults who are exiting "the life", (common colloquial term for involvement in CSE) or survivors of CSE. Though the presented programs cover a wide range of topics, there are a few common themes. Many of the programs include material on what human trafficking is, recruitment tactics, safety when using technology, healthy relationships, empowerment, and coping skills.

The majority of the prevention programs for specialized populations have not yet been empirically validated, but a few have used surveys to collect feedback from program participants and practitioners (see Table 7.2). One program has been empirically validated and found to have significant positive results across multiple measured outcome areas, and another is partnered with an organization to begin the process of validation. Further readings with detailed information on each of the presented intervention programs are provided in the corresponding references.

Take Away Points:

- The majority of the discussed programs (Table 7.2) are aimed at adolescents aged 12–18 and are generally intended to work directly with students or at-risk populations.
- Common themes from the programs include information about what human trafficking is, recruitment tactics, technology safety, healthy relationships, empowerment, and coping skills.
- The majority of prevention programs have not been empirically validated, and this should be an area of focus for future research.

Conclusion

This chapter provides an overview of three of the more commonly implemented human trafficking prevention modalities – victim screening tools, K–12 prevention education, and prevention programs for vulnerable groups. As found by other reviews of human trafficking prevention programs (Bryant & Landman, 2020), the great majority of human trafficking prevention programs have not been evaluated. Of those programs which have been evaluated, many evaluations are focused on the program implementation and process evaluations rather than evaluation of the program impact on the prevention of human trafficking (Bryant & Landman, 2020).

Recommendations toward more evidence-based human trafficking prevention include the collection of baseline and trend data of human trafficking at local, state, and national levels. Reliable data is necessary to measure and evaluate prevention program impacts. Due to a lack of human trafficking data, organizations are unable to demonstrate impact and discern what works to prevent human trafficking. Second, many human trafficking prevention efforts focus on intervention after exploitation in human trafficking though raising awareness of the signs or red flags of human trafficking or by training professionals to intervene to prevent continued exploitation rather than focusing on primary prevention (i.e., preventing trafficking before it occurs). While secondary and tertiary prevention efforts are needed to stem continued harms of human trafficking, we recommended greater emphasis on primary prevention strategies to reduce the incidence of human trafficking.

Summary of Recommendations:

- Baseline and trend data of human trafficking should be collected at local, state, and national levels.
- Primary prevention strategies should be emphasized in effort to prevent trafficking before it occurs.
- Further research should focus on the impact of human trafficking prevention programs, as many programs have not been evaluated.

References

Albert, L. S. (2021). Trauma informed strategies for human trafficking education in urban schools: An attachment theory perspective. *Education & Urban Society*. doi: 10.1177/00131245211048427

Bigelson, J., Vuotto, S., Addison, K., Trongone, S., & Tully, K. (2013). Homelessness, survival sex, and human trafficking: As experienced by the youth of Covenant House, NY. Retrieved from https://cfpic.org/wp-content/uploads/2020/12/Covenant-house-assessment.pdf

Blum, D., Benoiton, T., & Kinder, S. (2018). "This doesn't happen here": Child sex trafficking in rural Oklahoma. *Administrative Issues Journal*, *8*(2), 1–15. https://dc.swosu.edu/aij/vol8/iss2/2

Bryant, K., & Landman, T. (2020). Combatting human trafficking since Palermo: What do we know about what works? *Journal of Human Trafficking*, *6*(2), 119–140. https://doi.org/10.1080/23322705.2020.1690097

Carpenter, A., & J. Gates. (2016). The nature and extent of gang involvement in sex trafficking in San Diego County (Final Report Grant No.: NIJ-2012-R2-CX-0028). United States Department of Justice. Retrieved from www.ncjrs.gov/pdffiles1/nij/grants/249857.pdf

Chang, K. S., Lee, K., Park, T., Sy, E., & Quach, T. (2015). Using a clinic-based screening tool for primary care providers to identify commercially sexually exploited children. *Journal of Applied Research on Children: Informing Policy for Children at Risk*, *6*(1), Article 6. https://digitalcommons.library.tmc.edu/childrenatrisk/vol6/iss1/6

Chisolm-Straker, M., Baldwin, S., Gaïgbé-Togbé, B., Ndukwe, N., Johnson, P. N., & Richardson, L. D. (2016). Health care and human trafficking: We are seeing the unseen. *Journal of Health Care for the Poor and Underserved*, *27*(3), 1220–1233.

Chisolm-Straker, M., Sze, J., Einbond, J., White, J., & Stoklosa, H. (2019). Screening for human trafficking among homeless young adults. *Children & Youth Services Review*, *98*, 72–79. doi: 10.1016/j.childyouth.2018.12.014

Connecticut State Department of Children and Family. (2021). Child trafficking decision map. Retrieved from https://portal.ct.gov/-/media/DCF/HumanTrafficking/pdf/HART-Decision-Map-5-17–21.pdf

Florida Department of Children and Families (FLDCF). (2009). Human trafficking of children indicator tool. Retrieved from https://humantraffickinghotline.org/sites/default/files/HumanTrafficking OfChildrenIndicatoTool%20-%20FL%20DCF.pdf

Florida Department of Education (FLDOE). (2019, September 30). Florida first state in nation to teach K-12 child trafficking prevention. Retrieved from www.fldoe.org/newsroom/latest-news/florida-first-state-in-nation-to-teach-k-12-child-trafficking-prevention.stml

Gallagher, A. T. (2010). *The international law of human trafficking*. Cambridge University Press.

Gardner, M., & Steinberg, L. (2005). Peer influence on risk taking, risk preference, and risky decision making in adolescence and adulthood: An experimental study. *Developmental Psychology*, *41*(4), 625–635. doi: 10.1037/0012-1649.41.4.625

Girls Educational & Mentoring Services (GEMS). (n.d.). Get trained. Retrieved from www.gems-girls.org/get-trained

Greenbaum, J., Crawford-Jakubiak, J. E., Committee on Child Abuse and Neglect, Christian, C. W., Crawford-Jakubiak, J. E., Flaherty, E. G., . . . Sege, R. D. (2015). Child sex trafficking and commercial sexual exploitation: Health care needs of victims. *Pediatrics*, *135*(3), 566–574.

Greenbaum, V. J., Dodd, M., & McCracken, C. (2018). A short screening tool to identify victims of child sex trafficking in the health care setting. *Pediatric Emergency Care*, *34*(1), 33–37.

Hershberger, A., Sanders, J., Chick, C., Jessup, M., Hanlin, H., & Cyders, M. (2018). Predicting running away in girls who are victims of commercial sexual exploitation. *Child Abuse & Neglect*, *79*, 269–278. doi: 10.1016/j.chiabu.2018.02.023

International Labour Organization. (2017). *Global estimates of modern slavery: Forced labour and forced marriage*. ILO. Retrieved from www.ilo.org/wcmsp5/groups/public/---dgreports/---dcomm/documents/publication/wcms_575479.pdf

Jeffreys, S. (2009). *The industrial vagina: The political economy of the global sex trade*. Routledge.

Kabbash, L. A., & Ronis, S. T. (2021). Making a dent in human trafficking: investigating the effects of social institutions and policies across 60 countries. *Crime, Law and Social Change*, *76*(3), 321–336. doi: 10.1007/s10611-021-09964-z

Kruger, A. C., Harper, E., Zabek, F., Collins, S., Perkins, C., & Meyers, J. (2016). Facilitating a school-based prevention of commercial sexual exploitation of children. *Health Promotion Practice*, *17*(4), 530–536. doi: 10.1177/1524839916628863

Lesak, A. M., Rizo, C. F., Franchino-Olsen, H., Jenkins, M. R., Winslow, H., Klein, L. B., . . . Dunkerton, C. (2021). Recommendations for educating youth about sex trafficking. *Journal of Human Trafficking*, 1–15. doi: 10.1080/23322705.2021.1951552

Long, E., Reid, J., McLeigh, J., Stoklosa, H., Felix, E., & Scott, T. (2019). Preventing human trafficking using data-driven, community-based strategies. Retrieved from www.communitypsychology.com/preventing-human-trafficking/

Love 146. (n.d.). Not A number: A child trafficking and exploitation prevention curriculum. Retrieved from www.love146.org/notanumber

Murphy, D. (2016). Commercial sexual exploitation of children and youth in a rural community: education for court dependent children and youth (Doctoral dissertation). Humboldt State University.

My Life My Choice: Empowering Youth, Ending Exploitation. (n.d.). My life my choice: Empowering youth, ending exploitation. Retrieved from www.fightingexploitation.org

National Center for Homeless Education (NCHE). (2014). Sex trafficking of minors: What schools need to know to recognize and respond to the trafficking of students. Retrieved from https://nche.ed.gov/wp-content/uploads/2018/10/trafficking.pdf

National Human Trafficking Training and Technical Assistance Center. (2018). Adult human trafficking screening tool and guide. Retrieved from www.acf.hhs.gov/sites/default/files/documents/otip/adult_human_trafficking_screening_tool_and_guide.pdf

New Jersey Department of Children and Families (NJDCF). (n.d.). Rapid human trafficking assessment (RHTA). Retrieved from www.state.nj.us/dcf/policy_manuals/CPP-X-A-1-9.3_issuance.shtml

Pascual-Leone, A., Kim, J., & Morrison, O. P. (2017). Working with victims of human trafficking. *Journal of Contemporary Psychotherapy*, *47*(1), 51–59. doi: 10.1007/s10879-016-9338-3

Peck, J. L., Meadows-Oliver, M., Hays, S. M., & Maaks, D. G. (2021). White paper: Recognizing child trafficking as a critical emerging health threat. *Journal of Pediatric Health Care*, *35*(3), 260–269. doi: 10.1016/j.pedhc.2020.01.005

Peters, S. (2012). Unbound Waco. Retrieved from http://unboundwaco.org

Pierce, A. (2012). American Indian adolescent girls: Vulnerability to sex trafficking, intervention strategies. *American Indian and Alaska Native Mental Health Research: The Journal of the National Center, 19*(1), 37–56. doi: 10.5820/aian.1901.2012.37

Polaris Project. (2010). Human trafficking assessment for medical professionals. Retrieved from https://humantraffickinghotline.org/sites/default/files/Assessment%20Tool%20-%20Medical%20Professionals.pdf

Polaris Project. (2011a). Comprehensive human trafficking assessment. https://humantraffickinghotline.org/sites/default/files/Comprehensive%20Trafficking%20Assessment.pdf

Polaris Project. (2011b). Human trafficking assessment for domestic workers. https://human trafficking-hotline.org/sites/default/files/Assessment%20Tool%20for%20Domestic%20Workers.pdf

Pooler, C., Sykora, J., & Pooler, D. (2022). The impact of assembly trainings on awareness of human trafficking among middle school and high school age youth. *Journal of Human Trafficking*, 1–9. doi: 10.1080/23322705.2020.1850141

Prevention Project. (n.d.). Human trafficking prevention education. Retrieved from www.prevention-project.org/home/

Project STARFISH. (n.d.). Retrieved from http://projectstarfish.education/

PROTECT. (n.d.). An educated student is a PROTECTed student. Retrieved from https://protectnow.org/

Reed, S. M., Kennedy, M. A., Decker, M. R., & Cimino, A. N. (2019). Friends, family, and boyfriends: An analysis of relationship pathways into commercial sexual exploitation. *Child Abuse & Neglect*, *90*, 1–12. doi: 10.1016/j.chiabu.2019.01.016

Reid, J., & Fox B. (2020). Human trafficking and the darknet: Technology, innovation, and evolving criminal justice strategies. In B. Fox, J. Reid, & A. Masys (Eds.), *Science informed policing. Advanced sciences and technologies for security applications*. Springer. doi: 10.1007/978-3-030-41287-6_5

Rizo, C. F., Chesworth, B. R., Franchino-Olsen, H., Klein, L., Villodas, M. L., Martin, S. L., & Macy, R. J. (2021). The state of programs for educating youth about sex trafficking in the united states: A nationwide scoping scan survey. *Journal of Human Trafficking*, 1–19. doi: 10.1080/23322705.2021.1943944

Rizo, C. F., Klein, L. B., Chesworth, B. R., O'Brien, J., Macy, R. J., Martin, S. L., Crews, M. E., & Love, B. L. (2019). Educating youth about commercial sexual exploitation of children: A systematic review. *Global Social Welfare, 6*, 29–39. https://doi.org/10.1007/s40609-018-0119-7

Rothman, E. F., Farrell, A., Paruk, J., Bright, K., Bair-Merritt, M., & Preis, S. R. (2021). Evaluation of a multi-session group designed to prevent commercial sexual exploitation of minors: The "my life my choice" curriculum. *Journal of Interpersonal Violence, 36*(19–20), 9143–9166. doi: 10.1177/0886260519865972

Rothman, E. F., Preis, S. R., Bright, K., Paruk, J., Bair-Merritt, M., & Farrell, A. (2020). A longitudinal evaluation of a survivor-mentor program for child survivors of sex trafficking in the United States. *Child Abuse & Neglect, 100*, 104083. doi: 10.1016/j.chiabu.2019.104083

Salas, R. G., & Didier, K. A. (2020). California adds human trafficking prevention training to its 7–12 grade curriculum: Should other states follow? *The Clearing House: A Journal of Educational Strategies, Issues & Ideas, 93*(1), 12–18. doi: 10.1080/00098655.2019.1677546

San Luis Obispo County CSEC Collaborative Response Team. (2014). Commercially sexually exploited children (CSEC) screening tool. Retrieved from www.cwda.org/sites/main/files/file-attachments/slo-csec-screening-tool.pdf?1455665472

Shared Hope International. (2010). Domestic minor sex trafficking practitioner guide and intake tool. Retrieved from https://sharedhope.org/product/intervene-course/

Shared Hope International. (n.d.). Training tools. Retrieved from https://sharedhope.org/what-we-do/prevent/training/

Shelley, L. I. (2010). *Human trafficking*. Cambridge University Press.

Smith, L., Vardaman, S., & Snow, M. (2009). *The national report on domestic minor sex trafficking: America's prostituted children*. Shared Hope International. Retrieved from https://sharedhope.org/wp-content/uploads/2012/09/SHI_National_Report_on_DMST_2009.pdf

Taylor, K. (2018). Teaching decision making and building resilience in youth: A case study to reduce the supply of vulnerable youth to sex traffickers in Atlanta, Georgia. *European Journal of Operational Research, 268*(3), 960–970. doi: 10.1016/j.ejor.2017.11.067

U.S. Department of Education (DOE). (2021). *Human trafficking in America's schools: What schools can do to prevent, respond, and help students to recover from human trafficking*, 2nd ed. DOE Office of Safe and Supportive Schools. Retrieved from https://www2.ed.gov/documents/human-trafficking/human-trafficking-americas-schools.pdf

U.S. Department of Health & Human Services (DHHS). (2019). Definitions and principles to inform human trafficking prevention. DHHS Administration for Children & Families, Office on Trafficking in Persons. Retrieved from www.acf.hhs.gov/sites/default/files/documents/otip/im_definitions_and_principles_of_human_trafficking_prevention.pdf

Urban Institute. (2017). Pretesting a human trafficking screening tool in the child welfare and runaway and homeless youth systems. Retrieved from www.urban.org/sites/default/files/publication/93596/pretesting_tool_0.pdf

Usacheva, M., Smalley, C., Hafer, N., & Brooks, S. (2021). Ending the game®: a new psychoeducational curriculum for victims of commercial sexual exploitation. *Women & Criminal Justice*, 1–20. doi: 10.1080/08974454.2021.1885568

Vera Institute for Justice. (2013). Trafficking victim identification tool (TVIT). Retrieved from www.vera.org/downloads/publications/human-trafficking-identification-tool-and-user-guidelines.pdf

Walts, K., French, S., Moore, H., & Ashai, S. (2011). Building a child welfare response to child trafficking handbook. Retrieved from https://ecommons.luc.edu/chrc/3/

West Coast Children's Clinic. (2015). Memorandum summarizing the available screening tools to identify commercially sexually exploited children (CSEC). Retrieved from https://theacademy.sdsu. edu/wp-content/uploads/2016/02/csec-screening-tools-matrix.pdf

West Coast Children's Clinic. (n.d.). Commercial sexual exploitation-identification tool (CSE-IT). Retrieved from www.westcoastcc.org/cse-it/

Zhang, S. X. (2012). Trafficking of migrant laborers in San Diego County: Looking for a hidden population (Final Report Grant No.: 2009-IJ-cX-0011). United States Department of Justice. Retrieved from www.ojp.gov/pdffiles1/nij/grants/240223.pdf

Zhu, T., Crenshaw, C., & Scott, L. (2020). Curriculum in action: Teaching students to combat human trafficking. *Education & Urban Society*, *52*(9), 1351–1371. doi: 10.1177/0013124520911909

PART II

Juvenile Justice and Early Interventions

8

SCHOOL-BASED PREVENTION AND CRIMINAL JUSTICE

Ashley L. White

The Extension of Zero Tolerance Through School Policy and Practice

Originally used in relation to drug policy, zero tolerance has been defined as a "philosophy or policy that mandated the application of predetermined consequences, most often severe and punitive in nature, and applied regardless of the gravity of behavior, mitigating circumstances or situational context" (Skiba et al., 2006, p. 2). Policies and practices consistent with zero tolerance were identified in schools well before the formal emergence of the term in 1989 (see Goss v. Lopez, 1975; Curran, 2019). "By 1993 such policies had been openly adopted by schools across the country" (Skiba & Peterson, 1999 as cited in White et al., 2021). Since its emergence, the term "zero tolerance" has been used in a number of ways across different contexts, with many states now choosing not to "refer to their school discipline laws as zero tolerance" (Curran, 2019, p. 332–333). Still, despite states' resistance to accurately name such polices, zero-tolerance policies and practices, such as suspension and expulsion, are readily observed in schools across the nation, and "the number of secondary school students suspended or expelled over the course of a school year increased roughly 40 percent from one in 13 in 1972–73 to one in nine in 2009–2010" (Kang-Brown et al., 2013, p. 2 as partially cited in White et al., 2021). This chapter provides a brief overview of the proliferation of exclusionary discipline/zero-tolerance policies; their consequences; and the potential effectiveness of school-based preventative practices in minimizing these policies, practices, and the deleterious outcomes.

From Zero Tolerance to the Preschool to Prison Pipeline

The American Civil Liberties Union (ACL) describes the (preschool to) prison pipeline as "the policies and practices that push our nations' schoolchildren, especially our most at-risk children, out of classrooms and into the juvenile and criminal justice systems" (Jones, 2017 as cited in White et al., 2021). This epidemic most adversely impacts Black (African American) students, students with disabilities, and students who possess these intersectional identities. According to an Office of Civil Rights (OCR) 2014 data collection report, during the 2011–2012 school year, Black students constituted 18% of preschool enrollment but 49% of preschool children experiencing one suspension or more. These disparities extend

DOI: 10.4324/9781003219286-11

beyond preschool for Black students and become more prevalent in comparison to other marginalized groups (Ruiz, 2017). The 2015–2016 OCR data collection (2018) indicated that while Black male students in P–12 represented only 8% of the student population, these students accounted for 25% of students receiving out-of-school suspension. Likewise, Black female students accounted for 8% of the P–12 population while also accounting for 14% of out-of-school suspensions. Across all grade levels, 26% of students with disabilities received out-of-school suspensions while accounting for only 12% of the overall student population.

In June 2021, the Office for Civil Rights reported on the state of suspensions and expulsions in public schools. While overall disciplinary actions have decreased (e.g., expulsions under zero-tolerance policies and number of in and out-of-school suspensions), Black students, who accounted for a mere 15.1% of total student enrollment, received a disproportionate number of out-of-school suspensions and expulsions, more than twice their "share of student enrollment" (p. 12 & 16). Likewise,

> students with disabilities received 20.5% of one or more in-school suspensions and 24.5% of one or more out-of- school suspensions represented, despite representing only 13.2% of total student enrollment . . . when disaggregated by race, disparities worsened. . . . Black students with disabilities received 6.2% of one or more in-school suspensions and 8.8% of one or more out-of-school suspensions, despite accounting for only 2.3% of total student enrollment.
>
> *(p. 18)*

The preschool to prison pipeline, and the zero-tolerance policies which support it, disrupt the bonds between students and teachers in a way that creates a permanent chasm and reinforces the cultural disconnect for students before they gain any positive or beneficial experiences around schooling. This in turn perpetuates the historical dehumanization of Black American students, families, and communities in much the same way that slavery, convict leasing, and incarceration have disrupted the cohesiveness, social, political, and economic advancement of Black American families and communities. Furthermore, the "growing pattern of tracking students out of educational institutions and tracking them directly and/or indirectly into the juvenile and adult criminal justice systems contributes to the escalation in prison populations, which has increased tenfold or more since 1970" (Heitzeg, 2009, p. 1). Heitzeg (2009, p. 5) states further, "the policy shifts in juvenile justice are both consistent with and in furtherance of another significant phenomena related to the school to prison pipeline – mass incarceration and the emergence of the prison industrial complex".

In 2016, the Economic Policy Institute (2016) published a report, *Criminal Justice Policy Is Education Policy*. In this report, Rothstein and Morsy drew connections between high incarceration rates of African American adults and the proliferation and likelihood of African American children and youth entering the criminal justice system, particularly through the preschool to prison pipeline. Zero-tolerance policies and practices drive this pipeline and include the presence of school resource officers (SROs) and the arresting of children and youth, an action which is precipitated by discriminatory zero-tolerance policies and practices themselves. This pipeline serves as a direct contributor to the inequitable state of our nation's criminal justice system, creates outcomes for Black American and other marginalized student populations that maintain socioeconomic disparities, and perpetuates longstanding practices of incarceration. As Ruiz (2017, p. 11) explains, "zero tolerance regulations essentially ignore the suspension of due process safeguards because students automatically receive the punishment paired with their alleged misconduct" (as cited in White et al., 2021). In thinking about our nation's use of policing through zero-tolerance practices and policies, educational stakeholders must also think about methods for disrupting the current pipeline that directly supports the criminalization of marginalized students, families, and communities.

Preventative and Responsive Evidence-Based Policies and Practices

While criminal justice systems have attempted to improve their policies and practices related to the reduction of recidivism among offenders, educational stakeholders must take even more immediate action to prevent and respond to student needs so that school systems do not contribute to the proliferation of the criminal justice system but, rather, work toward implementing policies and practices that support students' varying needs through evidence-based approaches that support the whole child. The following examples may be used to help practitioners think about and implement preemptive support for students, families, and communities.

Discipline Reform Through Positive Behavioral Interventions and Supports

Funded by the U.S. Department of Education's Office of Special Education Programs (OSEP), the Positive Behavioral Interventions and Supports (PBIS) TA Center strives to enhance the socio-emotional experiences of all students by supporting schools, districts, and states with PBIS implementation and the subsequent improvement of school climate and safety (Positive Behavior and Intervention and Supports [PBIS], 2022d). PBIS involves "an evidenced-based three-tiered framework to improve and integrate all of the data, systems, and practices affecting student outcomes everyday" (PBIS, 2022d, para 1). This three-tiered framework includes establishing "a foundation of regular, proactive support while preventing unwanted behaviors" (PBIS, 2022a, para 1), behaviors that obstruct normative learning experiences, through a universal and school-wide support system. The second tier includes providing support for students who may be more "at-risk for developing more serious behaviors" before their onset, with the goal of helping these students develop skills and strategies to function successfully in core instructional settings (PBIS, 2022b, para 1). PBIS's third tier includes more centralized "intensive and individual support for students" to help them achieve both academic and behavioral success in core instructional settings (PBIS, 2022c, para 1). Schools implementing PBIS with fidelity have been reported as enacting exclusionary discipline on students with disabilities at lower rates (Simonsen et al., 2021) and, overall, PBIS practices have

> demonstrated effectiveness in supporting schools in improving various prosocial outcomes including improved social, emotional, and behavioral skills; increased academic outcomes and attendance; decreased exclusionary discipline (e.g., office referrals, suspensions); and reduced reports of bullying and substance abuse.
>
> *(Feinberg et al., 2021)*

The successful implementation of PBIS requires the support of all teachers, administrative persons, and other staff within a school setting; the maintenance of quality implementation that includes teaching, rewarding and prevention strategies; and, most importantly, a focus on students. When students feel supported by teachers, it enhances the connections between students and teachers and significantly increases the likelihood of success in schools. These connections are particularly important when considering factors that confound relationship building with marginalized student groups (e.g., students serviced under the Individual with

Disabilities Education Act (IDEA), ethno-racially marginalized students, bilingual students) (Molloy et al., 2013). Furthermore, student and teacher connections contribute to the overall improvement of school climate (Cox, 2019), including the ability to maintain consistent schoolwide implementation frameworks (Molloy et al., 2013).

While researchers, practitioners, and other educational stakeholders cannot undo the damage of the preschool to prison pipeline, they can consider the ways in which evidence-based practices might serve as more effective supports for such students who have been impacted by the epidemic. Although research is limited, scholars have suggested the implementation of PBIS frameworks in alternative school settings (Jolivette et al., 2012; Nelson et al., 2009; Simonson & Sugai, 2013). While specific considerations exist for these settings (Scott & Cooper, 2013), Simonson and Sugai (2013) note that PBIS frameworks can be very effective in alternative settings when implemented with the same fidelity and overall practice as general education settings, including the use of all tiers.

The context of the racialized criminal justice system and related practices heightens the importance of considering culturally responsive (CRPBIS) implementation. Like the consideration of PBIS in alternative settings, research on culturally responsive PBIS is sparse. However, as the nation's ethno-racially diverse student population increases, the consideration of CRPBIS is imperative. Bal and colleagues (2012) identified three key areas of consideration for CRPBIS implementation: collaboration with families and community to establish school-normed behavioral expectations for students, monitoring disparities in office discipline referrals (ODRs) between culturally diverse and nondiverse student groups, and consistently providing professional learning experiences for educators. Bal and colleagues (2012) also emphasized the importance of cultural mediation when implementing CRPBIS. This specific practice includes but is not limited to adhering to tenets of culturally responsive pedagogy; the development of mutual relationships between student, teachers, and families; and the full use of student and practitioners as social agents and continual learners.

Restorative Practices

The practice of restorative justice (RJ), also known as "community justice, transformative justice, peacemaking criminology, relational justice" (Bazemore & Walgrave, 1999), was first used in criminal justice systems as a practice of transitioning from traditional practices of punishment such as incarceration, probation, and court-ordered restitution to focusing on the act of recovery (Latimer et al., 2005). Zehr (1990) discusses the importance of focusing on the violation of relationships that must be restored and the inclusion of willingness, truth, and face-to-face encounters when using restorative justice practices (Llewellyn & Howse, 1998 as cited in Latimer et al., 2005). Related to criminal justice, RJ practices have proven moderately effective in reducing delinquent behavior in comparison to more juvenile court practices (Wilson et al., 2017). "Case studies and evaluations conducted in schools worldwide indicate that restorative practices improve relationships among students and teachers, reduce disciplinary problems and build community" (Porter, 2007, para 3). More importantly, RJ practices have the potential to productively reshape school culture and climate.

In schools, RJ practices allow school leaders, educators, and other stakeholders to reimagine school discipline by restoring relationships between students, educators, parents, and even communities, as opposed to nurturing punitive discipline. RJ also has the potential to impact overall school climate through creating environments that improve learning outcomes for students, school safety, and reduced rates of suspension and expulsion (Ashley & Burke, 2009).

In focusing on the repairing of harm due to conflict, RJ requires that the infraction be clearly identified; all parties impacted by the infraction be included in the process of restoring justice (Dignity in Schools, 2013), understand the harm done, work toward the development of empathy for one another, listen and respond to the needs of both the offender and the harmed; and accountability and responsibility for the restorative process be included through reflective practices (Ashley & Burke, 2009).

Of note, RJ practices should have the ultimate goal of fostering healing in schools, rebuilding relationships, reconciliation (between the harmed and the offender) (Dignity in Schools Organization, 2013), nurturing caring climates to support healthy communities, and changing the system when it contributes to harm (Ashley & Burke, 2009). The Dignity in Schools Organization (2013) released a report that outlined how to implement RJ in schools. This report included successful implementation examples from districts and schools in New York. The following table includes components from these examples:

Mental Health Supports and Services

The rate of mental health concerns among children and adolescents is increasing, and in some cases may be highest among those students most impacted by the school to prison pipeline. Using data taken from the 2016 National Survey of Children's Health, Whitney and Peterson (2019) found at least 16.5% of children surveyed (7.7 million) had at least one mental health disorder and that the percentage of children not receiving services for their mental health needs ranged anywhere from 29.5 to 72.2%. The state of mental health among children and adolescents is not the only concern, as these rates are ever increasing (American Psychological Association, 2019). Additionally, the rate of suicide among children has increased dramatically over the last decade (American Civil Liberties Union [ACLU], 2021).

Mental illness not only impacts the lives of adults but of children and youth, often affecting students' instructional experiences and overall social development (Association for Children's Mental Health, 2021; National Alliance on Mental Illness [NAMI], 2021; National Association of School Psychologists [NASP], 2021). As with other services, schools serve as viable settings for mental health supports and services (NASP, 2021; Substance Abuse and Mental Health Services Administration [SAMHSA], 2019), providing an optimal setting for prevention, intervention, development, and open consistent communication between schools and families (NASP, 2021). School-based mental health services delivered by trained professionals (e.g., school psychologists, counselors, social workers, nurses) can increase "early identification and effective treatment for children and their families" (NAMI, para. 4 & 5).

Scholars have investigated and documented the effectiveness of robust mental health supports and services for students and families (Atkins et al., 2010: Maggin & Mills, 2013; Reinke et al., 2020). A focus on mental health services in schools stands to improve outcomes for students, including issues related to behavior that may have otherwise been addressed by draconian measures that increase the preschool to prison pipeline and perpetuate inequities in the criminal justice system at large. Furthermore, in lifting mental health services and supports in schools through funding and practice, policy and other decision makers can help to mitigate specific issues of disproportionate discipline for ethno-racially marginalized students and students with disabilities, those who are most demonstratively impacted by inequitable policies and practices in schools, and address fundamental student concerns in a way that would increase the effectiveness of other preventative and responsive interventions.

Table 8.1 Ideas for Restorative Justice Implementation in Schools: Adapted from *Building Safe, Supportive, and Restorative School Communities in New York City, Dignity in Schools* Report (2013)

Strategy	*Details*
Parent Leadership	Engaging parents in RJ professional development opportunities (and the development of schools' systems and frameworks)
Student Leadership	Engaging students in producing videos, skits, posters, and other materials to promote restorative approaches among their peers (and in learning about RJ overall)
Fairness Committees	Developed by educators at Humanities Preparatory High School in the 1990s, utilizing a small group of students and adults, representative of the school community, to discuss violations of the school's disciplinary policies and values with anyone who violates a policy or core value
Data Monitoring	Collaboration with administrators, faculty, students, and parents to develop a common set of indicators and protocols for collecting data to help understand the implementation and results of restorative practices in the pilot schools
Effectiveness Evaluation	Engaging in systematic and routine RJ practice evaluation with researchers (in conjunction with data monitoring to determine characteristics of consistency and overall effectiveness)
Values Discussion	Explicitly defining school values, including mission and vision statements
Interventions First	Helping teachers and other staff to think about how to intervene in conflict with students in a restorative way before employing more punitive practices
Student Mentorship	Utilizing students to mentor other students (e.g., older students mentoring younger students) – developing workshops for students to help them become mentors – utilizing students to conduct peer mediation sessions
Justice Panels	A specific number of students who convene to discuss and recommend solutions for disciplinary incidents in the school
Coordinator	A designated position with the sole focus of coordinating a positive, restorative climate and approach to discipline at the school
School-Wide Planning	Done with participation of all school stakeholders that integrate pre-existing behavior-related strategies, such as Fairness Committees, conflict resolution, peer mediation, and peer mentoring, into a restorative framework and set of values, and integrates that framework into existing school structures
Professional Development	Including faculty, counselors and other school employees, school safety agents, and a core group of student and parent leaders who can develop the skills to train their peers

Conclusion

Policies and practices included under zero tolerance led to the creation of the preschool to prison pipeline. Similarly, policies and practices also have the power to deconstruct this pipeline and ensure practices which support marginalized students are implemented in schools. When considering the reality of successful policy implementation, proponents of reform should consider two questions.

How Do Current Legislation and Policy Impact Equitable School-Based Prevention Practices?

Several current legislative efforts seek to support the practices outlined in this chapter, including those aimed at advocating against the presence of school resource officers in schools and the rerouting of SRO funding. These include the Counseling not Criminalization in Schools Act ([CNC] H.R. 411/S. 2125) which "aims to decrease the number of arrests in schools through the reduction of School Resource Officers (SROs) and the increase of counselors, social workers, nurses, and other health professionals on campuses" (Murphy.senate.gov, 2021 as cited in White & Freeman, 2022). Advocacy organizations (e.g., Council of Parent Attorneys and Advocates [COPPA], National Disability Rights Network [NDRN]) also support the replacement of SROs and the harmful school practices that align with zero-tolerance policy (e.g., corporal punishment, suspension, expulsion, seclusion, school arrests) in favor of more sustainable evidence-based practices that equalize learning opportunities for students.

However, other current legislative efforts stand to strengthen zero-tolerance policies and work against evidence-based interventions and strategies, namely the advancement of mental health supports and services for students. For example, the Luke & Alex School Safety Act (H.R.750/S.111) and the EAGLES Act (S.391) include policies and practices that would further disenfranchise student groups most affected by zero-tolerance policies and the criminal justice system. These legislative efforts advocate for strategies such as the National Threat Assessment Center (NTAC) as a remedy to school violence even though such practices contribute to disproportionate identification and the maltreatment of marginalized and minoritized students, specifically Black (African American) and Latino males, students with disabilities, and students who possess these intersectional identities (Cornell et al., 2018; Cornell & Maeng, 2020; Rollin, 2019 as cited in White & Freeman, 2022). In some cases, these pieces of legislation assign the responsibility of school safety to the Department of Homeland Security (DHS), a federal agency whose mission does not include school and student safety (Coalition for Smart Safety, 2021 as cited in White & Freeman, 2022) and whose functions do not lend themselves to educational improvement (White & Freeman, 2022).

> This bill would also enhance the involvement of SROs in schools and maintain threat assessments, thereby increasing the overidentification of marginalized and minoritized students as threats to school safety and likely swelling the number of students funneled into the preschool to prison pipeline.
>
> *(White & Freeman, 2022)*

How Can Law Enforcement Work With Educational Stakeholders to Implement Evidence-Based Interventions That Improve Outcomes?

Disproportionate outcomes related to interactions with SROs and subsequent arrests and referrals to law enforcement mimic suspension and expulsion data. "In 2017–18, Black students accounted for 28.7% of all students referred to law enforcement and 31.6% of all students arrested at school or during a school-related activity", despite accounting for only 15.1% of total student enrollment (OCR, 2021, p. 21). Likewise, Black students with disabilities accounted for 8.4% of students referred to law enforcement and 9.1% of students who were arrested, despite accounting for only 2.3% of total student enrollment.

The Center for Policing Equity (2021) offers strategies to reduce the negative impact that policing has on public safety. This roadmap is particularly important for marginalized communities who face the brunt of primarily racist policing practices. The Center suggests an analysis of community need and officer-initiated activities, a mapping of ineffective police activity, targeted investment, and the inclusion of community input to reduce law enforcement footprint in targeted communities. While these strategies apply to law enforcement activity in local communities, such practices and reform efforts also stand to impact law enforcement practices, considering that such reform efforts indicate an attempted shift in overall policing practices, including the way that law enforcement personnel perceive the nature of their charge both in and out of schools.

SROs have not increased equitable learning or social experiences for marginalized student groups. Rather, their presence and form of practice have, by and large, widened the equity gap between select student groups (Javdani, 2019; King & Schindler, 2021). As proponents of school policing await legislative shifts, educational stakeholders can turn to immediate reform efforts to begin to mitigate disparate policing practices and outcomes in schools. Short-term reforms include emphasizing the resource role of officers through attention to relationship building between SROs and students as well as the establishment of detailed protocols for SRO behavior and interaction with students in schools while districts and states focus on the phasing out of school policing practices in favor of preventative and nurturing supports for students (King & Schindler, 2021).

Educational stakeholders should be implementing practices that can improve outcomes for students already interacting with the criminal justice system and prevent more student interaction with that system. Such implementation must include the initiation and maintenance of multi-tiered systems of support/PBIS, communication with individual schools, development of written and actionable plans for transitioning youth out of the juvenile justice system, creation of systems for restoring trust and honoring justice, explicitly defining crisis incidents between schools and law enforcement, increasing mental health services and supports, and, overall, working with districts and schools to create supportive systems of practice for students that prevent them from interacting with any part of the justice system. This type of wide-scale change can only be accomplished with the support of and strategic planning from state and local agencies that contend with grossly skewed discipline practices and the resulting data and that utilize extant research and research-based practices to achieve systems and practices that work favorably for all students.

References

American Civil Liberties Union. (2021). *Cops and no counselors*. American Civil Liberties Union.

American Psychological Association. (2019). *Mental health issues increased significantly in young adults over the last decade*. American Psychological Association.

Ashley, J., & Burke, K. (2009). *Implementing restorative justice: A guide for schools*. Illinois Criminal Justice Information Authority.
Association for Children's Mental Health. (2021). *Problems in school: Why does mental health matter in schools?* Association for Children's Mental Health.
Atkins, M. S., Hoagwood, K. E., Kutash, K., & Seidman, E. (2010). Toward the integration of education and mental health in schools. *Administration and Policy in Mental Health and Mental Health Services Research*, *37*(1), 40–47.
Bal, A., Thorius, K. K., & Kozleski, E. (2012). *Culturally responsive positive behavioral support matters*. The Equity Alliance.
Bazemore, G., & Walgrave, L. (1999). *Restorative juvenile justice: Repairing the harm of youth crime*. Criminal Justice Press.
Center for Policing Equity. (2021). A roadmap for exploring new models of funding public safety. Author.
Coalition for Smart Safety. (2021). Opposition letter to the Luke and Alex school safety act. Author.
Cornell, D., & Maeng, J. L. (2020). Student threat assessment as a safe and supportive prevention strategy, final technical report. National Criminal Justice Reference Service. Retrieved from https://nij.ojp.gov/library/publications/student-threat-assessment-safe-and-supportive-prevention-strategy-final
Cornell, D., Maeng, J. L., Burnette, A. G., Jia, Y., Huang, F, Konold, T., Datta, P., Malone, M., & Meyer, P. (2018). Student threat assessment as a standard school safety practice: Results from a statewide implementation study. *School Psychology Quarterly: The Official Journal of the Division of School Psychology*. doi: 10.1037/Spq0000220
Cox, C. (2019). Positive behavioral interventions and supports: How and why does it work according to students? (13) [Master's thesis]. Dominican University of California, Dominican Scholar.
Curran, C. F. (2019). The law policy, and portrayal of zero tolerance school discipline: Examining prevalence and characteristics across levels of governance and school districts. *Educational Policy*, *33*(2), 319–349.
Dignity in Schools Organization. (2013, Summer). Building safe, supportive and restorative school communities in New York City: Case study series (Vol. 2). Retrieved from www.nesri.org/sites/default/files/DSCNY_CaseStudy_2013.pdf
Feinberg, A. B., Meyer, K. A., Everett, S., Robbie. K., Pierce. A., Shor, R., Ricotta, A., & Fischer, S. (2021, April). PBIS academy model demo brief: Impact of statewide support model on high-needs schools. Center on PBIS, University of Oregon. Retrieved from www.pbis.org
Goss v. Lopez, 419 U.S. 565 (1975)
Heitzeg, N. A. (2009). Education or incarceration: Zero tolerance policies and the school to prison pipeline. *Forum on Public Policy*, *2009*(2), 1–21.
Javdani, S. (2019). Policing education: An empirical review of the challenges and impact of the work of school police officers. *American Journal of Community Psychology*, *63*, 253–269.
Jolivette, K., McDaniel, S. C., Sprague, J., Swain-Bradway, J., & Ennis, R. P. (2012). Embedding the positive behavior intervention and supports framework into the complex array of practices within alternative education settings: A decision-making process. *Assessment for Effective Intervention*, *38*, 15–29.
Jones, S. (2017, December). Preschool-to-prison pipeline. Huffington Post. Retrieved from https://www.huffpost.com/entry/preschooltoprison-pipelin_b_9773826
Kang-Brown, J., Trone, J., Fratello, J., & Daftary-Kapur, T. (2013, December). A generation later: What we've learned about zero tolerance in schools. VERA Institute of Justice. Retrieved from https://www.vera.org/publications/a-generation-later-what-weve-learned-about-zero-tolerance-in-schools
King, R., & Schindler, M. (2021, April). A better path forward on criminal justice: Reconsidering police in schools. Brooking Institute. Retrieved from https://www.brookings.edu/research/a-better-path-forward-for-criminal-justice-reconsidering-police-in-schools/
Latimer, J., Dowden, C., & Muise, D. (2005). The effectiveness of restorative justice practices: A meta-analysis. *The Prison Journal*, *85*(2), 127–144.
Llewellyn, J., & Howse, R. (1998). *Restorative justice: A conceptual framework*. Law Commission of Canada.
Maggin, D., & Mills, C. (2013). Interconnecting school and mental health data to improve student outcomes. *Advancing Education Effectiveness*, *58*.
Molloy, L. E., Moore, J. E., Trail, J., Van Epps, J. J., & Hopfer, S. (2013). Understanding real-world implementation quality and "active ingredients" of PBIS. *Prevention Science*, *14*(6), 593–605.

Murphy.senate.gov (2021). *Fact sheet: The counseling not criminalization in schools act*. Retrieved from Murphy.senate.gov

National Alliance of Mental Illness. (2021). Mental health in schools. National Alliance of Mental Illness.

National Association of School Psychologists. (2021). Comprehensive school-based mental and behavioral health services and school psychologists. National Association of School Psychologists.

Nelson, C. M., Sprague, J. R., Jolivette, K., Smith, C. R., & Tobin, T. J. (2009). Positive behavior support in alternative education, community-based mental health and juvenile justice settings. In G. Sugai, R. Horner, G. Dunlap, & W. Sailor (Eds.), *Handbook of positive behavior support* (pp. 465–496). Springer.

Porter, A. J. (2007). *Restorative practices in schools: Research reveals power of restorative approach Part 1*. IIRP Graduate School.

Positive Behavioral Interventions and Supports. (2022a). What is Tier 1 support? Retrieved from www.pbis.org/pbis/tier-1

Positive Behavioral Interventions and Supports. (2022b). What is Tier 2 support? Retrieved from www.pbis.org/pbis/tier-2

Positive Behavioral Interventions and Supports. (2022c). What is Tier 3 support? Retrieved from www.pbis.org/pbis/tier-3

Positive Behavioral Interventions and Supports. (2022d). Who are we? Retrieved from www.pbis.org

Reinke, W. M., Herman, K. C., Thompson, A., Copeland, C., McCall, C. S., Holmes, S., & Owens, S. A. (2020). Investigating the longitudinal association between fidelity to a large-scale comprehensive school mental health prevention and intervention model and student outcomes. *School Psychology Review*, *50*(1), 17–29.

Rollin, M. A. (2019, December 12). Here's how threat assessments may be targeting vulnerable students. Better Conversation. Retrieved from https://educationpost.org/heres-how-threat-assessments-may-be-targeting-vulnerable-students/

Rothstein, R., & Morsy, L. (2016). Mass incarceration and children's outcomes. Economic Policy Institute. Retrieved from https://www.epi.org/publication/mass-incarceration-and-childrens-outcomes/

Ruiz, R. R. (2017). School-to-prison pipeline: An evaluation of zero tolerance policies and their alternatives. *Houston Law Review*, *54*, 803.

Scott, T. M., & Cooper, J. (2013). Tertiary-tier PBIS in alternative, residential and correctional school settings: Considering intensity in the delivery of evidence-based practice. *Education and Treatment of Children*, 101–119.

Simonsen, B., Freeman, J., Gambino, A. J., Sears, S., Meyer, K., & Hoselton, R. (2021, November). Are fewer students with disabilities suspended when schools implement PBIS? Center on PBIS, University of Oregon. Retrieved from www.pbis.org.

Simonsen, B., Freeman, J., Gambino, A. J., Sears, S., Meyer, K., & Hoselton, R. (2022). An exploration of the relationship between PBIS and discipline outcomes for students with disabilities. *Remedial and Special Education*, *43*(5), 287–300. doi: 10.1177/07419325211063490

Simonsen, B., & Sugai, G. (2013). PBIS in alternative education settings: Positive support for youth with high-risk behavior. *Education and Treatment of Children*, 3–14.

Skiba, F., & Peterson, R. (1999). The dark side of zero tolerance. *Phi Delta Kappan*, 372–382.

Skiba, R., Reynolds, C. R., Graham, S., Sheras, P., Conoley, J. C, Garcia-Vasquez, E. (2006). Zero tolerance task force report: Are zero tolerance policies effective in the schools? An evidentiary review and recommendations. American Psychological Association.

Substance Abuse and Mental Health Services Administration. (2019). *Key substance use and mental health disorders in the United States: Results from the 2019 National Survey on Drug Use and Health*. Substance Abuse and Mental Health Services Administration.

U.S. Department of Education Office of Civil Rights. (2018). 2015–2016 office of civil rights data collection: School climate and safety. Data highlights on school climate and safety in our nation's public schools. U.S. Department of Education Office of Civil Rights.

U.S. Department of Education Office of Civil Rights Data Collection. (2014). *Data snapshot: Early childhood education*. U.S. Department of Education.

U.S. Department of Education Office of Civil Rights Data Collection. (2021). 2017–2018 state and national estimations. Retrieved from https://ocrdata.ed.gov/estimations/2017-2018

White, A. L., & Freeman, J. (2022). Using the every students succeeds act to pursue equitable school climate practice and policy. In T. P. LaSalle (Ed.), *A primer for creating positive school environments for minoritized and marginalized youth*. Routledge.

White, A. L., Hoppey, D., & Allsopp, D. H. (2021). Addressing discipline policies and practices for students with disabilities. In J. A. Rodriquez & W. W. Murawski (Eds.), *Special education law and policy: From foundation to application* (pp. 390–423). Plural Publishing.
Whitney, D. G., & Peterson, M. D. (2019). US national and state-level prevalence of mental health disorders and disparities of mental health care use in children. *JAMA Pediatrics*, *173*(4), 389–391.
Wilson, D. B., Olaghere, A., & Kimbrell, C. S. (2017). Effectiveness of restorative justice principles in juvenile justice: A meta-analysis. Retrieved from www.ncjrs.gov/pdffiles1/ojjdp/grants/250872.pdf
Zehr, H. (1990). *Changing lenses: A new focus for crime and justice*. Herald Press.

9

EVIDENCE-BASED CRIMINAL JUSTICE PRACTICES

Current Status and Strategies for Successful Youth Outreach and Enrichment Programming

McKenzie N. Berezin, Raquel E. Rose and Shabnam Javdani

The goal of this chapter is to synthesize the state of the literature on outreach and enrichment for young people involved in the legal system and describe evidence-based programs and practices of interest to researchers and practitioners working with criminal justice populations. For this, we employ a framework that attends to the individual, interpersonal, and broader socio-cultural factors that promote or inhibit youth outreach and enrichment efforts.

We define outreach as part of any intervention- or prevention based effort aims to include and promote effective delivery of services to an intended population, thereby promoting greater and sustained *access* to services and accumulating or maintaining consistent *engagement* while services are being provided (Dembo et al., 2011; Smith, 2013; Vera et al., 2005). We define enrichment as a concept rooted in the prevention literature encompassing practices or services that move beyond reducing risk exposure to also promoting strengths and protective factors by employing a variety of approaches to facilitate positive youth development (Kohler et al., 2019; Simmons-Horton, 2017). Although outreach and enrichment are often considered and studied as different from each other and from the core programmatic elements that constitute evidence-based care, we argue that they represent essential and connected aspects of service delivery and uptake. Integration of outreach and enrichment strategies is especially critical for youth and families not traditionally served successfully by legal systems, such as youth of color, who face a higher mental health burden and increased risk for individual and intergenerational incarceration. Moreover, the racial and ethnic disparities present across the legal system continuum – from arrest to community supervision to confinement and reentry – are worsened when programs and services do not take outreach and enrichment into consideration. This misalignment in approaches often results in high dropout and program failure rates that have negative legal and social consequences, especially among underserved youth from racial and ethnic backgrounds who already experience high levels of police contact and surveillance (Mallett, 2018).

Indeed, young people are more likely to need services but not receive them and face more difficulty accessing services compared to adults (Becker & Kleinman, 2013). Specifically, one in five youth experience mental health challenges that warrant treatment, yet four in five of these youth never access services (e.g., Bornheimer et al., 2018). Among youth who do

 DOI: 10.4324/9781003219286-12

begin services, between 50% and 80% drop out before receiving an effective amount of care (Chacko et al., 2016). High treatment needs, high dropout, and low access are especially prevalent among youth experiencing externalizing ("acting out") mental health challenges (Kazdin & Wassell, 2000). Despite their higher rates of referral to care within and outside of the legal system, these youth are at greatest risk of dropout and service underutilization, especially if they have two or more social vulnerabilities, such as low-income background, low education, immigration status, or experience discrimination based on their racial, ethnic, economic, and/or gender identity (Comer et al., 2013). This underutilization of care is not only costly and ineffective but also results in negative legal consequences for young people who are mandated to programs or otherwise monitored for compliance.

Thus, outreach and enrichment efforts embedded within, or supplemented on top of, existing programming are critical to promoting access and sustained engagement to services. Literature on outreach and enrichment has rarely examined these efforts as distinct and separate from larger programs and services, and this has made it difficult to pinpoint their additive effect on youth outcomes. That said, the clear consensus in the literature is that these elements are important cornerstones of successful youth programs. In the following sections, we identify effective outreach and enrichment principles, practices, and programming elements from the extant literature and illustrate exemplary program models.

To identify evidence-based outreach and enrichment approaches, we employed a multipronged literature and program review. First, we conducted a full database search of the Office of Juvenile Justice and Delinquency Prevention's (OJJDP) Model Programs Guide, which is a publicly available peer-reviewed database that documents youth programs across the juvenile justice and child welfare continuum. This database further classifies them based on the strength of research evidence supporting each program (i.e., effective, promising, or no evidence of effectiveness). We performed a keyword search on "outreach", "enrichment", "engagement", and their variants on the entire database and identified four evidence-based programs (Table 9.1, section A). Second, we reviewed the descriptions for all programs deemed effective through experimental designs for juvenile justice populations to identify additional programs incorporating outreach and enrichment practices, even if they were not labeled as such. All included programs enrolled youth involved in the legal system (including prevention, court, and probation), were community based, and reported on enrichment- or outreach-related outcomes. This search yielded an additional eight programs (Table 9.1, section B). Third, to expand our search beyond OJJDP model programs, we also conducted a broader literature review to identify meta-analyses, systematic reviews, and exemplary outreach and enrichment approaches from the broader literature but with potential to be very relevant for legal system-involved youth. Using GoogleScholar, we generated a list of keywords to specify the population of interest (i.e., juvenile justice, youth, and their variants) *and* combined these with keywords to identify the programming approach (i.e., outreach, enrichment, and their variants). This yielded a total of 37 articles, including 11 meta-analyses and systematic reviews, from which 5 non-duplicated programs and practices were extracted and are listed in Table 9.1, section C.

Description of and Recommendations for Outreach and Enrichment Programming

Within the juvenile justice literature, enrichment- and outreach-focused programs that have been evaluated are rare. However, enrichment- and outreach- focused practices are an increasingly important part of programming for youth in the legal system that can not only reduce risk but also promote youth's strengths and protective factors, such as self-efficacy, creativity, and civic engagement (Butts, 2010; Johnson, 2020). Most of the current enrichment-focused programming is available in community settings and focuses on promoting individual skills and healthy relationships. A smaller subset of programs focus on incorporating resources needs, community and social engagement, and broader community and socio-cultural contexts into its delivery and outreach. As described in Table 9.1, common outreach and engagement strategies include integrating flexibility into program content and delivery, promoting youth choice and voice, and leveraging community resources including critical individuals to support engagement and participation. In the following, we describe our findings and synthesize four promising outreach and enrichment strategies that emerged across the reviewed programs and practices.

Expand How Enrichment Is Defined to Support Young People's Socio-Cultural Identities and Contextual Realities

Of existing programs and practices, most solely target individual or relational change, with little focus on the broader socio-cultural contexts relevant for young people's lives. Indeed, the most common targets of change across programming include increasing self-efficacy, problem-solving, and social and emotional skills, and decreasing recidivism and substance use. Programming should therefore expand this focus to include socio-cultural and structural outcomes as part of program content. For instance, we recommend that programs build civic engagement (e.g., United Teen Equality Center [UTEC]) and promote a rights and equity focus to engage youths' intersecting social identities (e.g., racial and ethnic identity, sexual orientation and gender expression, and disability status) (Osher et al., 2002; Saleh, 2020).

Critical consciousness (the ability to analyze inequitable social systems, such as those that promote patriarchy, heterosexism, and racism, and engaging in civic action to dismantle such systems) is one promising approach that incorporates structural indicators to cultivate positive youth development, especially among adolescents who identify with multiple marginalized social identities (Diemer, 2016). Youth leadership and creative arts projects can further facilitate young people contributing or "giving back" to their communities through programming. While these types of programs tend to be more time intensive and incorporate more collaborative practices with youth, they also report much stronger engagement and lower dropout. Though it is not clear whether the greater "dose" of programming accounts for this stronger engagement, programs promoting access to self-determined goals and resources (e.g., ROSES Advocacy Project), addressing discrimination (e.g., Adolescents in the Making [AIM]), and incorporating youth choice and voice (Youth Advocates Project) are among the most promising to expand deep-end youth and families.

Programs should also ensure that young people can successfully engage with activities regardless of their familial context and consider ways to invite critical individuals in youth's life into programming as desired by youth. Indeed, we found that individually focused enrichment programs are most often paired with skills promoting healthy parenting (typically) and peer (more rarely) relationships (Office of Juvenile Justice and Delinquency Prevention [OJJDP], n.d.). This suggests that typical enrichment programs are intended for young people who have a stable enough familial context to engage in programs that require parental involvement (either directly through program enrollment or indirectly through parental support for engagement). Incorporating opportunities that allow young people to choose critical individuals in their lives to participate in their programming (especially those that require a family focus)

Table 9.1 Model Youth Outreach and Enrichment Programs

Section A – OJJDP Model Programs Guide Direct Search				
Program Name (Designation)	*Target Population*	*Setting of Delivery*	*Key Enrichment Activities*	*Outreach and Engagement Strategies*
SNAP Outreach Program (Effective) **Outreach* (Sewell, 2017; Sewell et al., 2020)	Juvenile justice; offenders (boys < 12y) with ASB	Community	Multisystemic therapy (MST); cognitive problem-solving, cognitive self-instruction, family management and parent training	Multimodal; flexible; engages multiple individuals
Cure Violence (Promising) **Outreach*	Child welfare; boys and girls 16–25 y	Community	Street violence interrupters, community outreach, education, and mobilization	Structural focus; community outreach; credible messengers
Wyman's Outreach Program (Promising) **Outreach*	Child welfare; youth grades 6–12	Schools	Individual skill development (e.g., goal-setting, decision-making, health and sex); adult support; service learning project	Multimodal; engages multiple individuals; community engagement
NEW VISTAS (Promising) **Enrichment*	Juvenile justice; boys and girls, 11–18 y, AOD	Community	Five services for families, including drug and alcohol treatment, gender-specific, and neighborhood enhancement programs	Multimodal; individualized; engages multiple individuals
Youth Advocate Programs (Promising) **Engagement*	Juvenile justice; young offenders (boys < 12 y)	Community	Advocates partnering with youth and family to create individualized service plans; work on court mandates; ~6 months, 8 hrs/wk	Multimodal; youth-led; individualized; intensive; system navigation

(*Continued*)

Section B – OJJDP Model Programs Guide Expanded Search

Program Name (Designation)	*Target Population*	*Setting of Delivery*	*Key Activities*	*Outreach and Enrichment Strategies*
Adolescent Diversion Project (Effective) **Engagement*	Juvenile justice; young offenders	Community	Strengths-based mentorship with university students; diversion from formal legal contact; access to community resources; attachment to family and positive adults	Individualized; system navigation; resources; relationships; strengths-based
Project Build (Effective) **Enrichment*	Juvenile justice; AOD offenders	Community detention, supervision	Violence prevention; problem solving, communication, self-esteem, goal setting, decision making and resource access	Multimodal; resource focused; multiple aspects of health and well-being
AIM (Effective) **Enrichment*	Juvenile justice; families; prevention	Community	Separate and joint group sessions; parent career skills, managing racial stress; youth racial discrimination, self-care	Racial socialization; resource access; youth-led
Big Brothers/Sisters (Effective) **Outreach*	Juvenile justice; children exposed to violence	Community	Individual mentoring (2–4 times a month for at least 1 year); goal-setting; healthy relationships for delinquency prevention	Healthy relationships; youth-led; intensive; individualized
Positive Action (Effective) **Enrichment*	Juvenile justice; families; prevention	Community	Structured curriculum focuses on cognitive-behavioral therapy, improving self-concept, nutrition, self-efficacy	Multimodal; varied content delivery
Great Life Mentoring (Effective) **Engagement*	Juvenile justice; outpatient mental health	Community	Individualized mentorship, 2–3 hours per week for at least 1 year; focused on support and community engagement	Individualized; focus on community engagement
Strong African American Families (Effective) **Enrichment*	Juvenile justice; families; prevention	Community	Separate and joint parents and youth sessions (7 total); caregiver topics on parenting practices, racial socialization; youth topics on goals, risk, acceptance	Multimodal; engages multiple individuals; racial socialization
FAST (Effective) **Engagement*	Juvenile justice; families; prevention	Community or schools	Joint family sessions (8 total); focus on youth connecting to parents and school, structured meal and family time	Target family; engage multiple individuals

(Continued)

Section C – Targeted Literature Review

Program Name (Design)	*Target Population*	*Setting of Delivery*	*Key Activities*	*Outreach and Enrichment Strategies*
ROSES Advocacy Project **Engagement*	Juvenile justice; prevention	Community	Individualized advocacy (6–8 hours per week, 12 weeks); mobilizing resources for self-determined goals	Multimodal; youth-led; individualized; intensive; resources
MSSI **Outreach & Enrichment*	Child welfare; prevention	Community	Separate and joint adolescent and foster caregiver group sessions (6 each) on goals and SEL, and individual youth coaching	Multimodal; multiple supports individualized; system navigation
UTEC Inc. **Outreach & Enrichment*	Juvenile justice; youth offenders (17–25)	Community and corrections	Transitional coaching; gang/street peacemaking; paid work experiences; civic engagement; education resources; parent training and family enrichment	Multimodal; individualized; youth-led; multiple supports; resource access
CUT (Center for Urban Transformation) **Enrichment*	Prevention; juvenile justice; families	Community	Individual counseling; case management; needs assessment/resource attainment; problem solving skills, goal setting	Multimodal; individualized; resources; system navigation
Hartford Youth Project **Enrichment & Engagement*	Juvenile justice; prevention	Community and residential	Individual and family advocacy, substance use counseling; case management; needs assessment, resource attainment	Individualized; collaborative; resource access; multiple supports

Note

**Denotes focus of the program.* Where relevant, inclusion of boys and girls is described under Target Population. Community settings include a variety of settings, including family homes, public and afterschool settings, and other variable community-based locations (e.g., libraries). Duplicate programs yielded from searches are included only once. ASB = Antisocial behavior; AOD = Alcohol and Other Drug offenses; SEL = Social and emotional learning; FAST = Families and Schools Together; AIM = Adolescents in the Making. MSSI = Middle School Success Intervention; UTEC = United Teen Equality Center.

can ensure success and flexibility for youth who have a less stable familial context. Moreover, this promotes youth choice and voice, which can sustain engagement. This enrichment-based practice is distinct from other approaches that focus on program compliance for families, which can inadvertently put caregiver and youth goals in competition against one another (Liebenberg et al., 2015).

Other structural targets that can facilitate effective outreach and enrichment include partnerships with neighborhoods and community organizations to increase safety (e.g., Cure Violence), as well as practices that directly address systemic racism and discrimination-related stress in their content (e.g., AIM). Though less utilized, community leaders or credible messengers to deliver programming can also be an important outreach strategy for system-involved youth. For example, as found in the Cure Violence program delivered nationally, using community leaders and credible messengers can facilitate connection, build community, and incorporate the expertise and experiences of those who are closest to the lived realities of system-involved youth (Wical et al. 2020).

Directly Address Legal Mandates, Logistical Barriers, and Structural Challenges

While enrichment programs show promise for targeting individual and relational outcomes, there are significantly fewer programs that target structural barriers or youth's contexts directly (Alegria et al., 2018). Among those identified as effective or promising, such as the Center for Urban Transformation (CUT) or the Adolescent Diversion Project, only ~20% had an explicit focus on increasing access to needed resources to mitigate economic deprivation, and even fewer (~10%) provided legal and child welfare system navigation support (e.g., attending court). Given that resources are often scarce for legal-impacted families and, because it is challenging to meet legal mandates for compliance, enrichment programs should be able to respond to the realities of legal system involvement. For example, supporting youth to identify and meet their terms of probation, attend court, and write court letters of progress, especially for youth with consistent or deeper system contact. We also contend that programs, not families, should be responsible for engagement and compliance. One effective approach to ensure that families can succeed in court programs across the legal system spectrum is to structure both content and delivery in ways that allow flexibility and choice for young people and their families. Across our review, several processes emerged as effective for facilitating participation and ensuring success of young people and families facing structural barriers to service access. First, most programs were individualized to some degree to reflect the needs of young people and their families to meet them "where they are." Individualized program flexibility was described in terms of program content (e.g., offering an array of "menu" options for program focus) and delivery, such as through protocols to meet youth and families where it is most convenient or safest for them or, through the provision of multiple options (e.g., days and times) for participation. This not only supports successful engagement for families navigating the legal system who may experience structural barriers to participation, but it also cultivates engagement and success by attending to the unique individual and contextual needs of each young person participating in such programming. Other humanizing engagement efforts, such as the strategy of "dropping a cookie" (a small token to build rapport and communicate that the youth and family are worthy of time and resources) or communicating understanding and care around missed appointments, have also been found to better sustain engagement and reduce chances of dropout for system-involved youth and families (Schlernitzauer et al., 1998; Javdani & Allen, 2016).

While not incorporated consistently across programs, promising approaches also assessed and monitored specific barriers to participation as part of program delivery. This allowed for the content of programming to be individualized (e.g., youth-led goal-setting), encouraged youth and families to take ownership of their involvement, and also helped to reduce logistical and access barriers through flexible program delivery. For instance, the Families and Schools Together program holds meetings in shared community spaces and explicitly incorporates mealtime into their programming. This allows for participation during mealtime (e.g., after work hours); directly provides meals to families; and engages families in strength-based, flexible, and culturally responsive practices. Enrichment programs and outreach strategies are more successful if they deliberately use culturally and developmentally appropriate strategies to sustain involvement (e.g., mealtime, extracurricular activities, organizing), reach out in appropriate community or online spaces (e.g., social media), and allow for self- and peer-referrals. Notably, two programs delivered content in developmentally appropriate ways, such as through practice-oriented vignettes, providing "refreshers," and individualized coaching – all of which linked to longer engagement.

Make Enrichment and Outreach Strategies More Widely Available for Young People Across the Legal System

We found that the majority of identified programs focus on prevention, leaving only a few enrichment-based programs available for youth at the deeper end of the legal continuum. Indeed, most programs readily available for youth at later points of the legal system focused heavily on reducing recidivism or other serious behaviors such as substance use or mental health needs. Though outcomes of health and well-being are important, there was a notable lack of enriching strengths within and around young people. As a result, most programs have a narrow emphasis on youth enrichment and engagement, with such outcomes either secondary or absent altogether from services. Enrichment programs that emphasize outcomes such as creative arts, self-efficacy, or access to needed resources should therefore be continuously available to youth across the full spectrum of the legal system.

This is especially important for young people involved in the deeper end of the legal system, including those who are confined, returning to home or school after confinement, or involved in multiple systems at once (e.g., child welfare and juvenile legal). We found that programs at deeper ends of the legal system also focused heavily on compliance rather than utilizing the previous outreach and engagement strategies that facilitated choice and flexibility in program delivery and participation to meet the needs of each family. For example, as described, effective prevention-based outreach approaches considered individual barriers to participation for youth and families. This is particularly important for families deeper in the legal system who often face multiple barriers to accessing resources such as limited transportation, inability to take time off from work or school, and/or involvement in other social systems (e.g., child welfare) that make additional court mandated programming difficult. Neglecting this aspect of program delivery and outreach may make it difficult for families to succeed and ultimately push young people and families with resource challenges deeper into the legal system for failure to succeed or comply.

Define and Evaluate Enrichment and Outreach

Given that few outreach and enrichment strategies were evaluated using strong methods, we recommend using clear definitions of enrichment and outreach and developing measures to capture these strategies. This can also ensure accountability for stakeholders delivering programs. For example, system stakeholders should consider and systematize how enrichment and success should be defined and incorporate ways to capture many forms of youth engagement as they are receiving programming. This simple strategy can reduce discretionary punishment for youth participating in court-mandated programs because, for instance, programs can report if youth have been in consistent contact with a program (e.g., via text messaging) even if they have missed a few group sessions. Enhanced and rigorous measures of outreach would also provide better understanding of the specific approaches which facilitate effective engagement and participation, particularly when applied across local communities. Moreover, standardizing and evaluating outreach and prevention strategies can help build a more concrete definition and understanding of the importance of enrichment programs, particularly as they relate to promoting youths' developmental skills outside traditional indicators of success within the legal system.

Conclusion

Programs and practices that deliberately define and incorporate efforts to reach out to young people and support their self-determined goals and needs will likely be more engaging, successful, and able to connect with underserved youth and families. It is especially important that such programming expand to serve youth in the deeper end of the legal system, pay attention to youth's social identities and experiences of discrimination, target change in youth's contexts, support youth to meet legal mandates, create opportunities for them to succeed, and find ways to measure and document those successes.

References

Alegría, M., NeMoyer, A., Bagué, I. F., Wang, Y., & Alvarez, K. (2018). Social determinants of mental health. *Current Psychiatry Reports*, *20*(11), 1–13.

Becker, A. E., & Kleinman, A. (2013). Mental health and the global agenda. *New England Journal of Medicine*, *369*(1), 66–73.

Bornheimer, L. A., Acri, M. C., Gopalan, G., & McKay, M. M. (2018). Barriers to service utilization and child mental health treatment attendance. *Psych Services*, *69*, 1101–1104.

Butts, J. A., Bazemore, G., & Meroe, A. S. (2010). *Positive youth justice: Framing justice interventions using the concepts of positive youth development*. Coalition for Juvenile Justice.

Chacko, A., Jensen, S. A., Lowry, L. S., Cornwell, M., Chimklis, A., Chan, E., . . . Pulgarin, B. (2016). Engagement in behavioral parent training. *Clinical Child and Family Psychology Review*, *19*(3), 204–215.

Comer, J. S., Chow, C., Chan, P. T., Cooper-Vince, C., & Wilson, L. A. (2013). Psychosocial treatment efficacy for disruptive behavior problems in very young children: A meta-analytic examination. *JAACAP*, *52*(1), 26–36.

Dembo, R., Gulledge, L., Robinson, R. B., & Winters, K. C. (2011). Enrolling and engaging high-risk youths and families in community-based, brief intervention services. *Journal of Child & Adolescent Substance Abuse*, *20*(4), 330–350.

Diemer, M. A., Rapa, L. J., Voight, A. M., & McWhirter, E. H. (2016). Critical consciousness: A developmental approach to addressing marginalization and oppression. *Child Development Perspectives*, *10*(4), 216–221.

Javdani, S., & Allen, N. E. (2016). An ecological model for intervention for juvenile justice-involved girls: Development and preliminary prospective evaluation. *Feminist Criminology*, *11*(2), 135–162.

Johnson, K., & Pechota, D. (2020). *Expanding the arts across the juvenile justice system*. Policy Brief. Education Commission of the States.

Kazdin, A. E., & Wassell, G. (2000). Therapeutic changes in children, parents, and families resulting from treatment of children with conduct problems. *JAACAP*, *39*(4), 414–420.

Kohler, P. D., Gothberg, J. E., & Coyle, J. (2019). *Taxonomy for transition programming for systems involved youth*, 2nd ed. Western Michigan University.
Liebenberg, L., Ungar, M., & Ikeda, J. (2015). Neo-liberalism and responsibilisation in social service workers. *The British Journal of Social Work*, *45*(3), 1006–1021.
Mallett, C. A. (2018). Disproportionate minority contact in juvenile justice: Today's, and yesterdays, problems. *Criminal Justice Studies*, *31*(3), 230–248.
Office of Juvenile Justice and Delinquency Prevention (OJJDP). (n.d.). Retrieved from https://ojjdp.ojp.gov/model-programs-guide/home
Osher, D., Rouse, J., Quinn, M., Kandizoria, K., & Woodruff, D. (2002). *Addressing invisible barriers*. CECP and American Institutes for Research.
Saleh, M. C., & Cook, L. (2020). Serving justice-involved youth with disabilities. Retrieved from https://ecommons.cornell.edu/bitstream/handle/1813/90130/YTAC_Serving_Justice_Involved_Youth_with_Disabilities.pdf?sequence=1
Schlernitzauer, M., Bierhals, A. J., Geary, M. D., Prigerson, H. G., Stack, J. A., Miller, M. D., . . . Reynolds III, C. F. (1998). Recruitment methods for intervention research in bereavement-related depression: Five years' experience. *The American Journal of Geriatric Psychiatry*, *6*(1), 67–74.
Sewell, K. M. (2017). Theoretically grounded, evidence-informed clinical supervision for the SNAP programs: A model in development. *The Clinical Supervisor*, *36*(2), 340–359.
Sewell, K. M., Fredericks, K., Mohamud, A., Kallis, J., & Augimeri, L. K. (2020). Youth experiences in evaluating Canadian SNAP®. *Child & Ad Social Work Journal*, *37*(3).
Simmons-Horton, S. Y. (2017). Providing age-appropriate activities for youth in foster care. *Children and Youth Services Review*, *82*, 383–391.
Smith, C. K. (2013). Nothing about us without us! The failure of the modern juvenile justice system and a call for community-based justice. *Journal of Applied Research on Children: Informing Policy for Children at Risk*, *4*(1).
Vera, E. M., Buhin, L., Montgomery, G., & Shin, R. (2005). Enhancing therapeutic interventions with people of color. In *Handbook of racial-cultural psychology and counseling* (pp. 477–491). John Wiley & Sons, Inc.
Wical, W., Richardson, J., & Bullock, C. (2020). A credible messenger: The role of the violence intervention specialist. *Violence and Gender*, *7*(2), 66–69.

10

JUVENILE RESIDENTIAL AND OUT-OF-HOME PLACEMENT

Programs and Interventions

Svetlana Yampolskaya

Introduction

A substantial number of youth involved with the juvenile justice system get placed in out-of-home settings, such as detention centers, residential treatment centers, group homes, and correctional institutions. Nationwide during 2019, an estimated 36,479 youth ages 10–17 were held in residential placements on any given day (Puzzanchera & Hockenberry, 2021). Although residential placements remain an essential component of juvenile rehabilitation, there is a debate about the overall effectiveness of residential care, and there is considerable evidence to suggest that there are often undesirable effects associated with these placements. One area of concern is the potential negative impact on parental attachment when a child is placed in a residential setting. Residential placement necessitates removal from home, often requires transition out of a community, and causes disconnection from familiar surroundings. Thus, it may increase the risk for youth to develop insecure attachment and, as a result, the risk for psychopathology, behavior problems, and other adverse outcomes (Cyr et al., 2010).

Youth placement with other delinquent youth is also considered problematic. Evidence shows that exposure to delinquent peers in out-of-home settings may increase delinquency and problem behaviors (Wilson & Woods, 2006). Another area of concern is youth victimization in residential delinquent settings. Studies indicate that when removed from established support systems, youth often face harsh conditions that in turn result in long-term negative consequences and that youth victimization in these settings is a serious problem (Dmitrieva et al., 2012). Further, research has demonstrated that having an out-of-home placement experience is a significant risk factor for later offending behavior. Some research has shown that youth who experience an out-of-home placement are more likely to report having engaged in subsequent delinquent behavior, and that between 70% and 80% of juveniles who have been in residential correction programs were subsequently rearrested within a 3-year period (Mendel, 2011). In addition, studies indicated that juvenile out-of-home placement history has also been associated with a higher risk of adult imprisonment (Collins et al., 2001). Finally, involvement in the juvenile justice system is extremely costly; it has been estimated that in the United States, up to $88,000 per year is spent on each youth placed in a juvenile justice facility (Millenky & Mage, 2016).

DOI: 10.4324/9781003219286-13

Taken together, these findings suggest that:

- Placement in juvenile residential facilities is generally ineffective in reducing recidivism and may even increase the risk for various adverse outcomes.
- Considering costs associated with these placements, potential detrimental impact on youth, and the lack of success with this approach, the development of effective interventions and the use of evidence-based practices are of paramount importance.
- Research indicated that diversion programs, trauma-focused interventions, and aftercare programs show promise for promoting positive juvenile justice-related outcomes.

Although recent juvenile justice policies that aimed at diverting young people from formal court processing and providing alternatives to detention have led to a 54% reduction in the number of youth placed in residential facilities (Hockenberry, 2018), residential placement remains a substantial component of juvenile justice practice. Essential to achieving successful outcomes in residential care is the identification and implementation of evidence-based interventions that have been shown to be effective in preventing further system involvement among these youth. A broad range of programs has been developed and implemented to prevent juvenile recidivism. Although many of these programs have focused on community-based interventions designed to keep youth offenders out of the juvenile justice system, a great number of them focus on the rehabilitation of youth when they are in juvenile justice facilities, while others facilitate the transition of youth from juvenile justice facilities to the community.

Responsive Evidence-Based Programs, Policies, and/or Practices

Much attention has been paid to programs and interventions that present alternatives to involvement in the juvenile justice system for youth who have been formally charged with a crime. Although all diversion programs share similar goals, they vary in their approaches or intervention philosophies (Farrell et al., 2018). In general, the overreaching goal of these programs is to help youth avoid further involvement in the justice system including out-of-home placement in juvenile justice facilities. These programs fall into three categories: (a) police-led programs; (b) service coordination models, and (c) counseling/skill-building or treatment programs. Police-led programs include the use of warnings and civil citations rather than formal prosecution, and they prevent formal justice involvement while holding youth accountable for their actions. An example of such programs is Redwood City (CA) Juvenile Diversion Program. These programs target first-time offenders who are arrested on misdemeanor or low-level offenses.

Service coordination models is another category of diversion programs. It includes case management, system of care model, and wraparound approaches. Typically, these programs target justice-involved youth with multi-faceted needs, including mental health problems, and involve coordination and provision of various services for youth in collaboration with family members and professionals. The primary goal of these models is to identify the youth's needs and provide appropriate services. Although this type of model is widely implemented, research to date has yielded mixed results, with some studies supporting these programs' effectiveness (Kamradt & Goldfarb, 2015) and others questioning their value (Bruns et al., 2015). The most notable wraparound program was implemented in Milwaukee, Wisconsin, which demonstrated significant improvements for delinquent youths (Kamradt & Goldfarb, 2015).

Several studies demonstrated positive effects of Counseling/skill-building and treatment type programs, such as multidimensional treatment foster care (MTFC), multisystemic therapy

(MST), and functional family therapy (FFT). MTFC is a home-based family treatment that was developed as an alternative to group homes and residential placement (Chamberlain et al., 2011). MTFC utilizes specialized foster homes where caregivers are trained to manage delinquent behaviors. Trauma-adapted multidimensional treatment foster care (TA-MTFC) is MTFC plus traumatic stress treatment, and it has been shown to reduce trauma-related mental health problems and delinquency among justice-involved girls (Smith et al., 2012).

MST is a family- and community-based intervention that uses intense contact with families to understand and address the causes of delinquent behavior. Parental involvement is an essential component of the treatment. This intervention has been shown to be effective in reducing delinquent behavior among justice-involved adolescents, and it is one of the most extensively validated and widely disseminated evidence-based psychosocial treatments (Butler et al., 2011). FFT is a family-based intervention program that has been successfully used for high-risk youth. FFT is also a multisystemic and multilevel intervention that focuses on family and individual functioning. Various studies have shown that FFT significantly reduces recidivism for a wide variety of juvenile offenders (Henggeler & Sheidow, 2012).

Despite advocacy for the use of diversion programs, youth who need more intensive services that cannot be provided in the community or youth who pose a threat to public safety are still sent to residential facilities. Several interventions have been identified as best practice treatments that enhance rehabilitation. Recognition of the high rates of trauma exposure among justice-involved youth has led to the implementation of various trauma-specific interventions (Branson et al., 2017). Growing research evidence supports the effectiveness of several such interventions, including: (a) trauma affect regulation: guide for education and therapy (TARGET) – a therapeutic intervention that helps youth manage trauma-linked reactions to current stressors and achieve better emotional and behavioral regulation (Ford et al., 2016); (b) trauma-focused cognitive–behavioral therapy (TF-CBT) – a model that aims to enhance adaptive coping skills for trauma symptoms and process traumatic memory (Cohen et al., 2016); (c) trauma and grief components therapy for adolescents (TGCTA) – an intervention with the goal of enhancing posttraumatic emotional and behavioral regulation, processing of trauma and grief/loss experiences (Olafson et al., 2016); (d) cognitive processing therapy (CPT) – an intervention designed to reduce PTSD symptoms related to a variety of traumatic events (Resick & Schnicke, 1993); (e) attachment, self-regulation, and competency (ARC) – an intervention for youth with complex trauma (Blaustein & Kinniburgh, 2010); and finally, (f) Sanctuary – a model that emphasizes recovery from the impacts of traumatic stress while simultaneously providing safety for all participants (Rivard et al., 2005). A recent review provided additional evidence of the effectiveness of these interventions in reducing trauma symptoms; it also suggested that they show promise for promoting positive juvenile justice-related outcomes (Baetz et al., 2021).

Similarly, programs such as Aggression Replacement Training (ART) and the Good Lives Model that target behavioral problems among justice-involved youth in residential care have been shown to have positive effects on aggression, anger control, and social skills (Ensafdaran et al., 2019). In addition, meta-analytic results involving over 500 quality intervention studies with juvenile samples suggested that cognitive-behavioral therapy interventions are among the most effective in reducing recidivism (Lipsey, 2009). Research on "shock incarceration" programs or correctional boot camps that are modeled after military basic training finds less support for their effectiveness at reducing recidivism (Parent, 2003).

Another type of intervention utilized to reduce recidivism is aftercare or reentry programs, that is, programs initiated either during the transition from a residential facility to the community or soon after reentry. These programs focus on reducing recidivism through the provision and coordination of services and have been shown to have small but positive effects on recidivism (James et al., 2013). Examples of such programs include family-integrated transitions (FIT) – an intervention that focuses on youth with mental health and substance use disorders – and the Boston Reentry Initiative (BRI) – a program that focuses on developing individualized transition plans and connections with the mentor. Evaluation of FIT demonstrated reductions in felonies, while BRI was shown to lower re-arrest rates (Trupin et al., 2011).

Although there are different interventions that have been shown to be effective in preventing recidivism, there are common implementation strategies necessary to achieve this goal, including:

- A needs assessment should be conducted as a part of the admissions process to determine the unique needs of youth in residential care.
- Promising interventions that target specific youth needs should be selected.
- Adequate resources should be allocated to adapt necessary interventions.
- Training should be conducted to assure that staff members acquire a common understanding of the program model and implementation activities.
- Practice guidelines should be created and disseminated.
- Regular fidelity checks and monitoring of outcomes should be done to maintain the integrity of the key components of the program.

Sustainability strategies should be developed, such as interagency collaborations.

Conclusion

Evidence continues to accumulate regarding the effectiveness of various programs aimed at prevention of further involvement in juvenile justice and recidivism. It has been recognized that diversion programs, treatments, and interventions delivered during youth stay in juvenile residential facilities and aftercare programs are of equal importance, and they all have shown promise in reducing future delinquency. Fundamental to reducing recidivism among juveniles is provision of trauma-focused interventions and utilization of trauma-informed care. Evidence-based trauma-focused treatments appear to be particularly important due to the high prevalence of youth entering the justice system with histories of prior exposure to traumatic events and youth with complex trauma. In addition to complex trauma, youth placed in residential juvenile facilities have various and often co-occurring needs. When identifying treatment and interventions delivered to detained youth, it is critical to recognize their unique needs and to develop strategies that aim to match services and interventions to youth individual characteristics and risks. Matching offender characteristics to the types of services youth need would allow for controlling costs and achieving more successful outcomes for these youth.

References

Baetz, C. L., Branson, C. E., Weinberger, E., Rose, R. E., Petkova, E., Horwitz, S. M., & Hoagwood, K. E. (2021). The effectiveness of PTSD treatment for adolescents in the juvenile justice system: A systematic review. *Psychological Trauma: Theory, Research, Practice, and Policy*. Advance online publication.

Blaustein, M., & Kinniburgh, K. (2010). *Treating traumatic stress in children and adolescents: How to foster resilience through attachment, self-regulation, and competency*. Guilford Press.

Branson, C. E., Baetz, C. L., Horwitz, S. M., & Hoagwood, K. E. (2017). Trauma-informed juvenile justice systems: A systematic review of definitions and core components. *Psychological Trauma: Theory, Research, Practice and Policy*, *9*(6), 635–646.
Bruns, E. J., Pullmann, M. D., Sather, A., Brinson, R. D., & Ramey, M. (2015). Effectiveness of wraparound versus case management for children and adolescents: Results of a randomized study. *Administration and Policy in Mental Health and Mental Health Services Research*, *42*, 309–322.
Butler, S., Baruch, G., Hickey, N., & Fonagy, P (2011). A randomized controlled trial of multisystemic therapy and a statutory therapeutic intervention for young offenders. *Journal of the American Academy of Child & Adolescent Psychiatry*, *50*(12), 1220–1235.
Chamberlain, P., Saldana, L., Brown, C. H., & Leve, L. D. (2011). Implementation of multidimensional treatment Foster Care in California: A randomized control trial of an evidence-based practice. In M. Roberts-DeGennaro & S. J. Fogel (Eds.), *Using evidence to inform practice for community and organizational change* (pp. 218–234). Lyceum.
Cohen, J. A., Mannarino, A. P., Jankowski, K., Rosenberg, S., Kodya, S., & Wolford, G. L. II. (2016). A randomized implementation study of trauma-focused cognitive behavioral therapy for adjudicated teens in residential treatment facilities. *Child Maltreatment*, *21*(2), 156–167.
Collins, M. E., Schwartz, I. M., & Epstein, I. (2001). Risk factors for adult imprisonment in a sample of youth released from residential childcare. *Children and Youth Services Review*, *23*(3), 203–226.
Cyr, C., Euser, E. M., Bakermans-Kranenburg, M., & Ijzendoorn, M. H. V. (2010). Attachment security and disorganization in maltreating and high-risk families: A series of meta-analyses. *Development and Psychopathology*, *22*(1), 87–108.
Dmitrieva, J., Monahan, K. C., Cauffman, E., & Steinberg, L. (2012). Arrested development: The effects of incarceration on the development of psychosocial maturity. *Development and Psychopathology*, *24*, 1073–1090.
Ensafdaran, F., Krahé, B., Njad, S. B., & Arshadi, N. (2019). Efficacy of different versions of Aggression Replacement Training (ART): A review. *Aggression and Violent Behavior*, *47*, 230–237.
Farrell, J., Betsinger, A., & Hammond, P. (2018). Best practices in youth diversion: Literature review for the Baltimore City Youth Diversion Committee. The Institute for Innovation & Implementation. Retrieved from https://theinstitute.umaryland.edu/media/ssw/institute/md-center-documents/Youth-Diversion-Literature-Review.pdf
Ford, J. D., Kerid, P. K., Desai, N., & Feierman, J. (2016). Psychosocial interventions for traumatized youth in the juvenile justice system: Research, evidence base, and clinical/legal challenges. *OJJDP Journal of Juvenile Justice*, *5*(1), 31–49.
Henggeler, S. W., & Sheidow, A. J. (2012). Empirically supported family-based treatment for conduct disorder and delinquency. Journal of Marital and Family Therapy, 38(1), 30–58.
Hockenberry, S. (2018). Juveniles in residential placement, 2015. Office of Juvenile Delinquency and Prevention. Retrieved from https://ojjdp.ojp.gov/sites/g/files/xyckuh176/files/pubs/250951.pdf
James, C., Stams, G. J., Asscher, J. J., De Roo, A. K., & van der Laan, P. H. (2013). Aftercare programs for reducing recidivism among juvenile and young adult offenders: A meta-analytic review. *Clinical Psychology Review*, *33*(2), 263–274.
Kamradt, B., & Goldfarb, P. (2015). *Demonstrating effectiveness of the wraparound model with juvenile justice youth through measuring and achieving lower recidivism*. The Technical Assistance Network for Children's Behavioral Health.
Lipsey, M. W. (2009). The primary factors that characterize effective interventions with juvenile offenders: A meta-analytic overview. *Victims and Offenders*, *4*, 124–147.
Mendel, R. A. (2011). No place for kids: The case for reducing juvenile incarceration. Retrieved from www.aecf.org/OurWork/JuvenileJustice/~/media/Pubs/Topics/Juvenile%20Justice/Detentin%20Reform/NoPlaceForKids/JJ_NoPlaceForKidsEmbargoed.pdf
Millenky, M., & Mage, C. (2016). Preventing juvenile justice involvement for young women: An introduction to an evaluation of the PACE center for girls. *MDRC*. Retrieved from www.mdrc.org/sites/default/files/Preventing_Juvenile_Justice_Involvement_2016.pdf
Olafson, E., Goldman, J. H., & Gonzalez, C. (2016). Trauma-informed collaborations among juvenile justice and other child-serving systems: An update. *OJJDP Journal of Juvenile Justice*, *5*(1), 1–13.
Parent, D. G. (2003). *Correctional boot camps: Lessons from a decade of research*. U.S. Department of Justice, Office of Justice Programs. Retrieved from www.ojp.gov/pdffiles1/nij/197018.pdf

Puzzanchera, C., & Hockenberry, S. (2021). Trends and characteristics of youth in residential placement, 2019. Office of Juvenile Justice and Delinquency Prevention. Retrieved from www.ojjdp.gov/ojstatbb/snapshots/DataSnapshot_CJRP2019.pdf

Resick, E. A., & Schnicke, M. K. (1993). *Cognitive processing therapy for rape victims: A treatment manual.* Sage.

Rivard, J. C., Bloom, S. L., McCorkle, D., & Abramovitz, R. (2005). Preliminary results of a study examining the implementation and effects of a trauma recovery framework for youths in residential treatment. *Therapeutic Community: The International Journal for Therapeutic and Supportive Organizations*, *26*(1), 83–96.

Smith, D. K., Chamberlain, P., & Deblinger, E. (2012). Adapting multidimensional treatment Foster Care for the treatment of co-occurring trauma and delinquency in adolescent girls. *Journal of Child & Adolescent Trauma*, *5*(3), 224–238.

Trupin, E. J., Kerns, S. E. U., Walker, S. C., DeRobertis, M. T., & Stewart, D. G. (2011). Family integrated transitions: A promising program for juvenile offenders with co-occurring disorders. *Journal of Child and Adolescent Substance Abuse*, *20*(5), 421–436.

Wilson, M. N., & Woods, L. N. (2006). Iatrogenic outcomes of the child welfare system: Vulnerable adolescents, peer influences, and instability in foster care arrangements. In K. A. Dodge, T. J. Dishion, & J. E. Lansford (Eds.), *Deviant peer influences in programs for youth: Problems and solutions* (pp. 203–214). Guilford.

11
JUVENILE JUSTICE PRACTICES

Narim Lee and Jennifer H. Peck

Introduction

In the juvenile justice system, evidence-based practices (EBPs) are the most effective types of prevention and intervention efforts to decrease recidivism and increase prosocial outcomes in youth. An evidence-based practice "involves the use of scientific principles to assess the available evidence on program effectiveness and develop principles for best practices in any particular field" (Greenwood, 2013). They are programs, practices, and policies that have been evaluated and determined to prevent or reduce delinquency and involvement in the juvenile justice system. In other words, EBPs in juvenile justice refer to individual programs, interventions, or strategies which have sufficient and affirmative evidence on reducing youth recidivism and other problem behaviors in adolescence (Howell et al., 2014).

Over the last 20 years, there has been a substantial increase in the use of EBPs in juvenile justice settings. Most recently, several state juvenile justice systems have implemented EBPs for at-risk and justice-involved youth, their families, and communities (Howell et al., 2014). The Office of Juvenile Justice and Delinquency Prevention (OJJDP) houses the Model Programs Guide (MPG), which provides information about effective evidence-based juvenile justice (EBJJ) and youth prevention, intervention, and reentry programs. There are over 50 juvenile justice topics and 200 programs included in the MPG, which show that certain practices are not evidence based (e.g., specific yoga programs, the Drug Abuse Resistance Education (DARE) program) and could even be detrimental to youth outcomes (e.g., boot camps, wilderness camps, mandatory random student drug testing, domestic violence courts). Some of the more prominent programs, practices, and policies involving the juvenile justice system involve the following topics in particular: risk factors for delinquency, risk and needs assessments for youth, cognitive behavioral therapy (CBT), gang prevention, mentoring, and juvenile reentry. These topics provide some of the most consistent and reliable findings regarding EBJJ in the scientific literature.

State of the Literature on Key Topics

Risk factors for delinquency refer to constructs that predict an increased probability of delinquent behavior (Murray & Farrington, 2010). While static risk factors are unable to be changed (i.e., delinquent history), dynamic factors (also called "needs") in youth can be

 DOI: 10.4324/9781003219286-14

changed by prevention, intervention, services, and treatment (Resnick et al., 2004). Risk/need factors relate to a multitude of domains, such as individual (e.g., attitudes, values), peers (e.g., delinquency, attachment), family (e.g., management, bonding, abuse), school (e.g., attachment, performance, climate), and community (e.g., exposure to violence). Based on the three major principles of effective intervention (i.e., risk, needs, and responsivity) (see Andrews et al., 2011), EBPs in the juvenile justice system have predominantly focused on dynamic risk factors to ultimately decrease reoffending and increase positive short and long-term life outcomes for youth (McKee & Rapp, 2014). EBPs that focus on the promotion of children's emotional and social competencies have seen reductions in aggression and behavioral problems (Greenberg et al., 1995), along with increases in self-control and emotion regulation (Kam et al., 2003; Domitrovich et al., 2007). Additional EBPs that emphasize family, peers, school, and community-level risk factors have also been deemed effective at reducing a multitude of problem behaviors in youth (see Braga, 2008; Sexton & Turner, 2010).

Juvenile risk and needs assessments (JRNAs) are standardized tools that guide structured decision-making within the juvenile justice system, have implications for more effective decisions about justice-involved youth, and could reduce the presence of implicit or explicit biases in case outcomes. JRNAs and follow the "Risk-Needs-Responsivity" model, which is the dominant evidence-based framework for contemporary corrections policy and practice (Andrews et al., 2011). Utilized at multiple decision points in the juvenile justice system, JRNAs are integral EBPs by determining a youth's risk for recidivism (risk level), appropriate sanctions (e.g., probation, residential placement), and treatment services based on their needs (e.g., substance use, aggression, family conflict, etc.) The current juvenile justice literature supports the use of JRNAs as EBPs, as several JRNAs have been implemented and validated across the United States (i.e., Positive Achievement Change Tool (PACT), Youth Level of Service/Case Management Inventory (YLS/CMI), Structure Assessment of Violence Risk in Youth (SAVRY), etc.). These tools have high predictive validity, interrater reliability, and equity across a variety of juvenile justice outcomes and youth populations (Baglivio, 2009; Vincent et al., 2011).

Cognitive behavioral therapy as an EBP is a rehabilitative treatment that provides justice-involved youth with skills to identify and correct risky, biased, and deficient thinking patterns (Landerberger & Lipsey, 2005). CBT emphasizes behavior accountability and teaches individuals to understanding the thinking processes for delinquent behavior along with the choices and consequences of engaging in illegal/deviant activities. CBT is considered one of the strongest rehabilitative EBPs to effectively reduce recidivism (Lipsey et al., 2001). CBT is also incorporated into additional EBPs in juvenile justice, such as functional family therapy and multisystemic therapy, which are also proven successful/effective in reducing problem behaviors for youth (Sexton, 2000; Smith et al., 2004).

Gang prevention programs in the juvenile justice system are designed to prevent youth from joining gangs and interrupt gang formation (Howell, 2000). EBPs surrounding gang programs focus on prevention, intervention, and suppression, and they utilize multiple techniques, multiagency initiatives, and comprehensive approaches to gang problems. The literature has established that risk factors for youth gang involvement include antisocial behavior, alcohol and drug use, victimization, poor parental supervision, low commitment to school, and high community crime rates (Thornberry et al., 2003; Howell & Egley, 2005; Pyrooz et al., 2010).

Youth mentoring programs are EBPs that entail a prosocial relationship between youth and adults, which reduces delinquency through addressing family management problems, low commitment to school and also increases social support with positive youth–adult contact

(Miller et al., 2013). One of the benefits of youth mentoring programs is the ability to customize curricula to a wide range of risk factors and situations. Several studies, including meta-analyses, have confirmed the effectiveness of mentoring on youth outcomes such as delinquency, alcohol and substance use, and academic achievement (Newburn & Shiner, 2006; DuBois et al., 2002; Wood & Mayo-Wilson, 2012).

Juvenile reentry programs (also known as juvenile aftercare) provide justice-involved youth with a supportive transition back into their communities following placement in a residential facility (Spencer & Jones-Walker, 2004). These programs as EBPs are designed to meet the needs of youth that can impact the successful reintegration back into communities. Substance use treatment, family engagement, targeted educational, employment, and housing opportunities are components of juvenile reentry programs (Cusick et al., 2008), along with individual case management, CBT, wraparound services, family therapy, and mentoring programs (Abrams et al., 2014). Research on the effectiveness of reentry programs for justice-involved youth have shown mixed results, especially depending on the specific type of reentry program implemented (James et al., 2013; Weaver & Campbell, 2015).

Takeaway Points of the Scientific Literature

- EBPs that focus on a youth's dynamic risk factors/needs have resulted in increases in self-control, emotion regulation, social competence, and decreases in aggression and problem behaviors.
- Juvenile risk and needs assessments are structured decision-making tools that may reduce biases in the case outcomes of justice-involved youth compared to unstructured judgements by juvenile court actors.
- Cognitive behavioral therapy has been considered one of the most effective EBPs in reducing recidivism in at-risk and justice-involved youth.
- Specific juvenile gang prevention/intervention and mentoring programs have been deemed effective by OJJDP's MPG, although some evaluations only find a small (but beneficial) effect on youth outcomes.
- Research on the effectiveness of juvenile reentry programs has shown mixed results, which often depended on the type, intensity, and style of each specific program.

Responsive Evidence-Based Juvenile Justice Programs, Policies, and Practices

Since the 1990s, there has been a general consensus to make the juvenile justice system more evidence based. In fact, over the last 20 years, many federal and state government agencies have forced delinquency prevention and intervention programs to demonstrate their effectiveness, as the adoption of an EBJJ paradigm can increase our understanding of delinquency and responses to it. Research has established numerous solutions (i.e., EBPs) that can be implemented in the field to most effectively address key issues in the juvenile justice system. The specific EBPs discussed in the following include components that use research evidence in practice in the juvenile justice system. These prominent programs, practices, and policies focus on a youth's dynamic (changeable) risk/need factors, the use of JRNAs as structured decision-making tools in juvenile justice decision-making, CBT as one element of larger behavior modification interventions, the need for gang prevention/intervention, mentoring by prosocial role models, and a focus on "what works" in juvenile reentry.

First, the Comprehensive Strategy (CS) on Serious, Violent, and Chronic Juvenile Offenders (Howell, 2003) is based on five general principles: (1) strengthen families; (2) support core social institutions; (3) promote delinquency prevention efforts that are cost effective and reduce delinquency; (4) intervene with at-risk youth to prevent adolescents from becoming serious, violent, and chronic (SVC) offenders; and (5) identify and control SVC justice-involved youth who do not effectively respond to intervention efforts. The CS includes a system of graduated sanctions depending on a youth's risk level to recidivate (measured through a JRNA), where youth receive the least restrictive sanction available for their risk level, and residential placement (removal from the home) is only to be used for the highest risk of adolescents.

To illustrate, in Florida, a disposition recommendation matrix is used in juvenile case processing based on a youth's risk level to reoffend (low, moderate, moderate-high, high) and most serious current offense (civil citation eligible, minor, serious violent). The intersection of these categories delegates which type of outcome (i.e., disposition) youth will receive (i.e., probation, day treatment, secure residential commitment, etc.) The standardized program evaluation protocol (SPEP) is another CS component that evaluates how delinquency interventions align with the most effective EBPs in the juvenile justice field across service type (e.g., group counseling, CBT), quantity (e.g., duration and intensity of treatment), quality (e.g., protocols, manuals, fidelity monitoring), and youth characteristics (e.g., recidivism risk).

Second, there are multiple forms of evidence-based juvenile risk and needs assessments in the field, although not all of them are EBPs or have been validated. As of 2020, 42 states have adopted a single risk assessment tool that is either required or encouraged throughout juvenile court processing. JRNAs are administered to justice-involved youth at various stages of the juvenile justice process (i.e., intake, before disposition, within a juvenile commitment program, while on probation, etc.). Some examples of validated and evidence-based JRNAs include the YLS/CMI, SAVRY, and PACT. The YLS/CMI estimates a youth's risk of recidivism and services/treatment needs based on their history of antisocial behavior, antisocial personality pattern, antisocial cognition, antisocial associates, family/marital circumstances, school/work, leisure/recreation, and substance use (Hoge & Andrews, 2011). The SAVRY contains 24 items based on a youth's historical, social/contextual, and individual/clinical risk factors (Borum et al., 2006). The PACT is heavily adapted from the Washington State Juvenile Court Assessment (WSJCA). The full assessment includes 126 items of static, dynamic, and protective factors, along with a rank order of criminogenic needs to designate a youth's case plan.

Third, functional family therapy is both a prevention and intervention program for youth ages 11–18 who are either justice involved or at risk for delinquency, violence, substance abuse, or other problem behaviors. FFT can be conducted in inpatient/outpatient settings, home, or other community locations (i.e., halfway houses, group homes) across rural, urban, and suburban settings. As a strengths-based approach, FFT includes five phases (engagement, motivation, relational assessment, behavior change, generalization) that focuses on building relationships and interactions between children and families, enhancing prosocial values, providing skills training in communication and parenting, increasing problem-solving and conflict management, and eliminating problem behaviors. The implementation of FFT in the juvenile justice system has shown reductions in recidivism, substance use, anxiety, impulsivity, and depression, along with greater improvement in family and school domains (Gordon et al., 1988; Celinska et al., 2013).

Fourth, the group violence reduction strategy (GVRS) is a deterrence intervention EBP that is applicable to the juvenile justice system and has been shown to decrease persistent geographic patterns of violence, especially gun violence and homicide. GVRS identifies high-risk groups and key gang members who engage in a disproportionate share of serious violence. Individuals are advised that they will be under greater surveillance, scrutiny, enforcement, and prosecution by the justice system if violence continues. However, they are also provided access to social services. Together, GVRS is a three-pronged approach that includes law enforcement, threat of enhanced prosecution, and access to social services. After implementing GVRS, New Orleans, Louisiana, saw a reduction in overall homicide, firearm-related homicide, gang member-involved violence, and firearm assault (Corsaro & Engel, 2015). Similar GVRS strategies have been deemed effective in reducing violence across other geographical locations, such as Program Ceasefire in Oakland, California, and Operation Ceasefire in Boston, Massachusetts.

Fifth, Big Brothers Big Sisters (BBBS) is a community-based mentoring EBP with one-to-one mentoring to reduce risk factors and increase protective factors for at-risk youth ages 6–18 (Tierney et al., 2000). BBBS targets youth who reside in single-parent households, low-income neighborhoods, have a high risk of parental incarceration, and are exposed to violence in their home and community. The program currently serves over 250,000 children across 40 agencies and includes various types of social activities (e.g., shopping, attending a sports event, reading, hiking, etc.) The purpose of BBBS is to increase youths' positive adult contact, attachment to prosocial adults, commitment to goals, and trusting relationships between mentor and mentee. Mentored youth have reported a reduction in drug and alcohol use initiation and antisocial behavior, along with an increase in parental relationships and academic performance compared to their non-mentored counterparts.

Last, EBPs related to the rehabilitation and treatment of justice-involved youth in secure residential/correctional facilities aim at decreasing recidivism once adolescents are released back into their communities (see Garrido & Quinto, 2007). These reentry efforts have been deemed effective in decreasing overall recidivism and specifically serious recidivism for violent and chronic justice-involved youth. Practice types include behavioral treatment (i.e., token economy programs, behavior modification strategies), cognitive behavioral therapy (i.e., interpersonal cognitive problem-solving, social skills training, critical reasoning, anger control, etc.), group or individual therapy, educational assistance (i.e., increasing educational attainment through school programs), therapeutic communities, and violence prevention. These interventions (depending on the risk level and needs of youth) can include psychological approaches, environmental conditions, and social and educational methods, which focus on increasing resilience, prosocial attitudes, and positive behaviors.

Conclusion

Overall, the use of EBPs in juvenile justice has significantly grown in the last decade, as there has been a steady increase in applying research findings on outcomes of the juvenile justice system to implement programs, policies, and practices. Based on the previous description of responsive EBPs across numerous facets of the juvenile justice system, the following recommendations are provided:

- To truly address juvenile offending (especially youth violence and gun violence), the system needs to consider community factors and a holistic approach to change.
- Youth-serving agencies and communities must be cognizant of possible challenges to overcome with implementing EBPs, adapt accordingly, and focus on long-term benefits versus short-term constraints.
- Agencies need to modify their current operations, tasks, and responsibilities when applying EBPs to different geographic locations, settings, and target populations. A "one size fits all" approach is not effective.

- Organizations need strong leadership and support staff, buy-in from all participants (employees, youth, and families), training, funding, an appropriate match between the target population and specific programs/policies, evaluations of youth outcomes, and overall fidelity in the programs/policies.
- The juvenile justice system must continue an increased reliance on EBPs that focus on dynamic/changeable risk factors that are also tailored to each youth's individual needs.

References

Abrams, L. S., Mizel, M. L., Nguyen, V., & Shlonsky, A. (2014). Juvenile reentry and aftercare interventions: Is mentoring a promising direction?. *Journal of Evidence-based Social Work*, *11*(4), 404–422.

Andrews, D. A., Bonta, J., & Wormith, J. S. (2011). The risk-need-responsivity (RNR) model: Does adding the good lives model contribute to effective crime prevention? *Criminal Justice and Behavior*, *38*(7), 735–755.

Baglivio, M. T. (2009). The assessment of risk to recidivate among a juvenile offending population. *Journal of Criminal Justice*, *37*(6), 596–607.

Borum, R., Bartel, P., & Forth, A. E. (2006). *SAVRY, structured assessment of violence risk in youth: Professional manual*. Psychological Assessment Resources, Incorporated.

Braga, A. A. (2008). Pulling levers focused deterrence strategies and the prevention of gun homicide. *Journal of Criminal Justice*, *36*(4), 332–343.

Celinska, K., Furrer, S., & Cheng, C. C. (2013). An outcome-based evaluation of functional family therapy for youth with behavioral problems. Journal of Juvenile Justice, 2(2), 23–36.

Corsaro, N., & Engel, R. S. (2015). Most challenging of contexts: Assessing the impact of focused deterrence on serious violence in New Orleans. *Criminology & Public Policy*, 14(3), 471–505.

Cusick, G. R., George, R. M., & Bell, K. C. (2008). *From corrections to community: The juvenile reentry experience as characterized by multiple systems involvement*. Office of Justice Programs, Office of Juvenile Justice and Delinquency Prevention.

Domitrovich, C. E., Cortes, R. C., & Greenberg, M. T. (2007). Improving young children's social and emotional competence: A randomized trial of the preschool "PATHS" curriculum. *The Journal of Primary Prevention*, *28*(2), 67–91.

DuBois, D. L., Holloway, B. E., Valentine, J. C., & Cooper, H. (2002). Effectiveness of mentoring programs: A meta-analytical review. *American Journal of Community Psychology*, *30*(2), 157–197.

Garrido, V., & Morales, L. A. (2007). Serious (violent or chronic) juvenile offenders: A systematic review of treatment effectiveness in secure corrections. *Campbell Systematic Reviews*, 3(1), 1–46.

Gordon, D. A., Arbuthnot, J., Gustafson, K. E., & McGreen, P. (1988). Home-based behavioral-systems family therapy with disadvantaged juvenile delinquents. American Journal of Family Therapy, 16(3), 243–255.

Greenberg, M. T., Kusche, C. A., Cook, E. T., & Quamma, J. P. (1995). Promoting emotional competence in school-aged children: The effects of the PATHS curriculum. *Development and Psychopathology*, *7*(1), 117–136.

Greenwood, P. (2013). *Evidence-based practice in juvenile justice: Progress, challenges, and opportunities*. Springer Science & Business Media.

Hoge, R. D., & Andrews, D. A. (2011). *Youth level of service/Case management inventory 2.0 (YLS/CMI 2.0): User's manual*. Multi-Health Systems.

Howell, J. C. (2000). *Youth gang programs and strategies: Summary*. US Department of Justice, Office of Justice Programs, Office of Juvenile Justice and Delinquency Prevention.

Howell, J. C. (2003). Diffusing research into practice using the comprehensive strategy for serious, violent, and chronic juvenile offenders. *Youth Violence and Juvenile Justice*, *1*(3), 219–245.

Howell, J. C., & Egley, A. Jr. (2005). Moving risk factors into developmental theories of gang membership. *Youth Violence and Juvenile Justice*, *3*(4), 334–354.

Howell, J. C., Lipsey, M. W., Wilson, J. J., & Howell, M. Q. (2014). A practical approach to evidence-based juvenile justice systems. *Journal of Applied Juvenile Justice Services*, *1*, 1–21.

James, C., Stams, G. J. J., Asscher, J. J., De Roo, A. K., & Van der Laan, P. H. (2013). Aftercare programs for reducing recidivism among juvenile and young adult offenders: A meta-analytic review. *Clinical Psychology Review*, *33*(2), 263–274.

Kam, C. M., Greenberg, M. T., & Walls, C. T. (2003). Examining the role of implementation quality in school-based prevention using the PATHS curriculum. *Prevention Science*, *4*(1), 55–63.

Landenberger, N. A., & Lipsey, M. W. (2005). The positive effects of cognitive-behavioral programs for offenders: A meta-analysis of factors associated with effective treatment. *Journal of Experimental Criminology*, *1*(4), 451–476.

Lipsey, M. W., Chapman, G. L., & Landenberger, N. A. (2001). Cognitive-behavioral programs for offenders. *The Annals of the American Academy of Political and Social Science*, *578*(1), 144–157.

McKee, E. C., & Rapp, L. (2014). The current status of evidence-based practice in juvenile justice. *Journal of Evidence-based Social Work*, *11*(4), 308–317.

Miller, J. M., Barnes, J. C., Miller, H. V., & McKinnon, L. (2013). Exploring the link between mentoring program structure & success rates: Results from a national survey. *American Journal of Criminal Justice*, *38*(3), 439–456.

Murray, J., & Farrington, D. P. (2010). Risk factors for conduct disorder and delinquency: Key findings from longitudinal studies. *The Canadian Journal of Psychiatry*, *55*(10), 633–642.

Newburn, T., & Shiner, M. (2006). Young people, mentoring and social inclusion. *Youth Justice*, *6*(1), 23–41.

Pyrooz, D. C., Fox, A. M., & Decker, S. H. (2010). Racial and ethnic heterogeneity, economic disadvantage, and gangs: A macro-level study of gang membership in urban America. *Justice Quarterly*, *27*(6), 867–892.

Resnick, M. D., Ireland, M., & Borowski, I. (2004). Youth violence perpetration: What protects? What predicts? Findings from the National Longitudinal Study of Adolescent Health. *Journal of Adolescent Health*, *35*(5), 424. e1.

Sexton, T. L. (2000). Functional family therapy. US Department of Justice, Office of Justice Programs, Office of Juvenile Justice and Delinquency Prevention.

Sexton, T. L., & Turner, C. W. (2010). The effectiveness of functional family therapy for youth with behavioral problems in a community practice setting. *Journal of Family Psychology*, *24*(3), 339.

Smith, E. P., Wolf, A. M., Cantillon, D. M., Thomas, O., & Davidson, W. S. (2004). The adolescent diversion project: 25 years of research on an ecological model of intervention. *Journal of Prevention & Intervention in the Community*, *27*(2), 29–47

Spencer, M. B., & Jones-Walker, C. (2004). Interventions and services offered to former juvenile offenders reentering their communities: An analysis of program effectiveness. *Youth Violence and Juvenile Justice*, *2*(1), 88–97.

Thornberry, T. P., Krohn, M. D., Lizotte, A. J., Smith, C. A., & Tobin, K. (2003). *Gangs and delinquency in developmental perspective*. Cambridge University Press.

Tierney, J. P., Grossman, J. B., & Resch, N. L. (2000). Making a difference: *An* impact study of big brothers/big sisters. Public/Private Ventures.

Vincent, G. M., Chapman, J., & Cook, N. E. (2011). Risk-needs assessment in juvenile justice: Predictive validity of the SAVRY, racial differences, and the contribution of needs factors. *Criminal Justice and Behavior*, *38*(1), 42–62.

Weaver, R. D., & Campbell, D. (2015). Fresh start: A meta-analysis of aftercare programs for juvenile offenders. *Research on Social Work Practice*, *25*(2), 201–212.

Wood, S., & Mayo-Wilson, E. (2012). School-based mentoring for adolescents: A systematic review and meta-analysis. *Research on Social Work Practice*, *22*(3), 257–269.

12
YOUTH DECISION-MAKING AND JUVENILE JUSTICE POLICY

Lillian A. Rodriguez Steen and Lindsay C. Malloy

Adolescence is a period of great change hallmarked by exploration and risk-taking behaviors, a greater reliance on peers, and a growing desire for independence. These characteristics increase the likelihood that youth will become involved in legal proceedings as suspects or defendants. At the same time, these characteristics contribute to their vulnerabilities in legal contexts, including with respect to the decisions that they must make (see Steinberg, 2009). In this chapter, we discuss several characteristics of adolescence that impact youth decision-making in juvenile justice contexts – in the interrogation room and the courtroom. We conclude with a discussion of juvenile justice policy and recommendations. Though many of the concepts we discuss in this chapter largely apply to adolescents regardless of their geographic location, the recommendations we propose focus on amending current U.S. policies.

Characteristics of Adolescence Relevant to Their Legal Decision-Making

During adolescence, there are prominent changes in biology, cognition, and social relationships, as well as motivational and emotional functioning (Boyer, 2006). This period of development is typified by exploratory and risky behaviors, emerging peer relationships, and a drive for independence from parents and authority figures, all of which have implications for youths' decision-making in legal contexts. Before discussing these contexts, we review several key characteristics of adolescents relevant to their legal decision making. We note that our brief review is far from exhaustive. Indeed, our goal is to highlight a few developmental characteristics of adolescence that may shape their decisions in legal settings and, given our juvenile justice focus, to hone in on a few critical legal decisions that adolescent suspects and defendants are confronted with in particular.

First, during adolescence, youth become more independent as they begin to discover and develop their own identities. Exploration is an integral part of their emerging independence and allows youth to test new boundaries. For some adolescents, this includes engaging in risky or illegal activities, such as experimentation with alcohol or other substances (Steinberg, 2009). Exploratory behaviors are also motivated by their reward-seeking tendencies which increase during adolescence. For example, adolescents are more likely to make risky decisions that have the potential for high reward payouts, especially when those rewards are immediate as opposed to long-term (Braams et al., 2015). Second, as adolescents develop, they

DOI: 10.4324/9781003219286-15

rely less on parents and more on their increasingly important relationships with their peers. Thus, youth want to engage in behaviors endorsed by their peers, and their decisions often reflect their peers' values (van Hoorn et al., 2016). This can lead to a greater susceptibility to peer influence. Indeed, research shows that youth engage in more risky behaviors (e.g., driving recklessly) when peers are present than when they are alone (Albert et al., 2013). Last, as adolescents become increasingly independent from their parents, they place a higher emphasis on exerting and maintaining their autonomy (Steinberg & Silverberg, 1986) and their decision-making is impacted by this drive. Greater desire for autonomy may reduce adolescents' willingness to tell adults about risky experiences and may increase their likelihood of taking responsibility for those experiences even when they were pressured into doing them (Grandpre et al., 2003). Together, this constellation of characteristics, which are key for adolescent development, can have critical implications for their legal decision-making as suspects and defendants, as we review next.

Adolescents' Legal Decision-Making as Suspects and Defendants

Adolescents identified as suspects of criminal or delinquent behavior are tasked with making decisions that can have significant and long-lasting effects on their lives. They must typically decide whether to waive their Miranda rights and what they want to disclose to law enforcement, including whether to make admissions regarding their guilt to the police (a confession) or to a judge (guilty plea). These decisions, which can be difficult even for adults, may be influenced by the aforementioned developmental characteristics.

In the Interrogation Room

Research demonstrates that youth differ from adults in several critical ways when it comes to being questioned by the police as suspects – namely their willingness to talk to the police in the first place and what they say when questioned (e.g., whether to provide a true confession, false confession, or a denial). The first decision many adolescent suspects make regards their rights to remain silent and to an attorney. When adolescents (or adults) experience a "custodial" interrogation in the United States, they are required to be advised of their rights to both (i.e., their "Miranda rights"). Other countries may afford similar rights (e.g., the "police caution" in Canada). A large body of research, however, demonstrates that adolescents commonly (as in over 90% of them) waive these rights and allow questioning to take place (e.g., Cleary & Vidal, 2016; Grisso, 1980).

They may waive these rights at such a high rate because adolescents, especially younger adolescents, rarely fully understand or appreciate what these rights mean (Kelley et al., 2018). Furthermore, many adolescents involved in the legal system have learning disabilities, are delayed academically, or have cognitive deficits (Grigorenko, 2006). These difficulties can make them especially vulnerable to misunderstanding legal jargon, potentially complex topics, or discussions of personal rights (Lieser et al., 2019). Adolescents may struggle to request clarification when misunderstandings about their rights as suspects occur, wanting to appear independent. Their growing desire for autonomy may also influence their decisions to waive their right to have someone else (e.g., a parent or attorney) with them in the interrogation room (e.g., Grisso, 1980; Viljoen et al., 2005). Indeed, a study examining interrogations of youth charged with a felony offense in the United States found that parents were present in only 21% of interrogations, while defense attorneys were not present in any (Cleary, 2014).

The developmental characteristics of adolescence play an important role in increasing a youth's vulnerability to providing a false or coerced confession. Research clearly demonstrates that youth is a dispositional risk factor for false confession, and youth are overrepresented in proven false confession cases (see Cleary, 2017). Adolescents' reward-oriented thought processes may prompt youth to underemphasize the long-term significance of confessing to a crime while at the same time overemphasizing the short-term benefits of that confession. In some cases, youth may falsely confess believing that this may help to stop the interrogation and get them out of this unpleasant situation sooner, unsophisticated reasoning that is further fueled by their greater impulsivity. Grisso et al. (2003) showed youth and young adults vignettes of police interrogations and asked them whether the suspect's "best choice" was to remain silent, deny involvement, or confess to the crime. Nearly 60% of youth ages 11–13 and over 40% of youth ages 14–15 chose confessing as the best option, compared to only 20% of the young adults.

In field studies, many adolescents report having falsely confessed in order to protect someone else (e.g., Malloy et al., 2014; Viljoen et al., 2005), a potential consequence of adolescents' heightened peer orientation and susceptibility to peer influence. This tendency has been found in experimental research as well. That is, Pimentel et al. (2015) revealed that adolescents (ages 14–17) were significantly more likely (59%) than adults (39%) to take responsibility for another's act of wrongdoing by signing a confession statement claiming to have cheated on the study test. Furthermore, when deciding whether to sign the confession, significantly more adults (49%) than adolescents (32%) expressed concern about potential consequences to themselves for admitting to wrongdoing that they had not actually committed. Because of their greater sensitivity to rewards vs. risks and peer orientation, adolescents may have been thinking less in terms of the potential consequences of confessing and more about the benefits of protecting someone else. Or perhaps adolescents' growing desire for independence kept them from asking further questions about the consequences they might face, and they wanted to appear as though they understood and were "in charge" of the situation. Future research should examine the influence of reward sensitivity, peer relationships, and emerging autonomy on juveniles' false confessions.

In the Courtroom

Decision-making in the courtroom can also be affected by the key characteristics of adolescence – most notably whether to accept a plea deal. Pleading guilty is typically done to avoid facing a harsher charge and/or associated penalty if convicted at trial, yet pleas carry with them a number of "collateral" consequences. For example, in addition to surrendering their right to a trial, youth who plead guilty may also surrender their right to appeal, voting rights, and access to certain services or opportunities (see Edkins & Redlich, 2019). Yet pleading guilty may seem prudent even when one is innocent because plea agreements typically result in a sentence that is quantitatively (e.g., number of years in custody) and/or qualitatively (e.g., probation vs. custody) different from what is at stake if convicted at trial.

In the United States, juveniles typically must complete a plea colloquy that demonstrates their understanding of their admission and what it means for them. Largely, their understanding is determined by oral plea colloquies or written tender-of-plea forms. Plea colloquies are typically questions asked by the judge to determine whether any promises were made regarding accepting the plea, whether the defendant is incapacitated (e.g., on medication, intoxicated), and whether the defendant understands the legal rights they are waiving and the possible consequences of accepting the plea (American Bar Association, 1999). Little research has examined juveniles' understanding of plea colloquies or written tender-of-plea forms, but that which has been done generates concern about juveniles' understanding of these legal discussions and documents (e.g., Kaban & Quinlan, 2004; Redlich & Bonventre, 2015).

Research examining adolescents' plea decision-making demonstrates that some youth appear to deliberate in sensible ways when considering whether to accept a plea bargain. For example, in a hypothetical scenario, Peterson-Badali & Abramovitch (1993) found that even 10-year-olds knew not to take a plea when the evidence against them was weak. Viljoen et al. (2005) revealed that, among defendants ages 11–17, the older youth (ages 15–17) reported considering the evidence against them when deciding whether to accept a plea deal, whereas the younger youth (ages 11–14) did not. It seems rational to consider the evidence against oneself before deciding whether to plead guilty.

Although the research evidence concerning false confessions is now quite clear that juveniles are at a disproportionate risk for falsely confessing compared to adults, we do not yet know whether this is the case when it comes to false guilty pleas. Redlich (2009) outlined reasons why juveniles may be both *more* and *less* likely to take a false guilty plea than adults. Adolescents' differential emphasis on reward vs. risk may lead them to decide to take their chances at trial, for instance. Or, because adolescents are more sensitive to immediate rewards and less sensitive to long-term consequences, they may be excessively swayed by the more lenient treatment for admitting guilt typically afforded by making a guilty plea, even when it is false. Indeed, Redlich and Shteynberg (2016) found that when asked to assume innocence in a hypothetical situation, juveniles were more than twice as likely as young adults to falsely plead guilty.

Regardless of whether youth are at greater risk for making false guilty pleas than adults, research indicates that at least some youth make false guilty pleas. For example, Malloy et al. (2014) examined 193 male juveniles (ages 14–17) incarcerated for serious crimes and reported that 27.5% (n = 53) indicated that they had made a false guilty plea to a judge at least once in the past. Similarly, Zottoli et al. (2016) interviewed youth (ages 13–17) who pleaded guilty to felonies in New York City and found that 27% claimed they were completely innocent. Youths' greater compliance with authority figures and lack of legal knowledge may also be factors here. When Malloy et al. (2014) questioned incarcerated youth about their plea experiences, high-pressure tactics (e.g., threats) from lawyers were alarmingly common. Furthermore, such tactics were associated with self-reported false, but not true, guilty pleas. Finally, adolescents' desire for autonomy may affect their plea decision-making. For example, Redlich et al. (2021) observed plea hearings with juvenile defendants and found that they rarely asked questions; were often only minimally engaged; and provided brief, bare-minimum responses when asked questions. Youth may behave in this manner during plea hearings as a way of asserting their independence and demonstrating that they do not need help.

Key Takeaway Points

1. Adolescence is hallmarked by several characteristics, including risk-taking, reward orientation, emerging reliance on peers, and a drive towards autonomy.
2. These characteristics can affect the decisions that youth make and contribute to their vulnerabilities in legal contexts.
3. As suspects, adolescents often waive their Miranda rights without fully understanding them and submit to police questioning without an adult present.
4. As defendants, adolescents often must decide whether to accept a plea bargain, potentially without understanding the rights they might be waiving by accepting a plea or the long-term consequences of that acceptance.

5. Youths' developmental characteristics may put them at heightened risk for false confessions and false guilty pleas.

Juvenile Justice Policy

Empirical research on adolescent decision-making and experiences within the legal system has led to several changes in the policies and laws that impact justice-involved youth. Several critical legal cases, for example, appear to recognize the decision-making capacities of youth as they pertain to their decisions to commit a crime. For example, Roper v. Simmons (2005) eliminated the death penalty for 16- and 17-year-old defendants largely on the basis that youth are categorically different from adults who commit similar crimes. Psychological research on adolescent capabilities and limitations (e.g., the neuroscience of adolescence, their reward orientation and impulsivity, etc.) was featured prominently in this decision concerning adolescent culpability and sentencing. Next, we describe several recommendations for juvenile justice policy with regard to young suspects' and defendants' participation in the interrogation room and in the courtroom.

Developmentally-Informed Training

Perhaps the most straightforward policy suggestion in this area is the need for the legal community, including law enforcement, social services, and other legal professionals, to be trained on the various ways that development shapes adolescents' behaviors and decisions. This training is not only entirely possible, but, in some contexts, is already well underway. For example, attorneys and the courts regularly cite adolescents' immature brain circuitry and the prolonged development of neural systems across adolescence with regards to their criminal culpability. However, training must be expanded to ensure that professionals are aware of how the same developmental processes and characteristics shape decisions and behaviors throughout legal cases from the moment of arrest and questioning all the way to potential sentencing.

Recommendations for the Interrogation Room

There are several ways in which interrogations of juvenile suspects can be altered to better accommodate youths' developmental characteristics. For one, greater transparency via objective records of what occurred in the interrogation room would serve to help protect juveniles. For example, video recording interrogations can help to capture the tactics employed to obtain youths' statements. This will help ensure that any admissions of guilt are evaluated in the context of the tactics used without having to rely on the imperfect and potentially biased memories of those involved. Some states have mandatory policies for recording interrogations in place already. In California, for example, it is required to record all police interrogations with youth suspected of homicide offenses. However, this safeguard should, ideally, be extended to all police interrogations with juvenile suspects.

Given adolescents' tendency to waive their Miranda rights without fully understanding what waiving those rights means, another recommendation is that policy outlining the mandatory presence of or consultation with a professional adult advocate be established. This is standard in England and Wales, for example, where juveniles must be interrogated with an "appropriate adult" (e.g., parent, attorney, social worker) present. California, again, showcases that this can be implemented in the United States as well. In 2017, legislation passed requiring that youth 15 years and younger consult with attorneys before an interrogation.

Recommendations for the Courtroom

Legally, youth must decide to plead guilty knowingly, intelligently, and voluntarily (Godinez v. Moran, 1993). Yet, Redlich and Bonventre (2015) examined 208 tender-of-plea forms and found that the language used exceeded the reading comprehension of most defendants. Kaban and Quinlan (2004) found that court-involved juveniles (ages 9–17) defined correctly just 2–5 of 36 key words used in the Massachusetts tender-of-plea form and juvenile court colloquies. We recommend that plea colloquies and written tender-of-plea forms use language that is developmentally appropriate for youth. Furthermore, it is recommended that a knowledgeable adult advocate be present and available to help youth fully understand their plea decisions. We also recommend that future research focus on how attorneys counsel youth regarding accepting pleas, including how attorneys guide and influence adolescents through this process. A great deal remains to be learned about youths' plea decision-making including specifically how their various developmental characteristics influence their plea decisions and the ways in which lawyers and other potentially important sources of social influence (e.g., peers, parents) affect these decisions.

Summary and Conclusions

In sum, adolescence is a period of multifaceted change hallmarked by increased empowerment of youth as well as increased vulnerability. Decades of empirical research demonstrate how adolescents' characteristics may affect their legal decision making as suspects and defendants. This body of work should allow for more research-informed policies and laws in juvenile justice contexts.

References

Albert, D., Chein, J., & Steinberg, L. (2013). The teenage brain: Peer influences on adolescent decision making. *Current Directions in Psychological Science*, *22*(2), 114–120. doi: 10.1177/0963721412471347

American Bar Association. (1999). *ABA standards for criminal justice pleas of guilty*, 3rd ed. American Bar Association.

Boyer, T. W. (2006). The development of risk-taking: A multi-perspective review. *Developmental Review*, *26*(3), 291–345. doi: 10.1016/j.dr.2006.05.002

Braams, B. R., van Duijvenvoorde, A. C., Peper, J. S., & Crone, E. A. (2015). Longitudinal changes in adolescent risk-taking: A comprehensive study of neural responses to rewards, pubertal development, and risk-taking behavior. *Journal of Neuroscience*, *35*(18), 7226–7238. doi: 10.1523/JNEUROSCI.4764-14.2015

Cleary, H. M. D. (2014). Police interviewing and interrogation of juvenile suspects: A descriptive examination of actual cases. *Law and Human Behavior*, *38*, 271–282. doi: 10.1037/lhb0000070

Cleary, H. M. D. (2017). Applying the lessons of developmental psychology to the study of juvenile interrogations: New directions for research, policy, and practice. *Psychology, Public Policy, and Law*, *23*(1), 118–130. doi: 10.1037/law0000120

Cleary, H. M. D., & Vidal, S. (2016). Miranda in actual juvenile interrogations: Delivery, waiver and readability. *Criminal Justice Review*, *41*, 98–115. doi: 10.1177/0734016814538650

Edkins, V. A., & Redlich, A. D. (2019). *A system of pleas: Social science's contributions to the real legal system*. Oxford University Press. doi: 10.1093/oso/9780190689247.001.0001

Godinez v. Moran, 509 U.S. 389 (1993)

Grandpre, J., Alvaro, E. M., Burgoon, M., Miller, C. H., & Hall, J. R. (2003). Adolescent reactance and anti-smoking campaigns: A theoretical approach. *Health Communication*, *15*, 349–366. doi: 10.1207/S15327027HC1503_6

Grigorenko, E. L. (2006). Learning disabilities in juvenile offenders. *Child and Adolescent Psychiatric Clinics*, *15*, 353–371. doi: 10.1016/j.chc.2005.11.001

Grisso, T. (1980). Juveniles' capacities to waive Miranda rights: An empirical analysis. *California Law Review, 68*, 1134–1166.

Grisso, T., Steinberg, L., Woolard, J., Cauffman, E., Scott, E., Graham, S., . . . Schwartz, R. (2003). Juveniles' competence to stand trial: A comparison of adolescents' and adults' capacities as trial defendants. *Law and Human Behavior, 27*, 333–363. doi: 10.1023/A:1024065015717

Kaban, B., & Quilan, J. C. (2004). Rethinking a "knowing, intelligent, and voluntary waiver" in Massachusetts' juvenile courts. *Journal of the Center for Families, Children, and the Courts, 5*, 35–55.

Kelley, S., Zelle, H., Brogan, L., & Goldstein, N. E. (2018). Review of research and recent case law on understanding and appreciation of Miranda warnings. In M. Miller & B. Bornstein (Eds.), *Advances in psychology and law* (pp. 77–117). Springer. doi: 10.1007/978-3-319-75859-6_3

Lieser, A. M., Van der Voort, D., & Spaulding, T. J. (2019). You have the right to remain silent: The ability of adolescents with developmental language disorder to understand their legal rights. *Journal of Communication Disorders, 82*, 105920. doi: 10.1016/j.jcomdis.2019.105920

Malloy, L. C., Shulman, E. P., & Cauffman, E. (2014). Interrogations, confessions, and guilty pleas among serious adolescent offenders. *Law and Human Behavior, 38*, 181–193. doi: 10.1037/lhb0000065

Peterson-Badali, M., & Abramovitch, R. (1993). Grade related changes in young people's reasoning about plea decisions. *Law and Human Behavior, 17*, 537–552.

Pimentel, P. S., Arndorfer, A., & Malloy, L. C. (2015). Taking the blame for someone else's wrongdoing: The effects of age and reciprocity. *Law and Human Behavior, 39*, 219–231. doi: 10.1037/lhb0000132

Redlich, A. D. (2009). The susceptibility of juveniles to false confessions and false guilty pleas. *Rutgers Law Review, 62*, 943–957.

Redlich, A. D., & Bonventre, C. L. (2015). Content and comprehensibility of juvenile and adult tender-of-plea forms: implications for knowing, intelligent, and voluntary guilty pleas. *Law and Human Behavior, 39*(2), 162–176. doi: 10.1037/lhb0000118

Redlich, A. D., Domagalski, K., Woestehoff, S., Dezember, A., & Quas, J. A. (2021). What happens when suspects plea? An observational investigation of plea hearings in juvenile and criminal court (Unpublished manuscript).

Redlich, A. D., & Shteynberg, R. V. (2016). To plead or not to plead: A comparison of juvenile and adult true and false plea decisions. *Law and Human Behavior, 40*, 611. doi: 10.1037/lhb0000205

Roper v. Simmons, 543 U.S. 551 (2005)

Steinberg, L. (2009). Adolescent development and juvenile justice. *Annual Review of Clinical Psychology, 5*, 459–485. doi: 10.1146/annurev.clinpsy.032408.153603

Steinberg, L., & Silverberg, S. B. (1986). The vicissitudes of autonomy in early adolescence. *Child Development, 57*(4), 841–851.

van Hoorn, J., Fuligni, A. J., Crone, E. A., & Galvan, A. (2016). Peer influence effects on risk-taking and prosocial decision-making in adolescence: Insights from neuroimaging studies. *Current Opinion in Behavioral Sciences, 10*, 59–64. doi: 10.1016/j.cobeha.2016.05.007

Viljoen, J. L., Klaver, J., & Roesch, R. (2005). Legal decisions of preadolescent and adolescent defendants: Predictors of confessions, pleas, communication with attorneys, and appeals. *Law and Human Behavior, 29*, 253–277. doi: 10.1007/s10979-005-3613-2

Zottoli, T. M., Daftary-Kapur, T., Winters, G. M., & Hogan, C. (2016). Plea discounts, time pressures, and false-guilty pleas in youth and adults who pleaded guilty to felonies in New York City. *Psychology, Public Policy, and Law, 22*(3), 250–259. doi: 10.1037/law0000095

PART III

Predictors of Crime and Risk Assessment

13

ADVERSE CHILDHOOD EXPERIENCES AND OFFENDING

Strategies for Prevention, Intervention, Building Resiliency

Michael T. Baglivio

Introduction

Exposure to adverse childhood experiences (ACEs) represents a persistent and costly public health problem in the United States, with the total lifetime economic burden from *a single year's worth* of new cases of child maltreatment estimated at over $120 billion (Fang et al., 2012; see also Putnam, 2006). This enormous impact of both deleterious outcomes and fiscal repercussions necessitates not only policies targeting prevention of traumatic exposure but additionally effective interventions for exposed individuals. Nowhere is this need more essential than in the justice systems' responses to cumulative adversity among individuals who become system involved. This chapter serves to summarize the most consistent findings regarding the heightened exposure among those with justice system involvement and the traumatic exposure-offending relationship and to present a multi-tiered model of evidence-based and promising policies and practices to flatten the age–crime curve (Loeber, 2012) by reducing the proportion of those with extensive traumatic exposure becoming violent and life course persistent offenders.

Cumulative Traumatic Exposure

Historically, both public health and criminological research has focused on examining the prevalence and independent effects of individual traumatic exposures (i.e., neglect, sexual abuse; Browne & Finkelhor, 1986; Widom, 1989a, 1989b). The ACE study and subsequent investigations served to demonstrate the dose-response relationship of cumulative traumatic exposure with the leading causes of death, as more types of trauma exposures are related to increased odds of experiencing heart disease, cancer, chronic lung disease, skeletal fractures, and liver disease in adulthood (Felitti et al., 1998). The ten ACEs included three types of abuse (physical, sexual, emotional), two types of neglect (physical and emotional), and five household dysfunctions (household mental illness, substance abuse, incarceration history, parental separation/divorce, and domestic violence). Astonishingly, those exposed to six or more of the ten ACEs die on average 20 years earlier than those with no exposures (Brown et al., 2009).

ACE exposures are common, highly interrelated, and co-occur non-randomly such that exposure to any type of ACE dramatically increases the odds of exposure to others, leading

DOI: 10.4324/9781003219286-17

to the need to consider cumulative trauma (Anda et al., 2006; Baglivio & Epps, 2016; Dong et al., 2004). The predominant pathway by which ACE exposures manifests involves the disruption of neurodevelopment leading to social, emotional, and cognitive impairments (e.g., attention, impulsivity, decision-making, learning, emotion, response to stress), which in turn increase the odds of adopting risky behaviors (crime, violence, substance use, suicide attempts, risky sexual activity) that lead to disease, disability, and social problems and ultimately earlier death (Centers for Disease Control and Prevention, 2019). Critical to the current chapter is the relationship between ACE exposure and antisocial behavior. While ACE dose-response effects have been demonstrated across over 40 different physical health, mental health, and behavioral outcomes (CDC, 2019), a recent meta-analysis found the strongest associations between ACE and negative outcomes were with problematic drug use and interpersonal and self-directed violence (Hughes et al., 2017). Furthermore, while ACE prevalence within general populations were shocking revelations, even greater ACE exposure among individuals involved in the justice system has consistently been documented (Abram et al., 2004; Baglivio, Epps, et al., 2014; Cannon et al., 2016; Dierkhising et al., 2013; Evans-Chase, 2014; Reavis et al., 2013; Trulson et al., 2016; Vitopoulos et al., 2018).

ACEs and Antisocial Behavior

The link of childhood maltreatment to antisocial behavior is well elucidated (Widom, 1989b; Widom et al., 2018), increasing the odds of both self-reported and official delinquency, frequency of arrests, and seriousness of offending (Smith & Thornberry, 1995). Maltreatment increases the odds of violent juvenile offending in excess of 200% (Maxfield & Widom, 1996). Longitudinal meta-analytic work confirms abuse and neglect related to both general and aggressive antisocial behavior among juveniles (Braga et al., 2017). The effects of traumatic exposure on antisocial behavior include juvenile custodial settings, finding greater total incidents of institutional misconduct, suicidal attempts, and sexual misconduct (Trulson et al., 2016). While contradictory at times with respect to which sex demonstrates stronger effects, prior work indicates both males and females with traumatic exposures are at increased odds of violent offending (e.g., Chen et al., 2011; Herrera & McCloskey, 2001; Mass et al., 2008; Teague et al., 2008; Widom & Maxfield, 2001; Yu-Ling et al., 2011).

The measure of cumulative trauma vis-à-vis a composite ACE score to examine (re)offending and justice system-related outcomes has expanded greatly (Baglivio, 2018). Findings demonstrate higher ACE exposures related to increased risk of, and shorter time to, recidivism among juveniles involved in the justice system (Wolff et al., 2017; see also Craig et al., 2019; Kowalski, 2018). Such youth with higher ACEs are at increased odds of being victims of human trafficking and engaging in sex trading (Reid et al., 2019; Naramore et al., 2017), suicide attempts (Perez et al., 2016), psychopathic features (Baglivio et al., 2020), internalizing and externalizing behaviors (Muniz et al., 2019), substance abuse and delinquency (Leban & Gibson, 2020), and increasing interpersonal and self-directed violence by 35%–144% (Duke et al., 2010). Further, youth with violent offenses are more likely to have heightened ACE exposures than non-violent youth (Malvaso et al., 2019; see also Malvaso et al., 2018). Prospective work indicates higher ACE exposure by age 12 among justice-involved juveniles increases the odds of both gang involvement and juvenile justice residential placement by age 18 (Wolff et al., 2020; Zettler et al., 2018). Relatedly, higher ACEs among youth involved in the juvenile justice system are prospectively associated psychiatric symptoms and substance use (Folk et al., 2021).

ACE exposure in childhood and adolescence has implications on offending throughout the life course. Specifically, youth with substantiated maltreatment have an earlier age of onset of offending (Barrett et al., 2014; Dannerbeck & Yan, 2011; Rivera & Widom, 1990) are more likely to continue to offend into adulthood (Topitzes et al., 2011; Widom et al., 2018), 8.8 times more likely to be incarcerated in adulthood (Bellis et al., 2014; see also English et al., 2001; Fagan, 2005; Mersky & Topitzes, 2010), and 38% more likely to have a violent offending history (Widom, 1989b). Examining youth involved in the juvenile justice system, those with more than five (of the ten) ACEs experience dramatically greater odds of early onset, persistent offending (with an average of 18 arrests prior to age 18; Baglivio et al., 2015). Further, Fox and colleagues (2015) demonstrated each additional ACE exposure equated to a 35% increase in the likelihood of serious, violent, chronic (SVC) offending by age 18 compared to those adjudicated for only one nonviolent felony (see also Perez et al., 2018). Craig et al. (2017) demonstrated that as ACE scores increased, the average number of convictions from age 10 to 56 also tended to increase, with males having the highest scores accumulating substantially more convictions.

To summarize, the following critical takeaway points are pivotal to our understanding of the implications of traumatic exposure on crime and delinquency:

- Traumatic exposure is common and interrelated where exposure to one type greatly increases the odds of exposure to additional types;
- Heightened ACE exposure is consistently found among justice-involved individuals;
- Higher ACEs increases the odds of victimization, human trafficking victimization, substance use, internalizing and externalizing behaviors, and suicidal ideation/attempts;
- Heightened cumulative traumatic exposure is associated a variety of negative juvenile justice system outcomes, including higher odds of (re)offending, a shorter time to recidivism, and increased odds of residential placement and gang involvement by age 18;
- ACE exposure has life course implications for antisocial behavior and criminal offending.

Description of Responsive Evidence-Based Programs, Policies, and/or Practices

Tier 1: Prevention

ACEs are preventable. As such, a multi-tiered strategy should be centered first on the prevention of ACE exposure. Evidence-based programs with verified efficacy include nurse-family partnerships (Eckenrode et al., 2017; MacMillan et al., 2009), early parent training (Piquero et al., 2016), and universal prevention programs provided in early education settings (e.g., LifeSkills Training; Botvin & Griffin, 2004). As ACE exposure is heightened in areas of concentrated disadvantage (Baglivio et al., 2017; Coulton et al., 2007), targeting programs and ensuring adequate resources and access within such neighborhoods is pivotal. The CDC (2019) calls for prevention strategies including: strengthening household financial security, family-friendly work policy (paid maternity and sick leave, flexible work schedules), promoting norms against violence and adversity (public awareness campaigns), early home visitation programs, high-quality child care, and preschool. As prevention strategies will never eliminate ACE-exposed youth becoming system involved, strategies to address trauma-exposed youth in the juvenile justice/child welfare systems are key.

Among the first steps to evidence-based programs and practices for any sub-populations of individuals should be to first assess the efficacy of the predominant paradigm provided. As the current chapter is focused on ACEs and offending, that principal strategy under which juvenile and criminal justice systems operate is the risk-need-responsivity (RNR) model, calling for the individualized matching of services to assessed dynamic risk factors (Andrews & Bonta, 2003), with services delivered at sufficient dosage and quality (Lipsey, 2009). Recently, individual-level service matching and meeting treatment dosage targets established by Lipsey's Standardized Program Evaluation Protocol (SPEP) during residential placement were examined with respect to changes in dynamic risk during placement and recidivism post-release (Baglivio et al., 2021). Fortunately, while heightened ACE exposure was related to smaller dynamic risk reductions during placement and to an increased probability of reoffending, both low-ACE and high-ACE youth receiving matched services coupled with adequate dosage had greater treatment progress (dynamic risk reduction) and lower recidivism post-release. Essentially, the RNR model was equivalent in reducing recidivism for both low- and high-ACE-exposed youth. Nevertheless, the independent effect of ACE exposure on reoffending remained (Baglivio, Zettler, et al., 2021). This study demonstrated that following the RNR model and current justice system best practices may be necessary but is alone not sufficient. Trauma-exposed justice-involved youth need more.

Tier 2: Screening, Assessment, Staff Training, and Service Referrals

The second step of a multi-tiered best practice strategy includes screening, assessment, staff training, and service referrals. Arguments exist regarding universal screening of ACEs among the general population as well as using individual-level ACE scores as predictive tools (e.g., Anda et al., 2020). Arguably, however, best practices for individuals already involved in the justice system demand thorough understanding of the risk and protective factors and responsivity considerations to determine appropriate treatment and case planning. Traumatic exposure certainly fits within those concepts (as a responsivity "roadblock" to effective treatment at minimum, while recent prospective work indicates ACE exposure is more likely a risk factor for future system contact). Additionally, the ACE screening is preliminary, moving indicated individuals to assessment of clinical symptomology related to traumatic exposures. Clarity as to whether such exposure is underlying clinical issues such as flashbacks, difficulty sleeping/nightmares, arousal/reactivity, negative cognition/mood, or avoidance is clearly relevant. Assessment tools for children, adolescents, and adults are widely available, such as the UCLA Child/Adolescent PTSD Reaction Index for DSM-5 (e.g., Steinberg et al., 2013). Importantly, staff require adequate training on 1) universal precautions (assuming all justice-involved individuals are trauma exposed, because most are) and avoiding re-traumatization in custody settings (Miller & Najavits, 2012), 2) screening/assessment processes, and 3) making referrals or providing treatment "in house" related to clinical symptomology stemming from traumatic exposure (i.e., trauma-specific treatment).

Tier 3: Targeted Trauma-Specific Treatment Interventions, Coupled With a Resiliency-Building Focus

Service referrals or "in-house" treatment for justice-involved or "at-risk" individuals with indicated clinical symptomology related to ACE exposure should involve trauma-specific treatment. While, unfortunately, there is a paucity of research on the extent to which trauma-specific interventions reduce (re)offending (e.g., Zettler, 2020), a recent systematic review indicates such treatment reduces PTSD symptomology and trauma-related depressive symptoms and has promising indication of reductions in delinquency and recidivism (Baetz et al., 2021).

Considering trauma as a responsivity factor, reductions in associated symptomology should reduce roadblocks to effective interventions addressing prominent criminogenic dynamic risks.

The second element to reducing the deleterious effects of ACE exposure on crime and delinquency involves building resiliency among those who are already ACE-exposed. Early work focused on independent effects of singular promotive or protective factors in mitigating ACE effects on antisocial behavior. Promising strategies include increasing empathy (Narvey et al., 2021), preventing substance abuse (Craig et al., 2019), high school attainment, increasing self-control, and parental engagement (Craig, Piquero, et al., 2017). Recent work shows resiliency across multiple domains, termed cumulative "positive childhood experiences" (PCEs), mitigates the ACE effects on physical and mental health-related outcomes such as cardiovascular health in midlife, depression, substance use, body image, psychosocial problems, personality disorder symptoms, risky sexual behaviors, and teenage pregnancy (e.g., Banyard et al., 2017; Bethell et al., 2019; Chung et al., 2008; Crandall et al., 2019, 2020; Gunay-Oge et al., 2020; Hillis et al., 2010; Lenzi et al., 2015; Liu et al., 2020; Slopen et al., 2017). PCE exposures involve family–child communication, feeling supported by family, community/family traditions, a sense of belonging/engagement to school, support from friends, participating in organized activities, and having adult mentors (Baglivio & Wolff, 2020). Baglivio and Wolff (2020) replicated findings that higher ACEs increased reoffending but also that higher cumulative PCE decreased reoffending. More importantly, no significant effect of ACE exposure on recidivism remained among the youth with heightened positive experiences (i.e., cumulative PCE moderates the ACE-recidivism relationship). This is critical to juvenile justice policy, demonstrating ACEs do not lead to increased recidivism when youth concurrently have numerous PCEs.

Tier 4: System Alignment

The final tier to address the negative effects of ACEs on crime and delinquency is system alignment. A noteworthy portion of justice-involved youth are dually involved in the child welfare system. Such "crossover" youth have higher ACEs than the general population and single system-involved youth (c.f., Baglivio, Wolff, et al., 2016). Systems must better align. Best practices require early identification of dual involvement, sharing of data and information, single comprehensive care plans rather than a siloed approach, and a "one judge/one family" approach, in contrast to navigating separate courts (Stewart et al., 2010).

Conclusion

The ACE–offending relationship is well established. Heightened cumulative traumatic exposure increases the likelihood of both victimization (human trafficking, suicidal behavior) and justice system involvement/offending throughout the life course (earlier age at first arrest, greater frequency, severity, and duration of criminal "career"). Childhood maltreatment prevention remains critical, yet systems must be prepared and equipped to address the treatment needs of ACE-exposed individuals. Youth living in neighborhoods plagued by concentrated disadvantage are most at risk (CDC, 2019), including those adolescents with juvenile justice involvement (Baglivio et al., 2017), making ACE prevention and treatment integral to efforts at reducing ethnic disparities in the justice system. The best available evidence calls for a multi-tiered strategy of 1) prevention; 2) screening, assessment, staff training, and service referrals; and 3) targeted mental health and trauma-specific treatment, coupled with a resiliency-building focus and 4) ensuring systems alignment through information-sharing and coordinated care planning.

References

Abram K. M., Teplin, L. A., Charles, D. R., Longworth, S. L., McClelland, G. M., & Dulcan, M. K. (2004). Posttraumatic stress disorder and trauma in youth in juvenile detention. *Archives of General Psychiatry*, *61*, 403–410.

Anda, R. F., Felitti, V. J., Bremner, J. D., Walker, J. D., Whitfield, C., Perry, B. D., Dube, S. R., & Giles, W. H. (2006). The enduring effects of abuse and related adverse childhood experiences in childhood: A convergence of evidence from neurobiology and epidemiology. *European Archives of Psychiatry and Clinical Neuroscience*, *256*, 174–186.

Anda, R. F., Porter, L. E., & Brown, D. W. (2020). Inside the adverse childhood experience score: Strengths, limitations, and misapplications. *American Journal of Preventive Medicine*, *59(2)*, 293–295.

Andrews, D. A., & Bonta, J. A. (2003). *The psychology of criminal conduct*, 3rd ed. Anderson.

Baglivio, M. T. (2018). On cumulative traumatic exposure and violence/aggression: The implications of adverse childhood experiences (ACE). In A. T. Vazsonyi, D. J. Flannery, & M. DeLisi (Eds.), *The Cambridge handbook of violent behavior and aggression* (2nd ed., pp. 467–487). Cambridge University Press.

Baglivio, M. T., & Epps, N. (2016). The interrelatedness of adverse childhood experiences among high-risk juvenile offenders. *Youth Violence and Juvenile Justice*, *14*(3), 179–198.

Baglivio, M. T., Epps, N., Swartz, K., Huq, M. S., Sheer, A., & Hardt, N. S. (2014). The prevalence of Adverse Childhood Experiences (ACE) in the lives of juvenile offenders. *Journal of Juvenile Justice*, *3*, 1–23.

Baglivio, M. T., Wolff, K. T., DeLisi, M., & Jackowski, K. (2020). The role of adverse childhood experiences (ACEs) and psychopathic features on juvenile offending criminal careers to age 18. *Youth Violence and Juvenile Justice*, *18*(4), 337–364.

Baglivio, M. T., Wolff, K. T., Epps, N., & Nelson, R. (2017). Predicting adverse childhood experiences: The importance of neighborhood context in youth trauma among delinquent youth. *Crime & Delinquency*, *63*(2), 166–188.

Baglivio, M. T., Wolff, K. T., Piquero, A. R., & Epps, N. (2015). The relationship between adverse childhood experiences (ACE) and juvenile offending trajectories in a juvenile offender sample. *Journal of Criminal Justice*, *43*, 229–241.

Baglivio, M. T., Zettler, H., Craig, J. M., & Wolff, K. T. (2021). Evaluating RNR-based targeted treatment and intervention dosage in the context of traumatic exposure. *Youth Violence and Juvenile Justice*, *19*(3), 251–276.

Baetz, C L., Branson, C. E., Weinberger, E., Rose, R. E., Petkova, E., Horwitz, S. M., & Hoagwood, E. (2021). The effectiveness of PTSD treatment for adolescents in the juvenile justice system: A systematic review. *Psychological Trauma: Theory, Research, and Policy*. Advance online publication. doi: 10.1037/tra0001073.

Banyard, V., Hamby, S., & Grych, J. (2017). Health effects of adverse childhood experiences: Identifying promising protective factors at the intersection of mental and physical well-being. *Child Abuse & Neglect*, *65*, 88–98.

Barrett, D. E., Katsiyannis, A., Zhang, D., & Zhang, D. (2014). Delinquency and recidivism, A multicohort, matched- control study of the role of early adverse experiences, mental health problems, and disabilities. *Journal of Emotional and Behavioral Disorders*, *22*, 3–15.

Bellis, M. A., Lowey, H., Leckenby, N., Hughes, K., & Harrison, D. (2014). Adverse childhood experiences: Retrospective study to determine their impact on adult health behaviours and health outcomes in a UK population. *Journal of Public Health*, *36*, 81–91.

Bethell, C., Jones, J., Gombojav, N., Linkenbach, J., & Sege, R. (2019). Positive childhood experiences and adult mental and relational health in a statewide sample: Association across adverse childhood experiences levels. *JAMA Pediatrics*, *173*(11), e193007. doi: 10.1001/jamapediatrics.2019.3007

Botvin, G. J., & Griffin, K. W. (2004). Life Skills Training: Empirical findings and future directions. *The Journal of Primary Prevention*, *25*(2), 211–232.

Braga, T., Goncalves, L. C., Basto-Perpeira, M., & Maia, A. (2017). Unraveling the link between maltreatment and juvenile antisocial behavior: A meta-analysis of prospective longitudinal studies. *Aggression and Violent Behavior*, *33*, 37–50.

Brown, D. W., Anda, R. F., Tiemeier, H., Felitti, V. J., Edwards, V. J., Croft, J. B., & Giles, W. H. (2009). Adverse childhood experiences and the risk of premature mortality. *American Journal of Preventive Medicine*, *37*, 389–396.

Browne, A., & Finkelhor, D. (1986). Impact of child sexual abuse: A review of the research. *Psychological Bulletin*, *99*, 66–77.

Cannon, Y., Davis, G., Hsi, A., & Bochte, A. (2016). *Adverse childhood experiences in the New Mexico juvenile justice population*. New Mexico Sentencing Commission.

Centers for Disease Control and Prevention. (2019). *Preventing adverse childhood experiences: Leveraging the best available evidence*. National Center for Injury Prevention and Control, Centers for Disease Control and Prevention.

Chen, W. Y., Propp, J., deLara, E., & Corvo, K. (2011). Child neglect and its association with subsequent juvenile drug and alcohol offense. *Child & Adolescent Social Work Journal*, *28*, 273–290.

Chung, E. K., Mathew, L., Elo, I. T., Coyne, J. C., & Culhane, J. F. (2008). Depressive symptoms in disadvantaged women receiving prenatal care: The influence of adverse and positive childhood experiences. *Ambulatory Pediatrics*, *8*(2), 109–116.

Coulton, C. J., Crampton, D. S., Irwin, M., Spilsbury, J. C., & Korbin, J. E. (2007). How neighborhoods influence child maltreatment: A review of the literature and alternative pathways. *Child Abuse & Neglect*, *31*, 1117–1142.

Craig, J. M., Intravia, J., Wolff, K. T., & Baglivio, M. T. (2019). What can help? Examining levels of substance (non)use as a protective factor in the effect of ACEs on crime. *Youth Violence and Juvenile Justice*, *17*(1), 42–61.

Craig, J. M., Piquero, A. R., Farrington, D. P., & Ttofi, M. M. (2017). A little early risk goes a long way: Adverse childhood experiences and life-course offending in the Cambridge Study. *Journal of Criminal Justice*, *53*, 34–45.

Craig, J. M., Zettler, H. R., Wolff, K. T., & Baglivio, M. T. (2019). Considering the mediating effects of drug and alcohol use, mental health, and their co-occurrence on the adverse childhood experiences-recidivism relationship. *Youth Violence and Juvenile Justice*, *17*(3), 219–240.

Crandall, A., Broadbent, E., Stanfill, M., Magnusson, B. M., Novilla, M. L. B., Hanson, C. L., & Barnes, M. D. (2020). The influence of adverse and advantageous childhood experiences during adolescence on young adult health. *Child Abuse & Neglect*, *108*. doi: 10.1016/j.chiabu.2020.104644

Crandall, A., Miller, J. R., Cheung, A., Novilla, L. K., Glade, R., Novilla, M. L. B., Magnusson, B. M., Leavitt, B. L., Barnes, M. D., & Hanson, C. L. (2019). ACEs and counter-ACEs: How positive and negative childhood experiences influence adult health. *Child Abuse & Neglect*, *96*. doi: 10.1016/j.chiabu.2019.104089

Dannerbeck, A., & Yan, J. (2011). Missouri's crossover youth: Examining the relationship between maltreatment history and their risk of violence. *Journal of Juvenile Justice*, *1*, 78–97.

Dierkhising, C. B., Ko, S. J., Woods- Jaeger, B., Briggs, E. C., Lee, R., & Pynoos, R. S. (2013). Trauma histories among justice- involved youth: Findings from the National Child Traumatic Stress Network. *European Journal of Psychotraumatology*, *4*. doi: 10.3402/ejpt.v4i0.20274.

Dong, M., Anda, R. F., Felitti, V. J., Dube, S. R., Williamson, D. F., Thompson, T. J., Loo, C. M., & Giles, W. H. (2004). The interrelatedness of multiple forms of childhood abuse, neglect, and household dysfunction. *Child Abuse and Neglect*, *28*, 771–784.

Duke, N. N., Pettingell, S. L., McMorris, B. J., & Borowsky, I. W. (2010). Adolescent violence perpetration: Associations with multiple types of adverse childhood experiences. *Pediatrics*, *125*, 778–786.

Eckenrode, J., Campa, M. I., Morris, P. A., Henderson Jr., C. R., Bolger, K. E., Kitzman, H., & Olds, D. L. (2017). The prevention of child maltreatment through the Nurse Family Partnership Program: Mediating effects in a long-term follow-up study. *Child Maltreatment*, *22*(2), 92–99.

English, D., Widom, C., & Brandford, C. (2001). *Childhood victimization and delinquency, adult criminality, and violent criminal behavior: A replication and extension* (NCJ 192291). National Institute of Justice.

Evans-Chase, M. (2014). Addressing trauma and psychosocial development in juvenile justice- involved youth: A synthesis of the developmental neuroscience, juvenile justice and trauma literature. *Laws*, *3*, 744–758.

Fagan, A. A. (2005). The relationship between adolescent physical abuse and criminal offending: Support for an enduring and generalized cycle of violence. *Journal of Family Violence*, *20*, 279–290.

Fang, X., Brown, D. S., Florence, C. S., & Mercy, J. A. (2012). The economic burden of child maltreatment in the United States and implications for prevention. *Child Abuse & Neglect*, *36*, 156–165.

Felitti, V. J., Anda, R. F., Nordenberg, D., Williamson, D. F., Spitz, A. M., Edwards, V., Koss, M. P., & Marks, J. S. (1998). Relationship of childhood abuse and household dysfunction to many of the leading causes of death in adults: The Adverse Childhood Experiences (ACE) study. *American Journal of Preventive Medicine*, *14*(4), 245–258.

Folk, J. B., Ramos, L. M. C., Bath, E. P., Rosen, B., Marshall, B. D. L., Kemp, K., Brown, L., Conrad, S., & Tolou-Shams, M. (2021). The prospective impact of adverse childhood experiences on justice-involved youth's psychiatric symptoms and substance use. *Journal of Consulting and Clinical Psychology*, *89*(6), 483–498.

Fox, B. H., Perez, N., Cass, E., Baglivio, M. T., & Epps, N. (2015). Trauma changes everything: Examining the relationship between adverse childhood experiences and serious, violent, and chronic juvenile offenders. *Child Abuse and Neglect*, *46*, 163–173.

Gunay-Oge, R., Pehlivan, F. Z., & Isikli, S. (2020). The effect of positive childhood experiences on adult personality psychopathology. *Personality and Individual Differences*, *158*. doi: 10.1016/j.paid.2020.109862

Herrera, V. M., & McCloskey, L. A. (2001). Gender differences in the risk for delinquency among youth exposed to family violence. *Child Abuse and Neglect*, *25*, 1037–1051.

Hillis, S. D., Anda, R. F., Dube, S. R., Felitti, V. J., Marchbanks, P. A., Macaluso, M., & Marks, J. S. (2010). The protective effect of family strengths in childhood against adolescent pregnancy and its long-term psychosocial consequences. *Permanente Journal*, *14*(3), 18–27.

Hughes, K., Bellis, M. A., Hardcastle, K. A., Sethi, D., Butchart, A., Miktron, C., Jones, L., & Dunne, M. P. (2017). The effect of multiple adverse childhood experiences on health: A systematic review and meta-analysis. *Lancet Public Health*, *2*, e356–366.

Kowalski, M. A. (2018). Adverse childhood experiences and justice involved youth: The effect of trauma and programming on different recidivistic outcomes. *Youth Violence and Juvenile Justice*, *17*(4), 354–384.

Lenzi, M., Furlong, M. J., Dowdy, E., Sharkey, J., Gini, G., & Altoe, G. (2015). The quantity and variety across domains of psychological and social assets associated with school victimization. *Psychology of Violence*, *5*(4), 411–421.

Liu, S. R., Kia-Keating, M., Nylund-Gibson, K., & Barnett, M. L. (2020). Co-occurring youth profiles of adverse childhood experiences and protective factors: Associations with health, resilience, and racial disparities. *American Journal of Community Psychology*, *65*, 173–186.

Maxfield, M. G., & Widom, C. S. (1996). The cycle of violence: Revisited six years later. *Archives of Pediatric Adolescent Medicine*, *150*, 390–395.

Putnam, F. W., (2006). The impact of trauma on child development. *Juvenile and Family Court Journal*, *57*, 1–11.

Leban, L., & Gibson, C. L. (2020). The role of gender in the relationship between adverse childhood experiences and delinquency and substance use in adolescence. *Journal of Criminal Justice*. Advance online publication, doi.org/10.1016/j.jcrimjus.2019.101637.

Lipsey, M. W. (2009). The primary factors that characterize effective interventions with juvenile offenders: A meta-analytic overview. *Victims and Offenders*, *4*, 124–147.

Loeber, R. (2012). Does the study of the age-crime curve have a future? In R. Loeber & B. C. Welsh (Eds.), *The future of criminology* (pp. 11–19). Oxford University Press.

MacMillan, H. L., Wathen, C. N., Barlow, J., Fergusson, D. M., Leventhal, J. M., & Taussig, H. N. (2009). Interventions to prevent child maltreatment and associated impairment. *The Lancet*, *373*, 250–266

Malvaso, C. G., Delfabbro, P. H., & Day, A. (2019). Adverse childhood experiences in a South Australian sample of young people in detention. Australian and New Zealand *Journal of Criminology*, *52*(3), 411–431.

Malvaso, C. G., Delfabbro, P. H., Day, A., & Nobes, G. (2018). The maltreatment-violence link; Exploring the role of maltreatment experiences and other individual and social risk factors among young people who offend. *Journal of Criminal Justice*, *55*, 35–45.

Mass, C., Herrenkohol, T. I., & Sousa, C. (2008). Review of research on child maltreatment and violence in youth. *Trauma, Violence, & Abuse*, *9*(1), 56–67.

Mersky, J. P., & Topitzes, J. (2010). Comparing early adult outcomes of maltreated and non- maltreated children: A prospective longitudinal investigation. *Children and Youth Services Review*, *36*, 22–29.

Miller, N. A., & Najavatis, L. M. (2012). Creating trauma-informed correctional care: A balance of goals and environment. *European Journal of Psychotraumatology*, *3*, 1–8.

Muniz, C. N., Fox, B., Miley, L. N., DeLisi, M., Cigarran, G. P. II., & Birnbaum, A. (2019). The effects of adverse childhood experiences on internalizing versus externalizing outcomes. *Criminal Justice and Behavior*, *46*(4), 568–589.

Naramore, R., Bright, M. A., Epps, N., & Hardt, N. S. (2017). Youth arrested for trading sex have the highest rates of childhood adversity: A statewide study of juvenile offenders. *Sexual Abuse*, *29*(4), 396–410.

Narvey, C., Yang, J., Wolff, K. T., Baglivio, M. T., & Piquero, A. R. (2021). The relationship between empathy and adverse childhood experiences and their impact on juvenile recidivism. *Youth Violence and Juvenile Justice*, *19*(1), 45–67.

Perez, N. M., Jennings, W. G., & Baglivio, M. T. (2018). A path to serious, violent, chronic delinquency: The harmful aftermath of adverse childhood experiences. *Crime and Delinquency*, *64*, 3–25.

Perez, N. M., Jennings, W. G., Piquero, A. R., & Baglivio, M. T. (2016). Adverse childhood experiences and suicide attempts: The mediating influence of personality development and problem behaviors. *Journal of Youth and Adolescence*, *45*, 1527–1545.

Piquero, A. R., Jennings, W. G., Diamond, B., Farrington, D. P., Tremblay, R. E., Welsh, B. C., & Reingle Gonzalez, J. M. (2016). A meta-analysis update on the effects of early family/parent training programs on antisocial behavior and delinquency. *Journal of Experimental Criminology*, *12*, 229–248.

Reavis, J., Looman, J., Franco, K., & Rojas, B. (2013). Adverse childhood experiences and adult criminality: How long must we live before we possess our own lives? *The Permanente Journal*, *17*, 44–48.

Reid, J. A., Baglivio, M. T., Piquero, A. R., Greenwald, M. A., & Epps, N. (2019). No youth left behind to human trafficking: Exploring profiles of risk. *American Journal of Orthopsychiatry*, *89*, 704–715.

Rivera, B., & Widom, C. S. (1990). Childhood victimization and violent offending. *Violence and Victims*, *5*, 19–35.

Slopen, N., Chen, Y., Guida, J. L., Albert, M. A., & Williams, D. R. (2017). Positive childhood experiences and ideal cardiovascular health in midlife: Associations and mediators. *Preventive Medicine*, *97*, 72–79.

Smith, C., & Thornberry, T. P. (1995). The relationship between childhood maltreatment and adolescent involvement in delinquency. *Criminology*, *33*, 451–477.

Stewart, M., Lutz, L., & Herz, D. H. (2010). *Crossover youth practice model*. Center for Juvenile Justice Reform, Georgetown University McCourt School of Public Policy.

Stienberg, A. M., Brymer, M. J., Kim, S., Ghosh, C., Ostrowski, S. A, Gulley, K., Briggs, E. C., & Pynoos, R. S. (2013). Psychometric properties of the UCLA PTSD Reaction Index. Part 2: Investigating factor structure findings in a national clinic-referred youth sample. *Journal of Traumatic Stress*, *26*, 10–18.

Teague, R., Mazerolle, P., Legosz, M., & Sanderson, J. (2008). Linking childhood exposure to physical abuse and adult offending: Examining mediating factors and gendered relationships. *Justice Quarterly*, *25*, 313–348.

Topitzes, J., Mersky, J. P., & Reynolds, A. J. (2011). Child maltreatment and offending behavior: Gender-specific effects and pathways. *Criminal Justice and Behavior*, *38*(5), 492–510.

Trulson, C. R., Haerle, D., Caudill, J. W., & DeLisi, M. (2016). *Lost causes: Blended sentencing, second chances, and the Texas Youth Commission*. University of Texas Press.

Vitopoulos, N. A., Peterson-Badali, M., Brown, S., & Skilling, T. A. (2018). The Relationship between trauma, recidivism risk, and reoffending in male and female juvenile offenders. *Journal of Child & Adolescent Trauma*, *12*(3), 351–364.

Widom, C. S. (1989a). Child abuse, neglect, and adult behavior: Research design and findings on criminality, violence, and child abuse. *American Journal of Orthopsychiatry*, *59*, 355–367.

Widom, C. S. (1989b). The cycle of violence. *Science*, *244*(4901), 160–166.

Widom, C. S., Fisher, J. H., Nagin, D. S., & Piquero, A. R. (2018). A prospective examination of criminal career trajectories in abused and neglected males and females followed up into middle adulthood. *Journal of Quantitative Criminology*, *34*, 831–852.

Widom, C. S., & Maxfeld, M. G. (2001). *An update on the "cycle of violence."* National Institute of Justice, U.S. Department of Justice.

Wolff, K. T., Baglivio, M. T., Klein, H. J., Piquero, A. R., DeLisi, M., & Howell, J. C. (2020). Adverse childhood experiences and gang involvement among juvenile offenders: Assessing the mediation effects of substance use and temperament deficits. *Youth Violence and Juvenile Justice*, *18*(1), 24–53.

Wolff, K. T., Baglivio, M. T., & Piquero, A. R. (2017). The relationship between adverse childhood experiences and recidivism in a sample of juvenile offenders in community-based treatment. *International Journal of Offender Therapy and Comparative Criminology*, *61*, 1210–1242.

Yu-Ling Chiu, Y. L., Ryan, J. P., & Herz, D. C. (2011). Allegations of maltreatment and delinquency: Does risk of juvenile arrest vary substantiation status? *Children and Youth Services Review*, *33*, 855–860.

Zettler, H. R. (2020). Much to do about trauma: A systematic review of existing trauma-informed treatments on violence and recidivism. *Youth Violence and Juvenile Justice*, *19*(1), 113–134.

Zettler, H. R., Wolff, K. T., Baglivio, M. T., Craig, J. M., & Epps, N. (2018). The racial and gender differences in the impact of adverse childhood experiences on juvenile residential placement. *Youth Violence and Juvenile Justice*, *16*, 319–337.

14

EARLY PSYCHOSOCIAL RISK FACTORS AND IMPLICATIONS FOR PREVENTION

David P. Farrington

Introduction

This chapter aims to review important early psychosocial risk factors for offending and to derive implications for the prevention of offending. The emphasis is on risk factors that are explanatory and changeable. For example, early troublesome behavior is an important risk factor, but it is probably a measure of the same underlying construct as offending (e.g. an antisocial personality) rather than being a cause of offending. As another example, a criminal parent is an important risk factor, but it cannot be easily changed. It may be useful in risk assessment but would not be a feasible target for a prevention program.

The important early risk factors are as follows: 1) high impulsivity and attention deficit-hyperactivity disorder (ADHD), (2) low intelligence and low attainment, (3) low empathy, (4) poor child-rearing and poor parental supervision, (5) child maltreatment and harsh discipline, (6) parental conflict and disrupted families, (7) delinquent peers, (8) socioeconomic deprivation, and (9) poor housing and deprived areas. The most relevant research is based on prospective longitudinal studies, which measure the risk factors in childhood, before the offending occurs.

In discussing each topic, I will first report results from the Cambridge Study in Delinquent Development (CSDD), a prospective longitudinal study of 411 London boys from ages 8 to 61 (Farrington et al., 2021). I will review risk factors measured at age 8–10 that predict convictions between ages 10 and 17 (based on Farrington, 2012). Then I will summarize important narrative reviews of the topic. Then I will summarize important systematic reviews that include a meta-analysis and yield an effect size for the relationship between the risk factor and offending. The emphasis is on general offending, rather than on types of offending such as sex offending.

Unlike the more common narrative reviews, systematic reviews use rigorous methods for locating, appraising, and synthesizing evidence from studies, and they have explicit objectives, explicit criteria for including or excluding studies, and a structured and detailed report (Farrington & Petrosino, 2001). While there are important early reviews (e.g. Hoeve et al., 2009; Leschied et al., 2008), I will focus on relatively recent reviews (published from 2010 onwards). Within the very limited scope of this short chapter, it is only possible to mention a few of the more important findings; for more detailed narrative reviews, see Farrington (2021a), and for more information about systematic reviews of explanatory risk factors, see Farrington et al. (2017a).

DOI: 10.4324/9781003219286-18

Impulsivity and ADHD

In the CSDD, 40% of boys who were rated (by teachers) as lacking in concentration or restless in class were convicted, compared with 22% of the remainder (odds ratio or OR = 2.35; as a rule of thumb, any OR of 2 – a doubling of the odds – or greater indicates a strong effect). Also, 35% of boys who were the most impulsive on psychomotor tests were convicted, compared with 22% of the remainder (OR = 1.91; all ORs are statistically significant).

Aguilar-Carceles and Farrington (2017) published a narrative review of ADHD, impulsivity, and low self-control in relation to offending. Impulsive children are those who are very active and have difficulty in inhibiting behavior and deferring gratification. ADHD includes poor attention, physical restlessness, and acting without considering the consequences. Both are inter-related, and it was concluded that both are related to a variety of antisocial outcomes, including offending. It was argued that the psychological approach of studying risk factors such as impulsivity was preferable to defining a psychiatric syndrome such as ADHD.

Table 14.1 summarizes the results of meta-analyses of risk factors. Tanner-Smith et al. (2018) presented findings for impulsivity at different ages versus offending at different ages, and their average effect size was $r = .14$. Erskine et al. (2016) focused on ADHD, and their average effect size versus arrest was OR = 2.43. This was converted into Cohen's d using the equation Ln (OR) = $d/.5513$ (Lipsey & Wilson, 2001, p. 202) and then into r using $d = 2 \times r/\text{sqrt}(1 - r \times r)$ (Lipsey & Wilson, 2001, p. 200). The r value came to .24.

Table 14.1 Results of Meta-Analyses of Risk Factors

Study	*Risk Factor*	*Outcome*	N	*r*
Tanner-Smith et al. (2018)	Impulsivity	Offending	23	.14
Erskine et al. (2016)	ADHD	Arrest	10	.24
Tanner-Smith et al. (2018)	Low achievement	Offending	47	.11
Scott and Brown (2018)	Educational concerns (M)	Recidivism	5	.13
Scott and Brown (2018)	Educational concerns (F)	Recidivism	5	.10
Van Langen et al. (2014)	Low empathy (C)	Delinquency	30	.21
Van Langen et al. (2014)	Low empathy (A)	Delinquency	30	.09
Tanner-Smith et al. (2018)	Poor parenting	Offending	69	.20
Flanagan et al. (2019)	Poor supervision	Offending	18	.18
Derzon (2010)	Child maltreatment	Offending	8	.21
Braga et al. (2018)	Child maltreatment	Antisocial behavior	18	.18
Derzon (2010)	Parental conflict	Offending	11	.26
Derzon (2010)	Broken home	Offending	25	.10
Tanner-Smith et al. (2018)	Antisocial peers	Offending	100	.32
Scott and Brown (2018)	Antisocial peers (M)	Recidivism	12	.16
Scott and Brown (2018)	Antisocial peers (F)	Recidivism	12	.13
Derzon (2010)	Low SES	Offending	46	.13
Tanner-Smith et al. (2018)	Low SES	Offending	43	.06
Derzon (2010)	Urban housing	Offending	9	.13

Notes:

ADHD = Attention Deficit-Hyperactivity Disorder

(M) = males, (F) = females, (C) = cognitive, (A) affective

SES = socio-economic status

N = No. of effect sizes

These values of *r* indicate quite large effects. To a reasonable approximation, *r* is equal to the difference in proportions between risk and non-risk outcomes in a 2 × 2 table (Farrington & Loeber, 1989). Thus, if 30% of 100 impulsive boys became offenders, compared with 20% of 100 other boys, *r* = .115 (close to the .10 difference in proportions). The observed *r* value of .14 corresponds to 30% of 100 impulsive boys becoming offenders, compared to 18% of 100 other boys, which is a very big difference.

Low Intelligence and Attainment

In the CSDD, 37% of boys with low nonverbal intelligence (on the Progressive Matrices test) became offenders, compared with 21% of the remainder (OR = 2.20); 41% of boys with low attainment (on arithmetic, English, and verbal reasoning tests) became offenders, compared with 20% of the remainder (OR = 2.78). Farrington (2021a) reviewed research on these topics, revealing that, even when it is measured in the first few years of life, low intelligence predicts later delinquency. It was suggested that low IQ could lead to delinquency through the intervening factor of school failure and that a plausible explanatory factor underlying the link between low intelligence and delinquency was the ability to manipulate abstract concepts.

Table 14.1 summarizes the results of the systematic review by Tanner-Smith et al. (2018); the average *r* value for studies relating low achievement to offending was *r* = .11. Unusually, Scott and Brown (2018) reviewed risk factors for recidivism and presented results separately for males and females. For their risk factor of educational concerns, which included low achievement, truancy, and school problems, *r* = .13 for males and *r* = .10 for females.

Low Empathy

This was not measured in the CSDD when the original males were children, but it was measured in the children of the original males using the Basic Empathy Scale (BES) (Farrington & Jolliffe, 2021). The BES measures cognitive empathy, or the ability to understand the emotions of others, and affective empathy, or the ability to experience the emotions of others. Low cognitive and affective empathy scores significantly predicted both convictions and high self-reported offending of females. However, for males, only low cognitive empathy (almost) significantly predicted convictions and high self-reported offending.

The best recent review of empathy versus offending is the systematic review by Van Langen et al. (2014). Based on 30 studies, Cohen's *d* was .43 for cognitive empathy and .19 for affective empathy. These values were transformed into *r* = .21 for cognitive empathy and *r* = .09 for affective empathy. The researchers also found stronger relations for younger rather than older offenders and stronger relations for males rather than for females. Unlike other risk factors reviewed here, there have been few longitudinal studies on low empathy versus later offending.

Child-Rearing and Parental Supervision

In the CSDD, 40% of boys who were poorly supervised became offenders, compared with 21% of the remainder (OR = 2.50). Poor supervision identified parents who had lax rules and poor monitoring and who did not ensure that they knew what the boy was doing when he went out. Flanagan et al. (2019) published a systematic review of parental supervision versus later offending based on longitudinal studies. They reported that 13 out of 18 effect sizes were significant and that the weighted mean Cohen's *d* was .37. This was converted to *r* = .18 in Table 14.1. There was a larger effect size in studies that measured parental knowledge about the child's behavior than in studies that measured parental rules. Tanner-Smith et al. (2018) reviewed studies of poor parenting skills versus offending, and their mean r = .20.

Child Maltreatment and Harsh Discipline

In the CSDD, 36% of boys who received harsh and/or erratic discipline from their parents became offenders, compared with 20% of the remainder (OR = 2.29). Farrington and Malvaso (2019) reviewed ten key longitudinal studies on child maltreatment and physical punishment versus later offending. They went on to show that, in the CSDD, harsh discipline was the strongest predictor of violent offending by the original boys and that physical punishment was the second strongest predictor of violent offending by their sons. Most recently, Heilmann et al. (2021) published a narrative review of prospective studies on physical punishment versus child behavior problems.

In his meta-analytic review of family factors versus criminal and violent behavior, Derzon (2010) reported a weighted mean effect size of r = .21 for child maltreatment versus criminal behavior (see Table 14.1). Braga et al. (2018) published a meta-analysis of longitudinal studies on child maltreatment versus later antisocial behavior. Their weighted mean effect size was OR = 1.96, which translates into d = .37 and r = .18. Also, Carr et al. (2020) published a systematic review of 111 systematic reviews on outcomes of child maltreatment.

Parental Conflict and Disrupted Families

In the CSDD, 35% of boys brought up by disharmonious parents (defined as chronic tension or disagreement on many subjects or raging conflicts) became offenders, compared with 20% of the remainder (OR = 2.15). Also, 39% of boys who were separated from a parent became offenders, compared with 21% of the remainder (OR = 2.34). In his meta-analysis, Derzon (2010) reported a weighted mean effect size of r = .26 for parental discord versus criminal behavior, and r = .10 for broken homes versus criminal behavior. Many studies show that the cause of a broken home is important. For example, an early meta-analysis by Wells and Rankin (1991) found that broken homes were more strongly related to delinquency when they were caused by parental separation or divorce rather than by death.

Delinquent Peers

Peer delinquency was not measured in the CSDD at age 8–10, but the boys were asked about the delinquent acts of their friends at age 14. At this age, 48% of boys with delinquent peers were offenders, compared with 17% of the remainder (OR = 4.29). A very large effect size for delinquent peers is quite typical. However, the key issue is whether delinquent peers are a cause of a boy's delinquency or whether they merely reflect the fact that most offenses at young ages are committed in small groups (Reiss & Farrington, 1991). Because of co-offending, it is very likely that delinquent boys will have delinquent peers.

In the Pittsburgh Youth Study or PYS, which is a prospective longitudinal study from age 7 to age 38 (Ahonen et al., 2021), Farrington et al. (2002) compared predictions between individuals (e.g. comparing peer delinquency with delinquency over all boys at each age) with predictions within individuals (e.g. comparing changes in peer delinquency with changes in delinquency of each boy). If changes within individuals in peer delinquency predict changes within individuals in delinquency, we might conclude that peer delinquency is a cause of delinquency. However, in these analyses peer delinquency correlated with delinquency between individuals but did not predict delinquency within individuals, unlike family factors such as poor parental supervision and low parental reinforcement. Therefore, it was concluded that these family factors were most likely to be causes, whereas peer delinquency was most likely to be an indicator of the boy's offending. However, in similar analyses in Australia, peer delinquency predicted antisocial behavior both between and within individuals (Hemphill et al., 2015).

Tanner-Smith et al. (2018) reviewed research on antisocial peers versus offending. Not surprisingly, their average *r* value of .32 over 100 studies is the largest effect size in Table 14.1. Scott and Brown (2018) reviewed antisocial peers versus recidivism and reported *d* = .32 for males and *d* = .27 for females. These figures were translated into *r* = .16 for males and *r* = .13 for females.

Socioeconomic Deprivation

In the CSDD, 34% of boys from low socioeconomic status (SES) families (i.e. where the family breadwinner had an unskilled manual job) became offenders, compared with 23% of the remainder (OR = 1.73). Also, 41% of boys from low income families became offenders, compared with 21% of the remainder (OR = 2.66). Low income was probably a stronger predictor of offending because some manual jobs (e.g. dockers and printers) were quite well paid at that time in London. Derzon (2010) reviewed family factors and reported that the most extensively examined relationship in the literature was between low SES and criminal behavior, which was reported 533 times in 46 independent samples (total *N* = 133,525). The weighted average *r* = .13. Tanner-Smith et al. (2018) also reviewed studies of low SES versus offending, but their average *r* = .06, which is the weakest relationship in Table 14.1.

Poor Housing and Deprived Areas

In the CSDD, 34% of boys living in poor housing (dilapidated premises) became offenders, compared with 20% of the remainder (OR = 2.04). It has long been known that offenders disproportionately live in inner-city areas characterized by physical deterioration, neighborhood disorganization, and high residential mobility (e.g. Shaw & McKay, 1969). However, the key issue is to what extent the areas themselves influence antisocial behavior (e.g. because high population density causes tension or frustration) and to what extent it is merely the case that antisocial people tend to live in deprived areas (e.g. because of their poverty or public housing policies). In the longitudinal Chicago Youth Development Study, Tolan et al. (2003) concluded that the relationship between community structural characteristics (concentrated poverty, racial heterogeneity, violent crime rate) and individual violence was mediated by parenting practices, gang membership, and peer violence. Derzon (2010) reported an effect size of *r* = .13 for urban housing versus criminal behavior.

Implications for Prevention

After identifying nine major categories of risk factors for offending, the main implications for prevention are that programs should be implemented to try to reduce these risk factors. The principles of "risk-focussed prevention" were set out by Farrington (2000) and Farrington and Welsh (2007). Basically, key risk factors for offending should be identified in longitudinal studies and prevention methods to counteract them should be implemented in experimental studies. There should also be efforts to identify protective factors and to enhance them. Major longitudinal and experimental studies have been reviewed by Farrington (2013), studies designed to prevent offending have been reviewed by Farrington (2021b), and systemic reviews of the effectiveness of prevention programs have been reviewed by Farrington et al. (2017b).

The risk factors of high impulsivity and ADHD can be targeted in child skills training programs. These programs aim to encourage self-control, perspective-taking, and the internal inhibition of antisocial behavior using mainly cognitive-behavioral methods, including group discussions, individual instruction, role-playing exercises, feedback, and homework. Beelman and Lösel (2021) reviewed 113 evaluations of these programs and reported a weighted mean effect size of d = .27. This can be converted into OR = 1.63. If we assume 100 treated and 100 control children and that 25% of control children become offenders, this value of the OR corresponds to 17% of treated children becoming offenders. Therefore, we might conclude that child skills training causes a relative reduction in offending of 32% (8/25).

Low intelligence and low attainment can be targeted in preschool intellectual enrichment programs. The most famous of these programs is the Perry preschool program, carried out in Ypsilanti (Michigan) by Schweinhart and Weikart (1980). The aim of this "plan-do-review" program was to provide intellectual stimulation, to increase thinking and reasoning abilities, and to increase later school achievement. The experimental evaluation of this program found that it reduced arrests up to age 27 by half, and that $7 were saved for every $1 expended on the program (Schweinhart et al., 1993).

Low empathy can be targeted by empathy-enhancing interventions, which have been reviewed by Trivedi-Bateman and Crook (2022). These often include role-playing, modeling, perspective-taking, emotion regulation, prosocial reasoning, and other elements of social-emotional learning programs. Unfortunately, there seems to be no systematic review of the effects of empathy-enhancing interventions on later offending. The success of these interventions in increasing empathy depends on the timing, content, and length of the program, as well as on baseline levels of empathy. Jolliffe and Farrington (2021) reviewed relevant programs and concluded that there had been relatively few randomized trials and that the evaluations had generally not focused on persons with low empathy and had not studied antisocial outcomes. Clearly, more research on the effectiveness of empathy-enhancing interventions is needed.

Poor child-rearing and poor parental supervision can be targeted in parent training programs. These programs aim to train parents to notice what a child is doing, monitor the child's behavior over long periods, clearly state house rules, and make positive and negative reinforcements consistent and contingent on the child's behavior. Piquero et al. (2016) reviewed 76 evaluations of parenting interventions, mostly focusing on parents of children aged 3–8. They reported a weighted mean effect size of OR = 2.03. Assuming as before that there are 100 treated and 100 control children, and that 25% of control children become offenders, this value of the OR corresponds to 14% of treated children becoming offenders. Therefore, we might conclude that parent training causes a relative reduction in offending of 44% (11/25).

Child maltreatment and harsh discipline can be targeted in home visiting programs for women in pregnancy and the first 2 years of a child's life. In the most famous nurse–family partnership (NFP) program, the home visitors (nurses) gave advice about prenatal and postnatal care of the child, infant development, the importance of proper nutrition, and avoiding smoking, drinking, and drug use. The results of an experimental evaluation in Elmira (NY) showed that the home visits caused a decrease in recorded child abuse and neglect and a decrease in convictions, especially of daughters (Eckenrode et al., 2010). A replication experiment in Memphis (TN) yielded similar results, including fewer convictions, especially of daughters (Kitzman et al., 2019).

Parental conflict and disrupted families can be targeted by functional family therapy (FFT), which was developed to target families where there is a lot of conflict between individuals. This aimed to modify patterns of family interaction by modeling, prompting, and reinforcement; to encourage clear communication between family members of requests and solutions to problems; and to minimize conflict. Essentially, all family members were trained to negotiate effectively, to set clear rules about privileges and responsibilities, and to use techniques of reciprocal reinforcement with each other. Hartnett et al. (2017) published a meta-analysis of the effectiveness of FFT on offending and antisocial outcomes, based on 14 studies. My estimate is that the weighted average *d* value = .44, which transforms to OR = 2.22. Assuming as before that there are 100 treated and 100 control children, and that 25% of control children become offenders, this value of the OR corresponds to 13% of treated children becoming offenders. Therefore, it might be concluded that FFT causes a relative reduction in offending of 48% (12/25).

Delinquent peers could be addressed in mentoring programs. Community-based mentoring programs usually involve non-professional adult volunteers spending time with young people at risk of delinquency or other social problems. The mentors behave in a supportive, non-judgmental way while acting as role models. Tolan et al. (2014) carried out a systematic review of the effects of mentoring programs and estimated the effectiveness of mentoring on delinquency based on 25 evaluations. Overall, the effect on delinquency was summarized as *d* = .21, which converts into OR = 1.46, and a 25.6% relative reduction in offending, from 25% in the control group to 18.6% in the treated group. The effects were greater for programs that emphasized emotional support and advocacy rather than teaching and modeling.

Socioeconomic deprivation could be targeted by vocational education and training programs to improve employment prospects. The effects of these programs on offenders have been reviewed (e.g. Newton et al., 2018). However, I have not found a systematic review of the effects of these programs on the children of the targeted adults.

Finally, Communities That Care (CTC) can help people in poor housing or in deprived areas (Fagan et al., 2019). CTC is typically implemented in large public housing estates. The first step is to set up a community board that assesses key risk factors in the community that need to be tackled and key protective factors that need to be enhanced. Then the community board assesses existing resources and, with specialist technical assistance and guidance, develops a plan of intervention strategies. The strategies can include home visiting, preschool programs, parent training, child skills training, anti-bullying programs in schools, situational prevention, and policing strategies. The effectiveness of CTC has been demonstrated in a large-scale experiment in which 24 U.S. communities were placed into 12 matched pairs, and one community in each pair was chosen at random to receive CTC. Over 4,000 students were followed up from grade 5 (ages 10–11) to age 23. The program caused reductions in antisocial behavior and drug use, and $12.88 were saved for every $1 expended (Kuklinski et al., 2021).

Conclusions

This chapter has reviewed nine important categories of risk factors for offending and interventions that can target them in risk-focused prevention. The time is ripe for governments in all countries to mount an ambitious program of risk-focused prevention based on these results. Taking account of prior research (e.g. Welsh et al., 2015), I am confident that the financial benefits of such a program would greatly exceed its financial costs.

References

Aguilar-Carceles, M. M., & Farrington, D. P. (2017). Attention deficit hyperactivity disorder, impulsivity, and low self-control: Which is most useful in understanding offending? *Crime Psychology Review*, *3*, 1–22 [Reprinted in D. Canter & D. Youngs (Eds., 2021), *Reviewing crime psychology* (pp. 218–239). Abingdon, UK: Routledge].

Ahonen, L., Farrington, D. P., Pardini, D. A., & Stouthamer-Loeber, M. (2021). Cohort profile: The Pittsburgh Youth Study (PYS). *Journal of Developmental and Life-Course Criminology*, *7*, 481–523.

Beelman, A., & Lösel, F. (2021). A comprehensive meta-analysis of randomized evaluations of the effect of child social skills training on antisocial development. *Journal of Developmental and Life-Course Criminology*, *7*, 41–65.

Braga, T., Cunha, O., & Maia, A. (2018). The enduring effect of maltreatment on antisocial behavior: A meta-analysis. *Aggression and Violent Behavior*, *40*, 91–100.

Carr, A., Duff, H., & Craddock, F. (2020). A systematic review of reviews of the outcome of noninstitutional child maltreatment. *Trauma, Violence, and Abuse*, *21*, 828–843.

Derzon, J. H. (2010). The correspondence of family features with problem, aggressive, criminal, and violent behavior: A meta-analysis. *Journal of Experimental Criminology*, *6*, 263–292.

Eckenrode, J., Campa, M., Luckey, D. W., Henderson, C. R., Cole, R., Kitzman, H., . . . Olds, D. (2010). Long-term effects of prenatal and infancy nurse home visitation on the life course of youths: 19-year follow-up of a randomized trial. *Archives of Pediatrics and Adolescent Medicine*, *164*, 9–15.

Erskine, H. E., Norman, R. E., Ferrari, A. J., Chan, G. C. K., Copeland, W. E., Whiteford, H. A., & Scott, J. G. (2016). Long-term outcomes of attention-deficit/hyperactivity disorder and conduct disorder: A systematic review and meta-analysis. *Journal of the American Academy of Child and Adolescent Psychiatry*, *55*, 841–850.

Fagan, A. A., Hawkins, J. D., Catalano, R. F., & Farrington, D. P. (2019). *Communities that care: Building community engagement and capacity to prevent youth behavior problems*. Oxford University Press.

Farrington, D. P. (2000). Explaining and preventing crime: The globalization of knowledge – The American Society of Criminology 1999 Presidential Address. *Criminology*, *38*, 1–24.

Farrington, D. P. (2012). Childhood risk factors for young adult offending: Onset and persistence. In F. Lösel, A. Bottoms, & D. P. Farrington (Eds.), *Young adult offenders: Lost in transition?* (pp. 48–64). Routledge.

Farrington, D. P. (2013). Longitudinal and experimental research in criminology. In M. Tonry (Ed.), *Crime and justice in America 1975–2025* (pp. 453–527). University of Chicago Press.

Farrington, D. P. (2021a). The developmental evidence base: Psychosocial research. In D. A. Crighton & G. J. Towl (Eds.), *Forensic psychology* (3rd ed., pp. 294–329). Wiley.

Farrington, D. P. (2021b). The developmental evidence base: Prevention. In D. A. Crighton & G. J. Towl (Eds.) *Forensic psychology* (3rd ed., pp. 263–293). Wiley.

Farrington, D. P., Gaffney, H., Lösel, F., & Ttofi, M. M. (2017b). Systematic reviews of the effectiveness of developmental prevention programs in reducing delinquency, aggression and bullying. *Aggression and Violent Behavior*, *33*, 91–106.

Farrington, D. P., Gaffney, H., & Ttofi, M. M. (2017a). Systematic reviews of explanatory risk factors for violence, offending, and delinquency. *Aggression and Violent Behavior*, *33*, 24–36.

Farrington, D. P., & Jolliffe, D. (2021). Empathy, convictions and self-reported offending of males and females in the Cambridge study in delinquent development. In D. Jolliffe & D. P. Farrington (Eds.), *Empathy versus offending, aggression and bullying: Advancing knowledge using the Basic Empathy Scale* (pp. 77–88). Routledge.

Farrington, D. P., Jolliffe, D., & Coid, J. W. (2021). Cohort profile: The Cambridge Study in Delinquent Development (CSDD). *Journal of Developmental and Life-Course Criminology*, *7*, 278–291.

Farrington, D. P., & Loeber, R. (1989). Relative improvement over chance (RIOC) and phi as measures of predictive efficiency and strength of association in 2 × 2 tables. *Journal of Quantitative Criminology*, *5*, 201–213.

Farrington, D. P., Loeber, R., Yin, Y., & Anderson, S. J. (2002). Are within-individual causes of delinquency the same as between-individual causes? *Criminal Behaviour and Mental Health*, *12*, 53–68.

Farrington, D. P., & Malvaso, C. G. (2019). Physical punishment and offending in two successive generations of males. In I. Bryce, Y. Robinson, & W. Petherick (Eds.), *Child abuse and neglect: Forensic issues in evidence, impact and management* (pp. 203–224). Academic Press.

Farrington, D. P., & Petrosino, A. (2001). The Campbell collaboration crime and justice group. *Annals of the American Academy of Political and Social Science*, *578*, 35–49.
Farrington, D. P., & Welsh, B. C. (2007). *Saving children from a life of crime: Early risk factors and effective interventions*. Oxford University Press.
Flanagan, I. M. L., Auty, K. M., & Farrington, D. P. (2019). Parental supervision and later offending: A systematic review of longitudinal studies. *Aggression and Violent Behavior*, *47*, 215–229.
Hartnett, D., Carr, A., Hamilton, E., & O'Reilly, G. (2017). The effectiveness of Functional Family Therapy for adolescent behavioral and substance misuse problems: A meta-analysis. *Family Process*, *56*, 607–619.
Heilmann, A., Mehay, A., Watt, R. G., Kelly, Y., Durrant, J. E., Van Turnhout, J., & Gershoff, E. T. (2021). Physical punishment and child outcomes: A narrative review of prospective studies. *Lancet*, *398*(10297), 355–364.
Hemphill, S. A., Heerde, J. A., Herrenkohl, T. I., & Farrington, D. P. (2015). Within-individual versus between-individual predictors of antisocial behaviour: A longitudinal study of young people in Victoria, Australia. *Australian and New Zealand Journal of Criminology*, *48*, 429–445.
Hoeve, M., Dubas, J. S., Eichelsheim, V. I., Van Der Laan, P. H., Smeenk, W., & Gerris, J. R. M. (2009). The relationship between parenting and delinquency: A meta-analysis. *Journal of Abnormal Child Psychology*, *37*, 749–775.
Jolliffe, D., & Farrington, D. P. (2021). Empathy and offending, aggression and bullying: Taking stock and moving forward. In D. Jolliffe & D. P. Farrington (Eds.), *Empathy versus offending, aggression and bullying: Advancing knowledge using the Basic Empathy Scale* (pp. 239–254). Routledge.
Kitzman, H., Olds, D. L., Knudtson, M. D., Cole, R., Anson, A., Smith, J. A., . . . Conti, G. (2019). Prenatal and infancy nurse home visiting and 18-year outcomes of a randomized trial. *Pediatrics*, *144*, 82–94.
Kuklinski, M. R., Oesterle, S., Briney, J. S., & Hawkins, J. D. (2021). Long-term impacts and benefit-cost analysis of the communities that care prevention system at age 23, 12 years after baseline. *Prevention Science*, *22*, 452–463.
Leschied, A., Chiodo, D., Nowicki, E., & Rodger, S. (2008). Childhood predictors of adult criminality: A meta-analysis drawn from the prospective longitudinal literature. *Canadian Journal of Criminology and Criminal Justice*, *50*, 435–467.
Lipsey, M. W., & Wilson, D. B. (2001). *Practical meta-analysis*. Sage.
Newton, D., Day, A., Giles, M., Wokak, J., Graffam, J., & Baldry, E. (2018). The impact of vocational education and training programs on recidivism: A systematic review of current experimental evidence. *International Journal of Offender Therapy and Comparative Criminology*, *62*, 187–207.
Piquero, A., Jennings, W. G., Diamond, B., Farrington, D. P., Tremblay, R. E., Welsh, B. C., & Gonzalez, J. M. R. (2016). A meta-analysis update on the effects of early family/parent training programs on antisocial behavior and delinquency. *Journal of Experimental Criminology*, *12*, 229–248.
Reiss, A. J., & Farrington, D. P. (1991). Advancing knowledge about co-offending: Results from a prospective longitudinal survey of London males. *Journal of Criminal Law and Criminology*, *82*, 360–395.
Schweinhart, L. J., Barnes, H. V., & Weikart, D. P. (1993). *Significant benefits: The high/scope Perry preschool Study through age 27*. High/Scope Press.
Schweinhart, L. J., & Weikart, D. P. (1980). *Young children grow up: The effects of the Perry preschool program on youths through age 15*. High/Scope Press.
Scott, T., & Brown, S. L. (2018). Risks, strengths, gender, and recidivism among justice-involved youth: A meta-analysis. *Journal of Consulting and Clinical Psychology*, *86*, 931–945.
Shaw, C. R., & McKay, H. D. (1969). *Juvenile delinquency and urban areas*, Rev. ed. University of Chicago Press.
Tanner-Smith, E. E., Wilson, S. J., & Lipsey, M. W. (2018). Risk factors and crime. In F. T. Cullen & P. Wilcox (Eds.), *The Oxford handbook of criminological theory* (pp. 1–42). Oxford University Press.
Tolan, P. H., Gorman-Smith, D., & Henry, D. B. (2003). The developmental ecology of urban males' youth violence. *Developmental Psychology*, *39*, 274–291.
Tolan, P. H., Henry, D. B., Schoeny, M., Lovegrove, P., & Nichols, E. (2014). Mentoring programs to affect delinquency and associated outcomes of youth at risk: A comprehensive meta-analytic review. *Journal of Experimental Criminology*, *10*, 179–206.
Trivedi-Bateman, N., & Crook, E. L. (2022). The optimal application of empathy interventions to reduce antisocial behavior and crime: A review of the literature. *Psychology, Crime and Law*, *28*, 769–819.

Van Langen, M. A. M., Wissink, I. B., Van Vugt, E. S., Van Der Stouwe, T., & Stams, G. J. J. M. (2014). The relation between empathy and offending: A meta-analysis. *Aggression and Violent Behavior*, *19*, 179–189.

Wells, L. E., & Rankin, J. H. (1991). Families and delinquency: A meta-analysis of the impact of broken homes. *Social Problems*, *38*, 71–93.

Welsh, B. C., Farrington, D. P., & Raffan Gowar, B. (2015). Benefit-cost analysis of crime prevention programs. In M. Tonry (Ed.), *Crime and justice* (vol. 44, pp. 447–516). University of Chicago Press.

15

REVISITING THE ROLE OF SANCTION RISK PERCEPTIONS IN DETERRENCE POLICY

Timothy C. Barnum and Greg Pogarsky

> People do not make choices in a vacuum. They make them in an environment where many features, noticed and unnoticed, can influence their decisions.
>
> – *Thaler et al. (2010, p. 428)*

Introduction

The effectiveness of some crime control strategies depends on the fundamental assumption that people change their behavior in response to sanction threats. That is, differences in individual offending are related to differences in perceived arrest risk – as people perceive the chances of getting caught for offending increase, their likelihood or rate of offending should decrease. Research consistently demonstrates a negative correlation between sanction risk perceptions and lawbreaking (see Apel, 2022; Chalfin & McCrary, 2017; Nagin, 2013; Paternoster, 2010, for reviews). However, as Nagin (1998, p. 5) observed, "The conclusion that crime decisions are affected by sanction risk perceptions is not a sufficient condition for concluding that policy can deter crime. Unless the perceptions themselves are manipulable by policy, the desired deterrent effect will not be achieved". Put simply, sanction risk perceptions must be *grounded in reality* for deterrence to occur.

This straightforward idea has generated substantial debate, especially regarding the theoretical and practical meaning of a risk–crime relationship (see, e.g., Apel, 2013, 2022; Braga & Apel, 2016; Kleck, 2016; Lochner, 2007; Loughran et al., 2012; Nagin, 1998, 2016; Pickett & Roche, 2016; Pogarsky & Loughran, 2016). Adding to the challenges, research on interventions such as hotspot policing or situational crime prevention is often evaluative – it asks by how much, if at all, do certain interventions affect crime rates? To refocus attention on the influence sanction risk perceptions have on offending, we address two questions: Are sanction risk perceptions anchored in reality? And if so, how are recent insights on this issue leverageable to inform crime prevention efforts?

DOI: 10.4324/9781003219286-19

Are Sanction Risk Perceptions Grounded in Reality?

At its core, the deterrence perspective is grounded in information. Geerken & Gove (1974, p. 498) reasoned that:

> only analysis of all the sources of information about risk and severity of punishment and how they are related to social environment, crime rate, and the actual risk and severity of punishment will enable us to understand how punishment relates to crime in a real society.

Therefore, it is essential to understand the *formation and maintenance* of sanction risk perceptions to manipulate them for crime control.

Research has highlighted the responsiveness of sanction risk perceptions to two distinct sources of information as evidence for their grounding in reality. The first concerns personal and vicarious experience with avoiding or experiencing the consequences of crime (see Horney & Marshall, 1992; Pogarsky et al., 2005; Pogarsky & Piquero, 2003; Stafford & Warr, 1993). Empirical research consistently finds that apprehension for a crime increases perceived risk, whereas escaping apprehension for a crime reduces it, and in turn, these "updated" risk perceptions shape behavior (Anwar & Loughran, 2011; Lochner, 2007; Loughran et al., 2016; Wilson et al., 2017; see also Apel, 2013, 2022).

Beyond personal and/or vicarious experiences with punishment for a crime, contextual features of offending opportunities also influence risk perceptions. For example, Thomas et al. (2018) showed that people *coherently* rank the relative sanction risk of different crime types based on their severity. For example, the authors demonstrated that participants consistently rated the likelihood of apprehension higher for violent crimes such as assault and murder compared to lower-level crimes like marijuana use. Importantly, this pattern held even after exposure to arbitrary information that biased absolute risk estimates for each crime type. The key point for deterrence is not the error entailed in point estimates of risk but rather that people accurately *rank* crimes based on their potential for apprehension (see Pogarsky & Loughran, 2016). The groundedness of sanction risk perceptions becomes further evident from comparing sanction risk perceptions for the same offense but under different objective circumstances.

On this point, Barnum et al. (2021) extended Thomas et al.'s (2018) findings beyond comparisons across crime types to person-specific factors, such as the susceptibility to cognitive biases, personality characteristics, private information, *and* a coherence component defined by observable features of a criminal opportunity. To test this model, the authors surveyed experienced drivers who rated three videos of a car speeding on an interstate highway with a 70-mph speed limit. The videos manipulated three circumstances related to the probability of receiving a ticket: the driving speed (76, 82, and 86 mph), traffic flow (getting passed, driving with traffic, and passing traffic), and information regarding police activity (no information versus heightened enforcement). The results showed that estimates of the chances of getting ticketed were strongly tied to all three manipulated features of the videos. Specifically, participants perceived a low probability of being ticketed in situations where speeding was minimal, traffic conditions were favorable (e.g., getting passed or driving with traffic), and police enforcement was not mentioned. As circumstances became riskier for the driver – increased speeds, passing traffic, and heightened police presence – reported probabilities of sanctioning significantly increased. This pattern also emerged for perceptions of safety and intentions to speed.[1] The authors also had state troopers, who enforce the very traffic laws drivers must navigate, rate the same experimental videos based on the probability they would stop and ticket the car depicted in the video. There was substantial correspondence between civilian and officer evaluations such that *all* comparisons in risk estimates between groups were statistically insignificant. Given that sanction risk perceptions are grounded in reality, the next question is how to leverage this for public policy.

- Sanction risk perceptions relate negatively to personal experience with punishment avoidance, and positively with personal experience being punished.
- Sanction risk perceptions vary in common sense ways with observable features of an offending opportunity.
- Sanction risk perceptions of citizen drivers and police officers are strongly aligned, thus promoting the effectiveness of strategies to reduce speeding on highways.

Policy Implications for the Coherence of Sanction Risk Perceptions

The coherent, albeit imperfect, grounding of sanction risk perceptions in reality underlies various crime control strategies across different settings. Offenders are punished after committing a crime to deter future offending and motivate desistance, in part by raising their sanction risk perceptions (Thomas & Vogel, 2019). Area-based interventions such as hotspot policing and target hardening also seek to reduce crime by increasing the risks associated with offending (Braga et al., 2020; Clarke & Cornish, 1985). Although these interventions have had some success in reducing crimes, important criticisms remain. Foremost among these is that such interventions invariably target already disadvantaged persons, thus exacerbating friction between citizens and law enforcement while perpetuating further socioeconomic hardships.

Beyond this, closer attention is warranted to the *interrelated* influence of individual and contextual factors on deterrence. This often involves *ambiguity* in crime risk perception, which reflects second-order uncertainty over how sure someone is of their sanction risk estimate to begin with. (Casey & Scholz, 1991; Loughran et al., 2011; Nagin, 1998; Pickett & Bushway, 2015). Scholars have theorized that equivocation or ambiguity about the likelihood of punishment, all else constant, can enhance deterrent effects (Loughran et al., 2011; Nagin, 1998). For example, Sherman (1990) advocated for increasing police presence unpredictably in high-crime areas with no degradation in average sanction certainty to bolster deterrent effects.

Barnum and Nagin (2021) recently examined this question by integrating their model of idiosyncratically coherent risk perceptions from Barnum et al. (2021) with the model of target selection explicated in Nagin et al. (2015). The experimental paradigm was augmented to query respondents about their level of assuredness in estimating the risk of being sanctioned. The authors found that both sanction risk and perceived ambiguity independently deterred speeding. Interestingly, the effect of ambiguity on intent depended on the level of perceived risk, a phenomenon referred to as a *boundary effect* (Casey & Scholz, 1991; Loughran et al., 2011). The idea is that ambiguity prompts people to treat a sanction certainty estimate as if it were closer to the middle of the probability continuum than it objectively is. That is, ambiguity causes people to treat high-probability estimates as if they were lower and low estimates as if they were higher. Consistent with this, Barnum and Nagin (2021) found that participants who estimated a low probability of being sanctioned but were highly ambiguous about this estimate were the *least* likely to speed, demonstrating aversive behavior despite minimal risk. On the other hand, highly ambiguous estimates of higher sanction risk had the least deterrent impact, demonstrating *ambiguity seeking* behavior despite the relatively higher chance of being sanctioned (see also Casey & Scholz, 1991; Loughran et al., 2011). Thus, ambiguity about sanction certainty can lead to seemingly "irrational" behaviors – abstaining from crime when arrest risk is low while engaging in crime when arrest risk is very high.

The finding that ambiguity about perceived sanction threats produces a boundary effect on behavior has important implications for Sherman's (1990) original thesis. That is, generating ambiguity for prevention policies should be done only under certain circumstances. For example, the findings of Barnum and Nagin (2021) and others (Casey & Scholz, 1991; Loughran et al., 2011) suggest that generating ambiguity should be reserved for circumstances where the attendant level of arrest risk is ostensibly low, which is the case for many crime types (see Apel, 2013). Consider efforts aimed at deterring alcohol-impaired driving (DUI), a prototypical low-risk offending opportunity. Interventions to limit impaired driving in the United States are costly and typically involve many police officers, some on overtime status. Ambiguous messaging about sobriety checkpoints, regarding location, time of day, and day of the week can enhance such interventions without necessitating more time and resources.

In contrast, when the perceived detection rate is already high, Barnum and Nagin (2021; see also Casey & Scholz, 1991; Loughran et al., 2011) show that *reducing* ambiguity from the decision environment enhances deterrence. Midgette et al. (2021) recently evaluated the 24/7 Sobriety Program, which was designed to reduce alcohol and other drug consumption through high-frequency testing with the threat of incarceration for a failed test. The authors compared the program across two states with different implementation strategies. In South Dakota, *any* detected level of alcohol on a breathalyzer test was a violation, thus leaving no ambiguity about sanction risk. In Montana, the violation threshold is 0.02, producing greater ambiguity than in South Dakota about whether drinking will produce a failed test. Midgette et al. (2021) found that, compared to their South Dakota counterparts, Montana participants were 28% *more* likely to violate the terms of probation. This suggests that uncertainty around the breathalyzer test prompts participants to perceive they have "better" odds to successfully offend despite the near certain chance of apprehension.

- Generating ambiguity about sanction threats can be an effective and potentially less invasive crime prevention strategy.
- Additional deterrence is achievable for crimes with naturally low apprehension risk (e.g., DUI) by generating ambiguity through strategies such as randomized patrols.
- In contrast, for crimes with naturally high levels of apprehension risk (e.g., probation or parole violation, policies should minimize ambiguity in criminal justice messaging.

This research underscores that "blanket" policy interventions are often counterproductive because they disregard situational considerations. This is even evident from research on active offenders, such as burglars, terrorists, and drug dealers, who are both more skilled and more motivated than criminally less experienced respondents in studies of sanction risk perception. These atypical offenders tend to underestimate and are less sensitive to sanction threats during offending opportunities and thus respond differently to deterrence strategies (e.g., Nee et al., 2019; Deitzer et al., 2021). For example, Dugan et al. (2005) found that although efforts to deter hijacking such as metal detectors and law enforcement at passenger checkpoints generally reduced future attacks, the effects were strongest for *non-terrorist* hijackings.

Under such circumstances, interventions are needed that reinforce specific targets in which only certain types of offenders victimize (Clarke & Cornish, 1985; Clarke & Newman, 2006;

Nagin et al., 2015). Such specialized target hardening tactics could include impenetrable bank vaults to deter "professional" bank robbers or fulltime security guards to protect vandalization of targets by politically motivated offenders (e.g., farmhouses, abortion clinics, etc.). Large-scale deterrence tactics aimed at the public may keep perceived sanction threats high enough to deter the casual offender. But additional, targeted approaches are needed to increase the perceived sanction threats of experienced, skilled, and highly motivated offenders (Gibbs, 1975; Jacobs, 2010; Pogarsky, 2002). Put differently, to achieve deterrence among this population of offenders, the policy specifics must correspond to their level of motivation and skill.

Another suggestion for leveraging recent insights on sanction risk perceptions for broader but still "targeted" crime control involves *social interaction effects*, or "interdependencies among individuals in which the preferences, beliefs, and constraints faced by one person are directly influenced by the characteristics and choices of others" (Durlauf & Ioannides, 2010, p. 452). This notion offers an additional lever for crime control beyond directly targeting the objective risk for sanctioning (see, e.g., Barnum & Pogarsky, 2021; Pogarsky & Herman, 2019). Several social interventions have emphasized the potential harm certain behaviors have on other community members (e.g., the "don't mess with Texas" campaign against littering; see, e.g., Thaler and Sunstein, 2009, p. 61). Other campaigns highlight accurate statistics of problematic behaviors, such as the true incident rate of binge drinking on college campuses. These interventions indirectly affect behavior by attempting to "realign" perceptual correspondence and attitudes about specific crimes through changes in the way people interact and exchange information (e.g., Sirakaya, 2006). As well, such interventions may be less prone to perpetuate cumulative disadvantages (e.g., Sampson & Sharkey, 2008; Sampson & Laub, 1993).

- Policy makers should refrain from "blanket" or "one-size-fits-all" approaches to crime control.
- Characteristics of potential targets, such as those with politically charged elements, often motivate victimization despite intervention strategies, such as cameras and security guards, designed to increase apprehension risk.
- Experienced criminal offenders are often less responsive to sanction threats and thus less likely to be deterred by broad policy interventions.
- Crime control might also come from social nudges that realign people's perceptions by highlighting the potential social and personal consequences of their behavior.

Conclusion

When designing, implementing, and evaluating deterrence-based policy, it is important to remember that intentional action is best understood in *context* (e.g., Coleman, 1986; Matsueda, 2017; Nagin & Sampson, 2019). In this light, researchers should consider the way individual and situational factors shape sanction risk perceptions and decision processes generally rather than treating these two inputs as "ships that pass in the night" (Short, 1998, p. 3). Deterrence and rational choice perspectives offer a theoretical foundation to blend micro and macro-sociological concepts (Matsueda, 2017). This is likely to enrich our understanding of this critical decision mechanism – perceived sanction threats. All told, people are generally though imperfectly responsive to sanction threats, and the individual and contextual sources of these threats offer important avenues for manipulating sanction risk perceptions to reduce crime.

Note

1 Further underscoring the coherence of risk perceptions, the results showed that safety perceptions were unaffected by assignment to the heightened enforcement condition, a situational factor that, unlike risk of detection, is objectively unrelated to safety.

References

Anwar, S., & Loughran, T. A. (2011). Testing a Bayesian learning theory of deterrence among serious juvenile offenders. *Criminology*, *49*(3), 667–698.

Apel, R. (2013). Sanctions, perceptions, and crime: Implications for criminal deterrence. *Journal of Quantitative Criminology*, *29*(1), 67–101.

Apel, R. (2022). Sanctions, perceptions, and crime. *Annual Review of Criminology*, *5*, 205–227.

Barnum, T. C., & Nagin, D. S. (2021). Ambiguity and legal compliance. *Criminology & Public Policy*, *20*(4), 621–643.

Barnum, T. C., Nagin, D. S., & Pogarsky, G. (2021). Sanction risk perceptions, coherence, and deterrence. *Criminology*, *59*(2), 195–223.

Braga, A. A., & Apel, R. (2016). And we wonder why criminology is sometimes considered irrelevant in real-world policy conversations. *Criminology & Public Policy*, *15*, 813.

Braga, A. A., Barao, L. M., Zimmerman, G. M., Douglas, S., & Sheppard, K. (2020). Measuring the direct and spillover effects of body worn cameras on the civility of police-citizen encounters and police work activities. *Journal of Quantitative Criminology*, *36*(4), 851–876.

Casey, J. T., & Scholz, J. T. (1991). Boundary effects of vague risk information on taxpayer decisions. *Organizational Behavior and Human Decision Processes*, *50*(2), 360–394.

Chalfin, A., & McCrary, J. (2017). Criminal deterrence: A review of the literature. *Journal of Economic Literature*, *55*(1), 5–48.

Clarke, R. V. G., & Cornish, D. B. (1985). Modeling offenders' decisions: A framework for research and policy. *Crime and Justice*, *6*, 147–185.

Clarke, R. V. G., & Newman, G. R. (2006). *Outsmarting the terrorists*. Greenwood Publishing Group.

Coleman, J. S. (1986). Social theory, social research, and a theory of action. *American Journal of Sociology*, *91*(6), 1309–35.

Deitzer, J. R., Leban, L., Copes, H., & Wilcox, S. (2021). Criminal self-efficacy and perceptions of risk and reward among women methamphetamine manufacturers. *Justice Quarterly*, 1–24.

Dugan, L., LaFree, G., & Piquero, A. R. (2005). Testing a rational choice model of airline hijackings. *Criminology*, *43*(4), 1031–1065.

Durlauf, S. N., & Ioannides, Y. M. (2010). Social interactions. *Annual Review of Economics*, *2*(1), 451–478.

Gibbs, J. P. (1975). *Crime, punishment, and deterrence*. Elsevier.

Geerken, M. R., & Gove, W. R. (1974). Deterrence: Some theoretical considerations. *Law & Society Review*, *9*, 497.

Horney, J., & Marshall, I. H. (1992). Risk perceptions among serious offenders: The role of crime and punishment. *Criminology*, *30*(4), 575–594.

Jacobs, B. A. (2010). Deterrence and deterrability. *Criminology*, *48*(2), 417–441.

Kleck, G. (2016). Objective risks and individual perceptions of those risks. Criminology & Public Policy, 15, 767.

Lochner, L. (2007). Individual perceptions of the criminal justice system. *American Economic Review*, *97*(1), 444–460.

Loughran, T. A., Paternoster, R., Chalfin, A., & Wilson, T. (2016). Can rational choice be considered a general theory of crime? Evidence from individual-level panel data. *Criminology*, *54*(1), 86–112.

Loughran, T. A., Paternoster, R., Piquero, A. R., & Pogarsky, G. (2011). On ambiguity in perceptions of risk: Implications for criminal decision making and deterrence. *Criminology*, *49*(4), 1029–1061.

Loughran, T. A., Pogarsky, G., Piquero, A. R., & Paternoster, R. (2012). Re-examining the functional form of the certainty effect in deterrence theory. *Justice Quarterly*, *29*(5), 712–741.

Matsueda, R. L. (2017). Toward an analytical criminology: The micro–macro problem, causal mechanisms, and public policy. *Criminology*, *55*(3), 493–519.

Midgette, G., Loughran, T. A., & Tahamont, S. (2021). The impact of ambiguity-induced error in offender decision-making: Evidence from the field. *Journal of Research in Crime and Delinquency*, *58*(6), 635–665.

Nagin, D. S. (1998). Criminal deterrence research at the outset of the twenty-first century. *Crime and Justice*, *23*, 1–42.
Nagin, D. S. (2013). Deterrence in the twenty-first century. *Crime and Justice*, *42*(1), 199–263.
Nagin, D. S. (2016). What we've got here is failure to communicate. *Criminology & Public Policy, 15*, 753.
Nagin, D. S., & Sampson, R. J. (2019). The real gold standard: measuring counterfactual worlds that matter most to social science and policy. *Annual Review of Criminology*, 2, 123–145.
Nagin, D. S., Solow, R. M., & Lum, C. (2015). Deterrence, criminal opportunities, and police. *Criminology*, *53*(1), 74–100.
Nee, C., van Gelder, J. L., Otte, M., Vernham, Z., & Meenaghan, A. (2019). Learning on the job: Studying expertise in residential burglars using virtual environments. *Criminology*, *57*(3), 481–511.
Paternoster, R. (2010). How much do we really know about criminal deterrence?. *The Journal of Criminal Law and Criminology*, 765–824.
Pickett, J. T., & Bushway, S. D. (2015). Dispositional sources of sanction perceptions: Emotionality, cognitive style, intolerance of ambiguity, and self-efficacy. *Law and Human Behavior*, *39*(6), 624.
Pickett, J. T., & Roche, S. P. (2016). Arrested development: Misguided directions in deterrence theory and policy. *Criminology & Public Policy*, *15*(3), 727–751.
Pogarsky, G. (2002). Identifying "deterrable" offenders: Implications for research on deterrence. *Justice Quarterly*, *19*(3), 431–452.
Pogarsky, G., & Herman, S. (2019). Nudging and the choice architecture of offending decisions. *Criminology & Public Policy*, *18*(4), 823–839.
Pogarsky, G., Kim, K., & Paternoster, R. (2005). Perceptual change in the national youth survey: Lessons for deterrence theory and offender decision-making. *Justice Quarterly*, *22*(1), 1–29.
Pogarsky, G., & Loughran, T. A. (2016). The policy-to-perceptions link in deterrence: Time to retire the clearance rate. *Criminology & Public Policy*, *15*, 777.
Pogarsky, G., & Piquero, A. R. (2003). Can punishment encourage offending? Investigating the "resetting" effect. *Journal of Research in Crime and Delinquency*, *40*(1), 95–120.
Sampson, R. J., & Laub, J. H. (1993). Structural variations in juvenile court processing: Inequality, the underclass, and social control. *Law and Society Review*, 285–311.
Sampson, R. J., & Sharkey, P. (2008). Neighborhood selection and the social reproduction of concentrated racial inequality. *Demography*, *45*(1), 1–29.
Sherman, L. W. (1990). Police crackdowns: Initial and residual deterrence. *Crime and Justice*, *12*, 1–48.
Short, Jr., J. F. (1998). The level of explanation problem revisited – The American Society of Criminology 1997 presidential address. *Criminology*, *36*(1), 3–36.
Sirakaya, S. (2006). Recidivism and social interactions. *Journal of the American Statistical Association*, *101*(475), 863–877.
Stafford, M. C., & Warr, M. (1993). A reconceptualization of general and specific deterrence. *Journal of Research in Crime and Delinquency*, *30*(2), 123–135.
Thaler, R. H., & Sunstein, C. (2009). *Nudge: Improving decisions about health, wealth, and happiness.* Yale University Press.
Thaler, R. H., Sunstein, C. R., & Balz, J. P. (2010). Choice architecture (SSRN Working Paper Series No. 1583509). Retrieved from http://ssrn.com/abstract.1583509
Thomas, K. J., Hamilton, B. C., & Loughran, T. A. (2018). Testing the transitivity of reported risk perceptions: Evidence of coherent arbitrariness. *Criminology*, *56*(1), 59–86.
Thomas, K. J., & Vogel, M. (2019). Testing a rational choice model of "desistance:" Decomposing changing expectations and changing utilities. *Criminology*, *57*(4), 687–714.
Wilson, T., Paternoster, R., & Loughran, T. (2017). Direct and indirect experiential effects in an updating model of deterrence: A research note. *Journal of Research in Crime and Delinquency*, *54*(1), 63–77.

16

SEXUAL OFFENCE RECIDIVISM AND RISK ASSESSMENT

L. Maaike Helmus

Risk assessment is a core component of correctional decision-making, particularly for individuals charged or convicted of sexual offences. This chapter will briefly review recidivism and risk assessment for men convicted of sexual offences (women are a meaningfully different population, and preliminary research suggests existing risk assessment methods are not applicable; Marshall et al., 2021). Emphasis will be placed on the latest research advances and those that can inform evidence-based practice.

Sexual Offence Recidivism Rates

It seems simple to summarize sexual recidivism rates, but it is not. Rates differ for detected versus undetected reoffending. For detected recidivism, Hanson and colleagues (2018) examined 7,225 men across 20 samples and found 5-year sexual recidivism rates of 9%, 10-year rates of 13%, 15-year rates of 16%, 20-year rates of 18%, and 25-year rates of 18.5%. Recidivism is most likely to occur in the early years of release; the longer someone stays sex offence free in the community, the less the likelihood of sexual recidivism (for lifetime projections of recidivism, see Thornton et al., 2021). A complication, however, is that recidivism rates vary across studies. Obviously longer follow-ups are associated with higher recidivism, but variability persists beyond the more obvious differences in methodology and sample composition (for discussion, see Helmus, 2021). Comprehensive reviews will likely overestimate detected recidivism rates because research tends to disproportionately sample higher risk settings (e.g., higher stakes, more in-depth file information). Examining more representative samples, 5-year sexual recidivism rates are closer to 4% to 7% (Boccaccini et al., 2017; Lee & Hanson, 2021).

Recidivism rates based on new charges or convictions are underestimates because not all sexual offences are reported to police, much less prosecuted. But we do not know how much this underreporting influences recidivism rates. If only 10% of sex crimes are reported, it does not mean that real recidivism rates are 10 times higher than detected rates, for several reasons (see Helmus, 2021; Lave et al., 2021). Most individuals arrested for sexual offences have no detected sex offence history; those already detected and convicted might be more likely to be caught for future offences. Additionally, recidivists may commit multiple sex offences, increasing their likelihood of detection. Consequently, the detection rate per offence is lower than the detection rate per individual. Detection rates per individual will also vary based on risk and

DOI: 10.4324/9781003219286-20

offence type. There have been some attempts to extrapolate 'true' recidivism rates based on detected rates (e.g., Scurich & John, 2019). Unfortunately, there are too many unknowns in the underlying assumptions to have much confidence in such estimates (e.g., Helmus, 2021; Lave et al., 2021). But we can identify certain principles, such as for those who offend with higher frequency, the gaps between detected and undetected offending will be smaller.

Risk Assessment: Overview

Risk assessment scales synthesize risk factors, which are variables that are empirically related to recidivism. A common way of classifying risk factors is static versus dynamic (Bonta & Andrews, 2017). Static risk factors are historical or demographic factors that do not change (e.g., prior offenses, victim characteristics). Dynamic factors can change, and when changed, alter the likelihood of recidivism (Bonta & Andrews, 2017). Examples include procriminal attitudes, deviant sexual interests, and intimacy deficits (Mann et al., 2010). Dynamic factors can further be subdivided into those that change more slowly (stable factors) and those that change more rapidly, such as the individual's environment (acute factors). Risk scales may measure static and/or dynamic risk factors. Each has its own advantages depending on the context. Static risk factors can be scored quickly, reliably, and with minimal information (e.g., criminal history). Dynamic risk factors are harder to assess but guide treatment and re-assessments. Static and dynamic assessments add incrementally (Brankley et al., 2021).

We can also differentiate methods of structuring risk factors into an overall risk assessment (Hanson & Morton-Bourgon, 2009). In empirical-actuarial scales, items are included based on research, mechanically combined into a total score, and total scores are empirically linked to probability estimates of recidivism. Structured professional judgement (SPJ) scales are those in which a non-exhaustive list of items is specified (based on combinations of research, theory, and/or practice), and the overall risk appraisal is left to the discretion of the evaluator (Hanson & Morton-Bourgon, 2009). Mechanical scales look like actuarial scales (they have a total score) but do not meet all the evidence-based criteria of an actuarial scale (e.g., a total score from an SPJ scale). Last, unstructured clinical judgement is where the risk factors are not pre-specified, may or may not be empirically derived, and the combination into an assessment is left to the discretion of the evaluator. Different methods have different advantages. For example, actuarial scales have stronger empirical backing in item selection and structure but less flexibility to new situations, and they change more slowly in response to research advances compared to SPJ scales.

The most comprehensive meta-analysis of different methods of sexual recidivism risk assessments ($k = 118$, $n = 45{,}398$) found that empirical-actuarial and mechanical scales performed similarly with moderate predictive accuracy, and both had significantly higher accuracy than unstructured clinical judgement (Hanson & Morton-Bourgon, 2009). The accuracy of SPJ measures was intermediate between actuarial/mechanical and unstructured clinical judgment, not significantly different than any of them, although there were insufficient studies to draw strong conclusions because most validation studies of SPJ scales actually used them as mechanical scales.

Surveys on Scale Use

Several surveys have assessed what scales are most frequently used for sexual recidivism risk assessments (Blais & Forth, 2014; Doyle et al., 2011; Kelley et al., 2020; Neal & Grisso, 2014). Consistent findings are that Static-99R and its predecessor (Helmus et al., 2012) are the most frequently used by far. One exception is that Blais and Forth (2014) found the Psychopathy Checklist-Revised (PCL-R; Hare, 2003) was used more frequently for indeterminate sentences in Canada, although not all assessments were for individuals who had committed sexual offences. SPJ tools such as Sexual Violence Risk-20 (SVR-20; Boer et al., 2007) are regularly used but generally less often than actuarial scales. Dynamic scales are used with much lower frequency, and which tool is most commonly used varies across surveys (e.g., STABLE-2007 [Hanson et al., 2007] versus SVR-20). For example, in a recent survey Kelley et al. (2020) found that 22% of survey participants (e.g., forensic psychologists) did not routinely assess dynamic risk.

Summary of Recidivism and Risk Assessment Overview

- Detected sexual recidivism rates tend to be low (e.g., 4% to 9% after 5 years).
- Undetected sexual recidivism rates are difficult to estimate with much confidence.
- Different risk factors (e.g., static and dynamic) have different strengths and weaknesses, but comprehensive assessment would generally include both.
- Structured risk tools should be used over unstructured clinical judgement; empirical-actuarial, mechanical, and SPJ tools have different strengths and weaknesses.
- Static-99R is the most commonly used sexual recidivism risk tool worldwide.

Evidence-Based Practices and Advances

Assessment in Cases of Child Sexual Exploitation Material Offences

Individuals convicted for possession and distribution of child sexual exploitation material (CSEM) are becoming an increasingly sizable proportion of men convicted of sexual offences, with relatively little known about them (for a review, see Babchishin et al., 2018). Virtually all contemporary sexual recidivism risk scales were developed on samples that had few to no CSEM offences included. Consequently, best practices for assessment with this population are a topic of considerable interest. There is an important distinction between individuals who have committed both online and offline offences (mixed) and those whose only sexual offences are for CSEM (Babchishin et al., 2015). Those with mixed offences are higher risk and traditional sexual recidivism risk scales are appropriate to use.

Theoretically, the flexibility inherent in SPJ tools mean they can be used with those convicted of CSEM offences but there is no validation research on this application. To my knowledge, the only traditional actuarial or mechanical risk assessment tool that is explicitly suitable for CSEM-only individuals (and whose coding manual provides guidance for these cases) is the Risk Matrix-2000 (Thornton et al., 2003). Two non-overlapping samples support the predictive accuracy of the Risk Matrix in CSEM cases (Helmus, Eke, et al., 2022; Wakeling et al., 2011). Additionally, one specialized risk assessment scale has been developed and validated to predict reoffence among individuals with CSEM offences: The Child Pornography Offender Risk Tool (CPORT; Seto & Eke, 2015). There are six non-overlapping validations of the CPORT, and it has significant and moderate predictive accuracy (for a meta-analysis, see Helmus, Eke, et al., 2022). A primary disadvantage of the CPORT, however, is that it does not yet have sufficient normative data for credible estimates of recidivism probabilities.

Dangers of Overrides in Actuarial Scales

Actuarial scales do not include all relevant/possible risk factors. A key advantage of SPJ scales is their flexibility to include case-specific factors. That led many to presume that actuarial assessments could be improved by adjusting results based on external, empirical risk factors. This seems intuitive as it would draw on advantages of both methods, but research has consistently found that overriding actuarial results degrades their accuracy (Hanson & Morton-Bourgon, 2009; Schmidt et al., 2016), even when used sparingly (Guay & Parent, 2018) or by a multi-disciplinary team of experts (Duwe & Rocque, 2018). Possibly the largest and most informative study on overrides is from Wormith et al. (2012). They examined the Level of Service/Case Management Inventory (LS/CMI; Andrews et al., 2004) in predicting general, violent, and sexual recidivism among individuals convicted for non-sex offences ($N > 24{,}000$) and sexual offences ($N > 1{,}900$). For both offence types and all three recidivism outcomes, the overrides degraded the accuracy of the scale. Interestingly, the degradations were consistently more pronounced for individuals convicted of sexual offences.

So why don't overrides work? There are many possibilities. Just because we can identify external empirically supported risk factors does not mean we can integrate them effectively. This task is difficult given unknown incremental validity, uncertain weightings, and potential biases. Indeed, evaluators are far more likely to use overrides to increase than to decrease an individual's risk score (Hanson et al., 2015; Schmidt et al., 2016; Wormith et al., 2012). Also, increasing discretion increases room for bias (e.g., attending to irrelevant factors). This could be why degradation in accuracy was strongest for people convicted of sexual offences (Wormith et al., 2012); evaluators may have been influenced by the 'ick factor' inherent in the type of offence. Regardless of the reasons, it is clear that actuarial results should not be adjusted.

Assessing Changes in Risk Over Time

A surprisingly neglected area of research is how to assess when an offender's risk has changed. For nearly 30 years, people have talked about which risk factors are dynamic (i.e., changeable; Bonta & Andrews, 2017) and developed risk scales with putatively dynamic risk factors, but rarely examined whether lower scores upon reassessment are actually associated with reduced recidivism. Advances that have been made in this area have been dominated by the work of Mark E. Olver and colleagues with the Violence Risk Scale–Sexual Offender version (Olver, Beggs Christofferson, et al., 2014; Olver, Nicholaichuk, et al., 2014).

In addition to supporting the dynamic nature of risk, Olver and colleagues' work has demonstrated the importance of controlling for baseline risk when examining and using change information. A primary limitation of their research, however, is that it has focused on two timepoints: pre- and post-treatment. Although this is of interest in many correctional decisions, some contexts (e.g., community supervision) may involve regular reassessments over time, independent of treatment or well past completion of treatment. More recently, other research groups have examined how best to reassess risk over time in the community (Babchishin & Hanson, 2020; Hanson et al., 2021; Lloyd et al., 2020), offering significant advances both in terms of practical suggestions for evaluators as well as suggestions for statistical techniques to best capture the dynamic nature of risk. Important take-home messages from this line of research are that dynamic assessment should supplement (not replace) static risk assessment and that often the most recent assessment of dynamic risk is the most informative (as opposed to taking the best or worst result or averaging them across time).

Importantly, although treatment is likely the most effective and credible agent of change, it is not the *only* agent of change. Other research has explored how even relatively simple variables (i.e., the mere passage of time) can be used to reliable modify risk assessments. Risk for sexual recidivism roughly halves for every 5 years the individual is in the community without being charged for a new sexual offence, and this decline is relatively robust at all risk scores and age levels (Hanson et al., 2018). Most recently, this work has been used to develop a 'time-free calculator' (Thornton et al., 2021; calculator available from www.saarna.org). This calculator allows evaluators to input a recidivism estimate from any risk assessment scale and it will project 20-year recidivism estimates and provide residual risk estimates at any time-point, so evaluators can determine how much risk remains given that the individual has already been in the community for X years without reoffending. The calculator also accounts for non-sexual convictions and time in custody. This calculator is particularly useful for individuals who have been on community supervision for years (e.g., applying for removal from a sex offender registry, or loosening of supervision conditions) or adjusting assessments when the current offence they are being assessed for is not a sexual offence. One area in need of future research, however, is how to integrate time-free effects with re-assessments of dynamic risk factors.

Protective Factors

Risk scales contain items empirically related to recidivism, often called *risk factors*. Recent interest has focused on *protective factors* (de Vries Robbé et al., 2015) which may also be called promotive factors or strengths. Implicit or explicit in this literature is an assumption that these are different constructs than what is already considered in risk assessment. Evaluating this assumption is complicated by a dizzying array of vague and sometimes conflicting definitions (Harris & Rice, 2015; Helmus, 2018). Similar to potential overlap in static and dynamic risk factors, however, it is possible that measuring protective factors offers unique strengths (e.g., establishing rapport and motivation), even if the underlying constructs are similar. The biggest advance in the assessment of protective factors is the recent development of the SAPROF-SO (Structured Assessment of Protective Factors, Sexual Offence version; Kelley et al., 2022), which so far shows promising interrater reliability (Willis et al., 2020) and predictive accuracy (Nolan et al., 2022). Data collection on the SAPROF-SO is underway in several countries and it will be interesting to monitor its contributions to risk assessment.

Field Validity, Training/Implementation Issues, and the Importance of the Evaluator

Most studies of risk scales are conducted in research settings, where the scale is scored retrospectively based on file information by trained research assistants or clinicians. Coders are typically screened for high conscientiousness and required to demonstrate good calibration. In contrast, field studies examine the accuracy of scales under real-world conditions, scored by real staff for making real decisions with consequences for the individual being assessed and for public safety. Evaluators often have greater time pressures and likely vary in conscientiousness and commitment to scoring fidelity. Research studies show the potential of a scale; field studies show how it performs in practice, as implemented.

This raises the important question of whether findings from research studies can generalize to real-world settings, and some early discouraging results led to pessimism on this front (Boccaccini et al., 2009). However, a recent meta-analysis of field validity studies of Static-99R (the most widely used risk assessment scale) found predictive accuracy that was overall comparable to predominantly research studies (Helmus, Hanson et al., 2021). Although this demonstrates that risk scales *can* be implemented well in field settings, this should not always be taken for granted; in this meta-analysis, predictive accuracy was significantly higher in studies with appropriate training processes in place compared to studies where the training processes were unknown or not following the scale developers' recommendations. This suggests effective practice is dependent on fidelity to recommended training practices and scoring procedures.

At the individual level, another important factor influencing accuracy of risk scales is the conscientiousness or level of commitment of the evaluator. Specifically, in a prospective study of parole and probation officers across Canada, Hanson et al. (2015) found that Static-99R scores had significantly higher predictive accuracy for officers who completed every stage of the research process compared to officers who missed one or more steps. This was within a sample that had received appropriate training, suggesting that the benefits of appropriate training and staff commitment may be additive.

Conclusions

Sexual recidivism risk assessment is a field that advances rapidly. For risk tools to be evidence based, they must be regularly updated as new evidence accumulates, and it can be difficult to keep up with the literature. This chapter briefly reviewed some of the latest advances. If assessing individuals whose only sexual offences are for possessing or distributing CSEM, either the CPORT or Risk Matrix 2000 are defensible to use. Results of actuarial risk scales should not be overridden. Risk should be re-assessed not just post-treatment but after an individual has demonstrated the ability to remain in the community sex offence free for a period of time. When re-assessing dynamic risk, the last assessment is likely to be the most informative. We are beginning to see the development of risk assessment tools to assess protective factors, but research has yet to determine the added value of this type of assessment. Last, although most studies are in research settings, there is sufficient evidence (at least for Static-99R) to demonstrate that these tools can predict sexual recidivism with large accuracy when implemented in the field with appropriate training practices. Furthermore, even within jurisdictions with appropriate training, the conscientiousness of the evaluator is also important. Consequently, buy-in from staff, management, and administrators is needed to optimize the accuracy of risk assessment. Suggestions for high-quality implementations of risk assessment practices can be found in the coding manual for the STABLE-2007 (Fernandez et al., 2014).

References

Andrews, D. A., Bonta, J., & Wormith, S. J. (2004). *The level of service/case management* inventory (LS/CMI): User's manual. Multi-Health Systems.

Babchishin, K. M., & Hanson, R. K. (2020). Monitoring changes in risk of reoffending: A prospective study of 632 men on community supervision. *Journal of Consulting and Clinical Psychology*, *88*(10), 886–898.10.1037/ccp0000601

Babchishin, K. M., Hanson, R. K., VanZuylen, H. (2015). Online child pornography offenders are different: A meta-analysis of the characteristics of online and offline sex offenders against children. *Archives of Sexual Behavior*, *44*(1), 45–66. doi: 10.1007/s10508-014-0270-x

Babchishin, K. M., Merdian, H. L., Bartels, R. M., & Perkins, D. (2018). Child sexual exploitation material offenders: A review. *European Psychologist*, *23*(2), 130–143.

Blais, J., & Forth, A. E. (2014). Prosecution-retained versus court-appointed experts: Comparing and contrasting risk assessment reports in preventative detention hearings. *Law and Human Behavior*, *38*(6), 531–543. doi: 10.1037/lhb0000082

Boccaccini, M. T., Murrie, D. C., Caperton, J. D., & Hawes, S. W. (2009). Field validity of the Static-99 and MnSOST-R among sex offenders evaluated for civil commitment as sexually violent predators. *Psychology, Public Policy, and Law*, *15*(4), 278–314. doi: 10.1037/a0017232

Boccaccini, M. T., Rice, A. K., Helmus, L. M., Murrie, D. C., & Harris, P. B. (2017). Field validity of Static-99/R scores in a statewide sample of 34,687 convicted sexual offenders. *Psychological Assessment*, *29*(6), 611–623. doi: 10.1037/pas0000377

Boer, D. P., Hart, S. D., Kropp, P. R., & Webster, C. D. (2007). *Manual for the sexual violence Risk-20: Professional guidelines for assessing risk of sexual violence*. British Columbia Institute on Family Violence and Mental Health, Law, and Policy Institute, Simon Fraser University.

Bonta, J., & Andrews, D. A. (2017). *The psychology of criminal conduct*, 6th ed. Routledge. doi: 10.1080/14789949.2013.818162

Brankley, A. E., Babchishin, K. M., & Hanson, R. K. (2021). STABLE-2007 demonstrates predictive and incremental validity in assessing risk-relevant propensities for sexual offending: A meta-analysis. *Sexual Abuse*, *33*(1), 34–62. doi: 10.1177/1079063219871572

de Vries Robbé., Mann, R. E., Maruna, S., & Thornton, D. (2015). An exploration of protective factors supporting desistance from sexual offending. *Sexual Abuse*, *27*(1), 16–33. doi: 10.1177/1079063214547582

Doyle, D. J., Ogloff, J. R. P., & Thomas, S. D. M. (2011). An analysis of dangerous sexual offender assessment reports: Recommendations for best practice. *Psychiatry, Psychology and Law*, *18*(4), 537–556. doi: 10.1080/13218719.2010.499159

Duwe, G., & Rocque, M. (2018). The home-field advantage and the perils of professional judgment: Evaluating the performance of the Static-99R and the MnSOST-3 in predicting sexual recidivism. *Law and Human Behavior*, *42*(3), 269–279. doi: 10.1037/lhb0000277

Fernandez, Y., Harris, A. J. R., Hanson, R. K., & Sparks, J. (2014). STABLE-2007 coding manual – revised 2014 [Unpublished report]. Public Safety Canada.

Guay, J.-P., & Parent, G. (2018). Broken legs, clinical overrides, and recidivism risk. *Criminal Justice and Behavior*, *45*(1), 82–100. doi: 10.1177/0093854817719482

Hanson, R. K., Harris, A. J. R., Letourneau, E., Helmus, L. M., & Thornton, D. (2018). Reductions in risk based on time offense-free in the community: Once a sexual offender, not always a sexual offender. *Psychology, Public Policy, and Law*, *24*(1), 48–63. doi: 10.1037/law0000135

Hanson, R. K., Harris, A. J. R., Scott, T.-L., & Helmus, L. (2007). *Assessing the risk of sexual offenders on community supervision: The Dynamic Supervision Project* (User Report No. 2007–05). Public Safety Canada.

Hanson, R. K., Helmus, L. M., & Harris, A. J. R. (2015). Assessing the risk and needs of supervised sexual offenders: A prospective study using STABLE-2007, Static-99R, and Static-2002R. *Criminal Justice and Behavior*, *42*(12), 1205–1224. doi: 10.1177/0093854815602094

Hanson, R. K., & Morton-Bourgon, K. E. (2009). The accuracy of recidivism risk assessments for sexual offenders: A meta-analysis of 118 prediction studies. *Psychological Assessment*, *21*(1), 1–21. doi: 10.1037/a0014421

Hanson R. K., Newstrom, N., Brouillette-Alarie, S., Thornton, D., Robinson, B. B. E., & Miner, M. H. (2021). Does reassessment improve prediction? A prospective study of the Sexual Offender Treatment Intervention and Progress Scale (SOTIPS). *International Journal of Offender Therapy & Comparative Criminology*, *65*(16), 1775–1803. doi: 10.1177/0306624X20978204.

Hare, R. D. (2003). *The Hare Psychopathy Checklist-Revised technical manual*, 2nd ed. Multi-Health Systems.

Harris, G. T., & Rice, M. E. (2015). Progress in violence risk appraisal and communication: A commentary on hypotheses and evidence. Behavioral Sciences and the Law, 33(1), 128–145. doi: 10.1002/bsl.2157

Helmus, L. M. (2018). Sex offender risk assessment: Where are we and where are we going? *Current Psychiatry Reports*, *20*, 46. doi: 10.1007/s11920-018-0909-8

Helmus, L. M. (2021). Estimating the probability of sexual recidivism among men charged or convicted of sexual offences: Evidence-based guidance for applied evaluators. *Sexual Offending: Theory, Research, and Prevention*, *16*, 1–24. doi: 10.5964/sotrap.4283

Helmus, L. M., Eke, A. M., Farmus, L., & Seto, M. C. (2022). *Comparing the CPORT and Risk Matrix 2000 for men convicted of child sexual exploitation material (CSEM) offences: Predictive accuracy and a meta-analysis*. Manuscript Submitted for Publication.

Helmus, L. M., Hanson, R. K., Murrie, D. C., & Zabarauckas, C. L. (2021). Field validity of Static-99R and STABLE-2007 with 4,433 men serving sentences for sexual offences in British Columbia: New findings and meta-analysis. *Psychological Assessment*, *33*(7), 581–595. http://dx.doi.org/10.1037/pas0001010

Helmus, L., Thornton, D., Hanson, R. K., & Babchishin, K. M. (2012). Improving the predictive accuracy of Static-99 and Static-2002 with older sex offenders: Revised age weights. *Sexual Abuse*, *24*(1), 64–101. doi: 10.1177/1079063211409951

Kelley, S. M., Ambroziak, G., Thornton, D., & Barahal, R. M. (2020). How do professionals assess sexual recidivism risk? An updated survey of practices. *Sexual Abuse*, *32*(1), 3–29. doi: 10.1177/1079063218800474

Kelley, S. K., Willis, G. M., & Thornton, D. (2022). Clinical applications of the structured assessment of protective factors against sexual offending (SAPROF-SO), Version 1, *Journal of Sexual Aggression*. Advance online publication. doi: 10.1080/13552600.2021.2020345

Lave, T. R., Prescott, J. J., & Bridges, G. (2021). The problem with assumptions: Revisiting "the dark figure of sexual recidivism." *Behavioral Sciences and the Law*, *39*(3), 279–306. doi: 10.1002/bsl.2508

Lee, S. C., & Hanson, R. K. (2021). Updated 5-Year and new 10-Year sexual recidivism rate norms for Static-99R with routine/complete samples. *Law and Human Behavior*, *45*(1), 24–38. doi: 10.1037/lhb0000436

Lloyd, C. D., Hanson, R. K., Richards, D. K., & Serin, R. C. (2020). Reassessment improves prediction of criminal recidivism: A prospective study of 3,421 individuals in New Zealand. *Psychological Assessment*, *32*(6), 568–581. doi: 10.1037/pas0000813

Mann, R. E., Hanson, R. K., & Thornton, D. (2010). Assessing risk for sexual recidivism: Some proposals on the nature of psychologically meaningful risk factors. *Sexual Abuse: Journal of Research and Treatment*, *22*(2), 191–217. doi: 10.1177/1079063210366039

Marshall, E., Miller, H. A., Cortoni, F., & Helmus, L. M. (2021). The Static-99R is not valid for women: Predictive validity in 739 females who have sexually offended. *Sexual Abuse*, *33*(6), 631–653. doi: 10.1177/1079063220940303

Neal, T. M. S., & Grisso, T. (2014). Assessment practices and expert judgment methods in forensic psychology and psychiatry. *Criminal Justice and Behavior*, *41*(12), 1406–1421. doi: 10.1177/0093854814548449

Nolan, T., Willis, G. M., Thornton, D., Kelley, S. M., Christofferson, S. B. (2022). Attending to the positive: A retrospective validation of the Structured Assessment of Protective Factors-Sexual Offence Version. *Sexual Abuse*. Advance online publication. doi: 10.1177/10790632221098354

Olver, M. E., Beggs Christofferson, S. M., Grace, R. C., & Wong, S. C. P. (2014). Incorporating change information into sexual offender risk assessments using the Violence Risk Scale – Sexual Offender version. *Sexual Abuse*, *26*(5), 472–499. doi: 10.1177/1079063213502679

Olver, M. E., Nicholaichuk, T. P., Kingston, D. A., & Wong, S. C. P. (2014). A multisite examination of sexual violence risk and therapeutic change. *Journal of Consulting and Clinical Psychology*, *82*(2), 312–324. doi: 10.1037/a0035340

Schmidt, F., Sinclair, S. M., & Thomasdóttir, S. (2016). Predictive validity of the Youth Level of Service/Case Management Inventory with youth who have committed sexual and non-sexual offences. *Criminal Justice and Behavior*, *43*(3), 413–430. doi: 10.1177/0093854815603389

Scurich, N., & John, R. S. (2019). The dark figure of sexual recidivism. *Behavioral Sciences and the Law*, *37*(2), 158–175. doi: 10.1002/bsl.2400

Seto, M. C., & Eke, A. W. (2015). Predicting recidivism among adult male child pornography offenders: Development of the Child Pornography Offender Risk Tool (CPORT). *Law and Human Behavior*, *39*(4), 416–229. doi: 10.1037/lhb0000128

Thornton, D., Hanson, R. K., Kelley, S. M., & Mundt, J. C. (2021). Estimating lifetime and residual risk for individuals who remain sexual offense free in the community: Practical applications. *Sexual Abuse*, *33*(1), 3–33. doi: 10.1177/1079063219871573

Thornton, D., Mann, R., Webster, S., Blud, L., Travers, R., Friendship. C., & Erikson, M. (2003). Distinguishing and combining risks for sexual and violent recidivism. In R. A. Prentky, E. S. Janus, & M. C. Seto (Eds.), *Sexually coercive behavior: Understanding and management* (pp. 225–235). New York Academy of Sciences.

Wakeling, H. C., Howard, P., & Barnett, G. (2011). Comparing the validity of the RM2000 scales and OGRS3 for predicting recidivism by Internet sexual offenders. *Sexual Abuse*, *23*(1), 146–168. doi: 10.1177%2F1079063210375974

Willis, G. M., Kelley, S. M., & Thornton, D. (2020). Are protective factors valid constructs? Interrater reliability and construct validity of proposed protective factors against sexual reoffending. *Criminal Justice and Behavior*, *47*(11), 1448–1467. doi: 10.1177/0093854820941039
Wormith, J. S., Hogg, S., & Guzzo, L. (2012). The predictive validity of a general risk/needs assessment inventory on sexual offender recidivism and an exploration of the professional override. *Criminal Justice and Behavior*, *39*(12), 1511–1538. doi: 10.1177/0093854812455741

17

IMPLEMENTATION SCIENCE AND EVIDENCE-BASED VIOLENCE RISK ASSESSMENT

Kevin S. Douglas

Evaluating the risk of violence posed by people within various sectors of the criminal justice system is a complex undertaking. It requires not only well-researched, validated measures that suit the setting but also well-trained professionals to administer, communicate about, and act upon the assessments. Despite the absence of crystal balls, it asks professionals to make statements about the likelihood of future behavior. It is contentious, as it pits certain persons' rights against those of others (the right to freedom against the right to live free from violence). Moreover, often risk assessment transpires within large systems, with many moving parts, departments, professional groups, stakeholders, and personnel ranging from front-line staff, to unit managers, to site administrators, to system-level administrators. And, quite often, personnel within and across these levels and groupings have differing opinions about the best way to conduct risk assessments (if at all, for some).

There are plenty of opportunities to fail. Despite that, there are also plenty of success stories regarding the implementation of evidence-based violence risk assessment practice across various criminal justice settings (including, *inter alia*, for both adults and adolescents, sentencing; probation; prison-based risk classification; parole release decision-making; intake and discharge of persons found not guilty by reason of insanity or not criminally responsible on account of mental disorder).

This chapter will first present an overview of approaches to risk assessment and the state of the discipline for violence risk assessment research. It is not possible in this chapter to present this review of the research separately for each possible criminal justice setting. Rather, general trends will be described, focusing on findings shown to be robust and replicable. Second, the chapter will turn to issues of implementation – we know from research that risk assessment has solid empirical support, but how do we ensure that it is used in practice in a way that "works?"

State of the Discipline: Violence Risk Assessment Research

Approaches to Violence Risk Assessment

There are two approaches to risk assessment that have reasonable empirical support: structured professional judgment (SPJ) and actuarial. Both approaches reduce subjectivity and

DOI: 10.4324/9781003219286-21

enhance reliability through the imposition of structure on the decision-making task. Unstructured risk assessment – without the use of decision aids – has been demonstrated to be less reliable and of lower validity than structured approaches (see Guy et al., 2015, for a review). For this reason, it is not recommended for use.

There are important differences, though certainly some similarities, in the development, use, and assumptions between the SPJ and actuarial approaches, well discussed and debated in the field and not relitigated here (see, for example, Douglas et al., 2014; Hart et al., 2017; Quinsey et al., 2006). The primary, defining difference between these approaches is the use of algorithms (such as equations or cut-scores): actuarial approaches use them; SPJ approaches do not. Both approaches provide operationally defined risk factors to be rated, and both provide guidance to reach final decisions about risk. *All* SPJ instruments contain changeable, or dynamic, risk factors that are purportedly causal in nature and intended to capture change over time and serve as intervention/management targets to reduce risk (also referred to as criminogenic needs under the risk-need-responsivity or RNR model of risk assessment – see Andrews and Bonta, 2010). *Some* actuarial instruments do so, whereas others are static and do not allow for monitoring or managing change over time. SPJ approaches also systematically address *formulation* (Hart & Logan, 2011), or the task of determining the reasons *why* a person has been violent (both in terms of most relevant risk factors, as well as how these motivate, disinhibit, or destabilize people), whereas this typically is not addressed by actuarial approaches.

Summary of Predictive Validity Literature

There are hundreds of individual risk assessment studies. As such, the field is fortunate now to have many systematic reviews and meta-analyses, which are reviewed in detail elsewhere (Douglas et al., 2014; Guy et al., 2015; see also instrument-by-instrument literature reviews on leading risk assessment instruments contained in chapters within Douglas & Otto, 2021). Some meta-analyses focus on certain types of perpetrators, offenses, or settings, whereas some are broad. For instance, some focus on mentally disordered offenders (Bonta et al., 1998), offenders generally (Campbell et al., 2009), sexual offenders (Hanson & Morton-Bourgon, 2009), adolescent offenders generally (Koh et al., 2020), adolescent sexual offenders (Viljoen et al., 2012), female offenders (Geraghty & Woodhams, 2015), imminent violence (Dickens et al., 2020), or violence within forensic psychiatric hospitals (Ramesh et al., 2018). Others focus on specific instruments, such as the Short Term Assessment of Risk and Treatability (START; O'Shea & Dickens, 2014), the Psychopathy Checklist instruments (PCL; Leistico et al., 2008), or the Level of Service instruments (Olver et al., 2014). Others are intended to cover the field more broadly to compare instruments or approaches (Fazel et al., 2012; Singh et al., 2011; Yang et al., 2010). The trend over time is to become more specific.

The following is a list of cross-cutting, take-home findings supported by this meta-analytic research base:

- On average, most instruments have moderate to moderate-large associations with future violence or crime (correlation coefficients of around .30; AUCs around .65 to .70).
- Instruments focusing on specific forms of outcomes (violence, as opposed to crime broadly) have slightly larger effect sizes.
- Larger effect sizes tend to be found in studies that evaluate the outcomes that instruments were specifically intended to evaluate.

- Instruments containing dynamic (i.e., changeable) risk factors tend to produce larger effect sizes than those focused primarily on historical, static risk factors. Although meta-analyses have not addressed the link between actual changes in risk factors and subsequent violence, individual studies do tend to support this connection (de Vries Robbé et al., 2015; Hogan & Olver, 2016, 2019).
- Instrument-specific meta-analyses are consistent with the larger findings of meta-analyses in terms of average effect sizes.
- Meta-analyses of certain sub-groups (female offenders; people with intellectual disabilities) are consistent in their findings with those of the general meta-analyses.
- Evidence supports comparability of effect sizes across potential moderators (for instance, institutional compared to community violence; males compared to females).
- SPJ and actuarial instruments tend to perform comparably in terms of predictive validity, although SPJ instruments have not been tested as intended for use in practice in most studies or meta-analyses. Despite this, the majority of studies (39 of 45 published studies; see Heilbrun et al., 2021) support the predictive validity of SPJ's non-algorithmic risk communication method (summary risk ratings), with 16 of 18 studies that have specifically tested the predictive validity of this approach against an algorithmic combination of risk factors showing incremental validity of SPJ's summary risk ratings.

Implementation of Violence Risk Assessment Practice

There are hundreds if not thousands of violence risk assessment studies focusing on reliability and validity of instruments and decisions (that is, violence risk assessment practice). There are far, far fewer studies on implementation of violence risk assessment practice. There have been a number of published reports of implementation efforts gone awry. For instance, in a study of 12 courts that implemented risk assessment procedures in four states, only half of the court professionals (including probation officers) were using the tools regularly in their decision-making (Shook & Sarri, 2007). Most stopped using the tools within 2 years, and deviation from proper scoring and use of the tools was common. Flores et al. (2006) evaluated the implementation of a risk assessment measure across nine correctional facilities in a U.S. state. They found that the instrument was only predictive of recidivism when used by evaluators with adequate training, and in sites that had been using the instrument for more than 3 years. Young et al. (2006) reported that, in a pre-post study of the implementation of a risk assessment tool across five counties in Maryland, adherence to the policy for administering the instrument was only 55%.

How are such difficulties to be avoided? This section will outline practical suggestions and steps for implementation based on an integration of (a) the little that has been published on implementation of violence risk assessment, (b) the much larger field of implementation science, and (c) the observations of the author through his work with agencies and systems in different parts of the world. Implementation science is a broad, large field that cuts across and is applied in many disciplines (i.e., medicine, health, education, engineering, business). Its principles have been used within criminal justice with respect to programs and risk assessment instruments, but relatively infrequently. There are numerous principled approaches to aspects of implementation described in the field. The common aspect of all such approaches and models is to maximize the likelihood that new practices or policies are used as intended, and used effectively, by systems that adopt them. There are two models with particular utility for implementation of risk assessment instruments and practices (Damschroder et al., 2009;

Proctor et al., 2011). In this section, a summary of useful principles and practical suggestions, drawn from these models, is provided for those seeking to implement risk assessment instruments and practices.

Lessons from Implementation Science

Proctor et al. (2011) developed a framework for implementation that has been cited and used hundreds of times across broad domains. It contains a number of concrete principles that have been found to impact the success (or failure) of implementation attempts. Their principles, which are measurable and can serve as outcome goals for an implementation process, are as follows:

- *Acceptability:* Whether stakeholders perceive the implementation to be "agreeable, palatable, or satisfactory" (p. 67)
- *Adoption:* The "intention, initial decision, or action to try" the risk assessment instrument (p. 69)
- *Appropriateness:* The "perceived fit, relevance, or compatibility" of the instrument (p. 69)
- *Feasibility*: Whether the instrument is "successfully used or carried out within a given agency" (p. 69)
- *Fidelity:* The degree to which the instrument is "implemented as it was prescribed in the original protocol or as it was intended", such as whether assessors followed instructions in the manual (p. 69)
- *Penetration:* The "integration of the [instrument] within a service setting and its subsystems" (p. 70)
- *Sustainability:* Whether the implementation is "maintained or institutionalized within a service setting's ongoing, stable operations" (p. 70)

Vincent et al. (2012), drawing from Proctor's model, integrated with contemporary risk assessment principles, developed a guidebook for implementation of risk assessment instruments in juvenile justice settings. It contains eight steps, ranging from raising awareness among stakeholders, establishing buy-in, selecting a risk assessment instrument, identifying training needs, and developing policy and procedure manuals to monitoring quality over time. Viljoen and Vincent (2020) further expanded on how Proctor's model could be useful in the risk assessment context.

Damschroder et al. (2009) developed a broad framework for implementation research, that, like Proctor et al., 2011, has had widespread impact. Called the Consolidated Framework for Implementation Research, or CFIR, it proposes five primary areas within which to focus. Again, within each area, there are numerous measurable and important concrete principles to guide the various steps of implementation. These five areas of focus include:

- "*The intervention or object*", or, here, the risk assessment instrument or routine. Includes features such as validation status, complexity, adaptability, feasibility, cost, trialability.
- The *users or people* involved, such as staff, management, and stakeholders. Includes characteristics such as perceptions of the instrument, perceived efficacy or skills to do the proposed work, positive or negative views of the implementation, identification with the organization.
- The *inner setting*. Includes such factors as the culture, politics, communication style, readiness to change of the agency or organization.

- The *outer setting*. Includes factors such as the larger political and economic setting (i.e., a state government with certain correctional policies).
- The *process*. Includes features such as determining an implementation plan, choosing implementation team and opinion leaders, engaging stakeholders.

There is even a useful "barrier busting" online tool to help suggest solutions to barriers that might be encountered in any of these five areas (Waltz et al., 2019). Indeed, across these areas, up to 39 barriers, and proposed solutions based on a survey of 169 implementation experts, are included in this online tool. Experts provided up to seven solutions for each of the 39 barriers, and these are then provided in rank order, based on the percent of experts who provided the solution, upon querying solutions to the barrier.

As mentioned, there has been a relatively small number of implementation evaluations within the risk assessment field. In one way, all reliability and validity studies are relevant to implementation, as instruments should possess these characteristics in order to be considered viable "objects" to implement. There is a plethora of such studies, as reviewed earlier, but many fewer on whether these validated instruments are implemented successfully.

Levin et al. (2016) reviewed the state of the field in terms of risk assessment implementation studies, finding just 11 such studies. They attempted to estimate the importance of Damschroder et al.'s (2009) "determinants of practice" (barriers and facilitators) from their CFIR model with respect to implementation success. Their review of these 11 studies concluded that the following CFIR determinants were particularly important in terms of risk assessment implementation success:

- *The "object"/risk instrument:* involving staff in selecting the tool, adaptability of the tool to local needs, small-scale pilot-testing (trialability), complexity – too difficult or time-consuming (barrier).
- *Users/people involved:* staff opinions, beliefs, perceptions of the tool (positive or negative); perceived lack of experience, skills, efficacy to conduct assessments with the tool (barrier); sense of professional discretion maintained or enhanced; perceived need for change.
- *Inner setting:* size, complexity or poor communication within system (barrier); compatibility with existing workflows and systems; readiness to change among stakeholders; clear specification of goals, tasks, responsibilities, timeframes; communication and feedback to staff about progress; leader/management engagement in process, provision of learning climate, resources, training, education, support; treating staff as "knowledgeable participants" in the process.
- *Outer setting:* no studies identified a determinant in this category.
- *Process:* clear, predetermined though flexible and adjustable implementation plan; engaging stakeholders early in the process, and continuing throughout; formally appointing leaders of the implementation, who support it and are respected and authoritative; monitoring/evaluating fidelity to the plan and the instrument; reporting and discussing progress with stakeholders.

It is not possible in this chapter to provide lengthy illustrations of each of Proctor et al. (2011) and Damschroder et al.'s (2009) principles. However, several concrete examples are provided next, based also on the author's experience assisting agencies with implementation of the violence risk assessment and management policies and instruments.

The California Department of State Hospitals (DSH) has implemented two violence risk assessment instruments – the HCR-20 Version 3 (Douglas et al., 2013) and the START (Webster et al., 2009). DSH is a large system, with five main forensic and psychiatric state hospitals. As part of this, DSH needed to train hundreds of psychologists and deal with steady turnover and new staff. As such, they developed a training program consisting of foundational (introductory) training (basic introduction to risk assessment, the tools, how to complete them, practice cases), advanced training (more advanced cases and focus on risk formulation and treatment), and also a "train-the-trainer" model where a number of staff were trained to train others. This establishes local expertise, resources, and support for those conducting assessments.

Each hospital was responsible for establishing policies around which patients should receive which type of risk assessment, who should conduct it, and when. Auditing and monitoring processes were put into place. Further, DSH tested the interrater reliability of its staff – 70 clinicians each rated the same (paper) case and provided HCR-20 V3 and START ratings of risk factors. This provided useful feedback on level of agreement or disagreement at the risk factor level. Indeed, a few risk factors did not have high agreement, so that information can then influence subsequent training (ensure people are clearly understanding the definitions of those certain risk factors; extra attention paid to those risk factors in case reviews).

Vincent et al. (2016), applying their model that was informed by Proctor et al.'s (2011) principles, conducted a pre-post evaluation of six juvenile probation offices, including close to 1700 young offenders. They reported a number of positive findings – the instruments were administered as planned in five of six settings; the instruments were predictive of re-offending; the instruments were rated reliably; most probation officers had a positive attitude about the instruments; there was a reduction in the restrictiveness of dispositions after the instruments were implemented (in four of six sites); out-of-home dispositions decreased in several sites; supervision level and service referrals were related to risk level; there was no increase in recidivism, and it decreased in one site. In the one of six sites that did not achieve administration of the instruments as planned, it was attributed to low levels of buy-in from judges.

As another example, the author conducted an evaluation of the implementation of a violence risk assessment and reduction program that had been rolled out nationally in psychiatric and forensic facilities and hospitals in Norway (Douglas, 2022). Primarily this focused on "the object" (the "management of aggression program", MAP), and the perceptions of individuals involved. A survey – informed by concepts from Proctor et al. (2011) and Damschroder et al. (2009) – of roughly 120 MAP trainers was conducted, and results were the presented back to participants at a conference. The purpose was to identify areas of strength as well as barriers to successful implementation, so that the program could adjust as it proceeded.

Key areas of focus included perceptions of feasibility and usefulness; barriers to implementation; staff morale and resistance; support from management; self-efficacy; effectiveness of the program; adherence to program policies, time-frames, objectives; having the necessary time to fulfill one's responsibilities. A number of strengths were noted, and these will facilitate the implementation efforts: the program was not perceived as too complex or burdensome; it "fit" workflow and was seen as effective, feasible, and useful. However, barriers included lack of time, staff turnover, and less than optimal support from management (provision of time, resources, and knowledge). There was also variation in compliance with program policy expectations and adherence to program content. Further, a number of factors were statistically predictive of better compliance, adherence, and fidelity, as well as perceived benefits to patients (less aggression; less use of coercion). These factors included having time to train and support colleagues, receiving necessary information about one's roles and responsibilities, perceiving support from management and the larger organization (many aspects – time, resources, educational support, management knowledge), perceived useability of the program (low complexity), perceived feasibility and adaptability, proportion of staff having received training, established routines to carry out the program, perceived self-confidence in dealing with and de-escalating aggression, and job satisfaction.

The results of this evaluation have direct implications for those managing the program, in terms of areas to focus on and improve, moving forward. It also indicates that a number of implementation determinants were indeed influencing adherence and compliance with the program, and staff perceptions of its effectiveness. Program managers can then aim to resolve some of the problem areas with the goal of improving certain areas of lower compliance, adherence and perceptions of effectiveness. Of course, measurement of actual effectiveness is a necessary next step as well.

Conclusion

A great deal more attention to implementation of risk assessment instruments is needed. Table 17.1 provides a simple, concise set of "non-ignorable" areas to address when implementing a risk assessment instrument. These are drawn from the larger implementation science literature and the more limited risk assessment implementation literature and organized in three categories: people, process, and instrument. Each of these points should be considered when embarking on an implementation, and can be greatly expanded and unpacked depending on local needs. The Council of State Governments has recently released a report and set of guidelines for post-conviction risk and needs assessment that reflects implementation science principles (Desmarais et al., 2022), along with an online "self-assessment" tool (see: https://projects.csgjusticecenter.org/risk-assessment/self-assessment/) to help agencies select a risk assessment instrument that fits their needs. Such applied and concrete tools, founded upon decades of risk assessment research and drawing from implementation science, are invaluable (and free) resources for any agency (or practitioner) considering the implementation of evidence-based violence risk assessment tools.

At this point in history, there is no cogent rationale for failing to adopt an evidence-based risk assessment instrument, and to use the principles of implementation science to ensure its effective adoption. There are literally thousands of studies within both fields that, jointly, compel such an approach. Indeed, the marriage of evidence-based risk assessment with implementation science is a necessary condition of the responsible stewardship of criminal justice practices concerning risk assessment and management. It is the only approach that concurrently safeguards individual rights and freedoms, along with the protection of public safety.

Table 17.1 Risk Assessment Implementation Checklist

People	• Management is knowledgeable about the tool and respects evidence-based practice • Management respects staffs' opinions and skills • Opinion leaders ("local champions") raise awareness and positivity about the change • Staff perceive the instrument as useful to help them do their jobs and help clients • Stakeholders are engaged and aware of any changes in routines

(*Continued*)

Table 17.1 (Continued)

Process	• Identify perceived barriers amongst staff, management, site, and stakeholders
	• Develop policies and procedure manual, with management and staff input
	  • Who conducts the assessment? How is it communicated/recorded, and to whom?
	  • Clarify the use of assessment results (inform treatment? release decisions?)
	• Assess training needs; prepare foundational, advanced, and ongoing booster trainings
	• Develop local expertise, including training staff to train others ("train-the-trainer")
	• Evaluate interrater reliability locally; adjust/additional training for problem areas
	• Evaluate key validity questions
	  • Predictive validity; informing treatment and risk management; formulation quality
	• Establish quality assurance, adherence and fidelity checks, monitoring
	  • Completion rates; missing items; completed as intended; consistent with policy
	• Seek staff perceptions and input regularly (is it feasible, useful, helpful?)
	• Provide feedback and reinforcement to staff
	• Institutionalize the process, so it is not dependent on any single person

Instrument	• Peer-reviewed, independent evidence for interrater reliability and predictive validity • Feasible to use • Adaptable to local contexts

References

Andrews, D. A., & Bonta, J. (2010). *The psychology of criminal conduct*, 5th ed. LexisNexis/Matthew Bender.

Bonta, J., Law, M., & Hanson, R. K. (1998). The prediction of criminal and violent recidivism among mentally disordered offenders: A meta-analysis. *Psychological Bulletin*, *123*, 123–142.

Campbell, M. A., French, S., & Gendreau, P. (2009). The prediction of violence in adult offenders: A meta-analytic comparison of instruments and methods of assessment. *Criminal Justice and Behavior*, *36*, 567–590.

Damschroder, L. J., Aron, D. C., Keith, R. E., Kirsh, S. R., Alexander, J. A., & Lowery, J. C. (2009). Fostering implementation of health services research findings into practice: A consolidated framework for advancing implementation science. *Implementation Science*, *4*, 50.

de Vries Robbé, M., de Vogel, V., Douglas, K. S., & Nijman, H. L. I. (2015). Changes in dynamic risk and protective factors for violence during inpatient forensic psychiatric treatment: Predicting reductions in postdischarge community recidivism. *Law and Human Behavior*, *39*, 53–61.

Desmarais, S. L., D'Amora, D. A., & Tavárez, L. P. (2022). *Advancing fairness and transparency: National guidelines for post-conviction risk and needs assessment*. Lexington, Kentucky: The Council of State Governments Justice Centre.

Dickens, G. L., O'Shea, L. E., & Christensen, M. (2020). Structured assessments for imminent aggression in mental health and correctional settings: Systematic review and meta-analysis. *International Journal of Nursing Studies*, *104*, 103526.

Douglas, K. S. (2022, March). Implementation of the management of aggression program (MAP): Initial findings. In Invited presentation at the MAP annual conference. MAP.

Douglas, K. S., Hart, S. D., Groscup, J. L., & Litwack, T. R. (2014). Assessing violence risk. In I. Weiner & R. K. Otto (Eds.), *The handbook of forensic psychology*, 4th ed. John Wiley & Sons, Inc.

Douglas, K. S., Hart, S. D., Webster, C. D., & Belfrage, H. (2013). *Historical-clinical-risk management 20 (Version 3) violence risk assessment guidelines (HCR-20:V3)*. Mental Health, Law, and Policy Institute, Simon Fraser University.

Douglas, K. S., & Otto, R. K. (Eds.) (2021). *Handbook of violence risk assessment*, 2nd ed. Routledge: Taylor & Francis Group.

Fazel, S., Singh, J. P., Doll, H., & Grann, M. (2012). Use of risk assessment instruments to predict violence and antisocial behaviour in 73 samples involving 24,827 people: Systematic review and meta-analysis. *British Medical Journal*, *345*, e4692. doi: 10.1136/bmj.e4692

Flores, A. W., Lowenkamp, C. T., Holsinger, A. M., & Latessa, E. J. (2006). Predicting outcome with the level of service inventory-revised: The importance of implementation integrity. *Journal of Criminal Justice*, *34*, 523–529. doi: 10.1016/j.jcrimjus.2006.09.007

Geraghty, K. A., & Woodhams, J. (2015). The predictive validity of risk assessment tools for female offenders: A systematic review. *Aggression and Violent Behavior*, *21*, 25–38.

Guy, L. S., Douglas, K. S., & Hart, S. D. (2015). Risk assessment and communication. In B. Cutler & P. Zapf (Eds.), *APA handbook of forensic psychology* (Vol. 1, pp. 35–86). American Psychological Association.

Hanson, R. K., & Morton-Bourgon, K. E. (2009). The accuracy of recidivism risk assessments for sexual offenders: A meta-analysis of 118 prediction studies. *Psychological Assessment*, *21*, 1–21.

Hart, S. D., Douglas, K. S., & Guy, L. S. (2017). The structured professional judgment approach to violence risk assessment: Origins, nature, and advances. In M. Rettenberger & L. Craig (Series Eds.) and D. Boer (Volume Ed.), *The Wiley-Blackwell handbook on the assessment, treatment and theories of sexual offending: Volume 1. Assessment* (pp. 643–666). Wiley-Blackwell.

Hart, S. D., & Logan, C. (2011). Formulation of violence risk using evidence-based assessments: The structured professional judgment approach. In P. Sturmey & M. McMurran (Eds.), *Forensic case formulation* (pp. 83–106). Wiley-Blackwell.

Heilbrun, K., Yasuhara, K., Shah, S., & Locklair, B. (2021). Approaches to violence risk assessment: Overview, critical analysis, and future directions. In K. S. Douglas & R. K. Otto (Eds.), *Handbook of violence risk assessment* (2nd ed., pp. 3–27). Routledge/Taylor & Francis.

Hogan, N. R., & Olver, M. E. (2016). Assessing risk for aggression in forensic psychiatric inpatients: An examination of five measures. *Law and Human Behavior*, *40*, 233–243.

Hogan, N. R., & Olver, M. E. (2019). Static and dynamic assessment of violence risk among discharged forensic patients. *Criminal Justice and Behavior*, *46*, 923–938.

Koh, L. L., Day, A., Klettke, B., Daffern, M., & Chu, C. M. (2020). The predictive validity of youth violence risk assessment tools: A systematic review. *Psychology, Crime & Law*, *26*(8), 776–796.

Leistico, A. M. R., Salekin, R. T., DeCoster, J., & Rogers, R. (2008). A large-scale meta-analysis relating the Hare measures of psychopathy to antisocial conduct. *Law and Human Behavior*, *32*, 28–45.

Levin, S. K., Nilsen, P., Bendtsen, P., & Bulow, P. (2016). Structured risk assessment instruments: A systematic review of implementation determinants. *Psychiatry, Psychology and Law*, *23*, 602–628. doi: 10.1080/13218719.2015.1084661

Olver, M. E., Stockdale, K. C., & Wormith, J. S. (2014). Thirty years of research on the level of service scales: A meta-analytic examination of predictive accuracy and sources of variability. *Psychological Assessment*, *26*(1), 156.

O'Shea, L. E., & Dickens, G. L. (2014). Short-term assessment of risk and treatability (START): Systematic review and meta-analysis. *Psychological Assessment*, *26*(3), 990–1002. doi: 10.1037/a0036794

Proctor, E., Silmere, H., Raghavan, R., Hovmand, P., Aarons, G, Bunger, A., Griffey, R., & Hensley, M. (2011). Outcomes for implementation research: Conceptual distinctions, measurement challenges, and research agenda. *Administration and Policy in Mental Health*, *38*, 65–76. http://doi.org/10.1007/s10488-010-0319-7

Quinsey, V. L., Harris, G. T., Rice, M. E., & Cormier, C. (2006). *Violent offenders: Appraising and managing risk*, 2nd ed. American Psychological Association.

Ramesh, T., Igoumenou, A., Montes, M. V., & Fazel, S. (2018). Use of risk assessment instruments to predict violence in forensic psychiatric hospitals: A systematic review and meta-analysis. *European Psychiatry*, *52*, 47–53.

Shook, J. L., & Sarri, R. C. (2007). Structured decision-making in juvenile justice: Judges' and probation officers' perceptions and use. *Children and Youth Services Review*, *29*, 1335–1351.

Singh, J. P., Grann, M., & Fazel, S. (2011). A comparative study of violence risk assessment tools: A systematic review and metaregression analysis of 68 studies involving 25,980 participants. *Clinical Psychology Review*, *31*, 499–513.

Viljoen, J. L., Mordell, S., & Beneteau, J. L. (2012). Prediction of adolescent sexual reoffending: A meta-analysis of the J-SOAP-II, ERASOR, J-SORRAT-II, and Static-99. *Law and Human Behavior*, *36*, 423–438.

Viljoen, J. L., & Vincent, G. M. (2020). Risk assessments for violence and reoffending: Implementation and impact on risk management. *Clinical Psychology: Research and Practice*, e12378. doi.org/10.1111/cpsp.12378

Vincent, G. M., Guy, L. S., & Grisso, T. (2012). *Risk assessment in juvenile justice: A guidebook for implementation* (John D. & Catherine T. MacArthur Foundation). Retrieved from www.NYSAP.us

Vincent, G. M., Guy, L. S., Perrault, R. T., & Gershenson, B. (2016). Risk assessment matters, but only when implemented well: A multisite study in juvenile probation. *Law and Human Behavior*, *40*, 683–696. doi: 10.1037/lhb00 00214

Waltz, T. J., Powell, B. J., Fernández, M. E., Abadie, B., & Damschroder, L. J. (2019). Choosing implementation strategies to address contextual barriers: diversity in recommendations and future directions. *Implementation Science, 14*, 42. doi: 10.1186/s13012-019-0892-4

Webster, C. D., Martin, M. L., Brink, J., Nicholls, T. L., & Desmarais, S. L. (2009). *Manual for the short-term assessment of risk and treatability (START) (Version 1.1)*. British Columbia Mental Health & Addiction Services.

Yang, M., Wong, S. C., & Coid, J. (2010). The efficacy of violence prediction: A meta-analytic comparison of nine risk assessment tools. *Psychological Bulletin*, *136*(5), 740.

Young, D., Moline, K., Farrell, J., & Biere, D. (2006). Best implementation practices: Disseminating new assessment technologies in a juvenile justice agency. *Crime & Delinquency*, *52*, 135–158.

PART IV

Policing

18

EVIDENCE-BASED POLICE PATROL PRACTICES AT CRIME HOTSPOTS

Cory P. Haberman and Bradley J. O'Guinn

Introduction

Preventive patrol has been a staple of American policing since its inception. Early reformers believed random patrol deterred criminal activity by creating the impression of omnipresence (Kelling et al., 1974). This view was widely accepted until the 1970s, when a series of studies conducted by the Police Foundation found that both vehicle and foot patrol were ineffective at reducing crime *within geographically large patrol beats* (Kelling et al., 1974; Kelling, 1981). For many, these studies confirmed a growing sentiment within society: police could do little to prevent crime (Bayley, 1994; Weisburd & Braga, 2019). Others challenged this claim, suggesting that preventive patrol could reduce crime if it were targeted at *micro-level high crime locations*, or "hot spots" (Sherman & Weisburd, 1995). The key difference is that a hotspot might only be a single address, street block, or a "grid" of only a few streets. Research starting in the 1970s and 1980s (Sherman et al., 1989), and continuing today (Weisburd, 2015), has found that roughly 25% and 50% of crime is concentrated at just 1% and 3% of micro-locations. Importantly, over the past three decades, researchers have demonstrated that preventive patrol can reduce crime when targeted at high crime micro-locations (see Braga et al., 2019). This chapter's purpose is to examine these evidence-based patrol practices. In doing so, this chapter identifies some of the challenges associated with implementation and highlights avenues for future research.

The Theory Behind Patrol Effectiveness

Two theories underpin why directed patrols may reduce criminal activity at hotspots. Deterrence theory assumes rational actors alter their behavior when its costs outweighs any perceived benefits (see Sherman, 1990). The swiftness, severity, and certainty of punishment can be increased to change offenders' perceptions of risk, but certainty has been argued to be the most effective component of deterrence theory (Nagin, 2013; Nagin et al., 2015; Pratt et al., 2006). When police departments increase the number of officers patrolling at high crime locations, potential offenders may perceive that the certainty of apprehension has increased, even if the true risk of apprehension remains the same (Sorg et al., 2013). This is the idea of ecological deterrence, whereby the increased risks associated with police patrols are attributed

DOI: 10.4324/9781003219286-23

to the location where the patrols repeatedly occur (Cousineau, 1973). Alternatively, in the language of routine activities theory, increased police patrols represent increased guardianship (see Eck, 2003).

Second, patrols may also indirectly result in incapacitation (Haberman, 2016). Officers on directed patrols may engage in enforcement actions, like arrests. A small percentage of the population is responsible for most crime (Piquero et al., 2003). And it is well-known among officers that even a single high-rate offender can drive crime in an area. Thus, if directed patrols result in the arrest and incarceration of these prolific offenders, then an incapacitation effect could be generated.

Hotspot patrols

Hotspot patrols have been shown to be effective in multiple rigorous evaluations, including randomized controlled trials (see Braga et al., 2019). The first study of hotspot policing, the Minneapolis Hot Spots Experiment, showed total calls for service, "soft" crime calls for service, and observed disorder were reduced in the 55 hotspots that received police patrols relative to the 55 control hotspots that did not receive the patrols (Sherman & Weisburd, 1995). A long list of studies since have replicated the finding that calls for service or crime incidents decline when police patrol micro-level crime hotspots (e.g., see Sherman & Rogan, 1995; Weisburd & Green, 1995; Lawton et al., 2005; Ratcliffe et al., 2011; Telep et al., 2012; Piza & O'Hara, 2014; Haberman & Stiver, 2018). Of course, these studies had their own nuances, so readers are encouraged to read the originals, but the bottom line is that patrols in crime hotspots can be considered an evidence-based approach at this point.

But there are some practical considerations when implementing hotspot patrols: (1) the duration of the patrols and (2) the modality of patrols. There are two main variations on the duration of patrols. One is to have officers simply patrol a hotspot for a long period – such as an entire shift. In general, research finds shift-length patrols are associated with reductions in crime (see Sherman & Rogan, 1995; Lawton et al., 2005; Ratcliffe et al., 2011; Piza & O'Hara, 2014; Novak et al., 2016). However, long-duration patrols are resource intensive and may be disliked by some officers who find this assignment repetitive and uninteresting (Haberman & Stiver, 2020; Sorg et al., 2014).

Another option is to deploy hotspot patrols intermittently. Officers assigned to directed patrols periodically visit hotspots throughout their shift. While present at a high crime location, officers may remain stationary or travel throughout the hotspot for a limited time interval (e.g., 12–15 minutes). After this period, officers return to their normal work routine. This idea is based on the Koper curve (Koper, 1995). Koper (1995) used survival analysis to determine how long after a hotspot patrol a crime was likely to occur using data from Minneapolis Hot Spots Experiment (Sherman & Weisburd, 1995). The "curve" comes from a graph in the study, which showed that the number of minutes between a patrol and the next crime in a hotspot leveled off after about a 15-minute patrol, suggesting a diminishing return on patrols longer than 15 minutes. Again, research suggests intermittent patrols can reduce crime in hotspots (Telep et al., 2014; Haberman & Stiver, 2018).

Another nuance is whether to have officers patrol in vehicles or on foot. Foot patrol has increased in popularity since the proliferation of community-oriented policing (National Research Council, 2004). After the Newark Foot Patrol Experiment, however, the widespread view was that foot patrol might improve police–community relations but was ineffective for addressing crime (Ratcliffe & Sorg, 2017). Vehicle patrols have been most common (Rosenfeld et al., 2014; Sherman & Weisburd, 1995), but a growing body of research has now found that foot patrols can effectively reduce crime in hotspots (Ratcliffe et al., 2011; Novak et al., 2016; Piza & O'Hara, 2014; Haberman & Stiver, 2018). The key difference was foot patrol being deployed to geographically small areas, such as grids with no more than 1 mile of street network within them (see Ratcliffe et al., 2011). This is an important change because officers on foot can use the time to interact with citizens, gather intelligence, or improve police–community relations (Haberman & Stiver, 2020). Of course, foot patrol can be resource intensive and physically demanding and exacerbate officer safety risks (Haberman & Stiver, 2019). Foot patrol's crime reduction benefits also may decay over time (Novak et al., 2016; Sorg et al., 2013).

In addition to the patrol modality, it is worthwhile to think about the actions officers perform while patrolling crime hotspots. Some officers simply do nothing, using this time to catch up on paperwork or grab a bite to eat. Others conduct enforcement activity, like writing tickets, conducting vehicle checks, stopping and questioning suspicious people, and arresting individuals who have violated the law, and perhaps a high volume of enforcement is the key ingredient that makes hotspot patrols effective (e.g., see Ratcliffe et al., 2011; Groff et al., 2015). In general, prior research suggests that enforcement activities are associated with crime reductions (see Rosenfeld et al, 2014; Sherman & Rogan, 1995; Weisburd & Green, 1995; Weisburd et al., 2016). A recent meta-analysis conducted by Braga and Weisburd (2020) suggests that these "traditional" policing tactics were associated with a 14% reduction in crime (see also Braga et al., 2019).

Critiques of Hotspot Patrols

Despite the crime control benefits, hotspot patrols are not without limitations. First, some argue that intensive patrols can harm police–community relations (Rosenbaum, 2006; Kochel, 2010). Citizens are particularly concerned about increased enforcement (Brunson, 2007; Brunson & Miller, 2006), especially when the greatest burden is felt by people of color. Intensive patrol and enforcement may leave community members dissatisfied and harm police legitimacy (Gau & Brunson, 2010; Haberman et al., 2016). Two studies to date have not found that police–community relations worsen after hotspot patrols, among other tactics, but this is an area in need of vastly more research (Weisburd et al., 2011; Ratcliffe et al., 2015). Second, hotspot patrols may produce only short-term crime reductions (Sherman, 1990; Sorg et al., 2013). As such, patrol tactics may be seen as an early tactic for stabilizing crime hotspots as part of a long-term, comprehensive strategy (Haberman et al., 2016). Third, all place-based initiatives face concerns about spatial displacement. When displacement is measured in a roughly two-block area around the edge of hotspots, research suggests any displacement of crime is likely less than the amount of crime prevented by the initiative or a diffusion of crime control benefits is observed – where crime is actually also reduced in the surrounding area (Weisburd et al., 2006; Braga et al., 2019).

Takeaway Points

1. There is *strong evidence* to suggest that police patrol practices (e.g., stationary, vehicle, and foot patrol) can reduce crime if implemented in *micro-level* hotspots.
    - Directed patrols across geographically large areas, like police beats, are unlikely to be effective

2. There is some evidence that hotspot patrol's crime reduction benefits will decay over time.
3. Researchers and practitioners must consider how police patrol practices influence police–community relations and citizens' perceptions of procedural justice and police legitimacy. There is not enough research on the causal impacts of police patrol on police–community relations to know for sure.
4. Police patrol strategies require different decisions during implementation: (1) long vs. intermittent patrols, (2) vehicle vs. other types of patrol (i.e., foot), and (3) the role of enforcement in the strategy. No research comparing the relative benefits of each option exists.

Implementing Police Patrol Practices at Crime Hotspots

When implementing police patrol practices at crime hotspots, we recommend developing a plan based on the following five questions influenced by the previous research and our experience evaluating hotspot patrols:

1. What are the goals of the intervention?
2. What is the definition of a hotspot?
3. What are the components of the strategy?
4. How will officers be held accountable?
5. How will impact be assessed?

In the following, we consider each of these questions and provide recommendations supported by previous research.

What Are the Goals of the Intervention?

Prior to implementation, it is important that researchers define the goals of the hotspot intervention. This may seem like a simple question. Most hotspot policing initiatives are designed to reduce crime, minimize harm, or improve the quality of life for citizens living in a crime hotspot. But crime hotspots of different crime types may not overlap (see Haberman, 2017), and most agencies have enough resources to address only a few crime hotspots at once. Establishing a goal requires agencies to be specific about the certain *type(s)* of crime they wish to address (see Haberman et al., In Press). It follows that:

- Patrol strategies may not work for some crime types, like violence occurring indoors.
- Crime specific goals are often more attainable than those that seek to reduce an entire category of crime.
- Being deliberate about the crime types the initiative will focus on will help guide the analysis for identifying deployment areas.

Therefore, being specific in the early stages of the initiative helps set it up for success from the start.

Relatedly, realistic goals about the desired impact of patrol-based strategies at crime hotspots are needed. As noted, police patrol practices may have only short-term impacts that decay rapidly overtime (see Sorg et al., 2013). Longstanding and complex crime problems will often require a broader problem-solving strategy to address the underlying factors conducive to crime (Haberman et al., 2016). Being clear about what will be considered success over a given time frame will help know when to potentially end a resource intensive initiative or pivot to additional tactics, like problem solving.

What Is the Definition of a "Hotspot"?

Another factor to consider when designing a patrol-based policing intervention is deciding on the definition of a "hotspot". Past research has generally defined hotspots as specific addresses, specific street blocks or intersections, or collections of street blocks (i.e., grids; see Haberman, 2017). First, the size and location of crime hotspots may dictate the patrol deployment strategy. For example, if an agency is interested is reducing residential burglaries, then several grids spread out across a city for vehicle patrol is logical. Alternatively, foot patrols around an entertainment district may be reasonable if an agency plans to focus on nighttime street robberies in just the central business district. Second, the specific crime types can be intertwined with the hotspot definition used. For example, if single addresses are analyzed, large retail locations often will be the top-ranked hotspots in an analysis of all crime types due to high levels of theft and shoplifting that occur there, but those crime types may not be most amenable to patrol-based strategies. Alternatively, an address-level analysis of robbery will likely lead to stores that are repeatedly robbed being identified as hotspots. Of course, all of these examples may be appropriate in a given application, but the larger point is that the definition of hotspots used (and crime type analyzed) has implications for the population of hotspots ultimately available for deployment.

What Are the Components of the Strategy?

A successful patrol strategy should consider three components: (1) frequency and duration of patrols, (2) overall length of the intervention, and (3) types of activities required of officers when patrolling crime hotspots.

There is some research on the duration of individual patrols. Research suggests officers spend about 12 to 15 minutes at crime hotspots every 2 hours. After this, police patrols have diminishing deterrent benefits (Koper, 1995; Telep et al., 2014). This approach conserves resources, but some agencies may want to use patrols to build community relationships or gather intelligence (Haberman & Stiver, 2020); thus longer patrols spanning an entire shift may be more practical. No causal research exists comparing the relative effectiveness of different patrol lengths. In practice, patrol duration will depend on staffing levels, officer availability, and monetary resources (e.g., overtime pay).

Again, no research exists to guide how long an overall patrol initiative should last. Most initiatives typically stop when the grant funds supporting the work run out. However, there is some research to suggest the effects of hotspot foot patrols decay over time (Sorg et al., 2013; Novak et al., 2016). Sherman (1990) theorized deterrence decay was likely after offenders realized the risk of apprehension is lower than originally perceived (Sherman, 1990). Thus, hotspot patrol strategies should likely end after a few months or transition into a more robust strategy (Haberman et al., 2016).

A final consideration when developing a patrol strategy is to determine what officers will do while they are patrolling a crime hotspot. As noted, in studies showing hotspot patrol's effectiveness, officer activities have ranged from sitting in a patrol car to increased enforcement activity, like stopping vehicles and pedestrians, issuing citations, or making arrests. While each of these responses is likely to have *some* deterrent effect, there is no research on what actions are most effective relative to others. It is also possible enforcement tactics (e.g., pedestrian stops) can harm police–community relations and undermine citizens' perceptions of police legitimacy (Brunson, 2007). Enforcement actions are likely best if they focused precisely on the small number of people driving crime in a hotspot as opposed being applied broadly (Groff et al., 2015). As such, what officers are instructed to do (and held accountable for) while on hotspot patrols is extremely important and police executives should select enforcement activities that are consistent with the goals of the intervention but also align with the values of the community.

How Will Officers Be Held Accountable?

Based on the authors' experience, most patrol-based initiatives will fail to reach their potential or entirely without a process to hold officers accountable for conducting patrols. Agencies can monitor compliance in several ways – commonly referred to as "dosage" in academic studies. First, the simplest ways to measure patrols are using global positioning systems (GPSs) or automated vehicle location (AVL) systems. GPS may be included as part of officers' body-worn cameras (BWCs) or even embedded into radios. In that case, it can be assessed how often and for how long officers are in particular areas. BWC footage can also be used to see officers' behaviors while on patrol. AVL is particularly useful for vehicle-based patrol strategies, as only officers' vehicles will be tracked.

Second, designated call codes allow officers to manually alert dispatch when entering and leaving a crime hotspot on patrol. Any agency with computer-aided dispatch can easily generate a dataset on patrol dosage using this method. Similar processes could likely be developed in police records management systems too. Third, some police managers may prefer to monitor officers' actions during random spot checks. This strategy is obviously labor intensive but may be useful in different contexts. Nonetheless, incorporating hotspot patrol dosage analyses into accountability meetings or other mechanisms will help agencies ensure the initiative is being implemented with fidelity.

How Should Impact Be Assessed?

After implementation, it is crucial to assess the impact of the intervention. Hotspot interventions can have many goals, such as reducing calls for service or crime incidents or improving police–community relations. Of course, the previous research evidence suggests hotspot patrols are likely to be effective, but local variations in implementation, dosage, and so on may mean effects vary over sites and times. Standard evaluation methods can be used and adapted based on the goals established at the start of a hotspot patrol initiative, such as assessing changes in calls for service, crime incidents, or pre-post community surveys, but it is always best to confirm an agency's goals have been met when implementing hotspot patrols. Agencies that want a more rigorous evaluation might consider partnering with a university research partner, particularly in the planning phase of the initiative, which can help add to hotspot patrol's evidence base.

Conclusion

The purpose of this chapter was to (1) review of the evidence base for police patrol practices and (2) offer recommendations to aid in the implementation of patrol-based strategies. Overall, the evidence suggests that police patrol can reduce crime when targeted at high-crime locations for short amounts of time. These effects were observed for shift-length and intermittent patrols (12–15 minutes) as well as vehicle and foot patrol initiatives. The key component, however, is that patrol-based strategies are best suited for micro-level crime hotspots. Unfortunately, comparative evidence on which variations on patrol strategies (e.g., shift length vs. intermittent or vehicle vs. foot patrol) is not available, but all have been found to work in general and agencies can likely implement any variation with confidence. For police agencies implementing hotspot patrols, we recommend considering:

1. The goals of the intervention.
2. The size and scope of a crime "hotspot".
3. The frequency and duration of the response.
4. The mechanisms needed to hold officers accountable.
5. The best way to assess the impact of the intervention.

We stress that agencies should especially consider how hotspot patrols might impact police–community relations, be prepared for short-term crime reduction benefits, and consider integrating hotspot patrols into a larger crime reduction strategy (see Haberman et al., 2016). More research is needed comparing the effectiveness of different dosages, durations, and modalities of hotspot patrols.

References

Bayley, D. H. (1994). *Police for the Future*. Oxford University Press on Demand.

Braga, A. A., Turchan, B., Papachristos, A. V., & Hureau, D. M. (2019). Hot spots policing of small geographic areas effects on crime. *Campbell Systematic Reviews*, *15*(3), 1–88.

Braga, A. A., & Weisburd, D. L. (2020). Does hot spots policing have meaningful impacts on crime? Findings from an alternative approach to estimating effect sizes from place-based program evaluations. *Journal of Quantitative Criminology*. doi: 10.1007/s10940-020-09481-7

Brunson, R. K. (2007). "Police don't like Black people": African-American young men's accumulated police experiences. *Criminology & Public Policy*, *6*(1), 71–101. doi: 10.1111/j.1745-9133.2007.00423.x

Brunson, R. K., & Miller, J. (2006). Young Black men and urban policing in the United States. *British Journal of Criminology*, *46*(4), 613–640. doi: 10.1093/bjc/azi093

Cousineau, D. (1973). A critique of the ecological deterrence approach to the study of deterrence. *Social Science Quarterly*, *54*(1), 152–157.

Eck J. E. (2003). Police problems: The complexity of problem theory, research, and evaluation. In J. Knutsson (Ed). *Problem-oriented policing: From innovation to mainstream* (Crime prevention studies, Vol. 15, pp. 67–102). Criminal Justice Press.

Gau, J. M., & Brunson, R. K. (2010). Procedural justice and order maintenance policing: A study of inner-city young men's perceptions of police legitimacy. *Justice Quarterly*, *27*(2), 255–279. doi: 10.1080/07418820902763889

Groff, E. R., Ratcliffe, J. H., Haberman, C. P., Sorg, E. T., Joyce, N. M., & Taylor, R. B. (2015). Does what police do at hot spots matter? The Philadelphia policing tactics experiment. *Criminology*, *53*(1), 23–53.

Haberman, C. P. (2016). A view inside the "black box" of hot spots policing from a sample of police commanders. *Police Quarterly*, *19*(4), 488–517.

Haberman, C. P. (2017). Overlapping hot spots?: Examination of the spatial heterogeneity of hot spots of different crime types. *Criminology & Public Policy*, *16*(2), 633–660. doi: 10.1111/1745-9133.12303

Haberman, C. P., Clutter, J. E., Lee, H. (In Press). A robbery is a robbery is a robbery? Exploring crime specificity in official police incident data. *Police Practice and Research*.

Haberman, C. P., Groff, E. R., Ratcliffe, J. H., & Sorg, E. T. (2016). Satisfaction with police in violent crime hot spots: Using community surveys as a guide for selecting hot spots policing tactics. *Crime and Delinquency*, *62*(4), 525–557. doi: 10.1177/0011128713516840

Haberman, C. P., & Stiver, W. H. (2018). The Dayton foot patrol program: An evaluation of hot spots foot patrols in a central business district. *Police Quarterly*, *22*(3), 247–277. doi: 10.1177/1098611118813531

Haberman, C. P., & Stiver, W. H. (2020). Using officers' perspectives to guide the implementation of hot spots foot patrols. *Policing & Society*, *30*(8), 920–932. doi: 10.1080/10439463.2019.1611822
Kelling, G. L. (1981). *The Newark foot patrol experiment*. Police Foundation.
Kelling, G. L., Pate, T., Dieckman, D., & Brown, C. E. (1974). *The Kansas City preventive patrol experiment: A summary report*. Police Foundation.
Kochel, T. R. (2010). Constructing hot spots policing: Unexamined consequences for disadvantaged populations and for police legitimacy. *Criminal Justice Policy Review*, *22*(3), 350–374.
Koper, C. S. (1995). Just enough police presence: Reducing crime and disorderly behavior by optimizing patrol time in crime hot spots. *Justice Quarterly*, *12*(4), 649–672. doi: 10.1080/07418829500096231
Lawton, B. A., Taylor, R. B., & Luongo, A. J. (2005). Police officers on drug corners in Philadelphia, drug crime, and violent crime: Intended, diffusion, and displacement impacts. *Justice Quarterly*, *22*(4), 427–451. doi: 10.1080/07418820500364619
Nagin, D. S. (2013). Deterrence in the twenty-first century. *Crime and Justice*, *42*(1), 199–263. doi: 10.1086/670398
Nagin, D. S., Solow, R. M., & Lum, C. (2015). Deterrence, criminal opportunities, and police. *Criminology*, *53*(1), 74–100.
National Research Council. (2004). Fairness and effectiveness in policing: The evidence. Committee to review research on police policy and practices. In W. Skogan & K. Frydl (Eds.), *Committee on law and justice, division of behavioral and social sciences and education*. The National Academies Press.
Novak, K. J., Fox, A. M., Carr, C. M., & Spade, D. A. (2016). The efficacy of foot patrol in violent places. *Journal of Experimental Criminology*, *12*(3), 465–475.
Piquero, A. R., Farrington, D. P., & Blumstein, A. (2003). The criminal career paradigm. *Crime and Justice*, *30*, 359–506.
Piza, E. L., & O'Hara, B. A. (2014). Saturation foot-patrol in a high-violence area: A quasi-experimental evaluation. *Justice Quarterly*, *31*(4), 693–718.
Pratt, T. C., Cullen, F. T., Blevins, K. R., Daigle, L. E., & Madensen, T. D. (2006). The empirical status of deterrence theory: A meta-analysis. In F. T. Cullen, J. P. Wright, & K. R. Blevins (Eds.), *Taking stock: The status of criminological theory – Advances in criminological theory* (Vol. 15, pp. 367–395). Transaction.
Ratcliffe, J. H., & Sorg, E. T. (2017). *Foot Patrol: Rethinking the cornerstone of policing*. Springer.
Ratcliffe, J. H., Taniguchi, T., Groff, E. R., & Wood, J. D. (2011). The Philadelphia foot patrol experiment: A randomized controlled trial of police patrol effectiveness in violent crime hotspots. *Criminology*, *49*(3), 795–831. doi: 10.1111/j.1745-9125.2011.00240.x
Ratcliffe, J. H., Groff, E. R., Sorg, E. T., & Haberman, C. P. (2015). Citizens' reactions to hot spots policing: Impacts on perceptions of crime, disorder, safety and police. *Journal of Experimental Criminology*, *11*(3), 393–417.
Rosenbaum, D. P. (2006). The limits of hot spots policing. In D. Weisburd & A. A. Braga (Eds.), *Police innovation: Contrasting perspectives* (pp. 245–263). Cambridge University Press.
Rosenfeld, R., Deckard, M. J., & Blackburn, E. (2014). The effects of directed patrol and self-initiated enforcement on firearm violence: A randomized controlled study of hot spot policing. *Criminology*, *52*(3), 428–449. doi: 10.1111/1745-9125.12043
Sherman, L. W. (1990). Police crackdowns: Initial and residual deterrence. *Crime and Justice*, *12*, 1–48.
Sherman, L. W., Gartin, P. R., & Buerger, M. E. (1989). Hot spots of predatory crime: Routine activities and the criminology of place. *Criminology*, *27*(1), 27–55.
Sherman, L. W., & Rogan, D. P. (1995). Effects of gun seizures on gun violence: "Hot spots" patrol in Kansas City. *Justice Quarterly*, *12*(4), 673–693. doi: 10.1080/07418829500096241
Sherman, L. W., & Weisburd, D. (1995). General deterrent effects of police patrol in crime "hot spots": A randomized, controlled trial. *Justice Quarterly*, *12*(4), 625–648. doi: 10.1080/07418829500096221
Sorg, E. T., Haberman, C. P., Ratcliffe, J. H., & Groff, E. R. (2013). Foot patrol in violent crime hot spots: The longitudinal impact of deterrence and posttreatment effects of displacement. *Criminology*, *51*(1), 65–101. doi: 10.1111/j.1745-9125.2012.00290.x
Sorg, E. T., Wood, J. D., Groff, E. R., & Ratcliffe, J. H. (2014). Boundary adherence during place-based policing evaluations: A research note. *Journal of Research in Crime and Delinquency*, *51*(3), 377–393.
Telep, C. W., Mitchell, R. J., & Weisburd, D. (2014). How much time should the police spend at crime hot spots? Answers from a police agency directed randomized field trial in Sacramento, California. *Justice Quarterly*, *31*(5), 905–933. doi: 10.1080/07418825.2012.710645

Weisburd, D. (2015). The law of crime concentration and the criminology of place. *Criminology*, *53*(2), 133–157.
Weisburd, D., & Braga, A. A., (2019). Hot spots policing as a model for police innovation. In D. Weisburd & A. A. Braga (Eds.), *Police innovation: Contrasting perspectives* (2nd ed., pp. 347–365). Cambridge University Press.
Weisburd, D., & Green, L. (1995). Policing drug hot spots: The Jersey City drug market analysis experiment. *Justice Quarterly*, *12*(4), 711–735. doi: 10.1080/07418829500096261
Weisburd, D., Hinkle, J. C., Famega, C., & Ready, J. (2011). The possible "backfire" effects of hot spots policing: An experimental assessment of impacts on legitimacy, fear, and collective efficacy. *Journal of Experimental Criminology*, *7*(4), 297–320.
Weisburd, D., Wooditch, A., Weisburd, S., & Yang, S.-M. (2016). Do stop, question, and frisk practices deter crime? Evidence at microunits of space and time. *Criminology & Public Policy*, *15*(1), 31–56. doi: 10.1111/1745-9133.12172
Weisburd, D., Wyckoff, L. A., Ready, J., Eck, J. E., Hinkle, J. C., & Gajewski, F. (2006). Does crime just move around the corner? A controlled study of spatial displacement and diffusion of crime control benefits. *Criminology*, *44*(3), 549–592. doi: 10.1111/j.1745-9125.2006.00057.x

19

POLICING TECHNOLOGY

Silas Patterson and Kenneth J. Novak

Technological advances impact nearly every part of modern society, and technology (mainly information and digital) continues to evolve with staggering speed. This chapter focuses on three examples of police technology: National Integrated Ballistic Information Network (NIBIN), gunshot detection technology (GDT), and real-time crime centers (RTCCs). These are a relatively new evolution of police technology that focuses primarily (though not exclusively) on investigative functions. This chapter will highlight evidence-based approaches to understanding the efficacy of these technologies, highlighting what we know, what we don't know, and what we need to know as they become more predominant features within policing and society.

Several themes emerged from a review of the scientific literature:

- The implementation of NIBIN, GDT, and RTCC enhanced the efficiency of many police activities and efforts,
- It is unclear whether NIBIN, GDT, and RTCC produced measurable crime reduction benefits,
- It is unclear whether NIBIN, GDT, and RTCC produced a good return on investment, and
- Little is known about whether NIBIN, GDT, and RTCC impact equity in policing outcomes.

Introduction

There are many examples of how technological advancement has directly shaped the functions of policing. For instance, in its time, the installation of call boxes was viewed as cutting-edge technology and dramatically changed the day-to-day behaviors of street-level officers (Kelling & Moore, 1988). August Vollmer is responsible for integrating technology into police operations, including bicycles, motorcycles, automobiles, and two-way radios into patrol functions and polygraph tests into investigative procedures (Carte & Carte, 1975). Technology has impacted police accountability and transparency (e.g., body-worn cameras (BWCs)) and less-than-lethal weapons (e.g., conducted energy devices like TASER) and has affected investigative functions, including fingerprinting and DNA collection. It has become increasingly efficient to share personal information that could enhance criminal investigations between police departments

DOI: 10.4324/9781003219286-24

through the Advanced Fingerprint Identification Technology (AFIT) and the Combined DNA Index System (CODIS) (Cordner & Cordner, 2017; Schwabe et al., 2001).

When reflecting on the influence of technology on policing, it may be instructive to consider its impact across Bayley's (1994) framework of effectiveness, efficiency, and fairness. For example, the two-way radio allowed for centralized dispatching and communication between officers and supervisors, permitting strategic allocation of resources to enhance effectiveness and efficiency (as well as keeping track of what officers were doing within their environment). The automobile increased the efficiency in which police could respond to citizens' calls for assistance. BWCs shed new light on the low-visibility interactions between the police and the public, enhancing fairness and equity during encounters. AFIT and CODIS permit efficient information sharing across police departments, centralizing intelligence across decentralized police agencies. A systematic review of closed-circuit television (CCTV) indicated the technology could effectively lead to significant reductions of crime in public space (Piza et al., 2019).

National Integrated Ballistic Information Network

NIBIN is a database maintained by the Bureau of Alcohol, Tobacco, Firearms, and Explosives (ATF), whose purpose is to identify commonalities and connections between shooting events. The science is beyond the scope of this review, but the logic behind NIBIN to enhance investigations and prosecutions of gun crime is straightforward. When a gun is fired, it creates unique markings on the cartridge cases like the firearm's 'fingerprint'. Local or state police upload images of spent cartridges collected at crime scenes as part of the integrated ballistic identification system (IBIS) to a national database. Additionally, firearms seized as part of criminal investigations are 'test-fired,' and the images from those cartridges are added to the database. NIBIN technicians from the National Correlation and Training Center (NNCTC) compare (or correlate) images to identify possible *leads* – meaning two cartridges were likely fired from the same gun. The NNCTC notifies the police departments who recovered the cartridges of the lead, and correlation review specialists conduct an additional review of the physical cartridges to confirm a *hit* between the cartridges (King et al., 2013, 2017). Connections between shooting incidents can have investigative value by pooling intelligence gained from independent incidents.

ATF (2021) reported 258 NIBIN locations across the United States. Additionally, ATF has coordinated NIBIN technology-based process through Crime Gun Intelligence Centers (CGICs), inter-agency organizational arrangements between local police, ATF, and prosecutorial partners. CGIC is a business model designed to operationalize NIBIN across police departments. In fiscal year 2020, 25 CGICs were implementing a model based upon several key pillars: a comprehensive collection of ballistic evidence (e.g., cartridges), timely entry and correlation of ballistic evidence, timely analysis by ATF's NNCTC, assignment of leads and hits to local agencies for investigative follow-up, coordination of police (arrests) activities for state or federal prosecution, and providing feedback to partners to improve and sustain the CGIC model (ATF, 2021; PERF, 2017). In short, the goals of CGIC are improving investigative and prosecutorial effectiveness and efficiency, and if achieved, enhancing public safety.

Most evidence-based examinations of NIBIN have focused on jurisdictions implementing a CGIC, and because of this, the evidence of impact will focus on these CGIC evaluations. Related, little appears in the peer-reviewed scientific literature on the effects of NIBIN or CGIC; however, there have been several in-depth examinations of different CGICs – as such, we will focus our attention accordingly.

Examinations routinely note that inputs and activities increased after implementing the CGIC organizational arrangement. This included dramatic increases in the amount of ballistic evidence collected, consistent with the comprehensive collection goal within the CGIC model. Activities including ballistic examinations conducted and leads or hits produced also consistently increased (Flippin et al., 2021; Koper et al., 2019; Mei et al., 2019; PERF, 2017; Uchida et al., 2019). Additional, activities related to inputting ballistic evidence and timely correlation and analysis of leads or hits increased (Katz et al., 2021; Novak & King, 2020). Collectively, the research evidence strongly suggests that processes, inputs, and activities associated with the CGIC model were achieved. But evidence of impact or outcomes is far less clear. For example, in Phoenix, the implementation of CGIC was related to a 36% increase in homicide clearance rates, a 15% increase in aggravated assaults, 14% in carrying a weapon, and an 8% increase in discharging a firearm. Arrests for gun crimes were also 75% more likely when a NIBIN lead was produced (Flippin et al., 2021). At the same time, no increases in clearance rates were observed for armed robberies or drive-by shootings (Flippin et al., 2021; Katz et al., 2021). Tentative evidence exists that clearance rates increased in Milwaukee for nonfatal shootings, though there is less evidence of impact for other gun-related offenses (Koper et al., 2019).

Evidence of impact becomes scant at later stages of the CGIC model. There is an inconsistent indication that prosecutorial outcomes were enhanced (Katz et al., 2021). However, in Los Angeles, there was a corresponding increase in firearm possession court filings and convictions (Uchida et al., 2019). The outcomes on the environment are also inconsistent. For example, implementation of CGIC corresponded with about a 19% decrease in homicides and 7.7% decrease in firearm-related homicides in Los Angeles (Uchida et al., 2019). In Milwaukee, there were "tentative indications that NIBIN-related arrests reduced [fatal and nonfatal] shootings" (Koper et al., 2019, p. 48). In contrast, there was "no discernible effect on violent crime outcomes" in Washington, D.C. (Mei et al., 2019: p. 6).

Gunshot Detection Technology

GDT relies on strategically placed acoustic sensors that detect and locate gunshots and transfer information to a centralized computer system that informs law enforcement personnel promptly. GDT offers law enforcement various forms of intelligence centered on the detonation of a firearm. The strategically placed sensors detect acoustic soundwaves produced when a gun is detonated and use triangulation to identify the time of the gunshot and the spatial area in which it occurred (Choi et al., 2014; Doucette et al., 2021; Irvin-Erickson et al., 2017; Lawrence et al., 2018; Mares & Blackburn, 2012; Mares & Blackburn, 2021; Mazerolle et al., 1998; Ratcliffe et al., 2019; Watkins et al., 2002).

GDT emerged in the 1990s as an aid to law enforcement personnel in their dealings with rising cases of gun violence (Mazerolle et al., 1998). An escalating gun violence problem and the fact that most gun-related incidents are underreported to law enforcement created a market for the use of GDT, especially in high crime locations (Doucette et al., 2021; Mares & Blackburn, 2012; Lawrence et al., 2018). This technology aims to expedite law enforcement responses to gun-related crimes. Quick reactions to gun-related violence give police a chance to offer aid to victims, enhance the gathering of physical evidence (cartridges, bullets, and firearms), and increase the apprehension of shooters.

Evidence shows that GDT has impacted police processes. The first process of GDT is to activate or notify law enforcement of gunshot activity in the neighborhood or area of its placement. The implementation of GDT has shown to be an effective tool in increasing police awareness of shooting incidents and producing faster notifications for gunshot activity. Mares & Blackburn, 2021 found that the police in Saint Louis responded to 79% more gunshot incidents during the implementation and expansion of GDT compared to before implementation. Ratcliffe et al. (2019) found a 259% increase in gun-related incidents during the implementation of a GDT in Philadelphia. The evidence seems to support that the implementation of GDT in neighborhoods experiencing high rates of gun-related incidents increases police awareness of those incidents compared to traditional citizen reports or calls for service.

Some research reveals the effectiveness of GDT in reducing police response times to gun-related incidents compared to traditional responses to citizen reports. GDT has shown relatively minor reductions in police response times in terms of numbers, but many of these reductions have been deemed statistically significant. The decrease in response time ranges from about 30 seconds to 2 minutes. Choi and colleagues (2014) found a significant reduction of 31.67 seconds in police response times to gun-related incidents, while Goldenberg and colleagues (2019) found a 1.7-minute average reduction in police response times due to GDT activation. Mazerolle and colleagues (1998) observed around a 1-minute decrease in police response times to gun-related incidents.

Some collateral consequences of GDT exist. GDT has been shown to increase officer workload dramatically. Mazerolle and colleagues (1998) compared the number of "radio runs" (dispatches) stemming from citizen calls and GDT notifications over two months. Their findings revealed 39 citizen-initiated radio runs for gunfire and 151 extra radio runs arising from GDT notifications. These numbers indicated a 287% increase in responses to gun-related incidents. It makes logical sense that the implementation of GDT increases officer workload due to the significant increase in awareness of gun-related activity. Still, this workload needs to be juxtaposed against the measurable benefits realized.

Another consequence of the increased notification of gun-related incidents is that police response yields little to no evidence collection and witness identification results. Ratcliffe et al. (2019) found that although GDT's implementation increased notification and responsivity to gun-related incidents, a significant number of responses resulted in unfounded results. This finding indicated that officers had a workload increase but did not see a significant change in confirming gun-related incidents. This affirms that lacking confirmation of gun-related incidents by police does not indicate failure by the GDT but reveals the difficulty in locating substantial physical evidence that a gun crime occurred even after notification. These process-oriented findings guide us into the next section of what we do not know.

A large proportion of research on GDT is process focused, with little evidence on the actual effect these technologies have on gun crime, gun-related violence, and investigative closures and outcomes. The limited studies that have evaluated outcomes related to the implementation of GDT show minimal impact. Doucette and colleagues (2021) examined the effects of GDT on firearm homicides, murder arrests, and weapons arrests over 17 years and found no significant impact on gun-related homicides or arrests. Focusing on reporting outcomes, Mares and Blackburn (2012) found that GDT has no impact on gun-related crimes within the geographic location of their implementation.

The current state of research on GDT leaves much to be desired. The limited available research does not indicate any substantial impacts of GDT on law enforcement processes or outcomes. Increases in notifications and small reductions in police response times are the most consistent impacts of GDT. However, an uptick in notifications that do not lead to an increase in arrests or reduction in gun crime creates an increase in workload for officers with little tangible results. What is lacking in the research is comprehensive evaluations of GDT's impact on gun crime outcomes. Research that seeks to examine the impact of GDT's on arrests and rates of gun-related violence is necessary to understand the effectiveness of this technology.

Real-Time Crime Centers

RTCCs act as centralized command and control centers that use various police technologies to rapidly distribute information to police personnel in real-time responses to criminal incidents or investigations. Larger municipal agencies typically deploy RTCCs due to resource availability and the capability to compile various technologies and personnel into a centralized workgroup (Gurette et al., 2021; Hollywood et al., 2019). RTCCs possess various operational goals, the most prominent being crime reduction, offender accountability, officer safety, and timely responses to calls for service (Hollywood et al., 2019). Research on RTCCs is limited, with few studies examining their processes and outcomes (Gurette et al., 2021; Hollywood et al., 2019; Przeslowski et al., 2022).

Configuration of RTCCs varies based on agency characteristics; however, typically they are organizationally situated in support units such as intelligence or investigations and are made up of sworn personnel, crime analysts, and intelligence analysts. RTCCs are also considered their own operational units, separated from traditional intelligence or analyst units (Guerette et al., 2021). RTCCs are composed of a vast set of other supporting technologies. Guerette and colleagues (2021) found over 21 unique technologies used by the examined RTCC; however, they identified seven technologies used more consistently than others. These seven technologies were calls for service data, social media, CCTV footage, license plate readers, intelligence databases, open-source information, and criminal history information. An evaluation of a Chicago-based RTCC showed similar technological uses, including crime mapping software and GDT (Hollywood et al., 2019). An assessment of an RTCC housed in Chicago stated that crime mapping technologies offered the most situational awareness to officers in the field (Hollywood et al., 2019). RTCCs operate to provide real-time information to law enforcement personnel within their jurisdiction; many possess the ability to share information in real time to multiple agencies across various jurisdictions (city, county, state, federal).

RTCCs provide various functions, such as support for day-to-day decision making, answering information requests, monitoring various technologies (CCTV, GDT, radio feeds), offering field support, and engaging in cross-agency collaborations (Guerette et al., 2021; Hollywood et al., 2019). Real time refers to the information given to officers while they are responding to calls, during active surveillance activities, and during investigations following a criminal incident (Guerette et al., 2021). RTCCs are not crime specific and are designed to handle and distribute information connected to many crime types. RTCCs typically operate under limited hours; however, some function on 24/7 cycles (Guerette et al., 2021). The activation of RTCC services is typically a result of calls for service, investigations, individual officer requests, and system alerts stemming from technologies such as gunshot detection technologies (Guerette et al., 2021).

To date, the effectiveness of RTCCs on policing and justice-related outcomes is unclear. Lack of research on the impact of RTCCs could result from multiple factors. First, little empirical research examines the processes of RTCCs, and those that do reveal similar operational goals but significant variations in how they achieve those goals (Hollywood et al., 2019; Guerette et al., 2021). Operational processes may vary based on location, agency resources, and personnel. Outcome evaluations of RTCCs are even more limited. Hollywood and colleagues (2019) indicated that after the implementation of RTCCs in Chicago, crime was reduced overall, ranging in reductions of 3% to 17%. Although these findings are promising, the outcome evaluation conducted by Hollywood and colleagues (2019) is the only outcome-focused evaluation of RTCCs to date.

Moving forward, more research is needed in all areas of RTCCs. Evaluations of the processes are necessary to grasp operational procedures, primarily what consistencies exist in how RTCCs are operationalized. Second, research should examine the impact of RTCCs on crime, investigations, and law enforcement processes. Like any policing technology, RTCCs are an investment. It is important to understand the integrity of the investment, and extensive research is needed to arrive at any concrete conclusions.

Conclusion

The evolution of informational and digital technology will continue to impact policing. Technology that began as call-boxes, automobiles, and two-way radios has set the stage for modern incarnations, including NIBIN, GDT, and RTCCs. The evidence base on this technology's effectiveness, efficiency, and fairness is in its infancy. While a body of scientific literature has begun to develop, much remains unknown. We offer several observations from the current literature about what we know, what we don't know, and what we need to know to make evidence-based determinations on the efficacy of these technologies.

The implementation of NIBIN, GDT, and RTCCs has created efficiencies within the policing industry. The police can collect and analyze more ballistic evidence, are aware of more gunfire (thereby having a complete understanding of the nature of gun violence in their jurisdiction), and coordinate resources in real time to respond to emergencies or enhance investigations. However, it is unclear whether NIBIN, GDT, and RTCCs have led to consistent, measurable decreases in crime or other beneficial outcomes. This is likely because there is a dearth of rigorous scientific research that explicitly examines technology outcomes. Exploratory research on whether and how these technologies translate to measurable public safety or other justice-centered outcomes is an essential next step in the evolution of these technologies.

Further, little is known about whether NIBIN, GDT, and RTCCs represent a responsible return on investment. These technologies, and their maintenance, represent a financial barrier to many police organizations. Federal support (financial resources and inter-organizational partnerships) has made acquisition and operation accessible, but it is difficult to determine the ROI without more information on outcomes. For example, GDT systems, in particular, appear in small parts of jurisdictions, typically geographic areas with a disproportion of gun violence. These are often financial decisions because blanketing a city with GDT technology is cost prohibitive. The implementation of GDT is costly, ranging from 3.9 to 5.4 million dollars a year for large urban areas (Doucette et al., 2021). Implementing this technology at such a high price with little positive impact creates a need to reevaluate widespread investment in GDT. Also, as noted, the implementation of GDT was met with corresponding increases in street-officer workload (Mazerolle et al., 1998), which too represents a resource investment. Relatedly, Flippin et al. (2021) estimated the federal government had allocated over \$20 million to local jurisdictions to create and operate CGICs. The police, as stewards of the public dollar, should be aware of the return on investment this (or any) technology has.

Finally, little is known about whether NIBIN, GDT, and RTCCs alter the relationship between the police and the public. Much like the introduction of the automobile qualitatively changed the nature, frequency, and content of officer–citizen interactions, these technologies too can have unintended consequences. Suppose GDT is more likely to be in communities with disproportionate firearm violence, and these same areas are also characterized as a concentrated social and economic disadvantage. In that case, the frequency and nature of officers and citizens will be different. If RTCCs pool intelligence from GDT and other data sources (like CCTV and license plate readers), these areas will also be scrutinized differently than other areas. These consequences need not be inequitable, but when police transparency and accountability are increasingly central to their legitimacy, evidence-based inquires should explicitly consider these implications as part of technology's outcomes.

References

Alcohol, Tobacco, Firearms and Explosives (2021, September). Fact sheet – crime gun intelligence centers (CGIC). Retrieved from www.atf.gov/resource-center/fact-sheet/fact-sheet-crime-gun-intelligence-centers-cgic

Bayley, D. H. (1994). *Police for the future*. Oxford University Press.

Carte, G. E., & Carte, E. H. (1975). *Police reform in the United States: The era of August Vollmer, 1905–1932*. University of California Press.

Choi, K.-S., Librett, M., & Collins, T. (2014). An empirical evaluation: Gunshot detection system and its effectiveness on police practices. *Police Practice and Research, 15, 48–61.*

Cordner, A., & Cordner, G. (2017). Overview of law enforcement technology. In L. J. Moriarty (Ed.), *Criminal justice technology in the 21st century* (pp. 39–68). Charles C. Thomas Publishing.

Doucette, M. L., Green, C., Necci Dineen, J., Shapiro, D., & Raissian, K. M. (2021). Impact of Shotspotter technology on firearm homicides and arrests among large metropolitan counties: A longitudinal analysis, 1999–2016. *Journal of Urban Health: Bulletin of the New York Academy of Medicine, 98(5)*, 609–662.

Flippin, M. R., Katz, C. M., & King, W. R. (2021). Examining the impact of a crime gun intelligence center. *Journal of Forensic Sciences*. Advanced online publication. doi: 10.1111/1556-4029.14952.

Goldenberg, A., Rattigan, D., Dalton, M., Gaughan, J. P., Thomson, J. S., Remick, K., Butts, C., & Hazelton, J. P. (2019). Use of ShotSpotter detection technology decreases prehospital time for patients sustaining gunshot wounds. *The Journal of Trauma and Acute Care Surgery, 87*(6), 1253–1259.

Guerette, R. T., Przeslowski, K., Rodriguez, J., Ramirez, J., Gutierrez, A., & Lee-Silcos, J. (2021). *A national appraisal of real time crime centers in the United States*. Bureau of Justice Assistance.

Hollywood, J. S., McKay, K. N., Woods, D., & Agniel, D. (2019). Real-time crime centers in Chicago. Retrieved October, 1, 2021. https://www.rand.org/pubs/research_reports/RR3242.html

Irvin-Erickson, Y., La Vigne, N., Levine, N., Tiry, E., & Bieler, S. (2017). What does gunshot detection technology tell us about gun violence? *Applied Geography, 86*, 262–273.

Katz, C. M., Flippin, M., Huff, J., King, W. R., & Ellefritz, J. (2021). *Evaluation of the Phoenix crime gun intelligence center: Final report*. Center for Violence Prevention & Community Safety, Arizona State University.

Kelling, G. L., & Moore, M. H. (1988). *The evolving strategy of policing*. US Department of Justice.

King, W. R., Campbell, B. A., Matusiak, M. C., & Katz, C. M. (2017). Forensic evidence and criminal investigations: The impact of ballistics information on the investigation of violent crime in nine cities. *Journal of Forensic Sciences, 62*(4), 874–880.

King, W. R., Wells, W., Katz, C., Maguire, E. R., & Frank, J. (2013). *Opening the black box of NIBIN: A descriptive process and outcome evaluation of the use of NIBIN and its effects on criminal investigations*. National Institute of Justice.

Koper, C., Vovak, H., & Cowell, B. (2019). *Evaluation of the Milwaukee police department's crime gun intelligence center*. National Police Foundation.

Lawrence, D. S., La Vigne, N. G., Goff, M., & Thompson, P. S. (2018). Lessons learned implementing gunshot detection technology: Results of a process evaluation in three major cities. *Justice Evaluation Journal, 1*(2), 109–129.

Mares, D., & Blackburn, E. (2012). Evaluating the effectiveness of an acoustic gunshot location system in St. Louis, Mo. *Policing, 6*, 26–42.

Mares, D., & Blackburn, E. (2021). Acoustic gunshot detection systems: A quasi-experimental evaluation in St. Louis, MO. *Journal of Experimental Criminology, 17*(2), 193–215.

Mazerolle, L. G., Watkins, C., Rogan, D., & Frank, J. (1998). Using gunshot detection systems in police departments: The impact on police response times and officer workloads. *Police Quarterly, 1*(2), 21–49.

Mei, V., Owusa, F., Quinney, S., Ravishankar, A., & Sebastian, D. (2019). *An evaluation of crime gun intelligence center improvements implemented in Washington, DC, 2016–2019*. The Lab @ DC. Retrieved from https://crimegunintelcenters.org/wp-content/uploads/2019/12/DC-CGIC-Final-Evaluation-Report_10.30.19.pdf

Novak, K. J., & King, W. R. (2020). *Evaluation of the Kansas City Crime Gun Intelligence Center – Final Report*. Bureau of Justice Assistance.

Piza, E. L., Wesh, B. C, Farrington, D. P., & Thomas, A. L. (2019). CCTV surveillance for crime prevention: A 40-year systematic review with meta-analysis. *Criminology and Public Policy*, *18*(1), 135–159.

Police Executive Research Forum. (2017, May). *The "crime gun intelligence center" model: Case studies of the Denver, Milwaukee, and Chicago Approaches to investigating gun crime*. Retrieved from www.policeforum.org/assets/crimegunintelligencecenter.pdf

Przeszlowski, K., Guerette, R. T., Lee-Silcox, J., Rodriguez, J., Ramirez, J., & Gutierrez, A. (2022). The centralization and rapid deployment of police agency information technologies: An appraisal of real-time crime centers in the US. The *Police Journal*, 0032258X221107587.

Ratcliffe, J., Lattanzio, M., Kikuchi, G., & Thomas, K. (2019). A partially randomized field experiment on the effect of an acoustic gunshot detection system on police incident reports. *Journal of Experimental Criminology*, *15*.

Schwabe, W., Davis, L. M., & Jackson, B. A. (2001). *Challenges and Choices for crime-fighting technology federal support of state and local law enforcement*. RAND Corporation.

Uchida, C. D., Quigley, A., & Anderson, K. (2019). *Evaluating the Los Angeles crime gun intelligence center*. Bureau of Justice Assistance.

Watkins, C., Green Mazerolle, L., Rogan, D., & Frank, J. (2002). Technological approaches to controlling random gunfire: Results of a gunshot detection system field test. *Policing: An International Journal of Police Strategies & Management*, *25*(2), 345–370.

20

DRUG ENFORCEMENT AND ITS EFFECTIVENESS

Ojmarrh Mitchell and Alexander G. Toth

Introduction

Drug enforcement refers to law enforcement activities broadly defined aimed at controlling drug availability, use, and drug-related crime (e.g., crimes committed to obtain money for drugs). There are various kinds of drug enforcement strategies and tactics. However, the most common, traditional drug enforcement activities seek to disrupt the drug trade by: (1) reducing drug production, (2) interdicting drugs as they travel from their place of production to their final destination, (3) dismantling drug trafficking organizations (DTOs) by targeting their leaders (i.e., drug "kingpins"), (4) prosecuting those involved in middle-level and street-level drug transactions (seller, users, or both), or (5) seizing the proceeds of drug trafficking (e.g., anti-money laundering, civil/criminal asset forfeiture) (see e.g., Boyum & Reuter, 2005).

Drug enforcement activities are complicated by the fact that illicit drugs are driven by market forces. That is, drug markets are created by consumers seeking to obtain a desired product and sellers seeking to earn profits by supplying the product in demand. Unlike other types of crimes, drug offenses do not have an identifiable victim who could report the offense and potentially identify the offender. The market dynamics and lack of identifiable victims have important implications for drug enforcement. The absence of complaining victims and a dearth of available witnesses means that drug enforcement must use more intrusive tactics such as the use of informants, undercover police, wire taps, and searches of people and their possessions. Another implication is that as long as a society has a demand for psychoactive substances, all participants in drug markets and the specific substances sold in the market are *replaceable*. Drug sellers will be replaced by new sellers or existing sellers will expand their operations to meet demand. Individuals who desist from drug using invariably are replaced in time with new users. Strategies that successfully make one drug unavailable lead to that substance being replaced by another available psychoactive product. The replaceability of drug sellers and users means that drug markets are unlikely to be effectively controlled by deterring apprehended drug offenders (specific deterrence), incapacitating drug offenders, or rehabilitating those involved in drug markets. Instead, effective drug enforcement requires tactics that deter would-be participants in the drug economy (i.e., general deterrence) or minimize

DOI: 10.4324/9781003219286-25

the harms drug offenders do to themselves and others (Kleiman et al., 2011). Further, the financial incentives created by drug profits motivates drug traffickers and sellers to respond to new law enforcement tactics by innovating new methods of distribution. Collectively, these features make drug law enforcement, and controlling illicit markets more generally, exceedingly difficult.

Drug enforcement in absolute terms will inevitably fail. Even in the most secure communities, such as prisons, drugs are successfully trafficked into these facilities despite the many obstacles to drug markets operating in these tightly controlled institutions (e.g., armed guards patrolling the exterior, guards monitoring internal movements and activities). This implies that measuring the effectiveness of drug enforcement using drug availability is a logical but somewhat flawed measure because drug enforcement rarely is successful enough to make a drug unavailable or even very difficult to obtain for users with financial means.

Instead of evaluating drug enforcement in absolute terms, it is often more useful to think of drug law enforcement activities as a kind of "tax" that those involved in drug markets must pay to do business and the cost of these taxes are passed along to consumers. As a result of these taxes imposed on drug markets by drug enforcement, illicit drugs are much more expensive than they would be in the absence of law enforcement targeting drug trafficking. Thus, the price of drugs at the retail level is a key indicator of how much pressure drug law enforcement is placing on drug traffickers and drug markets.

Drug availability and retail drug prices are the two most prominent measures used to assess the effectiveness of drug law enforcement but they are not the only measures. In theory, effective drug enforcement will reduce drug availability causing drug prices to rise and drug use, rates of drug addiction, and drug-related crime to drop. As a result, drug enforcement can be evaluated by focusing on market factors (availability and price) or crime factors (drug use, drug addiction, drug-related crime).

Yet the ability of various drug enforcement strategies in achieving its goals must be weighed against the level of intrusiveness associated with a particular enforcement strategy. For instance, in the 1980s and 1990s many law enforcement agencies developed drug courier profiles to increase rates of domestic drug interdiction (Harris, 2003). These tactics undoubtedly led to more drugs and drug proceeds being indicted by law enforcement; however, these tactics at times morphed into racial profiling that disproportionately intruded into the lives of Blacks and Latinos (Harris, 2003). More recently, law enforcement has de-emphasized these tactics as they are now perceived too costly in terms of intrusiveness and deteriorated relations with minority communities (Mummolo, 2018). These tactics are being replaced by newer strategies that are consistent with harm reduction principles and show signs of effectiveness in achieving their stated goals without exacerbating racial/ethnic disparities.

Key Points:

- Drug crimes are driven by market forces created by users seeking an illicit drug and sellers seeking to profit by supplying this product.
- Traditionally, domestic and international law enforcement attempt to disrupt drug distribution networks at each stage of distribution.
- Drug enforcement activities cause the retail price of illicit drugs to be much higher than they would be in the absence of these activities.

Description of Evidence Base on Drug Enforcement Strategies

Traditional Drug Enforcement Strategies

The central question is: Are the five standard drug enforcement tactics effective in achieving their goals of increasing drug prices and reducing availability? Research assessing drug enforcement finds that collectively these five strategies clearly raise drug prices and reduce availability in comparison to if there were no drug enforcement (Kleiman et al., 2011). Boyum and Reuter (2005) estimate that the cost of producing the coca leaves necessary to produce 1 kilogram of cocaine is $300, and the price of 1 kilogram of pure cocaine in Colombia is $1500 or $1.50 per gram. It follows that in the absence of drug enforcement, a gram of cocaine would likely retail in the United States for less than $10 per gram – after adding transportation costs and dealer profits. Yet, because of drug enforcement, these authors estimate that a gram of 67% pure cocaine retails for more than $100. Further, the price of drugs increases sharply with each additional stage of drug production and distribution. These figures clearly illustrate that drug enforcement, in its totality, exerts considerable pressure on drug traffickers causing retail drug prices to be vastly more expensive than they would be without drug law enforcement.

Individually, however, increasing the intensity of any one of these drug enforcement practices, at best, is likely to have small marginal effects on drug prices and availability. That is, devoting additional law enforcement emphasis on any one of the five standard drug enforcement practices is likely to yield diminishing returns on the investment. The central problem making increased drug enforcement emphasis a poor investment is replacement. Crops destroyed in the fields can be regrown in another area. Regulating precursor chemicals may make these chemicals more difficult to obtain for a time, but inevitably new sources will be found. Apprehending drug kingpins may cripple a particular DTO, but other DTOs will fill the void. And so forth.

The empirical research assessing the effectiveness of intensifying each of the main drug enforcement strategy finds that intensification rarely produces a meaningful effect and oftentimes backfire in various ways. The research evaluating crop eradication is illustrative. Much of this research focuses on crop eradication and its intensification in Colombia. This body of research finds that the amount of land devoted to coca production *increased* after Colombian law enforcement stepped up crop eradication efforts (Moreno-Sanchez et al., 2003). This occurred because farmers whose coca crops were destroyed compensated by cultivating more coca to make up for their losses. In fact, another study conducted by Dion and Russler (2008) estimates that a 1% increase in eradication led to roughly a 1% *increase* in coca cultivation. Additionally, Angrist and Kugler (2008) found that a shock to the cocaine market, which caused a sharp increase in coca prices, led to increased coca cultivation in Colombia.

In turn, this increase in coca cultivation led to increased violence. Taken together, these studies demonstrate that intensified crop eradication not only is ineffective, but also it is likely to backfire by increasing coca cultivation, which leads to increased violence.

Research investigating the effects of interdiction efforts are rare. The research that does exist on this topic typically finds that interdiction efforts either increase drug prices temporarily or have no discernible effect. Weatherburn and Lind (1997) analyzed the effect of heroin seizures by law enforcement in Sydney, Australia on heroin prices. Their results found that heroin seizures were unrelated to heroin prices. In another study, Layne and colleagues (2002) measured the deterrent effect of drug interdiction on U.S. cocaine prices. These authors found that coordinated military operations had limited and temporary effects on drug prices. A qualitative study on the same issue interviewed high-level drug informants found that counter-drug interdiction efforts typically had temporary effects as drug traffickers quickly adopted new transportation routes in the face of stepped-up drug enforcement activities (Toth & Mitchell, 2018). These authors found a key factor in the ineffectiveness of coordinated interdiction efforts is corruption within local law enforcement, as corrupt agents frequently tipped off drug traffickers beforehand.

Apprehending high-level drug traffickers has also been determined to be a highly ineffective means of drug control that backfires by causing increased violence. Calderón and associates (2015) examined the effects of law enforcement captures or killings of drug kingpins and their lieutenants on drug-related violence. None of their findings indicate that taking down kingpins reduces drug-related violence; instead, these authors' results indicate that in the six-months after a high-level drug trafficker is captured or killed there is an increase in drug-related violence in cities in which the DTO operates and a general increase in homicides in the population (i.e., non-drug traffickers). Another, more recent study by Lindo and Padilla-Romo (2018) produced similar findings: arresting kingpins caused large and sustained increases in homicide rates in the area near the capture and smaller increases in violence in other locations in the DTO's drug route. These studies findings suggest that apprehending kingpins destabilizes DTOs, which leads to violence among suitors vying to become the new kingpin.

Perhaps the clearest demonstration of the limited value of increased drug enforcement comes from the war on drugs of the 1980s and 1990s. During this period, drug enforcement shifted emphasis from international operations (e.g., getting Turkey to stop growing opium poppies, disrupting the French Connection that supplied heroin to the United States) to domestic operations targeting retail level dealers and users. Police agencies throughout the United States made drug enforcement a priority. The end result of this new emphasis was a staggering increase in U.S. rates of drug arrests, convictions, and incarceration, despite the fact that drug use had been falling even prior to the launch of the drug war (National Research Council, 2014). If these tactics were effective, then drug prices should have increased due to these amplified drug enforcement activities. The research, however, finds that this massive increase in drug imprisonment affected the retail price of cocaine by only 5–15% (Kuziemko & Levitt, 2004). In fact, drug prices fell during the war on drugs (Office of National Drug Control Policy, 2016), perhaps due to increasing sophistication and efficiency among DTOs. In addition to the war on drugs' ineffectiveness in achieving its stated goals, its intrusive tactics were disproportionately deployed against minority suspects and in minority communities, which exacerbated racial disparities in drug arrests and incarceration and damaged the already tenuous relationship between police and minorities (Alexander, 2010; Tonry, 1995).

The final common set of strategies used in drug law enforcement is the seizure of illicit assets. The logic underlying this tactic is that drug traffickers are in business to earn profits, therefore, depriving traffickers of these profits may serve as a deterrent against continued participation in the drug economy. Several distinct activities are used by law enforcement to deprive illicit assets from drug traffickers, including civil asset forfeiture (e.g., seizing vehicles used to transport drugs without an accompanying criminal conviction), criminal asset forfeiture (e.g., seizing drug money or assets bought with drug money as part of a criminal conviction), and anti-money laundering activities. While such tactics, particularly anti-money laundering activities, have been pervasive, there is no research to our knowledge that assesses the effects of these drug enforcement activities on drug availability, drug prices, or drug-related crime (Reuter & Truman, 2005; Baumer, 2008).

- Collectively, traditional law enforcement strategies cause the prices of illicit drugs to be much higher than if they were legal, yet increasing the intensity of traditional drug law enforcement has little additional benefit in terms of drug prices or availability and may backfire by escalating violence and drug production.

Non-Traditional Strategies

The inability of traditional drug enforcement to effectively control drug crime has led to innovative police tactics that align with the philosophy of harm reduction. Harm reduction is an approach that acknowledges the market forces driving drug offenses, which limit the effectiveness of traditional law strategies in achieving its goals of reducing drug availability, increasing drug prices, and suppressing drug use. In lieu of focusing on these metrics, harm reduction seeks to develop strategies that minimize the harms caused by drug markets and the harms drug users do to themselves and others – but harm reduction does not necessarily seek to reduce drug consummation (Kleiman et al., 2011).

The Law Enforcement Assisted Diversion (LEAD) program is a prominent example of pioneering hard reducing drug enforcement strategy. LEAD was initiated in Seattle, Washington, in 2011 is aimed at reducing drug-related problems and drug use among non-violent low-level drug offenders. Instead of arresting and prosecuting low-level drug offenders, LEAD diverts these individuals from the criminal justice legal system and into harm reduction case management that provides legal assistance and non-coercive mental health and/or substance abuse counseling. This multi-faceted and multi-agency program aims to respond to the needs of individuals with substance use disorders. Early evaluations of the LEAD program indicate that individuals involved in LEAD had fewer jail bookings, spent fewer days in jail, and had considerably lower odds of imprisonment than a comparison group that was arrested and prosecuted as usual (Collins et al., 2017, 2019). Despite these findings being currently unreplicated, dozens of jurisdictions throughout the United States as well as in the United Kingdom and South Africa have adopted LEAD programs (Daugaard et al., 2021).

Another recent innovative approach to drug enforcement is the drug market intervention (DMI). DMI is a "focused deterrence" policing strategy that targets flagrant or overt drug markets in an effort to reduce the crime and disorder associated with open-air drug dealing. DMI attempts to close down overt drug markets by identifying such markets and the dealers operating in them. Law enforcement builds criminal cases against these dealers by using informants and undercover police officers to make controlled buys. Dealers with histories of violence are arrested and prosecuted based on the crimes documented by these enforcement activities. Non-violent dealers, however, are offered an opportunity to participate in a "call-in", in which law enforcement details the criminal cases built against each dealer, informs them that continued drug dealing will lead to aggressive prosecution, and offers a suite of social services to dealers to help redirect their activities towards lawful employment and other prosocial behaviors. Further, to prevent new sellers from conducting business in the targeted drug markets, police make it known that the area is under close surveillance and take aggressive actions against new sellers. Notice that DMI does not attempt to eliminate drug markets, per se; instead, DMI seeks to close overt drug markets and leaves undisturbed discreet, non-violent drug distribution networks. In this way, DMI is consistent with harm reduction principles as it addresses the crime and disorder problems associated with flagrant drug markets

DMI was first implemented in High Point, NC, in 2004, and an evaluation of this intervention found that violent crime declined significantly in the target areas in comparison to the same areas before the intervention to other areas of the city (Corsaro et al., 2012). DMI was implemented in several other cities with mixed but generally positive results (see Braga et al., 2018). Other research that followed a cohort of seven sites found that the sites had significant difficulty implementing DMI; in fact, three of the seven sites were unable to implement DMI, and there was significant variation in how well DMI as implemented in the four other sites (Saunders et al., 2017). Thus, DMI has been demonstrated to be effective if implemented well, but full implementation is often difficult.

While these newer approaches have not been extensively evaluated for their effects on racial/ethnic disparities, logically these less punitive and more targeted approaches are less prone to worsen disparities in criminal justice populations than traditional drug tactics.

- Non-traditional drug enforcement strategies targeting the harms of drug use and drug markets like LEAD and DMI are needed to supplement traditional anti-drug tactics. Evaluations of these strategies yield promising results.

Conclusion

Enforcing drug laws is different than law enforcement against other kinds of crime. Unlike other common crimes, drug crimes are driven by market forces involving seekers of illicit drugs and sellers willing to take the risks of supplying this illegal product. These simple market forces greatly complicate law enforcement and remove many of the levers used to control other types of crime. Specific deterrence, incapacitation, and rehabilitation are unlikely to be effective in suppressing drug use or drug markets, because new sellers and users replace those deterred, incapacitated, or rehabilitated. These factors undermine the effectiveness of the five traditional drug enforcement strategies.

Rather than focusing on suppressing drug use by making drugs expensive, drug law enforcement may need to pivot towards strategies that reduce the harms associated with drug markets and drug use. Non-traditional drug enforcement tactics like LEAD and DMI fit the harm reduction paradigm. While these programs may be difficult to implement well, the existing research suggests that these programs can be effective in reaching their goals if they are implemented well. Clearly, more drug enforcement strategies consistent with the harm reduction principle are necessary to combat the problems associated with drug use and drug markets.

References

Alexander, M. (2010). *The new Jim Crow: Mass incarceration in the age of colorblindness*. The New Press.

Angrist, J. D., & Kugler, A. D. (2008). Rural windfall or a new resource curse? Coca, income, and civil conflict in Colombia. *The Review of Economics and Statistics*, *90*(2), 191–215.

Baumer, E. P. (2008). Evaluating the balance sheet of asset forfeiture laws: Toward evidence-based policy assessments. *Criminology & Public Policy*, *7*, 245.

Boyum, D., & Reuter, P. (2005). *An analytic assessment of U.S. drug policy*. AEI Press.

Braga, A. A., Weisburd, D., & Turchan, B. (2018). Focused deterrence strategies and crime control: An updated systematic review and meta-analysis of the empirical evidence. *Criminology & Public Policy*, *17*(1), 205–250.

Calderón, G., Robles, G., Díaz-Cayeros, A., & Magaloni, B. (2015). The beheading of criminal organizations and the dynamics of violence in Mexico. *Journal of Conflict Resolution*, *59*(8), 1455–1485.

Collins, S. E., Lonczak, H. S., & Clifasefi, S. L. (2017). Seattle's Law Enforcement Assisted Diversion (LEAD): Program effects on recidivism outcomes. *Evaluation and program planning*, *64*, 49–56.

Collins, S. E., Lonczak, H. S., & Clifasefi, S. L. (2019). Seattle's law enforcement assisted diversion (LEAD): program effects on criminal justice and legal system utilization and costs. *Journal of Experimental Criminology*, *15*(2), 201–211.

Corsaro, N., Hunt, E. D., Hipple, N. K., & McGarrell, E. F. (2012). The impact of drug market pulling levers policing on neighborhood violence: An evaluation of the High Point drug market intervention. *Criminology & Public Policy*, *11*(2), 167–199.

Daugaard, L., Morris, N., & Cox, B. (2011). Lead National Support Bureau. Retrieved from leadbureau.org.

Dion, M. L., & Russler, C. (2008). Eradication efforts, the state, displacement and poverty: Explaining coca cultivation in Colombia during Plan Colombia. *Journal of Latin American Studies*, *40*(3), 399–421.

Harris, D. A. (2003). *Profiles in injustice: Why racial profiling cannot work*. The New Press.

Kleiman, M. A., Caulkins, J. P., & Hawken, A. (2011). *Drugs and drug policy: What everyone needs to know*. Oxford University Press.

Kuziemko, I., & Levitt, S. D. (2004). An empirical analysis of imprisoning drug offenders. *Journal of Public Economics*, *88*(9–10), 2043–2066.

Layne, M., Decker, S., Townsend, M., & Chester, C. (2002). Measuring the deterrent effect of enforcement operations on drug smuggling, 1991–1999. *Trends in Organized Crime*, *7*(3), 66–87.

Lindo, J. M., & Padilla-Romo, M. (2018). Kingpin approaches to fighting crime and community violence: evidence from Mexico's drug war. *Journal of Health Economics*, *58*, 253–268.

Moreno-Sanchez, R., Kraybill, D. S., & Thompson, S. R. (2003). An econometric analysis of coca eradication policy in Colombia. *World Development*, *31*(2), 375–383.

Mummolo, J. (2018). Modern police tactics, police-citizen interactions, and the prospects for reform. *The Journal of Politics*, *80*(1), 1–15.

National Research Council. (2014). *The growth of incarceration in the United States: Exploring causes and consequences*. The National Academies Press.

Office of National Drug Control Policy. (2016). *2015 national drug control strategy: Data supplement*. Executive Office of the President.

Reuter, P., & Truman, E. M. (2005). Anti-money laundering overkill? *International Economy*, *19*(1), 56–60.

Saunders, J., Robbins, M., & Ober, A. J. (2017). Moving from efficacy to effectiveness: Implementing the drug market intervention across multiple sites. *Criminology & Public Policy*, *16*(3), 787–814.

Tonry, M. (1995). *Malign neglect: Race, crime, and punishment in America*. Oxford University Press.

Toth, A. G., & Mitchell, O. (2018). A qualitative examination of the effects of international counter-drug interdictions. *International Journal of Drug Policy*, *55*, 70–76.

Weatherburn, D., & Lind, B. (1997). The impact of law enforcement activity on a heroin market. *Addiction*, *92*(5), 557–569.

21

EVIDENCE-BASED PRACTICES FOR POLICING DOMESTIC VIOLENCE

Tara N. Richards, Gillian M. Pinchevsky and Justin Nix

Introduction

Police respond to more incidents of domestic violence (DV) – defined here as violence between current or former intimate partners, family members, and household members – than any other violent offense (Sherman, 1992), so it is not surprising that police responses to these incidents have been extensively studied for decades. The police response to DV has shifted drastically throughout American history. Historically, DV – which was commonly referred to as "wife beating" – was seen as a societally accepted way for husbands to uphold stability in their households (Siegel, 1996). Despite its widespread criminalization before the end of the nineteenth century, the criminal justice system largely took a hands-off approach, as highlighted by Hirschel and colleagues' (1992) characterization that "spousal abuse has been considered more a problem of public order than a criminal matter" (p. 247). As recently as the late 1960s, informal and formal practices highlighted the resistance of the legal system to respond. For example, officers would often delay their arrival to incidents by driving slowly in hopes that the two parties would work out the issue by the time officers arrived (Black, 1980). Meanwhile, formal guidance from the International Association of Chiefs of Police (IACP) (1965) recommended that arrest only be made as a last resort (as cited by Parnas, 1967). Further, officers were restricted from making warrantless arrests for incidents they did not personally witness (Buzawa & Buzawa, 1996), lacked training to properly approach these incidents, and held long-standing negative perceptions about the dangers associated with DV and the system's ability to properly address these cases (e.g., Gover et al., 2011).

However, a "perfect storm" of events converged and changed the landscape of policing – and studying – domestic violence. In the late 1970s women in California and New York brought suits against police departments alleging unequal protection after police had failed to arrest their husbands for abuse (Goodmark, 2017). In 1984, research from the Minneapolis Domestic Violence Experiment (MDVE) – which found that arrest reduced DV recidivism – was published, leading policy makers to advocate for mandatory arrest policies in domestic violence incidents. In 1985, Tracey Thurman won more than $2 million in damages in a lawsuit against the City of Torrington, Connecticut, after the Torrington Police Department failed to protect her against a series of threats and assaults by her estranged husband, which culminated in a violent attack leaving her with serious, lifelong injuries (Goodmark, 2017).

DOI: 10.4324/9781003219286-26

Finally, the passage of the Violence Against Women Act (1994) – as part of the Violent Crime Control and Law Enforcement Act of 1994 – sent a clear message that DV must be taken seriously as a matter of criminal law. It provided new legal tools (e.g., affording full faith and credit to protection orders issued anywhere in the United States) and significant federal funds for law enforcement activities related to DV (e.g., for training, implementation of mandatory arrest laws). The convergence of landmark court cases, social science, and policy making significantly changed approaches to policing domestic violence.

Early changes in police responses to DV were primarily concerned with enforcing the law and reducing reoffending, with extensive attention placed on the role of arrest and officer behaviors toward compliance with mandatory arrest laws. More contemporary strategies aim to directly increase victim safety and/or victim satisfaction with police response. This chapter reviews the challenges of identifying evidence-based police responses to DV, briefly discusses four such responses, and concludes with considerations regarding the future of police interventions for DV.

The Challenge

Although the task of identifying "evidence-based police responses to DV" may seem straightforward, the sometimes-divergent goals of the police and larger criminal justice system and victims of domestic violence make it quite complex. Further, the goal(s) of the police response to DV may differ depending on which party – the victim or the perpetrator – is being prioritized. For example, prior research examining police responses to DV have examined efforts to reduce DV recidivism, reduce DV homicide, increase victim safety, increase victim reporting, and increase victim satisfaction with the system, to name a few. Although some of these goals may overlap (e.g., increasing victim safety and reducing recidivism), the approaches to achieve these goals may also compete with one another. Take, for instance, the goals of increasing victim satisfaction with police responses to DV (e.g., responsiveness to victim's wishes) and reducing DV recidivism. The practices intended to increase victim satisfaction (e.g., listening to the victim's preference in incident resolution) may be in direct contradiction to the primary way police attempt to reduce DV recidivism (e.g., through mandatory arrest). Thus, in this chapter we are mindful of the competing goals of different approaches to addressing DV and make note of the specific goal(s) of each response.

Take-Away Points

- The history of the criminal justice system's response to DV was characterized by a hands-off approach whereby family violence was considered a "private issue" and the system both formally and informally encouraged its actors (e.g., police) not to intervene.
- Social science research was a major contributor to widespread changes in the police response to DV.
- The police response to DV must be understood within the context of competing goals of police and victims of DV.

Approaches to Programs, Policies, and Practices

Mandatory Arrest

Arrest practices have received the most empirical attention regarding the criminal justice system's response to DV. The Minneapolis Domestic Violence Experiment (MDVE) – one of the most influential studies in criminology – randomized police response to misdemeanor DV incidents such that incidents were handled via officer mediation, brief separation of the victim and perpetrator, or arrest (Sherman & Berk, 1984). Findings showed that perpetrators who were arrested had lower DV recidivism rates over a 6-month follow-up period (measured by arrest and victim reports) than those who received mediation or separation (Sherman & Berk, 1984). Although Sherman and Berk strongly cautioned against policy changes before additional replication studies, advocates and policy makers were quick to call for reforms, and mandatory arrest laws were enacted across multiple states in the years following the MDVE (Goodmark, 2107; Sherman, 1992).

In the early 1990s, the National Institute of Justice supported a series of studies similar to the MDVE examining the impact of arrest on DV reoffending, collectively known as the Spousal Assault Replication Program (SARP; Buzawa & Buzawa, 1996; Sherman, 1992). Results from the SARP were inconsistent: in Colorado Springs and Miami arrest proved to be a significant deterrent to reoffending, while in Charlotte, Milwaukee, and Omaha arrest was not significantly related to reductions in reoffending (Sherman, 1992). Findings also suggested that the deterrent impact of arrest was strongly tied to employment (Sherman, 1992). Further, when the data across the SARP studies were pooled, arrest for the initial offense was not significantly associated with rearrest; however, it was associated with a significant decrease in victim-partner reports of repeat domestic violence (Maxwell et al., 2002). Taken together, Exum and colleagues (2014) summarize the evidence as follows: "MDVE found that arrest worked best, SARP found that arrest works sometimes, and a synthesis of SARP results found that arrest did not work at all – at least when using official measures of recidivism" (p. 1000).

Although proponents of mandatory arrest policies argue that symbolically they send the message that DV will not be tolerated (Goodmark, 2017), and substantively, they may have some deterrent effect on at least some individuals (e.g., those with stakes in conformity through employment; Berk et al., 1992; Pate & Hamilton, 1992), other research suggests that mandatory arrest policies may *increase* arrests for repeat DV (see Sherman, 1992 for an overview). Studies have also shown that mandatory arrest policies are associated with an increase in victim arrests for defensive violence and dual arrests (e.g., in cases where the officer does not or cannot decide who is the perpetrator of the violence) (see Goodmark, 2017). In addition, mandatory arrest policies have been criticized for taking away victims' agency and decision-making and mimicking coercive behaviors of abusive partners (see Hoyle & Sanders, 2000). As a result, mandatory arrest policies may deter victims of abuse from calling law enforcement for future violence. Finally, there is no evidence that mandatory arrest policies lead to higher *conviction* rates for DV (see Goodmark, 2017), and there is some evidence that mandatory arrest may lead to higher rates of DV homicide (see Ivengar, 2009; Sherman & Harris, 2013).

Take-Away Points:

- Mandatory arrest policies for DV are commonly used across the country but are not consistently found to be related to reduced recidivism.
- One-size-fits-all mandatory arrest policies may have unintended consequences relating to increased recidivism, arrest of victims, removal of victims' agency, reduction in victims' trust in the system, and increased risk of DV homicide.

Specialized Domestic Violence Units

Given the inconsistent evidence regarding mandatory arrest policies, police departments have adopted additional strategies to respond to DV. Since the early 2000s, many police agencies have implemented specialized domestic violence units (Reaves & Hickman, 2004; Townsend et al., 2005) which are staffed by officers with dedicated time and resources to follow-up with victims, investigate cases, and establish relationships with other criminal justice agencies and victim service providers. Rigorous research on the impact of DV units is scarce; however, the few available studies suggest these units reduce recidivism. For example, Farrell and Buckley (1999) examined the yearly number of repeat calls for service for DV before and after the implementation of a DV unit in one of seven police divisions. Findings showed that the DV unit division saw a decline in annual repeat calls, while the other six units saw an increase in repeat calls, suggesting that the specialized unit had a positive impact on offender recidivism for DV. However, further analysis showed that this deterrent effect was limited to offenders with fewer than eight prior DV arrests. More recently, Exum and colleagues (2014) examined nearly 900 misdemeanor DV cases in Charlotte, North Carolina, and found that after controlling for a host of offender and case characteristics, cases processed by Charlotte's specialized DV unit had lower rates of rearrest at 18- and 30-month follow ups than cases processed by standard patrol officers (Exum et al., 2014).

Take-Away Points:

- Limited research suggests that specialized domestic violence units within police departments may reduce DV recidivism.
- Additional studies on specialized domestic violence units is needed.

Second Responder Programs

In addition to specialized DV units within police departments, second responder programs combine police officers and social service providers (e.g., victims advocates) who work together to address a DV incident. The exact approach may vary by jurisdiction, but second responder programs generally involve officers and providers responding to the scene of a DV incident or following up with the victim (and in some cases, perpetrator) at a set time after the incident. In a meta-analysis of ten second responder programs involving in-person follow-ups, Davis and colleagues (2008) found that although these programs did not impact the likelihood of the DV recidivism, they did appear to increase victims' reports to police about future abuse when compared to a traditional officer-only response. Thus, Davis et al. (2008) concluded that seconder responder models may increase victims' confidence in the system. More recent research shows that victims who receive second-responder interventions call the police sooner and more often during 6- or 12-month follow-up periods compared to randomly assigned or matched controls (Davis et al., 2010; Stover et al., 2010).

The results of second responder programs underscore the dilemma of competing goals related to the police response to DV: evaluations of these programs do not suggest that they reduce recidivism, but they do appear to impact victims' confidence in using the system (Davis et al., 2008). Thus, the goals of fewer DV incidences and increased confidence in the system's response to DV are not necessarily both achieved by a given approach. As Davis and colleagues (2008) write: "Policy makers will have to decide whether the small gain in willingness to call the police is worth the cost of these programs".

Although second responder programs have typically focused on the safety of victims of DV, Davis et al. (2008) note that some programs do include perpetrators of the incident, mainly by warning them of additional sanctions if their behaviors continue. Arguing that such a deterrence-focused approach is not particularly effective, Scott et al. (2015) explored the impact of a perpetrator-focused second responder program that combines police and DV intervention treatment providers in a risk-needs-responsivity, therapy-based model. In this program, men who were charged with DV and considered a moderate-to-high risk to re-offend were quickly identified and recruited to voluntarily participate in an intervention program. Results showed decreased recidivism (both domestic and otherwise) and police involvement at 1- and 2-year follow-ups compared to men who did not participate in the second responder intervention. Although replication studies are needed, Scott et al. (2015) suggest that perpetrator-focused second responder programs could be a beneficial approach in addressing DV recidivism.

Take-Away Points

- The introduction of a victim advocate/social service provider into the police response to DV may mitigate long-standing concerns by victims that they will not be believed or that their concerns will not be taken seriously.
- Evidence suggests that coordination of police and social service providers increases victim confidence or trust in the system to call in the future but does not decrease recidivism.
- Perpetrator-focused second responder programs for medium and/or high-risk offenders show some promise for reducing DV recidivism.

Risk Assessments

Given the increased demand for police services for DV, police departments have also adopted strategies to identify the most high-risk cases to better direct finite resources, prevent an escalation of violence, or intervene prior to lethal DV. One of the most used DV risk assessments in the policing context is the Lethality Assessment Program (LAP), which aims to help law enforcement and other first responders identify victims of DV who are at the greatest risk for re-assault or lethality and connect them to victim service providers by phone at the time of a DV assault (Maryland Network Against Domestic Violence, n.d.). Specifically, law enforcement officers administer the Lethality Screen (i.e., an 11-item version of the Danger Assessment) with victims, and victims who endorse high-risk items or a series of items are connected via phone to a victim service provider who can assist with immediate safety planning and encourage victims to engage in follow-up services. Limited research on the impact of the LAP has been conducted. However, one quasi-experimental study demonstrated that victims who received the LAP were more likely to report having engaged in self-protective measures such as establishing a code with family/friends, applying for a protective order, or going somewhere her partner could not find her compared to victims who received a card with advocacy resources (Messing et al., 2015). Additional research on the LAP cautions that officer training is paramount, so that victims understand the limitations of the screen and do not consider failure to be designated as "high-risk" on the LAP as an indication that they are not in danger (Richards et al., 2020).

More generally, in Roehl et al.'s (2005) prospective study of the predictive validity of four instruments: the Danger Assessment (Campbell, 1986, 1995; Campbell et al., 2003), DV-MOSAIC (De Becker et al., 2000), the Domestic Violence Screening Instrument (Williams & Houghton, 2004), and the Kingston Screening Instrument for Domestic Violence (Gelles, 1998), findings showed the assessments were better than chance, but there was a high number of both false positives and false negatives across instruments. The most predictive instrument, the Danger Assessment, performed only slightly better than victims' own predictions of their likelihood of abuse. Further, research shows that officers tend to focus on a "small constellation of risk factors" (e.g., physical violence or the threat of violence, weapons, escalation in incidents) that they view as especially important in determining their response irrespective of these formal tools (Robinson et al., 2018; Trujillo & Ross, 2008). Further, police may simply not have time to complete a risk assessment in a crisis. Taken together, it may benefit police response to DV to provide consistent training to police on the most predictive risk factors for severe or lethal DV – strangulation, access to a firearm, previous threats to kill the victim (Campbell et al., 2003) – and encourage officers to consider victims' own self-assessments in making decisions in the field. More formal risk assessments can then be administered by victim service providers later when the victim is not in crisis.

Take-Away Points:

- Many police departments are using risk assessments to identify victims who are most at risk of severe DV or lethal violence.
- Evidence suggests that risk assessments may only be slightly more predictive than the victim's own perceptions about the likelihood of re-abuse.
- Implementations of risk assessments must include officer training on the limitations of these tools and victims' accounts should also be considered, particularly if they predict higher danger than the assessment.

Conclusion

Any discussion of evidence-based policing practices for responding to DV requires a deep dive into the various – and sometimes competing – goals of this response. Despite the extent of research that has been conducted on the topic, the evidence concerning the efficacy of system responses to DV is decidedly mixed, complex, and controversial. Recall that throughout much of American history, criminal justice system actors did not actively address DV (e.g., through policing, the courts), and it was not until abused women themselves *demanded* action that the criminal justice system began taking DV seriously. However, after decades of criminal justice reform and investment in policing and legislative practices regarding DV, some victims and victim advocacy groups have reconsidered these demands. Recent arguments suggest that in many situations, the system is simply ill equipped to appropriately respond to DV (Goodmark, 2018) and in some cases – particularly for victims of color – police responses may make families less safe and/or secure. Likewise, scholars argue that community-based forms of justice should be prioritized at least equally with a criminal justice response in order to give victims a choice regarding interventions (Goodmark, 2018).

In many ways, these concerns mirror those of the broader "Defund the Police" movement that proliferated after the murder of George Floyd in Minneapolis in May of 2020. That is, evidence in support of commonly used tactics is mixed at best, and questions remain about whether such tactics do more harm than good in some communities or for certain victims. Looking ahead, agencies must partner with subject matter experts and researchers who can help evaluate the impact of police approaches to DV. For their part, researchers must help design studies capable of measuring both successes *and* harms, so that communities and their elected officials can better understand the potential risks and rewards and decide whether costs are justified (Davis et al., 2008) or alternative programs would offer a better return on investment.

References

Berk, R. A., Campbell, A., Klap, R., & Western, B. (1992). The deterrent effect of arrest in incidents of domestic violence: A Bayesian analysis of four field experiments. *American Sociological Review*, *57*(5), 698–708.

Black, D. (1980). *The manners and customs of the police*. Academic Press.

Buzawa, E. S., & Buzawa, C. G. (1996). *Domestic violence: The criminal justice response*, 2nd ed. Sage Publications, Inc.

Campbell, J. C. (1986). Nursing assessment of risk of homicide for battered women. *Advances in Nursing Science*, *8*(4), 36–51.

Campbell, J. C. (1995). *Assessing dangerousness*. Sage.

Campbell, J. C., Webster, D., Koziol-McLain, J., Block, C., Campbell, D., Curry, M. A., Gary, F., Glass, N., McFarlane, J., Sachs, C., Sharps, P., Ulrich, Y., Wilt, S. A., Manganello, J., Xu, X., Schollenberger, J., Frye, V., & Laughon, K. (2003). Risk factors for femicide in abusive relationships: Results from a multisite case control study. *American Journal of Public Health*, *93*(7), 1089–1097.

Davis, R. C., Weisburg, D., & Taylor, B. (2008). Effects of second responder programs on repeat incidents of family abuse: A systematic review. *Campbell Systematic Reviews*, *4*, 1–38. doi: 10.4073/csr.2008.15

Davis, R. C., Weisburd, D., Hamilton, E. E. (2010). Preventing repeat incidents of family violence: A randomized field test of a second responder program. *Journal of Experimental Criminology*, *6*, 397–418.

De Becker, G., & Associates. (2000). Domestic violence method (DV MOSAIC). Retrieved from www.mosaicsystem.com/dv.htm

Exum, M. L., Hartman, J. L., Friday, P. C., & Lord, V. B. (2014). Policing domestic violence in the post-SARP era: The impact of domestic violence police unit. *Crime & Delinquency*, *60*(7), 999–1032.

Farrell, G., & Buckley, A. (1999). Evaluation of a UK police domestic violence unit using repeat victimization as a performance indicator. *Howard Journal*, *38*, 42–53.

Gelles, R. (1998, October). Lethality and risk assessment for family violence cases. Paper presented at the 4th International Conference on Children Exposed to Family Violence.

Goodmark, L. (2017). Innovative criminal justice responses to intimate partner violence. In C. Renzetti, J. Edelson, & R. K. Bergen (Eds.), *Sourcebook on violence against women*, 3rd ed. Sage.

Goodmark, L. (2018). *Decriminalizing domestic violence: A balanced policy approach to intimate partner violence*. University of California Press.

Gover, A. R., Paul, D. P., & Dodge, M. (2011). Law enforcement officers' attitudes about domestic violence. *Violence against Women*, *17*(5), 619–636.

Hirschel, J. D., Hutchinson, I. W., & Dean, C. W. (1992). The failure of arrest to deter spouse abuse. *Journal of Research in Crime and Delinquency*, *29*, 7–33.

Hoyle, C., & Sanders, A. (2000). Police response to domestic violence: From victim choice to victim empowerment? *British Journal of Criminology*, *40*, 14–36.

Ivengar, R. (2009). Does the certainty of arrest reduce domestic violence? Evidence from mandatory and recommended arrest laws. *Journal of Public Economics*, *93*(1), 85–98.

Maryland Network Against Domestic Violence. (n.d.). How LAP works. Retrieved from https://lethalityassessmentprogram.org/about-lap/how-lap-works/

Maxwell, C. D., Garner, J. H., &. Fagan, J. A. (2002). The preventive effects of arrest on intimate partner violence: Research, policy and theory. *Criminology & Public Policy*, *2*, 51–80.

Messing, J. T., Campbell, J. C., Webster, D. W., Brown, S., Patchell, B., & Wilson, J. S. (2015). The Oklahoma Lethality Assessment Study: A quasi-experimental evaluation of the Lethality Assessment Program. *Social Service Review*, *89*, 499–530.

Parnas, R. I., (1967). The police response to the domestic disturbance. Wisconsin Law Review, pp. 914–960.

Pate, A. M., & Hamilton, E. E. (1992). Formal and informal deterrents to domestic violence: The dade county spouse assault experiment. *American Sociological Review*, *57*(5), 691–697.

Reaves, B. A., & Hickman, M. J. (2004). *Law enforcement management and administrative violence against women act of 1994, Public Law 106-386 statistics, 2000: Data for individual state and local agencies with 100 or more officers*. U.S. Department of Justice.

Richards, T. N., Gillespie, L. K., Kafonek, K., & Johnson, M. (2020). An examination of the Lethality Assessment Program (LAP): Perspectives on implementation, help-seeking, and victim empowerment. *Violence against Women*, *26*(12–13), 1517–1537.

Robinson, A. L., Pinchevsky, G. M., & Guthrie, J. A. (2018). A small constellation: Risk factors informing police perceptions of domestic abuse. *Policing and Society*, *28*(2), 189–204.

Roehl, J., O'Sullivan, C., Webster, D., Campbell, J. (2005). *Intimate partner violence risk assessment validation study*. U.S. Department of Justice.

Scott, K., Heslop, L., Kelly, T., & Wiggins, K. (2015). Intervening to prevent repeat offending among moderate- to high-risk domestic violence offenders: A second-responder program for men. *International Journal of Offender Therapy and Comparative Criminology*, *59*(3), 273–294. doi: 10.1177/0306624X13513709

Sherman, L. W. (1992). *Policing domestic violence: Experiments and dilemmas*. Free Press.

Sherman, L. W., & Harris, H. (2013). Increased homicide victimization of suspects arrested for domestic assault: A 23-year follow-up of the Milwaukee Domestic Violence Experiment (MilDVE). *Journal of Experimental Criminology*, *9*, 491–514.

Sherman, L. W., & Richard, A. B. (1984). The specific deterrent effects of arrest for domestic assault. *American Sociological Review*, *49*, 261–272.

Siegel, R. B. (1996). "The Rule of Love": Wife beating as prerogative and privacy. *The Yale Law Journal*, *105*(8), 2117–2207.

Stover, C. S., Berkman, M., Desai, R., Marans, S. (2010). The efficacy of a police-advocacy intervention for victims of domestic violence: 12-month follow-up data. *Violence against Women*, *16*, 410–425.

Townsend, M., Hunt, D., Kuck, S., & Baxter, C. (2005). *Law enforcement response to domestic violence calls for service: Final report*. U.S. Department of Justice.

Trujillo, M. P., & Ross, S. (2008). Police response to domestic violence: making decisions about risk and risk management. *Journal of Interpersonal Violence*, *23*(4), 454–473.

Violence Against Women Act (1994). Public Law 106-386.

Williams, K. R., & Houghton, A. B. (2004). Assessing the risk of domestic violence re-offending: A validation study. *Law and Human Behavior*, 437–455.

Author Bios:

Tara N. Richards is a Distinguished Associate Professor in the School of Criminology and Criminal Justice at the University of Nebraska at Omaha and Co-Director of the Victimology and Victim Studies Research Lab. She received her Ph.D. in Criminology from the University of South Florida. Her research is centered in victimology, with recent articles appearing in *Criminology & Public Policy, Journal of Interpersonal Violence*, and *Psychology of Violence*.

Gillian M. Pinchevsky is a violence against women (VAW) scholar whose research primarily focuses on criminal justice and community responses to VAW. She received her Ph.D. in Criminology and Criminal Justice from the University of South Carolina. Her recent work has been published in *Feminist Criminology, Journal of Interpersonal Violence*, and *Criminal Justice Review*.

Justin Nix is a Distinguished Associate Professor in the School of Criminology and Criminal Justice at the University of Nebraska at Omaha. He received his Ph.D. in Criminology and Criminal Justice from the University of South Carolina. His research is centered on policing with a focus on legitimacy. His work has recently appeared in *Criminology & Public Policy, PLOS ONE*, and *Justice Quarterly*.

22

INTERVIEWING AND INTERROGATIONS

From the Third Degree to Science-Based Approaches

Amelia Mindthoff and Christian A. Meissner

Eliciting information from resistant individuals has long represented a challenge for interrogation professionals; however, the manner in which individuals are interviewed has transformed substantially over the past century. In this chapter, we provide a selective review of the evolution of interrogation practices, from coercive methods of the past that are prone to producing false confessions to rapport-based methods of the present and future. While we focus primarily on the adversarial interview context, readers interested in witness/victim interviewing (Hope & Gabbert, 2019) and the interviewing of children (Lamb et al., 2018; Nicol et al., 2017) are referred to other excellent reviews.

Interrogations of the Past

Through the first half of the twentieth century, it was customary for American police departments to practice the "third degree" – interrogation methods that involved physical and psychological coercion aimed at extracting confessions (Leo, 1992). Such methods included physical violence (e.g., whippings, punching) and torture (e.g., drilling into teeth), as well as coercive methods that were easily deniable given their lack of evidence (e.g., rubber hose beatings, being hung out of windows, being slapped if failing to stand up straight for hours). Although the use of such tactics had drastically decreased by the 1960s, they were ultimately replaced by techniques that apply psychological pressure, manipulation, and deception (Kassin et al., 2010). Such accusatorial tactics have also been widely used in other countries, including Canada (Snook et al., 2010) and the United Kingdom (Bull & Rachlew, 2020).

Central to modern accusatorial methods are the tenets of guilt presumption and confession elicitation (Kassin & Gudjonsson, 2004). As such, accusatorial interrogations are characterized by: (a) an interrogator-suspect dynamic in which the interrogator maintains control, (b) questioning approaches that focus on confirmation of guilt (in lieu of elicitation of information), (c) the presentation of interrogation "themes" that persuade suspects that it is in their best interest to confess, (d) the isolation of suspects meant to induce stress and a want to escape the interrogation context (via confession), and (e) a reliance on anxiety-based nonverbal cues to deception (Meissner et al., 2015). In this context, interrogators rely on methods including (but not limited to): *maximization* (harsh confrontations of guilt and exaggeration of consequences), *minimization* (providing face-saving excuses and downplaying

DOI: 10.4324/9781003219286-27

the consequences), and *false evidence ploys* (presenting fabricated incriminating evidence; see Kassin et al., 2010, for a comprehensive discussion of additional accusatorial methods). The use of such methods is inherently problematic, as accusatorial methods not only increase the rate of true confessions from the guilty but also increase the rate of false confessions from the innocent (Meissner et al., 2014).

The Problem of False Confessions

False admissions or confessions represent a leading cause of wrongful convictions in the United States. They are typically classified into one of three categories. *Voluntary false confessions* are those that arise without any prompting from law enforcement and are often seen in high-profile cases (e.g., the Black Dahlia case; Conti, 1999). *Compliant false confessions* are typically the product of accusatorial interrogation methods and represent the most typical form of false confessions. In such cases, individuals ultimately confess for positive rewards (e.g., escaping the interrogation context; in exchange for a promise of leniency) but internally maintain their innocence. Last, *internalized false confessions* are made by innocent, yet suggestible, individuals who are led to generate incriminating false memories that they come to believe, thereby lending credence to their false confession (see Gudjonsson, 2003; Kassin & Gudjonsson, 2004, for more on false confessions).

Factors Leading to False Confessions

Research indicates that several factors (both internal and external) can increase the likelihood of a false confession. *Dispositional risk factors*, such as intellectual/cognitive ability and youth, are often present in known cases of false confessions (Drizin & Leo, 2004) and have been experimentally demonstrated to increase false confession rates (see Kassin & Gudjonsson, 2004, for more on dispositional risk factors). It is likely that interrogative suggestibility mediates the effect of such characteristics on false confession rates (Otgaar et al., 2021). The detrimental impact of such vulnerabilities is often intensified by *situational risk factors* – factors that are imposed on the interrogation environment by an investigator. For example, the use of certain accusatorial tactics and prolonged detention/interrogation can significantly increase the likelihood of a false confession.

Accusatorial interrogations represent an inherently confirmatory process. Interviewers implementing this approach typically employ tactics designed to confirm a suspect's guilt. It is thus not surprising that such an approach fosters confirmation bias (i.e., actively seeking and using information that is in line with one's hypotheses/beliefs at the expense of ignoring conflicting information; Meissner & Kassin, 2004), which in turn exacerbates the use of accusatorial tactics aimed at confirming guilt, leading to an increased risk of false confession (Narchet et al., 2011). Furthermore, the confession-driven and confirmatory nature of accusatorial approaches often curtail the elicitation of additional information from suspects.

Innocence itself has also been shown to be a risk factor, as innocent suspects may waive their Miranda rights and agree to be questioned, believing that their innocence will be apparent (e.g., "didn't have anything to hide;" Kassin & Norwick, 2004). Such a belief may be naïve, particularly if investigators apply coercive, accusatorial methods. In such a context, an innocent suspect's persistent denials can increase the extent to which investigators utilize coercive tactics and increase the risk of false confession (see Kassin, 2005; Scherr et al., 2020).

Moving Towards Science-Based Interviewing

Interrogation practices and policies have experienced a paradigm shift as cases of wrongful convictions of false confessors began to emerge. Notably, a series of wrongful convictions in the United Kingdom (e.g., Guilford Four, Birmingham Six) gave rise to a series of reforms leading to the adoption of the PEACE model in 1992. The PEACE model, which is widely practiced in the United Kingdom, Wales, and several other countries, incorporates evidence-based interviewing techniques that include rapport-based approaches, productive questioning, and gradual presentation of evidence in combination with challenges to statement-evidence inconsistencies. Notably, the goal of the PEACE approach to interviewing is in stark contrast to that of traditional accusatorial methods: rather than being confession driven, PEACE methods are aimed at eliciting information (see Bull & Rachlew, 2020).

Since the introduction of PEACE, considerable research has led to the development and refinement of science-based interviewing in the United States (Meissner et al., 2017). Based on such work, scholars have proposed a framework that is built upon rapport-based, information-gathering techniques (Meissner et al., 2023). This framework has led to a shift from "interrogation" (a construct that induces a sense of guilt-presumption, a drive for confession, and is typically tied to the adversarial questioning of suspects) to "investigative interviewing" (questioning with the goal of eliciting accurate and detailed narratives, ultimately contributing to a broader investigative decision, and that can be used with various interviewees including witnesses, victims, suspects, and sources). Central to this science-based approach are productive questioning tactics, memory-based tactics, rapport-based approaches, strategic presentation of evidence, and strategic questioning to assess credibility.

Productive Questioning Tactics

The traditional accusatorial approach to questioning is characterized by closed-ended and leading questions (Snook et al., 2012), which can restrict the amount of information elicited from an interviewee and lead to memory errors (see Pickrell et al., 2016). In lieu of such unproductive questioning methods, scholars recommend that practitioners pose open-ended questions that facilitate recall and maintain the integrity of the interviewee's memory. Practitioners should consider implementing a funnel approach to questioning, by which they follow open-ended questions with probing questions and appropriate closed-ended questions that are based on previous statements made by the interviewee (Powell et al., 2005). Overall, these productive questioning strategies have been shown to increase the amount of information elicited from interviewees (Nunan et al., 2020).

Memory-Based Questioning Tactics

Eliciting information from interviewees can be impeded not only by their willingness to disclose, but also by their inability to retrieve the information from memory (Shepherd, 1993). In such instances, memory-based questioning tactics that were developed based on principles from cognitive psychology can help facilitate retrieval. Examples of memory-based tactics include instructing interviewees to close their eyes in order to facilitate mental-reinstatement of the context in which the memory being recalled was encoded, recall the event multiple times, recall the event in various temporal orders (e.g., reverse-order, from end to beginning), recall the event from a different perspective (e.g., from the perspective of a bystander), or recall sensory details in a manner that aligns with encoding (e.g., when asking about spatial details, having interviewees sketch what they remember). Such tactics are central to the cognitive interview (Fisher & Geiselman, 1992) – an evidence-based interview protocol that has been implemented in a variety of contexts (e.g., children and adult witnesses, suspects, sources). Attesting to the benefits of implementing memory-based tactics, the cognitive interview reliably increases the amount of correct information elicited from interviewees without reducing the accuracy of the information provided (Memon et al., 2010).

Rapport-Based Approaches

Rapport-based approaches to interviewing have been strongly endorsed as a necessary element to interviewing protocols (e.g., Army Field Manual; PEACE model; cognitive interview). Yet the literature has lacked a cohesive, comprehensive understanding of the rapport construct and the effectiveness of interviewing tactics meant to facilitate rapport. Recent systematic reviews of the rapport literature have begun to shed light on these issues.

Rapport is often described as "the quality of the interviewer-interviewee interpersonal interaction" (Neequaye & Mac Giolla, 2022, pp. 3), with a focus on at least one of the following attributes: positivity, mutuality, successful outcomes, respect, trust, or communication (see also Duke et al., 2018). Achieving rapport is often deemed beneficial, as rapport is believed to increase the amount of information an interviewee discloses. Research suggests that the effectiveness of rapport-approaches is a product of an interviewee's perceptions of rapport, as increased perceptions of rapport have been shown to facilitate an interviewee's decision to cooperate, leading to an increase in information disclosure (Brimbal et al., 2021; Brimbal et al., 2019; Dianiska et al., 2021).

Several tactics have been recommended to facilitate rapport (and ultimately information disclosure) and typically fall into one of three domains (Gabbert et al., 2021). First, *relationship-building tactics* can be used to promote a personal connection between the interviewer and interviewee. Examples include showing interest in the interviewee and finding common ground, which can be achieved via self-disclosure of personal information by the interviewer. Second, *demeanor-based approaches* can be used to characterize the interviewer as friendly and approachable. Such behaviors include a pleasant tone of voice, smiling, and open body language. Third, tactics that demonstrate that the interviewer is *paying attention* can be used, including active listening skills (e.g., nonverbal behaviors such as head nods and eye contact, and appropriate verbal responses such as reflective statements and summaries) and empathetic responses (i.e., responses that demonstrate authentic concern and understanding for the interviewee's perspective; see Meissner et al., 2023, for more on developing rapport).

Presentation of Evidence

Accusatorial forms of evidence presentation involve confronting a suspect with evidence early in the interview to overwhelm the suspect with incriminating information. Such evidence presentation, however, can be detrimental to the productiveness of the interview, as it can increase suspect resistance (Kelly et al., 2016) and offers deceptive individuals an opportunity to create a narrative that explains the incriminating evidence (Hartwig et al., 2005). Research has demonstrated the benefits of disclosing evidence towards the end of the interview or gradually throughout the interview (see more on the strategic use of evidence, Granhag & Hartwig, 2015, and the tactical use of evidence, Dando & Bull, 2011). Such evidence disclosure methods increase the number of statement-evidence inconsistencies made by guilty (vs. innocent) individuals (Oleszkiewicz & Watson, 2021).

Strategic Questioning to Assess Credibility

Interviewers can improve the accuracy of credibility assessments by implementing strategic questioning tactics that enhance the differences between truthful and deceptive statements (Vrij, 2015). Classifications of such tactics include (Vrij et al., 2017): (a) *imposing cognitive load* (increasing cognitive demands via tactics such as instructing interviewees to tell their narrative in reverse chronological order – instructions that prove difficult for liars, as fabricating information is already a cognitively taxing task), (b) *prompting interviewees to say more* (such an instruction can include a model statement that provides interviewees with an example of the level of detail the interviewer is seeking – a level of detail that may be difficult for liars to generate), and (c) *asking unanticipated questions* (questions that liars most likely would not have prepared for and, therefore, would have difficulty answering on the spot). Overall, strategic questioning leads to increased accuracy in distinguishing liars from truth-tellers, although this improved accuracy emerges only when individuals are trained in such methods (Mac Giolla & Luke, 2021).

Next Steps

Despite a general shift towards science-based interviewing approaches in recent years, accusatorial approaches continue to be taught and implemented in the interrogation of suspects/sources. For instance, a survey of active practitioners found that American and Canadian practitioners were more likely to endorse the use of accusatorial techniques, while practitioners from Europe, Australia, and New Zealand were more likely to adopt science-based approaches (Miller et al., 2018). In the transition to science-based approaches, seasoned practitioners may adopt a "toolbox" approach that includes the continued use of accusatorial tactics (Snook et al., 2020). Such an approach can undermine the investigative value of science-based techniques and highlights the need for a comprehensive model of science-based interviewing that can effectively address subject resistance (Meissner et al., 2023).

The refinement and adoption of such a comprehensive science-based interviewing model is most likely to come about via collaborations between researchers and practitioners. Although investigative interviewing studies conducted in the lab arguably lack a high level of ecological validity, they are crucial to determining a technique's *efficacy* (whether, and why, an interviewing technique results in desired outcomes). Furthermore, laboratory-based research is especially informative for understanding a technique's diagnosticity (whether a technique can increase the rate of true information/confessions without increasing the rate of false information/confessions), given that ground-truth can be controlled. To truly understand the real-world impact of an interviewing technique, however, it is critical to determine its *effectiveness* (testing the technique in the field and measuring desired outcomes). This is where collaborations with practitioners can be especially fruitful and facilitate the application and translation of research into training protocols that can be assessed for effectiveness (Bornstein & Meissner, 2023).

Overall, the science of interviewing and interrogation has evaluated practices from the third degree to modern rapport-based methods. Modern day science-based methods are derived from psychological theory and focus on the twin goals of gaining a subject's cooperation and eliciting investigation-relevant information (not confessions). This shift from a confession-focused approach to an information-gathering approach has been key to reducing the number of wrongful convictions based on false information or false confessions while ensuring that justice is served in an ethical and effective manner.

References

Bornstein, B. H., & Meissner, C. A. (2023). Influencing policy and procedure with law-psychology research: Why, when, where, how, and what. In D. DeMatteo & K. C. Scherr (Eds.), *Oxford handbook of psychology and law* (pp. 18–35). Oxford University Press. doi: 10.1093/oxfordhb/9780197649138.013.2

Brimbal, L., Dianiska, R. E., Swanner, J. K., & Meissner, C. A. (2019). Enhancing cooperation and disclosure by manipulating affiliation and developing rapport in investigative interviews. *Psychology, Public Policy, & Law*, *25*, 107–115. doi: 10.1037/law0000193

Brimbal, L., Meissner, C. A., Kleinman, S. M., Phillips, E. L., Atkinson, D. J., Dianiska, R. E., Rothweiler, J. N., Oleszkiewicz, S., & Jones, M. S. (2021). Evaluating the benefits of a rapport-based approach to investigative interviews: A training study with law enforcement investigators. *Law & Human Behavior*, *45*, 55–67. doi: 10.1037/lhb0000437

Bull, R., & Rachlew, A. (2020). Investigative interviewing: From England to Norway and beyond. In S. J. Barela, M. Fallon, & G. Gaggioli (Eds.), *Interrogation and torture* (1st ed., pp. 171–196). Oxford University Press.

Conti, R. P. (1999). The psychology of false confessions. *The Journal of Credibility Assessment & Witness Psychology*, *2*, 14–36.

Dando, C. J., & Bull, R. (2011). Maximising opportunities to detect verbal deception: Training police officers to interview tactically. *Journal of Investigative Psychology & Offender Profiling*, *8*, 189–202. doi: 10.1002/jip.145

Dianiska, R. E., Swanner, J. K., Brimbal, L., & Meissner, C. A. (2021). Using disclosure, common ground, and verification to develop rapport and elicit information. *Psychology, Public Policy, & Law*, *27*, 341–353. doi: 10.1037/law0000313

Drizin, S. A., & Leo, R. A. (2004). The problem of false confessions in the post-DNA world. *North Carolina Law Review*, *82*, 891–1007.

Duke, M. C., Wood, J. M., Bollin, B., Scullin, M., & LaBianca, J. (2018). Development of the Rapport Scales for Investigative Interviews and Interrogations (RS3i), Interviewee Version. *Psychology, Public Policy, & Law*, *24*, 64–79. doi: 10.1037/law0000147

Fisher, R. P., & Geiselman, R. E. (1992). *Memory-enhancing techniques for investigative interviewing*. Charles C Thomas Publisher.

Gabbert, F., Hope, L., Luther, K., Wright, G., Ng, M., & Oxburgh, G. (2021). Exploring the use of rapport in professional information-gathering contexts by systematically mapping the evidence base. *Applied Cognitive Psychology*, *35*, 329–341. doi: 10.1002/acp.3762

Granhag, P. A., & Hartwig, M. (2015). The strategic use of evidence technique: A conceptual overview. In P. A. Granhag, A. Vrij, & B. Verschuere (Eds.), *Detecting deception: Current challenges and cognitive approaches* (pp. 231–251). Wiley-Blackwell.

Gudjonsson, G. H. (2003). *The psychology of interrogations and confessions: A handbook*. John Wiley & Sons.

Hartwig, M., Granhag, P. A., Strömwall, L. A., & Vrij, A. (2005). Detecting deception via strategic disclosure of evidence. *Law & Human Behavior*, *29*, 469–484. doi: 10.1007/s10979-005-5521-x

Hope, L., & Gabbert, F. (2019). Interviewing witnesses and victims. In N. Brewer & A. B. Douglass (Eds.), *Psychological science and the law* (pp. 130–156). The Guilford Press.

Kassin, S. M. (2005). On the psychology of confessions: Does innocence put innocents at risk?. *American Psychologist*, *60*, 215–228.

Kassin, S. M., Drizin, S. A., Grisso, T., Gudjonsson, G. H., Leo, R. A., & Redlich, A. D. (2010). Police-induced confession: Risk factors and recommendations. *Law & Human Behavior*, *34*, 3–38. doi: 10.1007/s10979-009-9188-6

Kassin, S. M., & Gudjonsson, G. H. (2004). The psychology of confessions: A review of the literature and issues. *Psychological Science in the Public Interest*, *5*, 33–67. doi: 10.1111/j.1529-1006.2004.00016.x

Kassin, S. M., & Norwick, R. J. (2004). Why people waive their Miranda rights: The power of innocence. *Law & Human Behavior*, *28*, 211–221. doi: 10.1023/B:LAHU.0000022323.74584.f5

Kelly, C. E., Miller, J. C., & Redlich, A. D. (2016). The dynamic nature of interrogation. *Law & Human Behavior*, *40*, 295–309. doi: 10.1037/lhb0000172

Lamb, M. E., Brown, D. A., Hershkowitz, I., Orbach, Y., & Esplin, P. W. (2018). *Tell me what happened: Questioning children about abuse*. Wiley Blackwell.

Leo, R. A. (1992). From coercion to deception: The changing nature of police interrogation in America. *Crime, Law & Social Change*, *18*, 35–59. doi: 10.1007/BF00230624

Oleszkiewicz, S., & Watson, S. J. (2021). A meta-analytic review of the timing for disclosing evidence when interviewing suspects. *Applied Cognitive Psychology*, *35*, 342–359. doi: 10.1002/acp.3767

Otgaar, H., Schell-Leugers, J. M., Howe, M. L., Vilar, A. D. L. F., Houben, S. T., & Merckelbach, H. (2021). The link between suggestibility, compliance, and false confessions: A review using experimental and field studies. *Applied Cognitive Psychology*, *35*, 445–455. doi: 10.1002/acp.3788

Mac Giolla, E., & Luke, T. J. (2021). Does the cognitive approach to lie detection improve the accuracy of human observers?. *Applied Cognitive Psychology*, *35*, 385–392. doi: 10.1002/acp.3777

Meissner, C. A., & Kassin, S. M. (2004). You're guilty, so just confess!. In G. D. Lassiter (Ed.), *Interrogations, confessions, and entrapment* (pp. 85–106). Springer.

Meissner, C. A., Kelly, C. E., & Woestehoff, S. A. (2015). Improving the effectiveness of suspect interrogations. *Annual Review of Law & Social Science*, *11*, 211–233. doi: 10.1146/annurev-lawsocsci-120814-121657

Meissner, C. A., Kleinman, S. M., Mindthoff, A., Phillips, E. P., & Rothweiler, J. N. (2023). Investigative interviewing: A review of the literature and a model of science-based practice. In D. DeMatteo & K. C. Scherr (Eds.), *Oxford handbook of psychology and law* (pp. 582–603). Oxford University Press. doi: 10.1093/oxfordhb/9780197649138.013.34

Meissner, C. A., Redlich, A. D., Michael, S. W., Evans, J. R., Camilletti, C. R., Bhatt, S., & Brandon, S. (2014). Accusatorial and information-gathering interrogation methods and their effects on true and false confessions: A meta-analytic review. *Journal of Experimental Criminology*, *10*, 459–486. doi: 10.1007/s11292-014-9207-6

Meissner, C. A., Surmon-Böhr, F., Oleszkiewicz, S., & Alison, L. J. (2017). Developing an evidence-based perspective on interrogation: A review of the US government's high-value detainee interrogation group research program. *Psychology, Public Policy, & Law*, *23*, 438–457. doi: 10.1037/law0000136

Memon, A., Meissner, C. A., & Fraser, J. (2010). The Cognitive Interview: A meta-analytic review and study space analysis of the past 25 years. *Psychology, Public Policy, & Law*, *16*, 340–372. doi: 10.1037/a0020518

Miller, J. C., Redlich, A. D., & Kelly, C. E. (2018). Accusatorial and information-gathering interview and interrogation methods: a multi-country comparison. *Psychology, Crime & Law*, *24*, 935–956. doi: 10.1080/1068316X.2018.1467909

Narchet, F. M., Meissner, C. A., & Russano, M. B. (2011). Modeling the influence of investigator bias on the elicitation of true and false confessions. *Law & Human Behavior*, *35*, 452–465. doi: 10.1007/s10979-010-9257-x

Neequaye, D. A., & Mac Giolla, E. (2022). The use of the term rapport in the investigative interviewing literature: A critical examination of definitions. *Meta-Psychology*, *6*, 1–15. doi: 10.15626/MP.2021.2808

Nicol, A., La Rooy, D., & Lamb, M. E. (2017). Evidence-based and developmentally appropriate forensic interviewing of children. In L. Dixon, D. F. Perkins, C. Hamilton-Giachritsis, & L. A. Craig (Eds.), *The Wiley handbook of what works in child maltreatment: An evidence-based approach to assessment and intervention in child protection* (pp. 239–257). Wiley Blackwell.

Nunan, J., Stanier, I., Milne, R., Shawyer, A., & Walsh, D. (2020). Source Handler telephone interactions with covert human intelligence sources: An exploration of question types and intelligence yield. *Applied Cognitive Psychology*, *34*, 1473–1484. doi: 10.1002/acp.3726

Pickrell, J. E., McDonald, D., Bernstein, D. M., & Loftus, E. F. (2016). Misinformation effect. In R. F. Pohl (Ed.), *Cognitive illusions: Intriguing phenomena in judgement, thinking and memory* (1st ed., pp. 406–423). Routledge.

Powell, M. B., Fisher, R. P., & Wright, R. (2005). Investigative interviewing. In N. Brewer & K. D. Williams (Eds.), *Psychology and law: An empirical perspective* (pp. 11–42). Guilford Press.

Scherr, K. C., Redlich, A. D., & Kassin, S. M. (2020). Cumulative disadvantage: A psychological framework for understanding how innocence can lead to confession, wrongful conviction, and beyond. *Perspectives on Psychological Science*, *15*, 353–383. doi: 10.1177/1745691619896608

Shepherd, E. (1993). Resistance in interviews: The contribution of police perceptions and behaviour. *Issues in Criminological & Legal Psychology*, *18*, 5–12.

Snook, B., Eastwood, J., Stinson, M., Tedeschini, J., & House, J. C. (2010). Reforming investigative interviewing in Canada. *Canadian Journal of Criminology & Criminal Justice*, *52*, 215–229. doi: 10.3138/cjccj.52.2.215

Snook, B., Fahmy, W., Fallon, L., Lively, C. J., Luther, K., Meissner, C. A., Barron, T., & House, J. C. (2020). Challenges of a "toolbox" approach to investigative interview: A critical analysis of the RCMP's Phased Interview Model. *Psychology, Public Policy, & Law*, *26*, 261–273. doi: 10.1037/law0000245

Snook, B., Luther, K., Quinlan, H., & Milne, R. (2012). Let 'em talk! A field study of police questioning practices of suspects and accused persons. *Criminal Justice & Behavior*, *39*, 1328–1339. doi: 10.1177/0093854812449216

Vrij, A. (2015). A cognitive approach to lie detection. In P. A. Granhag, A. Vrij, & B. Verschuere (Eds.), *Detecting deception: Current challenges and cognitive approaches* (pp. 205–229). Wiley-Blackwell.

Vrij, A., Fisher, R. P., & Blank, H. (2017). A cognitive approach to lie detection: A meta-analysis. *Legal & Criminological Psychology*, *22*, 1–21. doi: 10.1111/lcrp.12088

23

EVIDENCE-BASED POLICING REFORM AND BUILDING POLICE–COMMUNITY RELATIONS

Lexi Gill and Bryanna Fox

Police–Community Relations and Calls for Evidence-Based Policing Reform

There is a long history of rifts between law enforcement and their local communities, which were only exacerbated by recent events involving (deadly) use of force by police. In 2014, former President Barack Obama commissioned the President's Task Force on 21st Century Policing to facilitate and enhance relationships between police departments and the communities they serve. Following publication of the Task Force's final report, police agencies across the country implemented new policies and practices suggested by the Task Force in hopes of reducing crime, police misconduct, and improving perceptions of trust and law enforcement's relationship with residents. Despite these efforts, there continues to be tension between police and communities, which has arguably increased since the Task Force convened in 2015. Indeed, recent events involving inappropriate and often deadly use of force and authority have resulted in a massive cultural flashpoint, in which communities nationwide vehemently called for an overhaul of the current policing system.

There are numerous viewpoints on how to reform police departments, with some advocating for abolishment, while others argue for more police funding and training, and everything in between. Regardless of the diverging opinions on how to reform policing, research indicates the importance of the community trust and support in order for police to be successful in their jobs (Tyler & Jackson, 2014; Walters & Bolger, 2019). How best to build community trust and support by police agencies is now the focus of much public and academic discussion. Therefore, two of the most effective approaches to improve police–community relations endorsed by the Task Force, and the evidence-based methods to achieve them, are reviewed in the following.

Trust, Legitimacy, and Procedural Justice

Building trust between police and the community is a foundational component to improving police-citizen relationships (President's Task Force, 2015). To that end, there has been an extensive focus on improving trust in police by addressing public perceptions of police legitimacy (Tyler, 1990, 2001, 2004; Sunshine & Tyler, 2003). Police legitimacy is the perception that police are a *legitimate* authority, which is developed by citizens believing police are

DOI: 10.4324/9781003219286-28

fair, just, and honest (Tyler, 1990; Sunshine & Tyler, 2003). Improving public views of police legitimacy is important because community residents are more apt to trust and comply with police officers and the law, as well as support their exercise of power, when they view police as being a legitimate authority (Beetham, 1991; Tyler & Jackson, 2014; Walters & Bolger, 2019). However, when police are viewed as being unjust, citizens are less likely to trust them, less compelled to obey laws, and less likely to support officers during enforcement duties (Jackson et al., 2012; Tyler, 1990).

Due to the implications of public perceptions of police, it is imperative that law enforcement consider citizens' views of police and take steps to bolster citizen perceptions of police legitimacy (Ramsey & Robinson, 2015). The President's Task Force on 21st Century Policing advocated for improving *procedural justice* as a way to build trust between police and communities. Procedural justice refers to when individuals feel they are treated fairly, are heard by authority, and trust and understand the legal process (Reisig et al., 2007; Sunshine & Tyler, 2003; Tyler, 1990). The procedural justice model has four sub-components: voice, neutrality, respect, and trustworthiness (Goodman-Delahunty, 2010; Tyler & Huo, 2002; Tyler & Murphy, 2011). This model contends that the way police act during an encounter with citizens has large notable implications such as shaping individuals' expectations about police behavior (Tyler, 1990, 2011). For instance, giving community members a 'voice' suggests community members are able to express their views to police and feel heard, which leads them to believe they are valued. Neutrality is demonstrated when police decisions are made with fairness, without bias, and with transparency. Respect is self-evident: police officers must treat community members with respect and act professionally. Last, trustworthiness embodies the perception that police are sincere and prioritize the community's needs while being honest and open.

In sum, procedural justice serves to build community trust and increase legitimacy by refocusing on carrying out officer duties in a way that is objectively fair, consistent, transparent, reflective of understanding of community concerns, and treating citizens with dignity and respect (Tyler, 1990). This leads individuals to feel that they are treated fairly and with respect, which, in turn, leads to higher levels of trust and legitimacy in police (Bolger & Walters, 2019; Donner et al., 2015; Hinds & Murphy, 2007; Lum et al., 2016; Tyler, 1990; Tyler & Huo, 2002; Walters & Bolger, 2019). Higher levels of trust and legitimacy in the police subsequently translates to greater compliance with the law and cooperation with the police, such as reporting crime, aiding in criminal investigations, and even cooperating during arrests (Jackson et al., 2012; Mazerolle et al., 2013; Murphy & Cherney, 2012; Sunshine & Tyler, 2003). Moreover, increasing perceptions of procedural justice is also associated with lower crime rates (Nagin & Telep, 2020), fewer arrests (Owens et al., 2018), and increased legal compliance (Nagin & Telep, 2017) – all of which are ideal outcomes in the mind of law enforcement and the communities they serve.

Furthermore, while minorities and individuals in poorer communities tend to have more negative views of procedural justice and subsequently less trust in police, research shows that the procedural justice–legitimacy link functions similarly for all individuals irrespective of race, gender, socioeconomic status, or neighborhood condition (Fox et al., 2021; Jackson et al., 2012; Wolfe et al., 2016). In other words, improving procedural justice will yield positive effects in terms of trust and legitimacy, even (or especially) in communities that have the most negative views of police. Therefore, it is vital for police to exercise procedural justice while engaging with all citizens they serve to positively impact citizens' perceptions of police, especially in communities that have more negative views on police officers.

Evidence-Based Training to Increase Trust, Legitimacy, and Procedural Justice

Despite these promising findings on the empirical link between procedural justice, trust, legitimacy, and positive police–community relations, there is only limited research on evidence-based practices to improve perceptions of procedural justice and ultimately citizens' trust and perceived legitimacy of police. As of this writing there is limited evidence-based and rigorously evaluated procedural justice training for law enforcement. These programs tend to be either script-based or skills-based training (Council on Criminal Justice Task Force on Policing, 2021). Script-based training provides officers a narrative for when they interact with citizens, while skills-based training involves four components: allowing citizens to have a voice, clarifying the purpose of their actions, treating citizens in a neutral and respectful manner, and communicating that officer motives address citizens' needs and interests (Council on Criminal Justice Task Force on Policing, 2021). Overall, the goal of these programs is to enhance officers' ability to be fair, transparent, respectful, and trustworthy in all of their interactions with citizens, particularly in situations that involve officer or citizen safety, enforcement of the law, and opportunities to build trust with residents (Polis Solutions, n.d.).

Evaluation research has shown that procedural justice training implemented in law enforcement agencies at various locations in the United States reduced officer use of force by 6% and citizen complaints by over 10% at these agencies over a 2-year time frame (Wood, Tyler, & Papachristos, 2020). Moreover, a similar evaluation in Chicago found that individual officers who received procedural justice training were 16–50% less likely to use force than similar officers who did not receive this training (Owens et al., 2018).

Two evidence-based procedural justice training programs are the Tact, Tactics, and Trust (T3) training (Council on Criminal Justice Task Force on Policing, 2021) and a training program that focuses on both the internal and external procedural justice practices developed by the U.S. Department of Justice Office of Community Oriented Policing Services (COPS) office and the Center for Public Safety and Justice (CPSJ) (Moe & Bradley, 2015). This training program focuses on implementing procedural justice principles in the organizational culture that will transfer to officer interactions with citizens (Moe & Bradley, 2015). While evaluations of these and other evidence-based programs are ongoing, we strongly recommend additional independent evaluations of training aimed at improving trust, legitimacy, and procedural justice to not only assess the fidelity and generality these programs' impact on various outcomes of interest to law enforcement and communities but also to assess the long-term effects on target outcomes to determine when and how often this training must be implemented (or 're-upped') to achieve maximum efficacy.

Trust, Legitimacy, and Procedural Justice Key Takeaways:

- Procedural justice includes four factors: voice, neutrality, respect, and trustworthiness (Goodman-Delahunty, 2010; Tyler, 1994; Tyler & Huo, 2002; Tyler & Murphy, 2011). Simply put, it describes how officers should engage with citizens. Interactions with police officers influence citizens' sentiment towards officers.
- Procedural justice practices lead to higher levels of police legitimacy, or trust and cooperation with police officers (Tyler & Huo, 2002).
- Race influences perceptions of procedural justice, as Black citizens tend to be less likely to experience an encounter where police use procedural justice (Mastrofski et al., 2016).

However, when officers display procedurally just behavior, it tends to improve trust and perceived legitimacy of police across race/ethnicity and other demographic features (Fox et al., 2021).

Community-Oriented Policing

Community-oriented policing has been increasingly utilized in police departments since the 1990s, as it is a policing philosophy focused on building relationships with the community in order to increase satisfaction and trust in police while also reducing crime (Office of Community Oriented Policing Services, 2012; Skogan, 2006; Weisburd & Eck, 2004). To do this, COP has three main components: community partnerships, organizational transformation, and problem solving, whereby police draw upon these elements to collaboratively work alongside local residents, businesses, organizations, media, and service providers to pinpoint and address local crime problems in order to reduce crime and build police–community relations (Office of Community Oriented Policing Services, 2012). Community partnership involves police working with local residents and organizations to prevent and solve crime problems (Office of Community Oriented Policing Services, 2012). The organizational transformation component involves reframing the internal structure of police departments to afford street-level officers more latitude in terms of decision making because they are more directly involved with the community (Office of Community Oriented Policing Services, 2012). The third component, problem solving, entails a four-part technique commonly associated with problem-oriented policing: scanning, analysis, response, and assessment (SARA), which is used to guide officers through the problem-solving stage and objectively identify methods to find, respond, and reduce crime (Eck & Spelman, 1987).

At its core, COP promotes a shift in policing from a 'warrior' to a 'guardian' mentality (Rahr & Rice, 2015; Stoughton, 2014), which has been shown to increase perceptions of police legitimacy and police–community relationships. The warrior mentality refers to an officer who views fighting crime as their main objective and focuses on law enforcement and officer safety above and beyond the needs and safety of citizens they serve (Rahr & Rice, 2015; Stoughton, 2016). This typically causes a division between officers and citizens because it heightens the perception of officers being superior to citizens, is perceived by citizens to be too aggressive and insensitive, and may cause destructive outcomes for citizens, including over-policing or unnecessary or unjust use of force (Rahr & Rice, 2015; Stoughton, 2016). Alternatively, the guardian mentality holds that it is an officer's duty is to protect citizens, which is accomplished through working with the community (Stoughton, 2016). Research indicates that guardian officers are more apt to collaborate with the community, focus on communication instead of physical control when interacting with citizens, and perceive their authority being based on citizen consent, all of which are consistent with COP (McLean et al., 2020). Not surprisingly, citizens prefer the guardian mentality, as it tends to generate greater trust and support for law enforcement compared to the warrior mentality (McLean et al., 2020). Therefore, altering officer attitudes and behaviors in line with a guardian mentality, in line with the principles of COP, will have positive implications towards building officers' relationships with the communities they serve (McLean et al., 2020).

While law enforcement agencies nationwide indicate that they engage in COP, the fidelity of these programs and their efficacy vary widely (Office of Community Oriented Policing Services, 2012; Skogan, 2006). This heterogeneity suggests a strong need for specific guidance regarding the optimal programming features and implementation of COP to achieve the most consistent and highest magnitude of success. Further, research on COP demonstrates only modest effectiveness in reducing crime and citizens' fear of crime (Gill et al., 2014; Sherman & Eck, 2006; Skogan & Frydl, 2004; Weisburd & Eck, 2004), while it is most effective in building police–community relations – a distinct but highly worthy goal. In sum, COP has been found to improve citizen satisfaction with the police and perceptions of police legitimacy, which is vital for building police–community relations (Gill et al., 2014). Even though COP has been less effective in decreasing crime in the short term, it may be effective long term because a critical component of police effectiveness is citizen cooperation, which can be enhanced through perceptions of police legitimacy (Gill et al., 2014). Consequently, COP is an effective evidence-based strategy recommended by the President's Task Force on 21st Century Policing to be included in a suite of policing reforms aimed at reducing crime and building police–community relations.

Evidence-Based Community-Oriented Policing Programs and Practices

As stated, many law enforcement agencies indicate participating in COP in some fashion, however, the quality and fidelity of these programs to the core concepts of COP tend to vary widely (Office of Community Oriented Policing Services, 2012; Skogan, 2006). As a result, the impact of these programs tends to vary greatly and summarizing evaluations of them as a whole would be unhelpful. Instead, it is best to highlight the best practices within community-oriented policing, which were developed from decades of research and summarized in a guide created by the U.S. Department of Justice's Office of Community Oriented Policing (Department of Justice, 2019). These best practices of COP include the following:

1. Devise an all-encompassing community policing strategic plan which includes the goals and mission for community policing and spell out how this will be carried out within the department.
2. All personnel should be trained on COP, which also includes how to overcome distrust. Improving trust among the community members can be accomplished through creating connections that extend beyond current relationships, developing relations in communities that currently do not have any connections, and distinctly showing their intention for open dialogue and collaboration.
3. Cultivate an environment of openness and transparency. Building off the previous principle, trust can be gained through transparency. As such, law enforcement should frequently share with the community, which should include data, policies, investigation results, and so on. Additionally, community sentiment to changes in law enforcement should be considered along with open dialogue between the community and agencies to gain an understanding of the agency's rationale.
4. Implement procedural justice as a leading principle. This encompasses the need to address the external issues that create crime though local partnerships in tandem with cultivating an internal cultural change centered on full trust and community engagement. Procedural justice internally influences how decisions are made and the implementation of policies.
5. Prioritize officers' wellness and safety. COP compels officers to be more empathetic, compassionate, and tolerant compared to the traditional policing style. In order for officers to fulfill these objectives, it is necessary for them to have good mental and physical health. Officers' jobs can be extremely stressful and taxing, therefore it is imperative they have resources to aid with their overall health.

6. Involve the community in a partnership to address issues of crime and disorder. The COPS Office suggests that law enforcement establish an advisory group that is representative of stakeholders in the community. Additionally, law enforcement should look to the community for guidance.
7. Act as though every contact is an opportunity to positively engage with a community resident. Positive interactions with community members improve legitimacy, trust, and community engagement. That said, officers should be assessed on procedural justice measures.
8. Measure social cohesiveness and build relationships. In communities with higher levels of crime, officers are more prone to using suppression strategies that create hostility between the community and officers. Often, these are also areas with lower levels of social cohesion, which refers to residents' sentiments toward community, magnitude of social interaction, and trust and willingness to interact with neighbors. Officers can facilitate social cohesion by helping the community members' capability for collaboration by helping establish safe environments for residents to build the social connections needed for social control or the ability to regulate behavior (Sampson & Groves, 1989).
9. Reevaluate the measures of community policing effectiveness. Agencies should evaluate strategies used in community policing along with the measures to indicate if they are reaching the department's standards.
10. Include community policing measures in performance evaluations, which will demonstrate the agency's progress in community policing.

Community-Oriented Policing Key Takeaways:

- Community-oriented policing aims to foster relationships between the community and citizens to address crime problems collectively (Office of Community Oriented Policing Services, 2012). Community-oriented policing can help mend relationships between communities and their residents, with an eye on reducing crime in the long-term.
- There should be shift from a warrior to guardian mentality, which emphasizes protecting citizens and is accomplished through working with the community, communication, and less favorable attitudes of force misconduct (McLean et al., 2020).
- The core principles and best practices of COP, as outlined by the U.S. Department of Justice Office of Community Oriented Policing, should be thoughtfully engaged to uphold program fidelity and have the greatest impact on police–community relations and crime.

Conclusion

The current state of police–community relationships in the United States clearly warrants responsive change in law enforcement and criminal justice practices in order to restore trust, improve functionality, and reduce negative outcomes through the use of evidence-based policy and practice. Specifically, it appears vital for police departments to thoughtfully integrate community-oriented policing and procedural justice principles, as recommended by the President's Task Force on 21st Century Policing. In sum, efforts to improve trust in police will be largely advanced by adoption of community-oriented policing, which aims to improve encounters between the community and police and creating partnerships between both entities to decrease crime. Moreover, efforts to improve citizens' perception of procedural justice can increase also public confidence and police satisfaction (Mazerolle et al., 2013). As such, the evidence clearly indicates that police departments should prioritize community-oriented policing and procedural justice to heal the current rift in police–community relations in the United States.

References

Beetham, D. (1991). Power and its need of legitimation. In *The legitimation of power* (pp. 42–63). Palgrave.
Bolger, P. C., & Walters, G. D. (2019). The relationship between police procedural justice, police legitimacy, and people's willingness to cooperate with law enforcement: A meta-analysis. *Journal of Criminal Justice*, *60*, 93–99.
Council on Criminal Justice Task Force on Policing. (2021). Procedural justice training – assessing the evidence. Council on Criminal Justice. Retrieved from https://counciloncj.foleon.com/policing/assessing-the-evidence/vi-procedural-justice-training/.
Donner, C., Maskaly, J., Fridell, L., & Jennings, W. G. (2015). Policing and procedural justice: A state-of-the-art review. *Policing: An International Journal of Police Strategies & Management*, *38*(1), 153–172.
Eck, J. E., & Spelman, W. (1987). *Problem-solving: Problem-oriented policing in Newport News*. US Department of Justice, National Institute of Justice.
Fox, B., Moule Jr, R. K., Jaynes, C. M., & Parry, M. M. (2021). Are the effects of legitimacy and its components invariant? Operationalization and the generality of Sunshine and Tyler's empowerment hypothesis. *Journal of Research in Crime and Delinquency*, *58*(1), 3–40.
Gill, C., Weisburd, D., Telep, C. W., Vitter, Z., & Bennett, T. (2014). Community-oriented policing to reduce crime, disorder and fear and increase satisfaction and legitimacy among citizens: A systematic review. *Journal of Experimental Criminology*, *10*(4), 399–428.
Goodman-Delahunty, J. (2010). Four ingredients: New recipes for procedural justice in Australian policing. *Policing: A Journal of Policy and Practice*, *4*(4), 403–410.
Hinds, L., & Murphy, K. (2007). Public satisfaction with police: Using procedural justice to improve police legitimacy. *Australian & New Zealand Journal of Criminology*, *40*(1), 27–42.
Jackson, J., Bradford, B., Hough, M., Myhill, A., Quinton, P., & Tyler, T. R. (2012). Why do people comply with the law? Legitimacy and the influence of legal institutions. *British Journal of Criminology*, *52*(6), 1051–1071.
Lum, C. M., Koper, C. S., Gill, C., Hibdon, J., Telep, C., & Robinson, L. (2016). *An evidence-assessment of the recommendations of the president's task force on 21st century policing: implementation and research priorities*. International Association of Chiefs of Police.
Mastrofski, S. D., Jonathan-Zamir, T., Moyal, S., & Willis, J. J. (2016). Predicting procedural justice in police-citizen encounters. *Criminal Justice and Behavior*, *43*(1), 119–139.
Mazerolle, L., Sargeant, E., Cherney, A., Bennett, S., Murphy, K., Antrobus, E., & Martin, P. (2013). *Procedural justice and legitimacy in policing*. Springer.
McLean, K., Wolfe, S. E., Rojek, J., Alpert, G. P., & Smith, M. R. (2020). Police officers as warriors or guardians: Empirical reality or intriguing rhetoric?. *Justice Quarterly*, *37*(6), 1096–1118.
Moe, C., & Bradley, M. (2015). Organizational change through decision making and policy: A new procedural justice course for managers and supervisors. *Dispatch*, *8*(4). Retrieved from https://cops.usdoj.gov/html/dispatch/04-2015/a_new_procedural_justice_course.asp
Murphy, K., & Cherney, A. (2012). Understanding cooperation with police in a diverse society. *The British Journal of Criminology*, *52*(1), 181–201.
Nagin, D. S., & Telep, C. W. (2017). Procedural justice and legal compliance. *Annual Review of Law and Social Science*, *13*, 5–28.
Nagin, D. S., & Telep, C. W. (2020). Procedural justice and legal compliance: A revisionist perspective. *Criminology & Public Policy*, *19*(3), 761–786.
Office of Community Oriented Policing Services. (2012). *Community-oriented policing defined*. U.S. Department of Justice, Office of Community Oriented Policing Services.
Owens, E., Weisburd, D., Amendola, K. L., & Alpert, G. P. (2018). Can you build a better cop? Experimental evidence on supervision, training, and policing in the community. *Criminology & Public Policy*, *17*(1), 41–87.
Polis Solutions. (n.d.). Polis Solutions: T3 – tact, tactics, and trust. Retrieved from www.polis-solutions.net/t3.
President's Task Force on 21st Century Policing. (2015). Final report of the president's task force on 21st century policing. Office of Community Oriented Policing Services.
Rahr, S., & Rice, S. K. (2015). *From warriors to guardians: Recommitting American police culture to democratic ideals*. US Department of Justice, Office of Justice Programs, National Institute of Justice.

Ramsey, C., & Robinson, L. (2015). *Interim report of the president's task force on 21st century policing*. Office of Community Oriented Policing Services
Reisig, M. D., Bratton, J., & Gertz, M. G. (2007). The construct validity and refinement of process-based policing measures. *Criminal Justice and Behavior*, *34*(8), 1005–1028.
Sampson, R. J., & Groves, W. B. (1989). Community structure and crime: Testing social-disorganization theory. *American Journal of Sociology*, *94*(4), 774–802.
Sherman, L. W., & Eck, J. E. (2006). Policing for crime prevention. In L. W. Sherman, D. P. Farrington, B. C. Welsh, & D. L. MacKenzie (Eds.), *Evidence-based crime prevention* (Revised ed., pp. 295–329). Routledge.
Skogan, W. G. (2006). Advocate: The promise of community policing. In *Police innovation: Contrasting perspectives* (pp. 27–43). Cambridge University Press.
Skogan, W., & Frydl, K. (2004). *Fairness and effectiveness in policing: The evidence*. National Academies Press.
Stoughton, S. (2014). Law enforcement's warrior problem. Harvard Law Review Forum, 128, 225.
Stoughton, S. (2016). Principled policing: Warrior cops and guardian officers. *Wake Forest Law Review*, *51*, 611.
Sunshine, J., & Tyler, T. R. (2003). The role of procedural justice and legitimacy in shaping public support for policing. *Law & Society Review*, *37*(3), 513–548.
Tyler, T. R. (1990). *Why people obey the law*. Princeton University Press.
Tyler, T. R. (1994). Governing and diversity: The effect of fair decisionmaking procedures on the legitimacy of government. *Law & Society Review*, *28*, 809.
Tyler, T. R. (2001). Public trust and confidence in legal authorities: What do majority and minority group members want from the law and legal institutions?. *Behavioral Sciences & the Law*, *19*(2), 215–235.
Tyler, T. R. (2004). Enhancing police legitimacy. *The Annals of the American Academy of Political and Social Science*, *593*(1), 84–99.
Tyler, T. R. (2011). Trust and legitimacy: Policing in the USA and Europe. *European Journal of Criminology*, *8*(4), 254–266.
Tyler, T. R., & Huo, Y. (2002). *Trust in the law: Encouraging public cooperation with the police and courts*. Russell Sage Foundation.
Tyler, T. R., & Jackson, J. (2014). Popular legitimacy and the exercise of legal authority: Motivating compliance, cooperation, and engagement. *Psychology, Public Policy, and Law*, *20*(1), 78.
Tyler, T. R., & Murphy, K. (2011). *Procedural justice, police legitimacy and cooperation with the police: A new paradigm for policing* (Australian Research Council Centre of Excellence in Policing and Security Briefing Paper). Griffith University.
U.S. Department of Justice. (2019). *Law enforcement best practices: Lessons learned from the field*. Office of Community Oriented Policing Services.
Walters, G. D., & Bolger, P. C. (2019). Procedural justice perceptions, legitimacy beliefs, and compliance with the law: A meta-analysis. *Journal of Experimental Criminology*, *15*(3), 341–372.
Weisburd, D., & Eck, J. E. (2004). What can police do to reduce crime, disorder, and fear?. *The Annals of the American Academy of Political and Social Science*, *593*(1), 42–65.
Wolfe, S. E., Nix, J., Kaminski, R., & Rojek, J. (2016). Is the effect of procedural justice on police legitimacy invariant? Testing the generality of procedural justice and competing antecedents of legitimacy. *Journal of Quantitative Criminology*, *32*(2), 253–282.
Wood, G., Tyler, T. R., & Papachristos, A. V. (2020). Procedural justice training reduces police use of force and complaints against officers. *Proceedings of the National Academy of Sciences*, *117*(18), 9815–9821.

PART V

The Courts

24

EVIDENCE-BASED PRACTICES IN PROSECUTION

Raquel A. Hernandez, Sean Houlihan, and Brian D. Johnson

Introduction

The capacious power of the prosecutor, and their far-reaching influence over criminal punishment, are difficult to overstate – American prosecutors arguably control a wider array of consequential decisions, with more discretion and less oversight, than any other criminal justice actor (Davis, 2019; Sklansky, 2018). Their power stems from the extensive control they wield over manifold, impactful decisions and from the fact that their discretion remains largely immune from public scrutiny and formal procedures of legal review (Johnson et al., 2016). Prosecutors typically decide what charges to file, how to amend them in plea negotiations, and whether to dismiss some or all counts. They have broad discretion over diversion and treatment options, and they make influential bail and sentencing recommendations. Court innovations, like sentencing guidelines and mandatory sentencing laws and the recent global pandemic, have substantially expanded prosecutorial power (Pfaff, 2017; Flanders & Galoob, 2020). Given their extensive influence and immense capacity to shape criminal case dispositions, it is imperative that prosecutorial discretion be guided by evidence-based policies. As Sklansky (2018, p. 452) recently opined, "There is a broad and growing sense" that policy efforts aimed at improving prosecution are "the most pressing challenge in American criminal justice" today. This chapter reviews the state of the literature on prosecutorial discretion, summarizes key empirical findings, and discusses the limited evidence base for guiding best practices before concluding with a discussion of essential steps to advance evidence-based practices in prosecution.

Empirical Research on Prosecutorial Discretion

For decades, academic research on the criminal courts has focused disproportionately on judges, with far less attention directed at public prosecutors. However, recent calls for greater scholarly work on prosecution has led to a modern resurgence in research on the causes and consequences of prosecutorial discretion (Johnson et al., 2016; Spohn, 2018). Though still in its nascence, this renaissance has begun to identify key insights related to prosecutorial discretion. The next section briefly outlines recent development in prosecution research and summarizes main findings from contemporary studies examining prosecutorial discretion.

DOI: 10.4324/9781003219286-30

Historical Developments in Research on Prosecution

Criminological research on prosecution has developed gradually over the past several decades. Seminal studies from the 1970s and 1980s provided comprehensive overviews of prosecution (e.g., Maynard, 1984; Nardulli et al., 1988; Rosett & Cressey, 1976), but subsequent research focused almost exclusively on judges as key reform efforts, like sentencing guidelines and mandatory minimums, were passed with the express goal of cabining in judicial discretion. This shift not only diverted academic attention away from prosecutors but also substantially enhanced their leverage to negotiate guilty pleas and craft final sentences (Sklansky, 2018). Scholarly efforts to collect prosecutor data also diminished as prosecutors became reticent to share their data with academics (Johnson et al., 2016).

Nevertheless, a number of small-scale studies based on independent data collections provided valuable insights about the exercise of prosecutorial discretion during the "tough on crime" era. This work was typically based on small samples that centered on select crime types, such as sexual assaults (Spohn & Spears, 1996) or intimate partner violence (Kingsnorth et al., 1999). Findings showed that charging decisions were influenced by key legal factors like offense severity, criminal history, and strength of evidence. Albonetti (1987), for example, demonstrated how these factors influenced the likelihood that a case would be filed and fully prosecuted. Another key finding from this era was that both defendant and victim characteristics impacted charging decisions. Research showed the victim's age, character, behavior (Spears & Spohn, 1997), relationship to the defendant (Spohn et al., 2001), and level of cooperation (Kingsnorth & MacIntosh, 2007; Spohn et al., 2001) all impacted prosecutorial assessments of case convictability (Frohmann, 1997), which shaped their decision-making in key ways. This early work had limited generalizability but was foundational for shaping contemporary scholarship.

In particular, a new wave of scholarship on prosecutorial discretion has arisen in recent years, being driven in part by a fundamental paradigm shift that reflects at least three emergent trends: 1) a growing dissatisfaction with mass incarceration in America, 2) the rise of social justice movements focused on racial equity and fairness in the justice system, and 3) a greater appreciation for the importance of researcher-practitioner partnerships in evidence-based policy. These trends are exemplified by the emergence of a novel class of "progressive prosecutors" across American cities (Davis, 2019; Sklansky, 2017) who typically eschew tough on crime approaches for reformist goals aimed at reducing disparity; improving fairness and transparency; decreasing reliance on incarceration; and emphasizing data-driven, evidence-based approaches to criminal justice (Sklansky, 2016). This shift has provided new opportunities for research grounded in collaborative partnerships designed to improve knowledge of prosecutorial discretion while also identifying effective policies to guide it. The following section details key findings from this contemporary work.

Contemporary Research on Prosecutorial Discretion

Advances in prosecutorial research have been guided by a growing recognition of the importance of early charging decisions and their subsequent effect on case outcomes. One key finding is that defendants of color are often more likely to have their cases dismissed (Barnes & Kingsnorth, 1996; Johnson et al., 2021; Petersilia, 1983). In a study of misdemeanor assaults in Ohio, Wooldredge and Thistlewaite (2004) found Black defendants were less likely to be charged and fully prosecuted compared to White defendants. Similarly, Kutateladze et al. (2014) found the odds of case dismissal were greater for Black and Hispanic defendants relative to White defendants in New York County, and Johnson et al. (2021) reported similar findings in Baltimore, Maryland. On the surface, this may suggest a putative advantage for defendants of color, but scholars argue that higher dismissal rates reflect evidentiary concerns that indicate these cases should not have been accepted for prosecution in the first place (e.g., Kutateladze et al., 2014; Kutateladze et al., 2016). Researchers also stress that quality indicators of evidentiary strengths are necessary to investigate these issues, though they note they are seldom available in analyses of prosecutorial discretion (Forst, 2010; Kutateladze et al., 2016; Ulmer, 2012).[1]

Given the ubiquity of guilty pleas in the criminal legal system, much of the present literature has also focused on the determinants and consequences of plea bargaining. One key finding from this work is that Black and Latino defendants benefit less when pleading guilty compared to Whites. This evidence is found at the county (Johnson & Larroulet, 2019; Kutateladze et al., 2016; Metcalfe & Chiricos, 2018), state (Stemen & Escobar, 2018), and federal levels (Shermer & Johnson, 2010). In Wisconsin, defendants of color were less likely to receive reduced charges and more likely to be given custodial pleas (Stemen & Escobar, 2018). Similar work in a Florida county found Black male defendants were less likely to enter a guilty plea and received less of a sentence discount when they did (Metcalfe & Chiricos, 2018; see also: Testa & Johnson, 2020). Additional studies have found plea disparities vary by offense. Minority defendants received custodial sentence offers more often when facing marijuana charges (Kutateladze et al, 2016), for example, and they benefit less from charge reductions for federal weapons charges (Shermer & Johnson, 2010). Research on racial disparities in guilty pleas is vital because a robust literature shows that pleading guilty routinely results in significant reductions in punishment severity (Johnson, 2019).

Another finding from extant research is that prosecutorial discretion is often influenced by decisions made at earlier stages, such as arrest and bail (Kurlychek & Johnson, 2019). For example, the probability of pleading guilty, and being convicted, is greater when a defendant is detained pretrial (Stevenson, 2018). This is because prosecutors hold greater bargaining in these cases and because accepting a guilty plea can often lead to pretrial release. Research shows that pretrial detention disproportionately affects poor defendants and defendants of color (Demuth, 2003) and that it also increases the probability of imprisonment (Wooldredge et al., 2015).

Similarly, early charging decisions also impact subsequent sentencing outcomes. Studies show that reductions in initial charge severity are strongly associated with less severe and shorter sentences (Bushway & Piehl, 2007; Shermer & Johnson, 2010) and that they tend to favor female and White defendants over male and minority defendants (Johnson & Larroulet, 2019). These findings suggest even small inequities in early case processing decisions may contribute to cumulative disadvantages in punishment (Kurlychek & Johnson, 2019). For example, Kutateladze and colleagues (2014) found that Black and Latino defendants were more likely to receive less favorable combinations of punitive decisions across multiple stages of criminal processing, producing harsher punishments for defendants of color. Taken as a whole, scholarly research on the exercise of prosecutorial discretion supports at least five core conclusions:

- Legal and evidentiary factors are strong predictors of charging outcomes
- Victim and offender characteristics also meaningfully shape case outcomes
- Minority defendants tend to be more likely to have their cases dismissed
- Male and minority defendants often receive less valuable plea deals
- Charging and plea disparities impact downstream sentence disparities

Evidence-Based Programs, Policies, and Practices

Extant research on prosecutorial discretion acutely highlights the need for policymakers and scholars to work together to develop better evidence-based practices. This need is accentuated by recent events, including the COVID-19 pandemic, rise of progressive-minded prosecutors, and modern acts of police violence that have sparked worldwide protests. Progressive prosecutors in several cities have initiated efforts to reckon with years of mass incarceration, systemic racial disparities, and the global pandemic (Flanders & Galoob, 2020), announcing diverse policy changes that include non-prosecution of low-level misdemeanors, increased use of prosecutorial diversion programs, and reduced reliance on lengthy terms of community supervision (Brennan Center for Justice, 2021; Hamann & Geisler, 2020). Some offices have also established "conviction integrity units" designed to investigate and overturn wrongful convictions (Levin, 2020).[2] Despite these sweeping policy reforms, there is a lack of empirical work on evidence-based prosecutorial practices. To address this, state's attorney's offices in select jurisdictions have begun to partner with researchers to improve their data infrastructures and to identify effective evidence-based policies in prosecution. This movement, however, is still in its infancy. As Sklansky (2017, p. 60) observed, there is still "no roadmap" and "no generally agreed-upon 'best practices' for prosecutors' offices". The American Bar Association (2017) publishes a useful guide for prosecutors, but it is not directly informed by empirical research. In the following, we consider current reform efforts, along with the available research evidence before offering tentative policy recommendations for prosecutors' offices.

Evidence-Based Reforms in Prosecution

One focus of evidence-based practices in prosecution has been how non-prosecution and shorter community supervision periods for low-level offenders impacts public safety. For example, in response to the global pandemic, the Baltimore City State's Attorney's Office announced the non-prosecution of warrants related to drug possession, prostitution, trespassing, minor traffic offenses, open containers, and urinating in public (Office of the State's Attorney for Baltimore City, 2021). John Hopkins researchers found this policy was associated with a decrease in 911 calls for drug use and sex work and no increase in public intoxication disturbances. Similarly, Suffolk County's District Attorney's Office limited enforcement of multiple nonviolent misdemeanor offenses, with preliminary evaluations showing decreases in criminal complaints, reductions in initial arraignment hearings, and no rise in serious crime (Agan et al., 2021). At the same time, the Philadelphia District Attorney's Office (DAO, 2019) implemented strategies to decrease supervision sentences for low-level misdemeanors in plea negotiations. The DAO encouraged prosecutors to limit probation terms to address mass supervision and racial disparities; results indicated support for shorter supervision sentences, no evidence of increased recidivism, and a decrease in the racial gap in punishment. All of this work is preliminary – it remains limited to particular offense types in single jurisdictions and lacks detailed information on plea offers, case evidence, and other factors like socioeconomic status – but early findings have been supportive of remedial policies for low-level misdemeanor offenses.

Some prosecutor offices have also expanded their use of pretrial diversion and alternative prosecution programs, with recent studies providing some support for these programs. A large, multisite evaluation funded by the National Institute of Justice, for instance, examined 16 prosecutor-led diversion programs across 11 offices and conducted impact evaluations of five specific diversion programs in three sites (Cook County, Illinois; Milwaukee, Wisconsin;

and Chittenden County, Vermont). The researchers found diversion significantly reduced the likelihood of conviction and incarceration, and in four out of five programs, it also lowered the odds of rearrest (Rempel et al., 2018). These programs were also associated with significant cost savings. Related work by the California Policy Lab examined pretrial data for seven diversion programs in San Francisco's courts over a 10-year period and found that diversion referrals increased time to disposition but significantly decreased the likelihood of reconviction (Augustine et al., 2021). These studies are not without limitations – there are variable program elements across jurisdictions and little information on how prosecutors select defendants for inclusion – but the preliminary evidence offers reason for optimism and suggests prosecutor-led diversion programs can successfully redirect defendants away from incarceration without significant costs for public safety.

Identifying and Addressing Racial Inequality

A burgeoning area of investigation in evidence-based work on prosecutorial discretion is identifying and addressing potential sources of racial inequality. Researchers and policymakers have long been concerned with persistent racial disparities in the justice system. Publicized events of racial injustice have encouraged more state's attorney's offices to partner with researchers to improve data capabilities, assess the efficacy of current practices, offer greater transparency, and conduct studies to identify sources of racial inequality (see Prosecutorial Performance Indicators, n.d.). Research in the Brooklyn District Attorney's Office, for example, found minority defendants had higher rates of dismissal, lesser reductions in top charges and higher odds of carceral sentence offers (Ferone et al, 2021; Bosick, 2021). Similarly, data from the San Francisco Public Defender's Office revealed that Black defendants were detained pretrial more often and had longer times to case resolution, though no race differences emerged in charge alterations (Owens et al., 2017). In Massachusetts, Harvard researchers found defendants of color were less likely than Whites to have their cases resolved through pretrial probation alternatives and more likely to have their cases sent to Superior Court where sentences are longer (Bishop et al., 2020). They also found racial differences in the application of mandatory minimum sentences and suggested disparities in initial charges were driving sentencing disparities. In Baltimore City, researchers likewise found that Black defendants were more likely than Whites to have their initial charges reduced and their cases dismissed, raising questions about arrest quality and initial charging decisions for Black defendants (Johnson et al., 2021).

Notably, a project known as Prosecution Performance Indicators (PPIs), created by professors at Florida International and Loyola University of Chicago and funded by the MacArthur Foundation, has examined racial disparities in multiple jurisdictions. Their series of reports suggest Black defendants are less likely to be selected for alternative prosecution and more likely to have their charges reduced, their cases dismissed, and receive custodial sentences in some jurisdictions (Kutateladze et al., 2018, 2019a, 2019b, 2019c, 2019d). This project uniquely connects prosecutors and researchers; provides a map for how district attorneys' offices can improve office performance along key policy dimensions, including racial justice; and includes more than 50 evidence-based indicators designed to identify prosecutorial strategies that can help promote fairness, efficiency, and public safety.[3] The PPIs are being adopted by dozens of prosecutors' offices across the nation and have proven a valuable tool for identifying racial inequalities and advising other data-driven reform efforts. Overall, research studies continue to reveal a number of ways that the race of the defendant and victim impact prosecution (see e.g. Wu, 2016; Kutateladze et al., 2012), but important policy steps are increasingly being pursued to address unwarranted sources of racial inequity in prosecution.

Although additional research is undoubtedly needed to investigate and establish best practices in prosecution, some preliminary policy recommendations can be offered that are consistent with available evidence on fair and effective prosecution. First, offices should expand their use of pretrial diversion and alternative prosecution programs while implementing procedures to guard against institutionalized bias in their application (Rempel et al., 2018). Research suggests diversion programs can be expanded without risk to public safety but also cautions that they can institutionalize bias if they are not guided by clear and principled procedures (Augustine et al., 2021). Second, prosecutors' offices should work to ensure that initial screening procedures identify cases early that are unlikely to be fully prosecuted (Kutateladze et al., 2019d; Ferone et al., 2021). Not accepting cases that will be dismissed or nol-prossed saves time and resources and prevents unnecessary criminal justice involvement (Stevenson & Mayson, 2021). Third, prosecutors should record detailed reasons for diversions, dismissals, charge reductions, and plea offers to help identify and address unintentional sources of bias (Bibas, 2009; Bosick, 2021). Inequalities can occur in highly discretionary decisions, and most decisions made by prosecutors involve broad discretion (Forst, 2010), so formalized procedures are needed to guide informal decision-making (Ashworth & Roberts, 2013; Pfaff, 2017). Fourth, there is growing consensus for the value of creating conviction integrity units within prosecutors' offices. Legal scholars argue that there is much to gain and little to lose from institutionalizing internal review units (Kroepsch, 2016). Fifth, detailed data should be collected and analyzed periodically to detect underlying patterns of inequality in charging and plea negotiations (e.g. Kutateladze et al., 2018). Data analysis is not only an essential step in identifying potential sources of unwarranted disparity but making it available to researchers and the public also increases transparency and accountability. As one legal scholar put it, "Justice is a noble goal, but how will you know if you are achieving it . . . unless you look – which is to say, unless you measure your performance objectively" (Sklansky, 2017, p. 31). All in all, extant work on recent innovations in prosecution supports the following preliminary policy recommendations:

- Expand pre-trial diversion options and ensure their fair and equal application
- Review and improve initial case screening procedures
- Create clear policies and procedures for guiding discretionary decisions
- Establish conviction integrity units if relevant and possible
- Periodically collect and analyze detailed data on key case processing decisions

Conclusion

Evidence-based policies in prosecution have lagged behind other areas of criminal justice reform. In part, this reflects prosecutors past reticence to partner with academics. However, this is rapidly changing and a new era of "progressive prosecutors" are redefining the goals of traditional prosecution to include the expansion of alternatives to incarceration, reduction in the reliance on carceral sentences, taking steps to address longstanding inequalities in punishment, and engaging the academic community to conduct data-driven evaluative research designed to identify best practices in prosecution (Davis, 2019). By partnering with researchers, prosecutors can more effectively investigate potential sources of inequality, assess the efficacy of key policy changes, and become active participants in ongoing efforts to advance knowledge on evidence-based policies in prosecution. In the end, we agree with David Sklansky (2017, p. 42), who observed: "A good district attorney can in fact do a great deal to improve the functioning of the criminal justice system. But the path is not well signposted; there is, as yet, no consensus set of 'best practices' for district attorneys", though developing them "is an urgent priority".

Notes

1 Kutateladze et al. (2015) have found some support for the salience of evidence-related variables in prosecutorial decision-making. Their research suggests more punitive charge offers are given in drug cases when certain evidence is available, including audio/video evidence, eyewitness identifications, and recovered currency from undercover "buy-and-bust" police operations.
2 Additionally, other reform efforts include discounted use of cash bail for low-level offenses, presumptive release of individuals on their own recognizance, virtual court appearances, dismissal of pending court cases, removal of outstanding warrants, and the early release of thousands of low-risk inmates (Sklansky, 2018).
3 Primary PPI domains include organizational and staff capacity, addressing serious crime, racial and ethnic disparity, time and resource prioritization, protecting and serving victims, minimizing unnecessary punitiveness, timely case processing, community outreach and engagement, and prosecutorial ethics and integrity (see https://prosecutorialperformanceindicators.org/).

References

Agan, A. Y., Doleac, J. L., & Harvey, A. (2021). Misdemeanor prosecution (No. w28600). National Bureau of Economic Research. Retrieved from www.nber.org/papers/w28600

Albonetti, C. A. (1987). Prosecutorial discretion: The effects of uncertainty. *Law & Society Review*, *21*(2), 291–314. doi: 10.2307/3053523

American Bar Association. (2017). Criminal justice standards for the prosecution function. Retrieved from www.americanbar.org/groups/criminal_justice/standards/ProsecutionFunctionFourthEdition/

Ashworth, A., & Roberts, J. V. (Eds.). (2013). *Sentencing guidelines: Exploring the English model*. Oxford University Press.

Augustine, E., Lacoe, J., Raphael, S., & Skog, A. (2021). The impact of felony diversion in San Francisco. (Working Paper No. 2021-1). *California Policy Lab*. Retrieved from www.capolicylab.org/wp-content/uploads/2021/04/The-Impact-of-Felony-Diversion-in-San-Francisco.pdf

Barnes, C. W., & Kingsnorth, R. (1996). Race, drug, and criminal sentencing: Hidden effects of the criminal law. *Journal of Criminal Justice*, *24*(1), 39–55. doi: 10.1016/0047-2352(95)00051-8

Bibas, S. (2009). Prosecutorial regulation versus prosecutorial accountability. *University of Pennsylvania Law Review*, *157*(4), 959–1016.

Bishop, E., Hopkins, B., Obiofuma, C., & Owusu, F. (2020). Racial disparities in the Massachusetts criminal system. A report submitted to the Supreme Judicial Court of Massachusetts. Criminal Justice Policy Program, Harvard Law School. Retrieved from https://hls.harvard.edu/content/uploads/2020/11/Massachusetts-Racial-Disparity-Report-FINAL.pdf

Bosick, S. J. (2021). *Racial disparities in prosecutorial outcomes*. University of Denver Colorado Evaluation and Action Lab. Retrieved from www.denverda.org/wp-content/uploads/news-release/2021/Racial-Disparities-in-Prosecutorial-Outcomes_March2021_final-002.pdf

Brennan Center for Justice. (2021). Prosecutors responses to Covid-19. Retrieved from www.brennancenter.org/our-work/research-reports/prosecutors-responses-covid-19

Bushway, S. D., & Piehl, A. M. (2007). Social science research and the legal threat to presumptive sentencing guidelines. *Criminology & Public Policy*, *6*(3), 461–482. doi: 10.1111/j.1745-9133.2007.00447.x

Davis, A. J. (2019). Reimagining prosecution: A growing progressive movement. *UCLA Criminal Justice Law Review*, *3*(1). Retrieved from https://escholarship.org/uc/item/2rq8t137

Demuth, S. (2003). Racial and ethnic differences in pretrial release decisions and outcomes: A comparison of Hispanic, Black, and White felony arrestees. *Criminology*, *41*(3), 873–908. doi: 10.1111/j.1745-9125.2003.tb01007.x

Ferone, J., Lawson, V., Spencer, K., & Bowling, J. (2021). *Justice in decision-making: studying racial & ethnic disparities in the Brooklyn District Attorney's Office. Technical Report*. CUNY Institute for State & Local Governance. Retrieved from https://islg.cuny.edu/resources/justice-in-decision-making

Flanders, C., & Galoob, S. (2020). Progressive prosecution in a pandemic. *Journal of Criminal Law and Criminology*, *110*(4), 685–706.

Forst, B. (2010). *Prosecution and courts: Oxford bibliographies online research guide*. Oxford University Press.

Frohmann, L. (1997). Convictability and discordant locales: Reproducing race, class, and gender ideologies in prosecutorial decisionmaking. *Law and Society Review*, *31*(3), 531–556.

Hamann, K., & Geisler, S. S. (2020, October). Prosecutors and the pandemic: Necessity is the mother of invention. Criminal Justice Magazine. Retrieved from https://www.americanbar.org/groups/criminal_justice/publications/criminal-justice-magazine/2020/fall/prosecutors-pandemic-necessity-mother-invention/

Johnson, B. D. (2019). Trials and tribulations: The trial tax and the process of punishment. *Crime and Justice*, *48*(1), 313–363. doi: 10.1086/701713

Johnson, B. D., Hernandez, R., Rackstraw, E., & Houlihan, S. (2021). Final report on racial justice in prosecution in Baltimore. Report published by the Office of the State's Attorney for Baltimore City. Retrieved from https://content.govdelivery.com/attachments/MDBALTIMORESAO/2022/03/16/file_attachments/2104881/FINAL_REPORT_ON_RACIAL_DISPARITY_FEB_2022.pdf

Johnson, B. D., King, R. D., & Spohn, C. (2016). Sociolegal approaches to the study of guilty pleas and prosecution. *Annual Review of Law and Social Science*, *12*, 479–495. doi: 10.1146/annurev-lawsocsci-110615-084755

Johnson, B. D., & Larroulet, P. (2019). The "distance traveled": Investigating the downstream consequences of charge reductions for disparities in incarceration. *Justice Quarterly*, *36*(7), 1229–1257. doi: 10.1080/07418825.2018.1529250

Kingsnorth, R. F., & MacIntosh, R. C. (2007). Intimate partner violence: The role of suspect gender in prosecutorial decision-making. *Justice Quarterly*, *24*(3), 460–495. doi: 10.1080/07418820701485395

Kingsnorth, R. F., MacIntosh, R. C., & Wentworth, J. (1999). Sexual assault: The role of prior relationship and victim characteristics in case processing. *Justice Quarterly*, *16*(2), 275–302. doi: 10.1080/07418829900094141

Kroepsch, D. (2016). Prosecutorial best practices committees and conviction integrity units: How internal programs are fulfilling the prosecutor's duty to serve justice. *Georgetown Journal of Legal Ethics*, 29(4), 1095–1110.

Kurlychek, M. C., & Johnson, B. D. (2019). Cumulative disadvantage in the American criminal justice system. *Annual Review of Criminology*, *2*, 291–319. doi: 10.1146/annurev-criminol-011518-024815

Kutateladze, B. L., Andiloro, N. R., & Johnson, B. D. (2016). Opening pandora's box: How does defendant race influence plea bargaining? *Justice Quarterly*, *33*(3), 398–426. doi: 10.1080/07418825.2014.915340

Kutateladze, B. L., Andiloro, N. R., Johnson, B. D., & Spohn, C. (2014). Cumulative disadvantage: Examining racial and ethnic disparity in prosecution and sentencing. *Criminology*, *52*(3), 514–551. doi: 10.1111/1745-9125.12047

Kutateladze, B. L., Lawson, V. Z., & Andiloro, N. R. (2015). Does evidence really matter? An exploratory analysis of the role of evidence in plea bargaining in felony drug cases. *Law and Human Behavior*, *39*(5), 431. doi: 10.1037/lhb0000142

Kutateladze, B. L., Lynn, V., & Liang, E. (2012). Do race and ethnicity matter in prosecution? A review of empirical studies. Vera Institute of Justice. Retrieved from https://www.vera.org/downloads/publications/race-and-ethnicity-in-prosecution-first-edition.pdf

Kutateladze, B. L., Meldrum, R., Richardson, R., Stemen, D., Webster, E., Ardnt, M., Matthews, D., & Soor, S. (2018). *Advancing Prosecutorial effectiveness and fairness report series: Prosecutorial attitudes, perspectives, and priorities: Insights from the inside*. Prosecutorial Performance Indicators. Retrieved from https://ppibuild.wpengine.com/wp-content/uploads/2020/09/FIU-Loyola-_MacAthruth-Prosecution-Project-Report-One-PDF.pdf

Kutateladze, B. L., Richardson, R., Meldrum, R., Stemen, D., Olson, D., Webster, E., Ardnt, M., Matthews, D., & Soor, S. (2019a). *Advancing prosecutorial effectiveness and fairness report series: Race, ethnicity & prosecution in Cook County, Illinois*. Prosecutorial Performance Indicators. Retrieved from https://ppibuild.wpengine.com/wp-content/uploads/2020/09/FIU-Loyola-Report-2-Cook-County-C-spreads-with-cover-small.pdf

Kutateladze, B. L., Richardson, R., Meldrum, R., Stemen, D., Olson, D., Webster, E., Ardnt, M., Matthews, D., & Soor, S. (2019b). *Advancing prosecutorial effectiveness and fairness report series: Race, ethnicity & prosecution in Milwaukee County, Wisconsin*. Prosecutorial Performance Indicators. Retrieved from https://ppibuild.wpengine.com/wp-content/uploads/2020/09/FIU-Loyola-Report-2-Milwaukee-Final-with-cover.pdf

Kutateladze, B. L., Richardson, R., Meldrum, R., Stemen, D., Olson, D., Webster, E., Ardnt, M., Matthews, D., & Soor, S. (2019c). *Advancing prosecutorial effectiveness and fairness report series: Race, ethnicity & prosecution in Hillsborough County, Florida*. Prosecutorial Performance Indicators. Retrieved from https://ppibuild.wpengine.com/wp-content/uploads/2020/09/FIU-Loyola-Report-2-Tampa-FINAL-with-cover-as-spreads.pdf

Kutateladze, B. L., Richardson, R., Meldrum, R., Stemen, D., Olson, D., Webster, E., Ardnt, M., Matthews, D., & Soor, S. (2019d). *Advancing prosecutorial effectiveness and fairness report series: Race, ethnicity & prosecution in Clay, Duval & Nassau Counties, Florida*. Prosecutorial Performance Indicators. Retrieved from https://ppibuild.wpengine.com/wp-content/uploads/2020/09/FIU-Loyola-Report-2-Jacksonville-Final-with-Cover-spreads.pdf

Levin, B. (2020). Imagining the progressive prosecutor. *Minnesota Law Review*, *105*(3), 1415–1452.

Maynard, D. (1984). *Inside plea bargaining: The language of negotiation*. Spring Science.

Metcalfe, C., & Chiricos, T. (2018). Race, plea, and charge reduction: An assessment of racial disparities in the plea process. *Justice Quarterly*, *35*(2), 223–253. doi: 10.1080/07418825.2017.1304564

Nardulli, P. F., Eisenstein, J., & Flemming, R. B. (1988). *The tenor of justice: Criminal courts and the guilty plea process*. University of Illinois Press.

Office of the State's Attorney for Baltimore City. (2021). *State's attorney, mayor's and community partners announce success of covid criminal justice policies*. Office of the State's Attorney for Baltimore City. Retrieved from https://www.stattorney.org/images/Newsletters/Spring_Newsletter_2021.pdf

Owens, E., Kerrison, E. M., & Da Silveira, B. S. (2017). Examining racial disparities in criminal case outcomes among indigent defendants in San Francisco. Quattrone Center for the Fair Administration of Justice, University of Pennsylvania Law School. Retrieved from www.issuelab.org/resources/28366/28366.pdf

Petersilia, J. (1983). *Racial disparities in the criminal justice system* (Vol. 2947). Rand Corporation. Retrieved from www.ojp.gov/pdffiles1/Digitization/127137NCJRS.pdf

Pfaff, J. (2017). *Locked in: The true causes of mass incarceration-and how to achieve real reform*. Basic Books.

Philadelphia District Attorney's Office (DAO). (2019). Ending mass supervision: Evaluating reforms in the Philadelphia District Attorney's Office. Retrieved from https://data.philadao.com/Research.html#reports

Prosecutorial Performance Indicators (PPIs). (n.d.). *Prosecutorial performance indicators: A suite of modern indicators for prosecutors committed to measuring effectiveness, efficiency, & fairness*. Retrieved from https://prosecutorialperformanceindicators.org/

Rempel, M., Labriola, M., Hunt, P., Davis, R. C., Reich, W. A., & Cherney, S. (2018). NIJ's multisite evaluation of prosecutor-led diversion programs. Center for Court Innovation. Retrieved from www.courtinnovation.org/sites/default/files/media/document/2017/Pretrial_Diversion_Overview_ProvRel.pdf

Rosett, A. I., & Cressey, D. R. (1976). *Justice by consent: Plea bargains in the American Courthouse*. Lippincott.

Shermer, L. O. N., & Johnson, B. D. (2010). Criminal prosecutions: Examining prosecutorial discretion and charge reductions in US federal district courts. *Justice Quarterly*, 27(3), 394–430. doi: 10.1080/07418820902856972

Sklansky, D. A. (2016). The nature and function of prosecutorial power. *Journal of Criminal Law Criminology*, *106*(3), 473–520.

Sklansky, D. A. (2017). The progressive prosecutor's handbook. *UC Davis Law Review Online*, *50*, 25–42.

Sklansky, D. A. (2018). "The problems with prosecutors." *Annual Review of Criminology*, *1*(1), 451–469. doi: 10.1146/annurev-criminol-032317-092440

Spohn, C. (2018). Reflections on the exercise of prosecutorial discretion 50 years after publication of the challenge of crime in a free society. *Criminology & Public Policy*, *17*(2), 321–340. doi: 10.1111/1745-9133.12367

Spohn, C., Beichner, D., & Davis-Frenzel, E. (2001). Prosecutorial justifications for sexual assault case rejection: Guarding the "gateway to justice". *Social problems*, *48*(2), 206–235. doi: 10.1525/sp.2001.48.2.206

Spohn, C., & Spears, J. (1996). The effect of offender and victim characteristics on sexual assault case processing decisions. *Justice Quarterly*, *13*(4), 649–679. doi: 10.1080/07418829600093141

Spears, J., & Spohn, C. (1997). The effect of evidence factors and victim characteristics on prosecutors' charging decisions in sexual assault cases*. *Justice Quarterly*, *14*(3), 501–524. doi: 10.1080/07418829700093451

Stemen, D., & Escobar, G. (2018). Whither the prosecutor? Prosecutor and county effects on guilty plea outcomes in Wisconsin. *Justice Quarterly*, *35*(7), 1166–1194. doi: 10.1080/07418825.2018.1548637

Stevenson, M. T. (2018). Distortion of justice: How the inability to pay bail affects case outcomes. *The Journal of Law, Economics, and Organization*, *34*(4), 511–542. doi: 10.1093/jleo/ewy019

Stevenson, M. T., & Mayson, S. G. (2021). Pretrial detention and the value of liberty (No. 2021–14). Virginia Public Law and Legal Theory Research Paper. Retrieved from https://ssrn.com/abstract=3787018

Testa, A., & Johnson, B. D. (2020). Paying the trial tax: Race, guilty pleas, and disparity in prosecution. *Criminal Justice Policy Review*, *31*(4), 500–531. doi: 10.1177%2F0887403419838025

Ulmer, J. T. (2012). Recent developments and new directions in sentencing research. *Justice Quarterly*, *29*(1), 1–40. doi: 10.1080/07418825.2011.624115

Wooldredge, J., Frank, J., Goulette, N., & Travis III, L. (2015). Is the impact of cumulative disadvantage on sentencing greater for Black defendants? *Criminology & Public Policy*, *14*(2), 187–223. doi: 10.1111/1745-9133.12124

Wooldredge, J., & Thistlethwaite, A. (2004). Bilevel disparities in court dispositions for intimate assault. *Criminology*, *42*(2), 417–456. doi: 10.1111/j.1745-9125.2004.tb00525.x

Wu, J. (2016). Racial/ethnic discrimination and prosecution: A meta-analysis. *Criminal Justice and Behavior*, *43*(4), 437–458. doi: 10.1177/0093854815628026

25

DEFENSE DECISION-MAKING AND PRACTICES

Kelsey S. Henderson and Jacqueline G. Lee

Introduction

In 1932, nine Black juveniles were convicted of sexually assaulting two white women in Alabama; their jury trials were combined and concluded in less than 1 day (*Powell vs. Alabama*, 1932). Despite having court-appointed counsel, the United State Supreme Court (USSC) ruled that the attorneys did not consult with their clients and did little to represent them at trial. The Court opined that, "the necessity of counsel [is] so vital and imperative that the failure of the trial court to make an effective appointment of counsel [is] likewise a denial of due process within the meaning of the Fourteenth Amendment". Because of this "vital and imperative" role, the American Bar Association (ABA, 2019) establishes an extensive list of standards for the defense function, which dictate defense attorneys' responsibilities and guide their conduct throughout all legal proceedings. The standards dictate defense attorneys' responsibilities to the client (e.g., "zealous representation", timely communication) and to the court and criminal justice system generally (e.g., "improve the administration of justice").

A wealth of research, some highlighted in the following, has examined defense attorneys' position within the courtroom workgroup, the differences between court-appointed and privately retained counsel, and defendants' perceptions of their attorneys. But less research has examined *defense attorney decision-making*, and defense attorneys' decisions are not the subject of empirical study as frequently as other legal actors (namely judges and prosecutors). Perhaps researchers have underestimated the role that defense attorneys play in the process? Perhaps there is an assumption of little variability between defense attorneys? It is also important to recognize the difficulty in examining defense attorney decision-making and possible data constraints with this population (e.g., attorney-client confidentiality). In the following, we highlight research on defense attorney decision-making and related factors and close with a discussion of evidence-based programs, policies, and/or practices that are ripe for empirical examination.

Brief Review of the State of the Literature

Defense Attorney Decision-Making

Rational decision-making models account for legal factors that impact decisions, specifically the influence of case factors such as strength of evidence, probability of conviction, and

DOI: 10.4324/9781003219286-31

expected sentence if the defendant is convicted at trial relative to the plea offer (see "Shadow of Trial" framework; Mnookin & Kornhauser, 1979; Redlich et al., 2016). Recently, scholars have called for an expansion of decision-making models to account for extra-legal factors such as structural influences (e.g., information deficits) and psychological processes (e.g., biases, heuristics) that undoubtedly impact decisions, in addition to further legal factors (Bibas, 2004; Redlich et al., 2017). Rational decision-making models have traditionally been used to account for defendant decisions, but research suggests they are applicable to defense attorneys as well (Henderson, 2020; Redlich et al., 2016). We briefly highlight relevant research on the impact of legal and extra-legal factors on defense attorney decision-making.

Much of the research examining the influence of legal factors on defense attorney decision-making has been in the context of plea-bargaining decisions and has utilized experimental methods (e.g., asking defense attorneys to evaluate a hypothetical case). Building off the Shadow of Trial framework, research has found that defense attorneys are cognizant of variations in evidence quality (e.g., eyewitness evidence, Pezdek & O'Brien, 2014) and the weight of various types of evidence (e.g., confession, eyewitness, and DNA evidence; Redlich et al., 2016). Defense attorneys' evaluation of the strength of evidence influences their estimates of the defendants' likelihood of conviction (Henderson, 2020), which ultimately drives their decisions and case recommendations (McAllister & Bregman, 1986; Helm et al., 2018). These studies exemplify how defense attorney decision-making involves weighing case characteristics and the defendant's likely trial outcome.

Extra-legal factors frame defense attorney decision-making and may even color how they weigh legal factors. When considering defense attorney decisions and practices, it is important to acknowledge that defense attorneys operate in an environment where they are forced to make quick decisions (e.g., pretrial release arguments), and operate at an information deficit compared to prosecutors (Bibas, 2004). As such, defense attorneys may rely on biases and heuristics (i.e., mental shortcuts) in decision-making. One examination of plea decision-making found that defense attorneys encouraged accepting guilty pleas that were less favorable for African American clients than Caucasian clients under equal case conditions (Edkins, 2011). Similarly, research demonstrates that self-serving biases can cause defense attorneys to overestimate their chances of winning at trial ("overconfidence"; Goodman et al., 2010). In some cases, heuristics aid in decision-making, but biases can also contribute to inappropriate decisions (e.g., disparities in judicial sentencing, Rachlinski et al., 2008).

Training for the Position

Even though approximately 90–95% of all cases are resolved with a guilty plea (as opposed to a trial; Pastore & Maguire, 2005), law school education historically has not included relevant skills training such as interpersonal skills, negotiation tactics, or client counseling strategies (Cramton, 1982; MacCrate, 1992; Sullivan et al., 2007). The more traditional approach to law school has instead been that law schools teach legal doctrine (Dolin, 2007; Lande, 2013), and then new lawyers develop more practical skills on the job. While the movement towards increased skills and clinical training in law schools has been gaining steady support, many pressures on law schools make this challenging (Lande, 2013). A recent report found that although a change by the ABA in 2014 to require 6 credit hours of "experiential training" was expected to meaningfully increase the attainment of practical skills while in law school, there has not been a significant increase in clinics or field placements (Kuehn, 2021). New attorneys may receive such training when they enter the workforce, but the quality and consistency of training is unclear. Though some law students receive quality instruction or practice in how to negotiate a plea offer and how to counsel a client, many new lawyers likely have little hands-on experience with the skills necessary to be an effective negotiator and counselor. This lack of training can further a reliance on biases and heuristics (discussed previously) and exacerbates the difficult environment in which defense attorneys work.

The Courtroom Workgroup

It is important to consider the defense attorney not as a unilateral actor with one goal in mind but to remember that they are part of the courtroom workgroup (Eisenstein & Jacob, 1977), which also includes the prosecutor, judge, and other actors such as court clerks and bailiffs. Within the workgroup, defense attorneys tend to be the most variable and least stable member, due to their larger numbers (e.g., all court-appointed and private criminal defense attorneys in a jurisdiction) and high numbers of clients. This means that some defense attorneys will have more knowledge of a courtroom's practices, procedures, and norms than others. Eisenstein and Jacob (1977) refer to defense attorneys who are consistently in a particular courtroom as "courtroom regulars" and argue that these frequently appearing attorneys (including public defenders) may thus be able to negotiate better deals for their clients.

Defense attorneys' goals and motivations may also vary based on their role within a particular workgroup. The external goals of a criminal court tend to include "justice" and expeditious case resolution, while internal goals focus on maintaining group cohesion and limiting uncertainty (Eisenstein & Jacob, 1977). A defense attorney's decisions may be affected by a desire to move through their own caseload, obtain the least severe and most certain sentence for their client, and avoid conflict with other workgroup members. At times, these goals may be in conflict; a defense attorney may have to weigh the implications of fervent advocacy for one client with the effect it may have on their other cases and relationships with other actors (see also Alschuler, 1975). For example, trials take much more time, energy, and resources than pleas, and an attorney might be aware that requesting a trial could irritate or cause other court actors to feel overburdened (Lynch, 1997). Balancing these goals and smoothly operating within a workgroup may impact defense attorney decision-making (i.e., structural influence).

Research exploring differences in case outcomes as a function of courtroom workgroup "regulars" versus "outsiders" has produced mixed results. Some research also suggests no differences between privately retained attorneys and public defenders; for example, Hartley and colleagues (2010) found no significant difference in bail decisions, plea bargaining, and sentencing outcomes between defendants represented by a public defender versus privately retained attorneys. Other research has identified differences; for example, in a Florida sample, clients represented by public defenders were more likely to be detained pretrial and convicted at trial and were less likely to have their case dismissed than defendants with privately retained attorneys (Williams, 2013). Despite mixed findings on outcomes, defendants perceive public defenders as lower quality than privately retained attorneys (Casper, 1970) and commonly have negative attitudes towards their court-appointed attorneys (Flemming, 1986). Defendants with court-appointed attorneys report lower levels of trust (Boccaccini & Brodsky, 2002) and satisfaction in their attorney than those with privately retained attorneys (Raaijmakers et al., 2015). Despite this, more recent qualitative research has found that many defendants recognize that public defenders are overworked and underfunded and feel empathetic towards "the institutional challenges that public defenders face" (Moore et al., 2019, p. 18). We highlight some of these challenges in the following (e.g., caseloads).

Caseloads, Incentives, and Burnout for Defense Attorneys

An additional factor influencing defense attorney decision-making is their caseload; this can be particularly true for those in public defense, who are likely balancing the needs of a great number of clients (Eight Guidelines of Public Defense Related to Excessive Workloads, 2009; Farole & Langton, 2010). Research has generally found that public defenders are overworked, and many public defender offices are underfunded (Langton & Farole, 2010) and do not have enough attorneys to represent all of their clients ("System overload", 2011; Furst, 2019). Simply put, many lawyers in public defense do not have the time or resources necessary to provide zealous advocacy to every single client. In addition, some emerging work has shown that the same defense attorney tracked over time may obtain more preferable outcomes (e.g., dismissal or a non-incarcerative sentence) when they are being paid by a private client as compared to a case where they are contracted and receiving state-mandated fees as assigned counsel (Agan et al., 2021). Together, this evidence suggests that many of the challenges in criminal defense, especially public defense, are related to resources – specifically time and money.

Tied in closely to being overworked and underfunded are the stress, burnout, and vicarious trauma associated with being a defense attorney. One study of public defenders in New York state identified a host of occupational stressors, including overly high caseloads, uncertainty over timing of trials, conflict with prosecutors, and dealing with unhappy clients and their families (Lynch, 1997). Importantly, some of these stressors may be exacerbated as a result of the COVID-19 pandemic and resulting case backlogs, which are contributing to uncertain court dates and difficulty counseling clients (Daftary-Kapur et al., 2021). Moreover, working in any "helping profession" can be associated with secondary trauma, which has been given various other labels such as compassion fatigue or vicarious trauma (Levin & Greisberg, 2003). Burnout is often an effect of continued secondary trauma and stress and is characterized by poor sleep, emotional changes, cynicism, substance abuse, poor job performance, and worsening of interpersonal relationships (Maslach & Leiter, 2017). There is surprisingly little research on this topic for defense counsel, but one survey examining burnout across various professions found that criminal defense attorneys experienced more secondary traumatic stress than mental health providers or social service workers (Levin & Greisberg, 2003). The authors of the study hypothesize that this may be due to defense attorneys carrying higher caseloads and a lack of training and guidance surrounding secondary trauma.

Key takeaways from the research presented:

- Defense attorney decision-making is influenced by a combination of legal factors (e.g., strength of evidence) and extra-legal factors (e.g., biases and structural influences).
- There are mixed findings regarding case outcomes between privately retained and court-appointed attorneys (i.e., public defenders and assigned counsel). Research has consistently found that clients of public defenders are less trusting of their attorney than clients of privately retained attorneys. Emerging research suggests some defendants are cognizant of the challenges public defenders face.
- Law schools' training focuses more on legal doctrine and less on skills surrounding negotiated dispositions, which account for the majority of case resolutions.
- Defense attorney decision-making can be impacted by their position within (or outside) of the courtroom workgroup.

- Defense attorney decision-making and practice is undoubtedly influenced by high caseloads, which can contribute to stress, burnout, and vicarious trauma.

Description of Responsive Evidence-Based Programs, Policies, and/or Practices

Unlike other areas in criminal justice (e.g., policing), there have been few randomized controlled trials on defense attorney decision-making and practices (to the authors' knowledge). Much of the research stems from experimental methodologies (highlighted previously), observations (e.g., Campbell & Henderson, forthcoming; Clair, 2020), and interviews with defense attorneys and/or clients (e.g., Clair, 2020; Lee & Ropp, 2020; Moore et al., 2019). In its totality, this research suggests practices that are "promising", but because of the previously mentioned concerns (i.e., access to data and/or practitioners), may not have been examined thoroughly. We include recommendations, and encourage further examination of these programs, policies, and practices.

Training Policy

Though it may seem an easy fix to simply increase skills training and courses in law school, extant research indicates that slow progress is being made in this effort (Lande, 2013; Kuehn, 2021). Law schools must be incentivized to provide these training courses and expand their clinical offerings. This might require increased oversight and involvement from the ABA to ensure that law students and their soon-to-be clients are set up for success.

Funding for Public Defense

Despite the fact that the vast majority of defendants are represented by court-appointed counsel (Harlow, 2000), "the structure, funding, quality, and breadth of the right to counsel varies dramatically" across the United States (Worden et al., 2011, p. 1424). From 2008–2012, state spending on public defense decreased an annual average of 0.2% and in 2012, states spent roughly $2.3 billion nationally on public defense (Herberman & Kyckelhahn, 2014), which represents a fraction of the nearly $6 billion spent on prosecutor's offices (Perry & Banks, 2011). The most obvious and critical improvement to public defense is allocating more funding (Furst, 2019). Such funding should support critical needs associated with delivering effective representation (e.g., hiring more attorneys; see the following for a discussion); additionally, a percentage could support research partnerships between agencies and researchers (e.g., see Campbell et al., 2015 for an example of such partnership to examine attorney–client communication).

Incentives

To improve outcomes for assigned counsel, states and counties should work to align assigned/contract counsel fees with local rates. This would create an increased moral imperative for attorneys to provide strong advocacy in all of their cases, not simply cases where they are being retained and paid by private clients (Agan et al., 2021).

Programs to Increase Trust

Building attorney–client trust is particularly important in public defense where defendants do not have the autonomy to choose their attorney, and may misunderstand the role of a court-appointed attorney as a "government agent", as opposed to their adversarial advocate. For example, in response to the question of whether their attorney was *on their side*, 100% of respondents with a privately retained attorney said yes, compared to 20.4% of those represented by a public defender (Casper, 1972). Recent qualitative research suggests that "choice of counsel" and "agency" are important to defendants (Moore et al., 2019), as such, one suggestion to counteract this question of allegiance is to allow defendants to choose their court-appointed attorney. Pilot projects that allow "client choice" have begun across the United States (see Iowa State Public Defender, n.d.; Nugent-Borakove & Cruz, 2017), with early findings suggesting positive outcomes (e.g., timeliness of first meeting).

Attorney Burnout Policy

Some occupational stressors may just be "part of the territory" for defense attorneys, and most entering the legal field are likely aware of the long work hours and challenges. There are, however, some avenues to decrease occupational stress and burnout for defense attorneys (particularly in public defense). An increase in funding would allow for higher salaries, recruitment of higher-quality attorneys, and hiring additional attorneys to ease caseloads. Lynch (1997) has also suggested that in addition to caseload reductions, increased judicial acceptance of trials would help lower stress for public defenders, as they would be able to provide zealous advocacy without fear of reprisals from other courtroom actors.

Conclusion

This chapter, while not exhaustive, provides an overview of important topics and issues to consider in understanding defense attorney decision-making and practices. The previously mentioned sections provide an overview of the influence of legal and extra-legal factors on defense attorney decisions, training and education, differences between court-appointed counsel and privately retained attorneys, and issues such as burnout and stress that influence defense attorney decision-making and practices. We then gave a brief overview of programs, policies, and/or practices that touch on some of the previously mentioned topics while hopefully providing researchers with ideas for future empirical research. We encourage readers to consider other, more detailed readings on some of the topics raised in this chapter (see Alschuler, 1975; Bibas, 2004).

References

Agan, A., Freedman, M., Owens, E. (2021). Is your lawyer a Lemon? Incentives and selection in the public provision of criminal defense. *The Review of Economics and Statistics*, *103*(2), 294–309. doi: 10.1162/rest_a_00891

Alschuler, A. W. (1975). The defense attorney's role in plea bargaining. *Yale Law Journal*, *84*, 1179–1315.

American Bar Association. (2019). Criminal justice section standards: Defense function. Retrieved from www.americanbar.org/groups/criminal_justice/standards/DefenseFunctionFourthEdition/

Bibas, S. (2004). Plea bargaining outside the shadow of a trial. *Harvard Law Review*, *117*, 2463–2547.

Boccaccini, M. T., & Brodsky, S. L. (2002). Attorney-client trust among convicted criminal defendants: Preliminary examination of the attorney-client trust scale. *Behavioral Sciences and the Law*, *20*, 69–87. Doi: 10.1002/bsl.469

Campbell, C. M., & Henderson, K. S. (forthcoming). Bridging the gap between clients and public defenders: Introducing a structured shadow method to examine attorney communication. *Justice Systems Journal.*

Campbell, C. M., Moore, J., Maier, W., & Gaffney, M. (2015). Unnoticed, untapped, and underappreciated: Clients' perceptions of their public defenders. *Behavioral Sciences & the Law, 33*(6), 751–770. doi: 10.1002/bsl.2182

Casper, J. D. (1970). Did you have a lawyer when you went to court – No, I had a public defender. *Yale Review of Law and Social Action, 1*(4).

Casper, J. D. (1972). *American Criminal Justice: The Defendant's Perspective.* Prentice-Hall.

Clair, M. (2020). *Privilege and punishment: How race and class matter in criminal court.* Princeton University Press.

Cramton, R. C. (1982). The current state of the law curriculum. Cornell Law Faculty Publications, pp. 321–335.

Daftary-Kapur, T., Henderson, K. S., & Zottoli, T. M. (2021). COVID-19 Exacerbates existing system factors that disadvantage defendants: Findings from a national survey of defense attorneys. *Law and Human Behavior, 45*(2), 81–96. doi: 10.1037/lhb0000442

Dolin, J. M. (2007). Opportunity lost: How law school disappoints law students, the public, and the legal profession. *California Western Law Review, 44*(6), 219–255.

Edkins, V. A. (2011). Defense attorney plea recommendations and client race: Does zealous representation apply equally to all? *Law and Human Behavior, 35*(5), 413–425. doi: 10.1007/s10979-010-9254-0

Eight Guidelines of Public Defense Related to Excessive Workloads. (2009). American Bar Association. Retrieved from www.americanbar.org/content/dam/aba/administrative/legal_aid_indigent_defendants/ls_sclaid_def_eight_guidelines_of_public_defense.pdf

Eisenstein, J., & Jacob, H. (1977). *Felony Justice.* Little, Brown.

Farole, D. J., & Langton, L. (2010). A national assessment of public defender office caseloads. *Judicature, 94*(2), 87–90. Retrieved from http://stats.lib.pdx.edu/proxy.php?url=http://search.proquest.com/scholarly-journals/national-assessment-public-defender-office/docview/808403163/se-2?accountid=13265

Flemming, R. B. (1986). Client games: Defense attorney perspectives on their relations with criminal clients. *American Bar Foundation Research Journal,* 11(2), 253–277. doi: 10.1111/j.1747-4469.1986.tb00241.x

Furst, B. (2019). *A fair fight: Achieving indigent defense resource parity.* Brennan Center for Justice. Retrieved from www.brennancenter.org/sites/default/files/2019-09/Report_A%20Fair%20Fight.pdf

Goodman-Delahunty, J., Granhag, P. A., Hartwig, M., & Loftus, E. F. (2010). Insightful or wishful: Lawyers' ability to predict case outcomes. *Psychology, Public Policy, and Law, 16*(2), 133–157. doi: 10.1037/a0019060

Harlow, C. W. (2000). Defense counsel in criminal cases. U.S. Department of Justice. Retrieved from www.bjs.gov/content/pub/pdf/dccc.pdf

Hartley, R. D., Miller, H. V., Spohn, C. (2010). Do you get what you pay for? Type of counsel and its effect on criminal court outcomes. *Journal of Criminal Justice, 38,* 1063–1070.

Helm, R. K., Reyna, V. F., Franz, A. A. Novick, R. Z., Dincin, S., & Cort, A. E. (2018). Limitations on the ability to negotiate justice: Attorney perspectives on guilt, innocence, and legal advice in the current plea system. *Psychology, Crime & Law, 24*(9), 915–934. doi: 10.1080/1068316X.2018.1457672

Henderson, K. S. (2020). Examining the Effect of Case and Trial Factors on Defense Attorneys' Plea Decision-making. *Psychology, Crime & Law, 27*(4), 357–382. doi: 10.1080/1068316X.2020.1805744

Herberman, E. J., & Kyckelhahn, T. (2014). State government indigent defense expenditures, FY 2008–2012 – Updated. U.S. Department of Justice. Retrieved from https://bjs.ojp.gov/library/publications/state-government-indigent-defense-expenditures-fy-2008–2012-updated

Iowa State Public Defender (n.d.). Client choice pilot project. Office of the State Public Defender. Retrieved from https://spd.iowa.gov/contract-attorneys/client-choice-pilot-project

Kuehn, R. (2021, April 28). Implementation of the ABA's new experiential training Requirement more whimper than bang. Best Practices for Legal Education. Retrieved from https://bestpracticeslegaled.com/2021/04/28/implementation-of-the-abas-new-experiential-training-requirement-more-whimper-than-bang/

Lande, J. (2013). Reforming Legal Education to Prepare law students optimally for real-world practice. *Journal of Dispute Resolution, 2013*(1), 1–17.

Langton, L., & Farole, D. (2010). State public defender programs, 2007. U.S. Department of Justice. Retrieved from https://bjs.ojp.gov/content/pub/pdf/spdp07.pdf

Lee, J., & Ropp, J. (2020). "Sometimes I'm just wearing the prosecutor down": An exploratory analysis of criminal defense attorneys in plea negotiations and client counseling. *Qualitative Criminology*, 9. doi: 10.21428/88de04a1.2168ad3e

Levin, A. P., & Greisburg, S. (2003). Vicarious trauma in Attorneys. *Pace Law Review*, *24*(1), 245–252. Retrieved from https://digitalcommons.pace.edu/cgi/viewcontent.cgi?article=1189&context=plr

Lynch, D. R. (1997). The Nature of Occupational Stress Among Public Defenders. *Justice System Journal*, *19*(1), 17–35.

Maslach, C., & Leiter, M. P. (2017). Understanding burnout: New models. In C. L. Cooper & J. C. Quick (Eds.), *The handbook of stress and health: A guide to research and practice* (pp. 36–56). Wiley Blackwell. doi: 10.1002/9781118993811.ch3

McAllister, H. A., & Bregman, N. J. (1986). Plea bargaining by prosecutors and defense attorneys: A decision theory approach. *Journal of Applied Psychology*, *71*, 686–690. doi: 10.1037/0021-9010.71.4.686

McCrate, R. (1992). *Task force on law schools and the profession: Narrowing the gap*. American Bar Association.

Mnookin, R. H., & Kornhauser, L. (1979). Bargaining in the shadow of trial: The case of divorce. *The Yale Law Journal*, 88(5), 950–997.

Moore, J., Plano Clark, V. L., Foote, L. A., & Dariotis, J. K. (2019). Attorney-client communication in public defense: A qualitative examination. *Criminal Justice Policy Review*, 1–31. doi: 10.1177/0887403419861672

Nugent-Borakove, M. E., & Cruz, F. (2017). The power of choice: Implications of a system where indigent defendants choose their own counsel. Texas Indigent Defense Commission. Retrieved from www.tidc.texas.gov/media/8d87c73b45a851e/client-choice.pdf

Pastore, A. L., & Maguire, K. (Eds.). (2005). Sourcebook of criminal justice statistics. Retrieved from www.albany.edu/sourcebook/pdf/t5462002.pdf

Perry, S. W., & Banks, D. (2011). Prosecutors in state courts, 2007 – Statistical tables. U.S. Department of Justice. Retrieved from www.bjs.gov/content/pub/pdf/psc07st.pdf

Pezdek, K., & O'Brien, M. (2014). Plea bargaining and appraisals of eyewitness evidence by prosecutors and defense attorneys. Psychology, Crime, and Law, 20(3), 222–241. doi: 10.1080/1068316X.2013.770855

Powell v. Alabama. (1932). 287 US 45.

Raaijmakers, E., de Keijser, J. W., Nieuwbeerta, P., & Dirkzwager, A. J. E. (2015). Criminal defendants' satisfaction with lawyers: Perceptions of procedural fairness and effort of the lawyer. *Psychology, Crime & Law*, *21*(2), 186–201. doi: 10.1080/1068316X.2014.951646

Rachlinski, J. J., Johnson, S. L., Wistrich, A. J., & Guthrie, C. (2008). Does unconscious racial bias affect trial judges? *Notre Dame Law Review*, *84*, 1195–1246.

Redlich, A. D., Bibas, S., Edkins, V. A., & Madon, S. (2017). The psychology of defendant plea decision making. *American Psychologist*, *72*(4), 339–352. doi: 10.1037/a0040436

Redlich, A. D., Bushway, S. D., & Norris, R. J. (2016). Plea decision-making by attorneys and judges. *Journal of Experimental Criminology*, *12*, 537–561. doi: 10.1007/s11292-016-9264-0

Sullivan, W. M., Colby, A., Wegner, J. W., & Shulman, L. S. (2007). Educating lawyers: Preparation for the profession of Law. The Carnegie Foundation for the Advancement of Teaching, pp. 1–16.

System Overload: The Costs of Under-resourcing Public Defense (2011). Justice Policy Institute. Retrieved from https://justicepolicy.org/wp-content/uploads/justicepolicy/documents/system_overload_factsheet_final.pdf

Williams, M. R. (2013). The effectiveness of public defenders in four Florida counties. *Journal of Criminal Justice*, *41*(4), 205–212. doi: 10.1016/j.jcrimjus.2013.05.004

Worden, A. P., Davies, A. L. B., & Brown, E. K. (2011). A patchwork of policies: Justice, due process, and public defense across American states. *Albany Law Review*, *74*(3), 1423–1463.

26
COMPETENCE TO STAND TRIAL
Evaluation and Restoration Services

Daniel C. Murrie, Neil Gowensmith, and Marcus T. Boccaccini

Competency to Stand Trial

Every criminal defendant has the right to a fair trial, but a trial is only fair if the defendant can understand legal proceedings and pursue a defense strategy. Defendants must understand the charges against them, understand the process to determine guilt, and be able to help their attorneys. The United States Supreme Court established the formal standard for competence to stand trial in *Dusky v. United States* (1960) when the Court held:

> It is not enough for the district judge to find "the defendant [is] oriented to time and place and [has] some recollection of events," but that the "test must be whether he has sufficient present ability to consult with his lawyer with a reasonable degree of rational understanding – and whether he has a rational as well as factual understanding of the proceedings against him."
>
> *(p. 402)*

All U.S. states have modeled their competence standard on this *Dusky* language. Essentially, it is unconstitutional for the government to conduct criminal proceedings against a defendant who is *not* competent to stand trial. Therefore, courts may order competence evaluations for defendants who may not have the capacities to understand and participate in proceedings. Although any party (defense, prosecution, judge) can raise the question of competence, typically defense counsel prompts the court to order an evaluation. Once ordered by the court, a forensic evaluator – usually a psychiatrist or a clinical psychologist – performs the evaluation and submits a written report of findings.

Competency Evaluations

Evaluators typically review defendant records and interview defendants to gauge the degree to which defendants understand the legal process and can approach their own proceedings with rational understanding and rational decision-making. Competency evaluations consider any symptoms of psychiatric illness, intellectual deficits, or other mental health conditions that may undermine the capacities necessary for competence. Most defendants opined incompetent

DOI: 10.4324/9781003219286-32

manifest either psychosis or cognitive deficits (Murrie & Zelle, 2015; Kivisto et al., 2020; Pirelli et al., 2011). For example, defendants with severe psychotic illness may be so grossly disorganized or distracted by hallucinations that they cannot understand or converse with counsel, or they may be so paranoid that they do not trust counsel enough to discuss their case. After an evaluator completes their evaluation, the court will read the report – or perhaps hear the evaluator's testimony in a formal hearing – and rule on the matter of competency.

The evidence base underlying competence evaluations is strong, at least with respect to reliability. The fields of forensic psychology (Melton et al., 2018; Zapf & Roesch, 2009) and forensic psychiatry (e.g., Mossman et al., 2007) have disseminated procedures for competency evaluations that are now commonly accepted. Structured instruments to aid in competency assessments are well researched and widely available (Grisso, 2006), though surveys of evaluators reveal that few use the instruments in routine practice (Neal & Grisso, 2014).

Research reveals that different evaluators examining the same defendant usually reach the same conclusions about competence. A comprehensive meta-analysis found "moderate" agreement rates among evaluators at around 70–85% (Guarnera & Murrie, 2017). At the same time, some variability exists among evaluators in their patterns of finding defendants incompetent (Murrie et al., 2020; Murrie & Boccaccini, 2023). So the field has some room for improvement in terms of improving training and practice to foster greater consistency and agreement among competency evaluators (Guarnera et al., 2017).

- *Main Point:* The guidelines and evidence base underlying competency evaluations – particularly their reliability and validity – are well established and fairly strong.

Competence Restoration

If an evaluator opines a defendant is incompetent to stand trial (IST), the court may hold a formal hearing to adjudicate competence. If a defendant is adjudicated as IST, the court must determine the next step, which is typically either dismissing the charges or ordering the defendant to competency restoration services with expected future hearings on competency. The latter is far more common. The process of "restoring competence" – providing psychiatric treatment to defendants until they can understand and meaningfully participate in proceedings – is a common form of public mental health treatment. Yet the evidence base underlying this common treatment is surprisingly slim (Heilbrun et al., 2019).

Common Restoration Services

Considering that competence restoration services are commonplace and legally mandated, it is remarkable how little empirical evidence base underlies them. Surveys reveal that most restoration still takes place within state psychiatric hospitals and usually relies on two processes: psychotropic medication for the underlying symptoms of mental illness and didactic education about the legal process (Miller, 2003; Noffsinger, 2001; Pinals, 2005; Policy Research Associates, Inc., 2020).

Restoration Treatments

Psychiatric medications (particularly antipsychotics) are often the most crucial component of restoration services, and there is a strong scientific evidence base underlying the effectiveness of psychiatric medications in treating symptoms of severe mental illness generally. Once some defendants are prescribed appropriate medications and take them regularly, their symptoms decrease enough they can meaningfully engage in legal proceedings. Some defendants who refuse medication may be required to take medication involuntarily to restore competence, according to the U.S. Supreme Court, but only under exceptional circumstances (Cochrane et al., 2013; *Sell v. United States*, 2003). In addition, psychiatric hospitals provide some didactic and/or psychoeducational services to teach about court proceedings. However, no uniform standards guide this type of educational intervention, and no conclusive research finds one particular method better than others (Heilbrun et al., 2021). Education has often been most effective with cognitively or developmentally impaired IST defendants, presumably because these are the defendants most likely to have deficits in basic factual understanding (Danzer et al., 2019; Wall & Christopher, 2012). But education alone is rarely effective for those with severe psychiatric illness that requires medication.

Most defendants who are initially found incompetent are restored to competency within 6 months, and the vast majority within 12–18 months (e.g., Morris & DeYoung, 2012; Morris & Parker, 2008; Nicholson & McNulty, 1992). Overall, at least 75–90% of defendants with mental illness are eventually "restored" and face their criminal charges (Pinals, 2005; Samuel & Michals, 2011; Zapf & Roesch, 2011). Of course, "restoration" means only that their symptoms improve enough to meaningfully participate in trial; it does not often entail a complete remission of symptoms or recovery from the underlying illness. Upon meta-analysis of more than 13,000 defendants in 56 studies from 1975–2013, Pirelli and Zapf (2020) reported a mean restoration rate of 81% and a mean length of stay to restoration of around 147 days. A study from one Virginia hospital showed an average length of stay of 73 days (Wolber et al., 2011), and more recent data from that broader state system revealed an average length of restoration services of 92 days (Virginia Department of Behavioral Health and Developmental Services internal report, December 2021).

Although research is limited, a few factors appear to be associated with unsuccessful restoration. Defendants that are the *least likely* to be restored to competence are often older, have more prior hospitalizations or incompetence findings, carry diagnoses of intellectual disability or comorbid intellectual disability and serious psychiatric illness, show poor treatment response overall, and face less serious charges (e.g., Colwell & Gianessi, 2011; Morris & Parker, 2008; Mossman, 2007; Zapf & Roesch, 2011).

- *Main Point:* The vast majority of defendants who are originally adjudicated incompetent will be "restored to competence," usually within 6 months.

The Recent Competency Crisis

Restoration services now face new challenges that may call for new approaches. Most state forensic administrators report increased competence restoration orders (Warburton et al., 2020), with many reporting increases of more than 100% within just a few years (see Gowensmith, 2019 for review). In short, more defendants are being ordered to competency restoration than ever (Gowensmith & Murrie, 2022; Pinals & Callahan, 2020). However, over the past seven decades, while orders for competence restoration have risen dramatically, the number of state psychiatric hospital beds has decreased roughly 90% in the broad process known as de-institutionalization (Parks & Radke, 2014; Torrey et al., 2010). Though there is no single reason for the dramatic increase in court orders for competence evaluation, most authorities speculate it is due to the increase in untreated mental illness, particularly among the increasing proportion of people without housing.

Consequently, many defendants are now placed on "waitlists" for transfer from jail to inpatient restoration services. For example, the waitlist in California more than tripled from 426 people in 2014 to 1,428 in 2020 (Clendenin et al., 2021). Defendants on these waitlists can wait from several weeks to more than 1 year detained in jail, depending on context, before they receive mental health services. Indeed, some waitlists have grown so lengthy, and wait times so long, that defendants might spend more time in jail awaiting competency services than they would have otherwise spent incarcerated if had they been found guilty of their charges.

As a result, several states face class action lawsuits and consent decrees to resolve these waitlists (Gowensmith, 2019; Heilbrun et al., 2019). Recently, more than a dozen states have faced litigation initiated by advocacy groups concerned about the long waits that incompetent defendants face in jail (Locklair, 2016; Shannon, 2017). Media coverage has described serious harm and suicide among those awaiting competency services in jail (e.g., Harki, 2018; McGuinness, 2017; Shafer, 2015; Sherry, 2021; Swaine, 2015). Most jails are unable to provide the mental health services necessary for the IST population, making quick transfer to psychiatric facilities crucial.

Emerging Evidence for New Approaches to Competency Restoration

Amid this crisis, states are implementing new approaches to restoration services. These include outpatient (or community-based) restoration programs, jail-based restoration programs, and triage systems to prioritize the most acutely ill defendants for inpatient restoration.

Community-Based Competence Restoration

Outpatient restoration – restoration service outside the state psychiatric hospital – is an increasingly common alternative to inpatient restoration. Even before the recent crisis, inpatient restoration was not the best approach for all defendants. First, many defendants, particularly those who are incompetent primarily due to intellectual deficits, do not benefit from inpatient hospitalization for medication or stabilization. Second, inpatient hospitals are inevitably the most expensive sites for restoration. Third, hospitals may be located quite far from a defendant's home community. So, although crucial for certain defendants, hospitalization may be unnecessary, or even inappropriate, for others. But state hospitals have been the default site for restoration, until overwhelming demand prompted some states to consider other options.

A recent survey revealed 16 U.S. states operating formal outpatient competency restoration programs (OCRPs) in at least one of their jurisdictions (Gowensmith et al., 2016). Most OCRPs operate in urban areas and focus on defendants facing low-level charges. However, there was substantial variability among programs; some offered only restoration education, while others offered broader psychosocial services (e.g., case management, housing, treatment services). Colorado operates a robust statewide OCRP and has attempted to provide additional professional positions to serve as liaisons and navigators for defendants in the OCRP to troubleshoot barriers in accessing services, attend to crises, and ensure compliance with court-mandated requirements (Colorado Department of Human Services, 2020). Virginia also provides statewide outpatient restoration. Proponents of OCRPs affirm the lower costs of community-based services, quicker access to outpatient services, and greater freedoms for participants; critics raise concerns about potential risks to community safety (Gowensmith et al., 2016).

OCRPs generally demonstrate positive outcomes (Gowensmith et al., 2016). Although restoration rates are often lower than those in state hospital inpatient programs, and lengths of stay are often slightly longer, these findings seem reasonable in light of the different populations they serve. Restoration rates from the 2016 OCRP national survey revealed an average of 70% (Gowensmith et al., 2016). Average lengths of treatment are longer than in inpatient restoration programs, averaging 149 days (Gowensmith et al., 2016). However, revocations, terminations, and arrests of OCRP participants are fairly rare.

Increased supervision and monitoring of OCRP participants likely decrease the rates of negative outcomes (e.g., re-arrest). OCRPs are also less expensive than inpatient settings, saving nearly $400 per defendant per day in many programs (Gowensmith et al., 2016). Early studies reveal that good continuity of care from inpatient to outpatient settings, as well as consistent session attendance, improve restoration outcomes (Musgrove, 2018). Lower restoration rates were associated with previous revocations of release and co-occurring mental illness and developmental disability (Mikolajewski et al., 2017).

- *Main Point:* Emerging evidence reveals that defendants can be restored to competence in the community, within reasonable time frames and without undue risk to public safety.

Jail-Based Competence Restoration

Restoration in jail is another alternative to inpatient hospital-based restoration (Danzer et al., 2019; Heilbrun et al., 2019). The exact number of jail-based restoration programs is unknown, though at least ten states offer at least one jail-based restoration program. Jail-based restoration, as compared to OCRP, is more often operated by for-profit corporations that operate other jail-based mental health services. Some are specific to one county jail (e.g., Georgia), while others span multiple jails (e.g., Colorado) or are even statewide (e.g., Virginia). Programs vary in scope; some operate much like inpatient restoration units (e.g., dedicated mental health staffing, intensive and frequent restoration services, group and individual treatment), but others simply provide restoration services (e.g., medication and/or psychoeducation) to defendants in standard jail housing. Jail-based restoration offers quick access to some mental health services, relatively low costs, and the ability to keep defendants closer to their communities. It raises fewer concerns about community safety compared to outpatient programs. But critics argue that jail-based restoration lacks the resources to offer meaningful mental health care; jails are no substitute for psychiatric hospitals (Kapoor, 2011).

The evidence addressing jail-based restoration programs is sparse. Studies show a range of restoration rates from 44% in Louisiana programs to 87% in a specific Arizona program (Morenz & Busch, 2011; Wik, 2018). Lengths of stay averaged 57 days in one California county (Carabello, 2013; Rice & Jennings, 2014); Virginia's statewide jail-based restoration program averaged 67 days (Virginia Department of Behavioral Health and Developmental Services, internal report, December 2021). Other programs from local jurisdictions in Colorado and Georgia report average lengths of stay between 2 and 4 months, with restoration rates ranging from 34% to 71% (Colorado Department of Human Services, 2015; Georgia Department of Behavioral Health & Developmental Disabilities, 2014).

- *Main Point:* Emerging evidence suggests that many defendants who cannot be treated in the community can be restored to competence in jails when provided with robust psychiatric treatment.

Triaging Defendants Based on Clinical Needs

The competency system has always been equitable, in the sense that defendants receive restoration services on a chronological "first come, first served" basis (i.e., in the order they were adjudicated incompetent). But in the era of a competency crisis, certain defendants with severe symptoms may be waiting many months in jail before admission to a psychiatric hospital, sometimes waitlisted behind defendants with less severe symptoms. This contrasts with other medical services that address acute emergencies. For example, hospital emergency departments always rely on a triage model to prioritize patients with the most urgent needs. A triage system that identifies and prioritizes inpatient restoration for those most acutely ill may improve the competency system. Not all IST defendants are in acute crisis; some may be stabilized through medications and jail mental health interventions. Those who are acutely unstable, even to the extent that they are suicidal or at great risk of harm due to psychotic symptoms, should be prioritized in a triage system.

For example, Colorado adopted a triage-style system to prioritize inpatient restoration for defendants with the most acute mental health needs (*Center for Legal Advocacy v. Barnes*, 2019; Gowensmith & Murrie, 2019, 2022). When evaluators opine a defendant is not competent, they must consider whether the defendant is suitable for outpatient restoration (the default) or whether the defendant requires inpatient restoration. If inpatient restoration is necessary, the evaluator opines whether the defendant is Tier 1 (i.e., in more urgent need of inpatient services) or Tier 2 (i.e., requiring inpatient services, but less urgently). In keeping with a formal Consent Decree, Tier 1 defendants must be admitted within 7 days, and Tier 2 defendants must be admitted within 28 days (*Center for Legal Advocacy v. Barnes*, 2019).

Two caveats are crucial in a triage system. First, triage is dynamic. Defendants' symptoms can worsen after several weeks in jail or improve as they respond to jail-based mental health interventions. Triage systems must regularly monitor all defendants waiting in jails for inpatient restoration so that decisions about changing psychiatric needs can be addressed quickly. Second, defendants who are *not* prioritized for admission must still be admitted within a reasonable period. More stable defendants cannot perpetually wait at the bottom of the list; at some point, time spent waiting for admission must be weighed against clinical need for inpatient care.

- *Main Point:* For those waiting for inpatient restoration, a triage system with careful monitoring can help ensure those who need treatment most urgently receive it first.

Avoiding the Default to Inpatient Restoration

As states have initiated competency restoration programs in settings other than inpatient state hospitals (e.g., jail-based restoration, outpatient or community restoration), evaluators are more frequently required to offer opinions about *where* competency restoration should occur. For example, Colorado and Virginia have identified outpatient restoration as the default practice, and evaluators must recommend inpatient restoration *only if clinically necessary*. Miami Dade County utilizes a robust diversion and deflection system to "re-route" defendants away from the competency system and into settings for clinical care and psychosocial services; outcomes are uniformly strong, with both jail days and recidivism decreasing and cost savings and treatment effects increasing (Iglehart, 2016; Leifman & Coffey, 2020).

Treating Misdemeanor Charges Differently

Recent research reveals that defendants facing only misdemeanor charges are disproportionately likely to be found incompetent and require restoration services (Katz, 2016; Murrie et al., 2022; Wik et al., 2020). Incompetent misdemeanants, as a group, tend to have more severe mental illness than incompetent felony defendants, often experiencing higher rates of psychosis (Murrie et al., 2022). Psychosis appears particularly associated with low-level, non-violent crimes common among chronically ill persons, who are often homeless (Pope et al., 2021; Treatment Advocacy Center, 2011). Given long waitlists for restoration and short sentencing options, courts often drop charges or allow a plea of time-served; in such cases, the individual returns to the community, often without any guarantee of maintaining treatment. Indeed, these defendants appear disproportionately likely to be re-arrested, often on similar minor charges, perpetuating the dilemma (Tansey et al., 2021).

How might systems respond to this dilemma? First, some states (Florida, New York) do not allow any competency restoration for misdemeanants, but they may be prioritized for community mental health care while their charges are dismissed (Igelhart, 2016). Second, other states (Hawaii, Ohio) shortened their time limits for competency restoration for defendants charged with misdemeanors, allowing just 60 days for restoration. Third, some states have restricted *inpatient* competency restoration only to persons who are either facing felony charges or who meet civil commitment criteria, so IST misdemeanants who do not meet civil commitment criteria can only be restored in outpatient settings.

Finally, diverting misdemeanor (or other low-level) incompetent defendants into treatment – and out of the competency system – appears to have the greatest potential impact on restoration wait lists and the broader competency crisis (Obikoya, 2021). A few jurisdictions are now beginning to utilize diversion early in the criminal justice process for misdemeanants with mental illness (Pinals & Callahan, 2020). There is good reason for persons with serious mental illness and non-serious charges to be diverted into community mental health services in lieu of raising and adjudicating competency, thereby addressing the primary mental health needs. Regardless of how the misdemeanor competency question is resolved – through dismissal or diversion – it does appear policies *must* begin managing these low-level cases outside of the traditional competency system.

- *Main Point:* Defendants with major mental illness, arrested for minor charges, should be diverted from the competency process and into robust community treatment.

Conclusions and Evidence-Based Recommendations

Competency restoration is a critical part of the legal and public mental health systems. But these services have received little empirical study, so the evidence base underlying restoration has been meager (Gowensmith, 2019; Pirelli & Zapf, 2020). However, as the competency crisis worsens in many states, the need for evidence-based practice becomes more dire. An emerging, evidence-based approach to competency services would prioritize the following:

- Abandon the historical practice of sending all incompetent defendants, by default, to a state psychiatric hospital for inpatient services.
- For those with serious mental illness arrested for minor crimes, divert from the competency system (and criminal justice system) and into community treatment. Diversion is a faster path to more appropriate treatment, which reduces strain on the competency system.

- Deliver restoration services in the community for any defendants who can be released on bond. These should follow the evidence base for general community psychiatric treatment.
- Begin psychiatric treatment in jails for any incompetent defendant who cannot receive restoration services in the community (due to severity of charge, for example).
- Reserve inpatient psychiatric hospital restoration for only those who need this intensive level of care.
- Implement a triage approach to provide these hospital services first to those who need them most urgently (i.e., with most severe and acute symptoms of illness).

These steps all play important roles in addressing and mitigating the nation's "competency crisis".

References

Carabello, K. (2013). Jail-based restoration of competency program fact sheet. Retrieved from www.leg.state.nv.us/Session/77th2013/Exhibits/Senate/JUD/SJUD623F.pdf

Center for Legal Advocacy v. Barnes. (2019). (Consent Decree) (Civil Action No. 11-CV-02285-NYW; D. Colo. 2019).

Clendenin, S., Edens, C., & Warburton, K. (2021, August). *DSH overview: Felony incompetent to stand trial challenges, data, and efforts* [Presentation]. IST Solutions Workgroup, California. Retrieved from www.chhs.ca.gov/wp-content/uploads/2021/08/DSH_IST_Overview.pdf

Cochrane, R. E., Herbel, B. L., Reardon, M. L., & Lloyd, K. P. (2013). The Sell effect: involuntary medication treatment is a "clear and convincing" success. *Law and Human Behavior*, *37*(2), 107–16. doi: 10.1037/lhb0000003

Colorado Department of Human Services. (2015). *Needs analysis: Current status, strategic positioning, and future planning*. National Association of State Mental Health Program Directors Research Institute.

Colorado Department of Human Services. (2020). Forensic services. Retrieved from www.colorado.gov/pacific/cdhs/obh-forensic-services#SB19-223

Colwell, L. H., & Gianesini, J. (2011). Demographic, criminogenic, and psychiatric factors that predict competency restoration. *The Journal of the American Academy of Psychiatry and the Law*, *39*(3), 297–306.

Danzer, G. S., Wheeler, E., Alexander, A. A., & Wasser, T. D. (2019). Competency restoration for adult defendants in different treatment environment. *The Journal of the American Academy of Psychiatry and the Law*, *47*(1), 1–19. doi: 10.29158/JAAPL.003819-19

Dusky v. United States. (1960). 362 U.S. 402. Retrieved from https://supreme.justia.com/cases/federal/us/362/402/

Georgia Department of Behavioral Health and Developmental Disabilities. (2014, July). From waiting lists to recovery. Presented at the Annual Conference of the National Association of State Mental Health Program Directors. Georgia Department of Behavioral Health and Developmental Disabilities.

Gowensmith, W. N. (2019). Resolution or resignation: The role of forensic mental health professionals amidst the competency services crisis. *Psychology, Public Policy, and Law*, *25*(1), 1–14. doi: 10.1037/law0000190

Gowensmith, W. N., Frost, L. E., Speelman, D. W., & Therson, D. E. (2016). Lookin' for beds in all the wrong places: Outpatient competency restoration as a promising approach to modern challenges. *Psychology, Public Policy, and Law*, *22*(3), 293–305. doi: 10.1037/law0000088

Gowensmith, W. N., & Murrie, D. M. (2019). *Groundswell services' response to the State of Colorado's Department of Human Services compliance plan*. State of Colorado's Department of Human Services.

Gowensmith, W. N., & Murrie, D. C. (2022). Competence restoration in an era of a competency crisis. In B. Bornstein, M. Miller, & D. DeMatteo (Eds.), *Advances in psychology and law* (Vol. 6, pp. 215–239). Springer.

Grisso, T. (2006). *Evaluating competencies: Forensic assessments and instruments* (Vol. 16). Springer.

Guarnera, L., & Murrie, D. C. (2017). Field reliability of competence and sanity opinions: A systematic review and meta-analysis. *Psychological Assessment*, *29*, 795–818.

Guarnera, L., Murrie, D. C., & Boccaccini, M. T. (2017). Why do forensic experts disagree? Sources of unreliability and bias in forensic psychology evaluations. *Translational Issues in Psychological Science*, *3*, 143–152.

Harki, G. A. (2018, August 23). Horrific deaths, brutal treatment: Mental illness in America's jails. *The Virginian-Pilot*. Retrieved from https://pilotonline.com/news/local/projects/jail-crisis/article_5ba8a112-974e-11e8-ba17-b734814f14db.html

Heilbrun, K., Giallella, C., Wright, H. J., DeMatteo, D., Griffin, P. A., Locklair, B., & Desai, A. (2019). Treatment for restoration of competence to stand trial: Critical analysis and policy recommendations. *Psychology, Public Policy, and Law*, *25*(4), 266–283. doi: 10.1037/law0000210

Heilbrun, K., Giallella, C., Wright, H. J., DeMatteo, D., Griffin, P. A., Gowensmith, W. N., Locklair, B., Ayers, D., Desai, A., & Pietruszka, V. (2021). Jackson-based restorability to competence to stand trial: Critical analysis and recommendations. *Psychology, Public Policy, and Law*, *27*(3), 370–386. doi: 10.1037/law0000307

Iglehart, J. K. (2016). Decriminalizing mental illness – The Miami model. *The New England Journal of Medicine*, *374*, 1701–1703. doi: 10.1056/NEJMp1602959

Kapoor, R. (2011). Commentary: Jail-based competency restoration. *Journal of the American Academy of Psychiatry and the Law*, *39*(3), 311–315.

Katz, M. H. (2016). Examination of increase in mental health competency cases. Los Angeles County Health Agency. Retrieved from http://file.lacounty.gov/SDSInter/bos/supdocs/102162.pdf

Kivisto, A. J., Staats, M. L. P., & Connell, R. (2020). Development and validation of the typology of criminal defendants admitted for inpatient competency restoration: A latent class analysis. *Law and Human Behavior*, *44*(6), 449–460. doi: 10.1037/lhb0000398

Leifman, S., & Coffey, T. (2020). Jail diversion: The Miami model. *CNS Spectrums*, *25*, 659–666.

Locklair, B. (2016, March). *Due process problems with civil commitment of incompetent defendants: The current round of litigation and the next* [presentation]. American Psychology-Law Society Annual Conference.

McGuinness, C. (2017, May 31). No place to go: Inmates declared mentally unfit to stand trial languish in jails. *New Times SLO*. Retrieved from www.newtimesslo.com/sanluisobispo/no-place-to-go-inmates-declared-mentally-unfit-to-stand-trial-languish-in-jails/Content?oid=2978784

Melton, G. B., Petrila, J., Poythress, N. G., Slobogin, C., Otto, R. K., Mossman, D., & Condie, L. O. (2018). *Psychological evaluations for the courts: A handbook for mental health professionals and lawyers*, 4th ed. Guilford.

Mikolajewski, A. J., Manguno-Mire, G. M., Coffman, K. L., Deland, S. M., & Thompson, J. W., Jr. (2017). Patient characteristics and outcomes related to successful outpatient competency restoration. *Behavioral Sciences and the Law*, *35*(3), 225–238. doi: 10.1002/bsl.2287

Miller, R. (2003). Hospitalization of criminal defendants for evaluation of competence to stand trial or for restoration of competence: Clinical and legal issues. *Behavioral Sciences and the Law*, *21*(3), 369–391. doi: 10.1002/bsl.546

Morenz, B., & Busch, K. (2011). Pima County Jail. *American Academy of Psychiatry and the Law Newsletter*, *36*(1), 25–31. Retrieved from www.aapl.org/docs/newsletter/AAPL%20Newsletter%20January%2011.pdf

Morris, D. R., & DeYoung, N. J. (2012). Psycholegal abilities and restoration of competence to stand trial. *Behavioral Sciences and the Law*, *30*(6), 710–728. doi: 10.1002/bsl.2040

Morris, D. R., & Parker, G. F. (2008). Jackson's Indiana: State hospital competence restoration in Indiana. *Journal of the American Academy of Psychiatry and the Law Online*, *36*(4) 522–534.

Mossman, D. (2007). Predicting restorability of incompetent criminal defendants. *Journal of the American Academy of Psychiatry and the Law*, *35*(1), 34–43.

Mossman, D., Noffsinger, S. G., Ash, P., Frierson, R. L., Gerbasi, J., Hackett, M., . . . Zonana, H. V. (2007). AAPL practice guideline for the forensic psychiatric evaluation of competence to stand trial. *Journal of the American Academy of Psychiatry and the Law*, *35*, S3–S72.

Murrie, D. C., & Boccaccini, M. T. (2023). How reliable and objective are forensic mental health evaluators? In D. DeMatteo & K. C. Scherr (Eds.), *The Oxford handbook of psychology and law* (pp. 343–364). Oxford University Press.

Murrie, D. C., Gardner, B. O., & Torres, A. N. (2020). Competence to stand trial evaluations: A statewide review of court-ordered reports. *Behavioral Sciences and the Law*, *38*(1), 32–50. doi: 10.1002/bsl.2436

Murrie, D.C., Gardner, B.O., & Torres, A.N. (2022). The impact of misdemeanor arrests in forensic mental health services: A state-wide review of Virginia Competence to Stand Trial evaluations. *Psychology, Public Policy, and Law, 28*(1), 53–66.
Murrie, D. C., & Zelle, H. (2015). Criminal competencies. In B. Cutler and P. Zapf (Eds.), *The APA Handbook of forensic psychology* (pp. 115–158). American Psychological Association.
Musgrove, L. M. (2018). Program evaluation and outcomes of an outpatient competency restoration program. [Doctoral dissertation]. University of Denver, Digital Commons. Retrieved from https://digitalcommons.du.edu/capstone_masters/329
Neal, T. M. S., & Grisso, T. (2014). Assessment practices and expert judgment methods in forensic psychology and psychiatry: An international snapshot. *Criminal Justice and Behavior, 41*, 1406–1421. doi: 10.1177/0093854814548449
Nicholson, R. A., & McNulty, J. L. (1992). Outcome of hospitalization for defendants found incompetent to stand trial. *Behavioral Sciences and the Law, 10*(3), 371–383. doi: 10.1002/bsl.2370100307
Noffsinger, S. G. (2001). Restoration to competency practice guidelines. *International Journal of Offender Therapy and Comparative Criminology, 45*(3), 345–362. doi: 10.1177/0306624X01453007
Obikoya, K. (2021). Jail diversion for misdemeanors can be a first step to improve the competency to stand trial process. *Journal of the American Academy of Psychiatry and the Law, 49*(4), 473–477. doi: 10.29158/JAAPL.210124-21
Parks, J., & Radke, A. Q. (2014). *The vital role of state psychiatric hospitals*. National Association of State Mental Health Program Directors. Retrieved from www.nasmhpd.org/sites/default/files/The%20Vital%20Role%20of%20State%20Psychiatric%20HospitalsTechnical%20Report_July_2014(6).pdf
Pinals, D. A. (2005). Where two roads meet: Restoration of competency to stand trial from a clinical perspective. *New England Journal on Criminal and Civil Confinement, 31*(1), 81–108.
Pinals, D. A., & Callahan, L. (2020). Evaluation and restoration of competence to stand trial: Intercepting the forensic system using the sequential intercept model. *Psychiatric Services, 71*(7), 698–705. doi: 10.1176/appi.ps.201900484
Pirelli, G., Gottdiener, W. H., & Zapf, P. A. (2011). A meta-analytic review of comparative competency to stand trial research. *Psychology, Public Policy, and Law, 17*(1), 1–53. doi: 10.1037/a0021713
Pirelli, G., & Zapf, P. A. (2020). An attempted meta-analysis of the competency restoration research: Important findings for future directions. *Journal of Forensic Psychology Research and Practice, 20*(2), 134–162. doi: 10.1080/24732850.2020.1714398
Policy Research Associates, Inc. (2020). Quick fixes for effectively dealing with persons found incompetent to stand trial, 2nd ed. Retrieved from www.prainc.com/wp-content/uploads/2020/09/ISTRebrand-508.pdf
Pope, L. G., Boswell, T., Zern, A., Erickson, B., & Compton, M. T. (2021). Failure to appear: Mental health professionals' role amidst pretrial justice reform. *Psychiatric Services*. Retrieved from appi-ps.
Rice, K., & Jennings, J. L. (2014). The ROC program: Accelerated restoration of competency in a jail setting. *Journal of Correctional Health Care, 20*(1), 59–69.
Samuel, S. E., & Michals, T. J. (2011). Competency restoration. In E. Y. Drogin, F. M. Datillio, R. L. Sadoff, & T. G. Gutheil (Eds.), *Handbook of forensic assessment* (pp. 79–96). John Wiley & Sons, Inc.
Sell v. United States, 539 U.S. 166. (2003). Retrieved from https://supreme.justia.com/cases/federal/us/539/166/
Shafer, S. (2015, October 20). Long, dangerous wait for hospital beds for those incompetent to stand trial. KQED. Retrieved from https://ww2.kqed.org/stateofhealth/2015/10/20/long-dangerous-wait-for-hospital-beds-for-those-incompetent-to-stand-trial/
Shannon, B. D. (2017). Competency, ethics, and morality. *Texas Tech Law Review, 49*(4), 861–880.
Sherry, A. (2021, November 12). Colorado doesn't have enough resources to treat people deemed incompetent to stand trial, so the state is turning to private hospitals. Colorado Public News. Retrieved from https://www.cpr.org/2021/11/12/colorado-jails-mental-health-competency-treatment-private-hospitals/
Swaine, J. (2015, August 28). Young Black man jailed since April for alleged $5 theft found dead in cell. The Guardian. Retrieved from www.theguardian.com/us-news/2015/aug/28/jamycheal-mitchell-virginia-jail-found-dead
Tansey, A., Brown, K. P., & Wood, M. E. (2021). Characteristics and outcomes for defendants charged with misdemeanors referred for court-ordered competency evaluations. *Psychological Services*. Retrieved from https://psycnet.apa.org/doi/10.1037/ser0000535

Torrey, E. F., Kennard, A. D., Eslinger, D., Lamb, R., & Pavle, J. (2010). More mentally ill persons are in jails and prisons than hospitals: A survey of the states. Treatment Advocacy Center. Retrieved from https://knox.oh.networkofcare.org/library/final_jails_v_hospitals_study.pdf

Treatment Advocacy Center. (2011). Consequences of non-treatment. Retrieved from www.treatmentadvocacycenter.org/problem/fast-facts-/1384.

Wall, B. W., & Christopher, P. P. (2012). A training program for defendants with intellectual disabilities who are found incompetent to stand trial. *Journal of the American Academy of Psychiatry and the Law*, *40*(3), 366–373.

Warburton, K., McDermott, B. E., Gale, A., & Stahl, S. M. (2020). A survey of national trends in psychiatric patients found incompetent to stand trial: Reasons for the reinstitutionalization of people with serious mental illness in the United States. *CNS Spectrums*, *25*(2), 245–251. doi: 10.1017/S1092852919001585

Wik, A. (2018). Alternatives to inpatient competency restoration programs: Jail-based competency restoration programs. *NRI: Analytics Improving Behavioral Health*. Retrieved from www.nri-inc.org/media/1500/jbcr_website-format_oct2018.pdf

Wik, A., Hollen, V., & Fisher, W. (2020). Forensic patients in state psychiatric hospitals: 1999–2016. *CNS Spectrums*, *25*(2), 196–206. doi: 10.1017/S1092852919001044

Wolber, G., Goldenberg-Blavens, R., Torres, A., Stredny, R. V. (2011). An approach to competency restoration. *American Journal of Forensic Psychology*, *29*(4), 17–31.

Zapf, P. A., & Roesch, R. (2009). *Evaluation of competence to stand trial*. Oxford University Press.

Zapf, P. A., & Roesch, R. (2011). Future directions in the restoration of competency to stand trial. *Current Directions in Psychological Science: A Journal of the American Psychological Society*, *20*(1), 43–47. doi: 10.1177/0963721410396798

27

EYEWITNESS IDENTIFICATION

Margaret Bull Kovera and Eliana Aronson

Starting in the late 1980s, new methods of forensic DNA testing resulted in the identification and exoneration of a number of defendants who had been wrongfully convicted. To date, DNA testing has exonerated 375 innocent people in the United States, with countless other wrongful convictions remaining undetected, likely forever, because there is no DNA evidence to test in those cases. As exonerations accumulated, experts who sought common threads among the wrongful convictions uncovered systemic failures that contributed to these miscarriages of justice (e.g., Garrett, 2012; Scheck et al., 2000). One commonality seemed to overshadow the rest: more than two thirds of the exoneration cases relied on eyewitness misidentifications (Innocence Project, 2019). As the evidence mounted for the critical role that mistaken eyewitness identifications played in wrongful conviction, so too did the body of research examining the factors that contribute to eyewitness misidentification grow exponentially. As eyewitness identifications remain an evidentiary staple of the criminal justice system, legal practitioners need to understand why witnesses make mistakes and must take proactive steps to preserve the integrity of eyewitness evidence.

The State of the Literature

Generally, researchers have distinguished two types of variables that can influence eyewitness accuracy: *system* and *estimator* variables (Wells, 1978). The main distinction between these variables is that system variables are under control of the justice system, whereas estimator variables are not. Instead, estimator variables are typically related to witnessing conditions that vary across events, moderating the quality of perception and memory encoding. Low lighting (Wagenaar & Van Der Schrier, 1996), long distances (Loftus & Harley, 2005), brief exposure times (Sporer, 1992), intoxication (Flowe et al., 2016), stress (Deffenbacher et al., 2004), witnesses and victims of different races (i.e., cross-race identification; Young et al., 2011), and weapon presence (Steblay, 1992) can all hinder memory (for a review, see Beaudry et al., 2018). Although knowledge of the effects of these factors may allow actors in the criminal legal system (e.g., police, prosecutors, defense attorneys, judges, jurors) to postdict the reliability of an eyewitness identifications, these factors cannot be changed to improve witness reliability. System variables, in contrast, are a function of the specific procedures used to

DOI: 10.4324/9781003219286-33

obtain eyewitness identifications that can be changed to improve witness reliability and thus are the central focus of this chapter.

Police interviews of witnesses to a crime are typically the first point of contact between investigators and eyewitnesses and, if conducted immediately following the crime, allow police to document the witnesses' descriptions of what they saw unfold during the crime. However, if improperly conducted, these interviews can directly influence the quality and accuracy of witnesses' statements. Witnesses adjust their memory for an event to accommodate post-event information, which interviewers can implicitly impart by using suggestive language during questioning (see Berkowitz & Loftus, 2017). For instance, witnesses estimated that cars were driving at higher speeds when interviewers referenced the cars "smashing into" (rather than hitting) one another (Loftus & Palmer, 1974). Similar misinformation effects can emerge from a diverse array of sources, such as discussions with co-witnesses (Gabbert et al., 2003) and exposure to media coverage (Crombag et al., 1996).

Interviews are most effective at eliciting accurate information when they prioritize non-suggestive open-ended prompts. Closed ended questions can be limiting and leading, whereas open-ended questions encourage more complete and accurate narratives while also minimizing the potential for the influence of interviewer expectancies (e.g., Lamb et al., 2007). Widely accepted interviewing protocols include the Cognitive Interview (Fisher & Geiselman, 1992), the Person Description Interview (Demarchi & Py, 2009), and the Self-Administered Interview (Hope et al., 2011). Scholars have also developed unique child interviewing guidelines to account for children's heightened suggestibility (La Rooy et al., 2015).

Just like interviews, identification procedures affect witness accuracy. There are two main types of identification procedures: lineups and showups. Lineups involve placing a single suspect into an array of known innocent fillers, whereas showups present the suspect alone. Both can be administered either live or photographically. Research consistently and unequivocally demonstrates that lineups are superior to showups, partly because fillers siphon witness errors away from innocent suspects (Smith et al., 2017). Fillers therefore allow investigators to identify and discount many eyewitness errors when they occur (e.g., when a witness positively identifies a filler as the culprit), thus reducing the likelihood that charges will be pressed against an innocent person.

The way lineups are constructed also can affect witness decision-making about whether the culprit is in the lineup. Although it does not seem to matter whether lineups are conducted with live people versus photographs of those people (Fitzgerald et al., 2018), low similarity between the suspect and fillers (i.e., known innocent lineup members) increases the rate at which witnesses make mistaken identifications (Fitzgerald et al., 2013). Witnesses disproportionately select suspects who stand out from fillers in any noticeable way, regardless of whether they are actually the culprit (Lindsay et al., 1987). For instance, if a culprit wore a red t-shirt while committing a crime, witnesses will be more likely to identify an innocent suspect if he is dressed in a red t-shirt and embedded among fillers dressed in black. Any visual cue that distinguishes the suspect from the fillers has potential to draw the witness's attention, from clothing, to lighting, to photographic background.

The way lineups are administered also affects the accuracy of witness identifications. Pre-lineup instructions that fail to warn witnesses that the culprit may not be present among the lineup members or photos increase the likelihood that witnesses will positively identify someone from the lineup (Clark, 2005) and consequently produce more false identifications when the culprit is absent (Steblay, 2013). Demonstrating the power of expectancy effects, lineup administrators privy to which lineup member is the suspect and which are fillers tend to send cues to witnesses, which cause witnesses to pick suspects at higher rates, irrespective of whether they are innocent or guilty. For instance, an administrator might inadvertently smile or lean in closer when a witness is looking at the suspect, in turn facilitating a positive identification of the suspect. Experts thus advocate for double-blind procedures in which neither administrators nor witnesses know which lineup member is the suspect (Kovera & Evelo, 2017, 2020).

Although it may be tempting to use witnesses' confidence statements as an indicator of their identification accuracy, just like memory, confidence can be contaminated by information the witness encounters post-identification (Steblay et al., 2014). Indeed, many defendants later exonerated by DNA cases were convicted, at least in part, because they were identified by highly confident, yet inaccurate, witnesses (Garrett, 2012). Positive post-identification feedback from administrators ("Good, you identified the suspect!") can induce artificial inflation of confidence (Wells & Bradfield, 1998). Similarly, social media searches, conversations with co-witnesses, or even the mere fact that a case proceeds to trial can all provide confirmatory feedback and boost witness confidence (Douglass & Smalarz, 2019). In general, confidence statements are far more diagnostic of witness accuracy when they are obtained immediately after the identification is made (Brewer & Wells, 2006), using pristine lineup conditions, including a suspect who does not stand out from the fillers in the lineup, a witness who is properly instructed that the culprit may not be present in the lineup, and an administrator who does not know which lineup member is the suspect (Wixted & Wells, 2017).

Main Takeaways

- Eyewitness evidence is often unreliable, and eyewitness misidentifications have contributed significantly to wrongful convictions in the United States.
- Although both estimator and system variables influence eyewitness accuracy, system variables are directly under the control of the criminal justice system, whereas estimator variables are not.
- Eyewitness judgments are not only a function of witness memory but also depend on contextual and social cues present during identification and interviewing procedures.
- Post-event information can influence eyewitness identification accuracy and witness confidence. Consequently, police officers should interview witnesses using open-ended, non-suggestive questions to protect against memory contamination, and an officer who does not know which lineup member is the suspect should collect confidence statements from witnesses immediately after the identification.
- The way an identification procedure is formatted, constructed, and administered affects the accuracy of eyewitness identifications.

Recommendations for Collecting Eyewitness Identification Evidence

In 2020, a group of leading eyewitness experts updated the American Psychology-Law Society's official recommendations for evidence-based best practices for the collection of eyewitness identification evidence (Wells et al., 2020). The following guidelines are drawn directly from these recommendations.

Pre-Lineup Interviews

Investigators should interview witnesses as soon as possible and prior to conducting any identification procedure. Witnesses should first provide descriptions of the culprit, before self-reporting viewing conditions, attentiveness during the crime, and prior familiarity with the culprit. To avoid contamination, witnesses should be instructed not to discuss the event with co-witnesses and to avoid attempting to identify the culprit on their own.

Evidence-Based Suspicion

Given that the ratio of guilty to innocent suspects in lineup procedures has more of an effect on the rate of misidentifications than any other system variable (Wells et al., 2015), investigators should never include a suspect in an identification procedure without evidence-based grounds to assume they were involved in the crime under investigation. Officers should document this evidence in writing before conducting the identification procedure.

Double-Blind Procedures

To prevent administrators from, consciously or unconsciously, steering the witness toward choosing the suspect, lineup administrators should always be blind to which lineup member is the suspect (Kovera & Evelo, 2017).

Lineup Fillers

Each lineup should only contain one suspect and at least five known-innocent fillers. The suspect should not stand out from the fillers in any way. In addition to ensuring that the fillers match the description of the culprit given by the witness, investigators should consider whether characteristics including facial tattoos, backgrounds, clothing, lighting, and photo size cause the suspect to stand out from among the fillers. If the suspect has a distinctive feature, it should either be consistently concealed or replicated on all fillers.

Prelineup Instructions

Prior to conducting an identification procedure, officers should avoid telling the eyewitness any extraneous information about the investigation and should not disclose whether the suspect has been arrested. In addition, officers should never suggest that the culprit will be present in the identification procedure. Lineup administrators should inform witnesses that: (a) they do not know who the suspect is, (b) the culprit might not be in the lineup at all, and the witness can say "not present", or "none of these", or "I don't know" if they cannot decide, (c) after making a decision they will be asked to state their confidence in their decision, and (d) the investigation will continue even if no identification is made.

Confidence Statements

To avoid post-identification feedback effects, investigators should collect confidence statements immediately after the identification decision.

Video Recording

To preserve a record of what happened during the interview and identification procedure, investigators should video-record all pre-identification interviews, witness instructions, identification procedures, and confidence statements.

Avoid Repeated Identifications

Investigators should never administer repeated identification procedures with the same suspect to a witness, even if the witness identified the suspect in the initial procedure. Familiarity judgements are vulnerable to source-monitoring errors (Johnson et al., 1993). Repeated exposure to a suspect can cause witnesses to commit to identifications of suspects who they were initially unsure or mistaken were the culprit (Deffenbacher et al., 2006). Witnesses may also infer that a suspect who has appeared repeatedly in an identification procedure is the suspect, which can bias decision-making (Wells & Luus, 1990) and artificially inflate confidence (Shaw, Garven, & Wood, 1997; Shaw & McClure, 1996).

Showups

As a general rule, investigators should use lineups instead of showups as lineups produce more accurate identifications (Colloff & Wixted, 2020). Showups should only be used when officers have no other probable cause for detaining a suspect, and that suspect has been immediately detained near or at the scene of the crime. Photographic showups should therefore never be conducted; if investigators had the ability to obtain a photo of the suspect, they can embed the photo among fillers before showing it to the witness. Finally, if a showup must be conducted, it is especially important that investigators adhere to the lineup recommendations listed previously.

Conclusion

Exoneration data have revealed that misidentifications play a large role in the wrongful conviction of innocent people. In light of these findings, investigators and legal actors must take careful steps to minimize contamination of witness memory when collecting eyewitness evidence. A variety of factors influence eyewitness accuracy, including those which are under the control of the criminal justice system (system variables), and those which are not (estimator variables). These variables can restrict eyewitness accuracy by affecting the initial encoding of an event into memory, by contaminating memory after the event has occurred through the use of biased or suggestive investigative procedures (i.e., the misinformation effect), or by affecting the rate at which guilty (as opposed to innocent) suspects appear in lineups. In addition, there are some contexts in which witness identifications may not be based on their memories of the culprit at all but rather are the product of social influence on the part of police (Kovera & Evelo, 2021; Wells, 2020). Both eyewitness interviews and identification procedures can contaminate memory if they are administered in a manner which is inherently suggestive. Investigators should aim to minimize the suggestiveness of both eyewitness interviews and identification procedures by adhering to the best practice guidelines outlined here (see also Wells et al., 2020).

References

Beaudry, J. L., Bullard, C. L., & Dolin, J. R. (2018). Estimator variables and eyewitness identification. *Encyclopedia of Criminology and Criminal Justice*, 1384–1394. doi: 10.1007/978-1-4614-5690-2_668

Berkowitz, S. R., & Loftus, E. F. (2017). Misinformation in the courtroom. *Oxford Scholarship Online*. doi: 10.1093/oso/9780190612016.003.0002

Brewer, N., & Wells, G. L. (2006). The confidence-accuracy relationship in eyewitness identification: Effects of lineup instructions, foil similarity, and target-absent base rates. *Journal of Experimental Psychology: Applied*, *12*(1), 11–30. doi: 10.1037/1076-898x.12.1.11

Clark, S. E. (2005). A re-examination of the effects of biased lineup instructions in eyewitness identification. *Law and Human Behavior*, *29*(4), 395–424. doi: 10.1007/s10979-005-5690-7

Colloff, M. F., & Wixted, J. T. (2020). Why are lineups better than showups? A test of the filler siphoning and enhanced discriminability accounts. *Journal of Experimental Psychology: Applied*, *26*(1), 124–143. doi: 10.1037/xap0000218
Crombag, H. F., Wagenaar, W. A., & Koppen, P. J. (1996). Crashing memories and the problem of 'source monitoring'. *Applied Cognitive Psychology*, *10*(2), 95–104. doi: 10.1002/(sici)1099-0720(199604)10:23.0.co;2-#
Deffenbacher, K. A., Bornstein, B. H., & Penrod, S. D. (2006). Mugshot exposure effects: retroactive interference, mugshot commitment, source confusion, and unconscious transference. *Law and Human Behavior*, *30*(3), 287–307. doi: 10.1007/s10979-006-9008-1
Deffenbacher, K. A., Bornstein, B. H., Penrod, S. D., & Mcgorty, E. K. (2004). A meta-analytic review of the effects of high stress on eyewitness memory. *Law and Human Behavior*, *28*(6), 687–706. doi: 10.1007/s10979-004-0565-x
Demarchi, S., & Py, J. (2009). A method to enhance person description: A field study. In R. Bull, T. Valentine, & T. Williamson (Eds.), *Handbook of psychology of investigative interviewing: Current developments and future directions* (pp. 241–256). Wiley Blackwell. doi: 10.1002/9780470747599.ch14
Douglass, A. B., & Smalarz, L. (2019). Post-identification feedback to eyewitnesses: Implications for system variable reform. *Advances in Psychology and Law*, 101–135. doi: 10.1007/978-3-030-11042-0_4
Fisher, R. P., & Geiselman, R. E. (1992). *Memory-enhancing techniques for investigative interviewing: The cognitive interview*. Charles C. Thomas Publisher.
Fitzgerald, R. J., Price, H. L., Oriet, C., & Charman, S. D. (2013). The effect of suspect-filler similarity on eyewitness identification decisions: A meta-analysis. *Psychology, Public Policy, and Law*, *19*(2), 151–164. doi: 10.1037/a0030618
Fitzgerald, R. J., Price, H. L., & Valentine, T. (2018). Eyewitness identification: Live, photo, and video lineups. *Psychology, Public Policy, and Law*, *24*(3), 307–325. doi: 10.1037/law0000164
Flowe, H. D., Takarangi, M. K., Humphries, J. E., & Wright, D. S. (2016). Alcohol and remembering a hypothetical sexual assault: Can people who were under the influence of alcohol during the event provide accurate testimony? *Memory*, *24*(8), 1042–1061. doi: 10.1080/09658211.2015.1064536
Gabbert, F., Memon, A., & Allan, K. (2003). Memory conformity: Can eyewitnesses influence each other's memories for an event? *Applied Cognitive Psychology*, *17*(5), 533–543. doi: 10.1002/acp.885
Garrett, B. (2012). *Convicting the innocent: Where criminal prosecutions go wrong*. Harvard University Press.
Hope, L., Gabbert, F., & Fisher, R. P. (2011). From laboratory to the street: Capturing witness memory using the self-administered interview. *Legal and Criminological Psychology*, *16*(2), 211–226. doi: 10.1111/j.2044-8333.2011.02015.x
Innocence Project (2019, April 3). Retrieved from https://innocenceproject.org/all-cases/
Johnson, M. K., Hashtroudi, S., & Lindsay, D. S. (1993). Source monitoring. *Psychological Bulletin*, *114*(1), 3–28. doi: 10.1037/0033-2909.114.1.3
Kovera, M. B., & Evelo, A. J. (2017). The case for double-blind lineup administration. *Psychology, Public Policy, and Law*, *23*(4), 421–437. doi: 10.1037/law0000139
Kovera, M. B., & Evelo, A. J. (2020). Improving eyewitness identification evidence through double-blind lineup administration. *Current Directions in Psychological Science*, *29*(6), 563–568. doi: 10.1177/0963721420969366
Kovera, M. B., & Evelo, A. J. (2021). Eyewitness identification in its social context. *Journal of Applied Research in Memory and Cognition*, *10*(3), 313–327. doi: 10.1016/j.jarmac.2021.04.003
La Rooy, D., Brubacher, S. P., Aromäki-Stratos, A., Cyr, M., Hershkowitz, I., Korkman, J., . . . Lamb, M. E. (2015). The NICHD protocol: A review of an internationally-used evidence-based tool for training child forensic interviewers. *Journal of Criminological Research, Policy and Practice*, *1*(2), 76–89. doi: 10.1108/jcrpp-01-2015-0001
Lamb, M. E., Orbach, Y., Hershkowitz, I., Horowitz, D., & Abbott, C. B. (2007). Does the type of prompt affect the accuracy of information provided by alleged victims of abuse in forensic interviews? *Applied Cognitive Psychology*, *21*(9), 1117–1130. doi: 10.1002/acp.1318
Lindsay, R. C., Wallbridge, H., & Drennan, D. (1987). Do the clothes make the man? An exploration of the effect of lineup attire on eyewitness identification accuracy. *Canadian Journal of Behavioural Science/Revue Canadienne des Sciences du Comportement*, *19*(4), 463–478. doi: 10.1037/h0079998
Loftus, E. F., & Palmer, J. C. (1974). Reconstruction of automobile destruction: An example of the interaction between language and memory. *Journal of Verbal Learning and Verbal Behavior*, *13*(5), 585–589. doi: 10.1016/s0022-5371(74)80011-3

Loftus, G. R., & Harley, E. M. (2005). Why is it easier to identify someone close than far away? *Psychonomic Bulletin & Review*, *12*(1), 43–65. doi: 10.3758/bf03196348

Quinlivan, D. S., Wells, G. L., Neuschatz, J. S., Luecht, K. M., Cash, D. K., & Key, K. N. (2016). The effects of pre-admonition suggestions on eyewitnesses' choosing rates and retrospective identification judgments. *Journal of Police and Criminal Psychology*, *32*(3), 236–246. doi: 10.1007/s11896-016-9216-7

Scheck, B., Neufeld, P., & Dwyer, J. (2000). *Actual innocence*. Doubleday.

Shaw, J. S., Garven, S., & Wood, J. M. (1997). Co-witness information can have immediate effects on eyewitness memory reports. *Law and Human Behavior*, *21*(5), 503–523. doi: 10.1023/a:1024875723399

Shaw, J. S., & Mcclure, K. A. (1996). Repeated postevent questioning can lead to elevated levels of eyewitness confidence. *Law and Human Behavior*, *20*(6), 629–653. doi: 10.1007/bf01499235

Smith, A. M., Wells, G. L., Lindsay, R. C., & Penrod, S. D. (2017). Fair lineups are better than biased lineups and showups, but not because they increase underlying discriminability. *Law and Human Behavior*, *41*(2), 127–145. doi: 10.1037/lhb0000219

Sporer, S. L. (1992). Post-dicting eyewitness accuracy: Confidence, decision-times and person descriptions of choosers and non-choosers. *European Journal of Social Psychology*, *22*(2), 157–180. doi: 10.1002/ejsp.2420220205

Steblay, N. M. (1992). A meta-analytic review of the weapon focus effect. *Law and Human Behavior*, *16*(4), 413–424. doi: 10.1007/bf02352267

Steblay, N. K. (2013). Lineup instructions. In B. L. Cutler (Ed.), *Reform of eyewitness identification procedures* (pp. 65–86). American Psychological Association. doi: 10.1037/14094-004

Steblay, N. K., Wells, G. L., & Douglass, A. B. (2014). The eyewitness post identification feedback effect 15 years later: Theoretical and policy implications. *Psychology, Public Policy, and Law*, *20*(1), 1–18. doi: 10.1037/law0000001

Wagenaar, W. A., & Schrier, J. H. (1996). Face recognition as a function of distance and illumination: A practical tool for use in the courtroom. *Psychology, Crime & Law*, *2*(4), 321–332. doi: 10.1080/10683169608409787

Wells, G. L. (1978). Applied eyewitness-testimony research: System variables and estimator variables. *Journal of Personality and Social Psychology*, *36*(12), 1546–1557. doi: 10.1037/0022-3514.36.12.1546

Wells, G. L. (2020). Psychological science on eyewitness identification and its impact on police practices and policies. *American Psychologist*, *75*(9), 1316–1329. doi: 10.1037/amp00007

Wells, G. L., & Bradfield, A. L. (1998). "Good, you identified the suspect": Feedback to eyewitnesses distorts their reports of the witnessing experience. *Journal of Applied Psychology*, *83*(3), 360–376. doi: 10.1037/0021-9010.83.3.360

Wells, G. L., & Luus, C. A. (1990). Police lineups as experiments. *Personality and Social Psychology Bulletin*, *16*(1), 106–117. doi: 10.1177/0146167290161008

Wells, G. L., Yang, Y., & Smalarz, L. (2015). Eyewitness identification: Bayesian information gain, base-rate effect equivalency curves, and reasonable suspicion. Law and Human Behavior, 39, 99–122. doi: 10.1037/lhb0000125

Wixted, J. T., & Wells, G. L. (2017). The relationship between eyewitness confidence and identification accuracy: A new synthesis. *Psychological Science in the Public Interest*, *18*(1), 10–65. doi: 10.1177/1529100616686966

Young, S. G., Hugenberg, K., Bernstein, M. J., & Sacco, D. F. (2011). Perception and motivation in face recognition. *Personality and Social Psychology Review*, *16*(2), 116–142. doi: 10.1177/1088868311418987

28

IMPLICIT AND INGRAINED? REDUCING UNCONSCIOUS BIAS AMONG JURORS

Angela M. Jones and Christine L. Ruva

Implicit and Ingrained? Reducing Unconscious Bias in the Courtroom

Courts across the country have grown increasingly concerned about the impact of bias on jurors' decision making (Elek & Hannaford-Agor, 2014; Kang et al., 2011). Jurors holding explicit biases, that is biases that people consciously endorse, are easier for courts to effectively address because they can be directly measured. More problematic, however, are biases that evade traditional methods of detection. Implicit biases may stem from preferences for ingroup members, one's social environment, and/or personal experience (Greenwald & Lai, 2020).

In this chapter, we explain why bias is problematic, noting how different types of bias such as those stemming from race influence jurors' decisions. We also outline the failure of limited voir dire to protect defendants' constitutional right to a fair and impartial jury of one's peers. We shift focus to more effective strategies for identifying explicit bias such as through advanced questionnaires and extended voir dire. Finally, we provide examples of promising interventions to reduce bias, such as increasing jury diversity and implicit bias training.

Why Is Bias Problematic?

Every defendant has the right to a trial by a fair and impartial jury of their peers. Yet archival, experimental, and public opinion research all demonstrate the problematic nature of explicit and implicit biases for ensuring fairness in the American criminal justice system. For example, Black defendants receive harsher punishments than similarly situated White defendants (Mitchell et al., 2005; see Sommers & Marotta, 2014 for review). Racial biases in juror decision-making reflect the broader public opinion differences in punitiveness between White and Black Americans (Peffley et al., 2017). White Americans are less likely to see racial disparities in the criminal justice system as indicative of racial discrimination and more likely to attribute disparities to inherent criminality among Black Americans (Peffley et al., 2017).

Failed Remedies to Reduce Bias

Voir dire is designed to safeguard a defendant's right to a fair and impartial jury. While the process varies greatly, venirepersons are usually questioned as a group, by a judge, and in

DOI: 10.4324/9781003219286-34

a limited fashion with the purpose of identifying bias (Hans & Jehle, 2003). The judge will attempt to rehabilitate biased venirepersons by asking if they can set their bias aside and determine a verdict based solely on the facts of the case. Those who state they are unable may be struck for cause. Attorneys also have a limited number of peremptory challenges to remove jurors for any reason except to discriminate on the basis of race, ethnicity, or sex. Yet attorneys use peremptory challenges more often to strike minority jurors, even though race-neutral reasons are provided (see Sommers & Marotta, 2014 for review). Peremptory challenges have, therefore, been criticized as a means for excluding people of color from juries (Grosso & O'Brien, 2012).

Multiple assumptions are built into the process of voir dire, some of which overlap with the flexible correction model (FCM; Wegner & Petty, 1997). That is, venirepersons must be aware of their own biases, motivated to correct for it, and understand the size and direction of their bias. Yet venirepersons may not realize they harbor implicit bias nor the extent to which implicit bias affects their behavior (Greenwald & Lai, 2020). Further, even among those motivated to correct for bias, voir dire does little to assist venirepersons with accurately identifying the direction and magnitude of their own implicit biases (Crocker & Kovera, 2010).

Courts also assume that successful rehabilitation will render jurors impartial. However, rehabilitation has failed to reduce both implicit biases associated with pretrial publicity (see Ruva, 2018 for review) and more explicit biases related to civil trial attitudes (e.g., skepticism towards litigants; Salerno et al., 2021) and race (Schuller et al., 2009). Missing FCM criteria (Wegner & Petty, 1997) and social desirability effects (Hans & Jehle, 2003) may explain why rehabilitation fails. Judges expect jurors to be impartial, which pressures jurors to give answers they believe the judge wants to hear and avoid reporting explicit biases that may displease the judge (Crocker & Kovera, 2010). As a result, juries may be composed of those who promise to be impartial because they felt pressured to socially conform, or who may genuinely believe they can be impartial, but still harbor implicit bias. These issues demonstrate the ineffectiveness of voir dire to protect against juror bias and suggest alternative approaches are needed.

How Can We Identify Explicit Bias in Jurors?

We suggest courts focus on empirically supported ways of identifying explicit bias, such as with extended voir dire and questionnaires. In contrast to limited voir dire discussed previously, extended voir dire involves both judges and attorneys asking more probing questions (see Salerno et al., 2021). Such questions increase the effectiveness of voir dire for uncovering bias (Crocker & Kovera, 2010; Salerno et al., 2021). The use of pretrial surveys may be even more effective at identifying juror bias due to reduced social and time pressures as well as increased privacy. Even when responses are not anonymous, the act of privately self-administering a survey results in more honest and less socially desirable responses (Gnambs & Kaspar, 2015). This is perhaps the best reason for requesting a written juror questionnaire.

Significantly, survey respondents who disclosed relevant biases were more likely to convict (Crocker & Kovera, 2010; see also Salerno et al., 2021 for liability judgments) and endorsed harsher punishments (Peffley et al., 2017). These findings demonstrate the consequence of failing to properly identify and eliminate biased jurors. Notably, however, questionnaires and voir dire can only assess explicit biases. Jurors may appear unbiased on explicit measures due to possessing egalitarian views that motivate them to appear unprejudiced, while still holding implicit bias toward certain groups (Dovidio & Gaertner, 2004). Thus, explicit and implicit biases should be assessed and remedied via different methods (Forscher et al., 2019).

What Are Promising Implicit Bias Interventions?

Increasing Jury Diversity

Representative juries are crucial to ensuring the fairness of the criminal justice system (Ellis & Diamond, 2003). Supporting this expectation, racially diverse juries share more information in ambiguous cases (Bergold & Kovera, 2022) and deliberate longer and more thoroughly, resulting in less biased decisions (Sommers & Marotta, 2014). More broadly, racially diverse groups demonstrate higher comprehensive thinking skills (Antonio et al., 2004), generate more effective and feasible solutions, and make more accurate decisions (Manata, 2021) compared to racially homogeneous groups. Thus, increasing diversity shows promise for more thoughtful decisions and minimizing racial bias in deliberations (Sommers & Marotta, 2014).

Given the positive effects of jury-member diversity on the quality of deliberations and decisions, how can jury diversity and representativeness be improved? Efforts are underway in state courts to better manage how jurors are summoned to court and expanding the sources of jury lists (National Center for State Courts, 2021). These efforts ensure jury pools reflect the demographics of the community from which they are drawn, ultimately translating to more representative (and likely diverse) juries (Sommers & Marotta, 2014).

Some legal scholars have also called for the elimination of preemptory challenges as they threaten jury representativeness (Bennett, 2010; Grosso & O'Brien, 2012). This concern is what drove Arizona to become the first state to do away with the peremptory challenge (Arizona Supreme Court, 2021) and may motivate other states to follow suit. Finally, another way to increase jury diversity, specifically Black and Hispanic jurors, is by increasing jury size from 6 to 12 members (Diamond et al., 2009). Thus, the combination of changes to the number of sources to compile jury lists, ending peremptory challenges, and using 12-person juries has the potential to increase jury diversity, reduce juror bias, and improve the quality of deliberations.

Implicit Bias Instructions and Training

Implicit bias instructions are growing in popularity in courts across the country, including in Iowa (Kang et al., 2012), Washington (U.S. District Court, Western District of Washington, n.d.), and California (U.S. District Court, Northern District of California, n.d.). For example, jurors in the high-profile case against Derek Chauvin in Minnesota were recently instructed to reflect carefully about the evidence and how bias may influence their decision, and to use a "consider the opposite" strategy to determine if they would make the same decision if the defendant was of a different background (State of Minnesota, 2021). While promising, limited evidence speaks to the effectiveness of implicit bias instructions for reducing implicit biases associated with race (Elek & Hannaford-Agor, 2014) and pretrial publicity (Ruva et al., 2022). Yet current implicit bias instructions are a good starting point as they increase awareness, prompting jurors to think about their own biases. This proposed remedy, given to jurors at the end of a trial, may be more effective if combined with an implicit bias training that is offered at the outset of a trial. The instructions would then serve as a reminder to jurors to reflect on the implicit bias training and their responsibility to fairly evaluate evidence and determine a verdict.

In addition to providing implicit bias instructions, courts in Washington (U.S. District Court, Western District of Washington, n.d.), Oregon (Oregon State Courts, n.d.), and New York (New York State Unified Court Systems, n.d.) have implemented implicit bias training during juror orientation. Currently, this training consists of a single brief (e.g., 11 to 12 minutes) session administered via video that (1) provides a definition and examples of unconscious bias, (2) indicates everyone is influenced by unconscious bias ("even honest, intelligent, really good people"), (3) makes appeals to egalitarian values (e.g., "commit to your oath as a juror to be fair and impartial" and "be sure you're . . . treating everyone fairly"), (4) indicates that awareness is the first step to addressing unconscious bias, and (5) provides suggestions for correcting bias (e.g., "Don't rush to a conclusion" and "Carefully examine our decisions & judgments as jurors" & "Question our decisions by asking whether they would be different if the witness, lawyer, or person on trial were of a different race, age, or gender"). The implicit bias juror training consists of many components necessary to reduce bias: making people aware that everyone holds implicit bias, suggesting that such bias can be remedied, providing suggestions on how to address this bias, and promoting egalitarian goals (Vitriol & Moskowitz, 2021). However, only two studies to date have tested this training, showing little evidence that it reduces pretrial publicity bias (Jones et al., 2021) or racial bias (Ruva et al., 2022).

Some features of the training may explain why there is little empirical support. For example, the one-size-fits-all training content currently being used by these courts may contribute to its failure – training is more effective when it is case-specific (e.g., considers the races of the defendant and victim; Calanchini et al., 2020). Additionally, training that involves a brief single session may be ineffective at producing behavioral change. Forscher et al. (2019) conducted a meta-analysis of 492 studies ($N = 87{,}418$) that mostly included brief single-session remedies. They found that while changing people's responses on implicit bias measures is possible, such changes may not result in behavioral change. Consistent with these findings, Chang et al.'s (2019) field experiment ($N = 3{,}016$) found that, while a short empirically based online diversity training session changed gender attitudes of people who were not highly supportive of women, the training failed to produce behavioral change. Thus, single-session diversity training that is common in the workplace, and is being explored by some courts to combat implicit bias, is unlikely to effectively change behavior.

Broader research on debiasing strategies suggests ways to increase training efficacy. The components of implicit bias training that show the greatest promise include perspective taking (Dovidio et al., 2004; cf., Lai et al., 2014), employing counter-stereotypical exemplars (e.g., providing a story that depicts a White man who commits a crime and a Black man who protects the victim; Calanchini et al., 2020), active participation (Lai et al., 2014; Morewedge et al., 2015), and personalized feedback (Vitriol & Moskowitz, 2021). For example, White participants instructed to imagine a Black man's feelings in a situation involving racial discrimination (i.e., perspective taking) showed the greatest reduction in prejudice compared to participants given no instructions or instructions to remain objective (Dovidio et al., 2004). Perspective taking may also be effective at reducing bias because there is an active component (Morewedge et al., 2015). Active participation is effective at reducing biases associated with the fundamental attribution error and projection more so than passively watching a video (Morewedge et al., 2015). Personalized feedback during training also reduces bias (Vitriol & Moskowitz, 2021). Thus, combining the current implicit bias juror training with a measure of implicit bias, such as an implicit association test (Greenwald & Lai, 2020), may provide jurors with feedback on the extent of their bias, and improve the training's efficacy.

In summary, while some components of implicit bias training show promise in reducing bias, none are a panacea. There is no one-size-fits-all training method, and such training would need to be tailored to individual case characteristics and consist of more than a single training session. However, even if changes in implicit bias are possible, this may not translate into changed behavior (Forscher et al., 2019).

Conclusions

The courts place much faith in the effectiveness of voir dire to elicit a jury composed of fair and impartial jurors. However, the evidence to date suggests voir dire, as it is commonly employed, does not serve its intended purpose. Case-specific pretrial questionnaires and extended voir dire can better identify explicitly biased jurors, while representative juries ensure more thorough and accurate decisions. We encourage social scientists to continue exploring how implicit bias influences juror decisions. Given that implicit bias interventions are relatively new and mostly untested in real-world situations, social scientists and the courts should work together to pilot these remedies and carefully examine their efficacy before implementing on a large-scale basis. To assist social scientists and the courts in exploring effective remedies, we end this chapter by providing a summary of the necessary components of effective implicit bias training.

Effective implicit bias training must:

1. be case specific and include active participation;
2. include perspective taking or counter-stereotypical exemplars;
3. make people aware of unconscious bias and provide suggestions for ways to control bias;
4. engender personal responsibility and culpability for bias by emphasizing that bias, while pervasive, is not acceptable or normative; and
5. provide individualized feedback for bias reduction success.

References

Antonio, A. L., Chang, M. J., Hakuta, K., Kenny, D. A., Levin, S., & Milem, J. F. (2004). Effects of racial diversity on complex thinking in college students. *Psychological Science*, *15*(8), 507–510.

Arizona Supreme Court. (2021). Order amending rules 18.4 and 18.5 of the rules of criminal procedure, and rule 47(e)of the rules of civil procedure. Retrieved from www.azcourts.gov/Rules-Forum/aft/1208

Bennett, M. W. (2010). Unraveling the Gordian knot of implicit bias in jury selection: The problems of judge-dominated voir dire, the failed promise of Batson, and proposed solutions. *Harvard Law & Policy Review*, *4*, 149–171.

Bergold, A. N., & Kovera, M. B. (2022). Diversity's impact on the quality of deliberations. *Personality and Social Psychology Bulletin*, *48*(9), 1406–1420.

Calanchini, J., Lai, C. K., & Klauer, K. C. (2020). Reducing implicit racial preferences: III. A process-level examination of changes in implicit preferences. *Journal of Personality and Social Psychology*, *121*(4), 796–818.

Chang, E. H., Milkman, K. L., Gromet, D. M., Rebele, R. W., Massey, C., Duckworth, A. L., & Grant, A. M. (2019). The mixed effects of online diversity training. *Proceedings of the National Academy of Sciences*, *116*(16), 7778–7783.

Crocker, C. B., & Kovera, M. B. (2010). The effects of rehabilitative voir dire on juror bias and decision making. *Law and Human Behavior*, *34*, 212–226.

Diamond, S., Peery, D., Dolan, F. J., & Dolan, E. (2009). Achieving diversity on the jury: Jury size and the peremptory challenge. *Journal of Empirical Legal Studies*, *6*, 425–449.

Dovidio, J. F., & Gaertner, S. L. (2004). Aversive racism. In M. P. Zanna (Ed.), *Advances in experimental social psychology* (Vol. 36, pp. 1–52). Academic Press.

Dovidio, J. F., Ten Vergert, M., Stewart, T. L., Gaertner, S. L., Johnson, J. D., Esses, V. M., Riek, B. M., & Pearson, A. R. (2004). Perspective and prejudice: Antecedents and mediating mechanisms. *Personality and Social Psychology Bulletin*, *30*(12), 1537–1549.

Elek, J., & Agor, P. H. (2014). Can explicit instructions reduce expressions of implicit bias? New questions following a test of a specialized jury instruction. Retrieved from http://ssrn.com/abstract=2430438

Ellis, L., & Diamond, S. S. (2003). Race, diversity, and jury composition: Battering and bolstering legitimacy, *Chicago-Kent Law Review*, *78*, 1033–1058.

Forscher, P. S., Lai, C. K., Axt, J. R., Ebersole, C. R., Herman, M., Devine, P. G., & Nosek, B. A. (2019). A meta-analysis of procedures to change implicit measures. *Journal of Personality and Social Psychology*, *117*(3), 522–559.

Gnambs, T., & Kaspar, K. (2015). Disclosure of sensitive behaviors across self-administered survey modes: A meta-analysis. *Behavior Research Methods*, *47*, 1237–1259.

Greenwald, A. G., & Lai, C. K. (2020). Implicit social cognition. *Annual Review of Psychology*, *71*, 419–445.

Grosso, C. M., & O'Brien, B. (2012). A stubborn legacy: The overwhelming importance of race in jury selection in 173 post-Batson North Carolina capital trials. *Iowa Law Review*, *97*, 1531–1559.

Hans, V. P., & Jehle, A. (2003). Avoid bald men and people with green socks? Other ways to improve the voir dire process in jury selection. *Chicago-Kent Law Review*, *78*, 1179–1201.

Jones, A. M., Wong, K., Meyers, C. N., & Ruva, C. (2021). Trial by tabloid: Can implicit bias education reduce pretrial publicity bias? *Criminal Justice and Behavior*.

Kang, J., Bennett, M., Carbado, D., Casey, P., Dasgupta, N., Faigman, D., Godsil, R., Greenwald, A. G., Levinson, J., & Mnookin, J. (2012). Implicit bias in the courtroom. *UCLA Law Review*, *59*(5), 1124–1186.

Kang, J., Bennett, M., Carbado, D., Casey, P., & Levinson, J. (2011). Implicit bias in the courtroom. *UCLA Law Review*, *59*, 1124–1186.

Lai, C. K., Marini, M., Lehr, S. A., Cerruti, C., Shin, J. E. L., Joy-Gaba, J. A., Ho, A. K., Teachman, B. A., Wojcik, S. P., Koleva, S. P., Frazier, R. S., Heiphetz, L., Chen, E. E., Turner, R. N., Haidt, J., Kesebir, S., Hawkins, C. B., Schaefer, H. S., Rubichi, S., Sartori, G., Dial, C. M., Sriram, N., Banaji, M. R., & Nosek, B. A. (2014). Reducing implicit racial preferences: I. A comparative investigation of 17 interventions. *Journal of Experimental Psychology: General*, *143*(4), 1765–1785.

Manata, B. (2021). Investigating the impact of racial diversity in decision-making groups: The moderating role of relationship conflict. *Negotiation and Conflict Management Research*, *14*, 40–50.

Mitchell, T. L., Haw, R. M., Pfeifer, J. E., & Meissner, C. A. (2005). Racial bias in mock juror decision-making: A meta-analytic review of defendant treatment. *Law and Human Behavior*, *29*(6), 621–637.

Morewedge, C. K., et al. (2015). Debiasing decisions: Improved decision making with a single training intervention. *Policy Insights from the Behavioral & Brain Sciences*, *2*, 129–140.

National Center for State Courts. (2021). Are all of the right people making it into your jury pools? Retrieved from www.ncsc.org/newsroom/at-the-center/2021/are-all-of-the-right-people-making-it-into-your-jury-pools

New York State Unified Court Systems. (n.d.). Jury service and fairness. Retrieved from http://wowza.nycourts.gov/vod/vod.php?source=ucs&video=2021-JuryServiceFairness.mp4

Oregon State Courts. (n.d.). Jury service videos. Retrieved from www.courts.oregon.gov/courts/grant/jury/Pages/JuryServiceVideo.aspx

Peffley, M., Hurwitz, J., & Mondak, J. (2017). Racial attributions in the justice system and support for punitive crime policies. *American Politics Research*, *45*, 1032–1058.

Ruva, C. L. (2018). From the headlines to the jury room: An examination of the impact of pretrial publicity on jurors and juries. In B. H. Bornstein & M. K. Miller (Eds.), *Advances in psychology and law* (Vol. 3, pp. 1–39). Springer.

Ruva, C. L., Sykes, E. C., Smith, K. D., Deaton, L. R., Erdem, S., & Jones, A. M. (2022). Battling bias: Can two implicit bias remedies reduce juror racial bias? *Psychology, Crime & Law*, 1–28.

Salerno, J. M., Campbell, J. C., Phalen, H. J., Bean, S. R., Hans, V. P., Spivack, D., & Ross, L. (2021). The impact of minimal versus extended voir dire and judicial rehabilitation on mock jurors' decisions in civil cases. *Law and Human Behavior*, *45*(4), 336–355.

Schuller, R. A., Kazoleas, V., & Kawakami, K. (2009). The impact of prejudice screening procedures on racial bias in the courtroom. *Law and Human Behavior*, *33*(4), 320–328.

Sommers, S. R., & Marotta, S. A. (2014). Racial disparities in legal outcomes: On policing, charging decisions, and criminal trial proceedings. *Policy Insights from the Behavioral and Brain Sciences*, *1*, 103–111.

State of Minnesota. (2021). Jury instructions in Derek Chauvin trial. Retrieved from www.mncourts.gov/mncourtsgov/media/High-Profile-Cases/27-CR-20-12646/JuryInstructions04192021.pdf
U.S. District Court, Northern District of California. (n.d.). Civil jury instructions. Retrieved from www.justia.com/trials-litigation/docs/caci/100/113/
U.S. District Court, Western District of Washington. (n.d). Unconscious bias juror video, criminal jury instructions. Retrieved from www.wawd.uscourts.gov/jury/unconscious-bias
Vitriol, J. A., & Moskowitz, G. B. (2021). Reducing defensive responding to implicit bias feedback: On the role of perceived moral threat and efficacy to change. *Journal of Experimental Social Psychology*, *96*, 104–165.
Wegener, D. T., & Petty, R. E. (1997). The flexible correction model: The role of naive theories of bias in bias correction. *Advances in Experimental Social Psychology*, *29*, 141–208.

29

JUDICIAL CONSIDERATIONS IN SENTENCING

A Call for Evidence-Based Reform

Hon. John L. Badalamenti and Lindsay Holcomb

Introduction

There is bipartisan consensus that criminal justice reform is critically needed in the United States (Equal Justice Initiative, 2018). Since 1980, the incarcerated population in our country has increased more than 600 percent (Federal Bureau of Prisons, 2021).[1] The United States incarcerates more people per capita than any other country in the world (BBC News, n.d.), and today, roughly 1 in 20 Americans can expect to be incarcerated at some point during their lifetime (Bonczar & Beck, 1997). As the incarcerated population has grown, and funding for prison-based educational and vocational programs has been reduced, the line between warehousing and rehabilitation has grown increasingly blurry (Davis et al., 2013).[2] This problem is not poised to end soon. More than one third of the individuals currently incarcerated in federal correctional facilities are serving sentences between 10 and 20 years, and roughly one in six are serving sentences between 20 years and life (United States Sentencing Commission [USSC], 2019). The current criminal justice system is also extraordinarily expensive. In fact, in 2020, the Federal Bureau of Prisons – a single agency in the executive branch – had an operating budget exceeding that of *the entire* judicial branch, a co-equal branch of the government developed by the framers (U.S. Government Publishing Office, 2020).

The extraordinary growth, and associated financial costs, of the prison population can be traced back to a number of sources. One of them, as I will outline in this chapter, is a flawed system of federal overcriminalization (Heritage Foundation, n.d.),[3] which is exacerbated by the current federal sentencing framework. One study revealed that there are more than 300,000 federal criminal laws woven into the United States Code and various federal regulations (Coffee, 1991). That is a far cry from the three crimes expressly enumerated in the Constitution—treason, piracy, and counterfeiting (U.S. Const. art. I, §§ 3, 8).

And despite vigilant, well-intended efforts to decrease federal sentencing disparities throughout the 93 districts comprising the federal judiciary, such disparities, according to a recent report, remain prominent within the four major groupings of crimes—fraud, drug trafficking, firearm-related offenses, and illegal reentry offenses (Breyer & Reeves, 2021). It is undeniable that similarly situated offenders are sentenced differently, depending upon their sentencing judges, under the current federal sentencing framework.

 DOI: 10.4324/9781003219286-35

Since my appointment to the federal bench in 2020, I have sentenced approximately 100 criminal defendants.[4] I bring with me the diverse experiences gained from serving both as legal counsel to the Federal Bureau of Prisons during a period of extraordinary inmate population growth in the 1990s (Larkin, 2013) and as an assistant federal public defender for a nearly decade, where I represented hundreds of criminal defendants. In both roles, I observed various federal judges with different approaches toward sentencing, which sometimes resulted in disparities among similarly situated defendants across the country and even within the same federal district.

Among the many cases I litigated as an assistant federal public defender, one stands out as clearly demonstrating the need for criminal justice reform. In 2012, I represented a commercial fisherman, John Yates, who was issued a *civil* infraction ticket for harvesting for sale 72 fish that, under a federal regulation, were deemed too small to sell. A federal officer who encountered Mr. Yates on the water told him to separate those undersized fish from the others and continue with his fishing trip. When Mr. Yates returned to port, he was met by federal officers who identified 69 undersized fish, 3 fish fewer than the 72 identified 100 miles off the coast of Tampa, Florida. The federal government charged Mr. Yates with the destruction of these three fish, utilizing a statute that Congress passed in the wake of the Enron paper-shredding and computer hard drive-wiping scandal—the Sarbanes-Oxley Act of 2002. This act criminalized, among other things, an individual's destruction of a "record, document, or tangible object" in anticipation of a federal investigation (18 U.S.C. § 1519). Effectively comparing Mr. Yates's destruction of fish to the Enron employees' destruction of business records in anticipation of a federal government investigation for securities fraud, the government charged Mr. Yates with violating the Sarbanes-Oxley Act. Such a violation carries a statutory maximum sentence of 20 years' imprisonment. Prior to the Sarbanes-Oxley Act, the *typical* federal criminal statute utilized for the destruction of property to prevent government seizure had a statutory maximum of only 5 years' imprisonment (18 U.S.C. § 2232(a)). But with hundreds of thousands of *federal* criminal laws on the books, it is not surprising that the same conduct can fall within the scope of many federal criminal statutes with varying statutory maximums, allowing for a significant degree of ambiguity in sentencing.

Ultimately, a jury found Mr. Yates guilty. Despite the fact that the three missing fish were going to be destroyed by federal officers upon their arrival at port anyway, the government asked the trial judge to sentence Mr. Yates to between 21 and 27 months' imprisonment (Yates v. United States, 2015). This range was derived from the United States Sentencing Guidelines—a set of policies for those convicted of federal crimes, which are distilled into a table setting forth ranges of months of imprisonment. The sentencing judge rejected the government's request and instead exercised his discretion to vary below the advisory sentencing guideline range by sentencing Mr. Yates to 30 days' incarceration at the local jail.

Heeding my client's unwavering desire to challenge his conviction, I represented him in the federal appellate court and, ultimately, before the Supreme Court of the United States in 2015. The justices intensely questioned both sides for an hour, attempting to reconcile the use of the Sarbanes-Oxley Act (2002) to punish the destruction of *fish*, as opposed to electronic or paper records or documents. In one striking exchange, Justice Samuel Alito pressed the assistant solicitor general about the application of the 20-year statutory maximum sentence, inquiring if the total sentence for the destruction of three fish under that statute would be 20 years' total imprisonment or 20 years' imprisonment per each of the three-missing fish, that is, 60 years' imprisonment. Remarkably, the assistant solicitor general's response was *60 years*.

The *Yates* case illustrates, among other things, the need for a more uniform, regimented approach to fashioning punishment. Mr. Yates had the good fortune of having his case assigned to a sentencing judge, now one of my colleagues, who questioned the reasonableness of serious punishment for such a peculiar use of a criminal statute for the charged conduct. I recall the sentencing judge straining to understand the need to sentence Mr. Yates to the 2 years' imprisonment requested by the federal prosecutor, let alone the 20 years' imprisonment *per destroyed fish* suggested by the assistant solicitor general during the oral argument. Ultimately, the judge decided that a sentence of 30 days in the local jail was sufficient, but not greater than necessary, to serve the purposes of the federal sentencing set forth by Congress in 18 U.S.C. § 3553(a). But had Mr. Yates's case been assigned to a different judge, his punishment might have been very different. Without clear, simple guidelines within which all judges can systematically approach cases, pure chance—based on the randomly assigned sentencing judge—can have a determinative effect in whether an individual receives 30 days or 20 years for the same conduct. This and myriad other reasons underscore the need for evidence-based research to guide meaningful criminal justice reform in the United States.

The Role of a Federal Sentencing Judge

In Federalist No. 78, Alexander Hamilton stated that a judge has "neither FORCE nor WILL, but merely judgment". This refrain is no truer than in the realm of sentencing. When pronouncing the punishment of an offender, a sentencing judge is not at liberty to impose, for example, a lesser term of incarceration than that prescribed by Congress merely because the judge believes that such a term is what the sentence *should be*. Congress, through its passage of 18 U.S.C. § 3553(a), has provided federal judges one overarching parameter for fashioning a criminal sentence—that the sentence they impose must be "sufficient but not greater than necessary" to serve the statutory purposes of sentencing. This statutory directive is not so simple in practice, however, because Congress has arrayed many, often competing, purposes of sentencing. It mandates that the sentence imposed must reflect the seriousness of the offense; promote respect for the law; provide just punishment; afford adequate deterrence; protect the public from future crimes for the defendant; and provide the defendant with needed educational or vocational training, medical care, or other correctional treatment in the most effective manner (18 U.S.C. § 3553(a)(2)). Judges must also consider the nature and characteristics of the offense, the criminal history and characteristics of the defendant, the kinds of sentences that are available, the need to avoid unwarranted sentence disparities among defendants with similar records who have been found guilty of similar conduct, and the need to provide restitution to any victims of the offense (18 U.S.C. § 3553(a)(1)).

To satisfy this statutory mandate, federal sentencing judges review lengthy pre-sentence investigation reports prepared by the United States Probation Office, which lay out the personal history and criminal background of the defendants. The sentencing judges also review the applicable sentencing guideline calculation and corresponding guideline range and hear live testimony from relevant parties such as victims, those supportive of the defendant, and mental health professionals, where appropriate. It is a difficult task. It is doubtful that there is a single sentencing judge who would not say that he or she strives to fashion an even-handed, reasonable sentence based on the facts before him or her for every criminal defendant he or she sentences. But how one judge fashions a sentence for a particular offender may not be how another judge would fashion it, even if the judges are in the same courthouse, federal district, or state.

Consider, for example, the myriad ways in which a hypothetical federal judge might sentence someone similarly situated to Mr. Yates for the destruction of three fish, bearing in mind that the sentencing guidelines yielded a recommended range of 21 to 27 months' imprisonment. Would the judge issue a sentence of 30 days, like Mr. Yates received? How about a sentence of 5 years' imprisonment, the maximum penalty for the typical federal crime charged for the destruction of property to prevent its seizure by the federal government? Or perhaps the judge would sentence Mr. Yates to 20 years' imprisonment, the stated statutory maximum for the charged offense? Or maybe even 60 years' imprisonment—20 years' imprisonment per each of the three missing fish? And therein lies the central challenge: How do we address these potential sentencing disparities but allow for a sentencing judge's discretion?

Federal Sentencing Guidelines

Since 1987, the predominant solution to sentencing disparities has been the federal sentencing guidelines, a manual of non-binding recommendations from the U.S. Sentencing Commission that inform judges' sentencing practices. As a general matter, the guidelines advise judges to impose terms of incarceration, probation, supervised release, community confinement, home detention, community service, or some combination thereof. But the guidelines specify that only certain offenders may receive non-carceral alternatives depending on the category of offense with which they are charged. And under the current guidelines system, there is little room for individualization based on the characteristics of the offender or the unique circumstances of the offense. Probation, for example, is available only for those offenders whose offenses fall into the least serious category of the sentencing table – crimes like theft, fraud, forgery where the loss did not exceed $6500, trespass, criminal infringement of copyright, removing a vehicle's license plate, receipt of unauthorized compensation, or failing to report a campaign contribution. Once an offender crosses the threshold into a more serious area of the sentencing table based on category of offense and the defendant's criminal history the guidelines suggest that only incarceration is appropriate. This one-size-fits-all approach, however, often fails to adequately appreciate the complexities surrounding the individual offender and offense. Thus, there remains a need to reconsider this approach.

The intellectual roots of the sentencing guidelines date back to the early 1970s when U.S. District Judge Marvin E. Frankel delivered a series of influential lectures critiquing what he perceived as systemically unfair sentencing disparities. Judge Frankel was concerned that there was no uniform way for judges to select a sentence within the vast range of sentencing possibilities that existed, there were no laws acting as a check on a sentencing judge's decisions, and there was no manner of comparing sentencing disparities between defendants, judges, courts, and districts. To resolve these issues of ambiguity and unpredictability, Judge Frankel called for determinative sentencing, aided by the creation of an administrative body to promulgate, monitor, and revise presumptively applicable guidelines for sentencing (Tonry, 2019).

Judge Frankel's suggestions led to a bipartisan Congressional effort to push for the creation of a United States Sentencing Commission. Soon after, in 1987, the Sentencing Commission drafted the United States Sentencing Guidelines with the aim of standardizing the judicial decision-making process and limiting disparate and unequal treatment between defendants who had committed similar crimes and had similar criminal histories. As originally designed, the guidelines provided a *binding* range of punishments for judges to follow in sentencing, limiting the free-wheeling judicial discretion of which Judge Frankel had complained. Under that model, the guidelines limited judges both in terms of the length of the punishment they were required to impose, as well as the form such punishment was supposed to take.

The guidelines quickly came under intense scrutiny after more than 200 federal trial judges found the guidelines unconstitutional (Nagel, 1990). In a 1988 case, *U.S. v. Mistretta*, the guidelines were challenged by a criminal defendant, who alleged that the Commission's predetermined sentences were a violation of the separation of powers. The Supreme Court, however, held that the guidelines were constitutional because they did not grant the Commission excessive legislative power or "place the [C]ommission in the judicial branch". With the Supreme Court's stamp of approval, the guidelines were applied, perhaps reluctantly, by federal sentencing judges throughout the 1990s. Many criticized the guidelines as too severe, overly complicated, uncompromising, and difficult to apply. A 1991 study carried out by the U.S. Sentencing Commission found that more than 40 percent of judges believed that the guidelines were inflexible and that they overburdened the judiciary (General Accounting Office [GAO], 1992). One third of federal judges surveyed thought that the guidelines overburdened the federal prison system (USSC, 2018).

One of the most disturbing trends to emerge after *Mistretta* was the frequency with which judges took to imposing sentences greater than the guidelines' range based on facts not presented to the jury in the first instance. In one such case, *U.S. v. Booker*, a federal judge sentenced a convicted drug dealer to a 30-year sentence based on additional facts that had not been presented to a jury and proved beyond a reasonable doubt. If the judge had relied only on the facts presented to the jury, however, the maximum allowable punishment would have been 9 years less. The case made its way to the Supreme Court, and the Court found the sentence imposed to be an unconstitutional violation of the defendant's Sixth Amendment right to a jury trial. Writing for the majority, Justice Stephen Breyer, who was a member of the original U.S. Sentencing Commission, held that 18 U.S.C. § 3553(b)(1), which *mandated* that federal judges, absent a few exceptions, impose a sentence within the sentencing range prescribed by U.S. Sentencing Guidelines, was unconstitutional. To thwart the dissolution of the Sentencing Guidelines model, the Supreme Court remediated the sentencing statute by excising the provision that made the guidelines mandatory. It was this compulsory nature of the guidelines which the defendant in *Booker* claimed rendered the guidelines unconstitutional. The high end of the guidelines range should be merely *advisory*, Justice Breyer wrote, in order to maintain consistency with the Sentencing Commission's original intention to make it more difficult to adjust sentences *upward*. Justice Breyer then called on Congress to rework the sentencing statutes. Two decades have elapsed since *Booker*, and Congress has yet to revisit the federal statutory sentencing scheme.

As an assistant federal public defender, I initially viewed *Booker* as a positive development. I thought it freed up sentencing judges to use their discretion to fashion a sentence for the *individual* defendant rather than simply sentencing a defendant to a one-size-fits-all term of incarceration based on a range of months' incarceration specified within a box of a sentencing table. It allowed me to present to the sentencing judge—without the judge's hands being tied from a mandatory sentencing scheme—evidence about, for example, the criminal defendant's mental illness, lack of educational or employment opportunities, drug and alcohol addictions, or abusive upbringing while still acknowledging the harm that defendant's conduct had caused the victim and the public.

But, as it turned out, evidence-based research demonstrated that the post-*Booker* advisory Sentencing Guidelines scheme created even more sentencing disparities throughout the country, resurfacing many of the concerns that Judge Frankel outlined in the 1970s. Studies have found that even after application of the *advisory* sentencing guideline range mandated by the Supreme Court in *Booker*, Black offenders were receiving sentences 5 percent higher than white offenders, and the average length of federal sentences varied dramatically between districts for similarly situated offenders convicted of the same crimes under the advisory Sentencing Guidelines scheme (Department of Justice [DOJ], 2006).

Additionally, research has confirmed that 62 percent of federal trial judges believe that most mandatory minimum sentences set forth by Congress are too severe (Mauer, 2010). More than half of surveyed judges expressed agreement with the contention that Congress should amend the existing federal statutory framework to give judges more sentencing options and allow broader ranges on the Sentencing Table (USSC, 2010). It is not that mandatory minimum sentences should not be required for certain offenses or offenders. But instead, that, from a criminal justice reform standpoint, the criminal justice system may be better served if Congress specified additional circumstances that permit a sentencing judge to sentence an individual below that mandatory minimum sentence, if appropriate.

Today, nearly four decades after the Sentencing Guidelines were first implemented and two decades after *Booker*, evidence-based research has confirmed that neither mandatory nor advisory guidelines seem to deliver the fair, uniform sentences envisioned by Judge Frankel and the early proponents of the Sentencing Commission. The Sentencing Guidelines, as they stand today, are not the cure for disproportionality and sentencing disparities among federal judges and across federal jurisdictions. As Judge John Coughenour on the Western District of Washington aptly stated:

> The thing that really hit me hard with the Sentencing Reform Act was that this art form – I considered sentencing to be an art and not a science – Congress tried to convert it into a science. And it's not a science. It's a human being dealing with other human beings. And it shouldn't be done by computers (Van Meter, 2016, para. 34).

Possible Reforms

Having identified some challenges presented by criminal statutes attaching mandatory minimum and maximum incarcerative sentences, and the existing federal sentencing statutes and Sentencing Guidelines framework, this chapter now turns to potential changes to our federal sentencing scheme.

A. New Federal Sentencing Scheme

As an initial matter, it is important to stress that effective sentencing reform can be accomplished without discarding the existing Sentencing Guidelines framework in its entirety. To this end, one suggestion, proposed by Chief Judge William H. Pryor of the United States Court of Appeals for the Eleventh Circuit, a former commissioner of the Sentencing Commission, is to adopt simpler, presumptive guidelines, where sentences of incarceration above a guideline range would have to be proven to a jury beyond a reasonable doubt, should an offender plead not guilty and proceed to trial. As Chief Judge Pryor has explained, "To increase certainty and proportionality and avoid unwarranted disparities, we need guidelines that judges will follow except when substantial and compelling reasons based on offense or offender characteristics warrant a downward departure".[5] Noting Judge Frankel's original complaints about sentencing, Chief Judge Pryor suggests that many of the post-*Booker* sentencing disparities that have emerged demonstrate that sentencing judges' "unrestrained ability to consider offender characteristics," without any sort of standardized guidelines within which to evaluate these perceptions of mitigating or aggravating traits.

Some federal judges have critiqued Judge Pryor's suggestions. For example, retired United States District Judge Nancy Gertner has written that eliminating consideration of individualized offender characteristics would blur meaningful distinctions between offenders who might be juveniles, addicts, or mentally disabled (Gertner, 2016). Other federal judges have also challenged Judge Pryor's proposal, arguing that disparities in sentencing are not a result of excessive flexibility afforded to sentencing judges, but rather, are consequences of statutory mandatory minimums and maximums, which allow law enforcement and prosecutors to essentially determine the sentence imposed with their enforcement and charging choices

(Baron-Evans & Patton, 2017). These individuals argue that presumptive sentencing guidelines would fail in the same way as the original, mandatory guidelines scheme because mandatory minimum and maximum sentences effectively obviate judicial discretion to select within an otherwise applicable guideline range.

I, in this early stage of my role as a sentencing judge, agree that the most viable way to minimize sentencing disparities and maintain proportionality is to create a far less complicated and confusing Sentencing Guidelines scheme with wider sentencing ranges for my consideration. I believe that the impact of Congress's utilization of mandatory minimum and maximum sentences may impede the full impact of a more discretionary guidelines construct (Larkin, 2013).[6] But these are pure policy issues reserved to the elected representatives of Congress, not federal judges.

It is undeniable that Congress's prescription of mandatory minimum or maximum sentences for certain crimes and certain offenders with prior convictions has contributed to the upward trend of incarceration rates in federal correctional facilities. Turning back to my former client, Mr. Yates, consider the strain on the public's resources had he been sentenced to a statutory maximum of 20 or 60 years' imprisonment or to upwards of 27 months' imprisonment as recommended by the post-*Booker* advisory guidelines system. In the mandatory minimum sentence context, sentencing judges must, absent very limited circumstances, sentence an offender to no less than what Congress provides, even if the originally calculated guideline range resulted in a far lower minimum sentence. The result of such constraints is often a significant human toll. For example, I have found myself duty-bound to sentence a 50-year-old relapsed drug addict in renal failure and with severe mental deficiencies to 21 years' imprisonment under the mandatory minimum statutory penalties because he possessed a firearm during the commission of three convenience store robberies. At the cost of approximately $108 per day to incarcerate an offender in a federal correctional institution, the sentence I was statutorily mandated to impose will cost the taxpayers $826,665. This offender had no violent criminal history, and he stole less than a total of $200. His prior offenses included drug-related and property crimes to support his drug habit, and he had no prior drug or mental health treatment interventions. Again, I, like all federal judges, must follow the sentences mandated by the elected representatives of the citizens of the United States in Congress.

This is not to say that all mandatory minimum sentences are a bad thing; for example, the justice system might lose public trust if it were to allow judges to grant negligible sentences to individuals convicted of violent crimes, heinous sex trafficking, or child pornography offenses, to name only a few. And I have no problem sentencing individuals far above the mandatory minimum prescribed by Congress, where I have the discretion to do so and the situation calls for it. The point is simply that mandatory minimum sentences can unnecessarily tie up taxpayer dollars and constrain the sentencing judge to fashion a sentence appropriate for a particular individual, where other alternatives would protect the public and satisfy the other purposes of sentencing. In the following, a few such alternatives are laid out and assessed. I invite both federal and state sentencing judges to consider these options should their jurisdictions permit.

B. Implementation of Evidence-Based Sentencing Options

i. Work Release

Ample empirical research has found that work release programs – programs where offenders live in correctional or community-based facilities and work in the community – are one of the most effective means of reducing an offender's potential for recidivism. For example, a 2015 study of more than 40,000 inmates released from Florida Department of Corrections found that those who participated in work release programs had dramatically lower levels of recidivism as compared with a control group of inmates who did not participate in such a program (DOJ, 2015). Additionally, a study from the Federal Bureau of Prisons' Post Release Employment Project found that work release programs significantly reduced offender misconduct while incarcerated (Duwe & McNeeley, 2018). And a study of Minnesota's work release program found that the program tended to reduce the risk that an offender would reoffend by roughly 16 percent (Duwe, 2015; Northcutt-Bohmert & Duwe, 2012). By reducing the likelihood of recidivism, reducing the likelihood of offender misconduct in prison, and increasing an offender's employability and likely wages, work release programs have been estimated to have a return on investment of $11.19 per $1.00 spent on the program (Aos & Drake, 2013).

ii. Electronic Monitoring

Electronic monitoring programs are another cost-effective alternative to incarceration with positive impacts in reducing recidivism. Offenders are released into their communities with ankle bracelets tracking their GPS locations to conform with a schedule established by the sentencing judge and the probation office. In an assessment of electronic monitoring in Florida, which compared roughly 5,000 medium and high-risk offenders on electronic monitoring with 267,000 offenders not subject to electronic monitoring, researchers found that electronic monitoring reduced offenders' recidivism risk by roughly 31 percent (National Institute of Justice [NIJ], 2011). At least three studies have shown that electronic monitoring leads to reductions in re-arrest rates for high risk offenders placed on parole as well as for those placed on electronic monitoring as an alternative to incarceration in the first instance (Bales et al., 2010; Gies et al., 2013; Padgett et al., 2006). Other studies have found that for those under 30 years old, serving a sentence of electronic monitoring rather than imprisonment reduces the probability of reoffending by 43 percentage points. Each offender who serves his sentence under electronic monitoring rather than in prison saves the public nearly $30,000 on reduced supervision and future court and prison costs (Williams & Weatherburn, 2021).

iii. Alternatives for Offenders with Mental Illness

One of the sentencing areas most in need of reform is the realm of alternatives to incarceration for individuals with serious mental illness. At present, the Sentencing Guidelines provide that "community confinement", which includes residence in a mental health facility, can be imposed as a condition of probation or supervised release but not as an alternative to incarceration and not for a period of more than 6 months (United States Sentencing Guidelines [U.S.S.G] § 5F1.1). Thus, judges often have no choice but to sentence offenders with serious mental illness to a term of incarceration in a classic prison setting, even where such offenders might be better served by 24-hour confinement to an in-patient treatment center. Today, while people with serious mental illness make up .3 percent of the U.S. population, they make up 4 percent of the federal prison population (U.S. Government Accountability Office [U.S. GAO], 2018) and about 10 to 25 percent of state prisoners (Collier, 2014; Maurer, 2018).

Incarcerating these mentally ill, high-need individuals is both expensive for taxpayers and evidence-based research has found the results to be largely ineffective. In 2016, for example, the Federal Bureau of Prisons spent about $72 million on psychology services, $5.6 million on psychotropic drugs, and $4.1 million on mental health care in residential reentry centers. And, as countless studies have shown, prison can exacerbate the symptoms of serious mental illness, leaving those affected by disease more likely to reoffend when they are released from incarceration (Quant & Jones, 2021). Judges need more options for sentencing offenders with serious mental illness so that the recurring cycle of recidivism and associated financial costs to the public by those with serious mental illness can be avoided. If judges have the option for closely monitored in-patient or outpatient mental health treatment as part of an offender's sentence, the research supports that the treatment will be more impactful for that offender than mental health treatment received while incarcerated in a traditional prison setting.

Many states have attempted to remediate this problem by developing mental health courts, which are focused on directing offenders with serious mental illness toward court-supervised, community-based treatment programs. New York, for example, has a mental health court program allowing judges, with the assistance of mental health professionals, to perform complex risk assessments that take the offender's mental health into account, identify treatment options for the offender, and establish long-term connections to the mental health system rather than to prisons. The National Institute of Justice recently studied New York's mental health courts and found that an offender's participation in mental health courts reduces the likelihood of re-arrest by nearly 50 percent and the likelihood of reconviction by nearly 30 percent (Center for Court Innovation, n.d.).

Conclusion

In a sentencing, the criminal defendant, his or her family and friends, the victims and their families and friends, and members of the public come together in a courtroom to observe a sentencing judge make a complex decision that will deprive someone of liberty and protect the public, among other things. Sentencing judges are highly trained and experienced professionals who encounter individuals from all walks of life. They should be afforded discretion in fashioning a sentence in conformity with the applicable law, not hamstrung into doling out a one-size-fits-all, statutorily mandated sentence.

Still, I know that there are not superpowers sewn into the robe I wear while I perform my judicial duties. As such, judges cannot be left completely to their own devices to consider any factor that strikes them as salient at the time of sentencing an individual. There must be some sort of middle ground. Perhaps a simpler sentencing guidelines system with broader ranges of incarceration and options for non-incarcerative sentences for more categories of offenders is an appropriate fix. This is a difficult problem that will require Congressional intervention to ameliorate. But using the evidence-based research commissioned by the stakeholders of the criminal justice system, Congress and state legislatures have the information they need to make meaningful sentencing reforms.

Until that reform occurs, however, judges can strive to avoid unfair disparities in their sentencing practices by engaging in simple self-monitoring. By collecting data of their sentencing decisions and reviewing that data with an eye toward any unintended or aberrant sentencing trends, judges can try to self-correct and engage in more empirically grounded, equitable sentencing practices. It is incumbent upon all three branches of government to not delay on this issue any further. Otherwise, the warehousing of offenders will continue to eat away at taxpayers' dollars and divert increasingly greater percentages of both the federal and state governments' budgets from other valuable projects.

Notes

1 In 1980, the federal prison population was just 25,000. Today, it has ballooned to 156,000.
2 This is all the more troublesome considering that incarcerated individuals who receive educational and vocational training are significantly less likely to recidivate than those that do not.

3 Broadly speaking, over-criminalization is defined as the "abuse of criminal law to address every societal problem and punish every mistake." It is the overuse of the federal criminal code to reach an extremely broad range of conduct that most Americans would likely not recognize as criminal or deserving of sanction.
4 Although this article is authored by both John Badalamenti and Lindsay Holcomb, for syntax and overall readability purposes, the first person, I, is used throughout this chapter and refers to John Badalamenti's observations. Furthermore, John Badalamenti's observations are his alone and do not represent the opinion of the Federal Judiciary, other judicial officers, the U.S. government, or any other person or entity.
5 Remarks at Scalia Law School, George Mason University (ussc.gov).
6 The Sentencing Guidelines, however, must comply with acts of Congress. See, for example, Dorsey v. United States, 132 S. Ct. 2321, 2326 (2012); Neal v. United States, 516 U.S. 284, 289–90 (1996). One result of the 1986 statute was to tie the hands of the Sentencing Commission regarding the minimum sentences that could be imposed for trafficking in crack.

References

Aos, S., & Drake, E. (2013). *Prison, police and programs: Evidence-based options that reduce crime and save money*. Olympia, WA: Washington State Institute for Public Policy.

Bales, W., Clark, C., Scaggs, S., Ensley, D., Coltharp, P., Singer, A., & Blomberg, T. (2016). An assessment of the effectiveness of prison work release programs on post-release recidivism and employment. Washington, DC: U.S. Department of Justice, National Institute of Justice. Retrieved from https://www.ncjrs.gov/pdffiles1/nij/grants/249845.pdf.

Bales, W., Mann, K., Blomberg, T., Gaes, G., Barrick, K., Dhungana, K., & McManus, B. (2010). A quantitative and qualitative assessment of electronic monitoring. Washington, DC: U.S. Department of Justice, National Institute of Justice. Retrieved from www.ncjrs.gov/pdffiles1/nij/grants/230530.pdf

Baron-Evans, A., & Patton, D. (2016). A Response to Judge Pryor's Proposal to "Fix" the Guidelines: A Cure Worse than the Disease. *Federal Sentencing Reporter*, *29* (2–3), 104–125.

BBC News. (n.d.). *World Prison Populations*. http://news.bbc.co.uk/2/shared/spl/hi/uk/06/prisons/html/nn2page1.stm.

Bonczar, T. P., & Beck, A. J. (1997). Lifetime likelihood of going to state or federal prison (Report No. NCJ 160092).Washington, DC: U.S. Department of Justice, Bureau of Justice Statistics.

Breyer, C. & Reeves, D. (2021, January 13). *Inter-district Differences in Federal Sentencing Practices Across Districts from 2005–2017*. United States Sentencing Commission. Retrieved from https://www.ussc.gov/research/research-reports/inter-district-differences-federal-sentencing-practices.

Center for Justice Innovation. (n.d.). *Brooklyn Mental Health Court*. www.courtinnovation.org/programs/brooklyn-mental-health-court.

Coffee, J. C. (1991). Does "unlawful" mean "criminal"?: Reflections on the disappearing tort/crime distinction in American law. *Boston University Law Review*, *71*(2), 193–246.

Collier, L. (2014). Incarceration Nation. *Monitor on Psychology*, *45*(9).

Davis, L. M., Bozick, R., Steele, J., Saunders, J., & Miles, J. (2013, August 22). Education and Vocational Training in Prisons Reduces Recidivism, Improves Job Outlook. *Rand Corporation, 22*. www.rand.org/news/press/2013/08/22.html.

Department of Justice (2006). *Fact Sheet: The Impact of United States V. Booker on Federal Sentencing* [Fact sheet]. https://www.justice.gov/archive/opa/docs/United_States_v_Booker_Fact_Sheet.pdf

Duwe, G. (2015). The Benefits of Keeping Idle Hands Busy: An Outcome Evaluation of a Prisoner Reentry Employment Program. *Crime and Delinquency*, *61*(4), 559–586.

Duwe, G., & McNeeley, S. (2020). The Effects of Prison Labor on Institutional Misconduct, Postprison Employment, and Recidivism. *Corrections: Policy, Practice and Research*, *5*(2), 89–108.

Equal Justice Initiative. (2018, December 20). *Bipartisan Support for Criminal Justice Reform Still Strong*. https://eji.org/news/bipartisan-support-criminal-justice-reform-still-strong/.

Federal Bureau of Prisons. (2021). *Population Statistics*. www.bop.gov/mobile/about/population_statistics.jsp#old_pops.

Gertner, N. (2016). A Critique of Judge Pryor's Proposals. *Federal Sentencing Reporter, 29*(2/3), 131–133.

Gies, S. V., Gainey, R., Cohen, M. I., Healy, E., Yeide, M., Bekelman, A., & Bobnis, A. (2013) *Monitoring high-risk gang offenders with GPS technology: An evaluation of the California supervision*

program final report. Washington, DC: U.S. Department of Justice, National Institute of Justice. Retrieved from www.ncjrs.gov/pdffiles1/nij/grants/244164.pdf
General Accounting Office (1992). *Sentencing Guidelines: Central Questions Remain Unanswered.* Washington, D.C: U.S. General Accounting Office. (GAO/GGD-92-93).
Larkin, P. J. (2013). Clemency, parole, good-time credits, and crowded prisons: reconsidering early release. *Georgetown Journal of Law and Public Policy*, *11*(1), 1–49.
Larkin, P. J. (2014). Crack cocaine, congressional inaction, and equal protection. *Harvard Journal & Public Policy*, *37*(1), 241–294.
Mauer, M. (2010). The impact of mandatory minimums in federal sentencing. *Judicature*, *94*(1), 6–40.
Mistretta v. United States, 488 U.S. 361 (1989).
Nagel, I. H. (1990). Foreword: Structuring Sentencing Discretion: The New Federal Sentencing Guidelines. *The Journal of Criminal Law & Criminology*, *80*(4), 883–943.
National Institute of Justice (2011). *Electronic Monitoring Reduces Recidivism: In-short – Toward Criminal Justice Solutions*. Washington, D.C. U.S. Department of Justice, Office of Justice Programs, NCJ 234460.
Northcutt-Bohmert, M., & Duwe, G. (2012). Minnesota's Affordable Homes Program: Evaluating the Effects of a Prison Work Program on Recidivism, Employment and Cost Avoidance. *Criminal Justice Policy Review*, *23*(3), 327–351.
Padgett, K. G., Bales, W. D., & Blomberg, T. G. (2006). Under surveillance: An empirical test of the effectiveness and consequences of electronic monitoring. *Criminology & Public Policy*, *5*(1), 61–91
Quant, K. R., & Jones, A. (2021, May 13). Research Roundup: Incarceration can cause lasting damage to mental health. *Prison Policy Initiative*. https://www.prisonpolicy.org/blog/2021/05/13/mentalhealthimpacts/.
The Heritage Foundation. (n.d.). *Overcriminalization*. Retrieved (2022, June 16) at https://www.heritage.org/crime-and-justice/heritage-explains/overcriminalization
Tonry, M. (2019). Fifty years of American sentencing reform: Nine lessons. *Crime and Justice*, *48*, 1–34.
U.S. Const. art. I, §§ 3, 8.
U.S. Dept. of Justice, Office of Justice Programs, National Institute of Justice. (2011, September). *Electronic Monitoring Reduces Recidivism*. www.ojp.gov/pdffiles1/nij/234460.pdf.
U.S. Government Accountability Office (2018). *Federal prisons: Information on inmates with serious mental illness and strategies to reduce recidivism*. Washington, D.C: U.S. General Accounting Office. (GAO-18-182).
U.S. Government Publishing Office (2020). *A Budget for a Better America: Promises Kept. Taxpayers First*. U.S. Government Publishing Office.
U.S. Sentencing Commission (2010). *Results of Survey of United States District Judges January 2010 through March 2010*. Office of General Counsel United States Sentencing Commission. https://www.ussc.gov/sites/default/files/pdf/research-and-publications/research-projects-and-surveys/surveys/20100608_Judge_Survey.pdf
U.S. Sentencing Commission (2018). *An Overview of the Federal Sentencing Guidelines*. Office of General Counsel United States Sentencing Commission. https://www.ussc.gov/sites/default/files/pdf/about/overview/Overview_Federal_Sentencing_Guidelines.pdf
U.S. Sentencing Commission (2019). *Quick Facts: Federal Offenders in Prison* [Fact sheet]. www.ussc.gov/sites/default/files/pdf/research-and-publications/quick-facts/BOP_May2019.pdf.
U.S.S.G § 5F1.1.
United States v. Booker, 543 U.S. 220 (2005).
Van Meter, M. (2016, February 25). One judge makes the case for judgment. *The Atlantic*. https://www.theatlantic.com/politics/archive/2016/02/one-judge-makes-the-case-for-judgment/463380/
Williams, J. & Weatherburn, D. (2021). Can electronic monitoring reduce reoffending? *The Review of Economics and Statistics*, *104*(2), 232–245.
Yates v. United States, 574 U.S. 528, 569–570 (2015).
18 U.S.C. § 1519.
18 U.S.C. § 2232(a).
18 U.S.C. § 3553(a)(1), (3)-(7) (1987).
18 U.S.C. § 3553(a)(2)(A)-(D) (1987).

30
PROBLEM-SOLVING COURTS
A Brief Overview of Judicial Interventions

Kathleen A. Moore, Melissa Carlson and Kelsey Greenfield

Introduction

Overview of Problem-Solving Courts and Their Effectiveness

In 1989, Florida started the national problem-solving court movement by creating the first drug court in the United States in Miami–Dade County. Other types of problem-solving court dockets subsequently followed using the drug court model and were implemented to assist individuals experiencing a variety of issues such as substance use, mental illness, domestic violence, child abuse/neglect, and homelessness. Initially developed to address the problem of substance use, problem-solving courts have since expanded to address various concerns and treat an array of target populations with the goal to address underlying issues that may have caused an individual to commit a crime (Miller et al., 2020). Although not entirely a new concept, modern problem-solving courts are the product of the War on Drugs, causing prison over-crowding and an influx of repeat offenders (Miller et al., 2020; Rottman & Bowman, 2014; Thielo, Cullen, Burton, et al., 2019).

A clear definition of what constitute a problem-solving court does not exist (Rottman & Bowman, 2014); Miller et al., 2020); however, these courts typically address two categories: (1) a specific social issue (i.e., substance use) and (2) a specific target population (i.e., veterans). Problem-solving courts can be incorporated into criminal court as a diversionary program or a post-conviction sentence requirement. When compared to traditional courts, problem-solving courts can generate better and more cost-effective outcomes (Rottman & Bowman, 2014).

Problem-solving courts have also demonstrated significant reductions in the rate of recidivism (Miller et al., 2020). A meta-analysis of problem-solving courts found that participants within these courts experienced reduced recidivism rates relative to individuals who had not participated in a problem-solving court (Trood et al., 2021). There does not appear to be a specific type of problem-solving court that is more successful than others, and the success of the program is usually dependent on the individual program components itself (Kaiser, 2020). However, courts that offer more types of services have a higher rate of participant completion (Kaiser, 2020). Overall, findings suggest that problem-solving courts generally work, but variation of success can be seen based on the internal processes of individual courts. Table 30.1 highlights various examples of specialty court programs.

DOI: 10.4324/9781003219286-36

Table 30.1 Examples of Specialty Courts

Adult Drug Court (Florida Office of State Courts Administrator, 2021d)	Adult post-adjudicatory prison diversion drug courts address underlying substance use disorders for prison-bound participants to reduce crime and restore lives and families. These courts operate based on the national drug court model in efforts to reduce state prison costs by identifying and diverting felony offenders with a diagnosed substance use disorder into drug court. Some key components include: • Integration of alcohol and drug services into justice system case processing • Continuum of services • Testing for abstinence • Ongoing judicial interaction • Monitoring and evaluation for program effectiveness • Interdisciplinary education • Partnerships with stakeholders
Veterans Treatment Court (Florida Office of State Courts Administrator, 2021b)	Veterans treatment courts are designed to accommodate service members with complex treatment needs related to substance use, mental health, trauma and/or post-traumatic stress disorder (PTSD), and traumatic brain injury (TBI). This type of court offers a unique component to its participants by connecting participating veterans with a veteran mentor. Identified mentors are suggested to be matched by military service branch and related experiences.
Adult Mental Health Court (Florida Office of State Courts Administrator, 2021c)	Adult mental health courts were created after the realization that repeat offenders cycling through drug courts were left with untreated serious mental illness. Mental health courts share the following goals in monitoring and effectively treating repeat offenders: • Improve public safety by reducing criminal recidivism • Improve quality of life of people with mental illnesses and increase treatment participation • Reduce court-related costs by providing alternative to incarceration
Family Dependency Treatment Court (Florida Office of State Courts Administrator, 2021a)	Family dependency treatment courts recognize a combination of traditional dependency court (timeliness, safety, permanency, and the general well-being of children) and adult drug court requirements (early identification, substance use disorder treatment, a non-adversarial approach, services for co-occurring concerns, frequent drug and alcohol testing, options for medication-assisted treatment [MAT], frequent judicial interactions, and incentives and sanctions). This unique combination allows court participants to focus on reunifying with their children while receiving appropriate substance use treatment. Courts are advised to establish permanency for the child within 12 months and include: • Foster care system • Family member or guardian • Participating dependency drug court parent (pending program completion and graduation)

Juvenile Drug Court (SAMHSA, 2020)	Juvenile drug courts were created to divert adolescents from incarceration by creating a program that includes treatment, court supervision, drug testing, and family or community linkages. In addition, the court tends to involve family members, coordination with school systems, and community partnerships.
DUI/DWI Court (Twelfth Judicial Circuit Court, 2023)	DUI/DWI courts are designed to address the needs of multiple DWI offenders with alcohol and/or substance use issues. The program is a stage approach in which offenders move through four intense phases over the period of 1 year: • Phase I: Orientation & Engagement • Phase II: Early Recovery • Phase III: Maintenance & Relapse Prevention • Phase IV: Continuance of Care & Commencement
Adult Reentry Court (Wolf, 2021)	Adult reentry courts allow community-based programs to oversee the transition from prison to parole supervision and to establish a seamless system of offender accountability and support services throughout the reentry process. Reentry courts provide incentives and sanctions, evidence-based practices, a wide variety of community resources, and strategies for transitioning from incarceration to the community.
Juvenile Mental Health Court (Thirteenth Judicial Circuit Court, 2021)	Juvenile mental health courts assist juveniles that have been found incompetent to proceed or if to address juveniles with behavioral or mental health issues. Provided services usually involve: • Mental health, family, substance use, and grief counseling • Anger management • Other therapeutic interventions

Adult Drug Courts

There are over 3,800 drug courts operating in the United States, about half of which are adult drug courts (National Drug Court Resource Center, 2021). Adult drug courts employ a program designed to reduce substance use relapse and criminal recidivism among individuals charged with or convicted of a crime through risk and needs assessment, judicial interaction, monitoring and supervision, graduated sanctions and incentives, treatment, and various rehabilitation services (U.S. Department of Justice, 2021). These programs utilize a multidisciplinary team that can include judges, prosecutors, defense attorneys, and treatment service professionals.

Prior research has demonstrated that adult drug court participants are less likely to cycle through the criminal justice system, and adult drug court graduates are less likely to reoffend than those who did not graduate the program (DeVall et al., 2017; Gibbs et al., 2019). It is unclear whether drug court programs benefit individuals who do not complete the program in its entirety, and employment, education, and age are all factors in successful completion of a drug court program (Gibbs & Lytle, 2020; DeVall et al., 2017). However, severe sentencing for participants who do not graduate drug court programs might be undermining any residual benefit of having participated in the program (Gibbs & Lytle, 2020).

The amount of time spent in a drug court program can significantly impact the outcome for participants. Research suggests that participants should spend between 12 and 16 months in a drug treatment court program before successful transition to graduation (Gibbs et al., 2019). The first 30 days of a program are vital in predicting a successful outcome, and participants who have a violation within the first 30 days of the program are less likely to graduate (Gibbs et al., 2019). Understanding the factors that can predict the likelihood of graduation can maximize the benefits of the program for the participants and community stakeholders (Jewell et al., 2017).

To promote success for drug court programs and its participants, the National Association of Drug Court Professionals (NADCP) developed the Ten Key Components for drug courts to adopt. The Ten Key Components provided a flexible implementation framework on the basic structure of drug court programs and offered suggestions on how participants would need to navigate through the program (Lutze & Wormer, 2014). NADCP assembled a committee of experts across the country to create the original Ten Key Components, which included drug court practitioners, representatives from courts, prosecution, public defense, treatment, pretrial services, case management, probation, court administration, and academia (U.S. Dept. of Justice, 1997). Drug courts that did not follow the structure of the Ten Key Components model experienced lower graduation rates, higher criminal recidivism, and lower cost savings (NADCP, 2018); Kearley & Gottfredson, 2020).

After 25 years of empirical study, the NADCP transitioned to a new model entitled the Ten Best Practice Standards for Adult Drug Court. The standards were drafted by a diverse, multidisciplinary committee composed of drug court practitioners, subject matter experts, researchers and evaluators, and state and federal policymakers (NADCP, 2018). Lutze and Wormer (2014) suggested that individuals can ensure the integrity of the drug court model by effectively working and managing the Ten Key Components. These new Ten Best Practice Standards should likewise be adopted and dispersed among key stakeholders responsible for the day-to-day operation of drug courts nationwide. Table 30.2 details each of the Ten Best Practice Standards for adult drug courts.

Table 30.2 Ten Best Practice Standards for Adult Drug Courts

Standard I Target Population	Drug courts are most effective for people who are addicted to intoxicating drugs or alcohol and are at a substantial risk for reoffending or have struggled to succeed in less intensive supervision or treatment programs. Candidates for drug court are assessed for eligibility using validated risk- and clinical-assessment tools.
Standard II Equity and Inclusion	Assurance of equal opportunity for everyone to participate and succeed, regardless of race, ethnicity, or gender. Drug courts take affirmative steps to detect and correct disproportionate census, inequitable services, and disparate outcomes involving those who have historically faced discrimination
Standard III Roles and Responsibilities of the Judge	A reduction in both crime and substance use when the judge is informed, approachable, fair, respectful, attentive, open, and caring. Judges are not trained to make clinical diagnoses or to select treatment interventions, which require expert input from treatment professionals to make treatment-related decisions.
Standard IV Incentives, Sanctions, and Therapeutic Adjustments	Behavior change strategies are used that are evidence based, fair, and consistently administered. Jail is not used when participants who are fully compliant with treatment struggle to remain abstinent. Instead, therapeutic adjustments are used to respond to continued substance use.
Standard V Substance Use Disorder Treatment	A continuum of evidence-based treatment services is provided, including medication-assisted treatment in combination with counseling and other psychosocial therapies as recommended by a qualified clinician.
Standard VI Complementary Treatment and Social Services	Delivery of additional mental health treatment; trauma-informed services; criminal-thinking interventions; counseling; and medical, vocational, housing, and educational services are given as needed, along with education on ways to prevent and manage overdose, including by administering the overdose reversal medication naloxone.
Standard VII Drug and Alcohol Testing	The frequency of random drug testing is maintained as the participant advances through program phases. Frequency is only reduced during the latter part of the final phase, when the participant is preparing for program completion.
Standard VIII Multidisciplinary Team	The drug court team consists of a judge, program coordinator, prosecutor, defense attorney, community supervision officer, treatment representative, and law enforcement officer and when each of these members consistently attends drug court status meetings
Standard IX Census and Caseloads	If evidence suggests that program census or practitioner caseload sizes are preventing best practices from being consistently implemented, the drug court team develops a corrective action plan and timeline to correct deficiencies and evaluate the success of remedial actions.
Standard X Monitoring and Evaluation	Drug courts monitor and evaluate their adherence to best practice standards at least annually.

(NADCP, 2018)

Adult Drug Court Case Example: Hillsborough County, Florida

The state of Florida currently has 125 drug courts in operation, including 52 adult, 31 veteran, 20 juvenile, 13 dependency, 4 DWI, and 1 Marchman Act (National Drug Court Resource Center, 2021). Circuit Judge Donald C. Evans began the first post-adjudication drug court in Florida in May of 1994. This court was and still is designed to treat and help aid individuals within the community whose substance use or issues with alcohol have resulted in being charged with a third-degree felony.

The Thirteenth Judicial Circuit Court of Hillsborough County established its first adult drug court division (Division "Y") in 1994 and has continued to receive state funding through administrative orders in 1997, 1998, 2004, 2010, and 2020. These administrative orders have equipped key stakeholders with updated procedures related to court definitions, division processes, eligibility criteria, plea definitions, violation of probation (VOP) transfer methods and requirements, and identification of acting county court judge and the drug court oversight committee. The administrative office of the courts, the Thirteenth Judicial Circuit, has also funded three full-time employees working exclusively as court specialists within the Adult Drug Court Division.

The Hillsborough County adult drug court includes the following key stakeholders: (1) drug court judge, (2) drug court specialists, (3) Public Defender's Office, (4) State Attorney's Office, (5) Department of Corrections, and (6) community treatment providers. Each stakeholder is provided with the foundation of gaining the knowledge needed to initiate appropriate planning processes for the adult drug court participant, is aware of the serious impacts of substance use and mental health, and seeks to become an advocate by utilizing their role in the court and within the community.

Florida's problem-solving courts, including the Thirteenth Judicial Circuit, embody five defining elements within the justice system process. This includes providing a broad-based team of justice system stakeholders, commitment to offering alternative litigation process, continuum of individualized treatment services (evidence-based practices), judicial leadership and interaction for monitoring compliance and progress, and responses to participant compliance both for incentives and sanctions and to promote both public safety and participant success.

The Hillsborough County Adult Drug Court Division has continued its commitment to appropriately executing the Ten Key Components of Drug Court and has seamlessly adapted to using the Ten Best Practice Standards for Adult Drug Court. In 2017, The Florida Mental Health Institute (FMHI) at the University of South Florida (USF) was tasked by the Thirteenth Judicial Circuit to complete a needs assessment of its problem-solving courts. The purpose of this needs assessment was to identify gaps in services needed by court participants, to ensure that evidence-based practices were being utilized by providers, and to confirm that the Ten Key Components of Drug Courts were being followed.

A mixed methods approach was used that included a Qualtrics survey, focus group interviews, and court record reviews. This assessment represented the first step in examining the effectiveness of the Thirteenth Judicial Circuit problem-solving courts. Findings suggested overall favorable promise that the problem-solving courts program would have long-term effects in reducing criminal recidivism and substance use among program participants. It also found that each program was likely to maximize the impact on participant outcomes and cost savings by increasing rates of retention and graduation. Several recommendations were provided to address important issues and gaps.

Additionally, in 2022, the Thirteenth Judicial Circuit requested the first of potentially many individual process evaluations on each problem solving court division. The Adult Drug Recovery Court (ADRC) process evaluation was conducted by the Department of Mental Health law and Policy (MHLP) at USF. This included a mixed methods approach of quantitative data collection, qualitative key stakeholder interviews and focus groups, and program and court records review. The primary goal of this evaluation was to provide recommendations and feedback to all key stakeholders of ADRC based on the recently updated NADCP Ten Best Practice Standards of Adult Drug Court.

The collaborative relationship between USF and the Thirteenth Judicial Circuit shows promise that court administration, clinical providers, and academic researchers can partner together to enhance the framework and effectiveness of problem-solving court programs.

Recommendations for Future Implementation

Although prior literature related to problem-solving courts has provided a great wealth of insight, there is still much to be learned about the long-term effectiveness of these programs. Researchers must continue to investigate and evaluate factors that promote long-term reductions in reoffending. The following section highlights some examples of evaluation guidelines:

1. **Rigorous Methodology:** Evaluation of problem-solving courts should increase the utilization of more rigorous methodology. Ideally, a comprehensive evaluation should include a comparison group matched to the participant population. Without randomized control trials or studies using matched samples, it is difficult to truly understand whether courts produce desired outcomes.
2. **Longitudinal Evaluation:** Multiple meta-analyses have suggested that adult drug treatment courts are associated with reduced recidivism. However, as noted by two of those meta-analyses (Shaffer, 2011; Wilson et al., 2006), very few evaluations examine the long-term impact drug courts have on recidivism.
3. **Assessment of Program Components:** Evaluation of problem-solving courts should assess how each program component is related to each of the outcomes. Rather than simply reporting that "court works", problem-solving court evaluations should try to assess what it is about the program that is working.
4. **Assessment of How Components Impact Participants:** Evaluation of problem-solving courts should assess how various elements included in their programming impact participants differently. Analyses on how different types of problem-solving courts affect participants based on their characteristics, such as demographics, socioeconomic status, social support, and criminal justice factors.

In addition to the evaluation guidelines, practitioners and stakeholders in problem-solving courts should adhere to following recommendations when implementing problem-solving courts to ensure that their courts are successful:

1. **Identify Potential Target Population:** If a judicial circuit does not already have problem-solving courts, the first step should be to identify high needs populations within the community. A county's demographics can guide the decision as to which problem-solving court should be initiated. However, high-risk and high-need participants should be targeted regardless of problem-solving court type, as these are the individuals most likely to reoffend.

2. **Adopt an Effective Problem-Solving Court Model**: Successful problem-solving courts in counties with similar demographics can serve as a starting point. The problem-solving court model should reflect the needs of the jurisdiction's demographics while still adhering to best practices. This could look like having a separate drug court track for opioid use if a similar county found co-mingling different populations of substance users led to more cases of recidivism and relapse.
3. **Examine Participation in Problem-Solving Courts:** Examine the potential to increase the number of individuals participating in problem-solving courts. Identifying individuals that may be eligible for problem-solving courts is not always simple for attorneys. Therefore, governing bar associations for attorneys should consider offering more continuing legal education (CLE) training on identification of those who could benefit from problem-solving courts and which would be the most beneficial. Problem-solving courts that have adopted an "opt-out" procedure for enrolling participants may have higher enrollment rates than problem-solving courts that have an "opt-in" procedure.
4. **Evaluate Barriers to Problem-Solving Court:** Some problem-solving courts require defendants to plead guilty before they can enter a program, so individuals may be compelled to do so to access treatment and earn reduced or dismissed charges. While defense attorneys support the idea of providing treatment, many are frustrated that they do not have an opportunity to refute charges. This may contribute to low enrollment and should be addressed if necessary.
5. **Leverage Existing Resources and Apply Best Practices:** Many resources have been developed for problem-solving courts: (a) National Center for State Courts (2007) developed a toolkit that offers steps for PSC implementation, and (b) the Council of State Governments (2016) published several documents to inform the design and implementation of mental health courts, including a comprehensive online curriculum.
6. **Maintain Fidelity to Problem-Solving Court Model**: Jurisdictions who have fidelity to the established problem-solving court model are more successful at reducing recidivism and being cost effective (Finigan et al., 2007). Steps to ensure that community partners are also adhering to best practices should also be taken, such as including language about utilizing evidence-based practices in any service contracts between the parties. Inviting third-party evaluators to conduct process evaluations periodically ensures that the problem-solving court and its community partners are adhering to national standards.

Acknowledgements

The authors would like to acknowledge the collaboration of the Thirteenth Judicial Circuit Court for their critique of this chapter, specifically as it relates to the section on "Adult Drug Court: Hillsborough County FL". Thanks also to Drs. Bryanna Fox and Edelyn Verona for allowing us to contribute to this exciting body of work in their new book entitled *Routledge Handbook of Evidence-Based Criminal Justice Practices*.

References

Council of State Governments. (2016). Mental health courts. Department of Justice, Bureau of Justice Assistance, Office of Justice Programs. Retrieved from https://csgjusticecenter.org/mental-health-court-project

DeVall, K. E., Gregory, P. D., & Hartmann, D. J. (2017). Extending recidivism monitoring for drug courts: Methods issues and policy implications. *International Journal of Offender Therapy and Comparative Criminology*, *61*(1), 80–99. doi: 10.1177/0306624X15590205.

Finigan, M., Carey, S., & Cox, A. (2007). *The impact of a mature drug court over 10 years of operation*. NPC Research.

Florida Office of State Courts Administrator. (2021a, April 30). Dependency drug courts. FLCourts. Retrieved from www.flcourts.org/Resources-Services/Court-Improvement/Problem-Solving-Courts/Drug-Courts/Dependency-Drug-Courts

Florida Office of State Courts Administrator. (2021b, August 4). Veterans courts. FL Courts. Retrieved from www.citationmachine.net/apa/cite-a-website/confirm

Florida Office of State Courts Administrator. (2021c, August 13). Mental health courts. FL Courts. Retrieved from www.flcourts.org/Resources-Services/Court-Improvement/Problem-Solving-Courts/Mental-Health-Courts

Florida Office of State Courts Administrator. (2021d, July 27). Adult drug courts. FL Courts. Retrieved from www.flcourts.org/Resources-Services/Court-Improvement/Problem-Solving-Courts/Drug-Courts/Adult-Drug-Courts

Gibbs, B. R., & Lytle, R. (2020). Drug court participation and time to failure: An examination of recidivism across program outcome. *American Journal of Criminal Justice*, *45*(2), 215–235. doi: 10.1007/s12103-019-09498-0.

Gibbs, B. R., Lytle, R., & Wakefield, W. (2019). Outcome effects on recidivism among drug court participants. *Criminal Justice and Behavior*, *46*(1), 115–135. doi: 10.1177/0093854818800528.

Jewell, J. D., Rose, P., Bush, R., & Bartz, K. (2017). The long-term effectiveness of drug treatment court on reducing recidivism and predictors of voluntary withdrawal. *International Journal of Mental Health and Addiction*, *15*(1), 28–39. doi: 10.1007/s11469-016-9652-8.

Kaiser, K. (2020). An evaluation of successful program completions across types of problem-solving courts. *Justice Evaluation Journal (Online)*, *3*(1), 54–68.

Kearley, B., & Gottfredson, D. (2020). Long term effects of drug court participation: evidence from a 15-year follow-up of a randomized controlled trial. *Journal of Experimental Criminology*, *16*(1), 27–47. doi: 10.1007/s11292-019-09382-1.

Lutze, F. E., & van Wormer, J. (2014). The reality of practicing the ten key components in adult drug court. *Journal of Offender Rehabilitation*, *53*(5), 351–383. doi: 10.1080/10509674.2014.922155.

Miller, M. K., Block, L. M., & DeVault, A. (2020). Problem-solving courts in the United States and around the world: History, evaluation, and recommendations. In *Advances in psychology and law* (pp. 301–371). Springer International Publishing. doi: 10.1007/978-3-030-54678-6_9.

National Association of Drug Court Professionals (NADCP). (2018). Adult drug court best practice standards. Retrieved from www.nadcp.org/wp-content/uploads/2019/09/Best-Practice-Standards-Flyer-Final-3.pdf

National Center for State Courts. (2007). Problem-solving justice toolkit. Retrieved from http://cdm16501.contentdm.oclc.org/cdm/ref/collection/spcts/id/147

National Drug Court Resource Center. (2021). Interactive maps. Retrieved from https://ndcrc.org/interactive-maps/

Rottman, D., & Bowman, J. (2014). Problem-solving courts. In G. Bruinsma & D. Weisburd (Eds.), *The Springer encyclopedia of criminology and criminal justice* (pp. 4000–4010). Springer.

Substance Abuse and Mental Health Services Administration (SAMHSA). (2020, May 4). Juvenile drug courts help youth dealing with trauma. SAMHSA. Retrieved from www.samhsa.gov/homelessness-programs-resources/hpr-resources/juvenile-drug-courts-help-youth

Shaffer, D. K. (2011). Looking inside the black box of drug courts: A meta-analytic review. *Justice Quarterly*, *28*(3), 493–521. doi: 10.1080/07418825.2010.525222.

Thielo, A. J., Cullen, F. T., Burton, A. L., Moon, M. M., & Burton, J. (2019). Prisons or problem-solving: does the public support specialty courts? *Victims & Offenders*, *14*(3), 267–282. doi: 10.1080/15564886.2019.1595243.

Thirteenth Judicial Circuit Court. (2021). Court Programs. FLJud13. Retrieved from www.fljud13.org/CourtPrograms/ProblemSolvingCourts/JuvenileMentalHealthCourt/FAQs.aspx

Trood, M. D., Spivak, B. L., & Ogloff, J. R. (2021). A systematic review and meta-analysis of the effects of judicial supervision on recidivism and well-being factors of criminal offenders. *Journal of Criminal Justice*, *74*, 101796. doi: 10.1016/j.jcrimjus.2021.101796.

Twelfth Judicial Circuit Court. (2023). Sarasota DUI court program. Retrieved from https://www.jud12.flcourts.org/Programs/DUI-Court

U.S. Department of Justice (1997). *Defining drug courts*. Office of Justice Programs, Drug Courts Program Office.

U.S. Department of Justice (2021). *Drug courts*. Office of Justice Programs. Retrieved from www.ojp.gov/pdffiles1/nij/238527.pdf.

Wilson, D. B., Mitchell, O., & MacKenzie, D. L. (2006). A systematic review of drug court effects on recidivism. *Journal of Experimental Criminology*, 2(4), 459–487. doi: 10.1007/s11292-006-9019-4.

Wolf, R. (2021). *Round table reentry courts: Looking ahead, a conversation about strategies for offender reintegration*. Bureau of Justice Assistance, U.S. Department of Justice (BJA) and Center for Court Innovation. Retrieved from www.courtinnovation.org/sites/default/files/documents/Reentry_Courts.pdf.

PART VI

Corrections

31

CORRECTIONAL PROGRAMMING

Evidence-Based Programs, Policies, and Practices

Mark E. Olver and Keira C. Stockdale

Rehabilitative efforts to change and reduce criminal or other forms of antisocial behavior and to encourage its replacement with positive prosocial behavior are at the core of correctional programming. Correctional programming, however, has a number of parameters that vary its delivery and attainment of outcomes. Being correctional in nature, this features men, women, and youth processed through traditional routes in the criminal justice system, all of whom are diverse with respect to development, ethnocultural heritage, mental health functioning, literacy, and cognitive ability, among other areas.

Correctional programs can be delivered in custodial (e.g., prison) or community (probation or parole) settings. Some targets and interventions within correctional programs apply across groups, while others are specific to targeted populations such as sexual offending, violence, intimate partner violence (IPV), or drug involved. Programs can be comprehensive and multimodal, targeting a number of risk factors over a series of modules, while others may be focused and specific to a particular domain (e.g., criminal attitudes). Further, correctional programs differ in many aspects of their modality, where they can be offered in group vs. individual format; they may be psychoeducational or more traditionally therapeutic; and with the advent of technology and the COVID-19 pandemic, may be delivered remotely through telepsychology or telehealth, if not feasible or practicable to offer face to face (see Batastini et al., 2021). And while the mainstay of correctional programming has been the use of cognitive behavioral treatment (CBT) methods of change, within this framework there are several variations, including the incorporation of new wave psychotherapies (Olver & Stockdale, 2018).

This chapter focuses on some of the key elements of what works in correctional programming, with a focus on reducing returns to the criminal justice system (a.k.a. recidivism). We review the correctional programming research through the lens of Andrews and Bonta's (2010a) risk-need-responsivity (RNR) model and follow with some key recommendations from this literature about what works to decrease recidivism.

State of the Correctional Programming Literature: A Brief Review

The RNR model has been a cornerstone in effective correctional programming and has been adopted in correctional systems the world over. Briefly, the principles state that correctional programming intensity should be matched to client risk level (risk principle) and target

DOI: 10.4324/9781003219286-38

criminogenic need (need principle) and be tailored to individual client characteristics that can impact retention and gain (responsivity principle). The largest RNR meta-analysis to date (Andrews & Bonta, 2010b) of 374 effect sizes demonstrated successively larger reductions in recidivism as a greater number of principles were followed: no principles (r = –.02), one principle (r = .02), two principles (r = .18), and all three principles (r = .26). The results of meta-analysis have demonstrated greater adherence to the RNR principles to be associated with greater reductions in recidivism for sexual offense treatment programs (Gannon et al., 2019; Hanson et al., 2009), violence reduction programs (Dowden & Andrews, 2000; Papalia et al., 2019), and IPV programs (Gannon et al., 2019). Applied research developments with respect to "what works" in correctional programming will now be examined in greater detail through the RNR framework.

Who to Treat and How Much? The Risk Principle: Evidence, Applications, and Implications

The implications of the risk principle are that when correctional programs are appropriately matched in intensity to risk level, recidivism decreases, while failure to do so results in little gain or sometimes even iatrogenic effects. Andrews and Dowden's (2006) seminal meta-analysis examined the risk principle across 225 studies, which generated 374 effect sizes. Broad adherence to the risk principle (operationalized as treating high-risk offenders) generated an effect size of φ = .10, amounting to a 10% reduction in recidivism for treated high-risk offenders relative to comparison controls; by contrast, treating low-risk persons had an effect size of φ = .03. What was most illuminating, however, was that treating high-risk cases was associated with the greatest reductions in recidivism when programs targeted criminogenic need (φ = .22), adhered to general responsivity (φ = .26), or employed both (φ = .22). No effect was found, however, despite targeting high-risk individuals when programs did not treat criminogenic need (φ = .01) or provide appropriate services (φ = .00), and the effect was diminished considerably when general responsivity was not followed (φ = .09). Additional lines of research since Andrews and Dowden (2006) have found overtreating cases relative to their level of recidivism risk can be paradoxically associated with increased recidivism (Lovins & Lowenkamp, 2009) or at least yield little added benefit, constituting a suboptimal use of resources (Sperber & Lowenkamp, 2017), while heeding the risk principle results in a larger net gain in recidivism reduction, particularly if other components of effective correctional treatment are followed (Lowenkamp et al., 2006).

In recent years, a dosage movement has developed with recommended treatment dosage hours for low risk (0–99 hours), medium risk (100–199 hours), and high risk (200+ hours) (e.g., Hanson et al., 2016). Simourd and Olver (2019) caution, however, that more programming is not necessarily better, especially if other critical components (i.e., need and responsivity) are not also followed. Evaluations of treatment efficacy by dosage have generated mixed evidence for the dosage rule on its own (Lester et al., 2020; Sperber & Lowenkamp, 2017); the final arbiter is to what extent program content (need principle), style of service delivery (responsivity principle), and fidelity of implementation (program integrity) are adhered to following best established practices.

Program Content Matters: The Need Principle

The need principle states that potentially changeable social, psychological, and environmental characteristics linked to the origin and maintenance of criminal behavior, known as criminogenic needs (a.k.a. dynamic risk factors), should be prioritized for intervention (Andrews & Bonta, 1994, 2010a). The central eight covariates of criminal behavior, which include one static domain (offense history) and seven criminogenic need domains of antisocial attitudes, antisocial peers, antisocial personality pattern, employment/education, family/marital, leisure/recreation, and substance abuse, have robust and well-established links to criminal recidivism (Bonta et al., 2014; Gendreau et al., 1996; Olver et al., 2014). Meta-analytic reviews demonstrate that there are additional criminogenic need domains associated with other forms of antisocial behavior, such as anger problems with interpersonal violence (Chereji et al., 2012) and sexual deviance with sexual violence (Hanson & Morton-Bourgon, 2005; Mann et al., 2010). In turn, criminogenic needs can be contrasted with non-criminogenic needs, that is, personal, social, and emotional characteristics that could have clinical salience and merit intervention (e.g., on ethical and humanitarian grounds), such as personal distress (e.g., anxiety, depression), self-esteem, or locus of control, but that in and of themselves are not associated with criminal behavior.

As would be anticipated, research has demonstrated that risk relevant changes in criminogenic domains have been found to be associated with reductions in recidivism. In a review of the sexual offense treatment change literature, Olver and Stockdale (2020a) found that positive treatment-related changes in empirically associated domains such as sexual deviance, pro-offense attitudes and cognitions, intimacy and relationship skills, anger/hostility, hostility toward women, and substance abuse were associated with decreases in sexual offense recidivism. By contrast, improvements in non-empirically associated domains (e.g., personal distress, empathy) were not meaningfully associated with reductions in recidivism. Other lines of research have examined changes in risk from correctional programming on structured risk assessment and change measures, such as the Violence Risk Scale (VRS; Wong & Gordon, 1999–2016) and its Sexual Offense version (VRS-SO; Wong et al., 2003–2017), and their associations with decreased recidivism. Results from RNR-based high intensity violence reduction correctional programs (Coupland & Olver, 2020a; Lewis et al., 2013) and sexual offense correctional treatment programs (Beggs & Grace, 2011; Olver et al., 2007, 2020) have found risk changes on the VRS and VRS-SO to be associated with significant decreases in sexual and violent recidivism.

Treatment specifically involves learning new prosocial behaviors, skills, and problem-solving strategies in replacement of criminogenic needs (Simourd & Olver, 2019; Sperber & Lowenkamp, 2017). One effective means is via prosocial role modeling and subsequent role plays of prosocial behavioral responses to potentially criminogenic scenarios. Sperber and Lowenkamp (2017), for instance, in a large sample of 980 men successfully discharged from a community-based correctional facility in Ohio, found that the frequency of weekly role plays was significantly inversely related to subsequent recidivism. Lowest rates of recidivism were found for men who had done roleplays 3+ times per week (18%) vs. 1 or 2 times per week (51 and 57%, respectively) vs. 0 roleplaying (71%); effects were strongest for high-risk men compared to those who were moderate and lower risk. The findings build on previous literature demonstrating the use of roleplays to reduce recidivism (Latessa & Lowenkamp, 2006), including the results from meta-analysis (Andrews & Dowden, 2006; Jolliffe & Farrington, 2007).

The research to date also shows that programs targeting criminogenic needs through skills training have larger effect sizes for reducing criminal recidivism. For instance, results from meta-analysis (Dowden & Andrews, 2000; Joliffe & Farrington, 2007; Papalia et al., 2019) in the violence treatment literature demonstrate skills training such as anger control, cognitive restructuring of criminal thinking, relapse prevention, and assignment of homework to promote skills retention to have significant effects for reducing both and violent recidivism. Further, in the sexual offense treatment literature, programs that target deviant sexual interests and arousal through arousal reconditioning have larger effect sizes for the reduction of sexual recidivism than those programs that do not target this domain; by contrast, programs that reported employing the polygraph had smaller effect sizes than those sexual offense program that did not (Gannon et al., 2019).

In the general corrections literature, a recent updated meta-analysis by Lipsey (2019) of 634 studies found a positive overall effect for recidivism reduction (d = .203), with stronger effects associated with programs that employed CBT-based interventions, structured group treatment approaches, counselling, and drug treatment courts. Additional research has demonstrated that focused areas of correctional programming, such as criminal attitude programs, which target the ways individuals think, perceive events, and problem solve, have positive treatment outcomes (Juarez & Howard, 2021; Simourd et al., 2016). Further, a recent meta-analysis of correctional education programs in the United States across 57 studies found program completion to be associated with a 32% decrease in the odds of recidivism post release (Bozick et al., 2018). While such results are informative and promising, Hsieh et al. (2021) found that combining correctional programs (education, vocational training, and CBT) to address multiple needs is linked to even greater reductions in recidivism than completion of a single program in isolation.

The Skill and Art of Correctional Program Delivery: The Responsivity Principle

The responsivity principle's focus is on the individualized style of delivery of treatment and can be organized into general and specific responsivity. General responsivity entails the use of a warm, empathic, firm but fair, humane approach to service delivery within the context of CBT methods of change (Andrews et al., 1990), while specific responsivity involves adapting program content and delivery to the unique characteristics of clientele such as ethnocultural heritage, motivation, personality, and cognitive capability. When responsivity is practiced, program attrition is minimized and client program retention and therapeutic gain is maximized; however, failure to heed general and specific responsivity can amount to a loss of client gains and increased recidivism (Olver et al., 2011).

In a meta-analysis of 114 correctional treatment studies that examined predictors of program attrition, Olver et al. (2011) identified a number of significant correlates, including demographic (e.g., young age, ethnocultural minority, education, unemployment, single), criminal history (e.g., prior incarceration, prior offenses), clinical (e.g., personality disorder, psychopathy, psychosis, low intelligence), criminogenic (e.g., anger, impulsivity, criminal attitudes, substance abuse), and treatment behavior (disruptive, low motivation, poor treatment attitude, poor engagement). In turn, Olver et al. (2011) found that program attrition was associated with a 10–23% increase in recidivism, which they attributed to: 1) noncompleters failing to derive benefit and thus being more likely to reoffend and 2) noncompleters also being higher risk and hence also more likely to reoffend.

Per the responsivity principle, a common thread is that none of these variables need to inexorably lead to program noncompletion. Rather, programs can engage unmotivated clients, contain and manage disruptive treatment-interfering behaviors; adapt program content and style of delivery to client literacy skills and cognitive ability; match interventions to client readiness to change; and incorporate cultural healers, subject matter experts, and culturally relevant interventions to engage ethnoculturally diverse clientele. For instance, per the general responsivity principle, a growing literature on the working alliance between the correctional client and program provider has found stronger alliances to be positively associated with successful program completion (DeSorcy et al., 2016), therapeutic gain (Olver et al., 2021; Polaschek & Ross, 2010), probation success (Hartman & Collins, 2014), and ratings of therapist warmth (Watson et al., 2017). Moreover, per the specific responsivity principle, recent lines of meta-analytic inquiry demonstrate correctional programs adapted to incorporate special needs of justice-involved women (Gobeil et al., 2016) and culturally relevant programming for Indigenous persons (Gutierrez et al., 2018) to generate greater reductions in recidivism compared to standard mainstream programming.

Now What? The Importance of Treatment Fidelity and Program Evaluation

When it comes to correctional program implementation, the devil is in the details; that is, even the most promising program on paper will not yield satisfactory results without fidelity in implementation and adherence to evidence-based practices (EBPs). Measures such as the Correctional Program Assessment Inventory (CPAI; Gendreau & Andrews, 2000) and Correctional Program Checklist (CPC; Latessa, 2005) have been developed to assess to what extent correctional programs are implemented with fidelity and follow EBPs (e.g., program development and leadership, staff characteristics, quality assurance, treatment characteristics). Not surprisingly, the extant research demonstrates program fidelity to be associated with larger treatment effect sizes and better outcomes (Farringer et al., 2021). A classic evaluation of 38 correctional programs by Lowenkamp et al. (2006) found CPAI total score to be associated with decreases in recidivism and technical violations. Although most programs fell into the "unsatisfactory" category of implementation, the few programs that demonstrated satisfactory treatment fidelity had greater reductions in recidivism. An updated review by Duriez et al. (2018) examined more than 20 years of program assessment using the CPAI (643 evaluations, 1995–2005) and CPC (499 evaluations, 2005–2016). Although there was a trend for a slight improvement in most CPAI/CPC categories over time, most programs were evaluated as having low adherence (36%) to EBP; encouragingly, 38% still demonstrated high or very high adherence to EBP.

Responsive Evidence-Based Programs, Policies, and Practices: Some Key Recommendations

So, is RNR enough? While these principles have substantial empirical backing, their implementation within the context of correctional programming is more challenging. In the following, we list seven key recommendations stemming from the literature intended to serve as an action-oriented summary of solutions that can be implemented in the field to strengthen correctional programming initiatives.

1. **Linking assessment and treatment:** it is essential to view correctional programming through the lens of dynamic risk. Programs, whether they be specific and focused in their targets or multimodal and comprehensive, need to assess and evaluate the targeted domain(s) at baseline through some structured means (e.g., dynamic risk tool) and coordinate services. This includes matching treatment intensity and identifying treatment foci at top risk management priority.
2. **Reassessment of treatment progress:** a structured measure should be administered before and after correctional programming to evaluate progress, development of prosocial

competencies, and reduction of risk in the targeted domains. Psychometrically well substantiated self-report measures of criminogenic needs (e.g., attitudes, anger) and/or dynamic risk measures should be employed to track and measure change (Olver & Stockdale, 2020a).

3. **Core correctional practices (CCPs):** use effective interaction skills (e.g., relationship practices, dealing with resistance, effective reinforcement, disapproval, use of authority) and intervention strategies (e.g., anti-criminal modeling, skill building, problem solving, cognitive restructuring) to promote the development of new prosocial behaviors (Dowden & Andrews, 2004). There is evidence that frontline staff can be effectively trained in CCPs to make the most effective use of client contacts to improve reintegration and reduce recidivism, such as the Strategic Training Initiative in Community Supervision (STICS; Bonta et al., 2011, 2021).
4. **Evaluate, treat, and monitor offense analogue and replacement behaviors (OABs and ORBs):** when targeting criminogenic needs, staff should pay attention to offense linked proxy behaviors (OABs) in closely supervised or custodial settings and intervene accordingly to address dynamic risk factors using CCPs. Similarly, everyday interactions should be prosocial and therapeutic so that coupled with programming this can foster the development of prosocial replacement behaviors (ORBs) (Gordon & Wong, 2015; Olver & Stockdale, 2020b).
5. **Capitalize on protective factors and areas of strength:** while targeting prosocial skill deficits (i.e., criminogenic needs) is key, correctional programs should also capitalize on strengths, protective factors, and resiliencies (e.g., prosocial problem solving, positive coping, prosocial peers and supports). Emerging research has demonstrated that protective factors can change for the better with correctional programming and that such improvements are associated with decreased recidivism (e.g., Coupland & Olver, 2020b; Olver & Riemer, 2021).
6. **Staff training and supervision:** there is a growing literature to show that staff training and supervision within correctional programs are associated with greater reductions in recidivism both within the sexual offense treatment literature (Gannon et al., 2019) and general community corrections programming literature (Labrecque & Viglione, 2021). Training and supervision are important to help translating assessments into more effective intervention and case management plans, strengthen staff intervention skills and to prevent program drift and maximize treatment integrity (Dyck et al., 2018; Wong, 2016).
7. **Evaluate program fidelity:** even the best program on paper will be ineffectual without proper implementation and maintaining integrity in delivery. Use of a structured tool onsite or by an external consultant (e.g., CPAI, CPC) can be valuable in evaluating to what extent a program is maintaining fidelity and following EBPs and, if not, how it can be supported to do so (Latessa, 2018).

Conclusion

The RNR principles have been well established over decades of correctional programming research and practice. Recent meta-analytic advancements and ongoing lines of research affirm the wisdom of "what works" in correctional programming to reduce recidivism, but with some important caveats. Matching correctional programming dosage to risk level, particularly prioritizing greater services for higher risk clientele, not only nets the greatest gain in terms of recidivism but also avoids a costly waste of scarce resources or, even worse, having iatrogenic effects with lower-risk clientele. More services, however, do little if they are not the "right" services; that is program content and style of service delivery matter. As such, correctional programs that target empirically established criminogenic needs through prioritizing prosocial skill acquisition (e.g., cognitive restructuring, prosocial problem solving, anger control) have stronger associations with decreased recidivism. Moreover, programs that adopt the interpersonal and interaction skills of CCPs per the need and responsivity principles generate higher client retention, lower attrition, and greater reductions in recidivism. All of this is moot, however, without good fidelity in programming implementation and adherence to EBPs. Although formal surveys of correctional programs show that they frequently and historically have fallen short in implementation, recent trends suggest improvement and some room for cautious optimism. All of this has the potential to make the greatest use of correctional programming resources to improve community outcomes and enhance community safety and wellbeing.

References

Andrews, D. A., & Bonta, J. (2010a). *The psychology of criminal conduct*. Routledge. (Originally work published 1994).

Andrews, D. A., & Bonta, J. (2010b). Rehabilitating criminal justice policy and practice. *Psychology, Public Policy, and Law*, *16*, 39–55.

Andrews, D. A., Bonta, J., & Hoge, R. D. (1990). Classification for rehabilitation: Rediscovering psychology. *Criminal Justice and Behavior*, *17*, 19–52. doi: 10.1177/0093854890017001004

Andrews, D. A., & Dowden, C. (2006). Risk principle of case classification in correctional treatment. *International Journal of Offender Therapy and Comparative Criminology*, *50*, 88–100.

Batastini, A., Paprzycki, P., Jones, A. C. T., & MacLean, N. (2021). Are videoconferenced mental and behavioral health services just as good as in-person? A meta-analysis of a fast-growing practice. *Clinical Psychology Review*, *83*, 101944. doi: 10.1016/j.cpr.2020.101944

Beggs, S. M., & Grace, R. C. (2011). Treatment gains for sexual offenders against children predicts reduced recidivism: A comparative validity study. *Journal of Consulting and Clinical Psychology*, *79*, 182–192. doi: 10.1037/a0022900

Bonta, J., Blais, J., & Wilson, H. A. (2014). A theoretically informed meta-analysis of the risk for general and violent recidivism for mentally disordered offenders. *Aggression and Violent Behavior*, *19*, 278–287.

Bonta, J., Bourgon, G., Rugge, T. Pednault, C. L., & Lee, S. C. (2021). A system-wide implementation and evaluation of the Strategic Training Initiative in Community Supervision (STICS). *Journal of Criminal Justice*, *74*, 101816. doi: 10.1016/j.jcrimjus.2021.101816

Bonta, J., Bourgon, G., Rugge, T., Scott, T. L., Yessine, A. K., Gutierrez, L., & Li, J. (2011). An experimental demonstration of training probation officers in evidence-based community supervision. *Criminal Justice and Behavior*, *38*(11), 1127–1148. doi: 10.1177/0093854811420678.

Bozick, R., Steele, J., Davis, L., & Turner, S. (2018). Does providing inmates with education improve postrelease outcomes? A meta-analysis of correctional education programs in the United States. *Journal of Experimental Criminology*, *14*, 389–428. doi: 10.1007/s11292-018-9334-6

Chereji, S. V., Pintea, S., & David, D. (2012). The relationship of anger and cognitive distortions with violence in violent offenders' population: A meta-analytic review. *The European Journal of Psychology Applied to Legal Context*, *4*(1), 59–77.

Coupland, R. B. A., & Olver, M. E. (2020a). Assessing dynamic violence risk in a high risk treated sample of violent offenders. *Assessment*, *27*, 1886–1900. doi: 10.1177/1073191118797440.

Coupland, R. B. A., & Olver, M. E. (2020b). Assessing protective factors in treated violent offenders: Associations with recidivism reduction and positive community outcomes. *Psychological Assessment*, *32*, 493–508. doi: 10.1037/pas0000807

DeSorcy, D. R., Olver, M. E., & Wormith, J. S. (2016). Working alliance and its relationship to treatment completion, recidivism, and ancestry in a sample of treated sexual offenders. *Sexual Abuse: A Journal of Research and Treatment*, *28*, 291–313. doi: 10.1177/1079063214556360

Dowden, C., & Andrews, D. A. (2000). Effective correctional treatment and violent reoffending: A meta-analysis. *Canadian Journal of Criminology*, *42*, 449–476.

Dowden, C., & Andrews, D. A. (2004). The importance of staff practice in delivering effective correctional treatment: A meta-analytic review of core correctional practice. *International Journal of Offender Therapy and Comparative Criminology*, *48*, 203–214. doi: 10.1177/0306624X03257765

Duriez, S. A., Sullivan, C., Latessa, E. J., & Brusman Lovins, L. (2018). The evolution of correctional program assessment in the age of evidence-based practices. *Corrections: Policy, Practice, and Research*, *3*(2), 119–136. doi: 10.1080/23774657.2017.1343104

Dyck, H. L., Campbell, M., & Wershler, J. L. (2018). Real-world use of the risk-need-responsivity model and the level of service/case management inventory with community-supervised offenders. *Law and Human Behavior*, *42*(3), 258–268. doi: 10.1037/lhb0000279.

Farringer, A. J., Duriez, S. A., Manchak, S. M., & Sullivan, C. C. (2021). Adherence to "what works": Examining trends across 14 years of correctional program assessment. *Corrections: Policy, Practice, and Research*, *6*(4), 269–287. doi: 10.1080/23774657.2019.1659193

Gannon, T. A., Olver, M. E., Mallion, J. S., & James, M. (2019). Does specialized psychological treatment for offending reduce recidivism? A meta-analysis examining staff and program variables as predictors of treatment effectiveness. *Clinical Psychology Review*, *73*, 1–18. doi: 10.1016/j.cpr.2019.101752

Gendreau, P., & Andrews, D. A. (2001). *The correctional program assessment inventory 2000 (CPAI 2000)*. University of New Brunswick.

Gendreau, P., Little, T., & Goggin, C. (1996). A meta-analysis of the predictors of adult offender recidivism: What works! *Criminology*, *34*(4), 575–607. doi: 10.1111/j.1745-9125.1996.tb01220.x

Gobeil, R., Blanchette, K., & Stewart, L. (2016). A meta-analytic review of correctional interventions for women offenders. *Criminal Justice and Behavior*, *43*(3), 301–322. doi: 10.1177/0093854815621100

Gordon, A., & Wong, S. (2015). The use of a structured guide to assess proxies of offending behaviours and change in custodial settings. *Journal of Forensic Practice*, *17*, 83–100. doi: 10.1108/JFP-10-2013-0048

Gutierrez, L., Chadwick, N., & Wanamaker, K. A. (2018). Culturally relevant programming versus status quo: A meta-analytic review of the effectiveness of treatment of Indigenous offenders. *Canadian Journal of Criminology and Criminal Justice*, *60*(3), 321–353. doi: 10.3138/cjccj.2017-0020.r2

Hanson, R. K., Bourgon, G., Helmus, L., & Hodgson, S. (2009). The principles of effective correctional treatment also apply to sexual offenders: A meta-analysis. *Criminal Justice and Behavior*, *36*, 865–891. doi: 10.1177/0093854809338545

Hanson, R. K., Bourgon, G., McGrath, R. J., Kroner, D., D'Amora, D. A., Thomas, S. S., & Tavarez, L. P. (2016). *A five-level risk and needs system: Maximizing assessment results in corrections through the development of a common language*. Justice Center, Council of State Governments.

Hanson, R. K., & Morton-Bourgon, K. E. (2005). The characteristics of persistent sexual offenders: A meta-analysis of recidivism studies. *Journal of Consulting and Clinical Psychology*, *73*, 1154–1163.

Hartman, J., & Collins, K. (2014). A 'back to basics' approach to offender supervision: Does working alliance contribute towards success of probation? *European Journal of Probation*, *6*, 112–125. doi: 10.1177/2066220314543747

Hsieh, M., Chen, K., Choi, P., & Hamilton, Z. K. (2021). Treatment combinations: The joint effects of multiple evidence-based interventions on recidivism reduction. *Criminal Justice and Behavior*, 1–19. Ahead of print publication doi: 10.1177/00938548211052584

Jolliffe, D., & Farrington, D. P. (2007). *A systematic review of the national and international evidence on the effectiveness of interventions with violent offenders* (Series 16/07). Ministry of Justice Research.

Juarez, T., & Howard, M. V. A. (2021). Self-reported change in antisocial attitudes and reoffending among a sample of 2,337 males convicted of violent offenses. *Criminal Justice ad Behavior*, *49*(1), 3–19. doi: 10.1177/00938548211013576

Labrecque, R. M., & Viglione, J. (2021). The impact of a community supervision officer training program on client outcomes. *Criminal Justice and Behavior*, *48*(3), 315–331. doi: 10.1177/0093854820980788

Latessa, E. J. (2005). *The evidence-based correctional program checklist*. Center for Criminal Justice Research and University of Cincinnati.

Latessa, E. J. (2018). Does treatment quality matter? Of course it does, and there is growing evidence to support it. *Criminology & Public Policy*, *17*(1), 181–188. doi: 10.1111/1745-9133.12339

Latessa, E. J., & Lowenkamp, C. T. (2006). What works in reducing recidivism? *University of St. Thomas Law Journal*, *3*(3), 521–535.

Lester, M. E., Batastini, A. B., Davis, R., & Bourgon, G. (2020). Is risk-need-responsivity enough? Examining differences in treatment response among male incarcerated persons. *Criminal Justice and Behavior*, *47*(7), 829–847. doi: 10.1177/0093854820915740

Lewis, K., Olver, M. E., & Wong, S. C. P. (2013). The Violence Risk Scale: Predictive validity and linking treatment changes with recidivism in a sample of high risk offenders with psychopathic traits. *Assessment, 20*, 150–164. doi: 10.1177/1073191112441242

Lipsey, M. W. (2019). *Rehabilitation programs for adult offenders: A meta-analysis in support of guidelines for effective practice*. U.S. Department of Justice. Retrieved from www.ojp.gov/ncjrs/virtual-library/abstracts/rehabilitation-programs-adult-offenders-meta-analysis-support

Lovins, B., Lowenkamp, C. T., & Latessa, E. J. (2009). Applying the risk principle to sex offenders: Can treatment make some sex offenders worse? *The Prison Journal, 89*(3), 344–357. doi: 10.1177/0032885509339509

Lowenkamp, C. T., Latessa, E. J., & Smith, P. (2006). Does correctional program quality really matter? The impact of adhering to the principles of effective intervention. *Criminology and Public Policy, 5*, 575–594.

Mann, R. E., Hanson, R. K., & Thornton, D. (2010). Assessing risk for sexual recidivism: Some proposals on the nature of psychologically meaningful risk factors. *Sexual Abuse: A Journal of Research and Treatment, 22*, 191–217. doi: 10.1177/1079063210366039

Olver, M. E., Nicholaichuk, T. P., Kingston, D. K., & Wong, S. C. P. (2020). A prospective multisite examination of dynamic sexual violence risk: An extension and update to Olver, Nicholaichuk, Kingston, and Wong (2014). *Journal of Consulting and Clinical Psychology, 88*, 362–371.

Olver, M. E., & Riemer, E. K. (2021). High psychopathy men with histories of sexual offending have protective factors too: But are they risk relevant and can they change in treatment? *Journal of Consulting and Clinical Psychology, 89*(5), 406–420. doi: 10.1037/ccp0000638

Olver, M. E., & Stockdale, K. C. (2018). Assessment and treatment of violent offenders. In M. Ternes, P. Magaletta, and M. Patry (Eds.), *The practice of correctional psychology* (pp. 143–172). Springer.

Olver, M. E., & Stockdale, K. C. (2020a). Assessing and managing offense analogue and offense replacement behaviors in correctional settings. *Advancing Corrections, 10*(3), 42–55.

Olver, M. E., & Stockdale, K. C. (2020b). Evaluating changes in men who have sexually offended: Linkages to assessment and management. *Current Psychiatry Reports, 22*(22), 1–10.

Olver, M. E., Stockdale, K. C., & Riemer, E. K. (2021). Working alliance and its association with psychopathy, sexual violence risk, and treatment change. Manuscript under review.

Olver, M. E., Stockdale, K. C., & Wormith, J. S. (2011). A meta-analysis of predictors of offender treatment attrition and its relationship to recidivism. *Journal of Consulting and Clinical Psychology, 79*, 6–21.

Olver, M. E., Stockdale, K. C., & Wormith, J. S. (2014). Thirty years of research on the Level of Service scales: A meta-analytic examination of predictive accuracy and sources of variability. *Psychological Assessment, 26*, 156–176. doi: 10.1037/a0035080

Olver, M. E., Wong, S. C. P., Nicholaichuk, T., & Gordon, A. (2007). The validity and reliability of the Violence Risk Scale-Sexual Offender version: Assessing sex offender risk and evaluating therapeutic change. *Psychological Assessment, 19*, 318–329.

Papalia, N., Spivak, B., Daffern, M., & Ogloff, J. R. P. (2019). A meta-analytic review of the efficacy of psychological treatments for violent offenders in correctional and forensic mental health settings. *Clinical Psychology Science and Practice*. Adavnce online publication doi: 10.1111/cpsp.12282

Polaschek, D. L. L., & Ross, E. C. (2010). Do early therapeutic alliance, motivation, and stages of change predict therapy change for high-risk psychopathic violent prisoners? *Criminal Behaviour and Mental Health, 20*, 100–111. doi: 10.1002/cbm.759

Simourd, D. J., & Olver, M. E. (2019). Prescribed correctional treatment dosage: Cautions, commentary, and future directions. *Journal of Offender Rehabilitation, 58*, 75–91.

Simourd, D. J., Olver, M. E., Brandenburg, B. (2016). Criminal attitudes among incarcerated offenders: Examination of a structured treatment program. *International Journal of Offender Therapy and Comparative Criminology, 60*, 1425–1445. doi: 10.1177/0306624X15579257

Sperber, K. G., & Lowenkamp, C. T. (2017). Dosage is more than just counting program hours: The importance of role-playing in treatment outcomes. *Journal of Offender Rehabilitation, 56*(7), 433–451. doi: 10.1080/10509674.2017.1359222

Watson, R., Daffern, M., & Thomas, S. (2017). Impact of interpersonal style and interpersonal complementarity on the therapeutic alliance between therapists and offenders in sex offender treatment. *Sexual Abuse: A Journal of Research and Treatment, 29*, 107–127. doi: 10.1177/1079063215580969

Wong, S. C. P. (2016). Treatment of violence prone individuals with psychopathic personality traits. In J. Livesley, G. Dimaggio, & J. Clarkin (Eds.), *Integrated treatment of personality disorder: A modular approach*. Guildford.

Wong, S., & Gordon, A. (2016). *The Violence Risk Scale (VRS)*. Regional Psychiatric Centre and University of Saskatchewan (Originally published 1999).

Wong, S., Olver, M., Nicholaichuk, T., & Gordon, A. (2003, 2017). *The Violence Risk Scale-Sexual Offense version (VRS-SO)*. Regional Psychiatric Centre and University of Saskatchewan.

32
INCARCERATION
Rehabilitative Versus Iatrogenic Effects

Meghan A. Novisky and Meghan M. Mitchell

Introduction

Many U.S. residents experience incarceration each year. Current estimates include the incarceration of approximately 2.2 million adults across the country, with 1,599,000 and 735,600 incarcerated in prisons and local jails, respectively (Carson & Kluckow, 2023). Beyond the sheer volume of people who experience incarceration annually, correctional facilities are also highly transient or fluid institutions. More specifically, carceral "churn" is the process of filtering large numbers of people in and out of jails and prisons from month to month or year to year. In 2019, more than 11 million new admissions were processed in jails (Zeng, 2023), and more than 443,000 sentenced prisoners were released (Carson, 2022).

Prior to their incarceration, many of these individuals experience cumulative disadvantages. This includes housing insecurity and disparate access to education and employment (Wakefield & Uggen, 2010). Incarcerated individuals also tend to have worse health at baseline in comparison to their community-dwelling peers (Binswanger et al., 2009). Incarceration itself is a major life event that carries with it further stigmatization, social isolation, and removal of freedom. A growing body of literature has linked incarceration with a range of negative consequences, including health declines (Massoglia & Remster, 2019), violence exposure (Novisky & Peralta, 2020), disruption of family ties (Turney, 2015), and decreases in employment opportunities (Huebner, 2005).

Statistics that track those released from periods of incarceration are also troubling because recidivism rates remain high. For example, among individuals released from prisons across 24 states in 2008, 66% were arrested within 3 years and 61% returned to prison within 10 years (Antenangeli & Durose, 2021). These high recidivism rates, in combination with mounting concerns about the negative consequences of incarceration on individuals, families, and communities, have motivated a movement in corrections over the last couple of decades to identify "what works". The culmination of this research outlines multiple practices that are effective at helping to reduce risks for recidivism and minimize other negative outcomes. In this chapter, we set out to address several related aims. The first section provides a brief overview of (1) the complex needs of incarcerated individuals; and (2) emerging research on criminogenic (crime-producing) aspects of the prison experience. The next section addresses research-informed practices that are key to increasing rehabilitative effects and reducing iatrogenic or negative consequences. Finally, we conclude by identifying areas in need of further research.

DOI: 10.4324/9781003219286-39

Literature Review

The millions entering prisons and jails every year are not a homogenous group of people; rather, they have various life histories, which have resulted in a host of challenges and corresponding needs. Although variation exists, researchers have been able to summarize the most common needs of incarcerated people in two categories: systemic and personal needs. Systemically, incarcerated people have been left out of public systems designed to support citizens and their families. As such, most incarcerated people have an eighth grade or lower reading level and have not graduated from high school or obtained a general education development diploma (Harlow, 2003). Often, they reside in low-income communities that are ridden with crime, gangs, and a culture of violence and often void of economic and employment opportunities (Clear, 2007). Consequently, people often report limited job opportunities prior to incarceration, and those meager opportunities substantially decline once in contact with the criminal justice system (Looney & Turner, 2018). The combination of poor educational systems, limited economic opportunities, and deteriorating neighborhoods creates a trifecta of challenges that are difficult for justice-involved people to overcome.

Unmet systemic needs trickle down and result in a host of challenges at the personal level. Researchers have estimated that over 85% of the incarcerated population has a substance use disorder or were under the influence at the time of their crime (Center on Addiction and Substance Abuse, 2010) and over 37% have a mental health disorder (Bronson & Berzofsky, 2017). Related, incarcerated people also report a history of trauma – especially during childhood – which is likely associated with mental health and substance use outcomes (Messina et al., 2007). Overall, people entering the criminal justice system bring with them a host of unique challenges and needs, which unfortunately are exacerbated by time in prison.

In recent years, a growing body of research has identified aspects of the incarceration experience that may compromise any rehabilitative opportunities the correctional facility may otherwise provide. While incarcerated, people experience a host of deprivations – liberty, autonomy, and relationships – and this dehumanizing experience exposes them to a unique culture within prisons which prioritizes toughness, isolation from others, distrust for authorities, and strategically navigating the challenging dynamics of incarceration (Sykes, 1958). While incarcerated, individuals are also exposed (personally or vicariously) to a greater level of individual or gang-related violence (Steiner et al., 2014) and victimization perpetrated by other incarcerated people or correctional staff (Wooldredge & Steiner, 2013). Also, those in prisons and jails have lower-rated mental and physical health outcomes in comparison to non-incarcerated populations. For example, over 50% of people incarcerated report a chronic health condition (Maruschak et al., 2015). The mental and physical health challenges while incarcerated are exacerbated by limited healthcare options (Rich et al., 2015) and an increased exposure to infectious diseases such as tuberculosis and COVID-19 (Brick, 2007; Novisky et al., 2021). The overcrowded nature of many U.S. prisons and jails also limits the accessibility of many behavioral, physical, and mental health services. In sum, incarcerated people present with complex needs prior to incarceration; those needs are intensified by incarceration, which only increases the demand for responsive programs and policies.

Key Takeaways:

- Incarcerated people have complex treatment needs, of which some are a result of limited systemic and community supports.
- Researchers highlight the debilitating prison environment, limited healthcare, and lack of prison programs as particularly troubling aspects of the incarceration experience.

Responsive Evidence-Based Programs, Policies, and Practices

To increase opportunities for rehabilitation and reduce negative consequences of incarceration, the research points to several important suggestions. First, correctional programming should be guided by established principles of effective intervention. This includes adherence to the RNR model, a framework of correctional service intervention that is informed by the psychology of criminal conduct (Andrews et al., 1990). The RNR model draws attention to three key principles: risk, need, and responsivity.

The risk principle states that greater levels of correctional intervention must be reserved for individuals who score higher on risk classification instruments, while those who score lower on risk should appropriately receive more minimal levels of correctional intervention (Andrews et al., 1990). The idea is to match correctional interventions by criminogenic risk level, to provide those with greater risk enough dosage hours of intervention, and to ensure those with lower risks do not become higher risk due to the nature of the intervention. For example, employment is an important protective factor that helps to reduce criminal risk, but certain correctional interventions can disrupt employment.

The need principle focuses on individually matching correctional interventions to areas known to increase criminogenic risk (Andrews et al., 1990). Those whose criminogenic risks are tied to aggression, for example, should be matched with interventions that target anger and violence prevention. Per the need principle, it is also important to concentrate treatment efforts on dynamic aspects of risk (e.g., those capable of change) versus static risk factors that cannot be changed, such as criminal history (Dowden & Andrews, 2004).

The responsivity principle emphasizes that barriers that can interfere with the success of correctional interventions must be proactively anticipated and addressed at the individual level (Andrews et al., 1990). Responsivity factors can include anything from reading comprehension, to trauma exposure, to mental health symptoms. An individual who has difficulties with reading, for example, may need to be paired with a peer mentor or tutor when assignments are given during treatment. The idea is that without adequate policies in place to recognize and respond to such barriers, the correctional intervention itself is likely to be compromised.

Implementation of core correctional practices is also important. Core correctional practices include use of specific behavioral skills to increase the therapeutic potential of correctional interventions (Andrews & Keissling, 1980). Key core correctional practices include not only quality interpersonal relationships between correctional staff and those under correctional supervision but effective use of authority, anticriminal modeling, and effective reinforcement. Research has shown that use of core correctional practices – in combination with attention to the RNR model – is associated with significant reductions in reoffending rates (Dowden & Andrews, 2004). This means that all correctional staff should be trained on core correctional practices. Performance evaluations of correctional staff should also be based on their use of core correctional practices. Moreover, to reinforce the importance of core correctional practices, it is critical that correctional administrators prioritize detection of and appropriate responses to instances of correctional staff misconduct (Novisky et al., 2021).

Finally, any efforts at rehabilitation are likely to be undermined in environments where people are abused, dehumanized, and segregated and where basic needs are not met. Rather, there is a better way, using evidence-based programs and policies, to incarcerate and rehabilitate those who have committed a crime. In fact, Scandinavian penal systems have been extremely effective in managing their carceral population without dehumanizing or inhumanely punishing those within the system (Pratt, 2008). Changing the philosophy of incarceration will significantly impact all aspects of incarceration from access to medical care and sanitary living conditions to evidence-based programing and policies.

Conclusion

Use of the RNR model, in combination with the principles of effective intervention and efforts to ensure humane correctional living spaces, provide the best possible solutions for addressing the complex needs of incarcerated people. However, it is important to emphasize that these efforts would be aided with meaningful reductions in carceral population sizes, as current population sizes constrain the implementation of even well-designed policies. For example, one of the best lines of defense in reducing the spread of COVID-19 is social distancing, yet social distancing is impractical in prisons and jails that are overcrowded. Also, while correctional facilities may offer effective rehabilitation programming, there are often waitlists due to population size that lead to funneling effects, where services are merely concentrated among those nearing release. Thus, the policy recommendations offered in this chapter should be paired with reductions in both the frequency of carceral sanctions as well as incarceration lengths to best effect change (Frost & Clear, 2013).

It is also important to recognize the disparities linked to the American criminal justice system. People of color and the poor are more likely to experience incarceration, and this has been the case now for decades (Alexander, 2012). Due to these disparities, both explicit and implicit biases can influence things like risk assessments. Meaningful correctional policy, then, must include a reckoning of such disparities and efforts to restore trust in agents of the criminal justice system. Future research that targets (1) practical ways to reduce carceral population size, (2) policies that will reduce sentencing disparities by race and social class, and (3) efforts to retain humanity throughout the process of carceral sanctions is warranted.

References

Alexander, M. (2012). *The new Jim Crow: Mass incarceration in the age of colorblindness*. The New Press.

Andrews, D. A., Bonta, J., & Hoge, R. D. (1990). Classification for effective rehabilitation: Rediscovering psychology. *Criminal Justice and Behavior*, *17*(1), 19–52.

Andrews, D. A., & Kiessling, J. J. (1980). Program structure and effective correctional practices: A summary of the CaVIC research. In R. R. Ross & P. Gendreau (Eds.), *Effective correctional treatment*. Butterworth.

Antenangeli, L., & Durose, M. R. (2021). Recidivism of prisoners released in 24 states in 2008: A 10 year follow up period (2008–2018). U.S. Department of Justice, Bureau of Justice Statistics (NCJ # 256094). Retrieved from https://bjs.ojp.gov/BJS_PUB/rpr24s0810yfup0818/Web%20content/508%20compliant%20PDFs

Binswanger, I. A., Krueger, P. M., & Steiner, J. F. (2009). Prevalence of chronic medical conditions among jail and prison inmates in the USA compared with the general population. *Journal of Epidemiological Community Health*, *63*, 912–919.

Brick, J. A. (2007). Infection control in jails and prisons. *Clinical Infectious Diseases*, *45*(8), 1047–1055.

Bronson, J., & Berzofsky, M. (2017). Indicators of mental health problems reported by prisoners and jail inmates, 2011–12. U.S. Department of Justice, Bureau of Justice Statistics (NCJ #250612). Retrieved from https://bjs.ojp.gov/content/pub/pdf/imhprpji1112.pdf

Carson, A. E. (2022). Prisoners in 2021. U.S. Department of Justice, Bureau of Justice Statistics (NCJ # 305125). Retrieved from https://bjs.ojp.gov/sites/g/files/xyckuh236/files/media/document/p21st.pdf

Carson, E. A., & Kuckow, R. (2023). Correctional populations in the United States, 2021 statistical tables. U.S. Department of Justice, Bureau of Justice Statistics (NCJ # 305542). Retrieved from https://bjs.ojp.gov/document/cpus21st.pdf

Center on Addiction and Substance Abuse. (2010). Behind bars II: Substance abuse and America's prison population. Retrieved from www.centeronaddiction.org/addiction-research/reports/behind-bars-ii-substance-abuse-and-america's-prison-population

Clear, T. R. (2007). *Imprisoning communities: How mass incarceration makes disadvantaged neighborhoods worse*. Oxford University Press.

Dowden, C., & Andrews, D. A. (2004). The importance of staff practice in delivering effective correctional treatment: A meta-analytic review of core correctional practice. *International Journal of Offender Therapy & Comparative Criminology*, *48*(2), 203–214.
Frost, N., & Clear, T. (2013). *The punishment imperative: The rise and failure of mass incarceration in America*. NYU Press.
Harlow, C. W. (2003). Education and correctional populations. Bureau of Justice Statistics. Retrieved from http://eric.ed.gov/?id=ED477377
Huebner, B. (2005). The effect of incarceration on marriage and work over the life course. *Justice Quarterly*, *22*(3), 281–303.
Looney, A., & Turner, N. (2018). Work and opportunity before and after incarceration. Brookings Institution. Retrieved from https://mykairos.org/docs/conference/Work%20and%20opportunity%20before%20and%20After%20Incarceration.pdf
Maruschak, L. M., Berzofsky, M., & Unangst, J. (2015). *Medical problems of state and federal prisoners and jail inmates, 2011–12*. US Department of Justice, Office of Justice Programs, Bureau of Justice Statistics.
Massoglia, M., & Remster, B. (2019). Linkages Between Incarceration and Health. *Public Health Reports*, *134*(1), 8S–14S.
Messina, N., Grella, C., Burdon, W., & Prendergast, M. (2007). Childhood adverse events and current traumatic distress: A comparison of men and women drug-dependent prisoners. *Criminal Justice and Behavior*, *34*(11), 1385–1401.
Novisky, M. A., Narvey, C. S., & Piquero, A. R. (2021). The keepers: Returning citizens' experiences with prison staff misconduct. *Criminal Justice and Behavior*, online first.
Novisky, M. A., Nowotny, K. M., Jackson, D. B., Testa, A., & Vaughn, M. G. (2021). Incarceration as a fundamental social cause of health inequalities: Jails, prisons and vulnerability to COVID-19. *The British Journal of Criminology*, *61*(6), 1630–1646.
Novisky, M. A., & Peralta, R. L. (2020). "Gladiator School: Returning Citizens' Experiences with Secondary Violence Exposure in Prison". *Victims & Offenders*, *15*(5), 594–618.
Rich, J. D., Allen, S. A., & Williams, B. A. (2015). The need for higher standards in correctional healthcare to improve public health. *Journal of General Internal Medicine*, *30*(4), 503–507.
Steiner, B., Butler, H. D., & Ellison, J. M. (2014). Causes and correlates of prison inmate misconduct: A systematic review of the evidence. *Journal of Criminal Justice*, *42*(6), 462–470.
Sykes, G. M. (1958). *The society of captives: A study of a maximum security prison*. Princeton University Press.
Pratt, J. (2008). Scandinavian exceptionalism in an era of penal excess part I: The nature and roots of Scandinavian exceptionalism. *The British Journal of Criminology*, *48*(2), 119–137.
Turney, K. (2015). Liminal men: Incarceration and relationship dissolution. *Social Problems*, *62*(4), 499–528.
Wakefield, S., & Uggen, C. (2010). Incarceration and stratification. *Annual Review of Sociology*, *36*, 387–406
Wooldredge, J., & Steiner, B. (2013). A bi-level framework for understanding prisoner victimization. *Journal of Quantitative Criminology*, *30*(1), 141–162.
Zeng, Z. (2023). Jail inmates in 2021. U.S. Department of Justice, Bureau of Justice Statistics (NCJ # 304888). Retrieved from https://bjs.ojp.gov/sites/g/files/xyckuh236/files/media/document/ji21st.pdf

33

WHAT WORKS IN IMPROVING REENTRY OUTCOMES? EFFECTIVE PROGRAMS AND RECOMMENDATIONS

Edelyn Verona, Kendall Smith, Michelle Hua, and Bryanna Fox

High incarceration and recidivism rates reflect one of the most profound challenges to the American criminal justice system. In 2018, an estimated 6.4 million persons were held in U.S. prisons or jails or were on probation or parole (Maruschak & Minton, 2020). Conservative estimates indicate that 25% of people who go to jail are rearrested within the same year (Sawyer & Wagner, 2020), although others estimate re-arrest rates from jail at 42%–75% (Fox et al., 2019; Raggio, 2021). In short, the correctional system touches a large segment of society, but is essentially a "revolving door" for most justice-involved people.

One reason for the high rate of recidivism is that incarcerated persons present with higher rates of mental illness, substance abuse, trauma, cognitive disability (e.g., brain injury, cognitive decline), and they experience lower education and occupational skills for employability than those outside of the justice system, with meager support networks or living arrangements upon their return to society (Petersilia, 2004; Seiter & Kadela, 2003). Given the limited funding and resources available to support reentry efforts aimed at reducing recidivism, agencies and institutions at the local, state, and federal level must rely on empirical evidence to determine the most beneficial and cost-efficient practices and policies to invest in. Thus, there is a pronounced need to disseminate information on evidence-based reentry programs and their effectiveness in reducing recidivism and promoting successful reentry.

Reviews of Programs Targeting Reentry

A major finding from previous reviews of the literature is that rehabilitative programs work better than reentry interventions involving mostly sanctions. In 2006, a meta-analysis by Aos et al. (2006) found that on average, drug treatment, cognitive-behavioral treatment, education, and work programs led to a statistically significant reduction in future recidivism, while intermediate sanctions (i.e., sentencing alternatives such as intensive supervision, adult bootcamps, and electronic monitoring), jail diversion programs for mental illness, and domestic violence prevention programs generally had no effect on recidivism. Findings from Lipsey and Cullen's (2007) meta-analysis indicated that rehabilitative programs (i.e., interventions designed to reduce recidivism among offenders by improving their behaviors, skills, mental

DOI: 10.4324/9781003219286-40

health, social functioning, and access to education and employment) showed consistently positive and relatively large recidivism reduction effects (Lipsey & Cullen, 2007).

In the following, we review the most prominent evidence-based programs and policies for reducing recidivism and improving reentry success, including those that are offered in custody and/or during post-release community-based interventions or casework. This review focuses on programs that include follow-up periods and examine reentry outcomes, especially recidivism, as well as other key post-release outcomes (e.g., employment, drug use, and mental wellbeing).

Comprehensive Reentry Services

Reentry programs aim to successfully reintegrate incarcerated individuals back into the community, and often begin during incarceration and aid in the transition into the community once an inmate is released. Reentry programs tend to be diverse in the services they provide and often link individuals to resources once they are released, including assistance with housing, education, employment, healthcare, substance abuse, mental health, and personal documentation (e.g., driver's licenses and Social Security number).

Evidence from quasi-experimental and randomized control trial (RCT) designs for the effectiveness of general reentry programs on reducing recidivism has generally been mixed (Clark, 2015; Cook et al., 2015; Ndrecka, 2014; Willison et al., 2014). In Ndrecka's (2014) meta-analysis of 53 studies on the effect of reentry programs on recidivism, results revealed a modest weighted mean effect size r of .06. Findings from three individual evaluations showed a general decrease in the likelihood of recidivating for program participants as compared to non-participants (Clark, 2015; Cook et al., 2015; Willison et al., 2014). The meta-analysis by Ndrecka (2014) found several factors that enhanced effects of reentry programs, including early initiation (during incarceration), targeting high-risk offenders, and the inclusion of therapeutic community or counseling components. Regarding employment outcomes, reentry programs show generally positive effects in the couple of studies available (Duwe, 2012), although the follow up attrition rate was high in some studies.

Overall, the existing literature shows a general trend of reentry programs being associated with reduced recidivism and increased employment. However, the strength of effects in improving recidivism outcomes are mixed. Positive effects are generally observed for reducing rearrests and, to a lesser extent, reconvictions and reincarcerations.

Academic and Educational Programs

Given the negative correlation between crime and employment (Western et al., 2001), educational programming remains crucial in preparing inmates for reentry. These programs are often offered while participants are in custody. Meta-analyses of evaluations of prison-based general educational and high school/GED preparation programs showed meaningful reductions in recidivism (Davis et al., 2013; Wilson et al., 2000), with effect sizes of .21–.34. One study, however, found that participation in GED programs did not have an effect on reducing recidivism for prison inmates (Duwe & Clark, 2014). Research suggests that postsecondary education programs (e.g., college-level or vocational programs) show greater effects in comparison to GED programs (Duwe & Clark, 2014; Wilson et al., 2000). For example, compared to the recidivism reduction found for GED programs (ds = .22 and .21) in Wilson et al. (2000) and Davis et al. (2013), respectively, postsecondary education programs show larger decreases in recidivism rates (ds = .33 and .43).

Less research examines post-release employment outcomes as a function of in-custody educational programs. An individual evaluation by Duwe and Clarke (2014) found that while GED program participation significantly increased chances of obtaining employment post-release, it did not significantly affect wages or number of hours worked. In contrast, postsecondary education program participation failed to increase chances of obtaining employment post-release in comparison to the control group but increased general wages and number of hours worked.

Overall, the literature on the effect of secondary education and GED programs presents a consistent pattern of small to moderate effects on recidivism, with only a few exceptions, and on obtaining employment post-release (Duwe & Clark, 2014; Wilson et al., 2000). Moreover, findings demonstrate that longer participation in the GED program and completion of the program closer to an inmate's release date are both linked to more positive outcomes.

Employment Training and Assistance

Employment training and assistance programs address issues with budgeting, financial literacy, job search skills, employment applications, and interview skills. Research on employment assistance programs show a general trend of lowered recidivism rates and increased employment for individuals participating in the programs (Aos et al., 2006; Duwe, 2015; Rossman et al., 1999), although a more fine-grained examination of recidivism findings across studies suggests mixed results. Variations in findings in effects on recidivism may be attributed to the varying methodologies of the studies, with weaker effects for RCT (Rossman et al., 1999) than quasi-experimental designs (Duwe, 2015). In terms of employment outcomes, Duwe (2015) and Rossman et al. (1999) found that participation in employment programs increased the likelihood that justice-involved people obtained employment post-release compared to non-participants. In sum, existing research suggests there is evidence that employment programs are effective, with more consistent support for improving employment outcomes than reducing recidivism (Duwe, 2015; Rossman et al., 1999).

Social Support in Reentry

Poor social support among formerly incarcerated persons is a significant barrier for reentry. Positive social support has been associated with improved reentry-related outcomes including substance use, physical health, housing, employment, and recidivism reduction (Brunton-Smith & McCarthy, 2017; Fahmy & Wallace, 2019). Such evidence is consistent with social bond theory, which asserts that strong bonds with friends and family will prevent individuals from engaging in illegal behavior (Colvin et al., 2002). That said, support commonly comes from friends and family but may also include professionals (Bares & Mowen, 2020) and community volunteers (Duwe, 2018).

The majority of literature assessing effects of social support on recidivism has focused on visitation while incarcerated. A meta-analysis by Mitchell et al. (2016) indicates inmates receiving support through visitation demonstrate a 26% reduction in reincarceration and reconviction. Less is known about the overall impact of social support post-incarceration; however, several individual studies investigating support in the community have indicated successful outcomes. For example, programs that have examined positive social support from families (Spjeldnes et al., 2012), professionals (Bares & Mowen, 2020) and community volunteers (Duwe, 2018) have demonstrated reductions in recidivism ranging from 14%–57%. The type of support received is important to consider. While both instrumental support (e.g. housing, financial help, transportation, resources) and emotional support (e.g. listening, compassion) have been related to improved outcomes, instrumental support has been associated with larger reductions in recidivism (Bares & Mowen, 2020; Mowen et al., 2019).

The existing research suggests improved social support is associated with significantly lower rates of reincarceration and reconviction; although there is limited and mixed support for its effects on rearrests (Duwe, 2018; Mitchell et al., 2016). Notably, interventions to increase instrumental support, particularly housing, should be prioritized in comparison to emotional support.

Cognitive Behavioral Therapy Targeting Criminogenic Thinking

Cognitive behavioral therapy (CBT) helps change negative emotions and patterns of thinking. Although various types of programs are often delivered within a CBT framework to target mental health and substance use problems, CBT programs have also been applied specifically to help change criminal thinking and behavior among individuals in the criminal justice system. Among the most extensively evaluated CBT programs for offenders include Reasoning & Rehabilitation (R&R), Thinking for a Change (TFAC), and Moral Reconation Therapy (MRT), among others.

Results from a meta-analysis indicate that such CBT programs are effective in reducing recidivism rates for adult and juvenile offenders, yielding an 8%–10% point drop between treatment and control groups (Aos et al., 2006; Lipsey et al., 2007). Studies have found an 8%–14% decrease in recidivism for R&R (Tong & Farrington, 2006; Wilson et al., 2005), and Lowenkamp et al. (2009) found that TFAC significantly lowered rearrest rates for probationers participating in the program compared to a nontreatment group. Existing meta-analyses of MRT have reported small to moderate effect sizes (.16–.22) in reducing rearrest and reincarceration rates (Ferguson & Wormith, 2013; Little, 2005).

Overall, previous findings provide support for positive effects of CBT programs targeting criminogenic thinking on reducing recidivism (Aos et al., 2006; Ferguson & Wormith, 2013; Lipsey et al., 2007; Little, 2005; Lowenkamp et al., 2009; Tong & Farrington, 2006; Wilson et al., 2005). Although the effectiveness of CBT programs delivered in community settings varies (Little, 2005; Van Voorhis et al., 2013), the treatment setting (i.e., institution vs. community) in which CBT programming is implemented does not have an overall impact on effect size (Lipsey et al., 2007). Importantly, stronger effects on recidivism are observed when CBT programs focus on high-risk offenders; have high quality treatment implementation; include both individual and group counseling; and include components focusing on anger control, cognitive restructuring, skill building, and interpersonal problem solving (Lipsey et al., 2007).

Violence Reduction Programs

Domestic Batterer Programs

Treatment programs for domestic violence (DV) offenders most commonly involve a feminist psychoeducational approach reflecting the Duluth model that focuses on the perspective that violence is caused by patriarchal ideals and men's power and control over women. Other DV programs include a CBT component that promotes skills training and alternatives to violent behavior. An early meta-analysis by Davis and Taylor (1999) found evidence that DV programs had a moderate effect in reducing further violence among DV offenders, but most of the programs had inadequate control groups. In contrast, two later meta-analyses of DV programs, including those using the Duluth model and those delivered within a CBT framework, found non-significant positive effects or zero effects in reducing recidivism (Babcock et al., 2004; Feder et al., 2008). These later quantitative reviews relied heavily on controlled experimental and quasi-experimental studies that addressed the issue of selection bias through matched comparison groups or statistical controls. However, the most recent meta-analysis by Arce and colleagues (2020) found positive medium effects ($d = 0.43$) reminiscent of Davis and Taylor (1999), specifically under the Duluth model and CBT based programs. However, this was the case mostly when operationalizations of recidivism relied on official reports and not couple reports; unfortunately, official reports captured only approximately half of the recidivism incidents self-reported by the couples.

With a fairly substantial number of evaluations on the effectiveness of DV programs, overall findings are mixed but generally demonstrate none to small effects on recidivism (Babcock et al., 2004; Davis & Taylor, 1999; Feder et al., 2008). Attending a greater number of treatment sessions and successful completion of treatment are significant factors in lowering the risk of domestic violence recidivism (Gordon & Moriarity, 2003).

Anger Management Programs

Anger control programs are commonly used for offenders with histories of violence and aggression. CBT-based programs conducted in a group format are notably the most popular method of anger management in correctional settings (Henwood et al., 2015; Papalia et al., 2019; Rosenfield et al., 2019). These focus on CBT principles, including problem solving and communication skills, relaxation training, and cognitive restructuring techniques to reduce anger. Meta-analyses of anger management interventions by Henwood et al. (2015) and Papalia et al. (2019) have revealed significant reductions in both general and violent recidivism in adults in correctional and forensic mental health settings; however, recent individual evaluations show more modest effects (e.g., Rosenfield et al., 2019). The majority of the research has been conducted with male offenders and involved CBT-based anger management programs. In addition to these general findings, the research has indicated a treatment completion effect, another topic to consider in future research.

Mental Health and Substance Use Programs

Mental Health Treatments

Although many court or correctional programs attempt to link individuals to community-based mental health treatment (Barrenger & Draine, 2013), fewer evaluations examine the effects of individual and group *psychological* treatments for reducing recidivism as well as symptoms of mental health problems (e.g., depression, anxiety) among incarcerated or released individuals. Only two studies have examined the effects of CBT-based mental health treatments on recidivism outcomes. One study by Khodayarifard et al. (2010), which provided cognitive therapy for anxiety and depression, found a significant reduction in recidivism for program participants compared to those on a waitlist for individual counseling. Results from an RCT found that participating in a trauma-informed therapy decreased the likelihood of returning to prison for the treatment group compared to the control group (Zlotnick et al., 2009).

Symptom reduction is often an outcome of interest, as it is surmised that symptom reduction may mediate effects on recidivism. In two RCTs comparing differences between prisoners receiving cognitive treatment to a control group, cognitive group therapy and individual/group therapy were both associated with greater reductions in depression and anxiety symptoms than either a no treatment control group (i.e., waitlist for individual counseling; Eseadi et al., 2018) or individual counseling control group (Khodaryarifard et al., 2010). Trauma-focused treatments in correctional settings, especially for women, have also resulted in reductions in PTSD symptom severity and depression scores from pre- to post-assessment in incarcerated women (Zlotnick et al., 2009). However, only one study found significantly improved outcomes in the trauma-informed intervention group relative to the treatment as usual group (Lynch et al., 2012).

In sum, given that only two studies examined recidivism outcomes related to mental health treatments, there is a notable lack of evidence on these programs' importance for reentry success. While previous research has demonstrated that mental health programming (e.g., jail diversion, mental health courts, reentry and case management services) are generally unsuccessful in reducing recidivism (Duwe, 2017), further research is needed to address how improvements in mental health may correlate with subsequent recidivism.

Substance Use Treatments

Several modalities are available to address substance use problems in correctional settings and the community. Evaluations of existing correctional drug treatment programs have largely focused on assessing therapeutic communities (TCs), a widely used model of treatment for problematic substance use and addiction. With an emphasis on social learning and mutual self-help, TCs promote a sense of community to drive individual changes in attitudes and behavior related to substance use through active participation in individual and group counseling, group sessions with peers, and assuming roles based on a hierarchy of increasing responsibilities and privileges. Substantial research on the effectiveness of TCs on recidivism outcomes report meaningful reductions in subsequent recidivism for program participants, with greater positive effects observed for TC programs offering a continuation of care in the community post-release (Aos et al., 2006; Mitchell et al., 2012). While the effect of TC programs on drug use relapse outcomes is less extensively researched, Galassi and colleagues' (2015) systematic review found that in 7 out of 9 studies, TCs were effective in reducing rates of drug use among participants compared to non-participants. Program completion and a continuum of treatment in the community after release remain important factors contributing to the success of TC programs (Aos et al., 2006; Galassi et al., 2015).

Substance use programs are also often delivered in a CBT framework, especially in general population. CBT for substance use typically follows a relapse prevention model to address negative thoughts, emotions, and behaviors related to addiction. Although few studies have investigated CBT-based substance use interventions in correctional settings or involving offenders, Aos et al.'s (2006) meta-analysis of 8 studies evaluating in-prison CBT programs for drug-involved individuals found a 6.8% reduction in recidivism rates for program participants compared to a treatment as usual group. Future studies with longer follow-up periods are necessary to examine the long-term effects of CBT relapse prevention programs on substance use and recidivism outcomes.

Finally, 12-step substance use programs are very common. They are based on spiritual principles and support group format that focus on accepting one's loss of control over addiction, making amends, and taking steps towards recovery from addiction. Mitchell et al.'s (2012) meta-analysis of 26 studies of counseling programs that generally incorporated elements of 12-step group counseling found that these programs were effective in reducing recidivism but not drug use among offenders. In addition, 12-step substance use programs were not as successful as other interventions, like CBT and therapeutic communities, especially when considering the studies with the most rigorous methodological approaches (e.g., Mitchell et al., 2012; Zanis et al., 2003). Higher frequency of participation in the programs and successful completion of the programs seem to be associated with better outcomes (Zanis et al., 2003).

Discussion and Conclusion

Summary of Findings

Following the conclusion in the 1970s that "nothing works" to rehabilitate incarcerated individuals (Martinson, 1974), correctional policies shifted from a focus on rehabilitation to one of punishment and incapacitation to prevent crime (Seiter & Kadela, 2003). The result was mass incarceration policies leading to overcrowded jails and prisons, with little associated reduction in crime and recidivism. The evidence in this review is clear that rehabilitative programs work better than sanctions upon release (i.e., intensive supervision, adult bootcamps, and electronic monitoring). Money may be better spent on programs that address risks and needs and less on sanctions and heavy supervision of released persons.

A simple summary of the evidence for specific programs is that existing evaluations provide the most support for the effectiveness of secondary/post-secondary education programs, social support, CBT-based programs for substance use and criminogenic thinking, and therapeutic communities for substance use in reducing recidivism. Findings are less promising for the efficacy of comprehensive reentry programs, employment programs, domestic violence/batterer programs, and 12-step substance use programs in improving recidivism rates.

Factors Contributing to Reentry Success

Given the extensive literature demonstrating that certain correctional programs work in lowering recidivism and promoting successful reentry, the greater challenge is now to define what works best for whom and under which circumstances. Factors that improve success are high-quality treatment implementation or fidelity (Lipsey et al., 2007), completion of program (Anderson & Moore, 1995), and continuity of care in the community after release (Duwe, 2015; Rossman et al., 1999; Willison et al., 2014). Based on the details of the reviewed studies, the following are key take-home points and recommendations:

1. Studies suggest that programs are more effective when *adhering to the principles of the risk–need–responsivity (RNR) model*, which calls for 1) assessing an individual's level of risk for re-offending; 2) directing more intensive treatments to higher-risk individuals; and 3) addressing criminogenic risks and needs, including antisocial personality, education, employment, family/marital, leisure/recreation, substance abuse, and mental health issues (Andrews et al., 1990; Andrews & Bonta, 2010). This is not always done. As one example, domestic violence batterer programs most commonly adopt the Duluth model and focus on changing patriarchal beliefs; however, the evidence indicates that scholars may want to more specifically address known criminogenic needs such as antisocial attitudes, substance abuse, and social support (Radatz & Wright, 2016).
2. Given evidence of better outcomes associated with more time in and completion of the program, existing programs should work on *improving engagement and reducing drop out as a regular part of treatment planning*. As one specific recommendation, it may be useful

to incorporate motivational interviewing approaches prior to treatment to increase engagement and attendance among participants (Hettema et al., 2005).

3. The timing and continuity of services from custody to the community seem highly important. For example, education-based programs show better outcomes the closer the intervention occurs to release date (Anderson & Moore, 1995). Reentry programs seem to show the most effectiveness when there is *early program initiation (during incarceration) and continuity of engagement across incarceration and following release* (Ndrecka, 2014).
4. Sometimes a program does not cost very much to implement. For example, given the promising effects of social support for successful reentry thus far, future policies should also consider strategies to *increase social support for incarcerated and recently released individuals*, such as improved access to support networks while incarcerated and offering programs that connect released offenders with supports upon reentry.
5. Although there is substantial research on prison-based programming, this review identified only five studies that focused solely on jail-based programming, highlighting how *jails are a relatively understudied aspect of the criminal justice system* (Fox et al., 2019). Importantly, effect sizes for these jail evaluations were consistent, if not a bit higher, than those reported in evaluations of prison-based programs. Thus, despite the fact that jails house individuals serving sentences less than a year or awaiting trial (Zeng, 2018), some interventions can be applied successfully in brief or short-term formats (Center for Substance Abuse Treatment, 2005).

References

Anderson, S. V., & Moore, E. A. (1995). *Evaluation of the impact of correctional education programs on recidivism.* Ohio Department of Rehabilitation and Correction, Bureau of Planning and Evaluation.

Andrews, D. A., & Bonta, J. (2010). Rehabilitating criminal justice policy and practice. *Psychology, Public Policy, and Law, 16*, 39–55. doi: 10.1037/a0018362

Andrews, D. A., Zinger, I., Hoge, R. D., Bonta, J., Gendreau, P., & Cullen, F. T. (1990). Does correctional treatment work? A clinically relevant and psychologically informed meta-analysis. *Criminology, 28*(3), 369–404. doi: 10.1111/j.1745-9125.1990.tb01330.x

Arce, R., Arias, E., Novo, M., & Fariña, F. (2020). Are interventions with batterers effective? A meta-analytical review. *Psychosocial Intervention, 29*(3), 153–164. doi: 10.5093/pi2020a11

Aos, S., Miller, M., & Drake, E. (2006). *Evidence-based adult corrections programs: What works and what does not.* Washington State Institute for Public Policy. Retrieved from www.wsipp.wa.gov/ReportFile/924

Babcock, J. C., Green, C. E., & Robie, C. (2004). Does batterers' treatment work? A meta-analytic review of domestic violence treatment. *Clinical Psychology Review, 23*(8), 1023–1053. doi: 10.1016/j.cpr.2002.07.001

Bares, K. J., & Mowen, T. J. (2020). Examining the parole officer as a mechanism of social support during reentry from prison. *Crime & Delinquency, 66*(6–7), 1023–1051. doi: 10.1177/0011128719881599

Barrenger, S. L., & Draine, J. (2013). "You don't get no help": The role of community context in effectiveness of evidence-based treatments for people with mental illness leaving prison for high risk environments. *American Journal of Psychiatric Rehabilitation, 16*(2), 154–178. doi: 10.1080/15487768.2013.789709

Brunton-Smith, I., & McCarthy, D. J. (2017). The effects of prisoner attachment to family on re-entry outcomes: A longitudinal assessment. *The British Journal of Criminology, 57*(2), 463–482.doi: 10.1093/bjc/azv129

Center for Substance Abuse Treatment. (2005). Substance abuse treatment for adults in the criminal justice system. Substance Abuse and Mental Health Services Administration (US).

Clark, V. A. (2015). Making the most of second chances: An evaluation of Minnesota's high-risk revocation reduction reentry program. *Journal of Experimental Criminology, 11*(2), 193–215. doi: 10.1007/s11292-014-9216-5

Colvin, M., Cullen, F. T., & Ven, T. V. (2002). Coercion, social support, and crime: An emerging theoretical consensus. *Criminology*, *40*(1), 19–42. doi: 10.1111/j.1745-9125.2002.tb00948.x

Cook, P. J., Kang, S., Braga, A. A., Ludwig, J., & O'Brien, M. E. (2015). An experimental evaluation of a comprehensive employment-oriented prisoner re-entry program. *Journal of Quantitative Criminology*, *31*(3), 355–382. doi: 10.1007/s10940-014-9242-5

Davis, L. M., Bozick, R., Steele, J. L., Saunders, J., & Miles, J. N. (2013). *Evaluating the effectiveness of correctional education: A meta-analysis of programs that provide education to incarcerated adults*. RAND Corporation.

Davis, R. C., & Taylor, B. G. (1999). Does batterer treatment reduce violence? A synthesis of the literature. *Women & Criminal Justice*, *10*(2), 69–93. doi: 10.1300/J012v10n02_05

Duwe, G. (2012). Evaluating the Minnesota comprehensive offender reentry plan (MCORP): Results from a randomized experiment. *Justice Quarterly*, *29*(3), 347–383. doi: 10.1080/07418825.2011.555414

Duwe, G. (2015). The benefits of keeping idle hands busy: An outcome evaluation of a prisoner reentry employment program. *Crime & Delinquency*, *61*(4), 559–586. doi: 10.1177/0011128711421653

Duwe, G. (2017). The use and impact of correctional programming for inmates on pre-and post-release outcomes (Vol. 48). US Department of Justice, Office of Justice Programs, National Institute of Justice. Retrieved from www.ojp.gov/pdffiles1/nij/250476.pdf

Duwe, G. (2018). Can circles of support and accountability (CoSA) significantly reduce sexual recidivism? Results from a randomized controlled trial in Minnesota. *Journal of Experimental Criminology*, *14*(4), 463–484. doi: 10.1007/s11292-018-9325-7

Duwe, G., & Clark, V. (2014). The effects of prison-based educational programming on recidivism and employment. *The Prison Journal*, *94*, 454–478. doi: 10.1177/0032885514548009

Eseadi, C., Obidoa, M. A., Ogbuabor, S. E., & Ikechukwu-Ilomuanya, A. B. (2018). Effects of group-focused cognitive-behavioral coaching program on depressive symptoms in a sample of inmates in a Nigerian prison. *International Journal of Offender Therapy and Comparative Criminology*, *62*(6), 1589–1602. doi: 10.1177/0306624X16687046

Fahmy, C., & Wallace, D. (2019). The influence of familial social support on physical health during reentry. *Criminal Justice and Behavior*, *46*(12), 1738–1756. doi: 10.1177/0093854819870268

Feder, L., Wilson, D. B., & Austin, S. (2008). Court-mandated interventions for individuals convicted of domestic violence. *Campbell Systematic Reviews*, *4*(1), 1–46.

Ferguson, L. M., & Wormith, J. S. (2013). A meta-analysis of moral reconation therapy. *International Journal of Offender Therapy and Comparative Criminology*, *57*(9), 1076–1106. doi: 10.1177/0306624X12447771

Fox, B., Verona, E., & Fournier, L. (2019). Psychological assessment of risk in a county jail: Implications for reentry, recidivism and detention practices in the USA. *Journal of Criminal Psychology*, *9*(4),173–186. doi: 10.1108/JCP-11-2019-051

Galassi, A., Mpofu, E., & Athanasou, J. (2015). Therapeutic community treatment of an inmate population with substance use disorders: Post-release trends in re-arrest, re-incarceration, and drug misuse relapse. *International Journal of Environmental Research and Public Health*, *12*(6), 7059–7072. doi: 10.3390/ijerph120607059

Gordon, J. A., & Moriarty, L. J. (2003). The effects of domestic violence batterer treatment on domestic violence recidivism: The Chesterfield County experience. *Criminal Justice and Behavior*, *30*(1), 118–134. doi: 10.1177/0093854802239166

Henwood, K. S., Chou, S., & Browne, K. D. (2015). A systematic review and meta-analysis on the effectiveness of CBT informed anger management. *Aggression and Violent behavior*, *25*, 280–292. doi: 10.1016/j.avb.2015.09.011

Hettema, J., Steele, J., & Miller, W. R. (2005). Motivational interviewing. *Annual Review of Clinical Psychology*, *1*(1), 91111. doi: 10.1146/annurev.clinpsy.1.102803.143833

Khodayarifard, M., Shokoohi-Yekta, M., & Hamot, G. E. (2010). Effects of individual and group cognitive-behavioral therapy for male prisoners in Iran. *International Journal of Offender Therapy and Comparative Criminology*, *54*(5), 743–755. doi: 10.1177/0306624X09344840

Little, G. L. (2005). Meta-analysis of moral reconation therapy recidivism results from probation and parole implementations. *Cognitive-Behavioral Treatment Review*, *14*(1/2), 14–16.

Lipsey, M. W., & Cullen, F. T. (2007). The effectiveness of correctional rehabilitation: A review of systematic reviews. *Annual Review of Law and Social Science*, *3*, 297–320. doi: 10.1146/annurev.lawsocsci.3.081806.112833

Lipsey, M. W., Landenberger, N. A., & Wilson, S. J. (2007). Effects of cognitive-behavioral programs for criminal offenders. *Campbell Systematic Reviews*, *3*(1), 1–27

Lowenkamp, C. T., Hubbard, D., Makarios, M. D., & Latessa, E. J. (2009). A quasi-experimental evaluation of thinking for a change: A "real-world" application. *Criminal Justice and Behavior*, *36*(2), 137–146. doi: 10.1177/0093854808328230

Lynch, S. M., Heath, N. M., Mathews, K. C., & Cepeda, G. J. (2012). Seeking safety: An intervention for trauma-exposed incarcerated women? *Journal of Trauma & Dissociation*, *13*(1), 88–101. doi: 10.1080/15299732.2011.608780

Martinson, R. (1974). What works? Questions and answers about prison reform. *The Public Interest*, *35*, 22.

Maruschak, L. M., & Minton, T. D. (2020). *Correctional populations in the United States, 2017–2018*. Bureau of Justice Statistics. Retrieved from https://bjs.ojp.gov/content/pub/pdf/cpus1718.pdf

Mitchell, O., Wilson, D. B., & MacKenzie, D. L. (2012). The effectiveness of incarceration-based drug treatment on criminal behavior: A systematic review. *Campbell Systematic Reviews*, *8*(1), 76. doi: 10.4073/csr.2012.18

Mitchell, M. M., Spooner, K., Jia, D., & Zhang, Y. (2016). The effect of prison visitation on reentry success: A meta-analysis. *Journal of Criminal Justice*, *47*, 74–83. doi: 10.1016/j.jcrimjus.2016.07.006

Mowen, T. J., Stansfield, R., & Boman IV, J. H. (2019). Family matters: Moving beyond "if" family support matters to "why" family support matters during reentry from prison. *Journal of Research in Crime and Delinquency*, *56*(4), 483–523. doi: 10.1177/0022427818820902

Ndrecka, M. (2014). *The impact of reentry programs on recidivism: A meta-analysis*. University of Cincinnati.

Papalia, N., Spivak, B., Daffern, M., & Ogloff, J. R. (2019). A meta-analytic review of the efficacy of psychological treatments for violent offenders in correctional and forensic mental health settings. *Clinical Psychology: Science and Practice*, *26*(2), e12282. doi: 10.1111/cpsp.12282

Petersilia, J. (2004). What works in prisoner reentry? Reviewing and questioning the evidence. *Federal Probation*, *68*(2), 4–8.

Radatz, D. L., & Wright, E. M. (2016). Integrating the principles of effective intervention into batterer intervention programming: The case for moving toward more evidence-based programming. *Trauma, Violence, & Abuse*, *17*(1), 72–87. doi: 10.1177/1524838014566695

Raggio, A. L. (2021). Behavioral health and recidivism among Rural County jail inmates (Doctoral dissertation). Western Carolina University.

Rosenfeld, B., Galietta, M., Foellmi, M., Coupland, S., Turner, Z., Stern, S., . . . Ivanoff, A. (2019). Dialectical behavior therapy (DBT) for the treatment of stalking offenders: A randomized controlled study. *Law and Human Behavior*, *43*(4), 319. doi: 10.1037/lhb0000336

Rossman, S., Sridharan, S., Gouvis, C., Buck, J., & Morley, E. (1999). *Impact of the opportunity to succeed. OPTS aftercare program for substance-abusing felons: Comprehensive final report*. Urban Institute.

Sawyer, W., & Wagner, P. (2020, March 24). *Mass incarceration: The whole pie 2020*. Prison Policy Initiative. Retrieved from www.prisonpolicy.org/reports/pie2020.html

Seiter, R. P., & Kadela, K. R. (2003). Prisoner reentry: What works, what does not, and what is promising. *Crime & Delinquency*, *49*(3), 360–388. doi: 10.1177/0011128703049003002

Spjeldnes, S., Jung, H., Maguire, L., & Yamatani, H. (2012). Positive family social support: Counteracting negative effects of mental illness and substance abuse to reduce jail ex-inmate recidivism rates. *Journal of Human Behavior in the Social Environment*, *22*(2), 130–147. doi: 10.1080/10911359.2012.646846

Tong, L. S., & Farrington, D. (2006). How effective is the "reasoning and rehabilitation" program in reducing reoffending? A meta-analysis of evaluations in four countries. *Psychology, Crime & Law*, *12*(1), 3–24. doi: 10.1080/10683160512331316253

Van Voorhis, P., Spiropoulos, G., Ritchie, P. N., Seabrook, R., & Spruance, L. (2013). Identifying areas of specific responsivity in cognitive-behavioral treatment outcomes. *Criminal Justice and Behavior*, *40*(11), 1250–1279. doi: 10.1177/0093854813494182

Western, B., Kling, J. R., & Weiman, D. F. (2001). The labor market consequences of incarceration. *Crime & Delinquency*, *47*(3), 410–427. doi: 10.1177/0011128701047003007

Willison, J. B., Bieler, S. G., & Kim, K. (2014). *Evaluation of the Allegheny County jail collaborative reentry programs*. Urban Institute.

Wilson, D. B., Bouffard, L. A., & MacKenzie, D. L. (2005). A quantitative review of structured, group-oriented, cognitive-behavioral programs for offenders. *Criminal Justice and Behavior*, *32*(2), 172–204. doi: 10.1177/0093854804272889

Wilson, D. B., Gallagher, C. A., & MacKenzie, D. L. (2000). A meta-analysis of corrections based education, vocation, and work programs for adult offenders. *Journal of Research in Crime and Delinquency*, *37*, 347–368. doi: 10.1177/0022427800037004001

Zanis, D. A., Mulvaney, F., Coviello, D., Alterman, A. I., Savitz, B., & Thompson, W. (2003). The effectiveness of early parole to substance abuse treatment facilities on 24–month criminal recidivism. *Journal of Drug Issues*, *33*(1), 223–235. doi: 10.1177/002204260303300109

Zeng, Z. (2020). *Jail inmates in 2018*. Bureau of Justice Statistics. Retrieved from https://bjs.ojp.gov/content/pub/pdf/ji18.pdf

Zlotnick, C., Johnson, J., & Najavits, L. M. (2009). Randomized controlled pilot study of cognitive-behavioral therapy in a sample of incarcerated women with substance use disorder and PTSD. *Behavior Therapy*, *40*(4), 325–336. doi: 10.1016/j.beth.2008.09.004

34

SUPPORTING HEALING AND WHOLENESS

Evidence-Based Practices in Community Supervision

Alexander M. Holsinger

Introduction

Probation and parole agencies account for the largest number of people under some form of correctional control in the United States. Community supervision provides an important alternative to incarceration, avoiding a great deal of expense and in theory preventing the direct and indirect harm associated with prisons and jails. When a person is granted community supervision post-conviction, they are given an opportunity to engage in employment, remain connected to family and friends, and utilize resources such as counseling and substance abuse treatment that will help them lead more functional lives and avoid further trouble. In addition, there is likely an assumption on the part of the public that community supervision agencies hold clients accountable, keep communities safe from crime, and deliver or at least facilitate services that improves lives. When done well, community supervision holds the potential for harm reduction and can improve the lives of justice-involved people and the family and friends that surround them. When done poorly, the inevitable is merely delayed, with supervision serving as little more than a way station on a person's trip to (or back to) prison.

From the early 1990s forward the literature base that constitutes "evidence-based practices" in correctional intervention has grown exponentially. At the current time, for example, we know that punishment (such as incarceration) that is devoid of any sort of effective and appropriate rehabilitative effort does not work to change behavior in the long term. Correctional control alone, whether it be in the form of incarceration or community supervision, can alter behavior in the short term but does little if anything to address the core factors that compel and motivate antisocial behavior. In the case of probation and parole, the mere act of supervising a person in the community can create some accountability, most commonly in the form of meeting at appointed times, seeking or maintaining employment, making payments on fines or restitution, and submitting to drug tests. But without a human service and needs-based treatment approach, in addition to the supervision, the best we can hope for in the long term is a perpetual cycling of people being on and off supervision, which more than likely will result in confinement (incarceration) at some point. In short, it is necessary to address, and change, the risk and need factors that are active in a corrections-involved person, if we want any hope of changing behavior in the long term (Taxman & Caudy, 2015; Nelson & Vincent, 2018).

DOI: 10.4324/9781003219286-41

What follows is an examination of three broad areas in need of application and/or improvement in the practice of community supervision. In an effort to create lasting behavioral change for clients under supervision in the community, probation and parole agencies need to make sure they are: hiring the right people, conducting appropriate and effective assessment and classification, and ensuring officers and case managers are utilizing effective supervision strategies, which includes offering effective and comprehensive treatment programming.

Hiring

When it comes to hiring the right people, especially entry-level supervision officers, probation and parole administrators should seek people who have a high level of emotional intelligence, who are oriented toward human service and abide by a "social worker" framework, who understand the behavior-shaping power of the relationship, and who are willing to engage in specialized learning and training opportunities. As line-staff move into administrative positions, those traits will become increasingly part of the organization's culture and help shape its trajectory and activities.

High emotional intelligence may be related to several desired traits in community supervision staff and administrators. Like intelligence itself which is indicative of the ability to think in the abstract and engage in complex problem solving, emotional intelligence is indicative of being able to understand and manage emotion in the self and others, and likewise regard the importance of context when understanding people and the circumstances they find themselves in (Mayer et al., 2016). As such, a high level of emotional intelligence may assist in fully understanding a person's behavior (particularly their antisocial behavior), its origins, and the social contexts surrounding the person. Likewise, well-developed emotional intelligence would support the development of plans to intervene with behavior and shape behavioral change over time. Emotional intelligence has been found to be related to the self-efficacy of leadership in correctional environments, though these two constructs remain under-studied in the peer-reviewed literature (Harper, 2016). For example, leaders who are able to fully understand those who work for them are in a much better position to assess performance and offer constructive feedback. The same would hold true for community corrections officers and the people they supervise. It is no surprise that the National Institute of Corrections has included an emphasis on emotional intelligence in their correctional leadership competency training models (Campbell, 2006). Being emotionally literate may be related to effective human service practice, particularly in settings where a staff person needs to evoke both compassion and accountability (Knight et al., 2016). Likewise, emotional intelligence has been related to the prevention of burnout, which in turn impacts staff turnover, which is no small problem for any human-service agency (Gutierrez & Mullen, 2016).

In addition to applied emotional intelligence, a human service/social-worker perspective can increase success on probation or parole supervision. It is common for justice-involved people to present with many serious needs, both criminogenic (e.g., substance abuse, cognitive distortions, lack of education) and non-criminogenic (e.g., mental health needs, poverty, medical). In response, community correctional agencies should position themselves to treat the "whole person", which means being equipped to address both criminogenic and non-criminogenic needs, and an orientation toward human service would assist staff in doing so.

The involvement of actual social workers in correctional practice would prove beneficial as well in meeting any number of needs. Social workers have historically been closely aligned with efforts to support vulnerable populations, including those experiencing correctional sanctions. Over time, however, a division between social workers and corrections developed due to a number of reasons, such as the professionalization of probation and a desire on the part of social workers to serve populations who are free from the duress of a correctional system (Peters, 2011). It is time to bring correctional work in the community back together with social work. Doing so would increase correctional clients' access to needed resources and might change how community correctional officers are viewed by their charges (Doekhie et al., 2018). Possibilities include treating the whole person, as noted (via the addressing of non-criminogenic needs); providing cognitive-behavioral therapeutic (CBT) counseling; and clinically supervising probation and parole officers who also provide CBT and related therapies.

The strength and nature of the relationship between community supervision officer and client is another important thing to consider when staffing a correctional agency. As will be seen in the following, the delivery of correctional services has evolved far beyond the mere "checking of boxes" ensuring court obligations are met. Increasingly officers are required to deliver behavioral change services even during the context of brief meetings with their clients. This renewed focus on officer-as-change-agent underscores the need for there to be a warm and professional relationship between officer and client in order to maximize the engagement and responsiveness of the client. Research has shown that the quality of the relationship does matter, and officer attitudes influence community supervision outcomes (Vidal & Woolard, 2017; Lowenkamp et al., 2013). Likewise, it has been demonstrated that the quality of the relationship between officer and client can influence satisfaction with supervision, which in turn may influence engagement, accountability, and success. In addition to emotional intelligence, correctional administrators should consider relational style, and the extent to which potential line officers evoke warmth and professionalism. Specialized training should be a frequent part of professional development as well. Effective training has been shown to increase officer knowledge about effective behavioral change strategies and other evidence-based practices. In addition, knowledge about specialized needs, particularly in the areas of mental and behavioral health are improved, which is important in light of the increasing extent to which correctional clients present with co-occurring needs (Lowenkamp et al., 2013; Tomar et al., 2017).

Takeaways:

- Correctional administrators should consider utilizing tests of emotional intelligence in the hiring process to ensure supervision officers possess the desired level of maturity and the ability to address the complexities related to changing antisocial behavior.
- Supervision officers should have an orientation toward human service delivery and a belief in the potential for behavioral change in the clients they serve.
- Supervision agencies should consider utilizing social workers to address clients' non-criminogenic needs and in an effort to leverage non-criminal justice related resources. Social workers (e.g. LCSWs) could also play a role in training staff in counseling techniques and providing clinical supervision.

- Supervision officers should be willing to build a warm, compassionate, and professional relationship with their clientele and recognize the power that the relationship holds in shaping behavior.

Assessment and Classification

Community correctional agencies must have a robust assessment and classification protocol in order to facilitate effective case management and behavioral interventions. At the heart of any protocol is a valid actuarial instrument that dynamically assesses the major criminogenic risk and need domains (e.g., education and employment, substance abuse, social network, and cognitions to name a few). For example, much research, including meta-analyses have demonstrated the predictive validity of instruments such as the Level of Service Inventory-Revised (LSI-R) and its juvenile counterpart, the Youth Level of Service/Case Management Inventory (YLS/CMI), on general as well as specific populations (Wilson & Gutierrez, 2013; Pusch & Holtfreter, 2017; Ostermann & Herrschaft, 2013). Other instruments are available, with several having exhibited varying degrees of effectiveness when their predictive validity is tested. Any instrument needs to be put through localized validation, preferably prior to full adoption, with plans for regular re-validation research (e.g., biennially). In addition, localized regular validation should be applied to the entire population and all subgroups individually, in order to test whether the instruments work for everyone the agency serves, and specific analyses should be used to test for racial, ethnic, and sex bias.

Effective risk/need assessments allow an agency to implement the risk and need principles, so the highest risk individuals will more likely receive the most attention. Good assessments also ensure that appropriate services are delivered to the correct clients, reducing the likelihood of future antisocial behavior (Lowenkamp et al., 2006). Correctional resources, particularly treatment programming, tend to be scarce commodities and are sometimes wasted on individuals who will not benefit from them, because they do not need them. An effective assessment model will allow line staff to build comprehensive and dynamic case plans that will facilitate the delivery of appropriate resources, and chart progress as a client moves through programming. The dynamic nature of both assessment instruments and case plans are crucial so change over time can be measured. In short, if supervision strategies and treatment programming are effective, change in summary scores should be observable over time, and the changes in scores should correlate with changes in behavior in the long term.

In addition to choosing the right risk/need tool and ensuring it possesses predictive validity, there are several other things that should be kept in mind if correctional administrators wish to foster an effective assessment and classification protocol. There must be strong buy-in on the part of all staff, especially those who will be using the instruments. Virtually all of the current fourth-generation comprehensive risk/need assessment instruments require training often involving at least 2 if not more days. That means there is a very real and often steep learning curve that staff must surmount if they are going to emerge equipped to use the instruments effectively. Staff will be challenged, and may be apt to grow frustrated, which in turn can impact the likelihood they will learn the necessary skills. Staff need to believe in the tool, and its potential benefits, to be in the best position to use the tool effectively and administer their caseloads appropriately. In addition to the initial training, booster or brief re-training sessions should be a regular part of annual training plans as well. Plans should be made to test the inter-rater reliability of the tools to ensure that staff are all "seeing" risk and need factors the same way. Without comprehensive implementation that involves many different and regular empirical tests, there are many ways in which validity can break down over time (Latessa & Lovins, 2010).

In addition to a general risk/need assessment tool, agencies should adopt domain-specific tools particularly when domain-specific programming is in place. Effective comprehensive tools will at least touch on each of the major criminogenic domains, but a generalized instrument's individual domains rarely if ever should serve as a stand-alone assessment for a particular area or need. For example, if a community supervision agency utilizes a cognitive behavioral program to address criminogenic cognitions, in addition to a comprehensive global risk/need assessment tool, a specific tool that goes into depth regarding antisocial cognitions (e.g., the Psychological Inventory of Criminal Thinking Styles, or PICTS) should be used also (see Walters, 2011 for an example of how the PICTS can be used alongside the screening version of the LSI-R). The same protocol referred to previously (buy-in, validation/re-validation, tests for bias) applies to any tools that are chosen and put into use.

Finally, despite its importance being highlighted for decades, the incorporation of responsivity into an agency's assessment protocol remains largely elusive and under-researched. Assessing risk tells an agency who among their clientele needs the most services (and likewise who needs the least), assessing need indicates what specifically needs to be targeted and addressed via effective supervision and treatment strategies. Assessing responsivity should inform the best ways to go about interacting with someone (i.e. relationally), and the manner by which treatment activities should be delivered, in an effort to mitigate barriers that would ordinarily prohibit a client from benefiting.

In fairness, assessing responsivity at the agency level is not nearly as straightforward as risk, or need. Responsivity considerations span a wide range of contexts and forms. Taxman (2014) highlighted in detail what are referred to as "general", "specific", and "systemic" responsivity considerations. Briefly, agencies utilize general responsivity when they prioritize interventions that incorporate a social learning method that addresses cognitions (which in turn necessitates the need to assess both learning style, and cognitions themselves). Specific responsivity factors exist at the individual level and are put into use when the agency tailors an intervention as best it can to account for individual barriers to engaging in treatment, such as motivation, relational style, anxiety, or language barriers, to name just a few. Systemic responsivity refers to the need to have available all resources necessary to address an array of criminogenic needs that likewise accounts for the functionality of the individual (Taxman, 2014).

Despite being generally under-studied, there are some empirical inquiries into responsivity in action. One qualitative study found that individual-level responsivity principles can be applied by developing a constructive relationship with clients. Basic but important characteristics emerged such as clear and honest communication, taking relational style into account and adjusting for it, and incorporating what was termed a "relational but secure" approach (Ricciardelli & Perry, 2016).

Takeaways:

- Community supervision agencies should adopt, thoroughly pilot, and fully implement a fourth-generation risk/need assessment instrument and ensure that the instrument drives dynamic and meaningful case planning and assesses the progress of clients.
- All risk/need assessments should periodically (e.g., every 2 years) be subjected to tests of predictive validity, including tests using specific sub-groups of the client population and rigorous tests for racial, ethnic, and sex bias.

- Agencies should adopt a "graduated" assessment model, whereby the comprehensive risk/need instrument serves as the foundation and additional domain-specific instruments go into more depth (e.g. with substance abuse, antisocial cognitions, education).
- Agencies should commit to formally assessing responsivity and infusing responsivity-based strategies into all procedures in order reduce barriers to success and to make behavioral change efforts more effective.
- Officer buy-in regarding all assessment tools should be periodically assessed and addressed as needed.

New More Effective Supervision Strategies

In the most recent decades, important developments in community supervision strategies have emerged. Perhaps most notably, the community supervision officer has re-emerged as an agent of behavioral change. Probationary supervision as a concept – as an alternative to incarceration – was originally seen as a way to help people change their behavior through care, counseling, and the provision of treatment services. Over time, treatment and rehabilitation came to be seen as separate and distinct from supervision, and as a result supervision evolved into more of an administrative function, meant to ensure that at a minimum the court-ordered requirements such as remaining drug free, engaging in employment, paying fines, and avoiding co-defendants were met. Helping the offender change their behavior was viewed as the responsibility of the treatment program and not directly under the purview of the community supervision officer.

Due to perceptions regarding how large caseloads typically are, and the relatively short amount of time an officer might spend with a client, the prospect of creating behavioral change within the context of an office visit seemed impossible (Gleicher et al., 2013). Recently, however, some researchers and policy makers have questioned whether behavioral change within the context of an office visit is indeed a "lost cause" and new strategies have emerged. An immediate concern revolved around what may have been initially viewed as a de-emphasis on, or even ignoring of, court-ordered requirements. In reality, however, the amount of time required to check on whether court orders have been met is not as great as initially thought, and in turn that time, even if brief, may be better spent focusing on behavior.

Several new curricula and strategies have been developed and implemented that do just that, blending what we now know can help change behavior with "regular" office visits between officer and client. A change in professional identity for community supervision officers may be emerging alongside these new curricula and strategies, compelling administrators and officers to see themselves more as "coaches" as opposed to "referees" (Lovins et al., 2018). This change in perception compels correctional professionals to focus on human service rather than control, behavioral change over efficiency and procedure, adopt a more personal approach, and use encouragement rather than warnings about rule infractions and potential consequences (Lovins et al., 2018). It is not farfetched to view these changes as blending treatment components that are integral to cognitive behavioral therapies with regular supervision.

Effective Practices in Community Supervision (EPICS) is one such curriculum designed to improve community supervision practices. The goal of the EPICS curriculum is to teach community supervision officers how to make behavioral change aspects of the risk, need, and responsivity (RNR) model part of their everyday work with clients. For example, officers trained in EPICS use an intentional and structured approach to their meetings with clients, targeting criminogenic needs (including antisocial cognitions) with active exercises that result in constructive feedback.

Clients are often given homework as well that will provide some of the structure for the next meeting, and so on. Becoming certified in EPICS requires a multi day training, with ongoing follow-up and coaching of the officer (Gleicher et al., 2013). There is empirical evidence that officers trained in EPICS do become proficient in behavioral change skills and incorporate them into their regular supervision meetings (Smith et al., 2012). Likewise, there is some evidence demonstrating that EPICS-trained officers impact the prevalence of antisocial cognitions in their clientele compared to non-trained officers (Labrecque et al., 2013).

Another RNR-based training curriculum for supervision officers was developed in Canada and is known as the Strategic Training Initiative in Community Supervision, or STICS (Bonta et al., 2019). Like EPICS, STICS involves intensive officer training in an effort to teach them to infuse their day-to-day meetings with clients with cognitive behavioral techniques, addressing criminogenic needs, and building rapport (Bonta et al., 2021). It has been demonstrated that officers trained in STICS do utilize the desired behavioral change strategies and that doing so may impact recidivism (Bonta et al., 2011). On the U.S. federal level, the Administrative Office of the Courts developed Staff Training Aimed at Reducing Rearrest, or STARR. The STARR curriculum endeavors to train officers in the use of what have commonly been referred to as core correctional practices, much in the same way as EPICS and STICS. Also, like EPICS and STICS, there is promising evidence that officers trained in STARR do incorporate the behavioral change strategies as designed, within the context of regular meetings, and in turn, some reductions in failure rates have been observed (Robinson et al., 2012; Lowenkamp et al., 2014). More rigorous analyses have revealed still promising but mixed results for STARR (Labrecque & Viglione, 2021).

Takeaways:

- Supervision officers should be encouraged to view themselves as agents of change, engaging in much more than basic accountability checks with their clients.
- One or more core correctional practice curricula should be adopted, piloted, and fully implemented. The implementation of the new curricula and related training and activities should be viewed as a paradigm shift in the mission of the agency. Officers should be fully aware of the power even a brief supervision visit can have in effecting change.
- Once the curriculum is adopted plans should be made to execute empirical investigations in order to assess effectiveness via outcomes that are influenced by the new strategies.
- Periodic checks on officer buy-in and skill attainment should be conducted.

Conclusion

The history and practice of community supervision has evolved substantially. Like many professions, probation and parole supervision have been influenced by the political climate, resource constraints, philosophical shifts, and crisis. Currently, however, the field is at an exciting point, with the potential of becoming more humane, just, and effective in helping offenders change their behavior in the long term and becoming fully functional and productive members of their community. Outlined previously are three broad areas that need further consideration, implementation, and empirical testing in the field.

When hiring staff, correctional leaders should look for people who believe in the possibility of behavioral change. Entry-level staff who have a background in criminal justice and criminology, psychology, education, and social work should be prioritized. Just as important as educational background, however, is the level of maturity a new staff member brings, including their emotional intelligence, ability (and willingness) to empathize, and their relational style.

Correctional administrators should also regularly revisit their agency's assessment protocol. Offender assessment and classification provides the foundation upon which most every other intervention is built, and as such it is of paramount concern that the instrument that is in place is comprehensive and dynamic, has exhibited adequate if not excellent predictive validity, is devoid of bias, and has broad and sincere staff buy-in. It is likewise time for agencies to widely adopt a graduated assessment model whereby specific domains are assessed further than the initial assessment goes, and likewise where specific instruments are utilized for specialized populations such as sex offenders and those who exhibit chronic domestic violence. Further, the field is yet under-developed regarding the extent to which responsivity as a construct is assessed in a standardized fashion and helps drive all interventions. Finally, it is time to do away with the model of supervision that incorporates little more than perfunctory checks on court-ordered accountability measures. Core correctional practices have developed in a manner that allows supervision officers to re-frame the "officer/client" meeting structure and relationship, thereby delivering active and interactive behavioral change treatment.

Any change, perhaps especially at the agency level, requires good and transparent leadership that consistently communicates the reasoning behind the desired change. Good leadership should also include strategies to assess staff buy-in and address doubts when they are revealed. While the focus of this chapter has been increasing the capacity to affect offender change, it should also be widely understood that many of the changes outlined previously depend on staff changing their behavior too. As a result, in keeping with cognitive behavioral principles, administrators should be able and prepared to reward good performance on the part of staff. Agencies should also have a clear path upward, so staff who perform at peak levels of effectiveness can advance. This also means that agencies should collect data from both staff and clients so that staff effectiveness can be measured, with high performance rewarded, allowing for areas needing improvement to be addressed. It is an exciting time to practice and study community corrections. Many of the more recent developments, if implemented widely and with integrity, will make our correctional systems overall more humane and effective in eliciting long-term behavioral change.

References

Bonta, J., Bourgon, G., Rugge, T., Scott, T. L., Yessine, A., Gutierrez, L., & Li, J. (2011). An experimental demonstration of training probation officers in evidence-based community supervision. *Criminal Justice and Behavior*, *38*(11), 1127–1148.

Bonta, J., Bourgon, G., Rugge, T., Pedneault, C. I., & Lee, S. C. (2021). A system-wide implementation and evaluation of the Strategic Training Initiative in Community Supervision (STICS). *Journal of Criminal Justice*, *74*, 101816.

Bonta, J., Rugge, T., Bourgon, G., & Wanamaker, K. A. (2019). A conceptual replication of the Strategic Training Initiative in Community Supervision (STICS). *Journal of Experimental Criminology*, *15*(3), 397–419.

Campbell, N. M. (2006). *Correctional leadership competencies for the 21st century: Manager and supervisor levels*. U.S. Department of Justice, National Institute of Corrections.

Doekhie, J., van Ginneken, E., Dirkzwager, A., & Nieuwbeerta, P. (2018). Managing risk or supporting desistance? A longitudinal study on the nature and perceptions of parole supervision in the Netherlands. *Journal of Developmental and Life-Course Criminology*, *4*(4), 491–515.

Gleicher, L., Manchak, S., & Cullen, F. T. (2013). Creating a supervision tool kit: How to improve probation and parole. *Federal Probation*, *77*(1), 22–27.

Gutierrez, D., & Mullen, P. R. (2016). Emotional intelligence and the counselor: Examining the relationship of trait emotional intelligence to counselor burnout. *Journal of Mental Health Counseling*, *38*(3), 187–200.

Harper, D. S. (2016). Correctional executives' leadership self-efficacy and their perceptions of emotional intelligence. *American Journal of Criminal Justice*, *41*(4), 765–779.
Knight, C., Phillips, J., & Chapman, T. (2016). Bringing the feelings back: Returning emotions to criminal justice practice. *British Journal of Community Justice*, *14*(1), 45–58.
Labrecque, R. M., & Viglione, J. (2021). The impact of a community supervision officer training program on client outcomes. *Criminal Justice and Behavior*, *48*(3), 315–331.
Labrecque, R. M., Smith, P., Schweitzer, M., & Thompson, C. (2013). Targeting antisocial attitudes in community supervision using the EPICS model: An examination of change scores on the Criminal Sentiments Scale. *Federal Probation*, *77*(3), 15–20.
Latessa, E. J., & Lovins, B. (2010). The role of offender risk assessment: A policy maker guide. *Victims and Offenders*, *5*(3), 203–219.
Lovins, B. K., Cullen, F. T., Latessa, E. J., & Jonson, C. L. (2018). Probation officer as coach: Building a new professional identity. *Federal Probation*, *82*(1), 13–19.
Lowenkamp, C. T., Latessa, E. J., & Holsinger, A. M. (2006). The risk principle in action: What we have learned from 13,676 offenders and 97 correctional programs. *Crime and Delinquency*, *52*(1), 1–17.
Lowenkamp, C. T., Holsinger, A. M., Flores, A. W., & Koutsenok, I. (2013). Changing probation officer attitudes: Training experience, motivation, and knowledge. *Federal Probation*, *77*(2), 54–58.
Lowenkamp, C. T., Holsinger, A. M., Robinson, C. R., & Alexander, M. (2014). Diminishing or durable treatment effects of STARR? A research note on 24-month rearrest rates. *Journal of Crime and Justice*, *37*(2), 275–283.
Mayer, J. D., Caruso, D. R., & Salovey, P. (2016). The ability model of emotional intelligence: Principles and updates. *Emotion Review*, *8*(4), 290–300.
Nelson, R. J., & Vincent, G. M. (2018). Matching services to criminogenic needs following comprehensive risk assessment implementation in juvenile probation. *Criminal Justice & Behavior*, *45*(8), 1136–1153.
Ostermann, M., & Herrschaft, B. A. (2013). Validating the level of service inventory-revised: A gendered perspective. *The Prison Journal*, *93*(3), 291–312.
Peters, C. M. (2011). Social work and juvenile probation: Historical tensions and contemporary convergences. *Social Work*, *56*(4), 355–365.
Pusch, N., & Holtfreter, K. (2017). Gender and risk assessment in juvenile offenders: A meta-analysis. *Criminal Justice and Behavior*, *45*(1), 56–81.
Ricciardelli, R., & Perry, K. (2016). Responsivity in practice: Prison officer to prisoner communication in Canadian provincial prisons. *Journal of Contemporary Criminal Justice*, *32*(4), 401–425.
Robinson, C. R., Lowenkamp, C. T., Holsinger, A. M., VanBenschoten, S., Alexander, M., & Oleson, J. C. (2012). A random study of Staff Training Aimed at Reducing Rearrest (STARR): Using core correctional practices in probation interactions. *Journal of Crime and Justice*, *35*(2), 167–188.
Smith, P., Schweitzer, M., Labrecque, R. M., & Latessa, E. J. (2012). Improving probation officers' supervision skills: An evaluation of the EPICS model. *Journal of Crime and Justice*, *35*(2), 189–199.
Taxman, F. (2014). Second generation of RNR: The importance of systemic responsivity in expanding core principles of responsivity. *Federal Probation*, *78*(2), 32–40.
Taxman, F. S., & Caudy, M. S. (2015). Risk tells us who, but not what or how: Empirical assessment of the complexity of criminogenic needs to inform correctional programming. *Criminology & Public Policy*, *14*(1), 71–103.
Tomar, N., Ghezzi, M. A., Brinkley-Rubinstein, L., Wilson, A. B., Van Deinse, T. B., Burgin, S., & Cuddeback, G. S. (2017). Statewide mental health training for probation officers: Improving knowledge and decreasing stigma. *Health and Justice*, *5*(1), 1–5.
Vidal, S., & Woolard, J. (2017). Youth's perception of parental support and parental knowledge as moderators of the association between youth-probation officer relationship and probation non-compliance. *Journal of Youth Adolescence*, *46*(7), 1452–1471.
Walters, G. D. (2011). Predicting recidivism with the psychological inventory of criminal thinking styles and level of service inventory-revised: Screening version. *Law and Human Behavior*, *35*(3), 211–220.
Wilson, H. A., & Gutierrez, L. (2013). A meta-analysis examining the predictive ability of the Level of Service Inventory (LSI) with aboriginal offenders. *Criminal Justice and Behavior*, *41*(2), 196–219.

35

JUSTICE-INVOLVED PERSONS WITH OPIOID USE DISORDER

Reducing Overdose and Criminal Recidivism

Khary K. Rigg

Introduction

The number of people involved in the criminal justice system has ballooned over the last few decades. There are currently two million individuals in America's prisons/jails and another five million living in the community under some form of criminal justice supervision (Kaeble et al., 2016). This represents a 500% increase in the number of justice-involved persons (JIPs) over the last four decades. This increase is largely due to the expansion of stricter drug laws and stiffer penalties for drug offenses. In fact, the number of Americans incarcerated for drug offenses has skyrocketed from 40,000 in 1980 to 430,926 in 2019 (Sentencing Project, 2021). This has resulted in an overrepresentation of people with substance use disorders (SUDs) in the justice system.

It is estimated that 65% of the United States prison population has an active SUD (National Institute on Drug Abuse [NIDA], 2021). Opioid use disorders (OUDs), in particular, are among the most prevalent and problematic type of SUD among JIPs. One study estimated that over 15% of the incarcerated population has an OUD, but less than 10% receive evidence-based OUD treatment (Johnson et al., 2020; NIDA, 2018). JIPs also experience greater consequences (e.g., hospitalization, mental health problems) from their use of opioids than their non-justice-involved peers (Malta et al., 2019; Rigg & DeCamp, 2014). Perhaps most importantly, though, risk of overdose death can reach up to 40 times higher for people recently released from prison than it is for the general population (Ranapurwala et al., 2018).

Despite JIPs being at elevated risk for OUD and overdose, there is little discussion about the unique risks facing opioid-involved offenders and best practices for intervening with this population. The overall goal of this chapter, therefore, is to assist correctional agencies, law enforcement, and probation/parole agencies in better responding to the needs of JIPs with OUD. A discussion of effective interventions could be useful to criminal justice professionals and help guide treatment providers serving JIPs (Rigg & Murphy, 2013).

Unique Risks Facing JIPs

Rates of intravenous drug use are high among JIPs (Surratt et al., 2011). Intravenous routes of administration carry the highest risk of overdose because they bypass the digestive system

DOI: 10.4324/9781003219286-42

and allow the drug to pass into the blood–brain barrier with higher bioavailability. JIPs also experience high rates of polydrug use, which is another risk factor for opioid related death (Bunting et al., 2020). Another contributing factor is that JIPs receive medication treatment for OUD (e.g., buprenorphine, methadone) at much lower rates than the general public (Nunn et al., 2009). Medication treatment is considered the gold standard OUD treatment approach and is the only intervention known to cut overdose risk by up to 50% (Pierce et al., 2016). The justice system has been historically resistant to offering medication because of the outdated belief that offenders are simply replacing one addiction with another.

Another reason JIPs are especially vulnerable to overdose is their low tolerance to opioids when released from prison. National data show that over seven million people are released from prison/jail each year (Healthy People, 2020). Formerly incarcerated persons undergo forced drug withdrawal during incarceration and thus have lowered opioid tolerance when they are released. Opioid misuse during the first few weeks of re-entry is particularly susceptible to overdose due to the body suddenly being exposed to opioids after a prolonged period of abstinence. Risk of overdose is exacerbated even further by medical comorbidities, inadequate economic resources, and lack of available post-release support programs. Additionally, JIPs re-entering the community return to environments (e.g., drug using peers, stressful living arrangements) that can trigger bouts of heavy opioid misuse, putting them at risk for overdose (Binswanger et al., 2012; Rigg et al., 2018). Interventions aimed at the general population tend to overlook these unique risk factors and are thus less effective for JIPs (Rigg et al., 2014). The following section is a brief summary of interventions for reducing overdose and criminal recidivism among JIPs who are opioid involved.

Interventions for JIPs with OUD

Pre-Arrest Diversion Programs

The traditional law enforcement response to people with OUDs has relied on a criminal justice-driven approach (e.g., arrest, prosecution, incarceration). Pre-arrest diversion programs are a newer approach to policing aimed at breaking the cycle of addiction by offering treatment in lieu of arrest and prosecution. The idea behind these programs is that communities cannot "arrest their way out of the drug problem", and connecting people to treatment and other support services is a more effective way to reduce addiction-related harms, such as crime and overdose. Some of the more popular pre-arrest diversion programs such as Police-Assisted Addiction and Recovery Initiative (PAARI), Law Enforcement Assisted Diversion (LEAD), and the Angel program have received national attention. These programs have been shown to reduce criminal recidivism and overdoses among some JIPs (Bernard et al., 2020; Collins et al., 2017), but further research is needed to determine how best to structure and implement these programs for optimal results (McNeish et al., 2019).

The following expansions are recommended:

- Pre-arrest diversion programs should be adopted widely and not only in jurisdictions where the need is high.
- To maximize the effects of these programs, eligibility criteria should be expanded so that pre-arrest diversion programs are not just limited to individuals with first-time or low-level offenses (e.g., misdemeanors).
- Persons with substance use problems and/or criminal histories (who may be more likely to reoffend) should not be immediately excluded from diversion opportunities. Some

discretion should be allowed for permitting individuals with these backgrounds into pre-arrest diversion programs so that more people can benefit.

Drug Treatment Courts

Drug treatment courts (DTCs) are specialized courts where offenders are processed with their addiction in mind, unlike traditional courts that favor long prison sentences (Marlowe, 2010). These courts involve a multidisciplinary team of criminal justice and treatment professionals who work together in order to provide a comprehensive treatment plan for addicted offenders. DTCs can be effective at making treatment linkages, and lowering substance use and criminal activity for offenders who are drug involved (Moore et al., 2017; Wilson et al., 2006). Despite the widespread adoption of DTCs nationally, more work is still needed to perfect these interventions. Detractors of DTCs criticize them for requiring participants to plead guilty, prohibiting/restricting medication-based treatment, and disproportionately selecting participants who are financially solvent and White (Tyler, 2017). Thus, changes are needed.

With these data in mind, recommendations regarding drug courts include the following:

- All drug treatment courts should offer medication-based treatment for OUD.
- Participation in drug treatment courts should not be dependent on one's ability to pay fines or fees, nor should inability to do so be criminally sanctioned (Social Science Research Council, 2019).
- A recurrence of drug use (often referred to as relapse) should not be used as the basis for imposing sanctions because relapse is considered an accepted part of recovery.
- The existence of a criminal record or the nature of the offense should not render people ineligible, which often happens (Mehta, 2017).

Medication Treatment in Criminal Justice Settings

Medication treatment is the gold standard for treating OUD in criminal justice settings. Not only are they FDA approved, but they have been around for decades, have undergone rigorous efficacy testing, and are considered safe. Criminal justice settings (e.g., jails, prisons, probation, parole) have been historically opposed to offering this form of treatment to JIPs because of the belief that these medications simply replace one addiction with another. Even DTCs have been reluctant to offer medications as evidenced by 44% still prohibiting/restricting their use to treat OUD (Matusow et al., 2013). Research, however, shows that providing medication treatment to JIPs, both during and after incarceration, reduces post-release overdose mortality, HIV infection, illicit drug use, and criminal recidivism/rearrest (Hyatt & Lobmaier, 2020). It is the unequivocal position of the National Drug Court Institute and National Association of State Alcohol and Drug Abuse Directors that medication treatment should not only be made available to all JIPs but should be considered the front-line treatment for OUD in criminal justice settings (National Drug Court Institute, 2021).

Given these data, it is recommended that:

- OUD medications be made widely available across criminal justice settings, as JIPs should be entitled to treatment options similar to those who are not justice involved (Bruce & Schleifer, 2008). These medications have high safety profile and high efficacy.
- Jurisdictions consider using existing federal and state funding to create/expand access to medication-based treatments for JIPs (Substance Abuse and Mental Health Services Administration, 2019).

Distributing Naloxone Kits

Naloxone, known widely as the opioid antidote, is a medication used to reverse opioid overdoses. Naloxone works by binding to opioid receptors and blocks the effects of other opioids, which restores normal respiration and prevents death. It is safe, easily administered, and should be given as soon as possible to people believed to be overdosing on opioids such as heroin, oxycodone, and fentanyl (McLean et al., 2019). Naloxone kits are portable pouches containing an opioid antidote that can be administered by injection or through the nose to revive an unresponsive person who is overdosing (Hamilton Health Sciences, 2020). Inside these kits are instructions on how to administer the medication and an explanation of how it works. Research has found that distributing naloxone kits to JIPs upon their release is effective at decreasing opioid overdose mortality in the often precarious weeks following the release of prisoners (Malta et al., 2019). Distributing naloxone kits to recently released JIPs with an OUD is a low-cost evidence-based intervention that should become standard practice for jails/prisons. Research also supports equipping police with naloxone as they are often the first on the scene of overdose emergency calls (Walley et al., 2013).

It is recommended that:

- JIPs receive training on the use of naloxone upon release, but preferably pre-release. Potential venues for this training could be in jail or prison, within probation departments or re-entry programs, or in housing or addiction treatment programs specifically for people exiting incarceration (Wenger et al., 2018).
- Individuals who live or work with recently released JIPs can also be trained on the use of naloxone.

Behavioral Health Alternatives to Opioid-Related 911 Calls

Many 911 calls that police departments respond to are better addressed by behavioral health professionals. To address this need, several programs are being piloted that divert non-criminal/non-violent 911 calls away from police officers. One of the goals of these programs is to send a behavioral health response team (e.g., social worker, case manager) rather than a police officer to calls related to addiction and overdose. Because of these programs, an overdose may be avoided because the behavioral health team provided on-the-spot support to someone in crisis, a common precursor of drug overdose. These programs also have the potential to connect more people to addiction treatment and self-help groups (e.g., Narcotics Anonymous) and even reverse overdoses that may be occurring when they arrive by administering naloxone. Although it may be premature to label these programs evidence based, they have a strong theoretical basis and there is much enthusiasm about these programs among both criminal justice and behavioral health professionals. Some promising pilot programs include the Support Team Assisted Response (STAR) Program in Denver, Community Assistance and Life Liaison (CALL) Program in St. Petersburg, and Crisis Assistance Helping out on the Streets (CAHOOTS) Program in St. Louis (Verona et al., 2022; Enos, 2020; Braziel, 2021; Waters, 2021).

The following recommendations follow from information obtained from existing programs:

- While these programs tend to be disproportionately available in urban areas, it is recommended that rural jurisdictions also consider adopting these programs.
- Stronger partnerships between behavioral health agencies and law enforcement will be needed to coordinate workflows and staffing, but there are models across the country that can be adapted to fit the needs of specific jurisdictions.

- More research is needed to evaluate the efficacy of these programs in diverting individuals, reducing maltreatment in the hands of law enforcement, and providing life-saving care and substance use treatment services.

Conclusions

The PREVIOUS strategies are, unfortunately, not standard practice in criminal justice settings. More needs to be done to remove implementation barriers so that these interventions can be scaled up. For example, concerns remain that medications used to treat OUD are often diverted and misused, even though these fears are largely unfounded as there is no evidence of these issues occurring on a large scale. Instead, the benefits of providing OUD medications to JIPs are many. Research shows that medications reduce illicit drug use and overdose events, both fatal and nonfatal (Lee et al., 2015, 2016). Across criminal justice settings, OUD medications have also been found to reduce arrests, criminal activity, re-incarceration, and probation revocations (Schwartz et al., 2009; Cornish et al., 1997; Ball & Ross, 1991). Another underused strategy that can save lives is to provide individuals exiting incarceration with naloxone kits, as well as receiving training on how to administer it (Wenger et al., 2019). Because overdose risk is so high upon re-entry, and persons being released into the community are typically entering neighborhoods where drug use is high and may witness an opioid overdose, being trained on overdose prevention and having a naloxone kit on hand could save lives.

Likewise, although drug treatment courts remain an evidence-based practice, improvements to these programs are needed. An overarching problem is that the manner in which these courts are implemented is wildly inconsistent and many programs do not follow best practices. For example, access to medication-based treatments is still lacking in some courts (Farago et al., 2022). Further, eligibility restrictions that block people with complicated criminal or substance use histories from participating in drug treatment courts should be reconsidered because they prevent potential beneficiaries of these programs from participating.

Finally, programs that dispatch behavioral health teams (instead of law enforcement) to addiction/overdose-related 911 calls are relatively few and many are still in the pilot stage. However, early findings are very promising as these programs have already had a positive impact in several communities across the country. Wider adoption of these programs will require increased awareness of their benefits, greater buy-in across police departments, and stronger community support. Implementing these programs can come at a significant cost, but all agencies must make difficult budget decisions and when people's lives are on the line, an investment in innovative programs like these should take priority.

This chapter fills a gap in the literature by spotlighting factors that place JIPs at risk for overdose and describing effective (and promising) programs for intervening with this population. Law enforcement, courts, corrections, and probation/parole agencies may wish to consider the risks and programs described in this chapter when looking to reduce overdose and criminal recidivism among opioid-involved JIPs in their jurisdictions. The information presented in this chapter is particularly timely given the recent spike in rates of opioid misuse and overdoses due to the COVID-19 pandemic.

References

Ball, J., & Ross, A. (1991). *The effectiveness of methadone maintenance treatment: Patients, programs, services, and outcomes*. Springer-Verlag.

Bernard, C. L., Rao, I. J., Robison, K. K., & Brandeau, M. L. (2020). Health outcomes and cost-effectiveness of diversion programs for low-level drug offenders: A model-based analysis. *PLoS Medicine*, *17*(10), e1003239.

Binswanger, I. A., Nowels, C., Corsi, K. F., Glanz, J., Long, J., Booth, R. E., & Steiner, J. F. (2012). Return to drug use and overdose after release from prison: A qualitative study of risk and protective factors. *Addiction Science & Clinical Practice*, *7*(1), 1–9.

Bruce, R. D., & Schleifer, R. A. (2008). Ethical and human rights imperatives to ensure medication-assisted treatment for opioid dependence in prisons and pre-trial detention. *International Journal of Drug Policy*, *19*(1), 17–23.

Bunting, A. M., Oser, C., Staton, M., & Knudsen, H. (2020). Polysubstance use patterns among justice-involved individuals who use opioids. *Substance Use & Misuse*, *55*(13), 2165–2174.

Collins, S. E., Lonczak, H. S., & Clifasefi, S. L. (2017). Seattle's Law Enforcement Assisted Diversion (LEAD): Program effects on recidivism outcomes. *Evaluation and Program Planning*, *64*, 49–56.

Cornish, J. W., Metzger, D., Woody, G. E., Wilson, D., McLellan, A. T., Vandergrift, B., & O'Brien, C. (1997). Naltrexone pharmacotherapy for opioid dependent federal probations. *Journal of Substance Abuse Treatment*, *14*(6), 529–534.

Enos, G. (2020). Crisis response in Denver progresses, with many other communities watching. *Mental Health Weekly*, *30*(37), 1–6.

Farago, F., Blue, T. R., Smith, L. R., Witte, J. C., Gordon, M., & Taxman, F. S. (2022). Medication-assisted treatment in problem-solving courts: A national survey of state and local court coordinators. *Journal of Drug Issues*, *1*, 1–25.

Hamilton Health Sciences. (2020). How to use a naloxone kit. Retrieved from www.hamiltonhealthsciences.ca/share/how-to-use-a-naloxone-kit/

Healthy People. (2020). Incarceration 2020. Retrieved from https://health.gov/healthypeople/priority-areas/social-determinants-health/literature-summaries/incarceration

Hyatt, J. M., & Lobmaier, P. P. (2020). Medication assisted treatment (MAT) in criminal justice settings as a double-edged sword: Balancing novel addiction treatments and voluntary participation. *Health & Justice*, *8*(1), 1–10.

Johnson, K., Rigg, K. K., & Eyles, C. H. (2020). Receiving addiction treatment in the US: Do patient demographics, drug of choice, or substance use disorder severity matter? *International Journal of Drug Policy*, *75*, 102583.

Kaeble, D., Glaze, L., Tsoutis, A., & Minton, T. (2016). Correctional populations in the United States, 2016. Retrieved from https://bjs.ojp.gov/content/pub/pdf/cpus16.pdf

Lee, J. D., Friedmann, P. D., Kinlock, T. W., Nunes, E. V., Boney, T. Y., Hoskinson Jr, R. A., . . . O'Brien, C. P. (2016). Extended-release naltrexone to prevent opioid relapse in criminal justice offenders. *New England Journal of Medicine*, *374*(13), 1232–1242.

Lee, J. D., McDonald, R., Grossman, E., McNeely, J., Laska, E., Rotrosen, J., & Gourevitch, M. N. (2015). Opioid treatment at release from jail using extended-release naltrexone: A pilot proof-of-concept randomized effectiveness trial. *Addiction*, *110*(6), 1008–1014.

Malta, M., Varatharajan, T., Russell, C., Pang, M., Bonato, S., & Fischer, B. (2019). Opioid-related treatment, interventions, and outcomes among incarcerated persons: A systematic review. *PLoS Medicine*, *16*(12), e1003002.

Marlowe, D. (2010). *Research update on adult drug courts*. National Association of Drug Court Professionals.

Matusow, H., Dickman, S. L., Rich, J. D., Fong, C., Dumont, D. M., Hardin, C., . . . Rosenblum, A. (2013). Medication assisted treatment in US drug courts: Results from a nationwide survey of availability, barriers and attitudes. *Journal of Substance Abuse Treatment*, *44*(5), 473–480.

McLean, K., Monnat, S. M., Rigg, K., Sterner III, G. E., & Verdery, A. (2019). "You never know what you're getting": Opioid users' perceptions of fentanyl in southwest Pennsylvania. *Substance Use & Misuse*, *54*(6), 955–966.

McNeish, R., Rigg, K. K., Tran, Q., & Hodges, S. (2019). Community-based behavioral health interventions: Developing strong community partnerships. *Evaluation and Program Planning*, *73*, 111–115.

Mehta, C. (2017). How drug courts are falling short. Retrieved from www.opensocietyfoundations.org/voices/how-drug-courts-are-falling-short

Moore, K. A., Barongi, M. M., & Rigg, K. K. (2017). The experiences of young adult offenders who completed a drug court treatment program. *Qualitative Health Research*, *27*(5), 750–758.

National Drug Court Institute. (2021). Treatment court practitioner tool kit: Model agreements and related resources to support the use of medications for opioid use disorder. Retrieved from https://www.ndci.org/wp-content/uploads/2021/05/NADCP_MOUD_toolkit_Final.pdf

National Institute on Drug Abuse. (2018). How is opioid use disorder treated in the criminal justice system? Retrieved from www.drugabuse.gov/publications/research-reports/medications-to-treat-opioid-addiction/how-opioid-use-disorder-treated-in-criminal-justice-system

National Institute on Drug Abuse. (2021). Criminal justice drug facts. Retrieved from www.drugabuse.gov/publications/drugfacts/criminal-justice

Nunn, A., Zaller, N., Dickman, S., Trimbur, C., Nijhawan, A., & Rich, J. D. (2009). Methadone and buprenorphine prescribing and referral practices in US prison systems: Results from a nationwide survey. *Drug and Alcohol Dependence*, *105*(1–2), 83–88.

Pierce, M., Bird, S. M., Hickman, M., Marsden, J., Dunn, G., Jones, A., & Millar, T. (2016). Impact of treatment for opioid dependence on fatal drug-related poisoning: A national cohort study in England. *Addiction*, *111*(2), 298–308.

Ranapurwala, S. I., Shanahan, M. E., Alexandridis, A. A., Proescholdbell, S. K., Naumann, R. B., Edwards Jr, D., & Marshall, S. W. (2018). Opioid overdose mortality among former Carolina inmates: 2000–2015. *American Journal of Public Health*, *108*(9), 1207–1213.

Rigg, K. K., Cook, H. H., & Murphy, J. W. (2014). Expanding the scope and relevance of health interventions: Moving beyond clinical trials and behavior change models. *International Journal of Qualitative Studies on Health and Well-being*, *9*(1), 24743.

Rigg, K. K., & DeCamp, W. (2014). Explaining prescription opioid misuse among veterans: A theory-based analysis using structural equation modeling. *Military Behavioral Health*, *2*(2), 210–216.

Rigg, K. K., McLean, K., Monnat, S. M., Sterner III, G. E., & Verdery, A. M. (2018). Opioid misuse initiation: implications for intervention. *Journal of Addictive Diseases*, *37*(3–4), 111–122.

Rigg, K. K., & Murphy, J. W. (2013). Storylines as a neglected tool for mental health service providers and researchers. *International Journal of Mental Health and Addiction*, *11*(4), 431–440.

Schwartz, R. P., Jaffe, J. H., O'Grady, K. E., Kinlock, T. W., Gordon MS, Kelly, S. M., et al. (2009). Interim methadone treatment: Impact on arrests. *Drug & Alcohol Dependence*, *103*(3):148–154.

Sentencing Project. (2021). Criminal justice facts. Retrieved from www.sentencingproject.org/criminal-justice-facts/.

Social Science Research Council. (2019). How drug courts fall short: A new report investigates this policy model model's performance in the Americas. Retrieved from https://items.ssrc.org/from-our-programs/how-drug-courts-fall-short-a-new-report-investigates-this-policy-models-performance-in-the-americas/

Substance Abuse and Mental Health Services Administration. (2019). Retrieved from https://store.samhsa.gov/sites/default/files/d7/priv/pep19-matbriefcjs_0.pdf

Surratt, H., Kurtz, S. P., & Cicero, T. J. (2011). Alternate routes of administration and risk for HIV among prescription opioid abusers. *Journal of Addictive Diseases*, *30*(4), 334–341.

Tyler, J. (2017). Criminal justice reformers are hooked on drug courts, they should kick the habit. Retrieved from https://thehill.com/blogs/pundits-blog/crime/345371-criminal-justice-reformers-are-hooked-on-drug-courts-they-should.

Verona, E., Liller, K., McCarthy, A., & Copenhaver, K. (2022). *Community assistance and life liaison program equity and process evaluation: Protocol and data review*. Program Evaluation and Technical Reports Submitted to St. Petersburg Police Department, Gulf Coast Jewish Family Services Center, and Foundation for a Healthy St. Petersburg.

Walley, A. Y., Xuan, Z., Hackman, H. H., Quinn, E., Doe-Simkins, M., Sorensen-Alawad, A., . . . Ozonoff, A. (2013). Opioid overdose rates and implementation of overdose education and nasal naloxone distribution in Massachusetts: Interrupted time series analysis. *BMJ*, 346–359.

Waters, R. (2021). Enlisting mental health workers, not cops, in mobile crisis response. *Health Affairs*, *40*(6), 864–869.

Wenger, L. D., Showalter, D., Lambdin, B., Leiva, D., Wheeler, E., Davidson, P. J., . . . Kral, A. H. (2018). Implementation of overdose education and naloxone distribution in criminal justice settings: The NEXT study. Retrieved from www.accjh.org/sites/default/files/presentations/Implementation%20of%20Overdose%20Prevention%20and%20Naloxone.pdf

Wenger, L. D., Showalter, D., Lambdin, B., Leiva, D., Wheeler, E., Davidson, P. J., . . . Kral, A. H. (2019). Overdose education and naloxone distribution in the San Francisco County jail. *Journal of Correctional Health Care*, *25*(4), 394–404.

Wilson, D. B., Mitchell, O., & MacKenzie, D. L. (2006). A systematic review of drug court effects on recidivism. *Journal of Experimental Criminology*, 2(4), 459–487.

PART VII

Considerations for Policy Change

36
CRIMINAL JUSTICE INTERVENTIONS AGAINST DRUG USE AND HARMS

Greg Midgette, Jacob Scocca, and Anna Newell

Introduction

People who use drugs and the markets through which drugs are supplied have long been priority concerns in the U.S. criminal justice (CJ) system. Today the nation faces dual opioid and methamphetamine epidemics that claim the lives of thousands and generate on the order of $70 billion per year in illicit income from retail drug expenditures (Midgette et al., 2019), cost billions of dollars to the CJ system, and cause incalculable pain and suffering. Scholars and the public alike believe the country's tradition of enforcement and punishment-centered approaches to drug control is not well suited to the problem and may even exacerbate it (Caulkins & Reuter, 2017; Jensen et al., 2004).

In this chapter we discuss criminal justice policies and interventions that both deter problem drug use and mitigate its concomitant harms borne by individuals and society; we do not consider approaches based on the legal status of a particular drug. However, we note that potential links between alcohol, heroin, methamphetamine, and cocaine to violent and property crime are the basis for the U.S. approach to criminal justice drug policy over the twentieth century (MacCoun & Reuter, 2001), and this tradition informs the set of politically feasible drug policy interventions today.

Throughout the twentieth century, U.S. federal responses to social problems related to drug use were prohibition, "tough on drugs" enforcement practices, and draconian sentencing laws. Over the course of decades, a succession of laws directed drug policy actions and prioritized punishment. Among the most significant of these laws were the 1920 Volstead Act prohibiting alcohol production and consumption, the Boggs Act of 1951 and Boggs-Daniels Act of 1956 establishing federal mandatory minimum sentences for drug offenses and codifying the federal mandate to combat drug trafficking, the Rockefeller Drug Laws in 1973 in the wake of President Richard Nixon's declaration of an "all-out offensive" in a war on drug abuse, and the Anti-Drug Abuse Acts of 1986 and 1988 in response to the crack epidemic.

The nation's enforcement and punishment-centered drug control strategy can claim few victories. Federal alcohol prohibition eroded the tax base and generated large and often violent illicit markets. The law was quickly found to be untenable and repealed in 1933. The decades-long war on drugs swelled courts, jails, and prisons, generating racial disparities in

DOI: 10.4324/9781003219286-44

the risk of arrest, sentencing outcomes, and incarceration. Even after policy changes to reduce disparities including the Fair Sentencing Act of 2010, the U.S. remains among the most punitive countries toward people who use drugs and has higher rates of drug dependence and overdose risk than economically similar countries (MacCoun & Reuter, 2011).

For the sake of brevity, in this chapter we review criminal justice policies focused on people who use drugs, rather than enforcement and interdiction practices meant to disrupt drug supply (for treatment of the topic of police enforcement of drug trade, see Mitchell & Toth, this volume).[1] We highlight drug policies and programs for which a strong or promising evidence base exists and discuss the importance of implementation fidelity to policy effectiveness. We also briefly discuss the challenge of interpreting early evidence from drug legalization.

Measuring Drug Use and Its Impact in Criminal Justice Settings

Provisional data indicate that over 100,000 people in the United States died of suspected drug overdoses in the United States in both 2021 and 2022 (Centers for Disease Control and Prevention, 2023), driven by consumption of illicitly obtained synthetic opioids such as fentanyl (Hedegaard et al., 2020). This represents 2.4-fold increase in overdose mortality from a decade prior, from which a significant proportion stems from diversion from prescription opioids to illicit opioid markets (Alpert et al., 2018, 2021; Cicero et al., 2014). The direct cost of alcohol misuse on the CJ system is on the order of $25 billion per year, about 10 percent of the total social costs of excessive drinking (Bouchery et al., 2011; Sacks et al., 2015). As a legally regulated drug for adult consumption, alcohol often is considered independent of other drugs in the context of criminal justice drug policy. Heavy alcohol use, however, increases the risk of violence, including homicide, suicide, sexual assault, and intimate partner violence and contributes to overdose risk when use co-occurs with other substances (NCCDPHP, 2021).

Twenty years prior to this review, the National Academies found that the United States lacked the data to evaluate the effectiveness of drug-enforcement programs (National Research Council, 2001). Today, data systems are worse (Reuter et al., 2021). Attempts to triangulate estimates from a portfolio of imperfect data sources suggest the number of people who use cocaine, heroin, or methamphetamine at least 4 days per month are each on the order of one to five million persons per year, with point estimates around two to three million and disproportionate representation from persons with CJ system contact (Midgette et al., 2019).

The prevalence of drug use among people in the CJ system is estimated to be much higher than in the general population. According to the 2016 National Crime Victimization Survey (ICPSR, 2020), approximately half of incidents involved offenders who were believed to be under the influence of alcohol or other drugs. Thirty-nine percent of persons incarcerated in prisons reported using drugs, and 30 percent reported using alcohol at the time of the offense (Maruschak et al., 2021). In the year prior to incarceration, nearly half of persons incarcerated in U.S. prisons met the DSM-IV criteria for a substance use disorder. The opioid epidemic in the United States has brought a new challenge to the CJ system, with approximately 15–20 percent of inmates reporting recent use of these drugs (Bronson et al., 2017). Persons who use opioids are also at especially high risk of relapse, overdose, and reincarceration upon release (Gordon et al., 2014; Lee et al., 2016).

The Impacts of Incarceration on People Who Use Drugs

- There is little evidence to support punitive carceral policies to reduce drug crime recidivism or drug use beyond the effects of incapacitation

Criminal justice policies arising from the crack epidemic and earlier laws imposed severe penalties to deter drug possession and incapacitate people involved in illegal and illicit drug markets (Alexander, 2010; MacCoun & Reuter, 2001). Though long-term mass incarceration has been driven predominantly by long sentences imposed for violent offenses (Pfaff, 2017), criminalization of drug use has differentially increased CJ system contact in communities where drug enforcement is most concentrated and contributed to racial disparities.

Loeffler and Nagin (2022) summarize evidence from studies with strong quasi-experimental research designs to find limited evidence of a preventive effect of prison over probation generally, and no effect among individuals convicted of drug offenses. Among the quasi-experimental evidence, Green and Winik (2010) and Mitchell and colleagues (2017) find that neither incarceration nor community supervision impact the probability of re-arrest or re-conviction in studies of formerly incarcerated samples in Washington, D.C., and Florida. However, there is heterogeneity among the generally null effects of incarceration. Recent review articles find that programmatic incarceration is more likely to reduce recidivism than punitive incarceration (Loeffler & Nagin, 2022; MacKenzie & Farrington, 2015).

The promising effects of incarceration-based treatment programs literature are consistent with the evidence of promising rehabilitation-based incarceration. Reviews of experimental and quasi-experimental studies find that therapeutic communities in prison settings reduced both recidivism and drug use relapse (De Andrade et al., 2018; Holloway et al., 2006; Mitchell, Wilson, & MacKenzie, 2012). Mitchell and colleagues (2012) further find that group-based counseling reduced recidivism, and narcotic maintenance programs reduced relapse. These findings are more equivocal than the consistent evidence of treatment efficacy in the general population (Prendergast et al., 2002). Caulkins and colleauges (2021) posit that this disparity in effects may be due to the additional stressors faced by people with drug use disorders in the CJ system such as mental health challenges and lack of family support.

In the following section, we review the evidence of three promising CJ-based approaches to reduce the harms associated with drug use: CJ agency-facilitated substance use treatments and therapies, drug courts, and "swift, certain, and fair" programs.

Evidence-Based Interventions to Reduce Drug Use and Recidivism

Criminal Justice Agency-Facilitated Treatment and Therapy in the Community

- Therapeutic communities, cognitive behavioral therapies, and medication-assisted treatment in institutional and community corrections settings are associated with meaningful reductions in recidivism and drug use

The National Institute on Drug Abuse defines treatment, ongoing case management, and targeted cognitive behavioral therapies addressing criminal thinking to be integral to desistance and recovery from drug addiction for CJ populations (NIDA, 2020). Amid the general need for more accessible evidence-based treatments and therapies, it is perhaps most acute for formerly incarcerated individuals, who face a heightened risk of overdose in the period immediately after release from prison (Merrall et al., 2010; Seaman et al., 1998). However, among persons meeting clinical criteria for substance dependence or abuse, only 28 percent of persons incarcerated in prison, 22 percent of those in jail received any form of treatment (Bronson et al., 2017), and 38 percent of treatment facilities provide services tailored to CJ-involved clients (SAMHSA, 2021).

Treatment has been found to be effective at reducing substance use and crime (Prendergast et al., 2002), and quasi-experimental findings show the presence of substance treatment facilities reduces violent and acquisitive crime at the county level (Bondurant et al., 2018). Among available treatment modalities and therapies, therapeutic communities – group-based long-term residential self-help-oriented therapy – and medication-assisted treatment provide the most consistent evidence of crime reduction (Holloway et al., 2006; Perry et al., 2019). Most common among medication-assisted treatments in the United States are methadone maintenance treatment, naltrexone, and buprenorphine for opioid dependence, and each has been found to be effective against relapse. No comparable treatment exists for stimulant drug use disorders (e.g., cocaine and methamphetamine). While reviews of therapeutic communities and methadone maintenance treatment have yielded support for reducing recidivism for both interventions, the long-term effects on drug use relapse are less promising (Marsch, 1998; Martin et al., 1999; Wexler et al., 1999).

Cognitive behavioral therapies are commonly integrated with substance use treatment and have been studied extensively in the context of CJ populations. These therapies can take many forms, but well-implemented programs that incorporate mindfulness training to address criminal thinking and substance use are associated with fewer arrests and fewer days of additional sentencing (Landenberger & Lipsey, 2005; Little et al., 1993; Wilson et al., 2005). Effectiveness appears to be most evident among high-risk populations, and the success of programs is sensitive to client characteristics, including race/ethnicity and risk profile, and to the quality of implementation (Landenberger & Lipsey, 2005; Spiropoulos et al., 2018).

Drug Courts

- Drug courts are a promising means to reduce drug consumption and future criminal justice involvement, but effect heterogeneity and program expense are cause for caution

The first drug treatment court was established in 1989 in Dade County, Florida, and today there are over 3,500 in the United States addressing youth, parents, Indigenous populations, intoxicated drivers, reentry, veterans, mental health, and general adult populations who have alcohol or other drug dependency problems by coordinating programs across courts, corrections, and social welfare agencies (Office of Justice Programs, 2021). In principle, drug treatment courts include a portfolio of programming including cognitive behavioral therapy, psychosocial therapy, and pharmacological therapy to match the individual needs of each client. In practice, program design and resources vary considerably, but the general design combines compulsory treatment with judicial discretion to reward preferred behaviors like treatment compliance and clean drug tests and punish prohibited activities like crime and drug use.

Meta-analyses of experimental and quasi-experimental evaluations have found drug courts' impact on recidivism is promising, though effect sizes are associated with program design choices and participant profiles (Mitchell, Wilson, Eggers, et al., 2012; Wilson et al., 2006), and programs' impact on the aggregate amount of incarceration is negligible (Sevigny et al., 2013). Specific provisions show particular promise. Family therapy, for example, is commonly used in drug courts as an alternative to group-based therapy and has proven to be useful in reducing rates of relapse in juvenile and adult offenders (Rowe, 2012). A survey-based evaluation of 380 drug courts found that courts that use judicial status hearings, praise, case management, treatment, and sanctions as leverage after non-compliance were most effective (Rossman et al., 2011). Drug courts' ubiquity may also have unexpected consequences, though, as they can contribute to net-widening (Lilley, 2017) and generate racial disparities in completion rates, charge reductions, and dismissals (Mitchell, 2021).

Swift, Certain, and Fair

- Programs that compel sobriety through the threat of moderate sanctions reduce drug consumption and offer promise as a means to reduce misconduct, but existing evidence of these programs' impact on crime leaves questions about generalizability unanswered

Community-based programs that coerce sobriety through the threat of legal penalties, sometimes referred to as swift, certain, and fair (SCF; Kleiman, 2009), typically begin either after arrest or after the determination of a sentence to probation or parole for offenses that are linked to drug use. SCF supervision approaches are varied in their structure, but the core elements of such programs are clearly defined rules, frequent interaction between clients and their program officer, frequent drug or alcohol testing, and well-defined mild punitive repercussions for rule violations. Typically, sanctions include a judicial hearing and/or confinement for a period of 12–72 hours, with no other associated criminal penalty. Sustained non-compliance can result in revocation of probation or parole, but such failures have been found to be rare in extant evidence.

The most frequently implemented designs among SCF-type programs derive from the alcohol-focused 24/7 sobriety program or the illicit drug-focused Hawaii's opportunity probation with enforcement (HOPE) program. Quasi-experimental studies of 24/7 sobriety programs in Montana and the Dakotas have found large reductions in the probability of re-arrest at the individual level and reductions in intoxicated driving and domestic violence arrests as well as mortality at the community level (Kilmer et al., 2013; Kilmer & Midgette, 2020; Midgette et al., 2020; Midgette & Kilmer, 2021; Nicosia et al., 2016). Though the absolute rates of compliance are high in all three states, the difference in violations leads to more incarceration in those with more violations, thus greater cost to participants and the jurisdictions (Midgette et al., 2021).

An experimental evaluation conducted among probation clients assigned to HOPE in Honolulu, HI, and a quasi-experimental study of the Swift-and-Certain program in Washington state found reductions in drug use, arrest, probation revocation, and incarceration (Hamilton et al., 2016; Hawken & Kleiman, 2009), but the results from a four-site field experiment replicating HOPE yield little evidence of a reduction in re-arrest (Lattimore et al., 2016). The studies provide consistent evidence of a reduction in drug use (Hawken, 2018; Lattimore et al., 2018).

Despite mixed evidence on the impact of illicit drug-focused approaches on recidivism and a lack of evidence on alcohol-focused programs outside of Hawaii and the upper midwestern United States, SCF programs have consistently demonstrated effectiveness in reducing substance use, but the effect of SCF programs on re-arrest risk may depend greatly on implementation fidelity (Humphreys & Kilmer, 2020; Midgette et al., 2021).

Drug Legalization

- Given the heterogeneity over jurisdictions in drug use, enforcement practices, public health expenditures, and prevention infrastructure, there is insufficient empirical evidence on the impacts of legalization on crime or public safety from early adopting jurisdictions.

The theoretical links between drug use and crime are numerous (Goldstein, 1985), but the causal pathways may run in both directions (Caulkins et al., 2021). Illegal drugs are more expensive than they would be under a legal regime. This exacerbates some of the criminal justice costs associated with drug use, generates acquisitive crime among people who use drugs and potentially spurs violent competition among traffickers and dealers who are lured into risky but profitable markets (Reuter & Kleiman, 1986). However, potential losses to society associated with increased drug use under legalization – through lost productivity, illness, and other intangible social costs – may outweigh the reduction in harm associated with criminalization (MacCoun & Reuter, 2001, 2011).

The net benefit or cost to society of drug decriminalization or legalization will likely vary by drug, by jurisdiction, and by the particular characteristics of the laws allowing drug production, sales, and consumption (Caulkins et al., 2015). We are hesitant to extrapolate from the early evidence on recreational cannabis legalization generated in Colorado, Oregon, and Washington – all in the top decile of use prevalence prior to legalization – to other parts of the United States, and we are similarly reticent to forecast the impact of broad drug decriminalization from Portugal to the United States because of underlying differences in public health and safety policies, access to treatment and prevention programs, and norms. However, as more states and countries liberalize drug laws, evidence of impacts will quickly follow.

Summary Points and Conclusion

Criminal justice programs and policies to reduce drug use can mitigate its concomitant harms, improve the wellbeing of participants, and reduce the long-term costs of enforcement, incarceration, and supervision incurred by CJ agencies. The CJ system serves as point of contact with an otherwise hard to reach population of people who use drugs (Reuter et al., 2021). Where public health infrastructure is insufficient, CJ agencies may also serve as the primary point of contact between people who use drugs among marginalized populations and interventions from which they may benefit. The promising interventions highlighted here run the gamut of strategies, including social psychological therapies, pharmacotherapies, and deterrence. Each approach is different, but all attempt to reduce the use of punishment relative to the practices they replace. The following concluding points should be kept in mind when considering interventions for drug use:

- A massive expansion of treatment capacity and drug use surveillance systems could pay enormous dividends in public health and safety.
- As the most promising interventions extend beyond traditional CJ expertise, agencies must strengthen coordination with medical, social, and public health services with specialized training to increase the likelihood of success.

- Inconclusive and heterogeneous findings are a common refrain across all interventions reviewed in this chapter.
- The impacts of feasible interventions may be greatly affected by the choices made by program planners and implementers. Across evidence-based interventions, effectiveness appears to hinge heavily on implementation, and the core determinants of program and policy success are often not yet well understood.
- The data on which drug policy decisions are based and interventions are evaluated are often sparse and flawed.
- Drug policy is the realm of pragmatists; criminal justice drug interventions should be designed to address the specific conditions they will operate in, including coordination issues among affected agencies and stakeholders, capacity constraints imposed by budgets and staff, and the needs of the target population.

Note

1 See Caulkins et al. (2021).

Additional Readings

Caulkins, J. P., & Reuter, P. (2017). Dealing more effectively and humanely with illegal drugs. *Crime and Justice*, *46*(1), 95–158. doi: 10.1086/688458

MacCoun, R. J., & Reuter, P. (2001). *Drug war heresies: Learning from other vices, times, and places*. Cambridge University Press; Cambridge Core. doi: 10.1017/CBO9780511754272

National Institute on Drug Abuse (NIDA). (2020). Principles of Drug Abuse Treatment for Criminal Justice Populations – A Research-Based Guide. Retrieved from www.drugabuse.gov/publications/principles-drug-abuse-treatment-criminal-justice-populations-research-based-guide/principles

References

Alexander, M. (2010). *The New Jim crow: Mass incarceration in the age of colorblindness*. New Press ([Jackson, Tenn.]: Distributed by Perseus Distribution, 2010). Retrieved from https://search.library.wisc.edu/catalog/9910095136402121

Alpert, A., Evans, W. N., Lieber, E. M. J., & Powell, D. (2021). Origins of the opioid crisis and its enduring impacts*. *The Quarterly Journal of Economics*, qjab043. doi: 10.1093/qje/qjab043

Alpert, A., Powell, D., & Pacula, R. L. (2018). Supply-side drug policy in the presence of substitutes: Evidence from the introduction of abuse-deterrent opioids. *American Economic Journal: Economic Policy*, *10*(4), 1–35. doi: 10.1257/pol.20170082

Bondurant, S. R., Lindo, J. M., & Swensen, I. D. (2018). Substance abuse treatment centers and local crime. *Journal of Urban Economics*, *104*, 124–133. doi: 10.1016/j.jue.2018.01.007

Bouchery, E. E., Harwood, H. J., Sacks, J. J., Simon, C. J., & Brewer, R. D. (2011). Economic costs of excessive alcohol consumption in the US, 2006. *American Journal of Preventive Medicine*, *41*(5), 516–524.

Bronson, J., Stroop, J., Zimmer, S., & Berzofsky, M. (2017). *Drug use, dependence, and abuse among state prisoners and jail inmates, 2007–2009*. United States Department of Justice, Office of Juvenile Justice and Delinquency Prevention.

Caulkins, J. P., Gould, A., Pardo, B., Reuter, P., & Stein, B. D. (2021). Opioids and the criminal justice system: New challenges posed by the modern opioid epidemic. *Annual Review of Criminology*, *4*(1), 353–375. doi: 10.1146/annurev-criminol-061020-125715

Caulkins, J. P., Kilmer, B., Kleiman, M., MacCoun, R. J., Midgette, G., Oglesby, P., Pacula, R. L., & Reuter, P. H. (2015). *Considering marijuana legalization: Insights for Vermont and other jurisdictions*. Rand Corporation.

Caulkins, J. P., & Reuter, P. (2017). Dealing more effectively and humanely with illegal drugs. *Crime and Justice*, *46*(1), 95–158. doi: 10.1086/688458

Centers for Disease Control and Prevention. (2023). Provisional data shows U.S. drug overdose deaths top 100,000 in 2022. National Center for Health Statistics. Retrieved from blogs.cdc.gov/nchs/2023/05/18/7365/

Cicero, T. J., Ellis, M. S., Surratt, H. L., & Kurtz, S. P. (2014). The changing face of heroin use in the United States: A retrospective analysis of the past 50 years. *JAMA Psychiatry*, *71*(7), 821–826.

De Andrade, D., Ritchie, J., Rowlands, M., Mann, E., & Hides, L. (2018). Substance use and recidivism outcomes for prison-based drug and alcohol interventions. *Epidemiologic Reviews*, *40*(1), 121–133. doi: 10.1093/epirev/mxy004

Goldstein, P. J. (1985). The drugs/violence nexus: A tripartite conceptual framework. *Journal of Drug Issues*, *15*(4), 493–506. doi: 10.1177/002204268501500406

Gordon, M. S., Kinlock, T. W., Schwartz, R. P., Fitzgerald, T. T., O'Grady, K. E., & Vocci, F. J. (2014). A randomized controlled trial of prison-initiated buprenorphine: Prison outcomes and community treatment entry. *Drug and Alcohol Dependence*, *142*, 33–40. doi: 10.1016/j.drugalcdep.2014.05.011

Green, D. P., & Winik, D. (2010). Using random judge assignments to estimate the effects of incarceration and probation on recidivism among drug offenders*. *Criminology*, *48*(2), 357–387. doi: 10.1111/j.1745-9125.2010.00189.x

Hamilton, Z., Campbell, C. M., van Wormer, J., Kigerl, A., & Posey, B. (2016). Impact of swift and certain sanctions. *Criminology & Public Policy*, *15*(4), 1009–1072. doi: 10.1111/1745-9133.12245

Hawken, A. (2018). Economic implications of hope from the demonstration field experiment. *Criminology & Public Policy*, *17*(4), 901–906. doi: 10.1111/1745-9133.12415

Hawken, A., & Kleiman, M. (2009). *Managing drug involved probationers with swift and certain sanctions: Evaluating Hawaii's HOPE: Executive summary*. National Criminal Justice Reference Services.

Hedegaard, H., Miniño, A. M., & Warner, M. (2020). Drug overdose deaths in the United States, 1999–2019 (NCHS Data Brief No. 394). Centers for Disease Control and Prevention and National Center for Health Statistics. Retrieved from www.cdc.gov/nchs/products/databriefs/db394.htm#Data

Holloway, K. R., Bennett, T. H., & Farrington, D. P. (2006). The effectiveness of drug treatment programs in reducing criminal behavior: A meta-analysis. *Psicothema*, *18*(3), 620–629.

Humphreys, K., & Kilmer, B. (2020). Still hopeful: Reconsidering a "failed" replication of a swift, certain, and fair approach to reducing substance use among individuals under criminal justice supervision. *Addiction*. doi: 10.1111/add.15049

Inter-university Consortium for Political and Social Research (Ed.). (2020). National crime victimization survey, [United States], 2016. *Bureau of Justice Statistics*. doi: 10.3886/ICPSR36828.v4

Jensen, E. L., Gerber, J., & Mosher, C. (2004). Social consequences of the war on drugs: The legacy of failed policy. *Criminal Justice Policy Review*, *15*(1), 100–121.

Kilmer, B., & Midgette, G. (2020). Deterring Crime: Insights from an Individual-Level Analysis of 24/7 Sobriety. *Journal of Policy Analysis and Management*. Retrieved from www.rand.org/pubs/working_papers/WR1190.html.

Kilmer, B., Nicosia, N., Heaton, P., & Midgette, G. (2013). Efficacy of frequent monitoring with swift, certain, and modest sanctions for violations: Insights from South Dakota's 24/7 Sobriety Project. *American Journal of Public Health*, *103*(1), e37–e43.

Kleiman, M. A. (2009). *When brute force fails: How to have less crime and less punishment*. Princeton University Press.

Landenberger, N. A., & Lipsey, M. W. (2005). The positive effects of cognitive-behavioral programs for offenders: A meta-analysis of factors associated with effective treatment. *Journal of Experimental Criminology*, *1*(4), 451–476.

Lattimore, P. K., Dawes, D., MacKenzie, D. L., & Zajac, G. (2018). Evaluation of the honest opportunity probation with enforcement demonstration field experiment (HOPE DFE) (No. 25175). Retrieved from www.ncjrs.gov/pdffiles1/nij/grants/251758.pdf

Lattimore, P. K., MacKenzie, D. L., Zajac, G., Dawes, D., Arsenault, E., & Tueller, S. (2016). Outcome findings from the HOPE demonstration field experiment. *Criminology & Public Policy*, *15*(4), 1103–1141. doi: 10.1111/1745-9133.12248

Lee, J. D., Friedmann, P. D., Kinlock, T. W., Nunes, E. V., Boney, T. Y., Hoskinson, R. A., Wilson, D., McDonald, R., Rotrosen, J., Gourevitch, M. N., Gordon, M., Fishman, M., Chen, D. T., Bonnie, R. J., Cornish, J. W., Murphy, S. M., & O'Brien, C. P. (2016). Extended-release naltrexone to prevent opioid relapse in criminal justice offenders. *New England Journal of Medicine*, *374*(13), 1232–1242. doi: 10.1056/NEJMoa1505409

Lilley, D. R. (2017). Did drug courts lead to increased arrest and punishment of minor drug offenses? *Justice Quarterly*, *34*(4), 674–698.

Little, G. L., Robinson, K. D., & Burnette, K. D. (1993). Cognitive behavioral treatment of felony drug offenders: A five-year recidivism report. *Psychological Reports*, *73*(3_suppl), 1089–1090.

Loeffler, C. E., & Nagin, D. S. (2022). The impact of incarceration on recidivism. *Annual Review of Criminology*. doi: 10.1146/annurev-criminol-030920-112506

MacCoun, R. J., & Reuter, P. (2001). *Drug war heresies: Learning from other vices, times, and places*. Cambridge University Press; Cambridge Core. doi: 10.1017/CBO9780511754272

MacCoun, R. J., & Reuter, P. (2011). Assessing drug prohibition and its alternatives: A guide for agnostics. *Annual Review of Law and Social Science*, *7*(1), 61–78. doi: 10.1146/annurev-lawsocsci-102510-105442

MacKenzie, D. L., & Farrington, D. P. (2015). Preventing future offending of delinquents and offenders: What have we learned from experiments and meta-analyses? *Journal of Experimental Criminology*, *11*(4), 565–595.

Marsch, L. A. (1998). The efficacy of methadone maintenance interventions in reducing illicit opiate use, HIV risk behavior and criminality: A meta-analysis. *Addiction*, *93*(4), 515–532.

Martin, S. S., Butzin, C. A., Saum, C. A., & Inciardi, J. A. (1999). Three-year outcomes of therapeutic community treatment for drug-involved offenders in Delaware: From prison to work release to aftercare. *The Prison Journal*, *79*(3), 294–320. doi: 10.1177/0032885599079003002

Maruschak, L. M., Bronson, J., & Alper, M. (2021). Alcohol and drug use and treatment reported by prisoners (Statistical Tables, Issue NCJ 252641). Bureau of Justice Statistics. Retrieved from https://bjs.ojp.gov/sites/g/files/xyckuh236/files/media/document/adutrpspi16st.pdf

Merrall, E. L. C., Kariminia, A., Binswanger, I. A., Hobbs, M. S., Farrell, M., Marsden, J., Hutchinson, S. J., & Bird, S. M. (2010). Meta-analysis of drug-related deaths soon after release from prison: Drug-related deaths after release from prison. *Addiction*, *105*(9), 1545–1554. doi: 10.1111/j.1360-0443.2010.02990.x

Midgette, G., Caulkins, J. P., Davenport, S., & Kilmer, B. G. (2019). *What America's users spend on illegal drugs, 2006–2016* (Product Page No. RR3140). RAND Corporation.

Midgette, G., & Kilmer, B. G. (2021). Can novel 'swift-certain-fair' programs work outside of pioneering jurisdictions? An analysis of 24/7 Sobriety in Montana, USA. *Addiction*, *116*(12), 3381–3387.

Midgette, G., Kilmer, B. G., Nicosia, N., & Heaton, P. (2020). A natural experiment to test the effect of sanction certainty and celerity on substance-impaired driving: North Dakota's 24/7 Sobriety program. *Journal of Quantitative Criminology*, *37*, 647–670.

Midgette, G., Loughran, T. A., & Tahamont, S. (2021). The impact of ambiguity-induced error in offender decision-making: evidence from the field. *Journal of Research in Crime and Delinquency*, *58*(6), 635–665.

Mitchell, O. (2021). Book review: Enforcing freedom: Drug courts, therapeutic communities, and the intimacies of the state. *Race and Justice*, *11*(2), 247–250. doi: 10.1177/2153368720934535

Mitchell, O., Cochran, J. C., Mears, D. P., & Bales, W. D. (2017). The effectiveness of prison for reducing drug offender recidivism: A regression discontinuity analysis. *Journal of Experimental Criminology*, *13*(1), 1–27.

Mitchell, O., Wilson, D. B., Eggers, A., & MacKenzie, D. L. (2012). Drug courts' effects on criminal offending for Juveniles and adults. *Campbell Systematic Reviews*, *8*(1). doi: 10.4073/csr.2012.4

Mitchell, O., Wilson, D. B., & MacKenzie, D. L. (2012). The effectiveness of incarceration-based drug treatment on criminal behavior: A systematic review. *Campbell Systematic Reviews*, *8*(1), i–76.

National Center for Chronic Disease Prevention and Health Promotion. (2021). Excessive alcohol use fact sheet. Centers for Disease Control and Prevention National Center for Chronic Disease Prevention and Health Promotion. Retrieved from www.cdc.gov/chronicdisease/resources/publications/factsheets/alcohol.htm

National Institute on Drug Abuse (NIDA). (2020). Principles of drug abuse treatment for criminal justice populations – a research-based guide. Retrieved from www.drugabuse.gov/publications/principles-drug-abuse-treatment-criminal-justice-populations-research-based-guide/principles

National Research Council. (2001). *Informing America's policy on illegal drugs: What we don't know keeps hurting us.* The National Academies Press. doi: 10.17226/10021

Nicosia, N., Kilmer, B., & Heaton, P. (2016). Can a criminal justice alcohol abstention programme with swift, certain, and modest sanctions (24/7 Sobriety) reduce population mortality? A retrospective observational study. *The Lancet Psychiatry*, *3*(3), 226–232.

Office of Justice Programs. (2021). Drug courts (No. 238527). U.S. Department of Justice. Retrieved from https://ojjdp.ojp.gov/sites/g/files/xyckuh176/files/media/document/drug-courts.pdf

Perry, A. E., Martyn-St James, M., Burns, L., Hewitt, C., Glanville, J. M., Aboaja, A., Thakkar, P., Santosh Kumar, K. M., Pearson, C., Wright, K., & Swami, S. (2019). Interventions for drug-using offenders with co-occurring mental health problems. *The Cochrane Database of Systematic Reviews*, *10*(10), CD010901. doi: 10.1002/14651858.CD010901.pub3

Pfaff, J. (2017). *Locked in: The true causes of mass incarceration-and how to achieve real reform.* Basic Books.

Prendergast, M. L., Podus, D., Chang, E., & Urada, D. (2002). The effectiveness of drug abuse treatment: A meta-analysis of comparison group studies. *Drug and Alcohol Dependence*, *67*(1), 53–72.

Reuter, P., Caulkins, J. P., & Midgette, G. (2021). Heroin use cannot be measured adequately with a general population survey. *Addiction*, *116*(10), 2600–2609. doi: 10.1111/add.15458

Reuter, P., & Kleiman, M. A. (1986). Risks and prices: An economic analysis of drug enforcement. *Crime and Justice*, *7*, 289–340.

Rossman, S. B., Roman, J. K., Zweig, J. M., Rempel, M., & Lindquist, C. H. (2011). *The multi-site adult drug court evaluation: The impact of drug courts.* Urban Institute.

Rowe, C. L. (2012). Family therapy for drug abuse: Review and Updates 2003–2010. *Journal of Marital and Family Therapy*, *38*(1), 59–81. doi: 10.1111/j.1752-0606.2011.00280.x

Sacks, J. J., Gonzales, K. R., Bouchery, E. E., Tomedi, L. E., & Brewer, R. D. (2015). 2010 National and State costs of excessive alcohol consumption. *American Journal of Preventive Medicine*, *49*(5), e73–e79. doi: 10.1016/j.amepre.2015.05.031

Seaman, S. R., Brettle, R. P., & Gore, S. M. (1998). Mortality from overdose among injecting drug users recently released from prison: Database linkage study. *BMJ*, *316*(7129), 426–428. doi: 10.1136/bmj.316.7129.426

Sevigny, E. L., Fuleihan, B. K., & Ferdik, F. V. (2013). Do drug courts reduce the use of incarceration?: A meta-analysis. *Journal of Criminal Justice*, *41*(6), 416–425. doi: 10.1016/j.jcrimjus.2013.06.005

Spiropoulos, G. V., Van Voorhis, P., & Salisbury, E. J. (2018). Programmatic Moderators of CBT correctional treatment for whites and African Americans. *International Journal of Offender Therapy and Comparative Criminology*, *62*(8), 2236–2258. doi: 10.1177/0306624X17721523

Substance Abuse and Mental Health Services Administration (SAMHSA). (2021). *National survey of substance abuse treatment services (N-SSATS): 2020 data on substance abuse treatment facilities.* Department of Health and Human Services.

Wexler, H. K., Melnick, G., Lowe, L., & Peters, J. (1999). Three-year reincarceration outcomes for amity in-prison therapeutic community and aftercare in California. *The Prison Journal*, *79*(3), 321–336. doi: 10.1177/0032885599079003003

Wilson, D. B., Bouffard, L. A., & Mackenzie, D. L. (2005). A Quantitative review of structured, group-oriented, cognitive-behavioral programs for offenders. *Criminal Justice and Behavior*, *32*(2), 172–204. doi: 10.1177/0093854804272889

Wilson, D. B., Mitchell, O., & MacKenzie, D. L. (2006). A systematic review of drug court effects on recidivism. *Journal of Experimental Criminology*, *2*(4), 459–487. doi: 10.1007/s11292-006-9019-4

37

EFFECTIVE BAIL REFORM STRATEGIES DRAWN FROM A LIMITED EVIDENCE BASE

Evan M. Lowder, Ashley E. Rodriguez and Carmen Diaz

Bail has long been a primary mode of pretrial release. Bolstered by United States Supreme Court decisions (e.g., *United States v. Salerno*, 48 U.S. 739.1987) that gave local pretrial decision-makers wide latitude in setting bail to protect public safety, use of bail steadily increased around the turn of the century (Liu et al., 2018). Bail can come in two forms: secured and unsecured bonds. Secured bonds are the most common type of financial bail and require that some amount of financial leverage be provided by the defendant to secure financial release. Secured bonds include cash, surety (i.e., bondsperson provides payment on loan), commercial (i.e., third party such as an insurance company provides payment on loan), collateral (i.e., other form of property used as payment), and deposit (i.e., a portion of the total amount is paid. Unsecured bonds allow individuals to be released on their personal recognizance with no obligation to pay unless they fail to appear for a court appearance.

Despite its wide use, legal advocates have argued that bail is ineffective as a mechanism to prevent pretrial misconduct and worsens disparities in criminal case processing. Many of these claims are backed by research showing limited and low-quality evidence on the effectiveness of bail on re-arrest and failure to appear (FTA) outcomes during the pretrial period (Bechtel et al., 2017). Prior research also suggests that Black and Latino defendants are more likely to receive bail and more likely to be detained due to an inability to pay bail relative to White defendants (Arnold et al., 2018; Demuth, 2003; Demuth & Steffensmeier, 2004; Sacks et al., 2015; Schaefer & Hughes, 2019). The harmful effects of bail are most pronounced among young Black men in particular (Wooldredge, 2012). In light of these trends, state and local policymakers have advanced efforts to eliminate or greatly reduce the use of bail and replace it with other practices. State legislative efforts have broadly focused on setting limits on the use of money bail, requiring the use of pretrial risk assessments to guide release decisions, and setting limits on the length of pretrial detention before a release decision is rendered. Because many of these reforms have occurred in recent years, there is limited long-term evaluation. However, initial evidence on state-level policy reform is promising (Anderson et al., 2019).

In light of ongoing reform efforts, the purpose of this chapter is to provide local agencies and practitioners who are looking to implement bail reform efforts with evidence-based recommendations. We note that given the recency of many large-scale bail reform efforts, research on bail reform strategies is relatively nascent. We focus our chapter on three goals: first, to highlight existing evidence on the effectiveness and potential adverse effects of bail; second,

DOI: 10.4324/9781003219286-45

to describe bail reform efforts and the emerging evidence base on their effectiveness; and third, to provide concrete recommendations for agencies looking to implement bail reform strategies in practice. Our review of bail reform strategies focuses specifically on the use of risk assessments in pretrial decision-making, the use of supervised pretrial release, and the potential for supporting rehabilitative efforts during the pretrial period.

State of the Literature

Is Bail Effective?

A principal question driving bail reform efforts is whether bail is effective in reducing pretrial misconduct. Overall, there is some agreement across studies that secured bonds may result in a small reduction in FTA rates relative to less restrictive release mechanisms. However, there are mixed and inconclusive findings on whether bail can reduce re-arrest during the pretrial period. For example, a meta-analytic investigation of eight studies found more restrictive bond types were associated with lower FTA rates, but the size of this effect was quite small (Bechtel et al., 2017). The authors of this meta-analytic investigation noted that research on bail is characterized by low methodological rigor with many investigations that use inappropriate data sources and have not been subjected to the peer review process. Individual studies have shown that commercial bonds (i.e., with an insurance agency serving as a surety) may be most effective in decreasing FTA (Morris, 2013), though these mechanisms are not available in every state. Other investigations have found that unsecured bonds may provide similar effectiveness to secured bonds (Jones, 2013). Finally, at least one study suggests that financial release via bond may reduce violations of pretrial conditions relative to nonfinancial release (Cohen, 2012). Notably, however, there has been limited consensus in the literature regarding these trends.

Consequences of Bail

Although there has been limited research on the use of bail as a mechanism to reduce pretrial misconduct, there is a much larger evidence base on the harmful effects of bail on defendant outcomes. Bail has been linked to financial strain for justice-involved individuals and their families (Liu et al., 2018; Stevenson, 2018b) as well as poorer criminal justice outcomes (Gupta et al., 2016), particularly for low-risk individuals (Lowenkamp et al., 2013). Pretrial detention due to an inability to pay bail has been linked to a multitude of adverse consequences for individuals. These include job loss (Dobbie et al., 2018), greater likelihood of a guilty plea and conviction (Dobbie et al., 2018; Heaton et al., 2017; Stevenson, 2018b), and longer sentences to incarceration (Heaton et al., 2017; Sacks & Ackerman, 2014; Stevenson, 2018b).

Prior research has shown that the harmful effects of bail are disproportionately borne by racial and ethnic minorities. Compared to White individuals, Black and Latino individuals are more likely to be given bail over non-monetary release options (Arnold et al., 2018; Demuth, 2003; Sacks et al., 2015; Schaefer & Hughes, 2019). Although there is less consensus on whether Black and Latino individuals receive higher bond amounts, they are less likely to be able to afford bail (Demuth, 2003; Demuth & Steffensmeier, 2004; Schlesinger, 2005) and thus are more likely to be detained pretrial (Demuth, 2003; Demuth & Steffensmeier, 2004; Freiburger et al., 2010; Sacks et al., 2015). Black and Hispanic men receive the harshest bail decisions, resulting in cascading adverse effects (Demuth & Steffensmeier, 2004; Wooldredge, 2012).

Pretrial Reform Efforts

In light of these trends, states across the United States have enacted legislative reforms to reduce or eliminate the use of bail. These reform efforts have taken several actions. These include establishing presumptive release for defendants pending serious public safety or absconding concerns. Reforms have also sought to set limits on both use of bail for lower-level charges and on the time that individuals can be held in detention without a release decision. Many reforms have included use of pretrial risk assessments to guide conditional release and detention decisions. Importantly, most reforms provide for judicial review and discretion in overriding presumptive release or risk assessment recommendations. Few states have actually eliminated cash bail, with the exception of Illinois, which passed House Bill 3653 in 2021.

Due to the recency of many reform efforts, there is limited evaluative evidence on bail reform strategies in total. New Jersey is one exception. In 2014, New Jersey passed the New Jersey Criminal Justice Reform Act S-946 to reduce use of money bail through establishing presumptive release, implementing pretrial risk assessments, and setting a limit on the length of detention if a pretrial release decision has not been made (i.e., 48 hours). Preliminary evaluative evidence suggests the legislation reduced defendants' overall length of time incarcerated and increased release on own recognizance decisions. There was also evidence that total arrest events decreased as well (Anderson et al., 2019). Longer-term evaluation of this reform is in progress. Overall, bail reform efforts are fairly recent and the evidence base is still developing. One challenge to evaluating the effectiveness of such reforms in practice, particularly with respect to the elimination of bail, is that many jurisdictions continue to use bail and most statutory guidelines allow for judicial discretion in pretrial release decisions. In some states where legislation was proposed or enacted to eliminate bail, this provision was amended or retracted (e.g., see New York Senate Bill 1509C; California Senate Bill 10). Pretrial reform efforts, including the extent to which bail is used, also vary tremendously from jurisdiction to jurisdiction. Researchers and some policymakers seem to agree that bail reform is necessary and that cash bail should be eliminated, but there remains little evaluative research on these efforts.

- Bail is not an effective mechanism to decrease pretrial misconduct.
- Bail disproportionately harms racial and ethnic minorities, who are more likely to be detained due to an inability to pay bail.
- Bail reform efforts are underway, but evaluative research is still accumulating.

Evidence-Based Bail Reform Strategies

We turn our attention to specific bail reform strategies that have an emerging evidence base. We focus our recommendations on pretrial risk assessments, supervised pretrial release, and the potential for supporting rehabilitative efforts during the pretrial period.

Pretrial Risk Assessment

Nearly half of local jurisdictions have implemented or are planning to implement pretrial risk assessment tools (Lattimore et al., 2020). These tools are designed to estimate a defendant's risk of committing a new offense or failing to appear for a court appearance during the pretrial period. Pretrial risk assessments consider a variety of risk factors but most commonly criminal history, housing, employment, and substance use (Desmarais et al., 2021). A moderately sized body of evidence suggests assessments produced by these tools can predict pretrial misconduct outcomes with accuracy (Desmarais et al., 2021). There is less evidence on the effects of these tools in practice. However, existing evidence suggests pretrial risk assessment tools can increase rates of non-financial release and reduce the use of bond (Anderson et al., 2019; Lowder et al., 2021; Stevenson, 2018a). The effectiveness of risk assessment in reducing use of bond and days in pretrial detention may be amplified when decision-makers adhere to structured decision-making guidelines (Lowder et al., 2021), such as a matrix that incorporates risk assessment and charge information to guide decisions. At least one evaluation of a statewide pretrial reform effort found that the effects of pretrial risk assessments waned over time (Stevenson, 2018a); however, there are limited long-term evaluations. Despite positive effects of pretrial risk assessments on release decisions, there is inconsistent evidence on whether these tools decrease rates of misconduct in the community or mitigate racial disparities in pretrial decision-making (Anderson et al., 2019; Lowder et al., 2021, 2022; Stevenson, 2018a).

Recommendations

Pretrial risk assessments can be a tool to facilitate non-financial release. However, local agencies should ensure that tools are implemented together with structured guidelines. These guidelines should incorporate risk assessment information into existing criteria for pretrial release decisions to ensure risk assessment information is compatible with local policies for pretrial release. Prior to their use in pretrial decision-making, pretrial risk assessments should be piloted to allow for local validation without confounding influences on misconduct outcomes (Douglas et al., 2011).

Pretrial Supervision

Pretrial supervision is now a frequently used alternative to pretrial detention, with nearly half of local jurisdictions providing pretrial supervision to defendants (Lattimore et al., 2020). As a form of community supervision, pretrial supervision typically includes meeting (e.g., in-person, remote) or contact (e.g., phone, paper check-in) requirements with a pretrial services officer, court date notifications and criminal background checks, as well as other conditions as ordered by the judge (e.g., electronic monitoring, drug testing, etc.). Importantly, in many jurisdictions, pretrial supervision and bail requirements are not mutually exclusive and may be ordered together. Research generally shows that supervised pretrial release can reduce pretrial misconduct relative to release on bail alone, especially for FTA outcomes (Austin et al., 1985; Barno et al., 2020; Lowenkamp & VanNostrand, 2013). However, beyond a minimum reporting requirement (e.g., 1 contact per month), more frequent reporting has not been shown to decrease the likelihood of pretrial misconduct in supervised defendants and may be counterproductive in low risk defendants, in particular (Goldkamp & White, 2006; Lowder & Foudray, 2021; Lowenkamp & VanNostrand, 2013). Research on the use of electronic monitoring as an enhancement of pretrial supervision has generally shown inconsistent effects on pretrial misconduct with potentially higher rates of technical violations (Baumer et al., 1993; Cadigan, 1991; Sainju et al., 2018; Wolff et al., 2017).

Recommendations

Jurisdictions looking to provide an alternative to pretrial detention may consider using pretrial supervision. However, such supervision should be implemented with the minimum necessary reporting requirements. Caution is warranted when prescribing supervision for low risk individuals, particularly those charged with low-level, non-violent crimes. Caution is also warranted when using electronic monitoring for pretrial defendants.

The "Need" Principal and the Pretrial Context

Many criminal justice interventions are based on the risk-need-responsivity model of offender rehabilitation (Andrews et al., 1990). This model suggests agencies match intensity of services and supports risk, identify and intervene to address criminogenic needs, and deliver interventions in a responsive fashion. Pretrial reform efforts overwhelmingly focus on the risk principle without addressing the needs of pretrial defendants. There is clear evidence that rehabilitative approaches are more effective than punitive approaches in reducing criminal recidivism (Lipsey & Cullen, 2007). Although there is less evidence on the effectiveness of these approaches in the pretrial context, they are a direction for further research and practice.

Recommendations

In addition to implementing risk assessments and pretrial supervision, agencies should consider incorporating mechanisms to connect pretrial defendants with needed services in the community to address their criminogenic needs.

Conclusion

Overall, there are clear harms and disparities associated with pretrial detention and bail. These harms appear greater for racial and ethnic minorities involved in the criminal justice system relative to White individuals. Research has not kept pace with the rapid implementation of pretrial reform strategies. Given the recency of many statewide reform efforts, there is limited evidence of their long-term effectiveness. We have several recommendations for jurisdictions looking to implement reform efforts to improve rates of non-financial release while minimizing risk of pretrial misconduct. First, jurisdictions looking to increase pretrial release rates may look to implement pretrial risk assessments, provided such tools are implemented together with structured guidelines. Second, pretrial supervision can be an effective strategy for reducing risk of pretrial misconduct among higher risk defendants, but should be used minimally with low risk defendants. Third, there is a growing opportunity to provide more rehabilitative services in the pretrial context. This is an underutilized strategy but one with a large evidence base in correctional rehabilitation more broadly. As bail reform efforts grow, more rigorous research on a wider variety of pretrial reform strategies will allow researchers, practitioners, and policymakers to develop and implement stronger evidence-based guidelines for pretrial reform.

References

Anderson, C., Redcross, C., Valentine, E., & Miratrix, L. (2019). *Evaluation of pretrial justice system reforms that use the Public Safety Assessment: Effects of New Jersey's criminal justice reform*. MDRC Center for Criminal Justice Research. Retrieved from www.mdrc.org/sites/default/files/PSA_New_Jersey_Report_%231.pdf

Andrews, D. A., Bonta, J., & Hoge, R. D. (1990). Classification for effective rehabilitation: Rediscovering psychology. *Criminal Justice and Behavior*, *17*(1), 19–52. doi: 10.1177/0093854890017001004

Arnold, D., Dobbie, W., & Yang, C. S. (2018). Racial bias in bail decisions. *The Quarterly Journal of Economics*, *133*(4), 1885–1932. doi: 10.1093/qje/qjy012

Austin, J., Krisberg, B., & Litsky, P. (1985). The effectiveness of supervised pretrial release. *Crime & Delinquency*, *31*(4), 519–537. doi: 10.1177/0011128785031004004

Barno, M., Martínez, D. N., & Williams, K. R. (2020). Exploring alternatives to cash bail: An evaluation of Orange County's Pretrial Assessment and Release Supervision (PARS) program. *American Journal of Criminal Justice*, *45*(3), 363–378. doi: 10.1007/s12103-019-09506-3

Baumer, T. L., Maxfield, M. G., & Mendelsohn, R. I. (1993). A comparative analysis of three electronically monitored home detention programs. *Justice Quarterly*, *10*(1), 121–142. doi: 10.1080/07418829300091731

Bechtel, K., Holsinger, A. M., Lowenkamp, C. T., & Warren, M. J. (2017). A meta-analytic review of pretrial research: Risk assessment, bond type, and interventions. *American Journal of Criminal Justice*, *42*(2), 443–467. doi: 10.1007/s12103-016-9367-1

Cadigan, T. P. (1991). Electronic monitoring in federal pretrial release. *Federal Probation*, *55*(1), 26–30.

Cohen, T. H. (2012). Pretrial release and misconduct in Federal District Courts, 2008–2010 (NCJ 239243). U.S. Department of Justice. Retrieved from https://bjs.ojp.gov/content/pub/pdf/prmfdc0810.pdf

Demuth, S. (2003). Racial and ethnic differences in pretrial release decisions and outcomes: A comparison of Hispanic, Black, and White felony arrestees. *Criminology*, *41*(3), 873–908. doi: 10.1111/j.1745-9125.2003.tb01007.x

Demuth, S., & Steffensmeier, D. (2004). The impact of gender and race-ethnicity in the pretrial release process. *Social Problems*, *51*(2), 222–242. doi: 10.1525/sp.2004.51.2.222

Desmarais, S. L., Zottola, S. A., Duhart Clarke, S. E., & Lowder, E. M. (2021). Predictive validity of pretrial risk assessments: A systematic review of the literature. *Criminal Justice and Behavior*, *48*(4), 398–420. doi: 10.1177/0093854820932959

Dobbie, W., Goldin, J., & Yang, C. S. (2018). The effects of pre-trial detention on conviction, future crime, and employment: Evidence from randomly assigned judges. *American Economic Review*, *108*(2), 201–240. doi: 10.1257/aer.20161503

Douglas, K. S., Skeem, J. L., & Nicholson, E. (2011). Research methods in violence risk assessment. In B. Rosenfeld & S. D. Penrod (Eds.), *Research methods in forensic psychology* (pp. 325–346). John Wiley & Sons.

Freiburger, T., Marcum, C., & Pierce, M. (2010). The impact of race on the pretrial decision. *American Journal of Criminal Justice*, *35*(1/2), 76–86. doi: 10.1007/s12103-009-9069-z

Goldkamp, J. S., & White, M. D. (2006). Restoring accountability in pretrial release: The Philadelphia pretrial release supervision experiments. *Journal of Experimental Criminology*, *2*(2), 143–181. doi: 10.1007/s11292-006-9001-1

Gupta, A., Hansman, C., & Frenchman, E. (2016). The heavy costs of high bail: Evidence from judge randomization. *The Journal of Legal Studies*, *45*(2), 471–505. doi: 10.1086/688907

Heaton, P., Mayson, S., & Stevenson, M. (2017). The downstream consequences of misdemeanor pretrial detention. *Stanford Law Review*, *69*(3), 711–794.

Jones, M. R. (2013). *Unsecured bonds: The as effective and most efficient pretrial release option*. Pretrial Justice Institute. Retrieved from www.courts.ca.gov/partners/documents/pdr-nat-bail_unsecured_bonds_pji_2013.pdf

Lattimore, P. K., Tueller, S., Levin-Rector, A., & Witwer, A. (2020). The prevalence of local criminal justice practices. *Federal Probation*, *84*(1), 28–37.

Lipsey, M. W., & Cullen, F. T. (2007). The effectiveness of correctional rehabilitation: A review of systematic reviews. *Annual Review of Law and Social Science*, *3*(1), 297–320. doi: 10.1146/annurev.lawsocsci.3.081806.112833

Liu, P., Nunn, R., & Shambaugh, J. (2018). The economics of bail and pretrial detention (Economic Analysis). The Hamilton Project. Retrieved from www.brookings.edu/wp-content/uploads/2018/12/BailFineReform_EA_121818_6PM.pdf

Lowder, E. M., Diaz, C. L., Grommon, E., & Ray, B. R. (2021). Effects of pretrial risk assessments on release decisions and misconduct outcomes relative to practice as usual. *Journal of Criminal Justice*, *73*, 101754. doi: 10.1016/j.jcrimjus.2020.101754

Lowder, E. M., Diaz, C. L., Grommon, E., & Ray, B. R. (2022). Differential prediction and disparate impact of pretrial risk assessments in practice: A multi-site evaluation. *Journal of Experimental Criminology*. doi: 10.1007/s11292-021-09492-9

Lowder, E. M., & Foudray, C. M. A. (2021). Use of risk assessments in pretrial supervision decision-making and associated outcomes. *Crime & Delinquency*, *67*(11), 1765–1791. doi: 10.1177/00111287211022642

Lowenkamp, C. T., & VanNostrand, M. (2013). *Exploring the impact of supervision on pretrial outcomes*. Laura and John Arnold Foundation. Retrieved from http://craftmediabucket.s3.amazonaws.com/uploads/PDFs/LJAF_Report_Supervision_FNL.pdf

Lowenkamp, C. T., VanNostrand, M., & Holsinger, A. (2013). The hidden costs of pretrial detention. Laura and John Arnold Foundation. Retrieved from https://nicic.gov/hidden-costs-pretrial-detention

Morris, R. G. (2013). *Pretrial release mechanisms in Dallas County, Texas: Differences in failure to appear, recidivism/pretrial misconduct, and associated costs of FTA*. University of Texas at Dallas.

Sacks, M., & Ackerman, A. R. (2014). Bail and sentencing: Does pretrial detention lead to harsher punishment? *Criminal Justice Policy Review*, *25*(1), 59–77. doi: 10.1177/0887403412461501

Sacks, M., Sainato, V. A., & Ackerman, A. R. (2015). Sentenced to pretrial detention: A study of bail decisions and outcomes. *American Journal of Criminal Justice*, *40*(3), 661–681. doi: 10.1007/s12103-014-9268-0

Sainju, K. D., Fahy, S., Hamilton, B. A., Baggaley, K., Baker, A., Minassian, T., & Filippelli, V. (2018). Electronic monitoring for pretrial release: Assessing the impact. *Federal Probation*, *82*(3), 3–10.

Schaefer, B. P., & Hughes, T. (2019). Examining judicial pretrial release decisions: The influence of risk assessments and race. *Criminology, Criminal Justice, Law & Society*, *20*, 47.

Schlesinger, T. (2005). Racial and ethnic disparity in pretrial criminal processing. *Justice Quarterly*, *22*(2), 170–192. doi: 10.1080/07418820500088929

Stevenson, M. T. (2018a). Assessing risk assessment in action. *Minnesota Law Review*, *58*, 303–384. doi: 10.2139/ssrn.3016088

Stevenson, M. T. (2018b). Distortion of justice: How the inability to pay bail affects case outcomes. *The Journal of Law, Economics, and Organization*. doi: 10.1093/jleo/ewy019

Wolff, K. T., Dozier, C. A., Muller, J. P., Mowry, M., & Hutchinson, B. (2017). The impact of location monitoring among U.S. pretrial defendants in the district of New Jersey. *Federal Probation*, *81*(3), 8–14.

Wooldredge, J. (2012). Distinguishing race effects on pre-trial release and sentencing decisions. *Justice Quarterly*, *29*(1), 41–75. doi: 10.1080/07418825.2011.559480

38

EXAMINING DILEMMAS ABOUT THE STATE OF AMERICA'S DEATH PENALTY

Anna R. Dixon and Ali Shakoor

On July 14, 2020, while the country was in the grips of the displacement, suffering, and death associated with the unprecedented COVID–19 pandemic, the government engaged in a practice it had abandoned since 2003 (Federal Board of Prisons [FBP], 2003). The macabre episode was reported on by Ruth Friedman, an attorney for Daniel Lee and the Director of the Federal Capital Habeas Project:

> It is important for everyone to understand exactly what happened last night to our client, Daniel Lewis Lee. At 2 AM on July 14, while the country was sleeping, the Supreme Court issued a 5–4 decision vacating the injunction that had been in place against the first federal execution in 17 years. Within minutes, the Department of Justice moved to re-set Danny Lee's execution – for 4 AM, summoning media and witnesses back to the prison in the very middle of the night. When it was brought to the government's attention that a court stay still remained in place, the DOJ first maintained that that stay presented no legal impediment to executing Danny Lee, but then filed an "emergency" motion to lift the stay.
>
> Over the four hours it took for this reckless and relentless government to pursue these ends, Daniel Lewis Lee remained strapped to a gurney: a mere 31 minutes after a court of appeals lifted the last impediment to his execution at the federal government's urging, while multiple motions remained pending, and without notice to counsel, he was executed.
>
> It is shameful that the government saw fit to carry out this execution during a pandemic. It is shameful that the government saw fit to carry out this execution when counsel for Danny Lee could not be present with him, and when the judges in his case and even the family of his victims urged against it. And it is beyond shameful that the government, in the end, carried out this execution in haste, in the middle of the night, while the country was sleeping. We hope that upon awakening, the country will be as outraged as we are.
>
> *(Defender Services Office [DSO], 2020)*

The execution of Mr. Daniel Lee was the first conducted by the federal government since the execution of Louis Jones on March 18, 2003 (FBP, 2003). The Daniel Lee execution

 DOI: 10.4324/9781003219286-46

was the first of 13 conducted by the federal government during the chaos and despair of the COVID–19 pandemic. Why the rush in executions under such dire conditions and misplaced resources? On July 25, 2019, former United States Attorney General William Barr stated: "The Justice Department upholds the rule of law – and we owe it to the victims and their families to carry forward the sentence imposed by our justice system" (Kennedy, 2019).

A Brief History of Capital Punishment in the United States

The death penalty has been an accepted punishment in the United States since before the adoption of our Constitution. The belief in and acceptance of capital punishment was carried over from Britain and early American colonies established the punishment for crimes such as witchcraft, perjury, adultery, theft, and idolatry, among other enumerated capital crimes (Reggio, 1999). Though death by hanging was most common, methods of execution included being burned alive, beheadings, and being crushed with stones (Jrank, 2023). Some national leaders have always been concerned about issues like morality, severity, and proportionality pertaining to the use of capital punishment. In 1764, an Italian criminologist and philosopher named Cesare Beccaria released a foundational treatise titled *On Crimes and Punishments* (Beccaria & Voltaire, 1764). The book theorized that capital punishment should be abolished, as it was not an efficacious way to prevent crime (Bessler, 2012, pp. 48–49). The influential work was published in 22 languages and had a strong influence on America's "founding fathers" (Bessler, 2014, pp. 245–47).

Though the idea of completely abolishing the death penalty was not persuasive, Beccaria's work did influence other aspects of early American attitudes about the implementation of capital punishment. George Washington ordered a copy of the book for his stepson in 1769 and later wrote a letter to Congress in 1781 highlighting the need for a "proper gradation of punishments . . . intermediate punishments short of the destruction of life" (Bessler, 2012, pp. 130–131). Beccaria's seminal piece also greatly affected the thoughts of John Adams, Thomas Jefferson, and James Madison, among other founding leaders directly influential in drafting our Constitution (Bessler, 2014, pp. 248–49). The full text of the Eighth Amendment reads: "Excessive bail shall not be required, nor excessive fines imposed, nor cruel and unusual punishments inflicted". Though the text does not explicitly mention "death", capital punishment was understood as an acceptable punishment, with limitations on the methodology of the punishment regulated by the clause forbidding those practices deemed "cruel and unusual". After the U.S. Constitution was ratified, capital punishment was established in law by the United States Supreme Court in case after case and most state legislatures for almost 200 years, until the 1972 decision in *Furman v. Georgia* (1972).

Furman v. Georgia *and the Eighth Amendment*

"In the 181 years since the enactment of the Eighth Amendment, not a single decision of this Court has cast the slightest shadow of a doubt on the constitutionality of the capital punishment" (*Furman v. Georgia*, 1972, p. 309). That was a correct assertion by then Chief Justice Burger, dissenting to the majority's 5–4 per curium decision in *Furman*, which had essentially invalidated capital punishment nationwide. The *Furman* decision consisted of nine separate opinions, as even the majority could not agree on a controlling rationale. But what was decided was that capital punishment violated the Eighth Amendment at the time of the opinion, based on the consideration of the three cases before the Court. *Furman*, involving a Black man convicted of murder, had two companion cases, also with Black male defendants: *Branch v.*

Texas (*Furman v. Georgia*, 1972, p. 253) and *Jackson v. Georgia* (*Furman v. Georgia*, 1972, p. 252), which were capital sentences following rape convictions, as opposed to murder.

The justices in the majority offered different perspectives about their position. Justices Brennan and Marshall considered the death penalty unconstitutional in all circumstances (U.S. Const., amend. VIII, 1972). The other three justices in the majority did not agree with full abolishment of capital punishment, but the reasoning of Justices Douglas and Stewart provided the most influential explanations of *Furman*'s rationale. Justice Douglas discussed the complete discretion jurors had in determining life and death and how such discretion allowed the death penalty to be applied arbitrarily and in a discriminatory manner against "the poor, the Negro, and the members of unpopular groups" (*Furman v. Georgia*, 1972 p. 250). Justice Douglas said of the death penalty statutes before the Court: "They are pregnant with discrimination and discrimination is an ingredient not compatible with the idea of equal protection of the laws that is implicit in the ban on 'cruel and unusual' punishments" (*Furman v. Georgia*, 1972, p. 257). Of all the rationales, Justice Stewart's assessment is perhaps the most resonating:

> These death sentences are cruel and unusual in the same way that being struck by lightning is cruel and unusual. For, of all the people convicted of rapes and murders in 1967 and 1968, many just as reprehensible as these, the petitioners are among a capriciously selected random handful upon whom the sentence of death has in fact been imposed. My concurring Brothers have demonstrated that, if any basis can be discerned for the selection of these few to be sentenced to die, it is the constitutionally impermissible basis of race. But racial discrimination has not been proved, and I put it to one side. I simply conclude that the Eighth and Fourteenth Amendments cannot tolerate the infliction of a sentence of death under legal systems that permit this unique penalty to be so wantonly and so freakishly imposed.
>
> *(Furman v. Georgia, 1972, p. 309–10)*

As *Furman* implicitly allowed for the administering of capital punishment only if it could be conducted pursuant to constitutional protections, state legislatures quickly got to work. For example, Florida passed a new capital statute on December 1, 1972, called the Florida Capital Punishment Act, directly in response to *Furman* (Thornton, 1974, pp. 108–09).

The time soon proved ripe for the United States Supreme Court to revisit capital punishment after flurries of legislation and litigation across the nation attempted to make sense of *Furman*. In 1976, with *Gregg v. Georgia*, along with the accompanying *Proffitt v. Florida* (1976) and *Jurek v. Texas* (1976), the Supreme Court considered the constitutionality of new state capital punishment schemes, which were enacted to overcome the constitutional inadequacies of the death penalty, as applied, found in *Furman*. In *Gregg*, the majority held that new Georgia death penalty scheme passed Eighth Amendment scrutiny (*Gregg v. Georgia*, 1976, pp. 195–97).[1]

After *Gregg*, there were other encouraging decisions from the Court about protecting the constitutional rights of capital defendants. At the same time *Gregg* was decided, the Court rejected a statutory scheme that neglected to practice "individualized sentencing determinations", by mandating the death penalty mandatory for all first-degree murderers, in *Woodson v. North Carolina*, 428 U.S. 280 (1976) (304–05).[2] In 1977, the Court decided *Coker v. Georgia*, 433 U.S. 584, 592 (1977), which held that the death penalty was "grossly disproportionate" for the crime of rape.[3] An impactful case decided in 1978 was *Lockett v. Ohio*, 438 U.S. 586 (1978), which struck down an Ohio statute which restricted the type and manner of mitigation that could be considered by the courts (p. 604).[4] The Court later decided that a "jury is entitled to, and indeed *must*, hear all relevant mitigating evidence (*Eddings v. Oklahoma*, 1982; *Skipper v. South Carolona*, 1986, 4).[5] In the years after *Gregg*, capital jurisprudence demonstrated more of a focus on mitigation in pursuit of "individualized sentencing" considerations and the need to "narrow" the class of individuals eligible for the death penalty (*Zant v. Stephens*, 1983, p. 876).[6]

Gregg is the blueprint case that supports the nationwide use of capital punishment today, and the rest of this chapter will explain why it should be revisited, as the current state of capital punishment falls short of constitutional standards. The current state of capital jurisprudence is just as arbitrary and unconstitutional as during the time of *Furman*.

Studies on Arbitrariness in Selection/Racial Disparities Based on Victims

The problems in *Furman* regarding the arbitrary and capricious use of the death penalty remain today. Since *Gregg*, 80% of U.S. counties have not executed a single soul (Death Penalty Information Center [DPIC], 2023e). Fewer than 2% of U.S. counties account for more than 50% of the total death row population in the country (DPIC, 2023e). Once we account for regions of the country, the arbitrariness is even more stark. Post-*Gregg*, 82% of all U.S. executions have occurred in southern states (DPIC, 2023e). Taking a closer look at executions within a state, Texas shows that only 3 counties account for more than half of the nearly 200 people on its death row, while only 50 out of 254 counties provide the entire death row population (Texas Coalition Against the Death Penalty [TCADP], 2023).

Another problem with discretion (Sharon, 2011, p. 227),[7] when it comes to the death penalty, is that the arbitrariness contributes to unconstitutional racial disparities. Race was in the DNA of *Furman*. In the notorious and detrimentally influential *McCleskey v. Kemp* (1987), the Court formally addressed racism in capital punishment. The case involved a challenge brought by a Black capital defendant from Georgia based on how its capital punishment scheme violated the Equal Protection Clause (*McCleskey v. Kemp*, 1987, p., 291). The proof of discrimination derived from an empirical study conducted by University of Iowa research professor David Baldus and colleagues, which showed that people convicted of killing White victims were four times as likely to be sentenced to death as those accused of killing Black victims (Baldus et al., 1983). Cases involving White victims and Black defendants received the death penalty 21% of the time, while White defendants were sentenced to death only 8% of the time for cases involving fellow White victims (Civil Liberties in the U.S., 2022). Yet the Court was unmoved to find a constitutional violation (*McCleskey v. Kemp*, 1987, pp. 312–20). Renowned attorney and professor Anthony G. Amsterdam, who argued the monumental *Furman* case before the Court, has called *McCleskey* "the Dred Scott decision of our time" (Liptak, 2020).

Emboldened by the Court's rejection of the Baldus Study in *McCleskey*, legal scholars used a larger single-county study to determine whether capital punishment was discriminatory in its practice in violation of the Equal Protection Clause (Shatz et al., 2020). The San Diego County study covered data from 1081 cases over a 14.5-year period and found substantial disparities where prosecutors used their discretion to issue capital charges more often when there were Black defendants with White victims (Shatz et al., 2020, p. 1073). Out of the 1,081 cases in which prosecutors filed charges where they intended to prove first-degree murder, they obtained first-degree convictions from the jury only 269 times, less than a 25% rate (Shatz et al., 2020, p. 1087). The data also showed how prosecutorial discretion, as opposed to the statutory scheme, "narrowed" the class of death-eligible defendants, as the county district attorney decided not to pursue the death penalty against over 85% of death-eligible defendants (Shatz et al., 2020, p. 1089). This empirical evidence demonstrates the following:

- The death penalty was rarely imposed, irrespective of the death-eligible class of defendants.
- When it was imposed, the race of the victims and defendants *appeared* to be substantial factors in how prosecutors exercised their discretion. Nationwide, problems remain regarding capital punishment used as retribution for White victims, disproportionally correlated with Black defendants (DPIC, 2023c).

As we will discuss later, racial problems from *Furman* regarding unfettered prosecutorial discretion and arbitrariness in sentencing have not been resolved.

A Retreat from "Evolving Standards of Decency"

The legal concept of "evolving standards of decency" as applied to the Eighth Amendment predates *Furman*. The first time the Court used the term in an opinion within the context of the Eighth Amendment was *Trop v. Dulles*, 356 U.S. 86 (1958), which was not a capital case (100–01).[8] Specifically, the Court stated the "Amendment must draw its meaning from the evolving standards of decency that mark the progress of a maturing society" (*Trop v. Dulles*, 1958, pp. 100–01).[9] The phrase appears multiple times throughout the majority *Furman* opinion (p. 238, 242, 269, 327, 329), as well as in *Gregg v. Georgia* (1976, p. 173).[10]

The concept rose to profound significance when the Court issued two major decisions that protected the most intellectually and emotionally vulnerable, and thus the least culpable, people from execution. Until 2002, this country permitted states to execute people who were clinically diagnosed as intellectually disabled (ID) (*Atkins v. Virginia*, 2002). Three years later, the Court found that standards had evolved, and society had progressed, to find the execution of children to violate the Eighth Amendment (*Roper v. Simmons*, 2005). In response, states had to set out a criterion to determine which defendants may qualify for protected status and how. Regarding *Atkins*, courts have had to rely on scientific standards from experts in the field to determine the issue of intellectual disability.[11]

The treatment of *Atkins* in Florida is an example of how current trends are contrary to the philosophy behind why affected defendants need Eighth Amendment protections. *Hall v. Florida*, 572 U.S. 701 (2014), initially provided signs of progress, as the Court overturned Florida's "bright-line" for determining ID, which had required a defendant to score 70 or below on a qualified IQ test to be considered death ineligible (p. 704, 715, 723).[12] However, by not finding *Hall* retroactive to cases that were final at the time of the decision, Florida is setting arbitrary barriers and allowing intellectually disabled persons to be executed, contrary to *Atkins* and the Eighth Amendment (*Phillips v. State*, 2016).[13] It is unconstitutional to execute intellectually disabled people because the very nature of their condition diminishes their capacity to aid in their own defense, and common themes of punishment such as deterrence and retribution are not as applicable to those with cognitive and behavioral impairments (*Atkins v. Virginia*, 2002, pp. 318–21). Further supporting the decision in *Atkins*, empirical evidence, discovered after analyzing statutes across the country, has shown that a national consensus had trended against executing people with certain intellectual disabilities (*Atkins v. Virginia*, 2002, p. 317). Therefore, newer arbitrary laws that prevent intellectually disabled people avenues to relief are deeply concerning.

Like *Atkins*, the Court in *Roper* was persuaded that based on a review of trends across the nation and using the "evolving standards of decency" test, it would be "cruel and unusual" to execute defendants for crimes they committed when they were juveniles (*Roper v. Simmons*, 2005, pp. 567–68). The Court in *Roper* also relied on amici briefs citing sociological and scientific studies, explaining the mitigating characteristics and qualities of children, as compared to adults (*Roper v. Simmons*, 2005, 569–70).[14] However, since the time of *Roper*, studies have often indicated that the case should be revisited, as experts opine that the brain keeps developing into a person's early 20s (Jordan, 2019).

The concerns about culpability and narrowing the class of death eligible to the "worst of the worst" that supported the national trends in *Atkins* and *Roper* should apply to a litany of defendants suffering from severe psychiatric issues or brain damage. Due to the subjective nature of what is considered "severe mental illness", there has been nothing approaching any type of national consensus on the issue (DPIC, 2023b). However, there are signs of hope, as Ohio recently passed House Bill 136 into law, which bars the death penalty from being imposed on those who suffered from severe mental illness that "significantly impaired their judgment, capacity, or ability to appreciate the nature of their conduct" at the time of their offense (DPIC, 2023b).

"Evolving standards of decency that mark the progress of a maturing society" has had profound meaning in capital jurisprudence. What remains to be seen is what happens to this concept if the standards of decency begin to *devolve* in this country, state by state.

Methods of Execution and Risk of Executing the Actually Innocent

Today, execution by lethal injection is the most common method used in those states that still utilize the death penalty (DPIC, 2023d). Death by lethal injection raises its own Eighth Amendment considerations, most often with challenges to the procedure focused "as applied" to a condemned inmate's medical condition and the possibility of tortuous suffering during the execution (*Bucklew v. Precythe*, 2019, pp. 1126–31).[15] The Court in *Bucklew v. Precythe* (2019) made a point of stating that the "Eighth Amendment does not guarantee a prisoner a painless death" (p. 1124).

One reason some states have been offering alternatives to lethal injection is problems obtaining the chemicals needed to constitute the cocktails (Chammah & Meagher, 2016).[16] Capital defense attorneys face an oppressive state of the law when it comes to challenging methods of execution. The Court has yet to find that any state's method of execution qualifies as "cruel and unusual" (*Bucklew v. Precythe*, 2019, p. 1124).

The biggest concern when it comes to the death penalty is always that the government may execute someone who is factually innocent. With Florida leading the way with 30 exonerations, at least 186 people across the United States have been completely exonerated of all charges that led to their conviction and sentence to death row (DPIC, 2023a). Studies have indicated a significant correlation between official misconduct by government officials and death row exonerations (Vick et al., 2021, p. 33). Wrongful capital convictions also erode trust in the criminal justice system. Public opinion support for the death penalty has been shown to decrease when citizens are presented with evidence of wrongful capital convictions, particularly when presented with an individual narrative account of a wrongfully convicted individual (Norris & Mullinix, 2020, p. 323). Distressingly, the U.S. Supreme Court has a high threshold, with rigorous criteria, for capital defendants to present free-standing claims of actual innocence at the federal level (Herrera *v. Collins*, 1993).

Empirical Evidence for Ongoing Issues

Evidence-based solutions depend on the amount and quality of empirical evidence available (cf. Donohue & Wolfers, 2006). We reviewed the literature from the past few years to capture the impact that shifting public opinion, new death penalty legislation, and case law have had on the landscape of capital cases in the United States and what solutions might follow from these studies. While this review is not exhaustive, other authors have produced extensive reviews of the empirical literature on the death penalty to date, largely by state. For example, Gorman and Ravenscroft (2020) reviewed Florida, Robinson (2021) reviewed North Carolina, and Okpara et al. (2021) reviewed Colorado. Important county-level statistical data were also contributed from a national survey by Amidon and Eassy (2021) and in San Diego County by Shatz et al. (2020). Other empirical studies have focused on specific aspects of the death penalty issue, particularly the impact of racial and ethnic bias in charging and sentencing (Hoag, 2020; Johnson, 2020; Ramirez, 2021; Shatz et al., 2020) but also how economic considerations affect whether death penalty charges are brought in different jurisdictions (Bruce, 2020; Wilford & Bornstein, 2021; Vick et al., 2021). A timely article by Acker and Stull (2021) examines the key issue of what happens to individuals under sentence of death when capital punishment legislation is repealed or invalidated.

National and state level studies such as Gorman and Ravenscroft (2020) make a compelling argument for focusing on the state of Florida, which ranks in the top few states where death penalty convictions are overturned. Until 2016 and the passage of legislation following the *Hurst* decision, Florida also had the distinction of being one of few states that could impose the death penalty without a unanimous recommendation from a penalty phase jury. In an analysis of post-*Hurst* Florida capital cases, Gorman and Ravenscroft reviewed 1,051 first-degree murder cases comprising 347 death sentence cases, including 126 resentencings pursuant to *Hurst v. Florida* (2016). Their analysis found that despite *Hurst*, new death penalty cases since 2016 continued to show wide geographic disparities in the application of the death penalty, with just five circuits accounting for over half of cases where the death penalty was sought (Gorman & Ravenscroft, 2020, pp. 967–971). Further, although 75% of inmates on death row had non-unanimous verdicts, only 40% were eligible for *Hurst* relief following Florida Supreme Court rulings in *Mosley v. State* (2016) and *Asay v. State* (2016) regarding retroactivity (Gorman & Ravenscroft, 2020, pp. 972–973). Gorman and Ravenscroft (2020) recommend:

> Provided this [improvement in the FDLE database] is undertaken, there should be solid evidence to support extensive legislative change that could address the issues discussed above. The authors predict that this will demonstrate the need to: (1) redraft the Florida statute to redefine the aggravators and narrow the death-eligibility appropriately; (2) introduce a standardized system of filing death notices, involving a committee consisting of independent members of the legal and criminal justice communities responsible for reviewing information from the state and defendants; (3) grant resentencings to all those under a sentence of death at the time of Hurst; and, (4) standardize jury fact-finding forms with mitigators as well as aggravators and jury-selection questionnaires.
>
> *(p. 975)*

North Carolina's last execution was held in 2006, and there has been an unofficial moratorium on executions since that time given the furious debate over the morality of lethal injection. Robinson (2021) surveyed a variety of statistical data from 1977–present, finding that the death penalty was not a deterrent to capital crimes. The murder rate in North Carolina steadily decreased through the 1990s, while death penalty sentences were at an all-time high due to statutory requirements for prosecutors to seek the death penalty whenever aggravating factors were present (Robinson, 2021, p. 14). Robinson (2021) notes that recent polling data show that only 25% of North Carolinians surveyed support capital punishment (p. 8).

Although Colorado abolished the death penalty in 2020, Okpara et al.'s (2020) retrospective multivariate study of sentencing decisions in Colorado between 1999 and 2010 found that beyond individual aggravating and mitigating factors, "race was a consistent and persistent statistically significant predictors of death notices" (p. 23).

Race and Ethnicity

Issues articulated in *McCleskey* remain today. Inequities in charging and sentencing by race and ethnicity were a consistent finding in recent empirical investigations. Hoag (2020) conducted a diachronic study of the interaction between race in death penalty cases and found, as had others in the past, that racial prejudice played a role from the initial point of arrest through charging and sentencing for Black defendants (pp. 992–993). Further, when the race of the defendant vs. victim was considered, cases where the defendant was Black and the victim White resulted in a higher frequency of charges, convictions, and/or executions in jurisdictions ranging from North Carolina, Louisiana, and Georgia (pp. 992–994). "The Court's decision in *Furman* afforded state actors significant discretion at each of these points, enabling them to insert racism, bias, and prejudice into their decision making" (Hoag, 2020, p. 994). This issue was taken up in *McCleskey*, with the Court holding that such statistical findings did not persuade them to find a violation of the plaintiff's constitutional rights and that legislative action was the appropriate remedy. As legislative remedies have yet to resolve this pattern of discrimination, Hoag proposes that the death penalty should be abolished to protect Black lives.

Johnson's (2020) study on the role of ethnicity in the imposition of the death penalty on Latino defendants marshaled a smaller body of empirical data. The difficulties that Johnson encountered in finding data on Latino defendants point out how problematic simply framing a problem is in the absence of systematic data. In the case of Latinos, archival and controlled sample experimental data found bias towards individuals with "Latin" surnames and cultural stereotypes of appearance. However, Latin ethnicity is not consistently or accurately collected in criminal justice proceedings, so the extent of bias may be much larger than estimated. Johnson (2020) concluded that efforts to reduce ethnic bias in the justice system, particularly where the death penalty is involved, are imperative while admitting that it is difficult to determine exactly how to do this (p. 429).

A 2021 conjoint experiment study by Ramirez offers some clarification regarding the role of race in public sentiment towards the death penalty. Ramirez (2021) used a sample of 500 U.S. adults to gain a more nuanced view of attitudes towards the death penalty, accounting for a variety of factors, including gender, age, prior convictions, mental illness, gang affiliation, accomplices, premeditation, drug-related offenses, sexual assault, race and gender of the victim, and race of offender. Participants were presented with a pair of hypothetical defendants who possessed random configurations of characteristics and were asked which defendant was more deserving of the death penalty. Results showed that although race was not a primary factor among the study participants, it *was* a persistent factor. The greatest predictor of racial bias in sentencing was a pre-existing animus towards Latinos or Black people, and Ramirez (2021) concedes that

> it is possible that at least some of the seemingly non-racial factors (in the study) are indeed race laden. For instance, the typification of Black and Hispanic criminality would suggest that some of these factors are more likely to be associated with racial minorities than Whites.
>
> *(p. 1942)*

Ramirez (2021) concludes:

> The findings here can shed light into important public policy debates among criminal justice reformers. The public clearly finds offenders deserving of capital punishment who have a history of violent crime, preplan their crimes, and maintain full agency over their actions. Yet, many of the first-time offenders currently on death row for crimes that occur in the heat-of-the-moment might gain leniency among many Americans. Moving the discussion of death penalty reform away from factors unimportant to the public and focusing on alternative ways of keeping the most dangerous career criminals off the street could drastically help reduce the death row population in the United States or eliminate it altogether.
>
> *(p. 1943)*

Shatz et al. (2020) conducted a detailed regression analysis of the characteristics of death penalty defendants in 1081 cases spanning 14 years in San Diego County, California, and, like Ramirez (2021), found that a variety of considerations aside from race or ethnicity factor in the decision to seek the death penalty, concluding that:

> Beyond the risk of arbitrariness, the study documents discrimination. We found that, in murder prosecutions during the relevant time – particularly in cases with White victims and Black defendants – a substantial factor in prosecutors' decision whether to charge special circumstances and in the District Attorney's decision whether to seek the death penalty was the race/ethnicity of the victims and defendants.
>
> *(p. 1098)*

Economic Considerations

The disparity in death penalty charges across jurisdictions presented at the beginning of this section has at its root a simultaneously pragmatic and pernicious reason: the cost of litigating a death penalty case. The studies discussed in the following show that the threat of the death penalty is used in some cases to effectively induce defendants to take a guilty plea with a life sentence. Further, the concentration of death penalty cases in a handful of counties across the United States is attributable to over-zealous prosecutors and the purported ability and willingness of those jurisdictions to bear the cost that a death penalty case and succeeding litigation entails.

Alexandria Bruce's (2020) article states that "there's no money left for the monster's ball", trenchantly noting that McCleskey was not necessarily executed because of racial discrimination but because "he refused to accept an offer to plead guilty to a life sentence" (2020, p. 170). Post-*Furman* capital sentencing guidelines reduce the risk of "arbitrary infliction of severe punishments" by bifurcating the trial and penalty phases, which is costly, particularly in the trial phase. Death penalty trials in some jurisdictions cost three times as much as non-death penalty trials for the same offense (Bruce, 2020, p. 174), and death penalty trials have forced some communities to borrow money and raise taxes to bear that cost (Bruce, 2020, p. 175). Bruce (2020) also notes that some of the most heinous offenders have been able to avoid the death penalty by pleading guilty and that plea bargaining in capital cases inevitably leads to false confessions and fraudulent testimony (p. 178). Once a prosecutor has filed an intention to seek the death penalty, Bruce (2020) argues, the voluntariness of a guilty plea to avoid a death sentence is under question (pp. 180–181). Those defendants who take that plea receive life sentences without parole regardless of actual guilt and with limited possibilities for appeal, forfeiting constitutional rights afforded to those on death row (pp. 188 189). Bruce (2020) concludes that capital plea bargaining needs to be either procedurally barred or completely restructured to avoid the loss of a capital defendant's constitutional rights.

Bruce's (2020) concerns about the constitutionality of capital plea bargaining are echoed by Wilford and Bornstein (2021), who observe that jury trials are "disappearing" as plea bargaining is increasingly used in capital cases. Vick et al. (2021), like Bruce, found that false pleas and false confessions constitute "lethal leverage" where capital defendants lose valuable constitutional rights.

The research evidence indicates ongoing problems with the implementation of the death penalty. The following take-home points and recommendations are provided in light of the evidence:

- The state of the death penalty indicates that it is declining in use, but issues remain.
- Race is still an ongoing issue, as White victims are deemed most worthy of the state making capital charging decisions.
- Plea bargaining should be eliminated in capital cases. It creates arbitrary considerations when it comes to prosecuting "the worst of the worst." However, the cost of capital litigation has been a factor in some states reconsidering the efficacy of the death penalty in relation to expense.

Most of the studies reviewed in this section do not provide solutions *per se*, although clearly the tenor is one that calls for reform, "disciplined retention" (Griffin, 2021), or outright abolition of the death penalty in the United States. Implementing any of these schemes requires complete, current, and accurate empirical data to make sure that all persons on death rows throughout the country receive the same measure of justice (Acker & Stull, 2021).

Conclusion

Capital punishment in America has a long history, with no complete end in sight. Practitioners should understand the evidence-based considerations in this chapter as they consider the complicated field of capital punishment. Historically, America has placed a value on condemning certain criminals to death. The *Furman* pause on capital punishment lasted several years, until the Court decided *Gregg*, which, as this chapter has opined, has done little to solve the problems of arbitrariness and racial inequities rooted in capital jurisprudence. As the pandemic executions proved, certain actors in the American government will take full advantage of the ability to execute people when given the power and opportunity to carry it out. Readers should take these key points from this chapter:

- Arbitrariness in the implementation of capital punishment, particularly based on factors such as geography and race, needs to be consistently litigated by practitioners.
- "Evolving standards of decency" have encouraged some Eighth Amendment protections on mentally and emotionally vulnerable classes of people, but arbitrary procedural obstacles and a dilution of caselaw precedent has been deeply concerning.
- Litigating issues concerning the methods of execution are particularly challenging due to the state of the law. However, abolitionists' grassroots efforts in lobbying certain drug

manufacturers have made it difficult for some states to obtain the necessary drug cocktails for lethal injection.

- Economic issues create a dichotomy where some states have considered doing away with capital punishment because of the cost, while many jurisdictions are engaging in capital plea bargaining that often results in the loss of constitutional protections for defendants.
- Capital punishment is not only imperfect, but the errors have also caused actually innocent people to be placed on death row.

What history and evidence-based analysis have demonstrated is that practitioners will need to tackle complex issues at the state level, state by state, to provoke positive change and protections for capital defendants under the Eighth Amendment to the United States Constitution. As is, America's capital punishment prudence is fraught with ethical and constitutional concerns, and disciplined retention, if not abolition, should be the focus of practitioners in this field.

Notes

1 In Gregg, the majority explained that "the concerns expressed in Furman that the penalty of death not be imposed in an arbitrary or capricious manner can be met by a carefully drafted statute that ensures that the sentencing authority is given adequate information and guidance" (Id. at 195). For the majority, "[a]s a general proposition these concerns are best met by a system that provides for a bifurcated proceeding at which the sentencing authority is apprised of the information relevant to the imposition of sentence and provided with standards to guide its use of the information" (Id. at 195) (1976). The majority made clear that such procedures were not the only way to satisfy Furman and that any sentencing system constructed along these general lines would [not] inevitably satisfy the concerns of Furman" (Id. at 195) (1976). Rather, "each distinct system must be examined on an individual basis" (Id).

The majority held that the statutory system under which Gregg was sentenced to death does not violate the Constitution (Id. at 207). Importantly for the majority, the Georgia death penalty scheme narrowed "the class of murderers subject to capital punishment by specifying 10 statutory aggravating circumstances, one of which must be found by the jury to exist beyond a reasonable doubt before a death sentence can ever be imposed" (196–97). The jury was also allowed to consider "any other any other appropriate aggravating or mitigating circumstances" (Id. at 197). The majority observed that "[t]hese procedures require the jury to consider the circumstances of the crime and the criminal before it recommends sentence" (Id). The majority found it "an important additional safeguard against arbitrariness and caprice, [that] the Georgia statutory scheme provides for automatic appeal of all death sentences to the State's Supreme Court" (Id. at 198. Gregg, 428 U.S. 153, 195–97) (1976) (internal footnotes omitted).

2 While the prevailing practice of individualizing sentencing determinations generally reflects simply enlightened policy rather than a constitutional imperative, we believe that in capital cases, the fundamental respect for humanity underlying the Eighth Amendment (see Trop v. Dulles, 356 U.S., at 100, 78 S. Ct., at 597 (plurality opinion)) requires consideration of the character and record of the individual offender and the circumstances of the particular offense as a constitutionally indispensable part of the process of inflicting the penalty of death. This conclusion rests squarely on the predicate that the penalty of death is qualitatively different from a sentence of imprisonment, however long. Death, in its finality, differs more from life imprisonment than a 100-year prison term differs from one of only a year or two. Because of that qualitative difference, there is a corresponding difference in the need for reliability in the determination that death is the appropriate punishment in a specific case (Woodson, 428 U.S. 280, 304–05 (1976)).

3 The ruling in Coker was extended in Kennedy v. Louisiana, 554 U.S. 407, holding that the death penalty for even adult rape, without a death, is unconstitutional: "Nine States – Florida, Georgia, Louisiana, Mississippi, Montana, Oklahoma, South Carolina, Tennessee, and Texas – have permitted capital punishment for adult or child rape for some length of time between the Court's 1972 decision in Furman and today". See supra, at 2651; Coker, supra, at 595, 97 S.Ct. 2861 (plurality opinion). Yet

no individual has been executed for the rape of an adult or child since 1964, and no execution for any other nonhomicide offense has been conducted since 1963. See Historical Statistics of the United States, at 5–262 to 5–263 (Table Ec343–357). Also see Thompson v. Oklahoma, 487 U.S. 815, 852–853, 108 S. Ct. 2687, 101 L.Ed.2d 702 (1988) (O'Connor, J., concurring *434 in judgment) (that "four decades have gone by since the last execution of a defendant who was younger than 16 at the time of the offense . . . support[s] the inference of a national consensus opposing the death penalty for 15-year-olds") (Kennedy, 554 U.S. 407, 433–34 (2008), as modified (Oct. 1, 2008), opinion modified on denial of reh'g, 554 U.S. 945 (2008)).

4 "The Eighth and Fourteenth Amendments require that the sentencer, in all but the rarest kind of capital case, not be precluded from considering, as a mitigating factor, any aspect of a defendant's character or record . . . that the defendant proffers as a basis for a sentence less than death" (Lockett v. Ohio, 438 U.S. 586, 604 (1978)).

5 See also Skipper v. South Carolina, 476 U.S. 1 (1986), holding that even seemingly minimal mitigation, from jail staff and a visitor, about the capital defendant being "well-adjusted" to penal life, could not be excluded on relevance grounds. "There is no disputing that this Court's decision in Eddings requires that in capital cases " 'the sentencer . . . not be precluded from considering, as a mitigating factor, any aspect of a defendant's character or record and any of the circumstances of the offense that the defendant proffers as a basis for a sentence less than death." Eddings, supra, 455 U.S., at 110, 102 S. Ct., at 874 (quoting Lockett, supra, 438 U.S., at 604, 98 S. Ct., at 2964 (plurality opinion of BURGER, C.J.)) (emphasis in original). Equally clear is the corollary rule that the sentencer may not refuse to consider or be precluded from considering "any relevant mitigating evidence." 455 U.S., at 114, 102 S. Ct., at 877. "These rules are now well established, and the State does not question them" (Id. at 4).

6 Zant v. Stephens, 462 U.S. 862, 876 (1983): The approval of Georgia's capital sentencing procedure rested primarily on two features of the scheme: that the jury was required to find at least one valid statutory aggravating circumstance and to identify it in writing, and that the state supreme court reviewed the record of every death penalty proceeding to determine whether the sentence was arbitrary or disproportionate. These elements, the opinion concluded, adequately protected against the wanton and freakish imposition of the death penalty. This conclusion rested, of course, on the fundamental requirement that each statutory aggravating circumstance must satisfy a constitutional standard derived from the principles of Furman itself. For a system "could have standards so vague that they would fail adequately to channel the sentencing decision patterns of juries with the result that a pattern of arbitrary and capricious sentencing like that found unconstitutional in Furman could occur." 428 U.S., at 195, n. 46, 96 S. Ct., at 2935, n. 46. To avoid this constitutional flaw, an aggravating circumstance must genuinely narrow the class of persons eligible for the death penalty and must reasonably justify the imposition of a more severe sentence on the defendant compared to others found guilty of murder. (internal footnotes omitted).

7 Prosecutors exercise complete discretion in seeking the death penalty on certain individuals based on at least one statutory aggravating factor. Jurors also have the discretion to impose death based on their analysis of said aggravating factors. See Sharon (2011, p. 227).

8 In Trop, the defendant was convicted in a military court partial for the crime "desertion", based on a statute that was first passed during the Civil War. The Court stated in relevant part:

'cruel and unusual' has not been detailed by this Court. But the basic policy reflected in these words is firmly established in the Anglo-American tradition of criminal justice. The phrase in our Constitution was taken directly from the English Declaration of Rights of 1688, and the principle it represents can be traced back to the Magna Carta. The basic concept underlying the Eighth Amendment is nothing less than the dignity of man. While the State has the power to punish, the Amendment stands to assure that this power be exercised within the limits of civilized standards. Fines, imprisonment and even execution may be imposed depending upon the enormity of the crime, but any technique outside the bounds of these traditional penalties is constitutionally suspect. This Court has had little occasion to give precise content to the Eighth Amendment, and, in an enlightened democracy such as ours, this is not surprising. But when the Court was confronted with a punishment of 12 years in irons at hard and painful labor imposed for the crime of falsifying public records, it did not hesitate to declare that the penalty was cruel in its excessiveness and unusual in its character. Weems v. United States, 217 U.S. 349, 30 S.Ct. 544, 54 L.Ed. 793. The Court recognized in that case that the words of the Amendment are not precise, and that their scope is not static. The Amendment must draw its meaning from the evolving standards of decency that mark the progress of a maturing society. We believe, as did Chief Judge Clark in the court below, that use of denationalization as a punishment is barred by the Eighth Amendment. Trop, 386 U.S. 86, 100–101 (1958) (internal footnotes and page numbers omitted).

9 Id.

10 It is clear from the foregoing precedents that the Eighth Amendment has not been regarded as a static concept. As Chief Justice Warren said, in an oft-quoted phrase, "(t)he Amendment must draw its meaning from the evolving standards of decency that mark the progress of a maturing society" (Trop v. Dulles, Supra, 356 U.S. at 101, 78 S. Ct., at 598). See also Jackson v. Bishop, 404 F.2d 571, 579 (CA 8 1968). Cf. Robinson v. California, supra, 370 U.S., at 666, 82 S. Ct., at 1420. Thus, an assessment of contemporary values concerning the infliction of a challenged sanction is relevant to the application of the Eighth Amendment (Gregg, 428 U.S. 153, 173 (1976)).

11 The American Psychological Association, which publishes the Diagnostic and Statistical Manual of Mental Disorders, Fifth Edition (DSM-V), and the American Association on Intellectual and Developmental Disabilities, which publishes the American Association on Intellectual and Developmental Disabilities, Intellectual Disability: Definition, Classification, and Systems of Supports (11th ed. 2010) (AAIDD-11), provide scientific guidance in assessing intellectual disability cases. Both the DSM-V and AAIDD-11 definitions of intellectual disability are generally accepted in the psychological community. The DSM-V defines intellectual disability as follows:

A. Deficits in intellectual functions, such as reasoning, problem solving, planning, abstract thinking, judgment, academic learning, and learning from experience, confirmed by both clinical assessment and individualized, standardized intelligence testing.
B. Deficits in adaptive functioning that result in failure to meet developmental and sociological standards for personal independence and social responsibility. Without ongoing support, the adaptive deficits limit functioning in one or more areas of daily life, such as communication, social participation, and independent living, across multiple environments, such as home, school, work, and community.
C. Onset of intellectual and adaptive deficits during the developmental period.

(DSM-V at 33)

The AAIDD-11 defines intellectual disability as follows:

Intellectual disability is characterized by significant limitations both in intellectual functioning and in adaptive behavior as expressed in conceptual, social, and practical adaptive skills. This disability originates before age 18.

(AAIDD-11 at 5)

12 The Court explained how Florida's rigid bright-line test and similar statutes in other states which did not consider standard areas of measurements utilized in the scientific community created the unacceptable risk that intellectually disabled persons could be executed, in violation of Atkins (Hall, 572 U.S. 701, 704, 715, 723 (2014)). (See also Moore v. Texas, 137 S. Ct. 1039, 1052–53 (2017), which held that states may not deviate from legitimate medical standards and diagnostic criteria when diagnosing even mild intellectual disabilities.)

13 See Phillips v. State, 299 So. 3d 1013 (Fla. 2020) (receding from Walls v. State, 213 So. 3d 340 (2016)), overturning mere 4-year-old precedent which had previously found Hall v. Florida, 572 U.S. 701 (2014) should be retroactively applied to impacted defendants. See also Nixon v. State, 2021 WL 3778705 (Aug. 26, 2021), holding that appellant would not be afforded relief under Walls even though it was good law at the time of the initial remand, because Phillips v. State was subsequent, intervening, and controlling law, thereby denying relief.

14 Roper, 543 U.S. 551. at 569–70 (2005): "Three general differences between juveniles under 18 and adults demonstrate that juvenile offenders cannot with reliability be classified among the worst offenders. First, as any parent knows and as the scientific and sociological studies respondent and his amici cite tend to confirm, [a] lack of maturity and an underdeveloped sense of responsibility are found in youth more often than in adults and are more understandable among the young. These qualities often result in impetuous and ill-considered actions and decisions." Johnson, supra, at 367, 113 S. Ct. 2658; see also Eddings, supra, at 115–116, 102 S. Ct. 869 ("Even the normal 16–year–old customarily lacks the maturity of an adult"). It has been noted that "adolescents are overrepresented statistically in virtually

every category of reckless behavior" (Arnett, Reckless Behavior in Adolescence: A Developmental Perspective, 12 Developmental Rev. 339 (1992)). In recognition of the comparative immaturity and irresponsibility of juveniles, almost every state prohibits those under 18 years of age from voting, serving on juries, or marrying without parental consent. See Appendixes B–D, infra.

The second area of difference is that juveniles are more vulnerable or susceptible to negative influences and outside pressures, including peer pressure. Eddings, supra, at 115, 102 S.Ct. 869 ("[Y]outh is more than a chronological fact. It is a time and condition of life when a person may be most susceptible to influence and to psychological damage"). This is explained in part by the prevailing circumstance that juveniles have less control, or less experience with control, over their own environment. See Steinberg & Scott, Less Guilty by Reason of Adolescence: Developmental Immaturity, Diminished Responsibility, and the Juvenile Death Penalty, 58 Am. Psychologist 1009, 1014 (2003) (hereinafter Steinberg & Scott) ("[A]s legal minors, [juveniles] lack the freedom that adults have to extricate themselves from a criminogenic setting").

The third broad difference is that the character of a juvenile is not as well formed as that of an adult. The personality traits of juveniles are more transitory, less fixed. See generally E. Erikson, Identity: Youth and Crisis (1968)."

15 See Bucklew v. Precythe, 587 U.S.___, 139 S. Ct 1112 (2019): upholding Baze v. Rees, 553 U.S. 35 (2008) and Glossip v. Gross, 576 U.S. 863 (2015), that death by lethal injection was permissible under the Eighth Amendment, and any challenge based on any alleged risk of pain and suffering would need to offer an alternative available method of execution that would significantly reduce the substantial risk of pain. Id. at 1126–31.

16 See Death Penalty Information Center (2023d): various different types of chemicals utilized in executions, including such drugs as pentobarbital, midazolam, sodium thiopental, and etomidate. Some states, including the federal government, use a single-dose procedure, whereas other states are using two to four different drugs.

References

Acker, R., & Stull, B. W. (2021). Life after sentence of death: What becomes of individuals under sentence of death after capital punishment legislation is repealed or invalidated. *Akron Law Review*, *54*(2), 268–328. Retrieved from https://ideaexchange.uakron.edu/akronlawreview/vol54/iss2/3

Amidon, E., & Eassy, J. M. (2021). Examining the county-level political considerations associated with declining reliance on the death penalty from1990 to 2010. *Criminology*, *59*, 318–350. doi: 10.1111/1745–9125.12272.

Atkins v. Virginia, 536 U.S. 304 (2002).

Baldus, D. P., Pulaski, C., & Woodworth, G. (1983). Comparative review of death sentences: An empirical study of the Georgia experience. *Journal of Criminal Law & Criminology*, (74), 663–753.

Beccaria, C., & Voltaire, V. (1764). *An essay on crimes and punishments*. W.C. Little and Company.

Bessler, J. (2012). *Cruel and unusual: The American death penalty and the founders' eighth amendment*. Northeastern University Press.

Bessler, J. (2014). Forward: The death penalty in decline: From Colonial America to the present. *Criminal Law of Bulletin*, *50*, 245–262.

Bruce, J. A. (2020). Because there is no money left for the monster's ball. *Georgetown Journal of Legal Ethics*, *33*(2), 167–199.

Bucklew v. Precythe, 587 U.S.___, 139 S. Ct 1112 (2019).

Chammah, M., & Meagher, T. (2016, April 12). How the drug shortage has slowed the death penalty treadmill: Only 4 states are currently carrying out executions, and 10 are considering other methods. The Marshall Project. Retrieved from www.themarshallproject.org/2016/04/12/how-the-drug-shortage-has-slowed-the-death-penalty-treadmill

Civil Liberties in the U.S. (2022). Baldus study (capital punishment). Retrieved from https://uscivilliberties.org/3159-baldus-study.html

Coker v. Georgia, 433 U.S. 584, 592 (1977).

Cruel and Unusual Punishment. (1972). The death penalty cases: *Furman v. Georgia, Jackson v. Georgia, Branch v. Texas*, 408 U.S. 238 (1972). *Journal of Criminal Law, Criminology and Police Science*, *63*, 484–491.

Death Penalty Information Center (DPIC). (2023a). Innocence. Retrieved from https://deathpenaltyinfo.org/policy-issues/innocence
Death Penalty Information Center (DPIC). (2023b). Mental illness. Retrieved from https://deathpenaltyinfo.org/policy-issues/mental-illness
Death Penalty Information Center (DPIC). (2023c). Race. Retrieved from https://deathpenaltyinfo.org/policy-issues/race
Death Penalty Information Center (DPIC). (2023d). State-by-state execution protocols. Retrieved from https://deathpenaltyinfo.org/executions/methods-of-execution/state-by-state-execution-protocols
Death Penalty Information Center (DPIC). (2023e). The 2% death penalty: The geographic arbitrariness of capital punishment in the United States. Retrieved from https://deathpenaltyinfo.org/stories/the-clustering-of-the-death-penalty
Defender Services Office (2020). Daniel Lee attorney statement about Lee's execution this morning. Retrieved from https://www.fd.org/news/daniel-lee-attorney-statement-about-lees-execution-morning
Donohue, J. J., & Wolfers, J. (2006). Uses and abuses of empirical evidence in the death penalty debate (National Bureau of Economic Research Working Paper 11982). doi: 10.3386/w11982.
Eddings v. Oklahoma, 455 U.S. 104, 115 (1982).
Federal Board of Prisons. (2003). Capital punishment. Retrieved from www.bop.gov/about/history/federal_executions.jsp
Furman v. Georgia, 408 U.S. 238 (1972).
Gorman, H. L., & Ravenscroft, M. (2020). Hurricane Florida: The hot and cold fronts of America's most active death row. *Columbia Human Rights Law Review*, *51*(3), 935–982.
Griffin, T. (2021). Comparing expert versus general public rationale for death penalty support and opposition: Is expert perspective on capital punishment consistent with "disciplined retention"? *Punishment & Society*, 1–21. doi: 10.1177/14624745211029370.
Gregg v. Georgia, 428 U.S. 153 (1976).
Hall v. Florida, 572 U.S. 701 (2014).
Herrera v. Collins, 506 U.S. 390, 417 (1993).
Hoag, A. (2020). Valuing Black lives: A case for ending the death penalty. *Columbia Human Rights Law Review*, *51*(3), 983–1007.
Johnson, S. L. (2020). The influence of Latino ethnicity on the imposition of the death penalty. *Annual Review of Law and Social Science*, *16*, 421–431. doi: 10.1146/annurev-lawsocsci-042220–111211
Jordan, Z. (2019). The Roper extension: A California perspective. *Hastings Law Journal*, *71*(1), 197–227.
Jrank. (2023). Capital punishment. Retrieved from https://law.jrank.org/pages/12367/Capital-Punishment.html
Jurek v. Texas, 428 U.S. 262 (1976).
Kennedy, M. (2019, July 25). Federal government to resume capital punishment after nearly 20-year hiatus. Retrieved from https://www.npr.org/2019/07/25/745223284/federal-government-to-resume-capital-punishment-after-nearly-20-year-hiatus
Liptak, A. (2020, August 3). A vast racial gap in death penalty cases, new study finds: Defendants convicted of killing white people, the study found, were far more likely to be executed than the killers of Black people. The New York Times. Retrieved from www.nytimes.com/2020/08/03/us/racial-gap-death-penalty.html
Lockett v. Ohio, 438 U.S. 586 (1978).
McCleskey v. Kemp, 481 U.S. 279 (1987).
Norris, R. J., & Mullinix, K. J. (2020). Framing innocence: An experimental test of the effects of wrongful convictions on public opinion. *Journal of Experimental Criminology*, *16*(2), 311–334. https://doi.org/10.1007/s11292-019-09360-7.
Okpara, C., Hendricks, A. E., & Cobb, L. (2021). Beyond aggravating and mitigating factors: The analysis of Colorado's death penalty cases (1999–2010). *Justice Evaluation Journal* doi: 10.1080/24751979.2021.1877090.
Proffitt v. Florida, 428 U.S. 242 (1976).
Ramirez, M. D. (2021). Unmasking the American death penalty debate: Race, context, and citizens' willingness to execute. *Social Science Quarterly*, *102*, 1931–1946. doi: 10.1111/ssqu.13051.
Reggio, M. H. (1999, February 9). History of the death penalty. PBS Frontline. Retrieved from https://www.pbs.org/wgbh/frontline/article/history-of-the-death-penalty/

Robinson, M. (2021). The Death Penalty in North Carolina, 2021: A summary of the data and scientific studies. In Policy report prepared for the North Carolina general assembly. Appalachian State University.

Roper v. Simmons, 543 U.S. 551 (2005).

Sharon, C. C. (2011). The most deserving of death: The narrowing requirement and the proliferation of aggravating factors in capital sentencing statutes. *Harvard Civil Rights-Civil Liberties Law Review*, (46), 223–251.

Shatz, S. F., Pierce, G. L., & Radelet, M. L. (2020). Race, ethnicity, and the death penalty in San Diego County: The predicable consequences of excessive discretion. *Columbia Human Rights Law Review*, *51*(3), 1070–1098.

Skipper v. South Carolina, 476 U.S. 1 (1986).

Texas Coalition Against the Death Penalty. (2023). Death penalty at the county level. Texas Coalition Against the Death Penalty. Retrieved from https://tcadp.org/get-informed/death-sentences-by-county/death-penalty-at-the-county-level/

Thornton, T. (1974). Florida's legislative and judicial responses to *Furman v. Georgia*: An analysis and criticism. *Florida State University Law Review*, 2(1), 108–152.

Trop v. Dulles, 356 U.S. 86 (1958).

Wilford, M. M., & Bornstein, B. H. (2021). The disappearing trial: How social scientists can help save the jury from extinction. *Psychology, Crime & the Law*. doi: 10.1080/1068316X.2021.1984482

Woodson v. North Carolina, 428 U.S. 280, 304–05 (1976).

Vick, K., Cook, K. J., & Rogers, M. (2021). Lethal leverage: False confessions, false pleas, and wrongful homicide convictions in death-eligible cases. *Contemporary Justice Review*, *24*(1), 24–47. doi: 10.1080/10282580.2020.1755845.

Zant v. Stephens, 462 U.S. 862, 876 (1983).

39

FIREARM POLICY AND REGULATION IN AMERICA

Promising Avenues for Future Research

Emma E. Fridel

Gun violence is a public health epidemic in the United States. In 2019 alone, over 38,000 residents died from suicide and homicide involving a firearm, representing approximately 60% of all incidents (Centers for Disease Control and Prevention, 2019). In context, a single year of firearms fatalities is equivalent to all American casualties during the Korean War, with a decade of deaths exceeding the carnage of World War II. Indeed, the United States' firearm suicide and homicide rates are 8.0 and 25.2 times greater than those of similar high-income nations (Grinshteyn & Hemenway, 2016).

Despite the severity of the problem, there is little consensus on how to best prevent gun violence in the United States. This chapter reviews the state of the literature on four types of gun control legislation, including universal background checks and permit-to-purchase laws, "red flag" laws, concealed carry, and prohibitions for domestic violence. Each section begins with a brief summary of the law turning to the empirical evidence.

Universal Background Checks and Permit-to-Purchase Laws

As part of the Brady Handgun Violence Prevention Act of 1994, federal law requires licensed firearm dealers to conduct background checks on all purchasers, with the goal of blocking prohibited possessors from obtaining guns (see 18 U.S.C. § 922). Although over 3.5 million applications have been blocked by the Brady Act since its passage (Brooks, 2021), nearly one-quarter of gun owners in the United States acquired their most recent firearm without a background check (Miller et al., 2017). Even more concerning, approximately 90% of prisoners who used a firearm during their offense obtained the weapon through transactions without background checks (Alper & Glaze, 2019). A study examining the implementation of the Brady Act similarly found that the law had minimal effects on rates of firearm violence (Ludwig & Cook, 2000).

Several states have enhanced background check laws designed to close major loopholes in the Brady Act, including exemptions for private or unlicensed sellers (i.e., "the gun show loophole") and default proceeds for background checks that take longer than three days (i.e., "the Charleston loophole", named after the 2015 Charleston Church massacre). As of 2020, 14 states and Washington, D.C., required universal background checks at the point of sale for all firearms, including unlicensed or private sellers; Pennsylvania requires similar checks, but only for handguns (see Giffords Law Center, 2021). In addition to or in lieu of point of

DOI: 10.4324/9781003219286-47

sale background checks, some states have a permit-to-purchase system (PTP), which requires individuals to obtain a permit or license to purchase firearms from both licensed dealers and private sellers that is contingent upon passing a background check. Some states also require completion of a firearm safety course and/or an in-person application at a law enforcement agency as part of their PTP.

Research on the efficacy of point of sale background checks has been somewhat mixed, partially due to the extensive variability in state laws. While Siegel et al. (2019) found that universal background checks were associated with a 15% reduction in firearm homicides, similar population-level studies have found no effect (Crifasi et al., 2018; Gius, 2015; Kagawa et al., 2018). Wintemute (2019) suggests that these null findings are the result of implementation failures rather than evidence that background checks are ineffective. Known issues with the National Instant Criminal Background Check System (NICS) include voluntary reporting by state and local agencies, exclusive reliance on federal rather than state databases, premature release of firearms, and noncompliance and limited enforcement.

In contrast to universal background checks at point of sale, prior work on PTP laws has been consistent and promising (Crifasi et al., 2019). For example, Connecticut's PTP law was associated with a 40% reduction in firearm homicides (Rudolph et al., 2015) and a 15% reduction in firearm suicides (Crifasi et al., 2015), while Missouri's repeal of similar legislation has been linked to significant increases in both types of violence (Crifasi et al., 2015; Hasegawa et al., 2019; Webster et al., 2014). Even further, prior work shows that guns used in crime are substantially less likely to have been initially purchased in states with PTP licensing systems and mandatory registration of handguns (Webster et al., 2001).

"Red Flag" Laws

Popularized by the 2018 Marjory Stoneman Douglas High School shooting in Parkland, Florida, "red flag" laws allow law enforcement officers and family members to petition a state court to temporarily remove firearms from an individual deemed to be dangerous to themselves or to others. Formally known as extreme risk protection orders (ERPOs) or gun violence restraining orders (GVROs), "red flag" laws have been adopted in some form by 19 states and Washington, D.C., as of 2020 (Giffords Law Center, 2021). Provisions vary from state to state regarding who is allowed to petition, whether the order is temporary (ex parte), the duration of the order, and the standard of evidence required to obtain an order.

As only five states implemented "red flag" laws prior to 2017, research on their efficacy remains limited. Some anecdotal evidence suggests that "red flag" laws can prevent mass shootings by removing firearm access from those posing a credible threat, though it remains impossible to prove a counterfactual (Wintemute et al., 2019). Nevertheless, prior work suggests that "red flag" legislation in Connecticut and Indiana averted one suicide for every ten gun seizures (Swanson et al., 2019; Swanson et al., 2017). Some of the reduction in firearm suicides, however, may be offset by increases in suicides with other weapons (Kivisto & Phalen, 2018). Currently, only one study has considered the effect of "red flag" laws on homicide, finding no significant impact (Dalafave, 2021). More research is needed, however, to adequately evaluate "red flag" laws due to their relatively recent implementation.

Concealed Carry

The United States currently has three types of right-to-carry or concealed carry laws, including permitless carry, "shall-issue", and "may-issue" policies. As the name implies, permitless carry allows gun owners to carry concealed firearms without any additional permits or documentation. In contrast, both shall- and may-issue states require individuals to apply for an additional concealed carry permit but differ in the degree of discretion granted to the issuing law enforcement agency. In the more permissive shall-issue states, law enforcement has minimal discretion and must grant concealed carry permits to all applicants who meet certain basic requirements outlined by the state. In contrast, the more restrictive may-issue states grant additional latitude to law enforcement officers, who may require applicants to provide a heightened showing or establish good cause and can deny a permit application even if all pre-requites are fulfilled.[1] Although historically, most states maintained restrictive no-issue or may-issue policies, the United States has experienced a dramatic shift towards more permissive concealed carry legislation over the past 30 years. As of 2020, 15 states were permitless carry, 26 were shall-issue, and 9 were may-issue (Siegel, 2021). Approximately 7% of Americans have concealed carry permits, although this number varies considerably across states (Lott, 2018).

Empirical research on the impact of concealed carry policies has been controversial for decades. Lott and Mustard (1997) found a significant deterrent effect of shall-issue laws in their study of U.S. counties from 1977 to 1992, arguing that up to 1,500 homicides could be prevented annually by loosening restrictions in may-issue states. This widely debated study sparked the shift towards more permissive legislation and became the basis for the popular "more guns, less crime" position adopted by supporters of the Second Amendment (Lott, 2000). Following a flurry of inconclusive replication studies, the National Research Council reviewed the literature and found that "it is not possible to determine that there is a causal link between the passage of right-to-carry laws and crime rates" due to various methodological challenges (Wellford et al., 2005, p. 150). Nevertheless, recent research utilizing a longer time period, more control variables, and more advanced statistical methods has consistently indicated that permissive concealed carry laws significantly *increase* homicide rates (Donohue et al., 2019; Doucette et al., 2019; Fridel, 2021; Siegel et al., 2017). Similarly, there is little evidence to suggest that more permissive concealed carry laws significantly deter mass shootings (Fridel, 2021), despite the widespread belief among the public that a "good guy with a gun" can save lives.

Domestic Violence

In the United States, federal legislation prohibits the purchase and possession of firearms for individuals who are subject to a domestic violence restraining order or have been convicted of a misdemeanor crime of domestic violence (see 18 U.S.C. § 922 (g)(8), (9)). Despite the protections of the Violence Against Women Act (VAWA) and the Lautenberg Amendment, federal law has three major loopholes. First, violence between unmarried persons who do not cohabitate or have a child in common was excluded (i.e., "the boyfriend loophole") until the passage of the Bipartisan Safer Communities Act in 2022. Second, restrictions only apply after notice and a formal hearing, so persons subject to ex parte (temporary or emergency) restraining orders are not prohibited from purchasing firearms. Third, there are no enforcement provisions to ensure that prohibited possessors relinquish their guns or that batterers are reported to the NICS. As of 2020, 20 states included dating partners for domestic violence restraining orders and firearms prohibitions, 10 extended restrictions to ex parte restraining orders, 14 required law enforcement officers to remove at least some firearms from the scene of domestic violence, and 4 mandated reporting of misdemeanor crime of domestic violence to NICS (Siegel, 2021; Giffords Law Center, 2021).

While removing firearms from domestic abusers enjoys widespread public support, the research literature evaluating the efficacy of such laws is sparse due to the recency and variability of these policies. On the whole, states with a large number of domestic violence firearm laws experience substantial reductions in female intimate partner homicide, relative to their more permissive counterparts (Sivaraman et al., 2019). Regarding specific provisions, prior work indicates that state restraining orders and firearm prohibition laws significantly lower the firearm-related intimate partner homicide rate, with reductions ranging from 7% to 25% (Diez et al., 2017; Vigdor & Mercy, 2006; Zeoli & Webster, 2010). Zeoli and Webster (2010) also found that state laws allowing police to make warrantless arrests for restraining order violations resulted in a 16% decrease in firearms intimate partner homicide. In contrast to the literature on restraining orders, there is little evidence to support similar restrictions on persons convicted of domestic violence, as only one study found a significant reduction in firearm homicide of pregnant and postpartum women (Wallace et al., 2021). Regardless, it remains unclear if restraining order and/or domestic violence prohibition laws by themselves are sufficient to reduce firearm homicide. Some contend, for example, that the effect of these laws is contingent upon the adoption of mandatory firearm relinquishment policies (Diez et al., 2017; Wallace et al., 2021), while other studies find little support for confiscation laws (Vigdor & Mercy, 2006; Zeoli & Webster, 2010). More work is necessary to evaluate the impact of additional laws, including mandatory reporting of MCDVs to the NICS.

Summary

- Evidence on universal background checks at point of sale is mixed, likely due to implementation issues. Prior research provides strong support for permit-to-purchase laws in reducing firearm homicide and suicide.
- Studies on two states suggest that "red flag" laws are effective in preventing firearm suicide, but more research is needed to determine their impact on other forms of violence.
- There is little evidence to suggest that more permissive concealed carry legislation deters gun violence, and recent research suggests that such policies are actually associated with increases in the firearm homicide rate.
- State laws extending firearms prohibitions for persons subject to domestic violence restraining orders reduce rates of intimate partner homicide but may not be effective without additional policies mandating firearm relinquishment.

Discussion and Conclusion

The issue of gun control has polarized the United States for decades, with both sides of the political aisle clamoring for changes to help the thousands of Americans impacted by firearm violence each year. Much to the frustration of lawmakers and the public alike, scholarship on reducing gun violence has been decidedly mixed due to a plethora of challenges in this area of research. Some common-sense policies like "red flag" laws and closing the "boyfriend loophole" have only recently been adopted in many states, limiting the data available to examine their efficacy. Complicating the matter further, many laws related to background checks, permit-to-purchase, and domestic violence prohibitions have so many distinct variations across states that it is difficult to ascertain which parts of the law, if any, are beneficial in reducing gun violence. Similarly, some laws may only be effective when coupled with additional policies, such as state-level prohibitions for domestic violence restraining orders and mandatory firearm relinquishment. Finally, poor implementation and enforcement of existing legislation may mask its true effect, leading to inaccurate study results.

Considering all of these issues, the policy recommendations proffered previously are tentative at best, and future scholarship on firearms legislation is critical. Nevertheless, the research literature on the four broad policies reviewed in this chapter is promising, and on the whole suggests that preventing prohibited persons from accessing guns – whether it be through enhanced background checks, "red flag" laws, or restrictions for domestic violence – is an effective strategy to reduce firearm violence. Aside from their empirical support, these policies are extremely popular and do not unduly infringe upon a person's constitutional rights, making their adoption politically feasible in partisan waters.

Note

1 In NYSRPA v. Bruen (2022), the Supreme Court ruled "proper cause" requirements unconstitutional, making several may-issue states effectively shall-issue, including New Jersey, California, and Hawaii.

References

Alper, M., & Glaze, L. (2019). Source and use of firearms involved in crimes: Survey of prison inmates, 2016. Retrieved from https://bjs.ojp.gov/content/pub/pdf/suficspi16.pdf

Brooks, C. (2021). Background checks for firearm transfers, 2016–2017. Retrieved from https://bjs.ojp.gov/content/pub/pdf/bcft1617.pdf

Centers for Disease Control and Prevention. (2019). *Web-based injury statistics query and reporting systems: Fatal injury data*. Author.

Crifasi, C. K., McCourt, A. D., Booty, M. D., & Webster, D. W. (2019). Policies to prevent illegal acquisition of firearms: Ipacts on diversions of guns for criminal use, violence, and suicide. *Current Epidemiology Reports*, *6*, 238–247.

Crifasi, C. K., Merrill-Francis, M., McCourt, A., Vernick, J. S., Wintemute, G. J., & Webster, D. W. (2018). Association between firearm laws and homicide in urban counties. *Journal of Urban Health*, *95*(3), 383–390.

Crifasi, C. K., Meyers, J. S., Vernick, J. S., & Webster, D. W. (2015). Effects of changes in permit-to-purchase handgun laws in Connecticut and Missouri on suicide rates. *Preventative Medicine*, *79*, 43–49.

Dalafave, R. (2021). An empirical assessment of homicide and suicide outcomes with red flag laws. *Loyola University Chicago Law Journal*, *52*(3), 867–906.

Diez, C., Kurland, R. P., Rothman, E. F., Bair-Merritt, M., Fleegler, E., Xuan, Z., Galea, S., Ross, C. S., Kalesan, B., Goss, K. A., & Siegel, M. (2017). State intimate partner violence-related firearm laws and intimate partner homicide rates in the United States, 1991 to 2015. *Annals of Internal Medicine*, *167*(8), 536–543.

Donohue, J. J., Aneja, A., & Weber, K. D. (2019). Right-to-carry laws and violent crime: A comprehensive assessment using panel data and a state-level synthetic control analysis. *Journal of Empirical Legal Studies*, *16*(2), 198–247.

Doucette, M. L., Crifasi, C. K., & Frattaroli, S. (2019). Right-to-carry laws and firearm workplace homicides: A longitudinal analysis (1992–2017). *American Journal of Public Health*, *109*(12), 1747–1753.

Fridel, E. E. (2021). Comparing the impact of household gun ownership and concealed carry legislation on the frequency of mass shootings and firearms homicide. *Justice Quarterly*, *38*(5), 892–915.

Giffords Law Center to Prevent Gun Violence. (2021). Gun Laws. Retrieved from giffords.org/lawcenter/gun-laws/

Gius, M. (2015). The effects of state and federal background checks on state-level gun-related murder rates. *Applied Economics*, *47*(38), 4090–4101.

Grinshteyn, E., & Hemenway, D. (2016). Violent death rates: the US compared with other high-income OECD countries, 2010. *The American Journal of Medicine*, *129*(3), 266–273.

Hasegawa, R. B., Webster, D. W., & Small, D. S. (2019). Evaluating Missouri's handgun purchaser law: a bracketing method for addressing concerns about history interacting with group. *Epidemiology*, *30*(3), 371–379.

Kagawa, R. M., Castillo-Carniglia, A., Vernick, J. S., Webster, D. W., Crifasi, C. K., Rudolph, K. E., Cerda, M., Shev, A., & Wintemute, G. J. (2018). Repeal of comprehensive background check policies and firearm homicide and suicide. *Epidemiology*, *29*(4), 494–502.

Kivisto, A. J., & Phalen, P. L. (2018). Effects of risk-based firearm seizure laws in Connecticut and Indiana on suicide rates, 1981–2015. *Psychiatric Services*, *69*(8), 855–862.

Lott, J. R. (2000). *More guns, less crime: Understanding crime and gun control laws*. University of Chicago Press.

Lott, J. R. (2018). Concealed carry permit holders across the United States: 2018. Retrieved from https://papers.ssrn.com/sol3/papers.cfm?abstract_id=3233904

Lott, J. R., & Mustard, D. B. (1997). Crime, deterrence, and right-to-carry concealed handguns. *Journal of Legal Studies*, *26*, 1–68.

Ludwig, J., & Cook, P. J. (2000). Homicide and suicide rates associated with implementation of the Brady Handgun Violence Prevention Act. *Journal of the American Medical Association*, *284*(5), 585–591.

Miller, M., Hepburn, L., & Azrael, D. (2017). Firearm acquisition without background checks. *Annals of Internal Medicine*, *166*(4), 233–239.

Rudolph, K. E., Stuart, E. A., Vernick, J. S., & Webster, D. W. (2015). Association between Connecticut's permit-to-purchase handgun law and homicides. *American Journal of Public Health*, *105*(8), e49–e54.

Siegel, M. (2021). *State firearms laws*. Robert Wood Johnson Foundation.

Siegel, M., Pahn, M., Xuan, Z., Fleegler, E., & Hemenway, D. (2019). The impact of state firearm laws on homicide and suicide deaths in the USA, 1991–2016: A panel study. *Journal of General Internal Medicine*, *34*(10), 2021–2028.

Siegel, M., Xuan, Z., Ross, C. S., Galea, S., Kalesan, B., Fleegler, E., & Goss, K. A. (2017). Easiness of legal access to concealed firearm permits and homicide rates in the United States. *American Journal of Public Health*, *107*(12), 1923–1929.

Sivaraman, J. J., Ranapurwala, S. I., Moracco, K. E., & Marshall, S. W. (2019). Association of state firearm legislation with female intimate partner homicide. *American Journal of Preventative Medicine*, *56*(1), 125–133.

Swanson, J. W., Easter, M. M., Alanis-Hirsch, K., Belden, C. M., Norko, M. A., Robertson, A. G., Frisman, L. K., Lin, H.-J., Swartz, M. S., & Parker, G. F. (2019). Criminal justice and suicide outcomes with Indiana's risk-based gun seizure law. *Journal of the American Academy of Psychiatry and the Law*, *47*(2), 188–197.

Swanson, J. W., Norko, M. A., Lin, H.-J., Alanis-Hirsch, K., Frisman, L. K., Baranoski, M. V., Easter, M. M., Robertson, A. G., Swartz, M. S., & Bonnie, R. J. (2017). Implementation and effectiveness of Connecticut's risk-based gun removal law: Does it prevent suicides? *Law and Contemporary Problems*, *80*, 179–208.

Vigdor, E. R., & Mercy, J. A. (2006). Do laws restricting access to firearms by domestic violence offenders prevent intimate partner homicide? *Evaluation Review*, *30*(3), 313–346.

Wallace, M. E., Vilda, D., Theall, K. P., & Stoecker, C. (2021). Firearm relinquishment laws associated with substantial reduction in homicide of pregnant and postpartum women. *Health Affairs*, *40*(10), 1654–1662.

Webster, D. W., Crifasi, C. K., & Vernick, J. S. (2014). Effects of the repeal of Missouri's handgun purchaser licensing law on homicides. *Journal of Urban Health*, *91*(2), 293–302.

Webster, D. W., Vernick, J. S., & Hepburn, L. M. (2001). Relationship between licensing, registration, and other gun sales laws and the source state of crime guns. *Injury Prevention*, *7*, 184–189.

Wellford, C. F., Pepper, J. V., & Petrie, C. V. (2005). *Firearms and violence: A critical review*. The National Academies Press.

Wintemute, G. J. (2019). Background checks for firearm purchases: Problem areas and recommendations to improve effectiveness. *Health Affairs*, *28*(10), 1702–1710.

Wintemute, G. J., Pear, V. A., Schleimer, J. P., Pallin, R., Sohl, S., Kravitz-Wirtz, N., & Tomisch, E. A. (2019). Extreme risk protection orders indended to prevent mass shootings. *Annals of Internal Medicine*, *171*, 655–658.

Zeoli, A. M., & Webster, D. W. (2010). Effects of domestic violence policies, alcohol taxes, and police staffing levels on intimate partner homicide in large U.S. cities. *Injury Prevention*, *16*(2), 90–95.

40
MASS INCARCERATION

Bryan L. Sykes and J. Amanda Sharry

The United States makes up 5% of the global population but contains 25% of the world's prisoners (National Research Council, 2014), incarcerating a much larger fraction of its population than any other advanced industrialized nation (Pettit & Sykes, 2017; National Research Council, 2014). By the end of 2015, people living in the United States were more than 10 times as likely to be in prison or jail as people living in Denmark, Sweden, and the Netherlands and 4 times as likely to be incarcerated when compared to residents of the United Kingdom (Pettit & Sykes, 2017).

Mass incarceration – the systematic jailing and imprisonment of whole groups of the population – is the latest system of social control in America (Garland, 2001; Alexander, 2010). Historically, incarceration in America was largely uncommon. For much of the twentieth century, the incarceration rate hovered around 110 inmates per 100,000 (Garland, 2001). At the close of 2018, the national incarceration rate was 650 inmates per 100,000, dropping from 760 per 100,000 at the height of the prison boom in 2008 (Minton et al., 2021). Since the 1970s, the United States has been in a period of drift characterized by the increased use of incarceration and imprisonment to control specific demographic groups (Garland, 2001; National Research Council, 2014). By the end of 2019, 6.3 million adults were under correctional supervision, representing 1 in 40 adult residents (2.5%), with nearly 2.1 million incarcerated in prisons and jails (Minton et al., 2021).

The risk of incarceration is not uniform throughout the population. Men, young adults, and people with little education are disproportionately incarcerated in America's prisons and jails. By the end of 2015, 9.1% of young Black men (ages 20–34) were incarcerated, a rate that is 5.7 times that of young White men (1.6%) (Pettit & Sykes, 2017). On any given day, over one-third of young Black men who dropped out of high school are behind bars (Sykes & Pettit, 2014; National Research Council, 2014).

Mass incarceration extends beyond the individual behind bars and affects children and families. In 1980, approximately half a million minors (under the age of 18) had a parent behind bars, but by 2012, nearly 2.6 million children had a parent incarcerated (Sykes & Pettit, 2014). Like the risk of adult incarceration, the risks of having a parent incarcerated for at least 1 year falls disproportionately on people of color; the cumulative risk of experiencing parental incarceration by age 17 was 24.2% for non-Hispanic Black children, 10.7% for Hispanic children, and 3.9% for Non-Hispanic White children by the end of 2009 (Sykes & Pettit, 2014).

DOI: 10.4324/9781003219286-48

The rise of punitive penology – three strike laws, mandatory minimums, and longer prison terms – has led the United States to incarcerate more people per capita than any other nation in the world (National Research Council, 2014; Sawyer & Wagner, 2020). These shocking levels of confinement have brought the relationship between incarceration and crime to the forefront of public discourse and criminological debate (National Research Council, 2014).

Incarceration is theoretically intended to provide two very distinct crime prevention effects: deterrence and incapacitation. Evidence shows that there is no relationship between incarceration and violent crime, and very little relationship between incarceration and crime overall (Durlauf & Nagin, 2011; Lofstrom & Raphael, 2016; National Research Council, 2014; Stemen, 2017). Other research concludes that policies like California's three strikes law does not induce enough criminal deterrence to warrant the increased costs of incarceration (Helland & Tabarrok, 2007). In other words, lengthy prison sentences are associated with diminishing returns (Spelman, 1995). Larger deterrent effects are associated with shorter sentences (Hjalmarsson, 2009; Ludwig & Raphael, 2003; Nagin, 2013; National Research Council, 2014). Likewise, Liedka et al. (2006) suggests that the scale of incarceration also reaches a point of diminishing returns. Low rates of incarceration are associated with significant decreases in crime, but incapacitation may be more costly than beneficial at extremely high rates of incarceration.

Over a decade ago, with little empirical evidence to support claims of a substantial deterrent effect and rapidly diminishing returns for incapacitation, advocates began to call for reform, particularly in the wake of the Great Recession, when states could no longer afford to sustain the high budgetary costs of mass incarceration. After decades of steady increases in incarceration, the correctional population reached its zenith of 7.3 million people in 2008 (Maruschak & Minton, 2020). Since 2009, however, the number of people incarcerated or under other forms of community supervision (probation or parole) has consistently fallen, reaching its current level of 6.3 million at the end of 2019 (Maruschak & Minton, 2020; Minton et al., 2021).

Reformers have made progress in their pleas to lawmakers for a less retributive and more equitable system (National Research Council, 2014; Subramanian et al., 2020). Both federal and state decision-makers have started to implement policies that have moved away from more punitive, crime control interventions to more evidence-based practices aimed at reducing the over reliance on lengthy prison terms that have proven to be harmful to individuals, families, and communities. The following sections outline the most recent evidence-based criminal justice reforms and policies, including federal and state-level initiatives. We conclude with five major takeaways on the topic of mass incarceration, with suggestions for future research and practices that may further mitigate the use of incarceration in America.

Federal Reforms

On December 21, 2018, President Donald J. Trump signed into law the First Step Act (FSA) of 2018 (Public Law 115–391). The FSA is federal legislation that aims to improve criminal justice outcomes and to reduce the size of the federal prison population. The legislation also creates mechanisms to maintain public safety, many of which were contained in the Federal Sentencing Reform and Corrections Act (2015) that did not pass Congress ahead of the 2016 presidential election (Grawert, 2020).

The FSA addresses many areas of the carceral state in need of reform, including conditions of confinement within federal institutions, racial bias, and federal sentencing reform. This legislation allows all incarcerated persons in federal prisons to participate in evidence-based recidivism reduction programs and activities, including education, vocational training, employment, substance abuse training, trauma counseling, and faith-based classes (First Step Act, 2018). Evidence shows families experience tremendous financial and emotional strain when faced with the weight of having an incarcerated loved one. Not only do families incur increased financial obligations spurred by their absence and missed income, but families also accumulate the costs of staying in touch, like expensive phone bills and visiting costs. Thus, emotional bonds are left strained and hard to maintain (Comfort et al., 2016; Turney, 2015). Under the bill, program participants are issued 30 minutes of phone time per day and up to 510 minutes per month, including video visits, if available in their facility. Further, the bill calls for those incarcerated individuals who have successfully completed evidence-based programs to be transferred to an institution closer to the individual's home and family to provide a support network upon release and ease the burden of maintaining emotional and familial bonds (First Step Act, 2018).

The FSA also outlines and envisions more humane and proper healthcare for women. Many states with large correctional populations (e.g., California, Illinois, and New York) have banned the use of shackles on incarcerated women during labor and delivery, and a landmark decision in the U.S. Court of Appeals for the Eighth Circuit declared the use of shackles during childbirth unconstitutional (Griggs, 2011; *Nelson v. Correctional Medical Services*, 2009). Yet, the use of shackles persisted in federal prisons until the First Step Act was signed into law. Now, current legislation prohibits the use of restraints during childbirth in federal prisons and mandates the distribution of female sanitary products (First Step Act, 2018).

Perhaps most importantly, the First Step Act restored judicial discretion in federal criminal sentencing (Ryan, 2020). While research shows that deterrence is associated with shorter sentences (Hjalmarsson, 2009; Ludwig & Raphael, 2003; Nagin, 2013; National Research Council, 2014), federal judges were constrained in discretionary sentences and were compelled to impose mandatory minimums according to sentencing guidelines. The FSA offers an important change to this policy, reauthorizing judicial discretion in sentencing and extricating judges from federal mandatory minimum guidelines (Grawert, 2020).

Last, the FSA also address racial bias in the correctional system. The U.S. War on Drugs played a large role in the rise of mass incarceration and disproportionately affected African Americans and Latinos (National Research Council, 2014). Research by Al Blumstein indicated that racial disparities in prison were not spurred at the time of arrest but rather were due to the unexplained differences observed among those convicted of drug offenses (Blumstein, 1993; Nellis, 2021). Historically, individuals convicted of distributing 5 grams of crack received a mandatory minimum 5-year federal prison sentence, compared to someone who distributed 500 grams of powder cocaine receiving the same sentence. This 100-to-1 crack versus powder cocaine sentencing disparity produced substantial racial inequality in incarceration rates. The 2010 Fair Sentencing Act aimed to fix the sentencing disparity between crack and cocaine, reducing the disparity from 100 to 1 down to 18 to 1. The First Step Act, however, further reduced this disparity down to 10 to 1. The First Step Act has partially resolved the inequity between crack and cocaine, leading to the resentencing and reduced incarceration periods for 3,000 individuals (Grawert, 2020). Last, as literature suggests, small incremental sanctions produce larger effects on criminal deterrence than large sanctions (Ludwig & Raphael, 2003; Nagin, 2013). Thus, the bill calls for the reinstitution of time credits. Any federally incarcerated individual that participates in a rehabilitative program can earn time credits toward pre-release custody (First Step Act, 2018).

Reentry and Child Support

Prior to the First Step Act, the Obama Administration implemented several criminal justice reforms before leaving office. One noteworthy reform is Executive Order 13563 (2012). This order helped remove financial barriers and increased accessibility to affordable child support payments for incarcerated parents (Holifield, 2019). Given the United States' high rates of incarceration, between 450,000 and one million people behind bars are indebted to child support systems (Haney & Mercier, 2021; Holifield, 2019). Many jurisdictions carry adverse consequences for delinquent child support payments, amplifying existing disadvantages that exacerbate inequality for a population already facing barriers to reintegration, including driver's license suspension, employment discrimination, and familial reunification difficulties (Haney & Mercier, 2021). This executive order is meant to relieve financial pressures on many unemployed, formerly incarcerated people by changing 45 CFR 302.56(c)(3), which now states that incarcerated parents may not be treated as voluntarily unemployed, given the labor market discrimination that many face because of their criminal records. Thus, states must provide relief from child support payments during the time of incarceration. Furthermore, states must modify and set child support obligations upon release (Office of Child Support Enforcement, 2021). While this new rule does not eliminate criminal debt, like legally imposed monetary sanctions, it does alleviate the negative associations and barriers to employment that child support imposes upon release and paves the way for a more positive family reunification experience.

State Reforms

Recent policy changes at the state level have also affected the levels and distribution of incarceration. California serves as a particularly good case study, as it has the third largest correctional population (Minton et al., 2021), behind Texas and Georgia and has implemented a series of landmark reforms. Arguably the most significant criminal justice reform is Assembly Bill 109 (AB109), also known as The Public Health and Safety Realignment Act (2011). The California legislature passed AB109 in response to *Brown v. Plata*, a U.S. Supreme Court decision that legally ordered the California Department of Corrections and Rehabilitation (CDCR) to reduce the state prison population by approximately 33,000 people (to 137.5% of design capacity) over a 2-year time frame (Verma, 2016), alleviating prison overcrowding and poor medical health treatment behind bars. Other reforms reclassified some offenses that were once felonies to misdemeanors, thereby reducing the length of jail/prison terms; AB109 requires that the terms of incarceration for nonviolent, nonserious, and nonsex offenses ("the triple nons") be served in county jails instead of state prisons. This shifted responsibility for punishment from prisons, which in the United States are state or federal operations, to jails, which are run by counties and their elected sheriffs. Each of California's 58 counties is allocated funds by the state to develop its own programs aimed at rehabilitative services that target the needs of each county's population (Petersilia, 2014). Since the implementation of AB109, California's incarceration rates have steadily declined, making the Golden State a national blueprint for safe and effective decarceration (Petersilia, 2014).

According to recent reports, prior to the COVID-19 pandemic, in 2019, California's prison population had fallen by 27 percent from its peak in 2006. In December 2020, after increased decarceration to mitigate the spread of COVID-19 within its correctional walls, California's prison population had fallen by 45 percent from its 2006 peak (California Law Revision Commission, Committee on the Revision of the Penal Code, 2021).

Most recently, California passed a series of legislative reforms targeting racial disparities within its penal system. Research shows that people of color are disproportionately targeted as gang members, with 92% of individuals convicted of a gang enhancement being a person of color (California Law Revision Commission, Committee on the Revision of the Penal Code, 2021). Despite California's recent reductions in the prison population driven by AB109, gang enhancements increased by nearly 40% (California Law Revision Commission, Committee on the Revision of the Penal Code, 2021). California's new AB333, also known as the Step Forward Act, now limits the state's gang enhancement charging abilities. Before its passing, the law allowed for entire social networks to be charged with a gang enhancement simply based on the neighborhood in which one resided, including potential "affiliations" with people the defendant may have never met (Step Forward Act, 2021). The new law now requires that an enhancement may only be applied if the individual charged *knowingly* participates in gang activity. Further, the bill requires that the enhancement count be tried separately from all other counts that do not require gang evidence as an element of the crime (Step Forward Act, 2021).

Additionally, California passed Senate Bill (SB) 483, that is meant to repeal sentence enhancements. Previous legislation, SB136 and SB180, allowed for 1 additional year of incarceration for any previous prison or jail term a person served and an additional 3 years of incarceration for any prior drug convictions, respectively. Empirical studies show that these legal enhancements have been disproportionately applied to people of color (California Law Revision Commission, Committee on the Revision of the Penal Code, 2021; Schlesinger, 2011; Spohn et al., 2022). Research also reveals that modest sentencing reform has no effect on recidivism rates (Rhodes et al., 2018; United States Sentencing Commission, 2014; United States Sentencing Commission, 2018). In other words, modest reductions of criminal sanctions can be made without putting public safety at risk. Under SB 483, the state of California requires county jail and prison officials to identify any individual sentenced to such enhancements be released if he or she has served the base sentence, eliminating the need to serve time on the enhancement. Those who are still serving their base sentence shall have their sentence recalled and will be dutifully resentenced under the new law, restoring a more equitable application of the law.

Conclusions and Future Policy Reforms

There are five main takeaways about mass incarceration:

1. The national incarceration rate was historically stable, at around 110 inmates per 100,000 residents between 1920 and 1970. However, by the mid- to late twentieth century (i.e., around the early 1970s), the incarceration rate began to rise precipitously, reaching a zenith of 760 inmates per 100,000 residents in 2008 (Minton et al., 2021). The decline in incarceration since the Great Recession now means that the current national incarceration rate is around 650 inmates per 100,000 residents (Minton et al., 2021);
2. Mass incarceration is uniquely and exceptionally American. The United States incarcerates a significantly larger fraction of its population than any other developed nation in the world, with over 25% of all inmates on the planet in American jails and prisons, despite the U.S. accounting for only 5% of the world's population (National Research Council, 2014).

3. Inequality exists in who is incarcerated. Men, young adults, people of color, and those with low levels of education are disproportionately targeted by the criminal justice system. Mass incarceration is now the latest configuration of social control for African Americans – and young Black men who have dropped out of high school, specifically – since slavery and Jim Crow (Alexander, 2010).
4. National policy reforms, like the First Step Act, have reduced incarceration levels in federal prisons and provide federal judges with more discretion in sentencing. Additionally, changes in penal confinement have also moved in the right direction, particularly for women. However, federal laws should eradicate, fully, sentencing disparities between crack and cocaine in order to further reduce racial disparities in incarceration.
5. State policy changes have been instrumental in reducing the number of people in prisons and jails. In many ways, California serves a model reform state, decentralizing imprisonment and reclassifying a number of offenses from felonies to misdemeanors while providing resources to counties so that they can make incarceration decisions about low-level offenses.

While many of these reforms have led to appreciable reductions in the number of people incarcerated, there is still work to be done. Sentencing reform can be done without causing harm to public safety but more reform needs to take place to restore racial justice. Across the nation, African Americans are incarcerated in state prison 5 times the rate of White Americans, and seven states, including California, maintain a 9 to 1 Black-White disparity in incarceration (Nellis, 2021). California has already begun to tackle racial inequality in this criminal justice practices. In January 2020, the California Law Revision Commission's Committee on Revision of the Penal Code began its work to enumerate and evaluate legislative statutes, specifically within the Penal Code, that produce and exacerbate well- known racial disparities within the state's criminal legal system (California Law Revision Commission, Committee on the Revision of the Penal Code, 2021). Future policy at the state level must review and redress racial disparities within their criminal justice systems.

References

Alexander, M. (2010). *The new Jim Crow: Mass incarceration in the age of colorblindness*. New Press.

Blumstein, A. (1993). Racial disproportionality of the U.S. prison populations revisited. *University of Colorado Law Review*, *64*(3), 743–760.

California Law Revision Commission, Committee on the Revision of the Penal Code. (2021). Annual report and recommendations, 2020. California Law Revision Commission. Retrieved from www.clrc.ca.gov/CRPC/Pub/Reports/CRPC_AR2020.pdf

Comfort, M., McKay, T., Landwehr J., Kennedy, E., Lindquist, C., & Bir, A. (2016). The cost of incarceration for families of prisoners. *International Review of the Red Cross*, *98*(3), 783–798.

Durlauf, S. N., & Nagin, D. S. (2011). Imprisonment and crime: Can both be reduced? *American Society of Criminology*, *10*(1), 13–54.

Exec. Order No. 13563 3 C.F.R. (2012).

First Step Act. (2018). H.R. 5682, 115.

Garland, D. 2001. *The culture of control: Crime and social order in contemporary society*. University of Chicago Press.

Grawert, A. (2020). What is the first step act? – And what's happening with it? Brennen Center. Retrieved from www.brennancenter.org/our-work/research-reports/what-first-step-act-and-whats-happening-it

Griggs, C. L. (2011). Birthing barbarism: The unconstitutionality of shackling pregnant prisoners. *American University Journal of Gender, Social Policy & the Law*, *20*(1), 247–272.

Haney, L., & Mercier, M. D. (2021). Child support and reentry. National Institute of Justice. Retrieved from https://nij.ojp.gov/library/publications/child-support-and-reentry

Helland, E., & Tabarrok, A. (2007). Does three strikes deter? A nonparametric estimation. *Journal of Human Resources*, *56*(3), 309–330.
Hjalmarsson, R. (2009). Crime and expected punishment: Changes in perceptions at the age of criminal majority. *American Law and Economics Review*, *11*(1), 209–248.
Holifield, C. (2019). Executive order 13563 creates access to affordable child support for incarcerated parents. *Texas A&M Journal of Property Law*, *5*(3), 201–223.
Liedka, R. V., Piehl, A. M., & Useem, B. (2006). The crime-control effect of incarceration: Does scale matter? *Criminology & Public Policy*, *5*(2), 267–294.
Lofstrom, M., & Rafael, S. (2016). Incarceration and crime: Evidence from California's public safety realignment reform. *The Annals of the American Academy*, *664*, 196–220.
Ludwig, J., & Raphael, S. (2003). Prison sentence enhancements: The case of Project Exile. In J. Ludwig & P. J. Cook (Eds.), *Evaluating gun policy: Effects on crime violence*. Brookings Institution Press.
Maruschak, L., & Minton, T. (2020). Correctional populations in the United States, 2017–2018. Bureau of Justice Statistics. Retrieved from https://bjs.ojp.gov/content/pub/pdf/cpus1718.pdf
Minton, T., Beatty, L., & Zeng, Z. (2021). Correctional populations in the United States, 2019. Bureau of Justice Statistics. Retrieved from https://bjs.ojp.gov/sites/g/files/xyckuh236/files/media/document/cpus19st.pdf
Nagin, D. S. (2013). Deterrence: A review of the evidence by a criminologist for economists. *Annual Review of Economics*, *5*, 83–105.
National Research Council. (2014). *The growth of incarceration in the United States: Exploring causes and consequences*. J. Travis, B. Western, & S. Redburn (Eds.). The National Academies Press.
Nellis, A. (2021). The color of justice: Racial and ethnic disparity in state prisons. Sentencing Project. Retrieved from www.sentencingproject.org/issues/sentencing-policy/
Nelson v. Correctional Medical Services, 2009.
Office of Child Support Enforcement. (2021). Modification for incarcerated parents. Retrieved from www.acf.hhs.gov
Petersilia, J. (2014). California prison downsizing and its impact on local criminal justice systems. *Harvard Law & Policy Review*, *8*(2), 327–358.
Pettit, B., & Sykes, B. (2017). Incarceration. In *The state of the union: The poverty and inequality report*, special issue, Pathways Magazine. The Stanford Center on Poverty and Inequality.
Rhodes, W. Gaes, G. G., Kling, R., & Cutler, C. (2018). Relationship between prison length of stay and recidivism: A study using regression discontinuity and instrumental variables with multiple break points. *Criminal Public Policy*, *17*(731–69), 758–759.
Ryan, Sarah. (2020). Judicial authority under the first step act: What congress conferred through section 404. *Loyola University Chicago Law Journal*, *54*, 57–125.
Sawyer, W., & Wagner, P. (2020). Mass incarceration: The whole pie 2020. Prison Policy Initiative. Retrieved from www.prisonpolicy.org/reports/pie2020.html
SB 483 CAL 2021 (enacted).
Schlesinger, T. (2011). The failure of race neutral policies: How mandatory terms and sentencing enhancements contribute to mass racialized incarceration. *Crime & Delinquency*, *57*(1), 56–81.
Spelman, W. (1995). The severity of intermediate sanctions. *Journal of Research in Crime and Delinquency*, *32*(2), 107–135.
Spohn, C., Verhagen, M., & Walker, J. (2022). Revisiting sentencing reform. In *Transforming criminal justice* (pp. 124–148). New York University Press.
Stemen, D. (2017). The prison paradox: More incarceration will not make us safer. Vera Institute of Justice. Retrieved from Chromeextension://efaidnbmnnnibpcajpcglclefindmkaj/viewer.html?pdfurl=https%3A%p2F%2Farchive.icjia.cloud%2Ffiles%2Fspac%2Fmeetings%2F091517_SPAC_Meeting_Materials.df&chunk=true
Step Forward Act. (2021). AB 333, Cal 2021 (enacted).
Subramanian, R., Eisen, L. B., Merkl, T., Arzy, L., Stroud, H., King, T., Fielding, J., Nahra, A., & Waldman, M. (2020). *Transition 2020–2021: A federal agenda for criminal justice reform*. Brennan Center for Justice, New York University School of Law.
Sykes, B., & Pettit, B. (2014). Mass incarceration, family complexity, and the reproduction of childhood disadvantage. *The Annals of the American Academy of Political and Social Science*, *654*, 127–149.
Turney, K. (2015). Hopelessly devoted? Relationship quality during and after incarceration. *Journal of Marriage and Family*, 480–495.

United States Sentencing Commission. (2014). *Recidivism among offenders receiving retroactive sentence reductions. The 2007 crack cocaine amendment* (pp. 14–15). Author.
United States Sentencing Commission. (2018). *Recidivism among federal offenders receiving retroactive sentence reductions* (pp. 1, 3). Author.
Verma, A. (2016). A turning point in mass incarceration? Local imprisonment trajectories and decarceration under California's realignment. *Annals of the American Academy of Political and Social Science*, *664*(1), 108–135.

41

ANTI-RACISM AND RACIAL JUSTICE IN THE CRIMINAL JUSTICE SYSTEM

Micah E. Johnson and Skye C. Bristol

Introduction

There is a rich body of transdisciplinary work on the relationship between race and criminal justice, providing evidence that racism played a fundamental role in the early development of the criminal justice system in the United States. This historical context permeates throughout contemporary society. Compelling evidence shows racial injustices at every stage of the justice system, from initial contact with the police to sentencing. Historical and contemporary racial injustices have devastated many communities, which resulted in trauma, distrust, and deep wounds. Fortunately, there are policies, programs, and practices that can be implemented in the criminal justice system to achieve anti-racism, racial justice, and healing among the victims of these injustices.

Historical Context

Historians have linked modern-day policing to slave patrols who were charged with safeguarding the institution of chattel slavery of African people in the United States (Brucato, 2021). Slave patrols used violence and intimidation to deter protest, enforce white supremacy, and apprehend those who ran away seeking freedom and returned them to bondage. These informal policing units of the 1600s that were charged with maintaining the racial order evolved into police patrols.

Urbanization and population growth increased the need for more developed and sophisticated systems of law enforcement (Musgrave, 2020). Similar to slave patrols, early police departments were mandated to enforce racist, oppressive, and unjust policies, often using brutal tactics. Law enforcement officers came to embody the injustices in the criminal justice system and served on the front lines to safeguard the status quo. The badge became the scapegoat. However, while police officers routinely enforced laws and ideas with gross cruelties, their actions represented sentiments that were systemic and widely held by the overwhelming majority of White Americans (Hickman et al., 2008; Hyland, 2015; Reppetto, 2013). Moreover, since the inception of law enforcement, police units have comprised formal agents of the state and citizen volunteers, from historical volunteer slave patrols and lynch mobs to modern neighborhood watch and citizen calls to police. For example, an FBI Intelligence Assessment

 DOI: 10.4324/9781003219286-49

found that the Ku Klux Klan had strong ties to local law enforcement (FBI Counterterrorism Division, 2006). Many marginalized and vulnerable communities have unique and often traumatic histories and relationships with law enforcement. This includes Black, Indigenous, People of Color (BIPOC), women, sexual and gender minorities, people of lower socioeconomic status, and those with mental health issues or other disabilities.

Black Populations

Black communities have suffered atrocities at the hands of law enforcement entities throughout history (Alexander, 2010). For centuries, law enforcement and affiliated entities have perpetuated violence, oppression, and anti-Black racism. The murder of George Floyd in 2020 sparked widespread interest in racial justice (McLaughlin, 2020; Silverstein, 2021). However, racist policies, sentiments, and actions towards Black and other persons of color remain commonplace today.

Latinx Communities

Many Latinx communities have also suffered from racism enforced or perpetuated by law enforcement entities, including lynching, deportation, terror, and mass incarceration. For example, in the Porvenir massacre in 1918, Texas Rangers, U.S. Cavalry soldiers, and local vigilantes murdered 15 Mexican American unarmed boys and men during the Brite Ranch raid; yet, no evidence linked the murdered boys and men to the prior attacks that provoked the massacre (The Editors of Encyclopaedia Britannica, 2021). Despite legal efforts for justice, no individuals were held responsible for the killings of the Porvenir residents. Documented accounts of violence and police scrutiny were rooted in xenophobia, nationalist, and anti-immigration sentiments (Delgado, 2009).

Indigenous and Native Americans

Native Americans have historically faced various forms of conflict with American settlers and the U.S. Government. Additionally, Native Americans were upheld by racist ideologies that characterized the population as savage, subhuman, and inferior. U.S. policies were designed to deculturize Native American communities and were one of many forms of forced assimilation this population faced (Spring, 2016). Through colonization, Native Americans faced genocide, forced displacement, and biological warfare (Dunbar-Ortiz, 2014). Furthermore, they were denied citizenship and had Native American customs and values intentionally destroyed through education policies (Dunbar-Ortiz, 2014).

Intersectionality

WOMEN

Historical and current accounts of law enforcement demoralizing and objectifying girls and women are rooted in ideologies of misogyny, patriarchy, and hegemonic masculinity. Specifically, women of color experience harsher encounters with law enforcement. When minority women and girls report crimes, they often face harassment, ridicule, and scrutiny. For example, Black women were excluded from rape laws until 1861 (Pokorak, 2006). However, even after their inclusion, there was a lack of recourse for Black women, as filed cases were rarely investigated (Irving, 2008). This lack of care is demonstrated in modern-day cases such as Cyntoia Brown, Eisha Love, and Bresha Meadows.

LGBTQIA

The creation of sodomy laws, violence in police custody, informal three-piece law, and profiling trans women as sex workers were all efforts to criminalize LGBTQIA individuals (Jurisdiction, 2014). The spark of the Stonewall riot can be explained by the continuous violent raids of LGBTQIA welcoming establishments. LGBTQIA individuals of color faced increased police harassment because their identity intersects two marginalized identities. This harassment likely results/ed from homophobia or transphobia, and racism (Center for American Progress, 2016). Violent attacks and death cases, like Marsha P. Johnson, typically remain misreported, unreported, or under-investigated.

MENTAL HEALTH AND DISABILITY

The combination of the policing model and lack of mental health response agencies has resulted in law enforcement officers being the main point of contact for those with mental health disorders (Livingston, 2016). Having a mental health disorder or other disability, such as deafness, schizophrenia, bipolar disorder, or autism spectrum disorder, while also belonging to a racial or ethnic minority group increases the risk of arrest (Compton et al., 2006; Cuellar et al., 2007). The dangers of a police encounter are heightened when a handling officer lacks training and knowledge of symptoms associated with mental disorders and crises. Instances of this problem are highlighted by the police encounters that Daniel Prude and Willie N. Henley experienced, with Prude being fatally shot by the officer and Henley being shot and then charged with a crime. Teplin (2000) explains that arresting and wrongfully labeling a person with a mental disorder as a "criminal" increases the likelihood of re-arrest in future cases. Consequently, these individuals are criminalized instead of receiving proper care from a mental health facility.

Contemporary Issues

Historical injustices influence contemporary issues associated with policing and the criminal justice system. Racial disparities persist, as BIPOC individuals experience discrimination in every stage of the criminal justice system. The U.S. mass incarceration rates disproportionately affect people of color, with Black prisoners having the highest imprisonment rate at 1,096 Black prisoners per 100,000 Black residents in 2019 (Minton et al., 2021). Mass incarceration may be explained by racial profiling (i.e., "Driving While Black"), sentencing discrepancies, implicit biases of law enforcement, over-policing in minority communities, strict guidelines for probation and parole, harsh punishment for non-violent crimes, and the War on Drugs disproportionately affecting Black communities. The War on Drugs enabled substance misuse among Black populations to be criminalized and stigmatized, while White communities received behavioral health resources for the same types of substance misuse. Similar patterns continue to exist. Black people are more likely to be arrested for a marijuana offense and receive longer sentences than their white counterparts (Edwards & Madubuonwu, 2020). Additionally, despite the juvenile and adult criminal justice systems being modeled after each other, racial disparities among incarcerated adults are gradually narrowing, while the Black to White racial gap appears to be widening among juveniles (Balko, 2020). Hager (2015) explores the possible underlying causes of this racial disparity. Patterns of criminalization are translated into the school context with the school-to-prison pipeline. The school to prison pipeline disproportionately impacts youth of color due to racial disparities in school discipline, as Black students have an increased likelihood of being suspended than White students (Balko, 2020).

Summary of Action-Oriented Solution

As evident through the aforementioned historical and present-day injustices, further action is critical to anti-racism and racial justice in the criminal justice system. The current literature on effective, action-oriented solutions to address racism and these injustices show promise. Though, there is still a significant need for progress. The most consistent findings in the literature regarding evidence-based programs, policies, and practices are listed in the following:

- Improved efforts in community outreach and inclusion in decision-making
- Reducing racial disparities on an individual and organizational level through required training and education of racial injustices among the criminal justice system
- Reallocation of less punitive resources
- Addressing race-neutral policies and enforcing racial impact statements

Description of Responsive Evidence-Based Programs, Policies, and/or Practices

Improved Community Outreach Efforts

Incorporating a partnership with community members and criminal justice system professionals is vital to repair or build a relationship that would lead to an anti-racist system. The use of procedural justice principles has demonstrated a positive effect on public trust and confidence in the police by promoting accountability and community support (Tyler et al., 2015; Williams et al., 2021). An example of implementing procedural justice principles includes initiating police and community dialogue programs to improve community policing efforts. The most effective dialogue sessions are in an open and honest environment and allow community members to feel heard with an absence of hierarchy. Specific examples of effective police–community dialogue programs focused on the youth population are: 1) Bridging the Gap: Kids and Cops Program and 2) Santa Cruz's Youth Violence Prevention Task Force and Dialogues for Change. Additionally, implementing community police review boards may result in more transparency and accountability for law enforcement officers.

Individual and Organizational Efforts among Criminal Justice Professionals

To achieve racial justice in the criminal justice system, both individual and organizational efforts for professionals in the system are needed. So far, there have been more accountability and transparency efforts through internal affairs, body and dash cams, and implicit bias training. Though, evidence suggests that criminal justice professionals continue to use racial bias when making decisions that adversely impact people of color. These professionals include prosecutors (Crawford et al., 1998; Starr & Rehavi, 2013) and judges (Spohn, 2000; Steffensmeier & Demuth, 2000, 2001), who are more likely to charge and sentence people of color with a harsher sentence compared to White individuals who commit similar offenses. Similarly, police officers were more likely to use deadly force against armed Black suspects than White armed suspects (Correll et al., 2014). Some research suggests providing implicit bias training to address injustices in the criminal justice system. However, in developing and implementing implicit bias training, research findings recommend that these programs and initiatives be coupled with monitoring and accountability systems (Carter et al., 2020). Research also remains inconsistent on the long-term effects of implicit bias training programs, with many findings reporting small effect sizes on bias and behavior changes (Kovera, 2019). Implementing continuous implicit bias training, accompanied by more training hours for de-escalation tactics, may decrease deadly encounters, though more research is required (Pontzer, 2021). Furthermore, enforcing organizational policies in pre-trial and sentencing practices may aid in reducing racial disparities throughout the criminal justice system.

Reallocation of Resources

The death of George Floyd re-ignited the Black Lives Matter movement to denounce police brutality and call for reform by "defunding the police". Defunding the police means reinvesting in community resources to prioritize public health and focus on non-violent approaches for social issues. This would allow for more funds to be allocated towards schools, hospitals, housing, investment in evidence-based drug prevention and treatment approaches, and general and emergency mental health services involving trained specialists in de-escalation tactics to provide crisis support. Additionally, funding could be allocated to decriminalizing antiquated laws, improving traffic services, and decreasing over-policing in minority communities. Some articles have reported a direct correlation in cities that decreased funding to law enforcement and an increase in violent crimes. However, these reports are anecdotal as there is no substantial long-term research to support these claims (Cassell, 2020). The "Defund the police" conversations have also sparked attention toward the influence of school resource officers in public schools. Specifically, these conversations focused on the school-to-prison pipeline phenomena and its disproportional impacts on BIPOC students (Balko, 2018; Heise & Nance, 2021; Nance, 2016). Many studies report that the presence of school resource officers increase referrals to law enforcement and youth involvement in the juvenile justice system (Owens, 2017; Spence, 2020). Notably, a more detailed analysis is needed to establish a correlation. In response to the adverse effects of school resource officers, the President's Task Force on 21st Century Policing (2015) recommends 1) partnerships between law enforcement agencies and schools, 2) increasing funding towards alternative efforts, such as peer interventions, youth courts, and restorative justice, and 3) including a team of mental health professionals, social workers, and crisis counselors in the policing sector (see President's Task Force on 21st Century Policing, 2015 for more in-depth recommendations).

Addressing Race-Neutral Policies and Enforcing Racial Impact Statements

The exclusion of key socioeconomic and racial disparity considerations is a significant disadvantage of race-neutral policies. Using a color-blind approach when developing race-neutral policies that intend to decrease disparities often adversely impacts racial minorities. When developing or evaluating policies, it is best to use well-established risk assessment instruments (RAIs) that support evidence-based practices. RAIs allow researchers to analyze possible disparate racial consequences that would further increase racial inequities. Additionally, implementing racial impact statements may decrease the disproportionate effects of policies on BIPOC communities (Lewis, 2019). Racial impact statements evaluate the potential effect a criminal justice law or policy may have on racial minorities and requires policymakers and legislation to utilize a racial equity perspective. States that require a racial impact statement prior to adopting any new law or policy are Connecticut, Iowa, New Jersey, and Oregon. The research on the efficacy of racial impact statements is limited and inconclusive, with studies reporting varying degrees of effectiveness (Erickson, 2014; Jensen et al., 2019; Smith, 2017).

Implementation

Stakeholders have the challenge of implementing these programs in their communities, systems, and institutions. Specifically, these challenges involve empowering members of the community without diminishing the effectiveness of these interventions. Intervention efforts may benefit from community-based participatory research (CBPR) principles. CBPR refers to a collaborative approach that empowers community members to play important roles in research and equitably involves all partners in the research process (W.K. Kellogg, 2001). Israel and colleagues (1998) stated that the core principles of CBPR are:

- The community is the "unit of identity".
- CBPR builds on the community's strengths and resources.
- CBPR involves collaborative partnerships in all phases of research.
- The integration of knowledge and action mutually benefits all partners.
- The CBPR process is cyclical and iterative.
- Findings and knowledge gained through CBPR must be disseminated to all partners.

There are many ways in which CBPR can strengthen efforts in addressing racial justice in the criminal justice systems. CBPR can potentially improve the quality and validity of research and knowledge, improve trust and relationships among diverse groups, and bring together diverse skills and expertise of all the community stakeholders (See Israel et al., 1998 for more benefits). Many communities are addressing racial justice in the criminal justice system by developing strong partnerships between researchers, policymakers, law enforcement, judicial actors, and diverse communities. BIPOC and other communities that have suffered from racial injustice are key stakeholders that make valuable contributions to the research, decision-making, and planning processes. CBPR is a mechanism by which these individuals can be empowered and help to improve efforts to promote anti-racism and racial justice.

Conclusion

Racism and racial injustices continue to contaminate the criminal justice systems in the United States, devastating many families and communities. For centuries, Black and Indigenous people and people of color have suffered from stigma, profiling, violence, mass incarceration, the war on drugs, disproportionate minority contact, the school-to-prison pipeline, the criminalization of mental health, racial/ethnic disparities, disproportionate sentencing, and other injustices. Many folks downplayed, ignored, or were ignorant to these injustices. Not surprisingly, many anti-racism programs are underdeveloped among the justice community and lack the standard of evidence required for widespread implementation. However, several initiatives show promise. Community policing, body cameras, accountability programs, police dialogues, and others programs represent progressive steps towards addressing the injustices, strengthening the justice system, and helping victims of racial injustices to heal.

Acknowledgments

The National Institutes of Health National Institute on Drug Abuse supported the research reported in this publication under award numbers 1K01DA052679 (Dr. Micah E. Johnson, PI), R25DA050735 (Dr. Micah E. Johnson, PI), R25DA035163 (Dr. Micah E. Johnson, Sub-PI), and U01DA051039 (Dr. Micah E. Johnson, Sub-PI). The content is solely the responsibility of the authors and does not necessarily represent the official views of the National Institutes of Health or the Florida Department of Juvenile Justice.

References

Alexander, M. (2010). *The new Jim Crow: Mass incarceration in the age of colorblindness*. The New Press.

Balko, R. (2018). Putting more cops in schools won't make schools safer, and it will likely inflict a lot of harm. The Washington Post. Retrieved from https://www.washingtonpost.com/news/the-watch/wp/2018/02/22/putting-more-cops-in-schools-wont-make-schools-safer-and-it-will-likely-inflict-a-lot-of-harm/

Balko, R. (2020). There's overwhelming evidence that the criminal-justice system is racist. Here's the proof. The Washington Post. Retrieved from www.washingtonpost.com/graphics/2020/opinions/systemic-racism-police-evidence-criminal-justice-system/

Brucato, B. (2021). Policing race and racing police: The origin of U.S. police in slave patrols. *Social Justice*, *47*(3–4), 115–136.

Carter, E. R., Onyeador, I. N., & Lewis Jr, N. A. (2020). Developing & delivering effective anti-bias training: Challenges & recommendations. *Behavioral Science & Policy*, *6*(1), 57–70.

Cassell, P. G. (2020). Explaining the recent homicide spikes in U.S. cities: The "Minneapolis Effect" and the decline in proactive policing. *Federal Sentencing Reporter*, *33*(1–2), 83–127. doi: 10.1525/fsr.2020.33.1-2.83

Center for American Progress. (2016). *Unjust: How the broken criminal justice system fails LGBT people of color*. Author.

Compton, M. T., Esterberg, M. L., Druss, B. G., Walker, E. F., & Kaslow, N. J. (2006). A descriptive study of pathways to care among hospitalized urban African American first-episode schizophrenia-spectrum patients. *Social Psychiatry and Psychiatric Epidemiology*, *41*(7), 566–573. doi: 10.1007/s00127-006-0065-z

Correll, J., Hudson, S. M., Guillermo, S., & Ma, D. S. (2014). The police officer's dilemma: A decade of research on racial bias in the decision to shoot. *Social and Personality Psychology Compass*, *8*(5), 201–213. doi: 10.1111/spc3.12099

Crawford, C., Chiricos, T., & Kleck, G. (1998). Race, racial threat, and sentencing of habitual offenders. *Criminology*, *36*(3), 481–512. doi: 10.1111/j.1745-9125.1998.tb01256.x

Cuellar, A. E., Snowden, L. M., & Ewing, T. (2007). Criminal records of persons served in the public mental health system. *Psychiatric Services*, *58*(1), 114–120. doi: 10.1176/ps.2007.58.1.114

Delgado, R. (2009). The law of the noose: A history of Latino lynching. *Harvard Civil Rights-Civil Liberties Law Review*, *44*, 297–312.

Dunbar-Ortiz, R. (2014). *An indigenous peoples' history of the United States*. Beacon Press.

Edwards, E., & Madubuonwu, B. (2020). A tale of two countries: Racially targeted arrests in the era of marijuana reform. American Civil Liberties Union Research Report. Retrieved from www.aclu.org/report/tale-two-countries-racially-targeted-arrests-era-marijuana-reform

Erickson, J. (2014). Racial impact statements: Considering the consequences of raicla disproportionalities in the criminal justice system. *Washington Law Review*, *89*(4), 1425–1465.

FBI Counterterrorism Division. (2006). White supremacist infiltration of law enforcement (Intelligence Assessment, Issue). Retrieved from https://oversight.house.gov/sites/democrats.oversight.house.gov/files/White_Supremacist_Infiltration_of_Law_Enforcement.pdf

Hager, E. (2015). Our prisons in black and white. The Marshall Project. Retrieved from www.themarshallproject.org/2015/11/18/our-prisons-in-black-and-white

Heise, M., & Nance, J. P. (2021). "Defund the (school) police"? Bringing data to key school-to-prison pipeline claims. *Journal of Criminal Law & Criminology*, *111*(3), 717–772. https://search.ebscohost.com/login.aspx?direct=true&db=aph&AN=152155211&site=ehost-live

Hickman, M. J., Piquero, A. R., & Garner, J. H. (2008). Toward a national estimate of police use of nonlethal force. *Criminology & Public Policy*, 7(4), 563–604. doi: 10.1111/j.1745-9133.2008.00528.x

Hyland, S., Langton, L., Davis, E. (2015). Police use of nonfatal force, 2022–11 (Special Report NCJ249216). Retrieved from https://bjs.ojp.gov/content/pub/pdf/punf0211.pdf

Irving, T. (2008). Decoding Black women: Policing practices and rape prosecution on the streets of Philadelphia. *NWSA Journal*, *20*(2), 100–120. Retrieved from www.jstor.org/stable/40071277

Israel, B. A., Schulz, A. J., Parker, E. A., & Becker, A. B. (1998). Review of community-based research: Assessing partnership approaches to improve public health. *Annual Review of Public Health*, *19*, 173–202. doi: 10.1146/annurev.publhealth.19.1.173.

Jensen, E. L., Mosher, C., Gerber, J., & Angulski, K. (2019). Progress at the state level versus recent regress at the federal level: Changes in the social consequences of the U.S. war on drugs. *Contemporary Drug Problems*, *46*(2), 139–164. doi: 10.1177/0091450919829087

Jurisdiction, U. S. v. W.-U. S. D. R. b. o. (2014). U.S. supreme court, 12–307. Retrieved from www.aclu.org/legal-document/united-states-v-windsor-united-states-doj-reply-brief-jurisdiction

Kellogg, W. K. (2001). *Foundation community health scholars program stories of impact [brochure]*. Kellogg Foundation Community Health Scholars Program.

Kovera, M. B. (2019). Racial disparities in the criminal justice system: Prevalence, causes, and a search for solutions. *Journal of Social Issues*, *75*(4), 1139–1164. doi: 10.1111/josi.12355

Lewis, J. (2019). Racial impact statements are a legislative imperative. *Contexts (Berkeley, Calif.)*, *18*(3), 68–68. doi: 10.1177/1536504219864966

Livingston, J. D. (2016). Contact between police and people with mental disorders: A review of rates. *Psychiatric Services*, *67*(8), 850–857. doi: 10.1176/appi.ps.201500312

McLaughlin, E. C. (2020). How George Floyd's death ignited a racial reckoning that shows no signs of slowing down. Retrieved from www.cnn.com/2020/08/09/us/george-floyd-protests-different-why/index.html

Minton, T. D., Beatty, L. G., & Zeng, Z. (2021). Correctional populations in the United States, 2019 – Statistical tables. U.S. Department of Justice Bureau of Justice Statistics (NCJ 300655). Retrieved from https://bjs.ojp.gov/library/publications/correctional-populations-united-states-2019-statistical-tables

Musgrave, P. (2020). Bringing the state police in: The diffusion of U.S. statewide policing agencies, 1905–1941. *Studies in American Political Development*, *34*(1), 3–23. doi: 10.1017/S0898588X20000036

Nance, J. P. (2016). Dismantling the school-to-prison pipeline: Tools for change. *Arizona State Law Journal*, *48*(2), 314.

Owens, E. G. (2017). Testing the school-to-prison pipeline. *Journal of Policy Analysis and Management*, *36*(1), 11–37. doi: 10.1002/pam.21954

Pokorak, J. J. (2006). Rape as a badge of slavery: The legal history of, and remedies for, prosecutorial race-of-victim charging disparities. *Nevada Law Journal*, *7*, 1. https://ssrn.com/abstract=961877

Pontzer, D. (2021). Recommendations for examining police deescalation and use of force training, policies, and outcomes. *Journal of police and criminal psychology*, *36*(2), 314–332. doi: 10.1007/s11896-021-09442-1

President's Task Force on 21st Century Policing. (2015). *Final report of the president's task force on 21st century policing*. Office of Community Oriented Policing Services. Retrieved from https://cops.usdoj.gov/pdf/taskforce/taskforce_finalreport.pdf

Reppetto, T. A. (2013). *American police, a history: 1945–2012: The blue parade, Vol. II* (Vol. 2). Enigma Books.

Silverstein, J. (2021). The global impact of George Floyd: How Black Lives Matter protests shaped movements around the world. Retrieved from www.cbsnews.com/news/george-floyd-black-lives-matter-impact/

Smith, J. M. (2017). Racial impact statements, knowledge-based criminology, and resisting color blindness. *Race and Justice*, *7*(4), 374–397. doi: 10.1177/2153368716661223

Spence, R. N. (2020). Saved by the bell: Reclaiming home court advantage for at-risk youth funneled into the school-to-prison pipeline. *Family Court Review*, *58*(1), 227–242. doi: 10.1111/fcre.12464

Spohn, C. C. (2000). Thirty years of sentencing reform: The quest for a racially neutral sentencing process. *Criminal Justice*, *3*.

Spring, J. H. (2016). *Deculturalization and the struggle for equality: A brief history of the education of dominated cultures in the United States*, 8th ed. Routledge.

Starr, S. B., & Rehavi, M. M. (2013). Mandatory sentencing and racial disparity: Assessing the role of prosecutors and the effects of booker. *The Yale Law Journal*, 2–80.

Steffensmeier, D., & Demuth, S. (2000). Ethnicity and sentencing outcomes in US federal courts: Who is punished more harshly? *American Sociological Review*, 705–729. doi: doi.org/10.2307/2657543
Steffensmeier, D., & Demuth, S. (2001). Ethnicity and judges' sentencing decisions: Hispanic-Black-White comparisons. *Criminology*, *39*(1), 145–178. doi: 10.1111/j.1745-9125.2001.tb00919.x
Teplin, L. A. (2000). Keeping the peace: Police discretion and mentally ill persons. *National Institute of Justice Journal*, *244*, 8–15.
The Editors of Encyclopaedia Britannica. (2021). Porvenir Massacre. Encyclopedia Britannica. Retrieved from www.britannica.com/event/Porvenir-Massacre
Tyler, T. R., Goff, P. A., & MacCoun, R. J. (2015). The impact of psychological science on policing in the United States: Procedural justice, legitimacy, and effective law enforcement. *Psychological Science in the Public Interest*, *16*(3), 75–109. doi: 10.1177/1529100615617791
Williams, L. S., Kyle, J., Hegarty, T., Lockett, L., & Grube, J. (2021). The arc of procedural justice in a U.S. non-metro community: Traffic stops and policing in the age of disruption. *Police Practice & Research*, *22*(1), 657–677. doi: 10.1080/15614263.2019.1658580

Conclusion and Integration

42

TOWARD POLICY REFINEMENT

Multi-Systemic and Evidence-Based Approaches

Edelyn Verona, Emily Torres, and Bryanna Fox

The chapters in this edited volume have described the best research evidence for burgeoning and longstanding practices in the criminal justice system and provided specific recommendations to inform practitioners and academics and guide implementation. In this final chapter, we highlight the key themes evident across the sections of the book, to further inform policy change and implementation practices across varied segments of the criminal justice system. The focus on the various segments of the justice system is important, since the functioning of one element of the system (e.g. policing) can have reverberating effects on individuals as they proceed through other points in the system (e.g. courts). Thus, it is important to highlight the common threads, in terms of *content* (e.g. effective practices) and *process* (e.g. ways of approaching problems or reforming the system) that are backed by research. A few main themes abound across many of the chapters.

Role of Law Enforcement

First, deterrence enacted by enhanced law enforcement and sanctioning can play an important role in crime reduction, especially when evidence-based patrolling approaches and community policing practices are followed (Haberman & O'Guinn, Chapter 18).[1] However, the evidence indicates that deterrence-based practices can only do so much, given the pervasive psychological, structural, and social factors that promote crime or bring individuals in contact with the criminal justice system regardless of increased risk of apprehension or sanction. Further, a high reliance on strict enforcement or harsh sanctions can sometimes do more harm than good. For example, shorter sentences may have a more deterrent effect on crime than longer sentences (Hjalmarsson, 2009; Ludwig & Raphael, 2003; Nagin, 2013; National Research Council, 2014), while detention of low-level offenders typically has iatrogenic effects on recidivism (Loeffler & Nagin, 2022). Moreover, some individuals may not even be aware of the enhanced enforcement and sanctions, meaning the deterrent effect of these is not communicated until after the crime is committed (Barnum & Pogarsky, Chapter 15). In the area of drug enforcement, research indicates that while some enforcement strategies can be effective in apprehending high-level drug traffickers, there are diminishing returns when these enforcement practices are applied to low-level offenders, and evidence for long-term reductions in drug crime is minimal or nil (Mitchell & Toth, Chapter 20). On top of that, enforcement practices

DOI: 10.4324/9781003219286-51

do not reduce drug use problems or addiction in individuals who use drugs, who often require multiple rounds of treatment and rehabilitation before they enter recovery (McLellan, et al., 2000; National Institute on Drug Abuse, 2000). In other words, there is no silver bullet when it comes to policing and effective enforcement strategies, as modern practices emphasize nuance in how evidence-based and effective policing strategies are applied, communicated, and implemented over time.

In this regard, evaluations of policing and enforcement efforts should assess the crime reduction benefits as well as costs that may be incurred across a variety of outcomes. For instance, evaluations should consider not only money spent on enhanced enforcement and sanctions as well as crimes prevented but also the extent to which heighted and broad enforcement practices can come at the expense of community relations (Gill & Fox, Chapter 23). While evidence-based policing practices may produce crime reductions, it is important to assess and consider potential implications for police–community relations and hardships for already disadvantaged persons (Gau & Brunson, 2010; Haberman et al., 2016). As such, a major takeaway is that research can indeed improve the efficacy of policing in terms of crime reduction but also that we can weigh these gains against costs and mitigate the impact on police–community relations and public perceptions of police legitimacy, to truly gain maximum benefit.

Addressing Social and Structural Needs

The second major theme from the chapters in this book is that, alongside evidence-based policing and appropriate sanctions, it is important to address the larger issues that promote crime in communities. Indeed, the evidence clearly indicates that social service, mental health, and needs-based practices should be part of the larger picture (Goodmark, 2018; Kleimam et al., 2011; Kopak, 2015). In fact, a combination of appropriate sanctions and provision of services (i.e., stick and carrot approach) is embedded in some of the most successful programs available in reducing in violent crime in communities, including focused deterrence strategies (Braga et al., 2018; Bureau of Justice Assistance [BJA], 2022; Fox et al., 2022).

Consistent with this, an evidence-based approach that has received increasing attention is the risk-needs-responsivity (RNR) model (Andrews et al., 1990a, 1990b), which emphasizes that one-size-fits-all policies do not work in terms of policing, sentencing, or service provision (e.g., anger management or drug treatment programs applied to all). For instance, it is well established that there are a myriad of risk factors that increase the likelihood of offending, and a number of treatments and services are available to encourage desistance in response to specific risk factors. More recent research has specifically identified the role that early psychosocial risk factors, such as adverse childhood experiences (ACEs, see Baglivio, Chapter 13), have on increased risk of delinquency and criminal behavior. Responding to childhood trauma with anger management or drug treatment, while individuals may show signs of both drug use and anger/irritability, is ultimately not addressing the root cause and therefore will be less effective to reducing future offending.

Unfortunately, many criminal justice policies tend to discourage the tailoring of practices, services, treatments, and sanctions to the needs and risks of individuals, or even the community. As an example, federal and state sentencing guidelines, developed in an effort to be more objective and consistent across cases, actually limit judges from taking specific circumstances or characteristics of the individual into account when structuring their sanctions. State and local laws may also limit the use of diversion programs. Non-carceral alternatives (e.g., probation, supervised release, home detention, community supervision) are available, but one's eligibility to receive these alternatives are contingent on their charges (Badalamenti & Holcomb,

Chapter 29). For instance, probation is only available for those charged with offenses on the lower end of sentencing guidelines. A sign of change is the First Step Act, which reinstated judicial discretion in federal sentencing (Ryan, 2020; Sykes & Sharry, Chapter 40), which had previously been restricted by mandatory minimum guidelines (Grawert, 2020). However, how this new judicial discretion ultimately impacts disparities in sentencing, mass incarceration, and access to diversion programs should be closely followed and rigorously evaluated.

To that end, some well-intended policies meant to increase justice and reduce bias are limited by implementation that does not consider the specifics of the situation. One-size-fits-all diversity and implicit bias training for jurors does not seem to work, and evidence indicates that it is best when these training are case-specific (e.g., considers race of defendant and victim; Calanchini et al., 2020) and involve more than one training session (Jones & Ruva, Chapter 28). Similarly, mandatory domestic violence arrest policies that were supposed to be gender-neutral have been shown to produce unintended consequences, often for victims (Richards, Pinchevsky & Nix, Chapter 21). For instance, evidence shows that mandatory and dual arrest policies, in which all parties that engaged in violence are arrested, are associated with increasing the arrests of victims, even if they were acting in self-defense (see Goodmark, 2018). These policies have actually been shown to lead to higher rates of domestic violence homicide, which is extremely concerning (see Iyengar, 2009; Sherman & Harris, 2013).

Instead, highly tailored and social service-based programs are most effective, particularly for youth and younger adults who are at risk or have had contact with the justice system. A top priority across criminal justice agencies has been on diversion, family and community-based interventions, and enrichment programs for youth, whose adjustments may deteriorate further the more time they spend in detention or in repeated contact with law enforcement (Cyr et al., 2010; Dmitrieva et al., 2012; Wilson & Woods, 2006). The chapters in this book call for a different approach to addressing youth conduct or disciplinary problems, including moving away from an enforcement-based approach to school and discipline problems to avoid the school to prison pipeline (White, Chapter 8). Reforming these practices in the schools, as a starting point, are likely to curb the cycle of incarceration in families and reduce the blight of mass incarceration.

Related to this, several chapters champion taking a harm reduction and public health approach to addressing the many social ills that often fall on the lap of the criminal justice system. This approach targets the behaviors or practices surrounding drug use that increase harm to self or the public. Several chapters in this book highlight how needle exchange programs, distribution of naloxone, and medical-based approaches to addressing addiction show promise in preventing overdose deaths, spread of infectious diseases, and crime among individuals who use drugs, although more research is needed to determine what are the actual outcomes from participating in those programs (Rigg, Chapter 35; Wilson & Henderson, Chapter 5). Given the success of these harm reduction campaigns in relation to drug use, public health approaches have also been proposed or implemented to address family or community violence, child welfare, sex work, gang-related violence, and other behaviors that bring individuals into contact with the criminal justice system (Butts et al., 2015; Lim et al., 2015; Parker et al., 2007; Shlonsky et al., 2007).

Multi-Systemic Approach

The third major theme, while related to the prior two, is the idea that we need a multi-agency and multi-systemic approach to most effectively address crime, public safety, and positive outcomes for those who encounter the criminal justice system. Despite the promise of service and health treatment programs, the interventions that have been studied so far focus largely on individual change, rather than structural and community changes which play a large role in crime and life outcomes as well. For instance, poverty, neighborhood disorganization, and lack of employment and resources all contribute to crime, and therefore should be considered to best remediate it (Fisher et al., 2014). Moreover, collaborations across domains can help address multiple risk factors such as therapy for childhood trauma, resources for poorly funded education programs, access to health care and mental health treatment, and more. By addressing only one of these at once, the maximum benefit for the individual and community cannot be reached.

When multi-agency collaborations occur, they are most commonly seen in the area of juvenile justice. Interventions that target family and community factors and take a holistic approach to change have shown the most effectiveness, including functional family therapy (Butler et al., 2011; Henggeler & Sheidow, 2012; Sexton, 2000; Smith et al., 2004, 2012). Further, community-based interventions that target social disorganization, such as community violence outreach programs, mentoring or after school programs, and physical environment improvement strategies have shown growing promise (Berezin et al., Chapter 9; Kubrin & Tublitz, Chapter 2; Lee & Peck, Chapter 11; Yampolskaya, Chapter 10), especially when these programs involve community-police collaborations (Farrell et al., 2018).

"One-stop shop" service organizations and practices may be the most helpful for persons who experience issues across multiple domains (George et al., 2020). Comprehensive care, trauma support services, and assistance with medical and basic necessities are the foci of these organizations (George et al., 2020). Similarly, many justice-involved youth are involved in the child welfare system and face greater treatment needs and system navigation support, such as attending court and meeting legal mandates (Baglivio, Chapter 13; Berezin et al., Chapter 9). As such, data sharing across systems, single comprehensive care plans, and the "one judge/one family" approach should be implemented rather than having to navigate separate courts (Baglivio, Chapter 13; Lutz & Stewart, 2015; Stewart et al., 2010). Youth enrichment programs can also help address multiple needs at once and coordinate across agencies. These programs can assist youth and families involved in the legal system by identifying and assisting with the compliance of probation terms, providing letters of progress, and increasing engagement through program flexibility (e.g., offering an array of options for program focus and delivery; Berezin et al., Chapter 9).

Researcher–Agency Collaborations

In many cases, as outlined in the chapters, the evidence base on a number of central issues is meager or not enough to make informed practice recommendations. That is why need more collaborations between practitioners and researchers, and to reconcile different approaches. Researchers can provide more rigorous evaluations of agency initiatives and potentially identify unintended systemic biases. For example, the research on interrogation practices has led to a shift towards science-based interviewing, which includes rapport-building and information gathering tactics (Kassin et al., 2010). However, coercive, accusatorial tactics of the past are still used (Mindthoff & Meissner, Chapter 22; Snook et al., 2020). Researcher and practitioner collaborations at the local level can lead to the proper implementation of science-based practices, including the use of more objective risk assessment strategies that work and reduce bias (Douglas, Chapter 17).

Similarly, in the court system, collaborations between prosecutors and researchers can provide much needed evidence-based practices in prosecution, considering the high levels of prosecutorial discretion allowed in the system (Hernandez et al., Chapter 24). Select state attorney's offices have started to partner with researchers to identify evidence based policies and refine their databases. Such partnerships can improve knowledge of prosecutorial discretion, identify the sources of racial disparities in sentencing and plea negotiations (see Kutateladze et al., 2018), and evaluate the efficacy of policy changes. In the area of public defense, one salient recommendation is to allocate more funding to facilitate effective counseling (Furst, 2019; Henderson & Lee, Chapter 25), a portion of which is encouraged to go towards supporting agency and researcher partnerships (e.g., Campbell et al.,2015).

Racial Justice and Equity

Many of the chapters in this handbook highlight how a history of inequitable treatment in the criminal justice system, including in policing, incarceration, and implementation of the death penalty, need to be addressed before citizens experience the justice system as legitimate and fair. As noted throughout, inequality exists in who is incarcerated and in the severity of sanctions (Berezin et al., Chapter 9; Dixon & Shakoor, Chapter 38; Johnson & Bristol, Chapter 41; Lowder et al., Chapter 37; Midgette et al., Chapter 36; Novisky & Mitchell, Chapter 32; Sykes & Sharry, Chapter 40). Often, those disproportionally incarcerated will be men, young adults, people of color, and undereducated populations (see Pettit & Sykes, 2017; Sykes & Pettit, 2014; National Research Council, 2014). Evidence-based programs, policies and practices aimed at reducing punitiveness and creating a more equitable system include providing training and education of racial injustices among the criminal justice system, such as implicit bias training, de-escalation training, and coupling training with monitoring and accountability systems (Carter et al., 2020). Importantly, one recommendation is the use of well-established risk assessment instruments during policy development to avoid inadvertently increasing racial disparities with laws that appear to be "race-neutral" (Johnson & Bristol, Chapter 41).

More recently, criminal justice reform efforts call for the reallocation of funding towards supporting public health approaches and prevention of crime, rather than toward law enforcement and sanctioning after crime occurs. This includes funding housing, hospitals, mental health services, and evidence-based drug prevention and treatment (Johnson & Bristol, Chapter 41). Indeed, partnerships between criminal justice professionals and communities are essential towards addressing injustices and inequalities in the criminal justice system. In particular, police reform efforts have been aimed at improving public perceptions of police legitimacy using procedural justice practices to foster trust and confidence in police by promoting community support and accountability (Gill & Fox, Chapter 23; Tyler & Huo, 2002; Tyler et al., 2015; Williams et al., 2021).

Navigating the System in Evidence-Based Ways

Although the previous themes provide recommendations for future practice, it is less clear how these practices have a direct impact on the individuals and communities affected. As such, we provide examples of how evidence-based practices can change the quality, duration, and trajectory of involvement in the criminal justice system. These examples are informed by the literature reviewed and recommendations from various chapters within this handbook.

Example 1: A juvenile with an extensive history of school suspensions eventually becomes justice involved as a function of zero-tolerance policies at their school. After numerous in-school arrests and being placed in out-of-home settings, including detention centers, correctional institutions, and group homes, the initial behavioral problems present are exacerbated. The involvement in detention and the juvenile justice system's out-of-home settings often lead to under-education, exposure to delinquent peers, and heightened exposure to adverse childhood experiences (e.g., abuse, victimization). The following policies and practices can curtail some of the adverse impacts associated with current common practices:

- Reducing the number school resource officers in schools and increasing the number of counselors, social workers, nurses, and other mental health support professionals for students to increase early identification and treatment for children (White, Chapter 8).
- Implementing positive behavioral interventions and supports (PBIS) to decrease exclusionary discipline and increase attendance, behavioral skills, and prosocial and academic outcomes (Feinberg et al., 2021; White, Chapter 8).
- Using detention diversion programs, such as counseling/skill-building or treatment programs (e.g., multidimensional treatment foster care [MTFC], functional family therapy [FFT], and multisystemic therapy [MST]; Yampolskaya, Chapter 10). These programs can help youth cope with trauma symptoms and provide intensive treatment for their co-occurring needs, which typically cannot be provided in the community or in residential facilities.

Example 2: An individual with serious mental health problems has frequent interactions with police during mental health crisis calls for service or after engaging in violent behaviors. Interactions with police often results in either no action or in multiple arrests and short-term jail stays. Their mental health problems continue to go unaddressed while in jail, and this individual experiences little to no engagement in community mental health services after release. Over time, their repeated contact with law enforcement and the increasing level of crimes leads to long-term incarceration in prison, where their symptoms of mental illness go unaddressed and are exacerbated by multiple experiences of victimization and isolation.

- At the community level, diversion programs involving behavioral or mental health professionals responding to mental health and non-criminal/non-violent 911 calls may have diverted criminal justice involvement early on and provided linkage to mental health services in the community (Torres et al., Chapter 4; Rigg, Chapter 35).
- After arrest, mental health courts (MHCs) involving court – supervised mental health treatment could be used to reduce recidivism (Canada et al., 2019; Dean, 2017; Fox et al., 2021; Lowder et al., 2018)
- While in prison and during reentry, cognitive behavioral therapy-based (CBT) programs that target violence and mental health problems, in combination with adherence to the risk-need-responsivity model, could be used to reduce symptoms of mental illness (Eseadi et al., 2018; Khodaryarifard et al., 2010) and recidivism (Aos et al., 2006).

Example 3: An individual experiencing substance use disorder is frequently in and out of various institutions (e.g., hospital and jail). Despite frequent interaction with both the healthcare and criminal justice system, they are not able to engage in long-term, comprehensive and continuous treatment/services. Thus, they commit various non-violent crimes as a result of their substance use disorder and other co-occurring risk factors associated with offending.

- Community harm reduction approaches in the community can provide a continuum of care, including needle exchange, naloxone distribution and leave-behind programs for first responders, and emergency department-based infectious disease screening programs (e.g., HIV and HCV; Wilson & Henderson, Chapter 5).

- Non-traditional policing strategies to address drug use and drug markets, such as law enforcement assisted diversion (LEAD) and drug market intervention (DMI) can divert individuals involved in drug use or trafficking away from the criminal justice system and into social services (Mitchell & Toth, Chapter 20).
- Medication assistance treatment (MAT) programs and naloxone distribution integrated in hospitals and criminal justice system encounters (e.g., drug treatment courts, jails, and prisons) can be used to decrease overdose mortalities and reduce recidivism (Rigg, Chapter 35; Wilson & Henderson, Chapter 5).

These examples highlight a few evidence-based programs recommended throughout this book and illustrate how they can affect the trajectory and quality of criminal justice system outcomes.

Conclusions

In summary, the latest research calls for the implementation of sanctions and enforcement strategies that are shown to increase deterrence and decrease reoffending and avoid disrupting community relations, multisystemic and multiagency approaches to crime and societal problems, and tailored public health and social services that provide individualized support. Since many traditional practices that are not evidence based persist, and new approaches require evidence of their effectiveness, we believe the path toward effective evidence-based practices requires researcher and practitioner collaborations and the involvement of and reinvestment in impacted communities. The totality of the evidence leads us to the following take home points:

- Evidence-based patrolling tactics, community policing, and less punitive sanctions provide the best results in terms of cost-benefit analyses (i.e., crime reduction and legitimacy).
- Social services and needs-based practices, in combination with appropriate sanctions, are key to successful programs in reducing crime and preventing further involvement in the system.
- There needs to be a shift towards structural and community change to address crime and criminal justice outcomes, as the problem of crime and justice involvement is multi-determined and broadly systemic.
- Inequities in the criminal justice system are often addressed when using evidence-based policies and programs, including implementing the principles of procedural justice, community-based patrol practices, and research-based interrogation practices.
- Because implementation of evidence-based practices is difficult and requires tailoring to the individual jurisdiction, researcher-practitioner collaborations are essential to demonstrate which policies "work" for whom. The rigorous evaluations provided by researchers can also identify potential inequities and bolster agency accountability.

Note

1 All chapters referenced are in this volume.

References

Andrews, D. A., & Bonta, J. (2010). Rehabilitating criminal justice policy and practice. *Psychology, Public Policy, and Law*, *16*(1), 39–55.

Andrews, D. A., Bonta, J., & Hoge, R. D. (1990a). Classification for effective rehabilitation: Rediscovering psychology. *Criminal Justice and Behavior, 17*(1), 19–52.
Andrews, D. A., Zinger, I., Hoge, R. D., Bonta, J., Gendreau, P., & Cullen, F. T. (1990b). Does correctional treatment work? A clinically relevant and psychologically informed meta-analysis. *Criminology, 28*(3), 369–404.
Aos, S., Miller, M., & Drake, E. (2006). *Evidence-based adult corrections programs: What works and what does not*. Washington State Institute for Public Policy. Retrieved from www.wsipp.wa.gov/ReportFile/924.
Badalamenti, J. L., & Holcomb, L. (Ch. 29, this volume). Judicial considerations in sentencing: A call for evidence-based reform. In E. Verona & B. Fox (Eds.), *Handbook of evidence-based criminal justice practices*. Routledge.
Baglivio, M. T. (Ch. 13, this volume). Adverse childhood experiences & offending: Strategies for prevention, intervention, and building resiliency. In E. Verona & B. Fox (Eds.), *Handbook of evidence-based criminal justice practices*. Routledge.
Barnum, T. C., & Pogarsky, G. (Ch. 15, this volume). Revisiting the role of sanction risk perception in deterrence policy. In E. Verona & B. Fox (Eds.), *Handbook of evidence-based criminal justice practices*. Routledge.
Berezin, M. B., Rose, R., & Javdani, S. (Ch. 9, this volume). Evidence-based criminal justice practices: Current status and strategies for successful youth outreach and enrichment programming. In E. Verona & B. Fox (Eds.), *Handbook of evidence-based criminal justice practices*. Routledge.
Braga, A. A., Weisburd, D., & Turchan, B. (2018). Focused deterrence strategies and crime control: An updated systematic review and meta-analysis of the empirical evidence. *Criminology & Public Policy, 17*(1), 205–250.
Bureau of Justice Assistance (2022, June 9). Project Safe Neighborhoods (PSN). Bureau of Justice Assistance. Retrieved from https://bja.ojp.gov/program/project-safe-neighborhoods-psn/overview
Butler, S., Baruch, G., Hickey, N., & Fonagy, P (2011). A randomized controlled trial of multisystemic therapy and a statutory therapeutic intervention for young offenders. *Journal of the American Academy of Child & Adolescent Psychiatry, 50*(12), 1220–1235.
Butts, J. A., Roman, C. G., Bostwick, L., & Porter, J. R. (2015). Cure violence: A public health model to reduce gun violence. *Annual Review of Public Health, 36*, 39–53.
Calanchini, J., Lai, C. K., & Klauer, K. C. (2020). Reducing implicit racial preferences: III. A process-level examination of changes in implicit preferences. *Journal of Personality and Social Psychology, 121*(4), 796.
Campbell, C., Moore, J., Maier, W., & Gaffney, M. (2015). Unnoticed, untapped, and underappreciated: Clients' perceptions of their public defenders. *Behavioral Sciences & the Law, 33*(6), 751–770.
Canada, K., Barrenger, S., & Ray, B. (2019). Bridging mental health and criminal justice systems: A systematic review of the impact of mental health courts on individuals and communities. *Psychology, Public Policy, and Law, 25*(2), 73–91.
Carter, E. R., Onyeador, I. N., & Lewis Jr., N. A. (2020). Developing & delivering effective anti-bias training: Challenges & recommendations. *Behavioral Science & Policy*, 6(1), 57–70.
Cyr, C., Euser, E. M., Bakermans-Kranenburg, M., & Ijzendoorn, M. H. V. (2010). Attachment security and disorganization in maltreating and high-risk families: A series of meta-analyses. *Development and Psychopathology, 22*(1), 87–108.
Dean, R. (2017). What is the impact of mental health courts? A systematic literature review. Retrieved from https://sophia.stkate.edu/msw_papers/721
Dixon, A. R., & Shakoor, A. (Ch. 38, this volume). Examining Dilemmas about the State of America's Death Penalty. In E. Verona, & B. Fox (Eds.), *Handbook of evidence-based criminal justice practices*. Routledge.
Dmitrieva, J., Monahan, K. C., Cauffman, E., & Steinberg, L. (2012). Arrested development: The effects of incarceration on the development of psychosocial maturity. *Development and Psychopathology, 24*, 1073–1090.
Douglas, K. (Ch. 17, this volume.) Implementation Science and Evidence-Based Violence Risk Assessment. In E. Verona & B. Fox (Eds.), *Handbook of evidence-based criminal justice practices*. Routledge.
Eseadi, C., Obidoa, M. A., Ogbuabor, S. E., & Ikechukwu-Ilomuanya, A. B. (2018). Effects of group-focused cognitive-behavioral coaching program on depressive symptoms in a sample of inmates in a Nigerian prison. *International Journal of Offender Therapy and Comparative Criminology*, 62(6), 1589–1602.

Farrell, J., Betsinger, A., & Hammond, P. (2018). Best practices in youth diversion. The Institute for Innovation & Implementation. Retrieved from https://theinstitute.umaryland.edu/media/ssw/institute/md-center-documents/Youth-Diversion-Literature-Review.pdf

Feinberg, A. B., Meyer, K. A., Everett, S., Robbie, K., Pierce, A., Shor, R., . . . Fischer, S. (2021). PBIS academy model demo brief: Impact of statewide support model on high-needs schools. *Center on Positive Behavioral Intervention and Supports*(First Step Act. (2018) H.R), 5682, 115.

Fisher, W. H., Clark, R., Baxter, J., Barton, B., O'Connell, E., & Aweh, G. (2014). Co-occurring risk factors for arrest among persons with opioid abuse and dependence: implications for developing interventions to limit criminal justice involvement. *Journal of Substance Abuse Treatment*, *47*(3), 197–201.

Fox, B., Allen, S. F., & Toth, A. (2022). Evaluating the impact of Project Safe Neighborhoods (PSN) initiative on violence and gun crime in Tampa: Does it work and does it last? *Journal of Experimental Criminology*, *18*(3), 543–567.

Fox, B., Miley, L. N., Kortright, K. E., & Wetsman, R. J. (2021). Assessing the effect of mental health courts on adult and juvenile recidivism: a meta-analysis. *American Journal of Criminal Justice*, *46*(4), 644–664.

Furst, B. (2019). A fair fight: Achieving indigent defense resource parity. *Brennan center for justice*. Retrieved from www.brennancenter.org/sites/default/files/201909/Report_A%20Fair%20Fight.pdf

Gau, J. M., & Brunson, R. K. (2010). Procedural justice and order maintenance policing: A study of inner-city young men's perceptions of police legitimacy. *Justice Quarterly*, *27*(2), 255–279.

George, J. S., Malik, S., Symes, S., Caralis, P., Newport, D. J., Godur, A., . . . Potter, J. E. (2020). Trafficking healthcare resources and intra-disciplinary victim services and education (THRIVE) clinic: A multidisciplinary one-stop shop model of healthcare for survivors of human trafficking. *Journal of Human Trafficking*, *6*(1), 50–60.

Gill, L., & Fox, B. (Ch. 23, this volume). Evidence-based policing reform and building-community relations. In E. Verona & B. Fox (Eds.), *Handbook of evidence-based criminal justice practices*. Routledge.

Goodmark, L. (2017). Innovative criminal justice responses to intimate partner violence. In C. Renzetti, J. Edelson, & R. K. Bergen (Eds.). *Sourcebook on violence against women*, 3rd ed. Sage.

Goodmark, L. (2018). *Decriminalizing domestic violence: A balanced policy approach to intimate partner violence*. University of California Press.

Grawert, A. (2020). What is the first step act? – And what's happening with it? Brennen Center. Retrieved from www.brennancenter.org/our-work/research-reports/what-first-step-act-and-whats-happening-it

Haberman, C. P., Groff, E. R., Ratcliffe, J. H., & Sorg, E. T. (2016). Satisfaction with police in violent crime hot spots: Using community surveys as a guide for selecting hot spots policing tactics. *Crime and Delinquency*, *62*(4), 525–557.

Haberman, C. P., & O'Guinn, B. J. (Ch. 18, this volume). Evidence-based police patrol practices at crime hotspots. In E. Verona & B. Fox (Eds.), *Handbook of evidence-based criminal justice practices*. Routledge.

Helseth, S. A., & Frazier, S. L. (2018). *Peer*-assisted social learning for diverse and low-income youth: Infusing mental health promotion into urban after-school programs. *Administration and Policy in Mental Health and Mental Health Services Research*, *45*(2), 286–301.

Henderson, K. S., & Lee, J. G. (Ch. 25, this volume). Defense decision-making & practices. In E. Verona, & B. Fox (Eds.), *Handbook of evidence-based criminal justice practices*. Routledge.

Henggeler, S. W., & Sheidow, A. J. (2012). Empirically supported family-based treatment for conduct disorder and delinquency. *Journal of Marital and Family Therapy*, *38*(1), 30–58.

Hernandez, R. A., Houlihan, S., & Johnson, B. D. (Ch. 24, this volume). Evidence-based practices in prosecution. In E. Verona & B. Fox (Eds.), *Handbook of evidence-based criminal justice practices*. Routledge.

Hjalmarsson, R. (2009). Crime and expected punishment: Changes in perceptions at the age of criminal majority. *American Law and Economics Review*, 11(1), 209–248.

Iyengar, R. (2009). Does the certainty of arrest reduce domestic violence? Evidence from mandatory and recommended arrest laws. *Journal of Public Economics*, *93*(1–2), 85–98.

Johnson, M. E., & Bristol, S. C. (Ch. 41, this volume). Anti-racism and racial justice in the criminal justice system. In E. Verona & B. Fox (Eds.), *Handbook of evidence-based criminal justice practices*. Routledge.

Jones, A. M., & Ruva, C. L. (Ch. 28, this volume). Implicit and ingrained? Reducing unconscious bias among jurors. In E. Verona, & B. Fox (Eds.), *Handbook of evidence-based criminal justice practices.* Routledge.

Kassin, S. M., Drizin, S. A., Grisso, T., Gudjonsson, G. H., Leo, R. A., & Redlich, A. D. (2010). Police-induced confession: Risk factors and recommendations. *Law & Human Behavior*, *34*, 3–38.

Khodayarifard, M., Shokoohi-Yekta, M., & Hamot, G. E. (2010). Effects of individual and group cognitive-behavioral therapy for male prisoners in Iran. *International Journal of Offender Therapy and Comparative Criminology*, *54*(5), 743–755.

Kleiman, M. A., Caulkins, J. P., & Hawken, A. (2011). *Drugs and drug policy: What everyone needs to know*. Oxford University Press.

Kopak, A. M. (2015). Breaking the addictive cycle of the system: improving US criminal justice practices to address substance use disorders. *International Journal of Prisoner Health*, *11*(1), 4–16.

Kubrin, C. E., & Tublitz, R. (Ch. 2, this volume). Social disorganization theory and community-based interventions. In E. Verona & B. Fox (Eds.), *Handbook of evidence-based criminal justice practices.* Routledge.

Kutateladze, B. L., Meldrum, R., Richardson, R., Stemen, D., Webster, E., Ardnt, M., Matthews, D., & Soor, S. (2018). *Advancing prosecutorial effectiveness and fairness report series: prosecutorial attitudes, perspectives, and priorities: Insights from the inside*. Prosecutorial Performance Indicators. Retrieved from https://ppibuild.wpengine.com/wp-content/uploads/2020/09/FIU-Loyola-_MacAthruth-Prosecution-Project-Report-One-PDF.pdf

Lee, N., & Peck, J. (Ch. 11, this volume). Juvenile justice practices. In E. Verona & B. Fox (Eds.), *Handbook of evidence-based criminal justice practices*. Routledge.

Lim, S., Peitzmeier, S., Cange, C., Papworth, E., LeBreton, M., Tamoufe, U., . . . Baral, S. (2015). Violence against female sex workers in Cameroon: Accounts of violence, harm reduction, and potential solutions. *JAIDS Journal of Acquired Immune Deficiency Syndromes*, *68*, S241–S247.

Loeffler, C. E., & Nagin, D. S. (2022). The Impact of Incarceration on Recidivism. *Annual Review of Criminology*, *5*(1), 133–152.

Lowder, E. M., Rade, C. B., & Desmarais, S. L. (2018). Effectiveness of mental health courts in reducing recidivism: A meta-analysis. *Psychiatric Services*, *69*(1), 15–22.

Lowder, E. M., Rodriguez, A., & Diaz, C. (Ch. 37, this volume). Effective bail reform strategies drawn from a limited evidence base. In E. Verona & B. Fox (Eds.), *Handbook of evidence-based criminal justice practices*. Routledge.

Ludwig, J., & Raphael, S. (2003). Prison sentence enhancements: The case of project Exile. In J. Ludwig, & P. J. Cook (Eds.), *Evaluating gun policy: Effects on crime violence*. Brookings Institution Press.

Lutz, L., & Stewart, M. (2015). *The crossover youth practice model: An abbreviated guide*. Center for Juvenile Justice Reform, Georgetown University.

McLellan, A. T., Lewis, D. C., O'Brien, C. P., & Kleber, H. D. (2000). Drug dependence, a chronic medical illness: Implications for treatment, insurance, and outcomes evaluation. *Journal of the American Medical Association*, *284*(13), 1689–1695.

Midgette, G., Scocca, J., & Newell, A. (Ch. 36, this volume). Criminal justice interventions against drug use and harms. In E. Verona & B. Fox (Eds.), *Handbook of evidence-based criminal justice practices.* Routledge.

Mindthoff, A., & Meissner, C. A. (Ch. 22, this volume). Interviewing and interrogations: From the third degree to science-based approaches. In E. Verona, & B. Fox (Eds.), *Handbook of evidence-based criminal justice practices*. Routledge.

Mitchell, O., & Toth, A. G. (Ch. 20, this volume). Drug enforcement and its effectiveness. In E. Verona & B. Fox (Eds.), *Handbook of evidence-based criminal justice practices*. Routledge.

Nagin, D. S. (2013). Deterrence: A review of the evidence by a criminologist for economists. *Annual Review of Economics*, *5*, 83–105.

National Institute on Drug Abuse. (2000). *Principles of drug addiction treatment: A research- based guide*. National Institute on Drug Abuse, National Institutes of Health.

National Research Council. (2014). In J. Travis, B. Western, & S. Redburn (Eds.), *The growth of incarceration in the United States: Exploring causes and consequences*. National Academies Press.

Novisky, M. A., & Mitchell, M. M. (Ch. 32, this volume). Incarceration: Rehabilitative versus iatrogenic effects. In E. Verona & B. Fox (Eds.), *Handbook of evidence-based criminal justice practices.* Routledge.

Parker, R. N., Luther, K., & Murphy, L. (2007). Availability, gang violence, and alcohol policy: Gaining support for alcohol regulation via harm reduction strategies. *Contemporary Drug Problems*, *34*(4), 611–633.

Pettit, B., & Sykes, B. (2017). Incarceration. In *State of the union: the poverty and inequality report*. Stanford Center on Poverty and Inequality.

Richards, T. N., Pinchevsky, G. M., & Nix, J. (Ch. 21, this volume). Evidence-based practices for policing domestic violence. In E. Verona & B. Fox (Eds.), *Handbook of evidence-based criminal justice practices*. Routledge.

Rigg, K. K. (Ch. 35, this volume). Justice-involved persons with opioid use disorder: Reducing overdose and criminal recidivism. In E. Verona & B. Fox (Eds.), *Handbook of evidence-based criminal justice practices*. Routledge.

Ryan, S. (2020). Judicial authority under the first step act: What congress conferred through section 404. *Loyola University Chicago Law Journal*, *54*, 57–125.

Sexton, T. L. (2000). Functional family therapy. US Department of Justice, Office of Justice Programs, Office of Juvenile Justice and Delinquency Prevention.

Sherman, L. W., & Harris, H. M. (2013). Increased homicide victimization of suspects arrested for domestic assault: A 23-year follow-up of the Milwaukee Domestic Violence Experiment (MilDVE). *Journal of Experimental Criminology*, *9*(4), 491–514.

Shlonsky, A., Friend, C., & Lambert, L. (2007). From culture clash to new possibilities: A harm reduction approach to family violence and child protection services. *Brief Treatment and Crisis Intervention*, *7*(4), 345.

Smith, D. K., Chamberlain, P., & Deblinger, E. (2012). Adapting Multidimensional Treatment Foster Care for the treatment of co-occurring trauma and delinquency in adolescent girls. *Journal of Child & Adolescent Trauma*, *5*(3), 224–238.

Smith, E. P., Wolf, A. M., Cantillon, D. M., Thomas, O., & Davidson, W. S. (2004). The Adolescent Diversion Project: 25 years of research on an ecological model of intervention. *Journal of Prevention & Intervention in the Community*, *27*(2), 29–47.

Snook, B., Fahmy, W., Fallon, L., Lively, C. J., Luther, K., Meissner, C. A., Barron, T., & House, J. C. (2020). Challenges of a "toolbox" approach to investigative interview: A critical analysis of the RCMP's Phased Interview Model. *Psychology, Public Policy, & Law*, *26*, 261–273.

Stewart, M., Lutz, L., & Herz, D. H. (2010). *Crossover youth practice model*. Center for Juvenile Justice Reform, Georgetown University.

Sykes, B., & Pettit, B. (2014). Mass incarceration, family complexity, and the reproduction of childhood disadvantage. *The Annals of the American Academy of Political and Social Science*, *654*, 127–149.

Sykes, B. L., & Sharry, J. A., (Ch. 40, this volume). Mass incarceration. In E. Verona & B. Fox (Eds.), *Handbook of evidence-based criminal justice practices*. Routledge.

Tyler, T. R., Goff, P. A., & MacCoun, R. J. (2015). The impact of psychological science on policing in the United States: Procedural justice, legitimacy, and effective law enforcement. *Psychological science in the public interest*, *16*(3), 75–109.

Tyler, T. R., & Huo, Y. (2002). *Trust in the law: Encouraging public cooperation with the police and courts*. Russell Sage Foundation.

White, A. (Ch. 8, this volume). School-based prevention and criminal justice. In E. Verona & B. Fox (Eds.), *Handbook of evidence-based criminal justice practices*. Routledge.

Williams, L. S., Kyle, J., Hegarty, T., Lockett, L., & Grube, J. (2021). The arc of procedural justice in a U.S. non-metro community: Traffic stops and policing in the age of disruption. *Police Practice & Research*, *22*(1), 657–677.

Wilson, J. W., & Henderson, H. (Ch. 5, this volume). Opioid use disorder, infectious disease, and coordinated harm reduction in a medical setting. In E. Verona, & B. Fox (Eds.), *Handbook of evidence-based criminal justice practices*. Routledge.

Wilson, M. N., & Woods, L. N. (2006). Iatrogenic outcomes of the child welfare system: Vulnerable adolescents, peer influences, and instability in foster care arrangements. In K. Dodge, T. Dishion, & J. Lansford (Eds.), *Deviant peer influences in programs for youth: Problems and solutions* (pp. 203–214). Guilford.

Yampolskaya, S. (Ch. 10, this volume). Juvenile residential and out of home placement: Programs & interventions. In E. Verona & B. Fox (Eds.), *Handbook of evidence-based criminal justice practices*. Routledge.

INDEX

Note: Page numbers in **bold** indicate a table on the corresponding page.

MIX
Papier | Fördert gute Waldnutzung
FSC® C083411

Kolibri 360 GmbH
Ferdinand-Jühlke-Straße 7
99095 Erfurt, Deutschland
produktsicherheit@kolibri360.de